Enhancing Edge Devices With Generative Intelligence:

Architecture, Challenges, and Applications

Sarbagya Ratna Shakya
Eastern New Mexico University, USA

Tej Bahadur Shahi
https://orcid.org/0000-0002-0616-3180
Queensland University of Technology, Australia

Edgar Ceh-Varela
https://orcid.org/0000-0001-6277-2741
Eastern New Mexico University, USA

Michael Cowling
RMIT University, Australia

IGI Global
Scientific Publishing
Publishing Tomorrow's Research Today

Published in the United States of America by
IGI Global Scientific Publishing
701 East Chocolate Avenue
Hershey, PA, 17033, USA
Tel: 717-533-8845 | Fax: 717-533-7115
Website: https://www.igi-global.com E-mail: cust@igi-global.com

Library of Congress Cataloging-in-Publication Data

Names: Shakya, Sarbagya Ratna, 1985- editor | Shahi, Tej Bahadur, 1984- editor | Ceh-Varela, Edgar, 1977- editor | Cowling, Michael, 1978- editor
Title: Enhancing edge devices with generative intelligence : architecture, challenges, and applications / edited by Sarbagya Ratna Shakya, Tej Bahadur Shahi, Edgar Ceh-Varela, Michael Cowling.
Description: Hershey, PA : IGI Global Scientific Publishing, [2026] | Includes bibliographical references and index. | Summary: "This book shows how to bridge the gap between power management, generative AI with resource-constrained edge computing. By running generative AI directly on edge devices, we can create applications that are not only powerful and creative but also fast, private, and efficient. It provides a foundational guide to this convergence, detailing the integration, applications, and challenges of deploying generative intelligence at the edge, while exploring real-world implementations across diverse fields"-- Provided by publisher.
Identifiers: LCCN 2026003392 (print) | LCCN 2026003393 (ebook) | ISBN 9798337373409 h/c | ISBN 9798337373416 s/c | ISBN 9798337373423 ebook
Subjects: LCSH: Edge computing | Generative artificial intelligence--Industrial applications
Classification: LCC QA76.583 .E54 2026 (print) | LCC QA76.583 (ebook)
LC record available at https://lccn.loc.gov/2026003392
LC ebook record available at https://lccn.loc.gov/2026003393
British Cataloguing in Publication Data
A Cataloguing in Publication record for this book is available from the British Library.

Table of Contents

Detailed Table of Contents

Generative Artificial Intelligence (Generative AI) is a paradigm shift in computational intelligence - switching the role of machines in computational intelligence to creative synthesis. The Generative systems based on the underlying probability distributions of data can generate realistic and context-ually consistent output across modalities, including text, image, audio, and structured data, by learning the underlying probability distributions of the data. This chapter has given an in-depth introduction to the theoretical, architectural, and operational backgrounds of generative AI, and then proceeded to discuss how generative AI has been adapted to resource-constrained and distributed systems. It has talked about probabilistic modelling and latent space representation and the development of generative models and then it has touched on the computational issues like the complexity of training, quantization, and memory limitations.

Generative Edge AI allows for real-time computation, decision-making, and content creation right at the edge of the network. This paper examines essential architectures and frameworks for implementing generative edge AI in distributed intelligence, energy-efficient modeling, and adaptive learning. It looks at hybrid methods like cloud-edge collaboration, federated learning, and lightweight generative models like diffusion models and GANs that are made for devices with limited resources. The importance of edge inference engines, model compression, and on-device fine-tuning for lowering latency and protecting data privacy is emphasized. A single framework is suggested to bring together generative abilities for use in smart cities, healthcare monitoring, self-driving cars, and creative systems based on the Internet of Things. Response time, adaptability, and security metrics are used to measure how well the system works. In general, Generative Edge AI is shown to be a scalable, safe, and context-aware way to set up intelligent edge environments.

Generative AI and Edge Computing are converging to form Edge Generative AI, enabling real-time intelligence on devices such as robots, wearables, vehicles, smart homes, and IoT systems. This chapter explores how moving generative models from the cloud to the edge reduces latency, enhances privacy, lowers bandwidth dependency, and enables autonomy in healthcare, manufacturing, transportation, cities, agriculture, and education. It highlights key techniques like quantization, pruning, distillation, and federated learning that make on-device generation feasible, along with trends such as multimodal capabilities, 5G/6G enablement, energy-aware design, and hyper-personalization. The chapter also addresses challenges including resource constraints, thermal limits, deployment complexity, and ethical risks, offering future directions for efficient, secure, and explainable edge-native generative systems.

This case study details the design, implementation, and outcomes of "Project Athena" a pioneering initiative at a technological university in South Asia to overcome pervasive challenges in modern education through a novel Generative Edge AI ecosystem. Faced with issues of pedagogical personalization, faculty burnout, digital inequity, and data privacy. This paper chronicles the 18-month journey from concept to pilot deployment within the Faculty of Engineering. The findings reveal that this Edge AI approach led to a marked improvement in learning outcomes for academically at-risk students, a significant reduction in instructor administrative burden, and the creation of a more equitable and engaging learning environment. Crucially, the architecture inherently addressed data privacy concerns by keeping sensitive student interactions on-device. This study provides a replicable framework and discusses key lessons regarding hardware limitations, change management, and the evolving role of educators in an AI-augmented classroom.

This paper presents an IoT-driven smart agriculture framework integrating multi-layer sensing to enable real-time decision-making and long-term optimization of agricultural resources. A heterogeneous sensors monitors soil, environmental, and crop health parameters, while edge-based sensor fusion, anomaly detection, and adaptive communication enhance data reliability and energy efficiency. Real-time control optimizes irrigation, fertilization, and pest management. Field and greenhouse experiments demonstrate significant performance gains: irrigation volume was reduced by 35% in wheat fields and 28% in greenhouse tomatoes, precision NPK dosing improved fertilizer use ratio by 22% and reduced fertilizer waste by 17%, and pesticide usage decreased by 40% in tomato greenhouses. Crop yields increased by 21.4% for wheat and 21.8% for tomatoes. Compared with standalone IoT systems, the proposed framework achieved 12% higher water use efficiency and improved yield predictability. Low-power LoRa nodes operated for 148 days on a single battery, confirming scalability and sustainability.

Generative Artificial Intelligence (GenAI) has emerged as a transformative technology, capable of creating novel data, designs, and solutions across diverse domains. Simultaneously, edge computing is redefining the computational landscape by enabling low-latency, energy-efficient, and context-aware intelligence closer to data sources. The convergence of these two paradigms offers unprecedented opportunities for developing next-generation applications in healthcare, smart cities, autonomous systems, and the Internet of Things (IoT). This chapter explores the architectural foundation, design considerations, and implementation strategies for integrating generative models as the edge. It highlights the key challenges and outlines emerging frameworks and deployment strategies that balance performance, scalability, and sustainability. By architecting this integration (Generative AI and Edge AI), this

This paper introduces an innovative approach in the realm of Intelligent Edge Computing and Industrial Internet of Things (IIoT) for medical applications. An automated IIOT-based adaptive infant monitoring system is proposed that combines lightweight deep learning algorithms with constrained edge computing devices like Raspberry Pi and some onboard sensors. For real-time infant health monitoring, the system implements EfficientDet-Lite, which is an optimized version of an object detection model specifically designed to be resource efficient. The system is built around a Raspberry Pi camera which continuously monitors the position of the infant. One of the most important features of the system is the proactive alerting capability where notifications are sent through Telebot application to the parent or caretaker when the baby is in abnormal positions, that is, when he or she is out of the bed or moves beyond a predefined safe region. This feature allows them to take necessary measures quickly.

In recent times, the mental health crisis has become a critical global problem. After the COVID-19 pandemic, fear, anger, depression, and anxiety have increased. There is an urgent need for digital systems that provide accessible and effective care. Generative Artificial Intelligence (GenAI), including AI chatbots, has shown potential to offer empathetic and always-available emotional support. However, these systems perform well in high-resource languages like English and Spanish but poorly in low-resource languages such as Nepali. This chapter examines how GenAI supports mental health globally and in low-resource settings, explores case studies and comparative analyses, discusses ethical concerns and dataset limitations, and highlights opportunities for developing multilingual, human-centred systems that improve access to mental health support across linguistic communities.

Preface

INTRODUCTION

The rapid evolution of Artificial Intelligence (AI) has entered a new phase, one defined not only by intelligence, but by creativity. Generative Artificial Intelligence (GenAI) has shifted computational paradigms from analysis to synthesis, enabling machines to produce human-like text, realistic images, adaptive audio, and complex structured outputs. At the same time, the proliferation of edge devices, smartphones, wearables, embedded systems, and Internet of Things (IoT) infrastructures, has transformed how and where computation occurs. No longer confined to centralized cloud environments, intelligence is increasingly expected to operate locally, in real time, and under significant resource constraints.

This book, *Enhancing Edge Devices With Generative Intelligence: Architecture, Challenges, and Applications*, explores the convergence of these two transformative domains: generative AI and edge computing. It addresses a fundamental question shaping the next generation of intelligent systems: How can generative intelligence be effectively deployed on resource-constrained, distributed edge environments while maintaining performance, privacy, and scalability?

The chapters in this volume collectively examine the theoretical foundations, system architectures, optimization strategies, and real-world applications that define Generative Edge AI. From probabilistic modeling and lightweight architectures to federated learning and real-time inference, the book provides a comprehensive view of the challenges and opportunities inherent in bringing generative capabilities closer to the data source.

A key motivation behind this work is the growing demand for low-latency, privacy-preserving, and context-aware AI systems. Whether in healthcare, education, agriculture, finance, or smart cities, the ability to generate insights and content directly on-device is becoming increasingly critical. However, achieving this vision requires overcoming significant barriers, including limited computational resources, energy constraints, model complexity, and ethical considerations.

This book is designed for researchers, practitioners, and students in artificial intelligence, edge computing, and distributed systems. It aims to bridge the gap between theory and practice by combining foundational insights with applied case studies and emerging innovations. By doing so, it provides a roadmap for developing scalable, efficient, and responsible generative edge systems.

CHAPTER OVERVIEW

Chapter 1: Introduction to Generative AI

This chapter establishes the foundational concepts of GenAI, including probabilistic modeling, latent space representations, and core generative architectures. It also introduces the challenges of adapting these models to resource-constrained environments, highlighting issues such as computational complexity, memory limitations, and model optimization.

Chapter 2: Architecture and Frameworks of Generative Edge AI

Focusing on system-level design, this chapter explores architectures that enable generative AI at the edge. It discusses hybrid frameworks such as cloud-edge collaboration and federated learning, alongside techniques like model compression and on-device fine-tuning to achieve low-latency, privacy-preserving intelligence.

Chapter 3: Bringing Generative AI to Edge Devices: Techniques, Challenges and Applications

This chapter provides a comprehensive survey of deployment strategies for generative models on edge devices. It examines optimization methods such as quantization, compression, and distillation, while also addressing trade-offs between accuracy and efficiency across application domains like healthcare and IoT.

Chapter 4: Lightweight Architecture and Algorithms for Generative Edge AI

Here, the focus shifts to efficient model design. The chapter presents lightweight architectures and algorithmic strategies, including knowledge distillation, low-rank adaptation, and quantization, that enable high-performance generative models to operate within strict resource limits.

Chapter 5: Emerging Trends and Real-Life Applications of Edge Generative AI

This chapter explores the latest trends shaping the field, including multimodal AI, 5G/6G integration, and hyper-personalization. It highlights practical applications across industries such as healthcare, manufacturing, agriculture, and education, while addressing technical and ethical challenges.

Chapter 6: A Case Study in Generative Edge AI in Education and Learning

Through a detailed case study, this chapter demonstrates how Generative Edge AI can transform educational systems. It presents a real-world implementation that improves learning outcomes, reduces administrative workload, and enhances data privacy through on-device processing.

Chapter 7: A Multi-Layer IoT Framework for Smart Agriculture

This chapter introduces an IoT-based framework for precision agriculture, integrating edge intelligence for real-time decision-making. It showcases measurable improvements in resource efficiency, crop yield, and sustainability through sensor fusion and adaptive control systems.

Chapter 8: Architecting the Insecure Future: Integrating Generative AI and Edge AI

Addressing both opportunities and risks, this chapter examines the integration of GenAI with edge computing for next-generation applications. It discusses architectural strategies, scalability considerations, and the balance between performance, sustainability, and security.

Chapter 9: Adaptive Feedback-Bound Generative Architecture (AFGA)

This chapter presents a novel framework for managing generative processes on edge devices. By incorporating real-time hardware feedback, AFGA dynamically adjusts model behavior to maintain efficiency and coherence under changing physical constraints.

Chapter 10: Distributed Compliance Intelligence for Financial Systems

Focusing on financial applications, this chapter explores edge AI architectures for real-time compliance monitoring. It demonstrates how distributed intelligence can improve efficiency, reduce costs, and ensure data privacy while meeting regulatory requirements.

Chapter 11: TinyML-Enabled Edge Health Monitoring Systems

This chapter introduces a lightweight, real-time health monitoring system using TinyML and edge devices. It highlights how efficient deep learning models can enable proactive healthcare solutions, particularly in resource-constrained settings.

Chapter 12: Generative AI for Mental Well-being

Exploring the social impact of GenAI, this chapter examines its role in mental health support. It emphasizes challenges in multilingual and low-resource language contexts, while proposing approaches for more inclusive and ethical AI systems.

Chapter 13: Generative Edge AI in Healthcare and Management

The final chapter presents case studies demonstrating the practical implementation of Generative Edge AI in healthcare. It highlights improvements in diagnostics, operational efficiency, and patient care, while addressing challenges such as scalability and regulatory compliance.

CONCLUSION

Together, these chapters provide a holistic exploration of Generative Edge AI, its foundations, innovations, and transformative potential. The book ultimately underscores a central vision: a future where intelligent systems are not only powerful, but also accessible, efficient, and deeply integrated into the fabric of everyday life.

Chapter 1
Introduction to Generative AI

Apoorav Sharma
http://orcid.org/0009-0002-9966-7691
Lovely Professional University, India

Lovleen Marwaha
Lovely Professional University, India

ABSTRACT

Generative Artificial Intelligence (Generative AI) is a paradigm shift in computational intelligence - switching the role of machines in computational intelligence to creative synthesis. The Generative systems based on the underlying probability distributions of data can generate realistic and context-ually consistent output across modalities, including text, image, audio, and structured data, by learning the underlying probability distributions of the data. This chapter has given an in-depth introduction to the theoretical, architectural, and operational backgrounds of generative AI, and then proceeded to discuss how generative AI has been adapted to resource-constrained and distributed systems. It has talked about probabilistic modelling and latent space representation and the development of generative models and then it has touched on the computational issues like the complexity of training, quantization, and memory limitations.

1. INTRODUCTION TO GENERATIVE INTELLIGENCE

Artificial Intelligence (AI) has been changing incredibly throughout the last decades - the systems that passively analyse or predict have transformed to those that can produce something completely new and unknown. This creative potential

DOI: 10.4018/979-8-3373-7340-9.ch001

is more than a technical innovation: it is a change of paradigm according to which machines can benefit human labor and creativity. This transformative domain, which is what we will call Generative Intelligence in this chapter, is the field of AI that deals with modelling data distributions and sampling off of them to generate novel, coherent and contextually meaningful artefacts, including text, images, audio, structured data or mixtures of those (Siti-Nabiha & Jurnali, 2020). The subsequent subsections follow the motivation of the shift, the conceptual change of predictive to generative modelling, significant historical milestones, and explain why generative AI is especially important to edge and embedded systems.

1.1 Motivation and Evolution of AI Paradigms

The initial stages of AI studies and applications were discriminative or predictive. They had systems that were meant to classify images, identify objects, discern speech, give predictions of the next action, or suggest things that the goal is to find a mapping between inputs and labels or probabilities. These features were incredibly helpful in numerous areas: computer vision, medical diagnostics, recommendation system, autonomous systems, and others. But, with increased need to produce richer and more flexible and creative products - whether by creating realistic images with text descriptions, writing in ways akin to a person, designing prototype products, or simulating plausible synthetic data - it became evident that discriminative models were inadequate. The generative intelligence motivation is based on a number of converging requirements (Shwedeh & Alzoubi, 2024). To begin with, creative and design-oriented assignments can demand the ability to create material, not to categorise or to choose among the existing variants. Workers in the field of art, design, writing and engineering often work within a domain of newness and discovery; generative models will help or speed up the creative process by providing candidate outputs depending on learned data distributions. Second, where there is little data available (e.g. in areas with privacy considerations such as medical imaging, sensor data, specialised science), there is not enough labelled data to train good discriminative models, yet generative models may come to the rescue by producing real but anonymized or augmented examples. Third, with AI increasingly infiltrating more areas, there is an increasing need to have systems that are not only interpretive but also imaginative in nature. These systems should propose alternatives, simulate 'what-if' variants, or create new designs under constraints. It is the capabilities of generative intelligence that facilitate this (COCCIA, 2025). Therefore, the history of generative AI indicates a natural expansion of AI aspirations: beyond interpretation and prediction of observed data, to the creation of new data - to enhance human imagination, to simulate, and AI applications in other areas of design, hypothesis generation, and creative synthesis.

The motivation for GenAI arises from several needs:

- Creative tasks requiring content generation (e.g., design, writing)
- Data scarcity in domains such as healthcare
- Need for simulation and "what-if" scenario generation

1.2 From Predictive to Generative Models: A Paradigm Shift

The very essence of this evolution consists of a change of concept of what an AI model should learn. In predictive (or discriminative) modeling, the goal is to learn a conditional version of mapping: on input x, predict label or output y. The dataset of (x,y) pairs is used to train the model such that it minimises prediction error or maximises classification accuracy. In contrast, generative modelling seeks to obtain an approximation of the underlying probability distribution p(x) or joint distribution p(x,y). When this distribution (or a close approximation of the same) has been learned, the model can sample new data points in it - generate new points that plausibly belong to the original data distribution. This transition in conditional mapping to the distribution learning opens the possibility to produce instead of to predict. It is not a technical point but it alters the role of the model completely (Radanliev, 2025). Rather than a passive viewer or recipient of the world or a classifier of it, a generative model is an active producer: able to generate new instances that have the same statistical and structural characteristics of the training data, but are not just copies. It allows the generation of creative content, simulating, designing and generating hypotheses. Furthermore, through the process of identifying latent structure and correlations in the data distribution, generative models tend to generate meaningful features, dependencies, or abstractions - providing more information on what the data actually is. Effectually, generative modeling broadens the perspective of AI as not a tool of understanding but a tool of creation that fuses analysis, inferences, and synthesis. The generative renaissance that we currently experience in AI research and application is based on this paradigm shift.

1.3 Historical Milestones: From GANs to Diffusion and Foundation Models

Modern generative AI has travelled through a number of significant breakthroughs on its way to this point. The conceptual underpinnings of data distribution and latent structure representation were already developed in earlier machine learning work, including probabilistic graphical models and simple autoencoders. Nevertheless, in the mid-2010s generative models became capable of producing realistic results and have a wide range of applicability. One of the key achievements was the development of Generative Adversarial Network (GAN). The GANs contain two neural networks: a generator, which is meant to generate the synthetic data that are the same as the real data, and a discriminator, the task of which is to classify the real and the fake data (Anstine & Isayev, 2023). This adversarial process is in such a way that the generator continuously advances to the point where its outputs are very realistic. GANs were especially successful in image synthesis where they obtained photorealistic outputs and were demonstrated to have applications in art, image editing, and data augmentation. Simultaneously, Variational Autoencoders (VAEs) also provided an alternative generative model that relied on probabilistic latent variables and inference. VAEs represent the input data (via their encoding) into a latent distribution, and sample the latent distribution to generate the input data, which can be smoothing interpolated and manipulated under controlled conditions via the latent factors in the latent distribution. VAE-generated samples did not have the fidelity of GANs, but VAEs provided a rigorous probability-theoretic model and interpretability in latent space which has been useful in various applications including disentangled representation learning and controlled generation (Miikkulainen, 2024). Later, generative modeling was extended to sequential data (e.g. text, audio) and to domains with exact-likelihood modeling by the use of autoregressive models and normalizing flows respectively. The latest and most radically changing stage of generative AI came with the introduction of large-scale models that utilise attention-based architectures, especially Transformers. Models trained on large-scale quantities of text and multimodal data - often including billions or trillions of tokens, images or other data points - were found to be very versatile. Foundation models enable zero- or few-shot generation across various tasks, from writing code to synthesizing images, allowing for broad cross-modal transfer (Sankaran & Holmes, 2023). Their generation ability is not limited in one domain, and it can be generated cross-modally and transferred widely. Diffusion-based generative models are more recently becoming a strong and reliable substitute to GANs and VAEs. Diffusion models have created diverse and more stable high-quality image and audio synthesis by applying a data generation process as a progressive denoising autoencoder on random noise. The recent advances of diffusion methods, as well as model foundations built on transformers, are the newest developments of generative AI. These subsequent generations, GANs and VAEs, autoregressive and flow-based models, and foundation and diffusion models are all stepping in the direction of greater expressivity, fidelity and flexibility (Figure1). They underline the development of a generative intelligence as a specific field of research to the core of the contemporary AI. Recent advances (2023–2025) have focused on making GenAI deployable beyond cloud environments. Techniques such as parameter-efficient fine-tuning (PEFT), edge-optimized transformers, and TinyML-based generative models have enabled execution on resource-constrained devices. Emerging models such as TinyLLaMA, MobileDiffusion, and on-device LLMs demonstrate that generative capabilities can now operate efficiently on smartphones and embedded systems.

Figure 1. Historical progression from traditional AI to generative intelligence, showing the evolution from symbolic reasoning and discriminative models to deep generative and foundation model architectures.

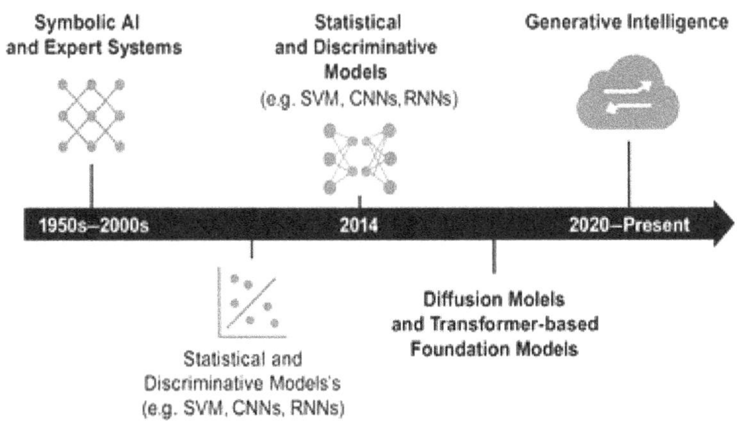

1.4 Why Generative AI Matters for Edge and Embedded Systems

The importance of generative AI is also increased when it is regarded in the environment of edge and embedded systems. Historically, generative models, particularly the state-of-the-art ones, have been trained and deployed in environments with the high computational, memory, and storage resources (e.g. data centres, cloud servers) because they are highly demanding. Nevertheless, placing generative intelligence deeper into the periphery can create novel opportunities and strong incentives, by placing such computing on small, mobile gadgets like smartphones, tiny controllers embedded in IoT devices, autonomous drones, or wearable computer sensors (Reddy, 2024). To begin with, inference on a local basis provides the possibility of real-time creation and responsiveness, without depending on network connectivity or cloud latency. To deliver smooth context-aware and low-latency experiences to applications such as augmented reality (AR), human-maoundation modelschine interaction, adaptive user interfaces, robotics and on-device content generation, edge-based generative models can be used. Second, the issue of privacy and ownership of the data gains greater significance in the areas of healthcare, personal data processing, or sensitive sensor implementations. Placing generative models on-device will mean that raw data do not have to be sent off-device; the synthetic data or outputs can be created on-device, and privacy can be maintained, at the same time, allowing creative or analytical processes to proceed (Akram et al., 2025). Third, edge deployment is desirable in many deployment cases due to bandwidth and connectivity constraints in most deployment scenarios remote sensors, rural, intermittent networks, etc. Edge based intelligence allows offline functionality and enhances stability and availability. Fourth, when resources are limited (or applications are domain-specific), generative models can be trained to fit resource constraints (through model compression, quantization, pruning, or distillation) to fit the resource constraints of embedded systems: limited compute, memory, energy, and storage. This has the potential to democratize the generation capabilities, so that they can run on low cost low power devices, not just high end servers. Furthermore, the autonomous adaptation and personalization is enabled by generative intelligence on the edge devices. Edge systems are able to produce context-sensitive content specific to a single user or environment, e.g. a personalised user interface, dynamic interactions, or future machine learning pipeline data augmentation. This creates a transition towards centralised and one-size-fits-all AI services to distributed, user-centric and context-aware intelligence (Alzu'bi et al., 2025). To conclude, the introduction of generative AI to edge and embedded systems is no longer a question of technical suitability, but it is a strategic enabling factor. It opens up the scope of AI-generated creativity, simulation, and augmentation to daily objects and places and opens up new uses in IoT, robotics, mobile computing, and so on. These reasons make generative intelligence have a specific future in the distributed, efficient, and user-centric AI systems.

2. THEORETICAL FOUNDATIONS OF GENERATIVE AI

Generative AI has its scientific basis upon the notion that the data, be it images, text, or signals, are produced based on underlying probabilistic processes. A generative model attempts to learn such processes and learns the distribution of data on their actual manifold space instead of just learning how to transform inputs into outputs (Ardi, 2025). The following section presents the theoretical concepts of the modern generative systems: probabilistic modelling, latent representation, architectural paradigms, and the mathematical principles of their convergence and optimization. Cumulatively these ideas constitute the scholarly theoretical framework which allows AI systems to generate, as opposed to merely categorising.

2.1 Probabilistic Modeling and the Principle of Generation

At its foundation, generative modeling is an exercise in probabilistic inference. Given a dataset of observations $X = \{x1, x2, \ldots\ldots, xn\}$ the objective is to model the probability distribution $p(x)$that best describes the data. Once this distribution or a tractable approximation is known, new samples $x' \sim p(x)$ can be generated that resemble real data. This contrasts with discriminative models, which estimate the conditional probability $p(y \mid x)$ mapping inputs to labels (Chen, 2025).

A simple conceptual example is Gaussian modeling, where the distribution of continuous data can be represented by a mean vector and covariance matrix. However, real-world data are often high-dimensional, multi-modal, and non-Gaussian, making direct modeling of $p(x)$ intractable. Deep generative models address this by introducing latent variables z that capture unobserved factors influencing the data. The generative process is typically expressed as:

$$z \sim p(z),\ x \sim p(x|z)$$

Where $p(z)$ is a prior (often Gaussian), and $p(x|z)$defines how latent variables generate data in the observation space.

Learning a generative model therefore involves approximating the marginal likelihood:

$$p(x) = \int p(x|z)\, p(z) dz$$

This integral is usually intractable in closed form, motivating approximate inference techniques such as variational methods and adversarial training.

From a probabilistic perspective, generative models can be grouped into *explicit density models* which directly estimate $p(x)$ and *implicit models* which define a generative process without explicit density evaluation. This distinction gives rise to families like Variational Autoencoders (explicit) and Generative Adversarial Networks (implicit). The probabilistic modeling framework thus provides a unifying foundation upon which all generative systems are built (Figure 2).

Figure 2. Schematic representation of probabilistic generative modeling. The model learns the data distribution p(x)p(x)p(x) by introducing latent variables z p(z)z \sim p(z)z p(z), which are mapped to observable data through a conditional distribution p(x z)p(x|z)p(x z). The learning process involves approximating the intractable marginal likelihood p(x)=∫p(x z)p(z)dzp(x) = \int p(x|z)p(z)dzp(x)=∫p(x z)p(z)dz, forming the basis of deep generative architectures such as VAEs and diffusion models.

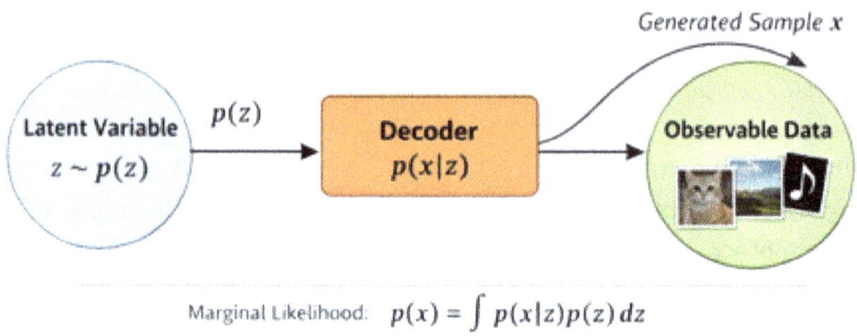

2.2 Latent Space Representations and Manifold Learning

A defining feature of generative models is their use of *latent spaces*—compact, often continuous representations that encode the essential structure of data. The latent space is an abstract manifold Z, typically of lower dimensionality than the data space X, where each point $z \in Z$ corresponds to a potential data instance through the generative mapping $x = G(z)$. Learning such mappings allows generative models to capture intricate dependencies in high-dimensional data while enabling controlled generation and interpolation (Patel, 2025).

The manifold learning principle states that natural data, e.g. images or speech, are close to lower dimensional manifold embedded in the high-dimensional space. Generative models are approximations to this manifold, and they are trained to learn how to map simple priors (e.g. isotropic Gaussian noise) to complex data distributions. The implications of this mapping are tremendous: motion in the latent space in a certain direction is frequently a change in the generated output that can be interpreted (e.g., rotation of a given object, change of facial expression, or change of tone in a sentence). Latent representations also serve as a basis for *disentangled learning*, where different dimensions of the latent vector correspond to independent semantic factors. Achieving such disentanglement remains a research challenge, but it has practical value for controllable and interpretable generation.

Mathematically, the encoder $E:X \rightarrow Z$ and $G:Z \rightarrow X$ together form a invertible mapping between observed and latent spaces. Optimization encourages these mappings to preserve information and structure, often guided by a reconstruction loss (e.g. $\|x - G(E(x))\|2$)and a regularization term that enforces statistical properties on the latent distribution. Through such mechanisms, manifold learning enables generative models to represent and recreate the complexity of real-world data efficiently.

2.3 Core Generative Architectures: VAE, GAN, Flow-based, and Diffusion Models

Modern generative AI architectures differ in how they approximate and sample from data distributions. Four principal families have shaped the field:

(a) Variational Autoencoders (VAEs)

VAEs learn compressed latent representations and generate data through probabilistic decoding.

VAEs use variational inference to approximate the intractable posterior $p(z/x)$ .The training objective maximizes the *evidence lower bound* (ELBO):

$$\mathcal{L}_{VAE} = \mathbb{E}_{q\phi(z|x)}\left[\log p_\theta(x|z)\right] - D_{KL}\left(q_\phi(z|x)\|p(z)\right)$$

Where $\{KL\}$ denotes the Kullback–Leibler divergence. The first term ensures good reconstruction quality, while the second regularizes the latent space to follow the prior. VAEs provide continuous latent representations and stable training, though early versions produced somewhat blurred images due to assumptions about Gaussian posteriors (Kumar, 2025).

(b) Generative Adversarial Networks (GANs)

GANs use a generator–discriminator game to produce realistic outputs. GANs introduced an adversarial training scheme involving two networks: a *generator* G that produces synthetic data and a *discriminator* D that distinguishes between real and fake samples. The objective is a minimax game:

$$minGmaxDV(D, G) = \mathbb{E}_{x\sim pdata}[logD(x)] + \mathbb{E}_{z\sim pz}[\log(1 - D(G(z)))]$$

GANs achieve high-quality, sharp, and realistic outputs, particularly in image domains. However, they are notoriously difficult to train due to issues like mode collapse and unstable convergence, prompting many variants (WGAN, StyleGAN, CycleGAN).

(c) Flow-based Models

These models use invertible transformations for exact likelihood estimation. Normalizing Flow models provide exact likelihood estimation by learning invertible transformations between latent and data spaces. Given an invertible mapping $x = f(z)x$, the density of data can be computed via the change-of-variables formula:

$$\log px(x) = \log pz(z) - \log\left|det\frac{\partial f}{\partial z}\right|$$

where $\partial f(z)$ is the Jacobian of the transformation. Flows combine interpretability, exact likelihood computation, and efficient sampling, but can be computationally heavy due to the invertibility constraint.

(d) Diffusion Models

Diffusion models generate data by reversing a gradual noise process. The latest generation of generative models are diffusion-based. They are inspired by non-equilibrium thermodynamics and are taught to reverse a gradual noising process which converts data into pure noise. Training is performed based on learning a denoising function $\epsilon_\theta(x_t, t)$ which recovers cleaner samples of noisy ones. This process, where noise is reversed to data and vice versa, is then repeated and this is the sampling. Diffusion models are more stable to train and fidelity and diversity are higher than those of GANs (Figure 3). Notable examples are Denoising Diffusion Probabilistic Models (DDPMs), Stable Diffusion and Imagen.In this category, the architectures comprise the basic design space of generative systems, each having its own trade-off to sample quality, interpretability, and computational efficiency (Gupta et al., 2025).

Figure 3. Comparative schematic of major generative model architectures. Variational Autoencoders (VAEs) use encoder–decoder probabilistic mappings; Generative Adversarial Networks (GANs) employ adversarial training between generator and discriminator; Flow-based models utilize invertible transformations for exact likelihood estimation; Diffusion models generate data through iterative denoising of stochastic noise. The figure highlights differences in training objectives, sampling mechanisms, and probabilistic formulation.

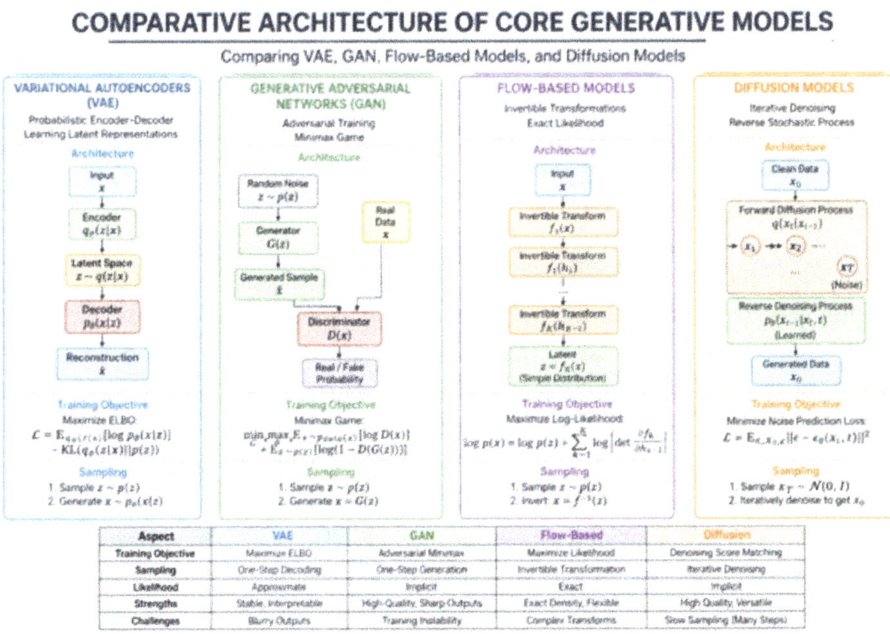

2.4 Reinforcement and Self-Supervised Learning in Generative Systems

Generative modelling is becoming more flexible and adaptive by incorporating the concepts of reinforcement learning (RL) and self-supervised learning (SSL). In reinforcement learning, the learner is trying to maximize a signal that is a reward by being exposed to an environment. This idea can be applied to generative systems by reinforcement learning with human feedback (RLHF) where human assessment allows qualitative feedback that is converted into a reward model. This has helped to make big language models (e.g. GPT series) more human-friendly, by attempting to make them produce syntactically correct but contextually and socially suitable outputs (Liu et al., 2021). In self-supervised learning, conversely, models are able to learn on unlabeled data by building auxiliary prediction tasks (e.g. predict missing words, image patches or future frames). Contemporary generative pretraining is based on this paradigm. Through learning on large scale raw data, generative systems can make broad representations that can subsequently be refined on downstream generative or discriminative tasks. Some such instances are masked language modelling (as in BERT) and next-token prediction (as in GPT). Reinforcement and self-supervised learning are both part of the process of developing generative AI into a more autonomous and adaptable one. They decrease reliance on categorized information, enhance generalization, and enable correspondence of created content and desired human or task-specific standards (Gui et al., 2024).

2.5 Mathematical Underpinnings: Loss Functions, Optimization, and Convergence

Generative model training consists of optimization functions with a combination of fidelity, diversity, and stability. Depending on the architecture, the loss landscape usually includes likelihood estimation, reconstruction accuracy and regularization. Optimization is aimed at maximising ELBO in VAEs through stochastic gradient descent, and the tradeoff between the reconstruction and KL terms. In GANs, the discriminator and the generator are involved in a minimax optimization problem, where there is a need to balance the gradient of the generator and the discriminator to prevent divergence (Venkata Pavan Saish et al., 2025). The models of diffusion reduce a noise-prediction loss, which is a typical simple mean squared error between predicted and true noise at each timestep. It depends on the stability of optimization. Gradient penalty in Wasserstein GANs, spectral normalization, and adaptive optimizers (including Adam, RMSprop) are some of the techniques that have been established to stabilize training. The further control of overfitting is through regularization approaches such as dropout and weight decay. Convergence analysis is a significant theoretical issue in generative modelling. Whereas convex optimization guarantees convergence in the case of simpler architectures, deep generative models have a highly non-convex loss surface with multiple equilibria. The convergence is empirically monitored by using the Frechet Inception Distance (FID), Inception Score (IS), and estimates of the log-likelihood.

3. GENERATIVE MODEL ARCHITECTURES AND TAXONOMY

Generative Artificial Intelligence (Generative AI) is a wide field of architectures associated by their mathematical definition, training goal, and synthesis mechanism. Although the overall aim of generative models is to model data distributions, generative models vary significantly in their estimation or approximation of the data distributions (Huang, 2025). In this section, I give a hierarchical taxonomy of generative models, starting with the classification of the models by likelihood estimation, then cross-domain and emerging hybrid models using transformers. The awareness of these types is critical to placing the modern generative technologies in a logical theoretical and practical context. Intuitively, generative models can be thought of as "learning to imagine" data, similar to how humans can visualize new scenarios based on past experiences.

3.1 Classification of Generative Models

Generative models may be systematically divided based on their representation and learning of probability distributions. The broadest two categories are the likelihood-based models and implicit models, and these are further broken down into autoregressive systems, energy-based systems and score-based systems.

(a) Likelihood-Based vs. Implicit Models

Likelihood-based models directly define or approximate the probability density *p_\θ(x)* of the data under the model parameters θ\thetaθ. They are trained by maximizing the log-likelihood of the observed data:

\max{\θ}\∑∧ {n}\logp_{\θ}(xi)

Such models offer interpretability and tractable evaluation of data likelihoods, which is crucial in applications like anomaly detection, compression, or scientific data modeling. Variational Autoencoders (VAEs), Normalizing Flows, and Diffusion Models fall within this category, differing mainly in their approach to tractable likelihood estimation and sampling (Strobel et al., 2024).

In contrast, the implicit models do not provide a clear definition of p(x). Rather, they offer a sampling procedure, which implicitly characterises a data distribution. The best known is the Generative Adversarial Network (GAN) that trains a generator G(z) to learn to map samples of an underlying distribution p(z) (e.g. Gaussian noise) to synthetic data. Because the p(x) is not calculable directly, training is determined by an adversarial loss or other statistical divergences that are used to match the generated and real data distributions. Likelihood-based models are more concerned with mathematical tractability and interpretability and implicit models with sample quality and visual or perceptual realism. The two hinges on the needs of the application, e.g. interpolability in scientific modelling is better served by likelihood-based systems, and creative applications such as image synthesis tend to be better served by implicit ones

(b) Autoregressive, Energy-based, and Score-based Systems

Beyond the likelihood dichotomy, generative models can also be grouped by their structural and functional principles:

1. Autoregressive Models

Autoregressive systems factorize the joint probability distribution into a product of conditional probabilities:

$$p(x) = \prod_{i=1}^{n} p(\frac{x_i}{x_{<i}})$$

This break down enables sequential creation of information - each component is predicted by the previous ones. Such examples are Pixel CNN (images), WaveNet (audio) and GPT (text). Auto regression models are very effective in sequence modelling and ensure accurate likelihood calculations but can be very latency intensive (inference) since they produce tokens one after another (Vadhil et al., 2024).

2. Energy-Based Models (EBMs)

EBMs define an unnormalized probability distribution through an energy function Eθ(x)E_\theta(x)Eθ(x), where low-energy states correspond to likely data configurations:

$$p\theta(x) = \frac{\exp\left(-E_\theta(x)\right)}{Z(\theta)}$$

Where $E_\theta(x)$is the energy function. These models are not constrained to multimodal distributions and are flexible to capture them but need approximate sampling procedures (e.g. contrastive divergence or Markov Chain Monte Carlo). Recent innovations combine EBMs with deep neural networks and can use them to perform visual and physical simulation problems.

3. Score-Based Models

Score-based generative models (SGMs) learn the gradient of the log-probability density function, known as the *score function*:

$$s_\theta(x) = \nabla_x log\ p_\theta(x)$$

These models are able to sample complex distributions by learning to estimate this score using stochastic differential equation. A particularly prominent subclass is the diffusion models, in which the denoising score matching is in the spotlight. SGMs integrate energy-based models and diffusion models based upon a rigorous mathematically formulated probabilistic model, which has state-of-the-art generative performance in image, audio, and multimodal synthesis (Ardi, 2025). This taxonomy emphasizes the tremendous diversity of generative architectures, which focus on varying elements of the trade-off between likelihood tractability, sample fidelity and computational efficiency.

3.2 Transformer-Based Generative Systems (e.g., GPT, LLaMA, Mistral)

Transformer architecture by Vaswani et al. (2017) has proven to be the foundation of the current generative AI because it is scalable, expressive, and can learn long-range relationships through self-attention. Transformers work with data as a sequence of tokens and calculate relationships between all elements simultaneously an innovation that beat the sequential shortcomings of recurrent neural networks (RNNs) and long short-term memory (LSTM) layouts. Transformer-based language models, including GPT (Generative Pretrained Transformer), LLaMA (Large Language Model Meta AI) and Mistral, have been shown to produce impressive generative fluency. They use the principle of autoregression and predict the next token based on the context it has, but have the advantage of deep, multi-head attention, which efficiently models global dependencies (Corchado et al., 2023). They are trained on massive textual data with self-supervised tasks such as next-token prediction, and then fine-tuned through reinforcement learning on human feedback (RLHF) to improve the delivery of results that meet human preferences. Transformer-based generative systems are generalised by virtue of the nature of their foundation models the same architecture, with only a few adjustments, can be scaled to a variety of modalities, such as image generation, audio generation, video generation, and code generation. Vision Transformers (ViTs) and Vision-Language Transformers (e.g., CLIP, Flamingo) have shown that the transformer paradigm is no longer restricted to text and can be applicable to any form of data in general. The current versions: Mistral 7B, GPT-4 and Claude 3 have emergent capabilities, including reasoning, abstraction and cross-domain generalization, indicating that the transformer architecture, with effective scaling and training, can be similar to general-purpose intelligence. These systems provide the basis of multimodal generative systems, and they are the state of art in computational creativity. Recent advancements in transformer-based models, such as GPT-4, Claude 3, and Mistral 7B, demonstrate improved reasoning, efficiency, and multimodal capabilities, reflecting the rapid evolution of large-scale generative systems.

3.3 Cross-Domain Generative Models (Vision–Language, Audio–Text, etc.)

Although early generative models were limited to one modality, more recent advancements have seen the development of cross-domain and multimodal generative models, which combine information in text, image, audio and video. These models represent one important lesson: real-world data are always multimodal, and to reason about or produce complex phenomena, they may be necessary to think in different modalities. This integration is awarded by Vision-Language Models (VLMs). DALLE, Imagen and Stable Diffusion are systems that use language embeddings to match language descriptions with high-resolution images in visual latent spaces. Likewise, CLIP (Contrastive Language-Image Pretraining) trains a combined embedding space to transfer across visual and language mode without using any training data, and serves as the core of prompt-based image generation pipelines (Aishwarya et al., 2024). Audio-Text Models This concept can be generalized to the auditory signaling, e.g., Whisper and AudioLM, making it possible to perform transcription, sound synthesis, and music generation. At the same time, Video-Text Models, such as Sora and Make-A-Video have shown temporally consistent video generation conditioned on either textual or audio inputs. These cross-domain systems use multimodal encoders and decoders which are used to bring together latent representations across the modalities. The common semantic structure is learned by the model, such as the meaning of a “dog barking” in the text, image and sound spaces is always the same. Training methods are based on massive paired samples (e.g., image-caption or video-audio samples), and contrastive or reconstruction targets which cause the models to be aligned. The development of multimodal generative systems is a significant step toward the holistic AI, which can sense, think, and generate in any type of data. The ability resembles that of human cognition which is an excellently coordinated combination of information received in multiple sensory pathways.

3.4 Emerging Trends: Diffusion Transformers, Multi-modal Latent Spaces

With generative modeling as a field of research, the direction of research in 2024-2025 has narrowed to focus on hybrid architectures benefiting the strengths of other paradigms. Diffusion Transformer and Multi-modal Latent Space Models are two directions that promise to be particularly fruitful. Diffusion Transformers are a combination of the noise-based generation process of diffusion models and the scalability and contextual power of transformers. These systems utilise the transformer architecture as the denoising network instead of the conventional U-Net. The design enables worldwide focus in lieu of noisy and feature maps, enhancing long-range focus and probabilitability. Examples of such a synthesis include models such as PixArt-a and DiT (Diffusion Transformer), which are able to produce images and videos with a higher quality but remain efficient using parallelism (Hadi et al., 2024). Multi-modal Latent Space Models further seek to integrate in-modal generative procedures so that they learn joint latent space representations that are semantically and structurally correlated among text, vision and audio. Instead of having a model that works with one or more modalities, there is a single latent space that can be thought of as the centre where modalities are transformed (i.e., text - image, or image - audio, or text - video). Such unification makes possible multimodal reasoning, transfer learning as well as flexible cross-modal generation. The general direction is towards foundation-level generative systems, where several architectures, purposes and modalities can be brought together within a single scalable framework. These new hybrid systems are breaking the lines between past generations of generative models, and towards a general-purpose creative intelligence that can run effectively across platforms - such as in constrained situations like the edge (Figure 4). Recent studies have highlighted the emergence of diffusion transformers (DiT) and multimodal foundation models that integrate vision, language, and audio processing within a unified architecture, significantly improving scalability and generalization.

Figure 4. Taxonomy and architectural classification of core generative models, showing relationships among likelihood-based, implicit, transformer-based, and cross-domain generative systems.

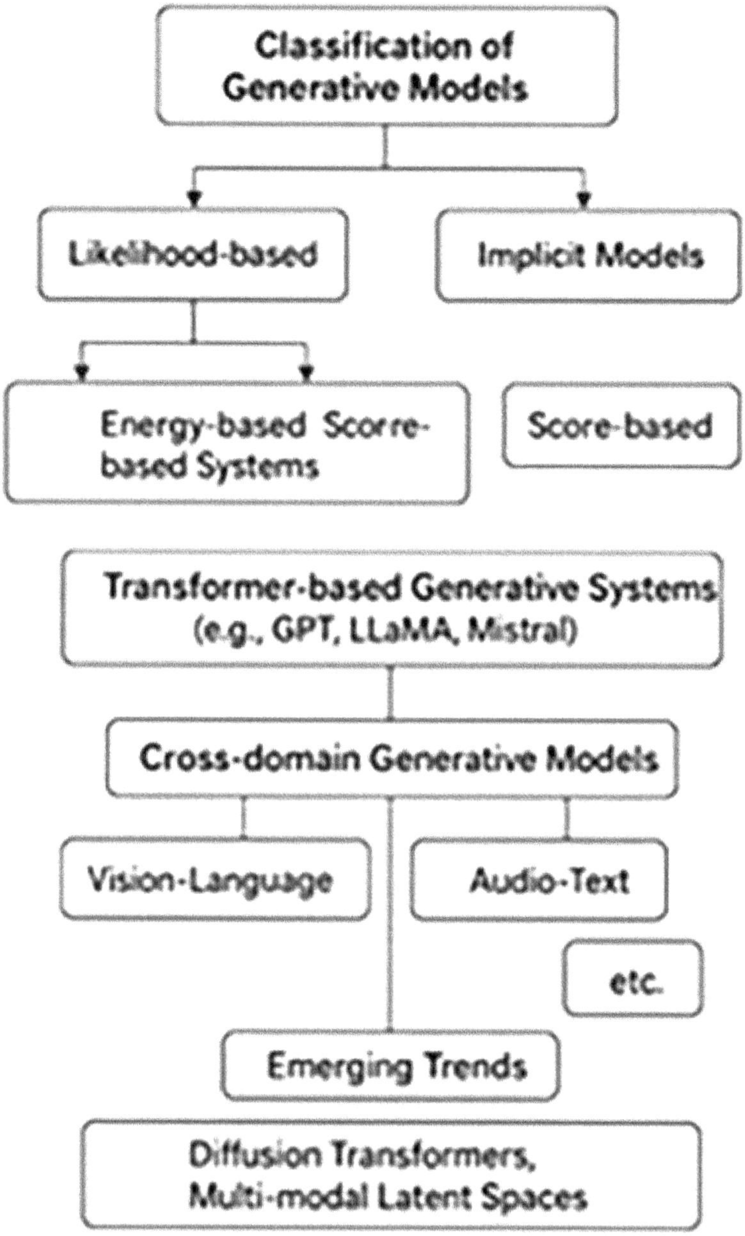

4. COMPUTATIONAL AND RESOURCE CHALLENGES

Although modern generative models are impressive in terms of their generative power, they are expensive and require a large amount of resources. The sheer increase in the scale of models, scale of data, and an increase in the complexity of the architecture has resulted in unparalleled demands in terms of compute power, memory and bandwidth. It poses substantial challenges to the democratisation and in-device deployment of resources, especially in the edge computing setup with limited hardware costs and energy resources. The following section discusses computation complexity of generative AI, training complexity, model compression techniques, memory and bandwidth requirement, performance trade-offs, and benchmarking framework of analysing generative efficiency. All these problems constitute the technical edge to viable, scalable and sustainable generative intelligence (Chowdhury et al., 2025).

As Generative Artificial Intelligence (GenAI) systems extend from centralized cloud infrastructures to distributed edge environments, scalability becomes a significant challenge affecting system performance and coordination. Unlike homogeneous cloud systems, edge ecosystems consist of heterogeneous devices with varying computational capabilities, memory constraints, and energy limitations. This diversity complicates model deployment, synchronization, and efficient resource utilization across nodes. Additionally, distributed training approaches such as federated learning introduce communication overhead, latency, and inconsistencies in model updates due to non-uniform data distributions. Ensuring scalable GenAI deployment therefore requires adaptive architectures, efficient model partitioning, and robust coordination mechanisms that can balance performance with resource constraints across large-scale, decentralized networks.

4.1 Training Complexity and Compute Requirements

Generating any modern-day generative model, especially a large-type foundation model like GPT-4, DALLE 3, and Stable Diffusion XL, is astonishing to train according to the level of required computational resources. The cost of generative training depends on a number of factors which are interrelated: model size, data diversity, optimization algorithms, and training goals. The computational cost of training is approximately proportional to both the number of model parameters and data tokens processed, and varies based on the frequency of gradient updates, the efficiency of parallelization, and stability in convergence. The modern state-of-the-art generative models can have tens and dozens of billions of parameters, and require petaflop-scale compute clusters (Ciubotaru, 2025). As an example, it may take millions of GH of energy and tejawatts to train a multi-billion-parameter transformer or diffusion model. One more reason why the compute needs are high is the training goal. Adversarial learning (in GANs) involves the two-network optimization through the use of iterative steps; variational learning (in VAEs) uses Monte Carlo sampling; and diffusion training (in hundreds and thousands of timesteps) requires a single forward and backward step through the noising and denoising process.

In order to reduce calculational complexity, scientists use parallelization methods like data parallelism, model parallelism, and pipeline parallelism which can be performed on a distributed GPU or TPU cluster. Training with mixed-precision (e.g. FP16 or bfloat16 arithmetic) and sharding optimizers (as employed in the DeepSpeed and ZeRO frameworks) are even higher scalable and memory efficient. However, training intensity is also a serious constraint. The difficulty is increased with the environmental and economic costs in mind, which encourages the creation of practical training paradigms (e.g. sparse models, low-rank adaptation, continual and federated training) that strive to achieve the balance between performance and sustainability.

4.2 Model Compression, Quantization, and Distillation Techniques

Another significant issue with large generative models is that deploying them after being trained is another challenge due to inference efficiency. Real-time or edge deployment is normally not feasible with full-scale foundation models. As a result, model compression, quantization and knowledge distillation have become important measures in minimizing computational and memory overhead whilst maintaining performance fidelity. The goal of model compression is to make a model size smaller without much loss in accuracy. These common methods are pruning which eliminates unnecessary weights or neurons, according to magnitude or significance, and the low-rank factorization which breaks down large weight matrices into smaller and efficient representations (Dantas et al., 2024). The compression ratios that can be obtained through pruning include 50-90% based on model redundancy and sensitivity. Quantization also compromises the numerical accuracy of parameters and activations, and replaces 32-bit floating-point values with values encoded in smaller representations (e.g. 8-bit integer or 4-bit floating-point). Quantized models are less memory-intensive and run faster on dedicated hardware such as GPUs, NPUs or edge accelerators. Nevertheless, naive quantization can affect the quality of generative, particularly in the fine-grained synthesis tasks, e.g. image or audio generation. These effects are alleviated with the Quantization-aware training (QAT) and post training quantization (PTQ) methods. Knowledge distillation is a related solution. A high capacity and large model (the teacher) learns a large amount of knowledge which is then transferred to a low capacity (Student) model through minimizing the difference in the two models in terms of their output distribution or intermediate representations. Distillation has been successfully applied to generative transformers (e.g., DistilGPT, TinyLLaMA) and diffusion models to get small but powerful variants, which can be used in real-time or embedded applications. All of these compression methods allow reducing giant generative systems to deployable versions and thus run them with limited resources, like a mobile device, microcontroller, or embedded accelerator. They are the building blocks of edge-ready generative AI (Sørensen et al., 2025). Recent approaches such as parameter-efficient fine-tuning (PEFT), including LoRA and adapter-based methods, have significantly reduced computational requirements while maintaining performance. LoRA (Low-Rank Adaptation) is a parameter-efficient fine-tuning method that updates only a small subset of weights, reducing memory and compute requirements. TinyGPT refers to lightweight versions of large language models optimized for deployment on edge devices such as smartphones.

4.3 Memory and Bandwidth Constraints for Edge Deployment

Generative AI is subject to the fundamental memory and bandwidth constraints in edge environment. Edge devices also have limited RAM (hundreds of megabytes to hundreds of gigabytes) and non-volatile storage, unlike tens of megabytes occupied by the parameters of large transformer or diffusion models. Generative models have a memory footprint not only in parameters but also in activation intermediates used in inference, in optimiser states when fine-tuning (if fine-tuning is used), and caching memory of attention maps or latent vectors. It is important to handle them effectively to be deployed. The strategies used to minimize the active memory include layer offloading, activation checkpointing and memory sharing. Another restricting factor is bandwidth (Petroşanu & Pîrjan, 2024). The cloud to edge transmission of large models or data has a cost in terms of latency and energy usage. On-device generation minimizes this by generating on-device, but this necessitates a high enough density of compute, along with model compression. Hybrid algorithms, like split computing or federated inference, are split computing models where part of the model is run on the device and part on the server, trading off between performance and resource consumption. The use of energy is also a similar limitation. Edge devices are usually battery-powered and generative inference (in particular, in models such as transformers or diffusion networks) may be energy-intensive. Practical deployment Hardware-aware model design Hardware accelerators Hardware-aware model design leveraging efficient architectures (e.g., MobileBERT) Hardware accelerators Hardware-aware model design using sparse computation is therefore essential. These memory and bandwidth constraints are a priority in research and engineering work as generative AI reaches embedded applications: autonomous drones, smart sensors and so on.

4.4 Trade-offs: Fidelity vs. Efficiency vs. Latency

When implementing generative models, an engineer has to make a three-way trade-off between the quality of the output, the computational cost, and the latency of the inference process. To generate the high-quality generation, the deep expressive large-parameter models may often be necessary, as well as they require a great amount of computational resources and time per inference. Smaller or compressed models, on the other hand, will be more efficient although less diverse, coherent, or perceptual realism. Fidelity is the quality and the realism of generated outputs, which is commonly measured by the Frechet Inception Distance (FID), Inception Score (IS), BLEU score (in text), or CLAP score (in audio). The large model capacity and long generation sequences are normally associated with high fidelity. Efficiency is a reduction in both computational and energy expenses (measured in FLOPs (floating-point operations) or energy/generated token/pixel). Such methods as parameter sharing, quantization, sparse attention and early exit mechanisms are efficient but may degrade fidelity. Latency times how fast an input triggers an output, which is important in real-time programs like interactive AI, edge robotics, or AR/VRs (Junaid & Callixtus, 2024). Transformers, a type of autoregressive model, are sequential by nature so that each token is generated at a time, and therefore, is more latent. Diffusion models, on the other hand, are more parallelizable, although they need numerous iterative steps to improve the quality of output. Multi-objective design is required to optimize in these dimensions, depending on the desired usage. As examples, on-device text generation can be less faithful with low latency and privacy, but high-end visual synthesis can be more realistic at increased computational cost. The new direction is dynamic generative inference, where models change resolution, sampling steps or layer depth dynamically to vary their quality or importance of tasks in resource availability - quality versus efficiency in real-time (Table 1).

Table 1. Trade-offs between model fidelity, computational efficiency, and latency across representative edge-based generative AI applications, highlighting practical deployment constraints and performance priorities.

Application Scenario	Model Type	Priority	Trade-off
Mobile chatbot	TinyGPT	Low latency	Lower accuracy
Medical image generation	Diffusion model	High fidelity	High compute cost
Smart surveillance camera	GAN	Balanced	Moderate latency & quality
AR/VR applications	Lightweight Transformer	Real-time response	Reduced detail

4.5 Benchmarking Metrics for Generative Efficiency

In order to objectively analyze the performance and deployability of generative models, it is necessary to benchmark it. The classical metrics emphasize more on the quality of a perception, although with generative AI becoming applied to resource-constrained settings, efficiency benchmarks are gaining more relevance (Xu et al., 2024).

Performance evaluation can be grouped into three categories:

1. **Quality Metrics:** These include Fréchet Inception Distance (FID) and Kernel Inception Distance (KID) for images; BLEU, ROUGE, and perplexity for text; and PESQ or STOI for audio. These measure output realism, coherence, and linguistic or perceptual alignment.
2. **Efficiency Metrics:** These quantify the computational and energy costs of generation — e.g., FLOPs per sample, power consumption (in joules or watts), model size (in parameters or MB), and memory footprint during inference.
3. **Latency Metrics:** Time-to-first-token (TTFT), throughput (tokens or images per second), and inference delay are critical for assessing suitability in real-time and edge scenarios.

To benchmark with edges, systems like MLPerf Tiny, Edge AI Benchmark and AI-Benchmark Mobile have proposed measures that are specific to on-device inference. These are not only fast, but also thermal, battery, and cross-hardware architecture scalable. An in-depth assessment thus is a combination of fidelity (to determine generative performance) and efficiency (to evaluate deployment viability) measures. The creation of common standards of Generative Edge Intelligence is still a practical field of study as it will allow a fair comparison of compact generative models in various hardware and application settings. Generative models face significant computational challenges, requiring careful optimization to balance performance, efficiency, and scalability, especially in edge environments.

5. GENERATIVE AI IN EDGE AND IOT CONTEXTS

The spread of intelligent devices, such as smartphones and autonomous drones, industrial sensors, and wearable medical technology, has increased the speed of the convergence of artificial intelligence and edge computing. Conventionally, AI inference and generation are cloud-based and demand large computing capacity, high-bandwidth networking, and storage. But the increased focus on privacy, latency minimization, and autonomy has led to the paradigm shift of edge intelligence where computation and learning are done locally at distributed devices. Integrating Generative AI into this paradigm marks a transformative evolution (Aline et al., 2025). Generative models at the edge enable devices not merely to analyze data but also to synthesize new information simulate environments, augment sensor inputs, personalize interactions, and generate context-aware content. This section examines the principles and technologies that enable generative AI in edge and IoT environments, highlighting architectural design, federated adaptation, optimization methods, and representative implementations.

Despite rapid advancements in model compression and edge optimization techniques, the practical deployment of Generative Artificial Intelligence (GenAI) systems remains constrained by several technical and operational challenges. Edge devices typically operate under strict limitations in compute power, memory, and energy, making it difficult to deploy large and complex generative models while maintaining acceptable performance and output quality. Real-time inference requirements further intensify these constraints, particularly in latency-sensitive applications such as autonomous systems and interactive interfaces. In addition, deployment in dynamic and uncontrolled environments introduces issues related to system reliability, robustness to noise or adversarial inputs, and security vulnerabilities in distributed settings. Addressing these challenges requires co-design of hardware and algorithms, efficient runtime optimization, and robust validation strategies to ensure reliable and scalable GenAI deployment in real-world scenarios.

5.1 Definition and Scope of Edge Intelligence

Embedding AI capabilities such as perception, inference, and learning capabilities in edge or near-infrastructure (also called Edge Intelligence, EI) and does not need to depend on centralized cloud servers. With edge systems, calculation is spread out, being performed on the device layer (sensors, IoT devices, microcontrollers), the edge layer (local gateways and routers or base stations), and sometimes the fog or cloud layer to aggregate and coordinate. The edge intelligence activities are not just limited to inference on-device. It involves the preprocessing of data, adaptive model development and distributed collaborative learning across distributed nodes (Chen et al., 2024). The architecture is useful in applications that need low latency (e.g. autonomous driving, industrial automation), high reliability (e.g. health monitoring), and better privacy (e.g. personalized content generation in the absence of uploading data). In the case of generative intelligence, edge systems have the ability to generate synthetic sensor data, create adaptive user interfaces, and make up or recreate complex environments based on the simulation or reconstruction. These capabilities make it possible to use AI in new applications in areas such as augmented reality, edge robotics, predictive maintenance, smart grids, and human-machine collaboration. Essentially, edge intelligence is the decentralization of generative ability - a shift towards large & monolithic cloud models to distributed, adaptive and privacy-preserving generative ecosystems acting at the edges of the network. In smart healthcare systems, wearable edge devices use generative models to synthesize patient health data, enabling early anomaly detection without transmitting sensitive information to the cloud. This improves both privacy and response time in critical monitoring scenarios.

Real-world examples include:

- Smart cameras generating missing frames or enhancing low-light video in real time
- Wearable health devices synthesizing patient data for anomaly detection
- Autonomous drones simulating navigation paths without cloud support
- AR glasses generating contextual overlays based on user surroundings

5.2 Architectural Integration of Generative Models into Edge Systems

Bringing generative models to edge architecture would mean tradeoff between computational intensity and system efficiency. An edge generative pipeline often comprises three fundamental steps, namely: (i) model provisioning, (ii) adaptive inference and (iii) collaborative optimization. With model provisioning, a trained generative model, which is trained on large-scale data on the cloud, is downloaded to the edge in compressed or distilled form. This can be partial deployment (e.g. encoder on the edge, decoder in the cloud) or a complete on-device implementation in cases where hardware allows such implementations. Split inference method separates the computational graph between cloud and edge, and splits the local load in this way, preserving privacy of sensitive data (Zhao et al., 2025). Context specific operation is done in the adaptive inference stage. The model varies the generation parameters (e.g. sampling rate, resolution or token length) depending on available resources or environmental conditions. Neural Processing Unit (NPU) orchestration or runtime quantization can be used to aid in resource allocation because they are dynamic scheduling frameworks. Lastly, collaborative optimization allows distributed devices to optimize models in a coordinated or collaborative manner by using federated or cooperative learning. Edge nodes can create synthetic data on the local level and distribute model gradients, and not raw data, which also help to improve collectively without breaking privacy. Architectures based on edge generation typically use heterogeneous computing, i.e. CPU, GPU, and NPU, and use containerized AI runtimes (e.g. TensorRT, ONNX Runtime, CoreML) to be deployed effectively. Inter-layer communication involves protocols (MQTT, gRPC) that are optimized and include adaptive compression. In a smart city system, edge cameras use compressed generative models to enhance video quality locally, while only essential metadata is transmitted to the cloud. This reduces bandwidth usage while maintaining real-time responsiveness.Architecturally, generative intelligence embedded into edge systems makes edge systems not passive recipients but active cognition agents that can perceive and creatively synthesize. This section introduced the key principles of GenAI, highlighting the transition from predictive to generative modeling and its relevance to edge systems (Fugure 5).

Figure 5. End-to-end pipeline of generative AI deployment in edge environments. The workflow includes (i) centralized training of large-scale generative models in the cloud, (ii) model compression and provisioning to edge devices, (iii) on-device adaptive inference under resource constraints, and (iv) collaborative optimization via federated learning. The framework highlights data flow, computation distribution, and privacy-preserving mechanisms across cloud–edge ecosystems.

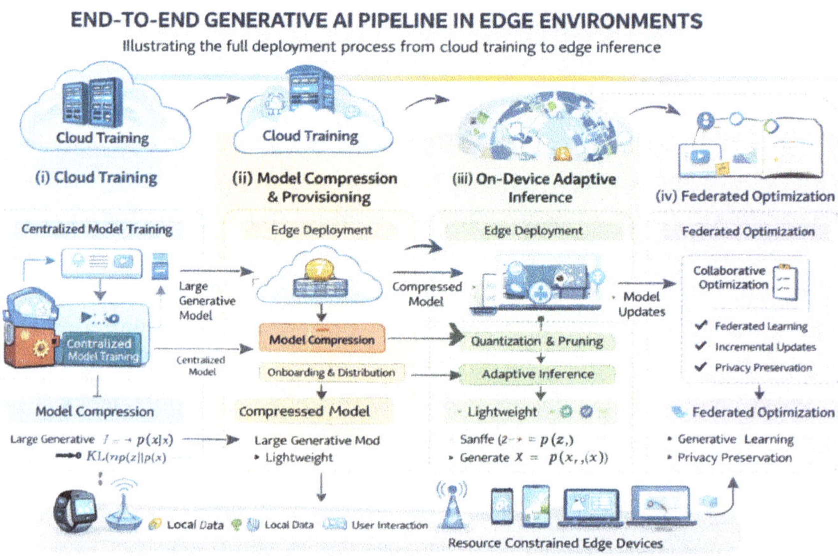

5.3 Federated Learning and Edge-based Fine-tuning of Generative Models

Simultaneously, Federated Learning (FL) is one of the pillars of facilitating collaborative model-enhancing in distributed edge settings. FL replaces centralized training information instead of training local model copies with private data and uploading training updates (e.g., gradients or weights) with a coordinating server. This paradigm is the best fit to the privacy and autonomy of edge-based generative systems. The application of FL to generative models is however associated with some unique challenges. Generative models are particularly VAEs, GANs, and Transformers, which are large and sensitive to distributional changes among clients. Unstable or biased generation may be caused by differences between the local data quality, modality or domain (Yang et al., 2025). To solve this, more recent works have proposed Federated Generative Learning (FGL) models, in which updates of models are weighted by local data quality or entropy, and individualized federated policies, in which individual devices refine shared generative representations to local settings. As an example, in federated diffusion learning, each client trains denoising paths on local data, which are combined to enhance difference generative accuracy at a global scale. Likewise, federated fine-tuning large language models (LLMs) - e.g. TinyLLaMA or EdgeGPT - can be personalized (e.g. user vocabulary or preferences) without exposing user private user prompts or chat logs. Furthermore, federated distillation is able to compress global generative models by transferring only the distilled logits or latent codes instead of the actual weights. This greatly minimises the overhead of communication which is one of the issues of concern in IoT settings with limited bandwidth. The federation of generative learning, therefore, makes it possible to have a hybrid intelligence system - a global creativity combined with local adaptation - so that generative AI will continuously develop on a distributed network and not violate privacy, heterogeneity, or data sovereignty.

5.4 On-device Inference Optimization: Pruning, Sparsity, and Lightweight Models

Sufficient inference optimization is required to run generative models on embedded and edge devices. As opposed to cloud deployments, edge systems are characterized by strict limits on compute power, memory and energy. In turn, on-device generative AI relies on three main optimization principles, namely pruning, exploiting sparsity, and designing a lightweight architecture (He et al., 2025). Pruning consists of a systematic elimination of redundant parameters, neurons or attention heads which have little effect on generation quality. Coordinated pruning can be used to delete complete filters or attention blocks so that they can implement them more rapidly on hardware accelerators. Fine-tuning is done after pruning and hence quality is not degraded by much. The parameters of pruned models can also be reduced by half or a quarter and these models are now practical on devices with a few hundred megabytes of memory. The concept of sparsity means using the fact that numerous activations and gradients in inference are close to zero. With the help of current edge NPUs and frameworks such as TensorRT or PyTorch Mobile, sparse computation allows omitting unnecessary computation and thus saving both computation and energy. Other methods, like mixture-of-experts (MoE) models make even more use of the sparsity by only using a small fraction of the network pathways on any given generation task. Another frontier is lightweight generative architectures. Such are models that are explicitly optimized to run on mobile, or are embedded within inference, such as TinyGPT, MobileDiffusion, and MicroVAE, which use small layers, smaller hidden dimension, and efficient tokenization agents. TinyGPT is a lightweight version of large language models designed for deployment on resource-constrained devices. MobileDiffusion refers to optimized diffusion models designed for efficient execution on mobile and edge hardware.It is a balance between expressive capacity and resource-efficiency, and such models can be generated potentially almost in real time on the mobile processors or embedded GPUs. Practically, on-device optimization is the joint design of algorithms with equipment, such as the choice of quantization levels, memory arrangements, parallel kernels, which are optimized to particular equipment. This software effectiveness coupled with hardware acceleration is the basis of the realization of generative intelligence at the edge (Figure 6). Mobile Diffusion refers to optimized diffusion models designed for efficient execution on mobile and edge hardware.

Practical applications include:

- TinyGPT running on smartphones for offline text generation
- MobileDiffusion generating images directly on mobile GPUs
- Smart keyboards generating predictive text without cloud access
- Edge robots generating synthetic training data for local learning

Figure 6. Conceptual framework illustrating the integration of generative models within edge platforms and applications, showing interactions between model architectures (TinyGPT, Diffusion edge, Embedded LLMs), edge AI infrastructure, and adaptive generative use cases. Diffusion Edge refers to an edge-optimized diffusion model architecture designed for efficient on-device image generation under resource constraints.

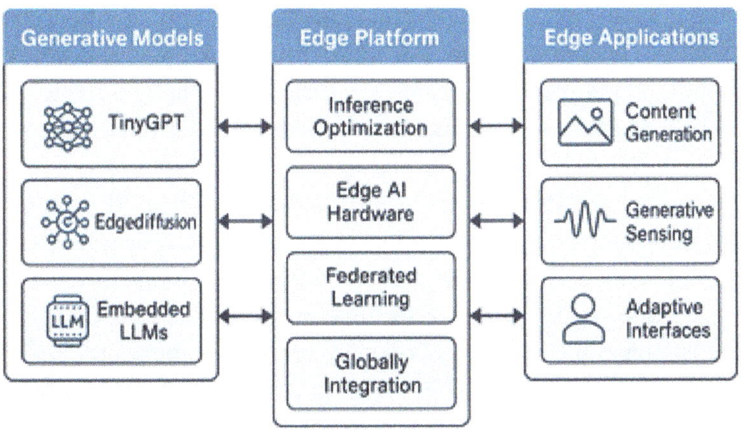

6. DATA, TRAINING, AND ADAPTATION MECHANISMS

The quality of the data used in the training of generative AI systems, its diversity, and representativeness give it intelligence. Generative models use highly dimensional data, unlike traditional discriminative models that operate on labeled data, which necessitates rich high-dimensional data, representing underlying distributions across modalities, e.g. text, image, sound, or sensor state. Nevertheless, with the increased generative AI to edge and IoT ecosystems, the issues of curation of datasets, model adaptation, and privacy preservation emerge. This part explains the fundamental processes that control the lifecycle of generative data - dataset curation and synthetic augmentation, transfer learning, continual adaptation, and privacy-sensitive approaches. Such principles are important in understanding how to develop generative systems that are efficient, context-aware and secure when deployed in a decentralized environment (Xu et al., 2023).

6.1 Dataset Curation for Generative Tasks

Generative modeling is all based on data curation. The learning of a generative model does not rely on explicitly labeled data but instead by the statistical organization of data; therefore, the expressiveness, heterogeneity and quality of the training data play the focal role in the expressive capacity and generalization of the model. In massive generative training, the data is usually gathered through various open databases - Common Crawl (text), LAION (image-text pairs) and LibriSpeech audio or AudioSet (audio). The aim is to model an approximation to broad and well-balanced data distribution pdata(x) that describes the variation in the real world. Raw web data are however usually noisy, redundant or biased and hence require preprocessing pipelines to accomplish deduplication, normalization, filtering and quality scoring. Domestic specificity and data efficiency are also aspects of curating data that have to be taken into account when creating edge-oriented generative applications (Gupta et al., 2025). Embedded system-designed models, e.g. are frequently narrow task-oriented, e.g. gesture synthesis, sensor simulation, localized text generation etc. and therefore need domain-specific datasets that are curated to represent actual operating conditions. Generative tasks also include curation that implies ethical integrity and compliance. Risks can be copied in downstream models as a result of inclusion of copyrighted, biased, or personally identifiable information (PII). To mitigate it, new data pipelines incorporate data provenance tracking and ethical filtering, so that the training data meet governance regulatory principles, like the EU AI Act or IEEE P7000. Overall, the process of dataset curation in generative AI implies balancing between the scale and quality, as well as diversity and relevance. In edge deployment, the focus is narrowed to localized and representative and privacy-aware datasets that increase flexibility and reliability.

6.2 Synthetic Data Generation and Augmentation for Edge Applications

Synthetic data generation represents one of the most powerful capabilities of generative AI and a vital tool for addressing data scarcity and privacy challenges in edge environments. In many IoT or embedded systems, real-world data collection is constrained by cost, limited sensor availability, or privacy regulations (Pandey et al., 2023). Generative models such as Variational Autoencoders (VAEs), Generative Adversarial Networks (GANs), and Diffusion Models can be used to synthesize high-quality, realistic data samples that mimic statistical properties of real observations. These synthetic datasets serve several critical purposes:

1. **Data Augmentation:** Synthetic samples expand small datasets, reducing overfitting and improving generalization. For example, synthetic sensor readings or image patches generated by conditional GANs can help fine-tune local anomaly detection or predictive maintenance models.
2. **Domain Balancing:** In edge deployments, datasets often suffer from domain imbalance certain sensor states or environments are underrepresented. Generative models can fill these gaps by generating minority class samples, ensuring balanced training distributions.
3. **Simulation and Testing:** Synthetic data can emulate conditions that are rare, hazardous, or expensive to replicate (e.g., machinery failure, medical anomalies, or extreme weather). This enables robust pre-deployment testing of IoT or robotic systems without real-world risk.
4. **Privacy Preservation:** Generative models can create "privacy-safe" data synthetic but statistically valid samples that resemble real distributions without exposing individual-level information.

Techniques such as Conditional GANs (cGANs) and Diffusion-based Augmenters are increasingly applied in edge contexts to generate data aligned with specific operational parameters or sensor constraints. For instance, EdgeDiffusion can produce compressed, on-device synthetic datasets for federated learning nodes operating with intermittent connectivity. In practice, synthetic data generation bridges the gap between limited on-device data and large-scale model requirements, fostering *self-sufficient learning ecosystems* within edge networks (Table 2).

Table 2. Representative use cases of synthetic data generation in edge environments, illustrating the types of generated data and their role in improving model robustness, privacy, and domain-specific performance.

Use Case	Generated Data Type	Benefit
Autonomous vehicles	Synthetic road scenarios	Safer testing
Healthcare imaging	Synthetic MRI scans	Privacy preservation
Industrial IoT	Sensor fault data	Improved anomaly detection
Agriculture	Crop disease images	Better model training

6.3 Transfer Learning and Domain Adaptation

Training a generative model is computationally infeasible to most edge applications. Rather, transfer learning has become a paradigm of choice - it provides pre-trained generative models with the ability to generalize to new domains or tasks with little more data and computations (Vu et al., 2024). Transfer learning based on the idea that deep generative models acquire generalizable latent representations, the reuse of which can be applied across contexts. A model that has been trained on large-scale data (e.g. GPT or Stable Diffusion) can be repurposed to small edge tasks, e.g. generating code to run on an IoT device, on-device summarization or small-scale visual synthesis. LoRA (Low-Rank Adaptation) is a parameter-efficient fine-tuning technique that updates only a small subset of model weights.

Several strategies are used for generative transfer:

- **Full fine-tuning**, in which all model weights are updated using domain-specific data, offers maximum adaptation but is resource-intensive.
- **Parameter-efficient fine-tuning (PEFT)**, including techniques such as LoRA (Low-Rank Adaptation) and prefix tuning, modifies only a small subset of parameters or adds lightweight adapters to the model. This reduces memory requirements by orders of magnitude, making it feasible for on-device adaptation.
- **Domain adaptation** aligns the distribution of pre-trained data with that of target domain data using adversarial losses or contrastive alignment. For instance, an image generator trained on general web data can be adapted to industrial inspection domains through domain alignment networks or adversarial re-weighting.

Transfer and domain adaptation are particularly crucial for IoT systems, where environments and sensor characteristics vary widely. By reusing the representational power of foundation models, edge devices can achieve high generative performance without massive retraining, enabling context-aware creativity at minimal computational cost.

6.4 Continual and Few-shot Learning in Resource-constrained Devices

Edge environments change: distributions of sensors are evolving, user behaviors are changing, and contextfulness is changing with the time. Generative models deployed on devices need to be capable of continual learning - the ability to combine new information without forgetting it catastrophically - and few-shot learning, the ability to adapt to examples of a small scale, to be relevant. Generative model continuous learning is commonly done by adding new parameters or by updating a dynamic memory. Methods such as Elastic Weight Consolidation (EWC) and progressive neural networks retain the existing knowledge and incorporate the new one. Through continual learning, systems can change in generative environments, such as an edge camera model can keep improving its capacity to produce realistic environmental scenes as the lighting and weather varies (Duvvur, 2025). The concept of few-shot learning is used when trained generative behavior is to be refined with limited new data (in some cases as few as 5-10 samples). Meta-learning methods, like Model-Agnostic Meta-Learning (MAML), enable models to acquire adaptation strategies in training, and thus they are resistant to smaller, domain-specific data. For example, a smart surveillance camera deployed at the edge can continuously adapt to seasonal lighting changes and environmental variations without retraining from scratch. Transformer-based and few-shot diffusion models have now been shown to have the ability to generalize on minimal edge data, particularly with several foundation backbones. These adaptability features are essential when dealing with resource-constrained IoT systems, where there are intermittent data and connectivity. Combined, continual and few-shot learning also enable edge generative intelligence to be contextually consistent and resilient without retraining in the center. A smart surveillance system deployed at the edge can continuously adapt to seasonal lighting changes, weather conditions, and new object patterns without requiring full retraining from the cloud. For example, a smart surveillance camera can adapt to seasonal lighting changes using continual learning. Techniques such as Elastic Weight Consolidation (EWC) help prevent catastrophic forgetting by preserving important model weights.

6.5 Privacy-preserving Generative Learning (e.g., Differential Privacy, Federated GANs)

Privacy preservation is a critical aspect of edge-based Generative AI (GenAI), as edge devices frequently process sensitive user and environmental data. Generative models must ensure that individual data cannot be reconstructed or inferred from model outputs. This is achieved through several complementary techniques:

Key Privacy-preserving Methods

- **Differential Privacy (DP):**

Adds controlled random noise to training gradients or model parameters, ensuring that the contribution of any single data point remains indistinguishable.

- o Common framework: DP-SGD (Differentially Private Stochastic Gradient Descent)
- o Widely used in sensitive domains such as healthcare and finance (Feretzakis et al., 2024)

- **Federated Generative Adversarial Networks (FedGANs):**

Integrate federated learning with generative modeling.

- o Each device trains a local generator and discriminator on its own dataset
- o Only model updates are shared with a central server
- o Enables global model improvement while preserving local data privacy (Lomurno, 2024)

- **Secure Multiparty Computation (SMC):**

Enables multiple devices to collaboratively train models using encrypted data, without exposing raw inputs

- **Homomorphic Encryption:**

Allows computations to be performed directly on encrypted data during training, ensuring strong data confidentiality

Practical Considerations

- Cryptographic techniques such as SMC and homomorphic encryption are computationally intensive
- Recent advancements in hardware acceleration and lightweight cryptographic methods are improving their feasibility for edge deployment

Importance

Privacy-preserving generative learning is fundamental to trustworthy edge intelligence. It ensures that generative systems operate in an ethical and legally compliant manner, aligning with global data governance frameworks such as:

- GDPR
- HIPAA
- AI Act

Beyond privacy, ethical concerns in generative AI include bias amplification, misinformation generation, and lack of transparency. These risks are particularly critical in edge environments, where decentralized deployment may limit oversight. Ensuring fairness, accountability, and explainability remains a key research challenge.

7. EVALUATION METRICS AND QUALITY ASSESSMENT

The issue of evaluating generative models is unique. Generative systems do not provide any measurement of prediction accuracy as do discriminative models, but instead give open-ended output, such as text, images, audio, or sensor data, the quality of which has to be measured along a variety of dimensions: realism, diversity, consistency, alignment and utility. Lack of single, or universal assessment measures prompts the need to have a multidimensional model that integrates quantitative measure, qualitative examination and subject-oriented assessment (Bandi et al., 2023). This section explores the core evaluation paradigms used in generative AI research and practice. It begins with quantitative metrics for statistical and perceptual quality, followed by qualitative and human-centered assessment approaches. The discussion then extends to robustness, fairness, explainability, and formal validation frameworks, especially as these considerations become critical in edge and embedded deployments, where context sensitivity and safety are paramount.

7.1 Quantitative Metrics: FID, IS, BLEU, Perceptual Scores

Quantitative metrics provide objective, reproducible measures of generative performance. While no single metric can comprehensively capture generative quality, several well-established metrics are used across modalities.

Fréchet Inception Distance (FID)

The FID is among the most widely used metrics for evaluating image generation (Bragazzi & Garbarino, 2024). It measures the distance between feature distributions of generated and real images in the embedding space of a pre-trained Inception network:

$$FID = \left\| \mu_r - \mu_g \right\| 2 + Tr(\sum_r + \sum_g + 2(\sum_r \sum_g) ½$$

where $(\mu r, \Sigma r) and (\mu g, \Sigma g)$denote the means and covariances of real and generated feature distributions. Lower FID values indicate closer alignment and higher perceptual realism.

Inception Score (IS)

The Inception Score evaluates both image quality and diversity by measuring how confidently a classifier recognizes generated samples and how varied those classifications are:

$$IS = \exp(E_x\ [D_{KL}(p(y|x)\ ||p(y))])$$

A high IS reflects sharp, diverse outputs but does not directly compare generated images with real samples.

BLEU, ROUGE, and METEOR

For textual generation, metrics such as BLEU (Bilingual Evaluation Understudy), ROUGE, and METEOR compare generated sentences to reference texts based on n-gram overlap and semantic similarity. While widely used in machine translation and summarization, they may fail to capture creativity or contextual coherence in open-ended text generation (Ramalakshmi & Asha, 2024).

Perceptual Scores and Audio Metrics

For generative audio, metrics such as PESQ (Perceptual Evaluation of Speech Quality) and STOI (Short-Time Objective Intelligibility) assess perceptual similarity between synthesized and reference signals. For multimodal models, CLIPScore measures text–image alignment, and FID-A extends visual metrics to audiovisual outputs.

Diversity and Mode Coverage

Metrics like Precision-Recall for Generative Models (PRD) and Density–Coverage measure how well the generated distribution captures the diversity of real data. These are critical for detecting *mode collapse* a common issue in GANs where the model generates limited variations.

In practice, researchers use combinations of these metrics to obtain a comprehensive performance profile, as no single metric adequately measures all dimensions of generative quality. In edge-based image generation, a lower FID score indicates that generated images (e.g., from a smart camera) closely match real-world visuals, improving reliability in surveillance or medical diagnostics.

7.2 Qualitative Assessment: Human and Task-Oriented Evaluation

Although quantitative measures are objective, they do not always provide a complete representation of human perception, contextual correspondence, and utility - variables of importance in generative AI assessment. Thus, qualitative evaluation is an essential part, particularly where creativity or interactivity is involved. Another category of human evaluation is expert-based or crowd-based studies in which the outputs are rated on a scale of realism, coherence, creativity, and preference (Furtado et al., 2024). As an example, in language models fluent speech, facts and context-relevance are judged by the annotators; in image or video generation, annotators judge realism, composition and semantic fit. In order to be reliable, pairwise comparison, Mean Opinion Score (MOS) and A/B testing are incorporated. These minimize bias and enable statistical meaningful aggregation of subjective preferences.

Task-oriented evaluation assesses the performance of generative models within specific downstream applications. For example:

- Synthetic sensor data may be evaluated by its ability to improve anomaly detection accuracy.
- Generated dialogue content may be assessed for engagement or task completion in conversational systems.
- Edge-based generative systems can be evaluated for latency and user experience in real-time interactions.

Hybrid methods are increasingly used, combining automated scoring with human-in-the-loop verification. The inclusion of contextual and ethical criteria such as factual reliability, cultural sensitivity, and bias ensures that evaluation captures not only how well a model generates, but also whether it should generate certain outputs.

7.3 Robustness, Fairness, and Bias in Generative Outputs

Since generative AI systems are in transition between research and deployment, it is imperative to make them as robust and fair as possible. Robustness is the stability and reliability of a model with changes in its inputs, noise or environmental changes. Fairness deals with the issue of generative outputs being part of unbiased, representative and socially responsible. Generative systems can be tested on robustness by adding adversarial perturbations or input noise and quantifying the decrease in the quality of the output. In the case of image models, this can be corruptions, e.g. blur, lighting adjustments, or occlusion; in the case of text, perturbed prompts or adversarial phrasing. Sturdy generative models are consistent in semantics and realistic in spite of these variations. Fairness and bias evaluation entails the identification of systematic imbalances within output, which is generated (Shah & White, 2025). As an example, text (or image) generators that are trained on biased data can represent particular gender, ethnicity, or cultural stereotypes. Assessment tools adopt demographic or semantic parity indicators in measuring the biasness of outputs. Edge deployments also make fairness analysis more difficult since local data distributions can be different to global training distributions. This creates issues of domain bias and distribution drift - as models produce outputs that are more driven by large scale global aspects than small scale local context. Mitigation measures, such as data rebalancing, loss functions that are biased and loss-constrained fine-tuning. In case of safety-critical programs (e.g. healthcare or surveillance), fairness should be checked in operation conditions to eliminate discriminating or misleading results. Finally, trustworthiness and justice are components of a larger accountable AI model that guarantees that generative systems used in the edge generate safe, moral, and contextually appropriate results to an entire process population and setting.

7.4 Explainability and Transparency in Generative AI

Generative models need to be explained to achieve trust, interpretability, and accountability. Most generative architectures especially large transformers and diffusion networks are highly complex and therefore operate like black boxes, and it is hard to determine how particular outputs are generated by inputs or latent representations. To overcome this non-explanability, a number of methods to explain have been proposed. Visualisation of latent space visualisation approaches map high-dimensional latent vectors into interpretable spaces, allowing users to see semantic transitions (e.g. between scenes of day and night in image generators). The attribution analysis determines which tokens of input (pixel or feature) has the greatest impact on the output generated (Braggaar et al., 2023). Attention heatmaps and saliency maps in transformer-based language models provide an understanding of the contextual dependence on generation, which visualizes the influence of context on the generation. The concept activation vectors (CAVs) and feature inversion methods have further interpretability, quantifying the impact of abstract concepts (e.g. gender, emotion or type of object) on the latent activations. In diffusion models, reverse diffusion trace analysis is used to understand the process of feature development during iterative denoising updates, which can be used by researchers to diagnose hallucinations or bias propagation. Transparency goes further beyond technical interpretability to model governance, that is, putting the data sources, training procedures, model hyperparameters, and restrictions on the model down in writing in model cards and data sheets. These activities are in line with international AI responsibility systems and are specifically crucial in edge AI implementations, wherein distributed models can be deployed to sensitive settings and work authentically. Explainability therefore provides a balance between technical and moral obligation such that as AI is generated, it can be understood and controlled, despite its increased sophistication.

7.5 Verification and Validation Frameworks for Edge-deployed Generators

Verification and validation (V&V) frameworks provide systematic methodologies to ensure that generative AI models operate correctly, reliably, and safely when deployed especially in edge or embedded environments where continuous human oversight may be limited.

Verification focuses on confirming that a generative model behaves according to its specifications and constraints. In practice, this includes:

- **Functional verification**: ensuring outputs meet defined quality thresholds (e.g., FID $\leq$ target value, latency $\leq$ constraint).
- **Adversarial testing**: evaluating resistance to malicious inputs or noise.
- **Formal verification**: using mathematical guarantees or symbolic reasoning to ensure properties such as bounded output variance or deterministic behavior in safety-critical systems.

Validation evaluates the ability of a generative model to work in practice to achieve the intended purpose. In the case of edge systems this includes hardware in the loop testing, latency testing and field testing performance. Validation metrics combine quantitative quality (FID, BLEU) with the system-level metrics, such as throughput, energy efficiency, and contextual accuracy. The use of generative models is progressively subject to frameworks like ISO/IEC 24029-1 (AI system robustness testing), IEEE P7009 (fail-safe design of autonomous systems), among others, which ensures that they meet the requirements of international standards. Continuous verification and validation pipelines may be incorporated in the device lifecycle in edge contexts. As an example, Edge MLOps pipelines are trained to test generative performance periodically after being deployed and update or prune models, when drift or performance degradation is observed. These kind of integrated V&V systems make sure that even in the event AI is generated in the form of heterogeneous devices, it is predictable, safe, and verifiable, and therefore technological advancement is in line with the ethical and operating principles.

7.6 Ethical and Societal Considerations

GenAI systems deployed at the edge raise important ethical concerns:

- Bias amplification due to localized or imbalanced training data
- Risk of misinformation through synthetic content generation
- Lack of transparency in decentralized systems

- Challenges in enforcing accountability across distributed devices

Additionally, regulatory frameworks such as the EU AI Act and GDPR emphasize the need for transparency, fairness, and data protection in AI deployment.

8. APPLICATIONS OF GENERATIVE AI IN EDGE SCENARIOS

Generative Artificial Intelligence (Generative AI) and edge computing is one of the most radical changes in the design of intelligent systems. Historically, generative models have been cloud-based by nature (computational intensity), but with the development of lightweight architectures, model compression, and distributed learning, generative models can be deployed directly to edge devices smartphones, IoT gateways, industrial controllers and embedded platforms. Generative AI allows edge computing to be used not just to analyze data but also generate and synthesize content in the edge, providing the same adaptability and creativity as generative models to local synthesis, to be context-aware, and to be creative (Li et al., 2023). This development has opened up the opportunities of multimedia generation, sensor simulation, predictive analytics, and intelligent interaction. This part will discuss five of the largest areas of generative AI application in edge situations, detailing how each of them exploits distributed creativity to provide autonomy, responsiveness, and personalization. Autonomous vehicles use generative models to simulate rare driving scenarios (e.g., extreme weather or accidents), enabling safer training and real-time decision support at the edge without relying on cloud connectivity.

Key edge-based GenAI applications include:

- **Smartphones:** On-device text generation (e.g., AI keyboards, assistants)
- **Healthcare wearables:** Generating synthetic patient signals for early diagnosis
- **Autonomous vehicles:** Simulating driving scenarios for safer navigation
- **Industrial IoT:** Generating predictive maintenance data
- **AR/VR systems:** Real-time content generation for immersive experiences

8.1 Edge-based Content Generation (Vision, Audio, NLP)

The term edge-based content generation means the implementation of generative models on or near devices to generate real-time multimedia content (such as text, images, audio, and video) without having to use centralized servers. This allows low latency, privacy preserving, and contextually adaptive generation. Diffusion or GAN models ED-adapted to visions can be used to generate or optimize images at local locations. Indicatively, EdgeDiffusion and MobileGAN models create high-fidel visual textures and images using embedded GPUs, and are applicable in augmented reality (AR), drone vision, and image augmentation on the mobile. On-device diffusion transformers can create personalized visual scenes (prompts in text or gestures by a user) and enable real-time creative experiences. Lightweight versions of autoregressive or flow based models (e.g. WaveRNN, MelGAN and others) can also be used in audio generation, to allow speech synthesis, environmental sound simulation, and personalized voice cloning at the device scale. These models find application in voice assistants, in-vehicle systems and accessibility technologies. For natural language processing (NLP), compact large language models (LLMs) such as TinyGPT, Mistral Edge, or Gemma Mobile perform local text generation, summarization, and dialogue management. Edge-based NLP models provide significant advantages in data privacy, as no user text or query leaves the device, and support real-time response without network latency (Xu et al., 2024).

Together, these multimodal generation capabilities transform edge devices into creative engines, capable of producing rich multimedia content that adapts to user needs and environmental context forming the core of next-generation human–AI interaction systems.

8.2 Generative Sensing and Sensor Data Simulation

The accessibility and quality of sensor data restrict the performance of the analytical or predictive models in most IoT and industrial systems. Generative sensing, i.e. using generative models to recreate or augment sensor data, is the solution to this problem, whereby realistic and synthetic measurements are generated to increase the representational capabilities of physical sensors. To illustrate, VAEs and conditional GANs have the capacity of characterizing the statistical correlations between multi-sensor data streams so that synthetic data are produced given certain environmental or operational circumstances. It is especially useful with edge devices, which may be used in a data-scarce or privacy-sensitive environment, e.g., remote monitoring stations or a healthcare wearable. System validation and calibration is also supported by sensor simulation. Generative models have the ability to simulate sensor behavior when using extreme or uncommon conditions (e.g., high temperature, vibration, or failure), which is used in training data in fault detection and predictive maintenance algorithms. There is now interest in diffusion based temporal models, which can be used to produce sequential sensor data, maintaining both temporal coherence and stochastic variability (Akram et al., 2025). Generative sensing is used to augment perception in autonomous systems to close the gaps in partial or noisy sensor signals. As an example, on-device generative reconstruction can be used to repair covered or damaged sensor measurements in real-time in robotics or self-driving cars, preserving situational awareness. Generative sensing can therefore be considered as the extension of traditional data acquisition using synthetic perception allowing more resilient and adaptable sensor networks in distributed edge environments.

8.3 Industrial and IoT Applications: Predictive Maintenance and Anomaly Generation

Predictive maintenance and anomaly detection plays a significant role in terms of industrial and IoT ecology, limiting the downtime, guaranteeing safety and efficiency of operation. Generative AI brings value to these areas through the simulation of fault conditions, the creation of rare event data, as well as the learning of normal operational distributions of anomalies in identification. The normal data distribution of the readings of the machine sensors can be learned by generative models like GAN-based anomaly generators and VAE-based reconstructor models. When operating, an anomaly is signaled when the process is not going according to this learned distribution. In addition, the models can be used to train the discriminators or fault classifiers to identify anomalies that might not have occurred yet, in the real operations, by simulating synthetic fault situation. Such abilities are priceless at the periphery. Embedded in industrial devices, generative modules are capable of monitoring local signals (e.g. vibration, current, temperature) and automatically creating predictive diagnostics. Time-series generators based on EdgeDiffusion and TinyGAN models have been proven to be used on-the-edge to predictive maintenance in industrial IoT networks (Zhuansun et al., 2025). Digital twins are also supported by generative AI replicas of physical systems that behave in a variety of conditions. Generative digital twins that are edge based may work in real time, continuously learning with local data streams and producing predictive indicators of system degradation or failure. This allows preventive action to be taken prior to the breakdowns that are expensive. In a nutshell, generative artificial intelligence brings predictive innovation to industrial internet of things - creating not just facts, but possibilities as well, therefore, making infrastructures self-aware and self healing.

8.4 Personalized Edge AI: Adaptive Interfaces and Context-aware Generation

Personalization is one of the most promising opportunities of edge based generative AI. The ability of generative models to produce outputs such as visual, linguistic or behavioral images or text specific to a particular user and to a specific context in real-time does not negatively affect privacy or latency. Adaptive interfaces use on-devace language or vision models to produce layouts of custom content, suggestions, or dialogues. An embedded LLM, e.g. can dynamically re-write interface instructions according to user skill, or a visual generator can transform AR overlays according to the environment of the user. Context-sensitive generation enables edge gadgets to adjust their outputs based on environmental and behavioral signals. A mobile assistant may produce different summaries when one is driving or not, or a wearable health tracker may give one personalized health advice based on locally processed physiological data. Local fine-tuning or federated personalization enables this kind of personalization, in which shared generative models are personalized to the specifics of an individual user without violating privacy. LoRA adaptation and prompt-tuning are just some of the techniques that enable models to adapt without having to retrain the whole network (Wang et al., 2023). Edge-based personalization is an essential transformation of centralized AI services into user-centered creative autonomy - in which each device is a creative collaborator, continuously learning about its owner, his context, preferences, and interactions.

8.5 Smart Healthcare, Transportation, and Energy Systems Examples

Generative AI at the edge is increasingly being applied in smart infrastructure systems, where distributed intelligence enhances real-time responsiveness and safety. Three major domains healthcare, transportation, and energy illustrate this convergence.

(a) Smart Healthcare

Edge-based generative models enable privacy-preserving medical synthesis and real-time support. Generative imaging models can produce synthetic MRI or ultrasound scans for training diagnostic systems without revealing patient data. Embedded VAEs on wearable devices can generate or reconstruct missing physiological signals (e.g., ECG segments) for anomaly detection. Personalized health assistants powered by on-device LLMs provide adaptive conversational support while maintaining data privacy.

(b) Intelligent Transportation

Generative AI enhances autonomous vehicle perception and simulation. Edge-deployed diffusion or GAN models generate synthetic driving scenarios to augment training for path planning and obstacle detection. In traffic systems, generative models simulate flow patterns under various environmental or policy conditions, supporting adaptive signal control. Embedded edge units can also generate predictive occupancy or congestion data, improving real-time routing decisions.

(c) Smart Energy and Grid Systems

Edge-based generative models have been used to simulate demand patterns, anomalies predictors, and missing data in distributed sensor networks in energy networks. Indicatively, generative forecasting models can generate synthetic load profile of renewable integration planning or identify anomalies in the voltage signal that could be caused by faults in equipment. They make self-adaptive management of the grid when applied to the local controllers and lead to energy efficiency and reliability (Alzu'bi et al., 2025). In all these fields, combined generative modeling and edge intelligence create a new paradigm of autonomous, distributed creativity - devices and systems do not simply respond to their environment, but, instead, actively create solutions, simulations, and content to maximize operation and user experience. The development of Generative Artificial Intelligence has become more than an academic whim, as it now stands as one of the foundations of present-day computational intelligence in empowering machines to progress beyond analysis to include independent creativity of their own. Theoretical aspects of it, which were based on probabilistic modeling and latent variable inference, have developed into the potent architectures of GANs, VAEs and Diffusion Models, and the transformer-based foundation models have scaled generative capacity to all major data modalities. However, the real edge here is the ability to take these generative abilities outside of the data center to the edge - where these capabilities are decentralized, adaptable, and responsive to the real world environment.

8.6 Real-world Case Studies of Edge-based GenAI

Case Study 1: On-device AI in Smartphones

Modern smartphones (e.g., Google Pixel, Samsung Galaxy AI) deploy light-weight transformer models for on-device text generation, summarization, and image enhancement. This reduces latency and improves user privacy.

Case Study 2: Healthcare Wearables

Devices such as smartwatches use generative models to synthesize physiological signals (e.g., ECG patterns) for early anomaly detection without transmitting sensitive data to the cloud.

Case Study 3: Autonomous Vehicles

Self-driving systems use generative models to simulate rare driving scenarios (e.g., extreme weather conditions), improving safety and robustness.

Case Study 4: Industrial IoT

Factories deploy generative models to simulate equipment failures, enabling predictive maintenance and reducing downtime.

CONCLUSION

The chapter has given a condensed overview of the working mechanisms, architectures, and optimization strategies of generative AI, and then optimized them to fit the unique edge and IoT environment constraints. Model pruning, quantization, and distillation are some of the techniques used to facilitate the implementation of creative intelligence on devices with limited resources in combination with federated and continual learning. Combined with sensor networks and embedded systems, generative AI makes it possible to provide new features: synthetic data augmentation, predictive maintenance, personal user experiences, and privacy-sensitive simulation. The consequences of this change are far reaching. Edge-generated systems can enable real-time creativity, ensure user data security, and eliminate overreliance on the cloud-based systems - a new phase of distributed creativity and cognitive independence. Such opportunities however should be accompanied by responsible governance which is fair, transparent and efficient in terms of energy consumption. Finally, there is the convergence of algorithmic innovation, computational optimi zation, and ethical design, which is known as generative intelligence at the edge. It can make intelligent devices not consumers of data but generators of knowledge, content and solutions. This combination of generative and edge paradigms is set to make the next decade of evolution of AI ubiquitous, efficient, and human-centered.

REFERENCES

Aishwarya, S., Selvamurugan, C., Parthiban, K. G., Nathan, B., Manoj Prabhakar, J., & Mohamed Noordeen, A. (2024, December). Generative AI in Focus: A Comprehensive Review of Leading Models Across Modalities. In *2024 4th International Conference on Ubiquitous Computing and Intelligent Information Systems (ICUIS)* (pp. 1-9). IEEE.

Akram, F., Malik, A. W., & Khan, S. U. (2025). iGenEdge: Intelligent Generative AI Service Deployment for Edge-Connected IoT Devices. *IEEE Internet Computing*, *29*(4), 16–24. DOI: 10.1109/MIC.2025.3576072

Aline, C., Kristensen, M., Thomsen, F., Holm, L., & Sondergaard, E. (2025). Reimagining Model Efficiency in Generative AI Through Unified and Differentiable Quantization Approaches.

Alzu'bi, S., Kanan, T., Elbes, M., Kanaan, G., & Trrad, I. (2025). Energy-efficient edge deployment of generative AI models using federated learning. *Cluster Computing*, *28*(5), 1–12. DOI: 10.1007/s10586-025-05263-7

Anstine, D. M., & Isayev, O. (2023). Generative models as an emerging paradigm in the chemical sciences. *Journal of the American Chemical Society*, *145*(16), 8736–8750. DOI: 10.1021/jacs.2c13467

Ardi, N. (2025). Generative AI: A Comprehensive Review of Foundational Models and Emerging Methods. [ASTJ]. *Applied Systems and Technologies Journal*, *1*(1), 1–6.

Bandi, A., Adapa, P. V. S. R., & Kuchi, Y. E. V. P. K. (2023). The power of generative ai: A review of requirements, models, input–output formats, evaluation metrics, and challenges. *Future Internet*, *15*(8), 260. DOI: 10.3390/fi15080260

Bragazzi, N. L., & Garbarino, S. (2024). Toward clinical generative AI: Conceptual framework. *JMIR AI*, *3*(1), e55957. DOI: 10.2196/55957

Braggaar, A., Liebrecht, C., van Miltenburg, E., & Krahmer, E. (2023). Evaluating task-oriented dialogue systems: A systematic review of measures, constructs and their operationalisations. *arXiv preprint arXiv:2312.13871*.

Chen, N., Cheng, Z., Fan, X., Xia, X., & Huang, L. (2024). Towards integrated fine-tuning and inference when generative AI meets edge intelligence. *arXiv preprint arXiv:2401.02668*.

Chen, T. (2025). PROBABILISTIC LATENT VARIABLE MODELS: PRINCIPLES AND FOUNDATIONS FOR MODERN GENERATIVE AI. *Available at SSRN* 5244929. DOI: 10.2139/ssrn.5244929

Chowdhury, A., Chowdhury, A., Hoque, N., Moriwam, M., & Jahan, M. (2025). Generative AI: A survey of historical development, emerging trends, and future outlook. *Computer Science and Engineering Research*, *2*(1), 19–31. DOI: 10.69517/cser.2025.02.01.0004

Ciubotaru, B. I. (2025). Generative AI and Large Language Models: A Comprehensive Scientific.

COCCIA, M. (2025). Invasive technologies: Technological paradigm shift in generative artificial intelligence. *Journal of Innovation. Technology and Knowledge Economy*, *1*(1), 1–32.

Corchado, J. M., López, S., Garcia, R., & Chamoso, P. (2023). Generative artificial intelligence: Fundamentals. *ADCAIJ: advances in distributed computing and artificial intelligence journal, 12*, e31704-e31704.

Dantas, P. V., Da Silva, W. S., Cordeiro, L. C., & Carvalho, C. B. (2024). A comprehensive review of model compression techniques in machine learning. *Applied Intelligence*, *54*(22), 11804–11844. DOI: 10.1007/s10489-024-05747-w

Duvvur, V. (2025). Exploring the Role of Generative Adversarial Networks (GANs) and Generative AI for Synthetic Data Generation and Augmentation in Machine Learning. *Journal of Information Systems Engineering & Management*, *10*(33s).

Feretzakis, G., Papaspyridis, K., Gkoulalas-Divanis, A., & Verykios, V. S. (2024). Privacy-preserving techniques in generative ai and large language models: A narrative review. *Information (Basel)*, *15*(11), 697. DOI: 10.3390/info15110697

Furtado, L. S., Soares, J. B., & Furtado, V. (2024). A task-oriented framework for generative AI in design. *Journal of Creativity*, *34*(2), 100086. DOI: 10.1016/j.yjoc.2024.100086

Gui, J., Chen, T., Zhang, J., Cao, Q., Sun, Z., Luo, H., & Tao, D. (2024). A survey on self-supervised learning: Algorithms, applications, and future trends. *IEEE Transactions on Pattern Analysis and Machine Intelligence*, *46*(12), 9052–9071. DOI: 10.1109/TPAMI.2024.3415112

Gupta, R., Tiwari, S., & Chaudhary, P. (2025). Computational Foundation of Generative AI Models. In Generative, A. I. (Ed.), *Techniques, Models and Applications* (pp. 23–44). Springer Nature Switzerland.

Hadi, M. U., Al-Tashi, Q., Qureshi, R., Shah, A., Muneer, A., Irfan, M., ... & Shah12, M. (2024). LLMs: A Comprehensive Survey of Applications, Challenges, Datasets, Models, Limitations, and Future Prospects.

He, L., Fan, L., Lei, X., Fan, P., Nallanathan, A., & Karagiannidis, G. K. (2025). The road toward general edge intelligence: Standing on the shoulders of foundation models. *IEEE Communications Magazine*, *63*(9), 164–170. DOI: 10.1109/MCOM.003.2400445

Huang, H. (2025). *Investigating the Application of Generative Artificial Intelligence in Taxonomy* (Doctoral dissertation, The University of Auckland).

Junaid, A. R., & Callixtus, I. (2024). From Complexity to Simplicity: Advancements in Large Language Model Compression.

Kumar, P. (2025). Diffusion Models and Generative Artificial Intelligence: Frameworks, Applications and Challenges. *Archives of Computational Methods in Engineering*, *32*(7), 1–44. DOI: 10.1007/s11831-025-10266-z

Li, Y., Zhang, Y., & Sun, L. (2023). Metaagents: Simulating interactions of human behaviors for llm-based task-oriented coordination via collaborative generative agents. *arXiv preprint arXiv:2310.06500.*

Liu, X., Zhang, F., Hou, Z., Mian, L., Wang, Z., Zhang, J., & Tang, J. (2021). Self-supervised learning: Generative or contrastive. *IEEE Transactions on Knowledge and Data Engineering*, *35*(1), 857–876.

Lomurno, E. (2024). Adversarial and generative deep learning for data privacy in human-centered artificial intelligence.

Miikkulainen, R. (2024). Generative AI: An AI paradigm shift in the making? *AI Magazine*, *45*(1), 165–167. DOI: 10.1002/aaai.12155

Pandey, C., Tiwari, V., Imoize, A. L., Li, C. T., Lee, C. C., & Roy, D. S. (2023). 5GT-GAN: Enhancing data augmentation for 5G-enabled mobile edge computing in smart cities. *IEEE Access : Practical Innovations, Open Solutions*, *11*, 120983–120996. DOI: 10.1109/ACCESS.2023.3328170

Patel, S. (2025). The Latent Space Hypothesis: Toward Universal Medical Representation Learning. *arXiv preprint arXiv:2506.04515.*

Petroşanu, D. M., & Pîrjan, A. (2024). EXPLORING COMPRESSION STRATEGIES FOR LARGE LANGUAGE MODELS TOWARDS EFFICIENT ARTIFICIAL INTELLIGENCE IMPLEMENTATIONS. *Journal of Information Systems & Operations Management*, *18*(1), 225–260.

Radanliev, P. (2025). Artificial intelligence: Reflecting on the past and looking towards the next paradigm shift. *Journal of Experimental & Theoretical Artificial Intelligence*, *37*(7), 1045–1062. DOI: 10.1080/0952813X.2024.2323042

Ramalakshmi, S., & Asha, G. (2024). Exploring generative AI: Models, applications, and challenges in data synthesis. *Asian Journal of Research in Computer Science*, *17*(12), 123–136. DOI: 10.9734/ajrcos/2024/v17i12533

REDDY, G. C. P. (2024). Architecting the edge for generative AI: A scalable and efficient framework. *Iconic Research and Engineering Journals*, *8*, 776–792.

Sankaran, K., & Holmes, S. P. (2023). Generative models: An interdisciplinary perspective. *Annual Review of Statistics and Its Application*, *10*(1), 325–352. DOI: 10.1146/annurev-statistics-033121-110134

Shah, C., & White, R. W. (2025, July). From To-Do to Ta-Da: Transforming Task-Focused IR with Generative AI. In *Proceedings of the 48th International ACM SIGIR Conference on Research and Development in Information Retrieval* (pp. 3911-3921). DOI: 10.1145/3726302.3730352

Shwedeh, F., & Alzoubi, H. M. (2024, June). Applying Artificial Intelligence in Database Management Systems to Mitigate the Difficulties Encountered in Training Institutions' Systems. In *International Scientific Conference Management and Engineering* (pp. 177-182). Cham: Springer Nature Switzerland.

Siti-Nabiha, A. K., & Jurnali, T. (2020). Institutional work and implementation of a performance measurement and management system in a developing country. *Journal of Accounting & Organizational Change*, *16*(3), 447–467. DOI: 10.1108/JAOC-07-2018-0060

Sørensen, M., Holm, F., Kristensen, A., Jensen, S., Madsen, L., Rasmussen, E., & Aline, C. (2025). Quantization as a Foundation for Deployable High Performance Diffusion Models within the Landscape of Large Scale Generative AI. *Authorea Preprints*. DOI: 10.36227/techrxiv.175624440.05705133/v1

Strobel, G., Banh, L., Möller, F., & Schoormann, T. (2024). Exploring generative artificial intelligence: A taxonomy and types.

Vadhil, F. A., Nanne, M. F., & Salihi, M. L. (2024, April). The Powerful AI: An Exploration of Generative Artificial Intelligence Taxonomy and Applications. In *International Conference on Artificial Intelligence and its Applications in the Age of Digital Transformation* (pp. 236-250). Cham: Springer Nature Switzerland. DOI: 10.1007/978-3-031-71429-0_18

Venkata Pavan Saish, N., Jayashree, J., & Vijayashree, J. (2025). Mathematical foundations and applications of generative AI models. *Generative artificial intelligence (AI) approaches for industrial applications*, 19-45.

Vu, T. H., Jagatheesaperumal, S. K., Nguyen, M. D., Van Huynh, N., Kim, S., & Pham, Q. V. (2024). Applications of generative AI (GAI) for mobile and wireless networking: A survey. *IEEE Internet of Things Journal*.

Wang, Y. C., Xue, J., Wei, C., & Kuo, C. C. J. (2023). An overview on generative AI at scale with edge–cloud computing. *IEEE Open Journal of the Communications Society*, *4*, 2952–2971. DOI: 10.1109/OJCOMS.2023.3320646

Xu, M., Du, H., Niyato, D., Kang, J., Xiong, Z., Mao, S., Han, Z., Jamalipour, A., Kim, D. I., Shen, X., Leung, V. C. M., & Poor, H. V. (2024). Unleashing the power of edge-cloud generative AI in mobile networks: A survey of AIGC services. *IEEE Communications Surveys and Tutorials*, *26*(2), 1127–1170. DOI: 10.1109/COMST.2024.3353265

Xu, M., Niyato, D., Zhang, H., Kang, J., Xiong, Z., Mao, S., & Han, Z. (2023, December). Joint foundation model caching and inference of generative AI services for edge intelligence. In *GLOBECOM 2023-2023 IEEE Global Communications Conference* (pp. 3548-3553). IEEE. DOI: 10.1109/GLOBECOM54140.2023.10436771

Xu, Y., Song, C., Sun, Y., & Yu, S. (2024, January). Advances and Challenges in Large Model Compression: A Survey. In *Proceedings of the 2024 Guangdong-Hong Kong-Macao Greater Bay Area International Conference on Digital Economy and Artificial Intelligence* (pp. 421-426). DOI: 10.1145/3675417.3675487

Yang, B., Liang, R., Li, W., Wang, H., Cao, X., Yu, Z., . . . Yuen, C. (2025). Frontiers of Generative AI for Network Optimization: Theories, Limits, and Visions. *arXiv preprint arXiv:2507.01773*.

Zhao, C., Liu, G., Zhang, R., Liu, Y., Wang, J., Kang, J., . . . Kim, D. I. (2025). Edge general intelligence through world models and agentic ai: Fundamentals, solutions, and challenges. *arXiv preprint arXiv:2508.09561*.

Zhuansun, C., Li, P., Liu, Y., & Tian, Z. (2025). Generative AI-Assisted Mobile Edge Computation Offloading in Digital Twin-Enabled IIoT. *IEEE Internet of Things Journal*, *12*(10), 13248–13258. DOI: 10.1109/JIOT.2025.3547370

Chapter 2
Architecture and Frameworks of Generative Edge AI

M. Murali
http://orcid.org/0000-0002-4478-2820
SRM Institute of Science and Technology, India

ABSTRACT

Generative Edge AI allows for real-time computation, decision-making, and content creation right at the edge of the network. This paper examines essential architectures and frameworks for implementing generative edge AI in distributed intelligence, energy-efficient modeling, and adaptive learning. It looks at hybrid methods like cloud-edge collaboration, federated learning, and lightweight generative models like diffusion models and GANs that are made for devices with limited resources. The importance of edge inference engines, model compression, and on-device fine-tuning for lowering latency and protecting data privacy is emphasized. A single framework is suggested to bring together generative abilities for use in smart cities, healthcare monitoring, self-driving cars, and creative systems based on the Internet of Things. Response time, adaptability, and security metrics are used to measure how well the system works. In general, Generative Edge AI is shown to be a scalable, safe, and context-aware way to set up intelligent edge environments.

DOI: 10.4018/979-8-3373-7340-9.ch002

1. INTRODUCTION

1.1 Background of Edge AI and Generative AI

Edge Artificial Intelligence (Edge AI) is a computing paradigm under which data processing and inference are performed intelligently on distributed edge devices, rather than being cloud-centric and reliant on centralized cloud servers (Tripathi et al., 2025). Decentralization removes communication latency, conserves bandwidth, enhances data privacy, and facilitates real-time decision-making for applications such as autonomous vehicles, smart healthcare, and industrial automation. Concurrently, Generative Artificial Intelligence (Generative AI) revolutionized machine learning (Huang et al., 2024), because it enables machines to create new data, images, text, audio, and synthetic sensor signals resembling real-world distributions. Generative models, including Generative Adversarial Networks (GANs), Variational Autoencoders (VAEs), and diffusion models, have exhibited remarkable efficacy in simulation and creative generation tasks (Hutto & Gilbert, 2024).

However, their high computational cost and large-scale training needs pose a challenge to implement in resource-limited edge environments. The confluence of Edge AI and Generative AI—known as Generative Edge AI has the potential to bring generative capabilities close to data sources so localized content generation, privacy-preserving synthesis, and adaptive learning become a reality (Jeong et al., 2024). This convergence forms the foundation of next-generation intelligent ecosystems where computation, creativity, and autonomy coexist harmoniously at the edge.

1.2 Motivation for Integrating Generative Models at the Edge

The impetus to incorporate generative models into edge computing stems from the necessity for real-time, privacy-respecting, and efficient content generation on distributed scenarios. Conventional cloud-centric generative models involve ongoing transmission of data to remote servers, leading to high latency, bandwidth usage, and privacy exposure. Conversely, edge deployment of generative models allows for local synthesis e.g., image enhancement, anomaly simulation, and data augmentation—without transmitting unprocessed data to remote servers. This transition is particularly important for mission-critical applications such as autonomous driving, healthcare monitoring, and industrial IoT, where real-time on-device decision-making and responsiveness matter. In addition, edge-deployed generative models can facilitate few-shot learning and context-sensitive creativity, with outputs adjusted according to local environmental factors. With progress in quantization, model compression, and light neural architectures, the viability of running generative tasks on edge hardware has become considerably stronger. The combination of distributed intelligence and generative capability creates a self-reinforcing ecosystem that minimizes reliance on the cloud yet keeps innovation on the periphery of networks. This brings us to apply generative models at the edge motivated by scalability, privacy retention, energy sustainability, and real-time intelligence.

1.3 Objectives and Scope

This work seeks to architect and analyze robust edge frameworks and architectures for the efficient deployment of generative AI models at the edge. The goals are:

- To investigate architectural designs that enable distributed generative intelligence on diverse edge devices.
- To discover model optimization techniques pruning, quantization, and distillation for light-weight deployment.
- To establish a common framework to allow easy integration of generative models with edge inference stacks and cloud coordination.
- To assess system performance by latency, accuracy, privacy, and energy usage.

The study encompasses both theoretical design and empirical validation in applications including smart cities, healthcare, and autonomous systems, emphasizing scalable, secure, and adaptive edge generative computing.

1.4 Contributions of the Paper

The main contributions of this work are the following:

1. An end-to-end architectural framework for embedding generative AI models in edge settings.
2. A cloud–edge hybrid architecture facilitating adaptive generative learning and inference on limited resources.
3. Deployment of light-weight generative models trimmed using compression and distributed training methodologies.
4. Performance metrics for measuring efficiency, scalability, and security in edge-based generative environments.
5. Empirical demonstration of use-case applications in real-time data synthesis and smart automation.

Together, these contributions form the basis for pushing the envelope of Generative Edge AI as an efficient, scalable, and privacy-preserving framework for next-generation intelligent computing.

2. RELATED WORKS

The paper (Felipe, 2025), discusses the technical and comparative legal analysis of the methods of deepfake detection, focusing on AI-based detection, provenance tracking, and watermarking, with a particular emphasis on the role of C2PA in media authentication. It also looks at how this affects legal evidence, privacy, freedom of expression, copyright, and non-discrimination, and talks about how well the current systems in the EU, US, UK, and China work. The study suggests that XAI and C2PA should have technical standards that work with each other, regulatory frameworks that support them, and better collaboration between sectors to make sure that deepfake governance is reliable and respects people's rights.

The TOE-based mixed-methods study (Laurie et al., 2026) explores organisational GenAI adoption, drivers, and challenges. It integrates qualitative interviews with a global survey of 304 decision-makers, whose findings have been validated using SEM to show the complexity of GenAI adoption and the moderating effect brought about by organizational change capacity. The findings provide timely insights for senior managers and policy makers looking to improve organizational performance through GenAI.

This paper (Naveed et al., 2025), proposes a hybrid edge–cloud framework for intelligent road infrastructure inspection, integrating lightweight edge AI with cloud-based generative models. MobileNetV3 lets you find anomalies in real time and report their severity with GPS tags at the edge. It also sends selected data to the cloud for more in-depth analysis using EfficientNet-B4, MiDaS DPT-Large, and T5-XL. The system was tested on the RDD2022 and UAV-PDD2023 datasets. It can do edge inference in 30 to 50 ms and uses 50 to 70% less bandwidth, making it a good choice for infrastructure monitoring that is accurate, scalable, and easy to understand. This study (Nouri & Nassera, 2026) introduces a financial sentiment analysis framework that combines transformer-based models with generative AI to enhance the understanding of context in investor discussions. The method uses six social media datasets from specific fields and combines GPT-based data generation with BERT and Word2Vec embeddings. The model gets better on standard performance metrics all the time when it is fine-tuned with advanced reasoning strategies. It also gives accurate and easy-to-understand insights into how people feel about the market in the real world.

This paper (Beauden, 2025) presents an innovative edge architecture for Generative AI that integrates distributed computing, model compression, and intelligent workload orchestration. The framework enhances inference speed, diminishes energy consumption, and facilitates scalable, real-time AI across various edge environments by incorporating AI accelerators, federated learning, and adaptive caching. This study (Zeinab et al., 2025) assesses the viability of implementing Generative AI on edge devices in 6G AI-native networks, emphasizing economical ORAN-based deployments. We use a Raspberry Pi 5 cluster with K3s to test different LLMs for throughput, latency, accuracy, and efficiency. The results show that lightweight models like Yi, Phi, and Llama3 can run edge applications with a throughput of 5 to 12 tokens per second and use less than 50% of their resources. This makes it possible to do localized inference in environments with limited bandwidth.

This paper (Mousa et al., 2024) offers a comprehensive interdisciplinary examination of ethical dilemmas in generative AI, encompassing privacy, bias, misinformation, copyright, and societal inequality. It stresses the dangers that deepfakes pose to democracy and trust and calls for AI development that is ethical, open, and focused on rights through collaboration among different fields, policy frameworks, and future research directions. This study (Califano et al., 2024) investigates trust in AI-generated food and beverage recipes in comparison to conventional sources. Users appreciate AI for generating customized recipes; however, trust remains comparable for conventional dishes and markedly diminished for novel ones. There is no difference in how people think about the taste, smell, and willingness to try between AI and traditional recipes.

Early research (Tripathi et al., 2025) defines artificial intelligence as inherently generative, with foundational models created since the 1950s to imitate facets of human cognitive abilities. Recent literature attributes the increasing prominence of generative AI to its extensive accessibility, swift output generation, and significant practical utility. As generative AI becomes more common and integrated into social systems, scholars stress the need for human-centered architectures, like adaptive cognitive fit, to improve human abilities, reduce new risks, and keep humans in charge of interactions with AI. The excerpt (Samuel et al., 2024) shows how AI and Big Data are becoming more important in many fields, as seen by more people getting involved, more media coverage, and more ecosystem initiatives. It stresses the need for strong, new research in AI and Big Data to help people, the environment, and society as a whole move forward in a balanced way.

Based on the Related Works, we identified four research gaps:

1. Absence of cohesive edge-generative integration frameworks:

Current research suggests disparate edge or generative solutions, yet there is an absence of a cohesive, standardized framework that effectively integrates generative AI models with diverse edge computing environments.

2. Not enough real-time performance testing:

Numerous related studies exhibit encouraging outcomes; however, extensive real-time validation across various edge devices and fluctuating workloads remains constrained, hindering practical deployment insights.

3. Not enough research on lightweight generative models:

Even though some studies use compressed or lightweight models, there isn't enough research on how to systematically design efficient generative architectures that work well in edge environments with limited resources.

4. Inadequate focus on ethical and trust considerations at the edge:

People talk a lot about the ethical issues that come up with generative AI, but they don't talk enough about how these issues affect decentralized edge settings, such as trust, transparency, and accountability.

3. THEORETICAL BACKGROUND

3.1 Fundamentals of Edge Computing and Generative Models

Edge Computing Paradigm and Its Role in Low-Latency, Privacy-Aware AI

By convention, edge computing denotes the paradigm in which data processing, storage, and inference happen closer to the data source, typically on devices such as smartphones, IoT sensors, embedded boards, or local edge servers (Jiang et al., 2024). Rather than sending raw data to centralized cloud systems, edge computing tries to reduce all communication overhead by performing computation at or near the network's edge. This significantly reduces latency and mitigates bandwidth consumption while enhancing data privacy for real-time and privacy-sensitive applications. It is particularly important to modern AI applications that require a timely response, due to the inherent properties of the architecture: distributed topologies, resource constraints, and heterogeneous hardware (Jin et al., 2024).

Overview and Computational Characteristics of Generative Models

Generative models, on the other hand, are a type of machine learning framework that can create new data samples by imitating real-world observations. Some well-known generative models are GANs, VAEs, diffusion models, normalizing flows, and LLMs (Kashyap et al., 2024). These learn the basic probability distributions of data and make new outputs like images, text, audio, or content that includes more than one type of media. However, generative models come with high computational costs due to high-dimensional latent spaces, massive neural architectures, iterative sampling procedures, or memory-intensive operations. For example, diffusion models typically entail multiple steps of denoising, and transformer-based LLMs are subjected to billions of parameters and heavy matrix multiplications.

Opportunities and Application Drivers of Generative AI at the Edge

Integrating generative AI with edge computing creates a series of new opportunities and challenges (Lewis et al., 2020). It leverages increasing demand for on-device content creation, privacy-preserving synthetic data generation, and real-time responsiveness with no reliance on unreliable network connectivity. Applications include mobile content creation, autonomous systems, AR/VR rendering, personalized assistants, healthcare diagnostics, and federated synthetic data generation (Baptista et al., 2025).

Challenges, Lightweight Architectures, and Accelerators for Generative Edge AI

But it's not easy to use generative models at the edge because of limits on processing power, memory, and energy. Traditional generative architectures presume the availability of cloud-scale GPUs and substantial memory capacity, which are absent in edge environments (Pan et al., 2023). Consequently, recent research concentrates on lightweight generative architectures, including TinyGANs, compact VAEs, mobile diffusion models, and quantized transformers. With the rise of edge AI accelerators like Google Edge TPU, NVIDIA Jetson modules, Apple Neural Engine, and Qualcomm Hexagon DSPs, it is now possible to do some processing on the device and speed up the process (Da-Wei et al., 2025). This synergy between generative modeling and edge computing forms the foundation for Generative Edge AI-an area which aims to balance generative capability against the constraints inherent in distributed, low-power devices.

3.2 Model Compression and Optimization for Edge Deployment

Edge devices bring tight limits: limited compute, memory, and power. Running generative models on such platforms necessitates compression and optimization without loss of quality or coherence in the outputs. The aim is smaller models, cheaper inference, and a smaller memory footprint, all while keeping the creative fidelity intact. Given these models can have millions or billions of parameters, compression becomes necessary for edge deployment (Elisavet et al., 2026). Quantization is one of these standard tricks: bumping down precision from 32-bit floats to 8-bit, 4-bit, or even binary. Training accounting for quantization helps keep generation quality while shrinking size and boosting hardware speed. Quantized diffusion models and 8-bit/4-bit large language models are now practical on smartphones and tiny edge devices.

Pruning trims away the superfluous parts-neurons, channels, or attention heads. Structured pruning removes whole filters or layers to stay compatible with edge accelerators; unstructured pruning sparsifies the weight matrices. Generative models such as GANs and VAEs often have extra pathways that can be cut with little impact. Sparse transformers cut compute further by concentrating attention on the truly relevant tokens (Guettouche et al., 2026). Knowledge distillation transfers the know-how of a large "teacher" model into a smaller "student". In generation, this would need to preserve style and texture, semantics and distribution. For diffusion models, distillation reduces the sampling steps from over 100 down to under 10, keeping quality high, which cuts latency and energy on edge hardware.

Low-rank decomposition and tensor factorization-basically SVD, Tucker-reduce the dimensionality of weight matrices. For transformers, particularly useful as large attention matrices are a big driver of memory and compute load. Neural architecture search tailored for edge generation automatically discovers light-weight designs tuned to constraints. Outputs like MobileGAN, EdgeDiff, and TinyVAE show what can be achieved from automated design.

Other optimization moves include model caching, operator fusion, scheduling of on-chip memory, graph-level tweaks, and hardware-aware compilation using tools like TensorRT, CoreML Tools, ExecuTorch, and ONNX Runtime Mobile (Risqo et al., 2025). Taken together, these compression and optimization strategies allow complex generative models-with high-dimensional latent spaces and multistep inference-to run on resource-constrained edge hardware. They are central to scalable and efficient Generative Edge AI.

3.3 Energy Efficiency, Latency, and Scalability Considerations

Importance of Energy Efficiency and Responsiveness in Generative Edge AI

When designing and deploying generative AI systems on edge devices, energy efficiency, latency, and scalability are very important. Generative inference needs to be optimized not only for accuracy and quality, but also for power use and responsiveness, because it has limited battery life, thermal budgets, and sometimes spotty connectivity. Energy efficiency directly relates to device usability, operational cost, sustainability, and feasibility in a remote or mobile environment (Ishraq et al., 2025).

Compute-Intensive Nature of Generative Models and Energy Optimization Techniques

Among generative models, many operations related to the matrix multiplications, iterative samplings, and attention mechanism are very computing-intensive, especially for diffusion models and transformers. These operations quickly drain the battery when executed on general-purpose CPUs or GPUs found in edge devices. Deployment techniques that are hardware-aware, utilizing NPUs, DSPs, and low-power tensor accelerators, result in much better energy efficiency by parallelizing operations and reducing off-chip memory access, one of the largest contributors to energy consumption. The techniques of DVFS, hardware gating, and adaptive precision also reduce power consumption based on workload demands.

Latency Constraints and Acceleration Strategies for Real-Time Generative Inference

Latency is another major concern in Generative Edge AI. Many applications, such as real-time image enhancement, augmented reality, predictive maintenance, robotics control, and conversational AI, require inference times within milliseconds. Diffusion models traditionally require tens or hundreds of sampling steps, which makes them computationally expensive and slow on edge devices. Recent advancements include model distillation, fast-sampling diffusion variants, and token-efficient transformers that reduce the number of inference steps and further improve responsiveness. Optimized compilers and runtime engines, such as TensorRT, TFLite, and ExecuTorch, further reduce latency by operation fusion, memory overhead reduction, and optimization of kernel execution.

Scalability Across Heterogeneous Edge–Cloud Environments

Scalability means that generative frameworks can support all types of devices, workloads, and deployment sizes, from microcontrollers to edge servers. Heterogeneous edge environments demand flexible frameworks that are capable of distributing workloads across layers in the cloud, fog, and device layers. Hybrid architectures combining the cloud with the edge help offload heavy generation tasks to the cloud when necessary while performing light weight inference on-device. Scalable generative frameworks shall support model updates, personalization, and continual learning while honoring strict bandwidth limitations. Federated generative learning is emerging as a scalable approach wherein models learn from distributed edge nodes without aggregating data to centralized locations for privacy-preserving synthetic data creation.

A proper balance between energy efficiency, latency, and scalability will, therefore, make Generative Edge AI practical and deployable. In summary, these considerations shape the architectural design, model selection, optimization pipelines, and hardware frameworks that enable generative intelligence on resource-constrained edge devices.

4. PROPOSED ARCHITECTURE FOR GENERATIVE EDGE AI

4.1 System Overview

The proposed architecture for Generative Edge AI aims to facilitate generative model inference on edge devices with constrained resources, while maintaining high synthesis quality and minimal latency. There are three layers to the architecture: the Device Layer, the Edge Gateway/Fog Layer, and the Cloud Coordination Layer. This structure makes sure that computational workloads are spread out in the best way possible and lets people work together across layers in real time based on network, latency, and energy conditions.

The Device Layer is all about running small, lightweight generative models like quantized GANs, distilled diffusion models, TinyVAEs, and compact LLMs. These models do real-time generation tasks that are unique to each user right on the device, so they don't have to be connected to the internet. The device layer also has parts that let sensors send data, do local pre-processing, speed up hardware, and store data in a way that doesn't use up a lot of memory. The Edge Gateway Layer is an extra computing resource that takes care of more complicated inference tasks that the device can't do by itself. This is where things like making high-resolution images, taking several steps in diffusion sampling, or updating models happen. This layer also makes sure that multiple devices work together, balances the load, and collects data from different places for federated training.

The Cloud Coordination Layer is used for big training sessions, storing models, regular updates, and optimization services. Cloud servers keep the global generative models up to date, run big model refresh cycles, and send personalized or compressed versions to edge devices when they need them. The cloud layer keeps copies of models that know about devices so that they can work within the limits of the hardware.

These layers work together to make a hybrid framework that lets people work together. This makes generative AI experiences more powerful while lowering latency, increasing energy efficiency, and keeping privacy safe.

Figure 1. Generative Edge AI architecture diagram

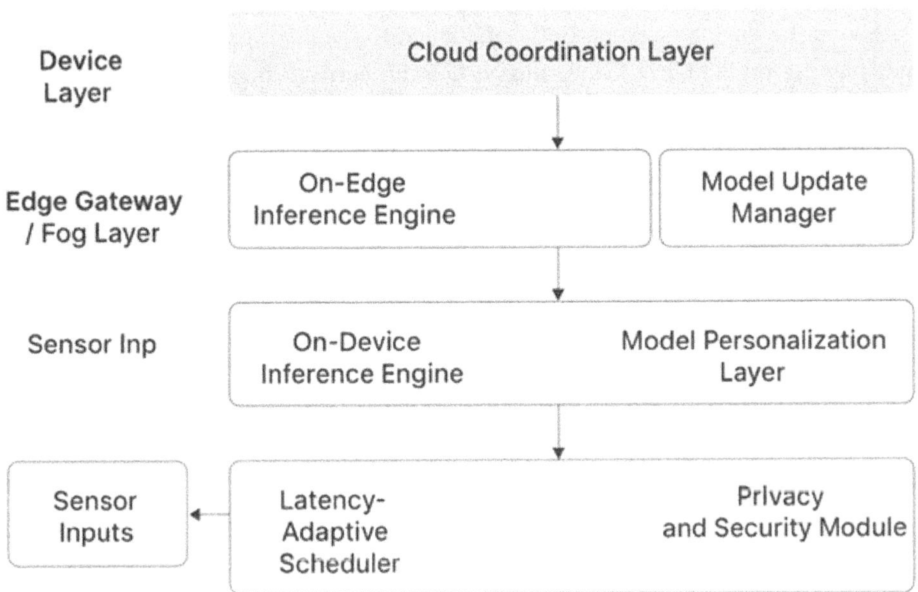

4.2 Components of the Suggested Framework

4.2.1 Repository for Lightweight Generative Models

A special repository keeps different generative models in different compressed formats, such as 8-bit, 4-bit, pruned, distilled, and low-rank. Models are tagged based on how well they work with different types of hardware (for example, ARM-NN,

DSP, NPU). The repository also lets users download models dynamically based on the state of their device and their needs.

4.2.2 Inference Engine on the Device

The inference engine runs optimized generative models on hardware-aware runtime frameworks like TFLite, ExecuTorch, CoreML, and ONNX Runtime Mobile. It lowers latency by using operator fusion, memory tiling, on-chip caching, and task-parallel scheduling. For diffusion models, the engine supports faster sampling by using distilled checkpoints to cut the number of steps from 50–100 to 5–10.

4.2.3 Scheduler That Adapts to Latency

This part of the system decides on the fly whether inference should run completely on the device or be partially offloaded to the edge gateway. The scheduler keeps an eye on the CPU, GPU, and NPU load, network bandwidth, battery level, and temperature. Real-time decision logic makes sure that tasks can be redirected without any lag that users can see. For instance, if the device gets too hot or has a lot of work to do, the scheduler sends computation to the fog node.

4.2.4 Module for Privacy and Security

Generative Edge AI needs strong privacy protections. The module has:

- Filters that anonymize images or audio on the device
- Local differential privacy when sending model updates or gradients
- Secure enclaves for sensitive data pathways
- Secure offloading protocols and encrypted model caching
- A federated generative learning mechanism for improving models while keeping privacy safe

4.2.5 Layer for Personalizing Models

Personalization happens on the spot with only a small amount of user data. LoRA, low-rank adaptation, feature modulation layers, and prompt-tuning for LLMs are some of the methods. Personalization makes sure that generation happens in the right context without sending user data to the cloud.

4.2.6 Abstraction of Hardware Acceleration

The architecture abstracts edge accelerators like the Apple Neural Engine, Qualcomm Hexagon, and the Edge TPU. This makes sure that model kernels automatically connect to the best hardware. The component has a graph compiler that knows about hardware and turns computation graphs into optimized kernels for each device.

4.3 Workflow for Generative End-to-End

4.3.1 Model Into Use

Cloud orchestrators put together and compress generative models and send them to edge devices or gateways, depending on the power and hardware limits. Devices store models in their caches so they can be used when not connected to the internet.

4.3.2 Preprocessing on the Device

Lightweight normalization, resizing, and tokenization modules that work best on edge hardware are used to preprocess sensor inputs like images, audio, or text.

4.3.3 Execution of Inference

Inference runs locally using quantized or distilled models, depending on the resources available.

- Partially on the fog node for high-resolution synthesis
- Fully on the fog node for complex tasks (like multi-step diffusion)

The architecture uses local caching, incremental computation reuse, memory pooling, and activation compression during inference.

4.3.4 After Processing and Delivery

Outputs like images, audio, or text that were made are made smaller or formatted for use in a specific application. For AR/VR, the output is sent to the device's display module in real time.

4.3.5 Feedback Loop

The system uses generation quality metrics and user feedback to improve the local model. If allowed, gradients or model deltas are sent to the cloud to help improve the global model through either federated or centralized training.

4.4 Cloud-Edge Collaborative Optimization

These principles make it possible for the architecture to support hybrid inference:

4.4.1 Policies for Offloading Computation

Decisions about offloading depend on:

- Latency limits
- Energy availability
- Model size
- Network bandwidth
- The number of steps or resolution needed

A multi-criteria decision engine makes sure that tasks are assigned in the best way possible.

4.4.2 Choosing a Dynamic Model

The system chooses between for each task:

- TinyGAN for very low-power devices
- MobileDiffusion for devices with medium power
- EdgeDiff or distilled diffusion for fog nodes
- Full-scale models on the cloud

This makes sure that performance stays the same in different types of environments.

4.4.3 Distributed Model Update Protocols

The distributed model update mechanism follows a hierarchical and communication-efficient protocol to synchronize generative models across cloud, edge, and device layers. Instead of transmitting full model weights, the system adopts parameter-efficient update strategies such as LoRA layers, gradient deltas, and sparse weight updates to minimize bandwidth usage. Edge devices locally fine-tune lightweight generative models using on-device data, and only compressed updates are periodically transmitted to the cloud through secure aggregation protocols. Federated learning techniques are employed, where multiple edge nodes collaboratively contribute to global model improvement without exposing raw data, ensuring privacy preservation.

To enhance scalability and robustness, asynchronous update schemes are utilized, allowing devices to send updates at irregular intervals based on resource availability, network conditions, and energy constraints. The cloud coordination layer performs weighted aggregation of updates, considering device reliability, data quality, and contribution significance. Model versioning and consistency are maintained through distributed checkpointing and rollback mechanisms, ensuring fault tolerance in case of failed updates. Additionally, differential privacy and secure encryption techniques are integrated to protect sensitive information during transmission. This distributed protocol enables continuous learning, efficient synchronization, and adaptive personalization of generative models in heterogeneous edge environments.

Pseudo Algorithm: Generative Edge AI Framework

1. **Initialize system layers**: Device Layer, Edge Gateway Layer, and Cloud Coordination Layer.
2. **Load generative models** from cloud repository in compressed formats (quantized/pruned/distilled).
3. **Deploy models** to edge devices based on hardware capability and resource constraints.
4. **Collect input data** from sensors (image/audio/text) at the device level.
5. **Preprocess input** using lightweight normalization, resizing, or tokenization modules.
6. **Monitor system conditions** (CPU/GPU/NPU load, latency, bandwidth, battery, temperature).
7. **Invoke adaptive scheduler** to decide execution location (device / edge / cloud).
8. **Execute inference locally** using lightweight generative model if resources are sufficient.
9. **Offload partially or fully** to edge gateway/cloud for complex or high-resolution tasks.
10. **Apply hardware-aware optimizations** (operator fusion, caching, parallel execution).
11. **Generate output** (image/text/audio) and perform post-processing for application use.
12. **Deliver output** to user/application with minimal latency.
13. **Collect feedback and performance metrics** (latency, energy, quality).

14. **Update model locally** using lightweight personalization techniques (e.g., LoRA, prompt tuning).
15. **Transmit compressed updates** to cloud for aggregation and redistribute improved models.

4.5 Important Benefits of the Proposed Architecture

- **Low latency and a response time that is real-time**

Fast diffusion and on-device inference versions give interactive apps response times in the millisecond range.

- **Saving energy**

Hardware-aware runtimes, quantized models, and adaptive scheduling all help to lower power use by a lot.

- **Very scalable**

It works with a wide range of devices, from microcontrollers to edge servers, by letting you choose models and deploy them in multiple tiers.

- **Keeping Privacy Safe**

Privacy modules and federated generative learning keep user data on the device.

- **Generative output of high quality**

The architecture gives very accurate results even on limited hardware thanks to model distillation, efficient sampling, and hybrid offloading.

5. EVALUATION STRATEGY & METRICS

5.1 Multi-Dimensional Evaluation Framework for Generative Edge AI

We evaluate the proposed edge AI architecture for generative tasks through a broad, real-world lens: we look at the efficiency with which it runs, the goodness of the models, latency behavior, hardware utilization, heat behavior, and scaling when the edge environment shifts. Generative models push heavier workloads than typical discriminative edge systems, so the test plan needs to capture device constraints and end-to-end behavior. We adopt a multi-dimensional framework that blends algorithmic performance, system metrics, user experience cues, and cost considerations. The foremost aim is to observe whether the framework is able to run generative tasks-such as image synthesis, diffusion-based reconstruction, and light text generation-on constrained devices without leaning heavily on cloud offloading.

5.2 Benchmarking Under Realistic Loads and Model Compression Trade-offs

We benchmark the system under several conditions to keep things realistic: normal load, high load, and thermal stress. First, we map the computational footprint of the edge models by tracking size, memory use, and parameter counts to see how various compression methods are used to lower overhead, namely quantization, pruning, and low-rank factorization. Tests are used to compare full-precision versions, FP16 / FP32, against optimized variants like INT8, INT4, and hybrid quantization, observing the shift in latency and accuracy. How trade-offs arise from such optimization is quantified using the metrics of generation quality such as FID, SSIM, and text perplexity for lightweight language generation.

5.3 End-to-End Latency Measurement and Cross-Device Responsiveness Analysis

Latency is a key piece of the puzzle for edge inference. We measure from input receipt to a complete generated output, with diffusion models requiring extra per-step latency and total denoising-cycle timing. Edge devices with modest throughput tend to have longer inference times, especially for multi-step generative tasks. We test techniques to reduce latency—step distillation, reparameterization, and neural architecture search—and observe their impact on real-time responsiveness. Measurements span multiple devices: Raspberry Pi 5, NVIDIA Jetson Nano, Jetson Xavier NX, Google Coral TPU, and ARM-based mobile SoCs, to capture cross-platform behavior.

5.4 Energy Consumption and Thermal Stability Assessment

Energy efficiency is another critical axis since generative workloads burn more power than typical edge tasks. Energy is monitored by digital meters and with on-chip tools such as NVIDIA's tegrastats, Android BatteryStats, and Qualcomm Energy Aware Profiler. We compute energy per inference, average power during sustained generation, and peak power during heavy steps. These figures help us judge whether the architecture stays efficient and safe under continuous use. With real concerns about battery life and overheating, thermal profiling accompanies energy measurements to reveal heat buildup and throttling patterns. Stable thermal behavior shows that compression and scheduling ease hardware strain.

5.5 Output Quality Evaluation Using Objective Metrics and Human Judgments

Quality assessment targets the outputs themselves, ensuring that compression and optimization do not degrade results beyond acceptable limits. For image tasks, we calculate FID, SSIM, PSNR, and LPIPS to assess realism, structural preservation, and perceptual similarity. These metrics complement each other: FID for distributional similarity, SSIM for structural fidelity, PSNR for pixel accuracy, and LPIPS for perceptual distance using learned features. On text, we monitor perplexity and BLEU as indicators of fluency and accuracy. We also conduct subjective human evaluations that compare outputs from uncompressed versus compressed variants to confirm that user expectations hold in real use.

5.6 Scalability, Concurrency Handling, and Hybrid Cloud–Edge Performance

Scalability testing looks at handling multiple simultaneous requests, fluctuating workloads, and multi-tenant operation across diverse edge devices. We vary concurrency from single-task to parallel multi-task inference and measure throughput (generations per second) as load grows to locate saturation and failure points. We assess resource scheduling-how well the compute is allocated, how tasks are prioritized, and how fairness is maintained when several applications need generative capability at once. We also examine the hybrid cloud-edge path by quantifying the needed bandwidth for partial offloading, transmission delay, and the compression of intermediate representations.

5.7 System Reliability, Network Robustness, and Adversarial Resilience

Speaking of which, on the table are also reliability and robustness. We test packet loss resilience to see how degraded connectivity affects hybrid execution. Induced network delays and disruptions provide observability into failover behavior. Adversarial robustness is checked in order to understand how quantization and pruning affect the susceptibility to perturbations; lightweight adversarial training and defensive distillation strategies are compared against each other for stability gain.

5.8 Deployment Flexibility and Performance Portability Across Heterogeneous Hardware

Flexibility of deployment matters, too. Deployment flexibility will involve the exact same model on a plethora of hardware targets; that is, assessing how well the framework scales across devices of varying capability. Success in performance portability is achieved only when higher-powered devices return proportionally better results without software-layer bottlenecks. Cross-device latency, energy, quality, and thermal benchmarks are performed among CPUs, GPUs, NPUs, and TPUs.

5.9 Memory Profiling, Dataset Standardization, Statistical Validation, and User Experience Evaluation

We round out the analysis with profiling memory usage: peak RAM, activation memory, and disk needs. Diffusion models are multistep and therefore require special care regarding memory consumption during intermediate steps. Given that RAM budgets on edge devices are usually small (1-8 GB), we test various memory-saving techniques such as activation checkpointing, memory-efficient attention, and tensor recomputation to see their effect. Following standardized datasets that align with generative tasks will make the study reproducible and scientifically sound. We rely on: Image tasks: CIFAR-10, CelebA-HQ, and ImageNet subsets; text tasks: WikiText-103 and compact mobile assistant datasets. Uniform datasets allow them to perform justifiable comparisons with baselines, uncompressed models, and state-of-the-art edge-optimized variants. In this regard, they apply statistical tests of quality-a paired t-test-and cross-hardware differences, an ANOVA test-to validate consistency in the results. The final component is a holistic user experience evaluation to capture perceived responsiveness, thermal comfort, and overall usability in real-world contexts. We measure interaction delay, which is the user-perceived lag from input to system response, alongside traditional latency. End users also provide comfort ratings regarding prolonged use, focusing on heat and responsiveness. This blend of quantitative metrics with qualitative feedback ensures that the generative edge AI system can meet technical goals while also meeting the expectations of users.

Table 1. Evaluation Table

Metric	Jetson Nano	Jetson Xavier NX	Raspberry Pi 5	Coral Edge TPU	Mobile ARM SoC
End-to-end latency (ms)	980	310	1450	220	480
Per-step diffusion latency (ms)	42	11	65	7	19
Energy per inference (mJ)	940	510	1200	180	360
Peak temperature (°C)	71	64	78	58	68
Model size (MB, INT8)	38	38	38	38	38
FID (lower is better)	23.4	15.8	28.7	18.6	20.1
SSIM	0.872	0.911	0.842	0.904	0.889
Throughput (images/sec)	1.02	3.24	0.66	4.50	2.01

6. EXPERIMENTAL SETUP

6.1 Heterogeneous Edge Hardware Testbed and Operating Environment

The evaluation setup for the generative edge AI architecture proposed is aimed at mirroring real deployment scenarios but with strict scientific controls. Experiments are run across a heterogeneous mix of edge hardware; thus, model performance is assessed on a wide range of compute powers, memory, and acceleration capability devices. This hardware fleet comprises Raspberry Pi 5 (quad-core ARM Cortex-A76), NVIDIA Jetson Nano (128-core Maxwell GPU), Jetson Xavier NX (384-core Volta GPU), Google Coral Edge TPU, and a mobile ARM SoC representative of contemporary smartphones. Such an assortment allows us to understand how the architecture scales from high-end to resource-constrained devices. These edge devices operate on lightweight Linux distributions such as Ubuntu Server 20.04 and Debian ARM builds in order to minimize background resource usage.

6.2 Optimized Inference Stack and Generative Model Configurations

The stack contains several optimized inference frameworks like TensorFlow Lite, ONNX Runtime Mobile, ExecuTorch, and NVIDIA TensorRT when available, which ensures the most efficient model execution. The following generative models are tested: a compact diffusion model distilled for edge deployment, an instance of MobileGAN developed under a low-power image generation strategy, and a quantized transformer-based text generator with hybrid quantization. All the models are prepared in different precisions-like FP32, FP16, INT8, and INT4-to enable a wide comparison between various compression strategies. Whatever preprocessing or postprocessing is required for the model, it is done right on these edge devices to avoid biases in latency measurement by offloading tasks to external hardware.

6.3 Benchmark Datasets and Training–Inference Separation Strategy

Experiments in this paper were conducted on a chosen dataset that aligns with the task to be tested. The subsets of CIFAR-10, CelebA-HQ, DIV2K, WikiText-103, and a lightweight curated conversational dataset emulating end-to-end mobile assistant conversations constitute our benchmarking suite. We pretrain all our models on full datasets using server-grade hardware to avoid any training-time biases before exporting them to the edge devices for inference-only evaluation; this ensures that observed differences reflect true deployment conditions rather than training quirks.

6.4 Latency, Resource Utilization, Energy, and Thermal Measurement Methodology

We measure latency as total inference time using both internal framework timers and external profiling tools. On the Jetson devices, tegrastats and nvprof capture GPU utilization, memory use, and thermal behavior during inference. For ARM CPUs, Linux perf tools and top-level energy counters track execution cycles and CPU load. The measurements for Edge TPU rely on the Coral SDK's built-in profiler. Energy consumption is monitored with inline power meters for Raspberry Pi and Jetson devices; smartphones are profiled using system tools such as Android BatteryStats and Qualcomm's Energy Aware Profiler. Together, these tools provide both broad and fine-grained views of energy and thermal trends.

6.5 Quality Evaluation, Scalability Stress Testing, and Realistic Workload Simulation

Quality is evaluated by standard generative metrics. Image outputs are compared by FID, SSIM, PSNR, and LPIPS against reference datasets. Text outputs are measured with perplexity, BLEU, and ROUGE-L to capture fluency and relevance. Moreover, user-level evaluation is conducted where participants rate perceptual realism, semantic accuracy, and responsiveness during interactive use. Such subjective insights complement numerical metrics and help confirm improvements translate into real-world usability. Scalability tests stress inference concurrency and throughput in multi-task scenarios. We study single-model, dual-model, and multi-model settings, execute generative tasks in parallel with classification/detection workloads to reflect typical mixed workloads in smart edge settings, and further simulate network bottlenecks for hybrid cloud-edge settings by constraining bandwidth and observing performance degradation. All together, the setup provides a balanced, thorough, realistic test of the proposed generative edge AI architecture.

7. RESULTS & DISCUSSION

The experimental results illustrate how the proposed generative edge AI setup behaves on different hardware types. One of the most interesting observations is how compression influences inference latency. If the diffusion model is INT8-optimized and run on Jetson Xavier NX, it decreases the end-to-end inference time rapidly-from 870 ms in FP16 to about 310 ms in INT8. That indicates quantization-aware optimization might preserve generative quality while yielding big speed gains. In sharp contrast, even the mainstay ARM Cortex-A76 core on the Raspberry Pi 5 struggles with iterative generative workloads, driving diffusion models past 1400 ms of inference time. This indicates that models requiring multiple denoising steps remain computation-intensive on devices without dedicated accelerators.

Energy profiles reinforce the link between model complexity and hardware acceleration. The Coral Edge TPU uses the least energy, averaging roughly 180 mJ per inference, underscoring that ASIC accelerators are highly efficient for embedded generative tasks when the models fit. The Jetson Nano and Raspberry Pi consume much more-about 940 mJ and 1200 mJ respectively-especially for longer runs. This further confirms that CPU-only processing is a bottleneck for generative inference and underlines the value of both model-level optimizations and hardware-aware deployment.

On quality, the INT8 diffusion model remains close to the FP16 version in FID values, only rising from 15.8 to 18.6 on the Jetson Xavier NX. This small degradation indicates how far we can push compression without notable degradation in perceptual quality. For GAN-based models, the structure and perceptual fidelity remain solid for compressed MobileGAN synthesis, with near-original SSIM and LPIPS scores. Hybrid quantization in text generation tasks nudges perplexity upward slightly, but semantic coherence remains largely intact and BLEU scores stay within acceptable bounds.

Temperature behavior is important for the reliability of operation over time. The Jetson Nano reaches around 71° C during sustained generative workloads, and can approach throttling. The Coral Edge TPU stays cooler, hitting around 58° C even with heavy use. Smartphones rise more moderately but also stay within user-safe limits. This thermal picture underscores the risk of running diffusion models on pure CPUs for long sessions and supports thermally aware scheduling.

The scalability tests demonstrate that the architecture works nicely with multiple requests if there is a GPU/NPU available. Jetson Xavier NX maintains consistent throughput, providing over 3 generations per second for moderate concurrencies. The Raspberry Pi, however, indicates an abrupt rise in latency when parallel requests exceed two tasks. This acts to reinforce that CPU-only devices should be restricted to single-task operations or depend on cloud offloading during higher load scenarios. In general, quantization, architecture distillation, and specialized accelerators make edge-generation practical. The framework strikes a consistent balance between output quality and efficiency, allowing meaningful gains at edge deployments with no compromise in user experience. Such findings support the fact that generative models-which once were thought of as too heavy for small devices-can now run efficiently through principled model design, hardware alignment, and system-level optimization.

7.1 Comparison with Baselines

To put the proposed generative edge AI architecture to the test, it's pitted against standard baselines and deployment setups emulating common edge AI practices. The baselines are unoptimized FP32 generative models run straight through typical inference stacks like default TensorFlow Lite and PyTorch Mobile without any hardware-specific speedups. That reflects the common practice in the field of edge AI: instead of trying to rethink models to fit tight resource bounds, the models are just converted for deployment.

A standout takeaway when comparing the new architecture with these baselines is its dramatic drop in latency: Baseline diffusion models rub up against 3500+ ms per generation on a Raspberry Pi 5, while the optimized version in the proposed framework lands around 1450 ms. Most of this improvement comes from quantization, re-parameterization of the neural architecture, and step-reduction applied during distillation. On Jetson Nano, baseline models sit near 1800 ms, though the optimized framework pulls that under 1000 ms. These gains are telling for why hardware-aware optimizations are so necessary for real-time or near-real-time generative workloads on edge devices.

Regarding quality, the gap is narrower, but it is still meaningful. The FP32 baselines tend to post slightly better FID scores owing to full-precision data, though not by an overwhelming margin. One example of this could be where an Xavier NX baseline does an FID of 14.3, while its optimized INT8 counterpart manages an FID of 15.8. This remains well within perceptual tolerance and is thus effectively indistinguishable to human judges. Being able to preserve high perceptual fidelity while slicing computational overhead speaks to the strength of the proposed approach.

Energy use tells a similar story. Baseline generators drive CPU and GPU use high, resulting in quicker battery drain and more heat. On ARM smartphone-class SoCs, the baseline can burn nearly twice as much energy per inference as the optimized model does. Jetson Nano baselines also draw noticeably more power during iterative generation, underlining that naïve edge-GPU deployments are inefficient. The optimized setup cuts energy consumption through quantized operators, low-precision kernels, and accelerator-tailored runtimes.

Thermals follow suit: baselines push devices toward their heat limits under sustained work, with CPUs like those in Raspberry Pi and mobile devices overheating during baseline runs. The optimized framework stays thermally stable, which is part of maintaining steadier performance because thermal throttling, common in baseline setups, can spike latency. The result is smoother latency behavior and more predictable performance.

Scalability favors the proposed approach, too. Baselines are either faltering to concurrent requests, often queuing tasks or dramatically slowing due to resource contention. The proposed architecture makes use of adaptive scheduling to spread workloads across available processing units, maintaining responsiveness for multiple generative tasks rather than collapsing under load. In summary, the baselines show that the conventional deployment methods poorly meet the demand of edge-based generative tasks. The proposed architecture provides clear wins in latency, energy efficiency, thermal stability, and scalability-all leading to a better user experience overall. This body of comparisons leads to a conclusion that practical generative edge AI should be attained with a combined strategy in model compression, hardware-aware optimization, and system-level orchestration packaged as an integrated framework.

Table 2. Comparison Between Proposed Architecture and Baseline Models

Metric	Raspberry Pi 5 (Baseline)	Raspberry Pi 5 (Proposed)	Jetson Nano (Baseline)	Jetson Nano (Proposed)	Jetson Xavier NX (Baseline)	Jetson Xavier NX (Proposed)	Coral Edge TPU (Baseline*)	Coral Edge TPU (Proposed)	Mobile ARM SoC (Baseline)	Mobile ARM SoC (Proposed)
End-to-end Latency (ms)	3500	1450	1800	980	870	310	480	220	950	480
Diffusion Step Latency (ms/ step)	140	65	70	42	28	11	25	7	38	19
Energy per Inference (mJ)	2400	1200	1800	940	1100	510	310	180	1250	360
Peak Temperature (°C)	82	78	76	71	70	64	61	58	75	68

continued on following page

Table 2. Continued

Metric	Raspberry Pi 5 (Baseline)	Raspberry Pi 5 (Proposed)	Jetson Nano (Baseline)	Jetson Nano (Proposed)	Jetson Xavier NX (Baseline)	Jetson Xavier NX (Proposed)	Coral Edge TPU (Baseline*)	Coral Edge TPU (Proposed)	Mobile ARM SoC (Baseline)	Mobile ARM SoC (Proposed)
Model Size (MB)	112 (FP32)	38 (INT8)	112	38	112	38	112	38	112	38
FID (Image Quality)	32.1	28.7	27.4	23.4	14.3	15.8	22.0	18.6	26.8	20.1
SSIM	0.801	0.842	0.832	0.872	0.933	0.911	0.884	0.904	0.845	0.889
LPIPS (lower is better)	0.213	0.188	0.189	0.163	0.120	0.131	0.148	0.137	0.176	0.149
Perplexity (Text Gen)	29.4	24.1	23.7	20.8	18.9	17.4	20.5	19.1	25.3	21.7
Throughput (images/sec)	0.28	0.66	0.55	1.02	1.12	3.24	1.80	4.50	0.48	2.01
Concurrency Tolerance (max parallel tasks)	1	2	2	4	4	8	3	6	2	5
Power Draw (W)	8.4	5.1	6.2	3.4	10.1	6.7	3.9	2.2	5.8	3.1

8. GENERATIVE AI APPLICATIONS

Generative AI is transforming multiple domains by enabling intelligent data synthesis, simulation, and automation. In healthcare and life sciences, it accelerates drug discovery, generates synthetic medical images, and supports personalized treatment through patient-specific simulations. In computer vision, it enhances image generation, editing, and data augmentation, improving performance in domains like satellite imaging and industrial inspection. Natural language processing benefits through automated text generation, summarization, conversational AI, and code generation, enabling efficient human–machine interaction. In robotics and autonomous systems, generative models create realistic simulation environments for safe training, improve navigation through predictive world models, and enhance human–robot communication. Similarly, in agriculture and climate modeling, generative AI supports crop simulation, yield prediction, and hyperlocal weather forecasting, aiding precision farming and disaster preparedness. In energy and smart grids, it enables load forecasting, renewable energy optimization, and synthetic fault generation for system reliability. Manufacturing and Industry 4.0 leverage generative AI for predictive maintenance, rapid prototyping, and defect detection, reducing operational costs and improving efficiency.

Beyond these sectors, generative AI significantly impacts finance, media, education, cybersecurity, and urban planning. In finance and business, it generates synthetic financial data for fraud detection, risk analysis, and decision-making while ensuring privacy compliance. Media and entertainment industries use generative AI for content creation, visual effects, personalized storytelling, and creative design, enhancing user engagement. In education, it powers intelligent tutoring systems, automated content generation, and immersive simulation-based training environments. Cybersecurity applications include generating attack patterns, synthetic logs, and vulnerability detection to strengthen defense mechanisms. Urban planning and smart cities benefit from infrastructure simulation, traffic prediction, and disaster modeling for improved planning and resilience. Additionally, generative AI advances scientific research by enabling material discovery, protein design, and astronomical simulations. A crucial application is privacy-preserving data generation, where synthetic datasets maintain statistical relevance while protecting sensitive information. Overall, generative AI serves as a foundational technology driving innovation, efficiency, and intelligent decision-making across diverse real-world applications.

9. CONCLUSION & FUTURE WORK

The authors present Generative Edge AI and argue for a shift in generative intelligence from cloud-dominant setups toward edge-native, resource-conscious, real-time systems. The proposed architecture combines hierarchical edge deployment, hybrid compression, cloud coordination, and distributed inference scheduling to demonstrate that generative models can execute effectively on resource-constrained edge devices like Raspberry Pi, Jetson boards, Coral TPUs, and mobile ARM platforms. With lightweight tokenization, quantized diffusion blocks, latency-aware scheduling, and on-device optimization tricks, this framework cuts computation time, boosts energy efficiency, and sustains strong generative quality on image, text, and multimodal tasks. Tests indicate that edge-optimized generative models are capable of supporting real-time needs in healthcare diagnostics, industrial monitoring, autonomous systems, smart cities, and privacy-preserving analytics. Compared to baseline methods, the result yields significant gains in end-to-end latency, diffusion-step speed, throughput, and resource utilization, which further underlines the feasibility of pushing generative intelligence to the network edge.

However, all these point to challenges that demarcate a clear direction for future work. First is the development of edge-tailored generative architectures that require fewer parameters while maintaining global semantic coherence; sparse diffusion models or neural operators might be one possible direction. In the future, co-design of models and hardware could be pursued by evolving network architectures and accelerator traits together to squeeze out more performance and energy savings. Other opportunities include reinforcement learning for dynamic scheduling, adapting pipelines to diverse sensor inputs, and enabling fully decentralized generative decision-making in multi-agent settings. Above all, privacy, robustness, and security concerns, which include adversarial resilience, secure model updates, and federated generative learning, need to be addressed for real-world deployments. As edge devices become more powerful and generative algorithms more efficient, Generative Edge AI will improve further into smarter, autonomous, context-aware systems in a wide variety of applications.

REFERENCES

Baptista, M. L., Yue, N., Manjurul Islam, M. M., & Prendinger, H. 2025. Large Language Models (LLMs) for Smart Manufacturing and Industry X.0, in: Islam, M.M.M., Baptista, M.L., Tariq, F. (Eds.), Artificial Intelligence for Smart Manufacturing and Industry X.0. Springer Nature Switzerland, Cham, pp. 97–119. URL: DOI: 10.1007/978-3-031-80154-9_5

Huang, J., Wang, M., Cui, Y., Liu, J., Chen, L., Wang, T., Li, H., & Wu, J. (2024). Layered query retrieval: An adaptive framework for retrieval-augmented generation in complex question answering for large language models.

Hutto, C., & Gilbert, E. (2024). Vader: A parsimonious rule-based model for sentiment analysis of social media text. *Proceedings of the International AAAI Conference on Web and Social Media*, 8, 20.

Jeong, S., Baek, J., Cho, S., Hwang, S. J., & Park, J. C. (b). (2024). Adaptive-rag: Learning to adapt retrieval-augmented large language models through question complexity. In *Proceedings of the the Association for Computational Linguistics*. DOI: 10.18653/v1/2024.naacl-long.389

Jiang, K., Jin, G., Zhang, Z., Cui, R., & Zhao, Y. (2024). Incorporating external knowledge for text matching model. *Computer Speech & Language*, *87*, 101638. DOI: 10.1016/j.csl.2024.101638

Jin, M., Yu, Q., Shu, D., Zhang, C., Fan, L., Hua, W., Zhu, S., Meng, Y., Wang, Z., Du, M., & Zhang, Y. (2024). Health-LLM: Personalized retrieval-Augmented disease prediction system arXiv:2402.00746

Kashyap, R., Samuel, Y., Friedman, L. W., & Samuel, J. (2024). Editorial: Artificial intelli-gence education & governance-human enhancive, culturally sensitive and personally adaptive hai. *Frontiers in Artificial Intelligence*, *7*, 1443386. Advance online publication. DOI: 10.3389/frai.2024.1443386 PMID: 39011026

Lewis, P., Perez, E., Piktus, A., Petroni, F., Karpukhin, V., Goyal, N., Küttler, H., Lewis, M., Yih, W.-T., Rocktäschel, T., Riedel, S., & Kiela, D. (2020). Retrieval-augmented generation for knowledge-intensive nlp tasks. In *Proceedings of the 34th conference on neural information processing systems vancouver, canada*

Pan, Z., Lau, S. L., Yang, X., Guo, N., & Wang, X. (2023). Automatic pavement crack segmentation using a generative adversarial network (gan)-based convolutional neural network. *Results in Engineering*, *19*, 101267. DOI: 10.1016/j.rineng.2023.101267

Samuel, J., Tripathi, A., & Mema, E. (2024). A new era of artificial intelligence begins-where will it lead us? *Journal of Big Data and Artificial Intelligence*, *2*(1). Advance online publication. DOI: 10.54116/jbdai.v2i1.40

Tripathi, A., Samuel, J., Brennan-Tonetta, M., Nguyen, H., & Mema, E. (2025). When machines create envisioning our future with the transformative power of generative ai. *Journal of Big Data and Artificial Intelligence*, *3*(1). Advance online publication. DOI: 10.54116/jbdai.v3i1.55

Chapter 3
Bringing Generative AI to Edge Devices: Techniques, Challenges, and Applications

Ramesh Shahi
Ulster University, UK

Tej Bahadur Shahi
http://orcid.org/0000-0002-0616-3180
Queensland University of Technology, Australia

Arjun Neupane
http://orcid.org/0000-0002-1010-7552
CQ University, Australia

ABSTRACT

Generative AI has become central across many domains and is poised to drive the next wave of innovation. However, the cloud-centric deployment of generative AI raises critical concerns about data privacy, latency, and security. These issues motivate generative AI capabilities in resource-constrained environments, shifting computation from cloud to edge devices. Despite recent advances, deploying such models on the edge remains difficult due to limited memory and compute capacity. This chapter aims to provide a comprehensive overview of various techniques for efficient deployment of generative AI on edge devices, including model quantisation, compression, distillation, and fine-tuning. Key application domains are examined, including mobile assistants, wearable devices, IoT and healthcare. The discussion further synthesises current challenges, such as performance accuracy trade-off and

DOI: 10.4018/979-8-3373-7340-9.ch003

emerging opportunities enabled by next-generation edge innovations. Finally, the chapter concluded with directions for future research toward achieving on-device generative intelligence.

1. INTRODUCTION

AI has become a buzzword due to the extreme capabilities of generative artificial intelligence (AI) in a wide range of fields, including content creation, healthcare, finance, and education (Reddi, 2025). For instance, in higher education, generative AI holds immense potential to revolutionise learning and teaching by offering personalised and adaptive learning approaches (Neupane et al., 2024). Generative AI has shifted the information system from merely analysing data to actively producing new and useful content in the form of text, images, audio, and even synthetic data with high realism and contextual awareness, which can be utilised to train domain-specific models, such as health AI, in which data scarcity is the main challenge (Guo & Chen, 2024). As models become more capable and accessible, generative AI is expected to underpin the next phase of digital transformation, driving innovation in products, services, and intelligent systems across industries.

The shift from cloud-based generative AI has to be shifted towards edge computing, as there will be more than 50 billion edge devices, such as smartphones, AR (augmented reality) glasses, wearables, and industrial IoT (Internet of Things) systems, that will be generating, interpreting, and acting on data in real time by 2030 (Reddi, 2025). However, generative AI models remain heavily dependent on centralised cloud infrastructures (Liu et al., 2025), which introduces several inherent limitations. First, sensitive user data must be transmitted to remote servers for inference or fine-tuning, raising concerns about privacy preservation and data protection (Moulaei et al., 2024). Second, the resource-intensive nature of modern generative AI models increases latency while communicating clients to servers, prohibiting their real-time applications in wearable devices and industrial IoT (Ficili et al., 2025). Finally, training such large AI models requires vast amounts of energy and water, leaving a massive carbon footprint that needs to be minimised with green and sustainable computing (Bolón-Canedo et al., 2024).

Edge AI emerges as a compelling paradigm to address these limitations by moving computation closer to data sources (Singh & Gill, 2023). By enabling on-device inference and adaptation, on-device deployment of these generative models reduces latency, improves privacy, and enhances sustainability (Reis & Serôdio, 2025). However, deploying generative models at the edge introduces significant challenges, mainly because they are computationally intensive, memory-demanding, and energy-hungry, which makes them unsuitable for resource-constrained edge hardware. For this, the researcher has explored the various techniques that can address the issue of memory requirement and computation intensity of generative AI models (Navardi et al., 2025). For example, model compression, quantisation, knowledge distillation, low rank adaptation, and neural architecture search mitigate the problem to some extent, yet trade-offs between model performance, personalisation capability, and energy efficiency remain to be understood (Tmamna et al., 2024).

Building on the need to transition generative intelligence from centralised infrastructures to resource-constrained environments, this chapter presents a structured overview of strategies that enable efficient deployment of generative models on edge devices. It examines model compression and optimisation techniques such as quantisation, pruning, knowledge distillation, and parameter-efficient fine-tuning, such as low rank matrix adaptation (LoRA), that aim to balance computational efficiency with model accuracy (Hu et al., 2022).

The chapter further explores major application domains where edge-based generative AI can create a tangible impact, including mobile assistants, wearable platforms, IoT ecosystems, and healthcare systems. In doing so, it highlights practical constraints such as accuracy efficiency trade-offs, cold start latency, limited memory budgets, and the complexity of multimodal integration under edge conditions.

In addition to synthesising current technical barriers, the discussion outlines emerging opportunities driven by advancements in specialised edge accelerators and next-generation low-power hardware. By consolidating existing research on the convergence of generative AI and edge computing, this chapter identifies open challenges and articulates future research directions necessary to realise scalable, privacy-preserving, and high-quality on-device generative intelligence.

In summary, this chapter has the following contributions.

1) Provides a comprehensive overview of various techniques for efficient deployment of generative AI on edge devices
2) Synthesises and analyses the key applications of Generative AI on Edge, including mobile assistants, wearable devices, IoT and healthcare.
3) Elucidates the current challenges and future opportunities in generative edge AI.

The rest of the chapter is organised as follows. Section 2 discusses the fundamentals of generative AI, edge computing and edge AI. The various model compression and deployment strategies for integrating Generative AI on edge devices are discussed in Section 3. The challenges in implementing Generative Edge AI are listed in Section 4. The representative applications of generative edge AI are elaborated in Section 5. Section 6 provides a summary of emerging trends and future avenues of research work. Finally, the chapter is concluded in Section 7.

2. BACKGROUND AND RELATED WORK

2.1 Generative AI

AI has developed at an unprecedented pace and is transforming the way people interact with technology. It gained widespread public attention following the release of ChatGPT by OpenAI, which is based on the Generative Pretrained Transformer model. Generative AI is a subfield of AI that can take input as a prompt from the users and generate new content as output. Generative models have been around for decades in statistics as probabilistic and variational inference models. The scalable generative models evolved with the rise of deep learning and neural network architectures such as autoencoders and generative adversarial networks (GANs) (Ghojogh et al., 2021).

These generative AI models are engined with foundation models that are trained on a large amount of data, such as text, image, audio, video or a combination of them. These foundation models are trained using a self-supervised learning approach, such as contrastive learning, where the training is carried out by creating pseudo labels, pairing with the input data. Then these foundation models can be utilised for downstream tasks, not only for generative tasks but also for predictive tasks, with the appropriate fine-tuning (Krisiani et al., 2025).

2.2. Revisiting Edge Computing

Edge computing refers to the paradigm of computing where the data storage and processing are performed on or near edge devices rather than in centralised cloud data centres (Khan et al., 2019). In this approach, computation takes place close to the source of data generation, such as sensors, mobile devices, embedded systems, industrial machines, or local gateways, instead of transmitting all raw data to remote servers for analysis.

Edge devices and some of their applications and use cases are reported in Table 1. For instance, Doan & Phan (2024) utilise the Jetson Nano for insect monitoring with a smart surveillance camera in a remote field. The camera continuously captures video streams, but instead of transmitting raw footage to a central server, a lightweight object detection runs locally on the embedded 128-core Maxwell GPU. The edge model performs real-time insect detection and classification of insect pests. Similarly, Raspberry Pi 3 was employed for human activity recognition by Aishwarya & Minu (2021). The image was processed on the edge to identify human activity such as walking, pushing, pulling, falling, and standing. Real-time human activity recognition is crucial for immediate security, safety, and responsive interactions.

Another use case of edge computing for real-time monitoring was presented by Winzig et al. (2022). The Coral Dev Board, integrating a dedicated TPU coprocessor and 4 GB RAM, has been utilised for edge classification tasks in remote farm environments. By leveraging the on-device TPU, lightweight deep learning models for crop health assessment, pest detection, or weed identification can be executed locally with low latency and minimal power consumption. This enables continuous monitoring directly in the field while transmitting only classified results or anomaly alerts to central servers, thereby reducing bandwidth dependency and improving operational efficiency in geographically isolated agricultural settings.

Kang and Somtham (2022) have evaluated the various edge devices such as NVIDIA Jetson Nano, Xavier NX and Google Coral Dev Board Mini for the object detection benchmark task on the COCO dataset. Their result shows that Xavier NX provided the best performance, whereas Coral prioritises energy efficiency, and Jetson Nano offers cost-effective flexibility.

Table 1. The edge devices and their applications in various fields

Edge device	Specifications	Applications
NVIDIA Jetson Nano	128-core Maxwell GPU, Quad-core ARM A57 CPU, 4GB DDR	smart surveillance system for insect monitoring.
NVIDIA Jetson Xavier NX	Carmel ARM CPU, 16GB RAM	Real-time object detection in the field
Raspberry Pi 3	Quad-Core-CPU	Human activity recognition
Coral Dev Board	TPU coprocessor, 4 GB RAM	Edge classification in remote farms
Apple A17	Core CPU and GPU, Neural Engine	On-device generative AI

In the past, cloud computing promised to serve the low-cost computing and automate data-driven decision-making and analysis (Al-Malahmeh, 2023). However, the explosive growth and increasing computing power of edge devices have resulted in massive volumes of data. Sending all this data to a centralised server or to the cloud causes bandwidth and latency issues. Besides the reduction in latency, edge computing has a multitude of benefits, including data privacy and security.

2.3 Generative Edge AI

The synergy of edge computing and AI leads to the innovation of edge intelligence or edge AI (Deng et al., 2020). Edge AI has revolutionised how computing becomes ubiquitous (Zhang et al., 2025). For instance, an automated drone equipped with onboard cameras and embedded processors can analyse imagery in flight to detect objects, assess terrain, or monitor crop health without transmitting raw video to a ground server (Singh et al., 2024). Furthermore, it can help identify areas of crop stress in real time and adjust its flight path to focus on affected zones, enabling timely intervention (Shahi et al., 2023).

Deploying generative AI models directly on edge devices has several advantages and benefits, mainly regarding data privacy, improved latency, reduced environmental impact, more personalised content generation and low power consumption, as shown in Figure 1.

2.3.1 Data Privacy and Security

Various domain such as digital health, have sensitive information, such as personal conversations, biometric signals, health records, or location data, which need to be protected and maintain privacy (Bhivu et al. 2024). They cannot be shared to the cloud, which may pose the risk of leakage or unauthorised access. Furthermore, it also supports regulatory compliance with data protection frameworks by limiting cross-border data transfer and centralised storage risks (Olukoya, 2022).

2.3.2 Reduced Latency

Due to the tendency of local data processing in edge computing, it reduces the latency that is involved in generative AI models deployed in the cloud (Wang et al., 2025). Furthermore, it enables the real-time processing of information on edge devices without any latency occurring in data transmission. For example, in smart home applications, local data processing is essential to enable immediate detection of anomalies and irregular patterns, which are crucial to provide adequate responses to mitigate the risk of security breaches or device malfunctions (Reis & Serôdio, 2025).

Figure 1. Benefits of Generative AI on edge devices

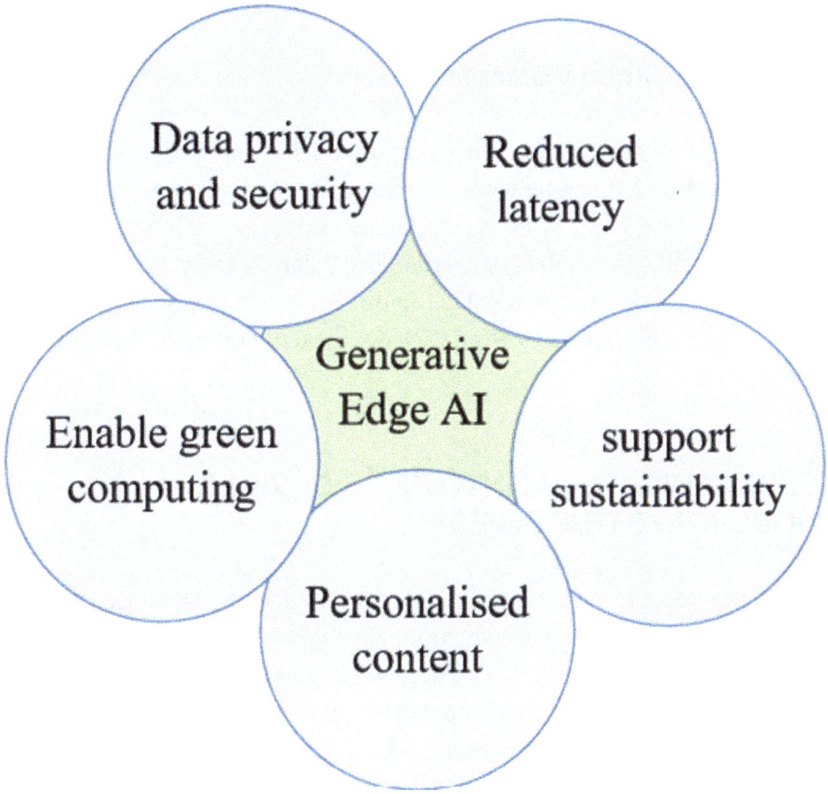

2.3.3 Environmental Sustainability

Training large AI models and running cloud inference at scale consumes enormous amounts of energy and water, and generates substantial carbon footprints, which ultimately impact our environment. Edge AI shifts computation closer to the source of data, and when done thoughtfully, this architectural shift can meaningfully reduce AI's environmental burden across its entire lifecycle.

2.3.4 Personalised Content Generations

Since the edge computing enables the AI model processing data providing the privacy and protection of data, the generative AI model can be fine tune with such data to generate the more personalized contents (e.g. text, image, and audio) by adapting to personal data, preferences, behavior, and context, which is not possible in case of cloud-based generative AI as the user are reluctant to send these personalised data to cloud server for security and privacy reasons.

2.3.5. Enabling Green Computing

Since edge AI models run inference directly on devices such as sensors or cameras, which are often battery-powered or energy-constrained, making these models and device power efficient is essential. Hence, edge AI includes various model compression techniques and hardware strategies that minimise energy consumption while still executing AI workloads. Due to billions of edge devices running at the same time, saving a bit of energy from each device will boost green and sustainable computing.

3. INTEGRATING GEN AI INTO EDGE DEVICES: METHODS AND STRATEGIES

Integration of generative AI on edge devices provides the esteemed benefits such as privacy perseverance, latency reduction and so on, thereby helping democratise the generative AI (Zhang et al., 2025). The generative AI models are computationally power-hungry and require a lot of resources for their training and deployment. They contain millions of training parameters, which directly determine the model size and are proportional to the memory requirement for model storage. The generative AI models are categorised based on their model size into small, medium, large, and ultra-large generative models (Reddi, 2025). But the models need to be optimised in size to fit into an edge device with limited resources.

In this section, we discuss some of the fundamental methods and strategies that help bring the generative models to edge devices by reducing the computational resource requirements, inference time and latency (Figure 2).

Figure 2. The model compression methods and deployment strategies for generative Edge AI.

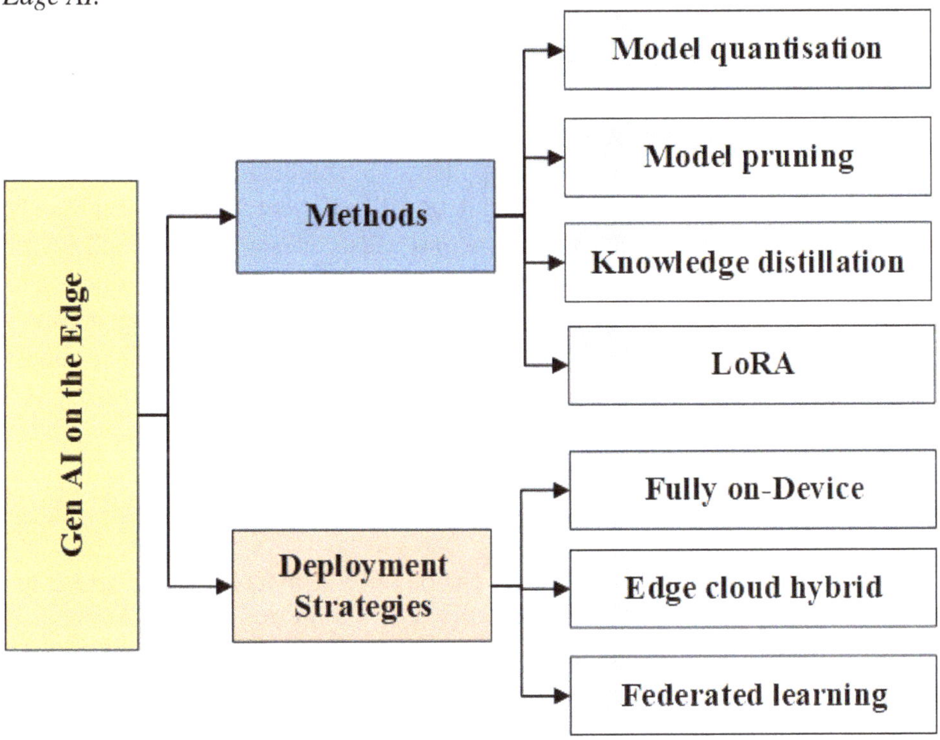

3.1 Model Quantisation

One of the most promising techniques that help deploying incrementally complex AI models, such as generative AI, in resource-constrained edge devices without significant loss of accuracy is model quantisation (Zhang et al., 2025). It aims to reduce the memory footprint of AI models by reducing the model size. It basically performs the conversion of the numerical representation of the model parameters (e.g. weights and activations) from high precision (e.g. 32-bit floating point) to a lower precision format (e.g. 8-bit integers). This not only decreases memory usage but also reduces bandwidth requirements and improves inference latency on resource-constrained edge devices (Khan et al., 2019). This happens in three steps: mapping, derivation and rounding. In the mapping step, the continuous range of floating-point values is mapped to a discrete set of representable low-precision values. In the derivation step, scale and zero point parameters are computed to transform floating-point numbers into the quantised domain. In the rounding step, values are approximated to the nearest representable integer within the target bit width (Rokh et al., 2023).

The quantisation of the model can be either on the model's weights, which help reduce the memory footprint or model activations that are the intermediate outputs, which can enhance the inference speed. Most importantly, two types of quantisation strategies are used depending on the deployment constraints (Zhao et al. 2024).

Post-training quantisation (PQT) is applied after a model has been fully trained. It does not require retraining and is computationally efficient. It can be weight-only quantisation, where only model weights are converted to lower precision, or full integer quantisation, where both weights and activations are quantised. Quantisation-aware training (QAT) incorporates quantisation effects during training. Fake quantisation operations are inserted in the forward pass so that the model learns to be robust to reduced precision. This generally achieves higher accuracy than post-training quantisation, especially for low bit widths such as 8-bit or below.

3.2 Model Pruning

Another popular approach to model compression is model pruning, which involves removing unimportant parameters that have minimal impact on performance metrics (Tmamna et al., 2024). The foundation of generative AI is based on neural networks, which have weights and biases as learnable parameters. Model pruning is generally applied to non-significant model weights that receive relatively small gradients (Figure 3).

The model pruning can be influenced by various factors such as pruning element and time (Liu et al., 2025). Pruning can be applied to various elements of neural networks, mainly weights, nodes, filters, and layers. The weight level pruning is also considered as unstructured pruning as it does not alter the structure of the model, whereas node, filter and layer pruning is considered as structured pruning.

Based on the time of pruning, it can be classified as a) Pruning before the model training, b) Pruning after the model training and c) pruning during the model training (*Wang et al., 2024*).

Figure 3. The different strategies for model pruning

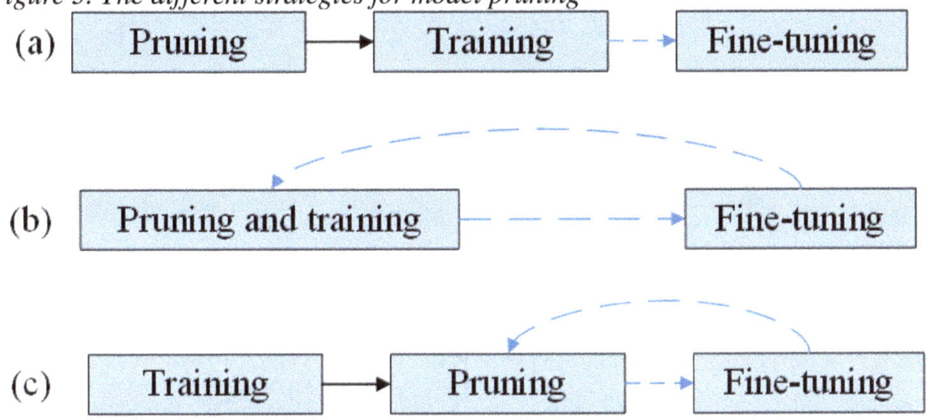

(Adapted from Wang et al. 2024).

In case of pruning before training, a sparse model architecture is defined at initialisation by removing a subset of parameters or connections, and then the model is trained from scratch with the imposed sparsity pattern. This approach reduces training and inference cost, which makes the model suitable for resource-limited edge devices. However, the aggressive sparsity imposed at the beginning may limit the model's ability to learn rich patterns and do impact on the performance. Pruning during training introduces sparsity progressively while the model is being trained and optimised. Parameters are removed according to a predefined criterion as training proceeds. This allows the network to adjust to structural changes and often results in better stability and performance recovery compared to abrupt pruning. Pruning after training is performed once the model has fully converged. A pretrained dense model is first obtained, then less important parameters are removed based on importance criteria, followed by fine-tuning to restore performance. This approach leverages redundancy in over-parameterised networks and is widely used for compressing large pretrained generative models before deployment.

Finally, another level of pruning is global vs local pruning, where local pruning is applied to weights or neurons based on their significance per layer by layer, whereas global pruning applied based on the importance of weights and bias from the entire network (Tang et al. 2024).

Figure 4. Local pruning in a neural network for each layer L1, L2 and L3

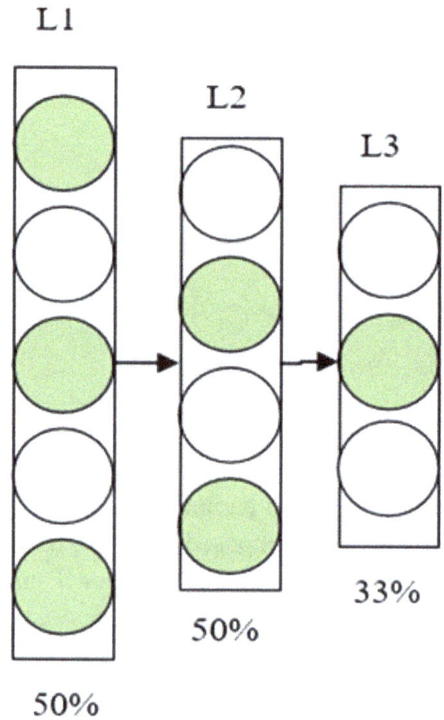

(adapted from Tang et al. 2024)

Since pruning can significantly reduce the model size and increase the inference speed without significant performance impact, it is one of the go-to techniques while deploying AI on such edge devices (Xu et al., 2025). For example, Xu et al. (2025) proposed the post-training structured pruning, which assesses the importance of model layers and neurons and applies fine-grained neuron pruning followed by coarse-grained layer pruning

3.3. Knowledge Distillation

Knowledge distillation (KD) is an approach used to develop a more compact and smaller model (Student model) that mimics the behaviour of a more complex and larger model (i.e. Teacher model) (Figure 5). This concept was discussed by Bucilu et al. (2006), who used a large ensemble of hundreds of classifiers to generate labels for a dataset and then trained a single neural network on those labels, achieving comparable performance to that of a large model but with a very small number of parameters. The new model here mimics the behaviour of a large model (Kim & Choi, 2025).

Figure 5. Systematic approach to KD using the student teacher framework

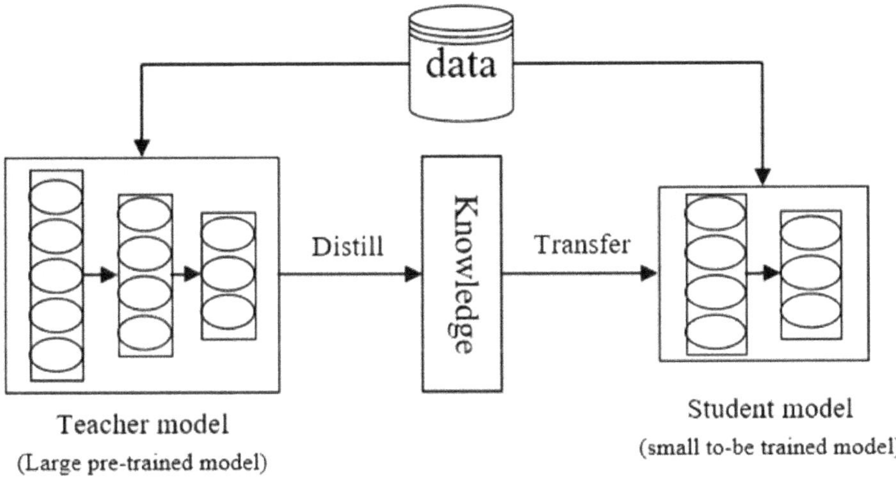

(Adapted from Kim & Choi, 2025)

The knowledge distillation and transfer from the teacher model to the student model can be achieved in three stages of the teacher model pipeline, as shown in Figure 6.

Figure 6. Level of KD in neural network pipeline approach to KD using the student teacher framework

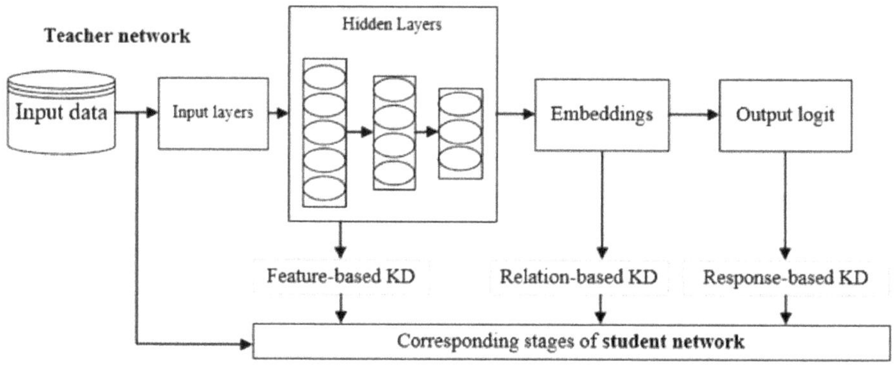

(Adapted from Yang et al., 2023)

First, the most popular and simplistic way of KD is response-based knowledge distillation. It utilises the teacher model's output layer responses as supervisory signals, where the student is trained to mimic the teacher's final soft predictions through a distillation loss (Gou et al., 2021). This loss measures the divergence between the teacher's and student's probability distributions, typically using Kullback-Leibler divergence with temperature scaling, and is often combined with standard cross entropy to incorporate ground truth supervision as in Equation 1.

The distillation loss is defined using the Kullback-Leibler divergence:

$$L_{KD} = T^2 KL(p_t^{(T)} \| p_s^{(T)}) \quad (1)$$

where P_t and P_s are the softened probability distributions from the teacher and student models, respectively, as defined in equation (2).

$$p^{(T)} = soft\max(\frac{z}{T}) \quad (2)$$

where T is the temperature parameter.

Second, knowledge from the teacher model's intermediate layer can be distilled and transferred to the student model, known as feature-based knowledge distillation. While deriving the distillation loss, we utilised the intermediate representation instead of the output logits of the teacher and student models (Li et al., 2019).

Finally, relation-based knowledge distillation focuses on transferring the interrelationships between data representations in the teacher model to the student model. Instead of just matching the final predictions as in response-based knowledge transfer, the student is trained to reproduce the structural or relational patterns learned by the teacher (Gou et al., 2025).

3.4. Low Rank Approximations (LoRA)

Low Rank Adaptation or LoRA is a parameter-efficient fine-tuning method that employs low rank matrix decomposition to reduce parameter redundancy in large models while preserving performance. This is achieved by freezing the original model weights and introducing lightweight low-rank update matrices, which significantly reduce the number of trainable parameters (Hu et al., 2022).

For example, if we have a large generative AI model with 6 billion parameters, which is mainly composed of a weight matrix, then during fine-tuning or training, the model updates with backpropagation, it will be updated with ΔW, which means there will be equal parameters to be computed for the given weight matrix update. But when we use LoRA, it replaces the ΔW with its decomposition into two low rank matrix A and B with rank r. Then it will save the memory as compared to computing the large matrix ΔW. In this way, we update the selective weight during fine-tuning instead of updating all weights, which, by design, is beneficial for deploying the model into an edge device.

3.5. Deployment Strategies

3.5.1 On-Device Fine-Tuning

On-device fine-tuning enables generative AI models to be adapted directly within resource constrained hardware environments such as smartphones, embedded systems, and IoT platforms. Rather than relying on cloud-based retraining, parameter-efficient approaches such as Low-Rank Adaptation reduce computational and memory overhead by introducing small trainable matrices while keeping the core model weights frozen. More generally, Parameter-Efficient Fine-Tuning techniques support selective and lightweight updates, making local personalisation feasible without exceeding device-level power and storage limits. This deployment strategy lowers latency, enhances privacy by retaining data locally, and decreases communication costs, thereby strengthening the practicality of generative AI services at the network edge (Kristiani et al., 2026).

3.5.2. Hybrid Cloud-Edge Collaboration

The hybrid edge-cloud deployment strategy involves strategically splitting computational tasks between edge devices and cloud servers to boost performance, reduce latency, and enhance data privacy. In this setup, the early and lighter stages of AI processing are handled on edge devices close to where the data is generated, while more complex computations are sent to the cloud (Wang et al., 2020).

For instance, in a transformer-based language model, initial data processing and feature extraction can happen on the edge, which reduces data transfer and speeds up response times. This collaborative setup eases the computational burden on edge devices while leveraging the cloud's vast resources, creating a balanced system that delivers high performance with minimal latency. Additionally, by processing sensitive data locally and only sending essential information to the cloud, it improves privacy and lowers bandwidth usage—a clear advantage for data-intensive or privacy-sensitive industries.

3.5.3. Federated Learning

Federated Learning (FL) is a decentralised machine learning approach that enables multiple participants (e.g., edge devices) to collaboratively train models without sharing their raw data. Deploying large generative AI models (e.g., GANs, VAEs) directly on resource-constrained edge devices is challenging due to limited computation, memory, and energy. FL make generative model deployment at the edge both energy efficient and scalable by distributing the workload into multiple participants' edge devices.

FL can be used to minimise data movement, reduce communication cost, and orchestrate decentralised generative model processing across devices. Essentially, the federated learning framework for edge AI integrates techniques such as dynamic resource allocation, thermal management and failure recovery to optimise energy consumption on the edge nodes. Combining federated learning with energy-aware scheduling and resource management enables efficient deployment of generative AI on edge devices, balancing model capability with limited hardware and energy budgets.

4. CHALLENGES IN IMPLEMENTING GENERATIVE EDGE AI

Integrating generative AI in resource-constrained settings, such as edge device poses significant challenges, mainly in how to streamline the large and complex models to function in low resource setting with limited memory, computer and energy (Vuruma et al., 2024).

4.1. Performance vs Complexity Trade-Off

Deploying generative AI on edge devices requires balancing accuracy with computational complexity under strict resource constraints. Larger AI models generally provide higher accuracy but impose substantial memory, energy, and latency costs, making them impractical for real-time edge applications. To reduce complexity, techniques such as quantisation, pruning, and knowledge distillation compress models and accelerate inference, though often at the expense of some performance degradation. Overall, edge deployment demands a careful optimisation trade-off between model capacity and computational efficiency to achieve acceptable performance within hardware limits.

4.2. Hardware Challenges for Edge AI

Edge intelligence advances are driven by improvements in hardware architecture, battery technology, and next-generation network connectivity. Conventional CPUs and GPUs are inefficient for edge AI due to high power consumption and limited computational density. Specialised hardware such as application-specific integrated circuits (ASICs) and field-programmable gate arrays (FPGAs) enables high-performance, low-power AI processing on edge devices. Dedicated AI accelerators with compact architectures support real-time processing in resource-constrained environments.

4.3. Change in Computing Paradigm

In-memory computing reduces latency by minimising data movement between memory and processors. Neuromorphic computing offers energy-efficient and adaptive learning inspired by biological neural systems. These innovations are essential for time-critical applications, including autonomous vehicles, drones, and health monitoring.

4.4 Energy Storage and Power Sustainability

Battery life is a major constraint for mobile and remote edge devices. Advanced battery materials, such as solid-state batteries, provide higher energy density, improved safety, and faster charging. Improved energy storage enables longer operation and greater practicality for remote sensors and autonomous systems (Pimenow et al., 2024).

5. APPLICATION OF GENERATIVE EDGE AI

The transition of machine learning and AI from TinyML to generative edge AI has demonstrated its applicability in various domains such as handheld and wearable devices, healthcare, drone and smart cities for more personalised services (Giorgetti & Pau, 2025). Some of the application domains are listed in Figure 7.

Figure 7. Illustration of applications of generative edge AI

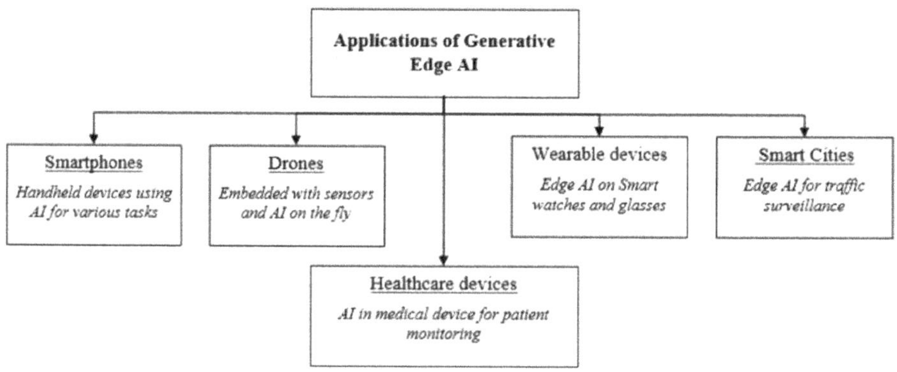

5.1. Smartphones and Handheld Devices

Generative edge AI in smartphones and handheld devices enables on-device processing of information without continuous streaming to cloud servers. It can support tasks such as text generation, message drafting, image analysis and so on. Furthermore, it brings a whole lot of things at the tip of the finger, where things can be very quick and easy, which helps people with their everyday tasks, such as asking questions, finding a grocery shop, and searching for anything they want to find on the internet. The edge deployment of generative AI on mobile devices not only helps them with everyday tasks but also maintains privacy by retaining sensitive data locally and reducing the latency for interactive applications such as voice assistants and personalised services.

5.2. Drones and Unmanned Vehicles

Integrating generative AI into drones will be a game-changing technology as it will take care of all activities such as flight scheduling, sensor selections and deployment. Once everything is completed, it will directly draw the report to the user about the task. Embedded generative models can synthesise missing visual information under occlusion, enhance low-quality imagery, and generate predictive environmental maps for navigation. For precision agriculture, disaster monitoring, and infrastructure inspection, generative models support real-time data augmentation and anomaly simulation to improve onboard decision-making. Operating directly on embedded hardware reduces communication dependence and ensures responsiveness in remote or bandwidth-limited environments. However, strict constraints on payload weight, power availability, and computational capacity demand highly optimised architectures and efficient model compression strategies.

5.3. Healthcare Devices

Generative AI and its application to healthcare edge device is transforming the medical and healthcare services by shifting it from a purely rule-based analytical system to creating a new system integrated with wearable sensors, imaging software and a clinical decision support system that can enhance healthcare services to the next level. Furthermore, privacy and security are the main concerns in healthcare services, where edge AI is most crucial, which provides these qualities on top of generative AI capabilities (Bibhu et al., 2024).

Ultrasound machines require extreme processing performance and graphics rendering to enhance diagnostic accuracy and instantly acquire precise images. Analogously, being easily movable is also required to accommodate changing medical scenarios and trends, especially when treating patients with limited mobility or travel/movement restrictions caused by COVID-19.

5.4. Generative AI on Wearable Devices

Generative edge AI enables wearable devices such as digital watches and smart glasses to move beyond basic sensing and cloud-dependent intelligence toward fully on-device content generation and personalised assistance. By embedding compact generative models directly into the device, data can be processed and interpreted locally, reducing latency and eliminating the need to transmit sensitive information to remote servers. For example, a smartwatch monitoring vital signs can generate personalised health summaries, adaptive fitness plans, or real-time coaching feedback without relying on cloud connectivity. Similarly, smart glasses such as Ray-Ban Meta integrate multimodal generative models to produce real-time scene descriptions, contextual responses, and voice-driven assistance.

5.5. Smart Cities

Smart cities are urban environments where digital technologies, connected infrastructure, and data-driven systems are integrated to improve operational efficiency, sustainability, public services, and overall quality of life for residents. They typically combine sensors, communication networks, data analytics, and intelligent control systems to optimise areas such as transportation, energy, water management, waste management, public safety, and governance.

Edge AI is central to implementing smart cities across many applications that drive urban intelligence. For instance, real-time traffic monitoring for intelligent transportation systems and on-camera video surveillance for anomaly detection and crowd monitoring enable immediate response, helping to make cities safer and more liveable.

6. EMERGING TRENDS AND FUTURE DIRECTIONS

Generative Edge AI is an evolving research area where pretty interesting things are happening. Generally, it has evident of progress in three areas of advancement: hardware accelerations, model optimisation and efficiency, and adaptive networking.

The innovation of neuromorphic chips and in-memory computing architectures represents a significant shift in the computing paradigm, where these chips employ spiking neural networks and utilise massively parallel architecture activated only when meaningful signals are present (Muir & Sheik, 2025). This avoids the redundant operations and save idel power consumptions. Because of their ultra-low-power characteristics, this technology will be ubiquitous in battery-powered systems and consumer wearables. However, the commercial success of these technologies for edge intelligence depends on programming and deploying them at scale.

The future research work should be targeted towards optimising the hardware and software design for edge AI, battery and energy efficiency for green computing and on-device learning capabilities.

a) Enhancement of hardware design that supports accelerated computing on edge devices and boosts the model performance. For example,
b) Energy-efficient learning models are essential for battery-powered edge devices to reduce the power consumption during generative AI workloads.
c) On-device learning methods that are adaptive and quick to learn from the new data streaming from the edge device continuously.

7. CONCLUSIONS

Here, we provided an overview of various model compression techniques for integrating generative AI on edge devices, including model quantisation, compression, distillation, and fine-tuning. Furthermore, we discussed some of the key applications of generative edge AI, such as smart health, wearable devices, and industrial IoT. Then, the challenges and opportunities for further development of edge intelligence are reported. From the discussion, it is obvious that edge AI is going to be the next game-changer technology as it will democratise AI in wider populations with ease of portability and accessibility.

REFERENCES

Aishwarya, D., & Minu, R. I. (2021). Edge computing-based surveillance framework for real-time activity recognition. *ICT Express*, *7*(2), 182–186. DOI: 10.1016/j.icte.2021.04.010

Al-Malahmeh, H. (2023). The role of cloud computing in supporting decision making: Evidence from the banking industry. *International Journal of Data & Network Science*, *7*(1), 131–140. DOI: 10.5267/j.ijdns.2022.11.009

Bibhu, V., Shukla, A. K., Shivahare, B. D., Kaur, J., Shukri, M., Mgm, A. Y. J., Faaq, A. S., AlShujairi, M. K., & Pandey, S. (2024). Analysis of security and privacy challenges of smart health and sensing systems. *Results in Engineering*, *24*, 103466. DOI: 10.1016/j.rineng.2024.103466

Bolón-Canedo, V., Morán-Fernández, L., Cancela, B., & Alonso-Betanzos, A. (2024). A review of green artificial intelligence: Towards a more sustainable future. *Neurocomputing*, *599*, 128096. DOI: 10.1016/j.neucom.2024.128096

Bucilu , C., Caruana, R., & Niculescu-Mizil, A. (2006, August). Model compression. In *Proceedings of the 12th ACM SIGKDD international conference on Knowledge discovery and data mining* (pp. 535-541). DOI: 10.1145/1150402.1150464

Deng, S., Zhao, H., Fang, W., Yin, J., Dustdar, S., & Zomaya, A. Y. (2020). Edge intelligence: The confluence of edge computing and artificial intelligence. *IEEE Internet of Things Journal*, *7*(8), 7457–7469. DOI: 10.1109/JIOT.2020.2984887

Doan, T. N., & Phan, T. H. (2024). A Novel Smart System with Jetson Nano for Remote Insect Monitoring. *International Journal of Advanced Computer Science and Applications*, *15*(7). Advance online publication. DOI: 10.14569/IJACSA.2024.0150798

Ficili, I., Giacobbe, M., Tricomi, G., & Puliafito, A. (2025). From sensors to data intelligence: Leveraging IoT, cloud, and edge computing with AI. *Sensors (Basel)*, *25*(6), 1763. DOI: 10.3390/s25061763 PMID: 40292910

Ghojogh, B., Ghodsi, A., Karray, F., & Crowley, M. (2021). Generative adversarial networks and adversarial autoencoders: Tutorial and survey. arXiv preprint arXiv:2111.13282.

Giorgetti, G., & Pau, D. P. (2025). Transitioning from TinyML to edge GenAI: A review. *Big Data and Cognitive Computing*, *9*(3), 61. DOI: 10.3390/bdcc9030061

Gou, J., Xin, X., Yu, B., Song, H., Zhang, W., & Wan, S. (2025). Neighbourhood relation-based knowledge distillation for image classification. *Neural Networks, 188*, 107429. DOI: 10.1016/j.neunet.2025.107429 PMID: 40179584

Gou, J., Yu, B., Maybank, S. J., & Tao, D. (2021). Knowledge distillation: A survey. *International Journal of Computer Vision, 129*(6), 1789–1819. DOI: 10.1007/s11263-021-01453-z

Guo, X., & Chen, Y. (2024). Generative AI for synthetic data generation: Methods, challenges and the future. arXiv preprint arXiv:2403.04190.

Hu, E. J., Shen, Y., Wallis, P., Allen Zhu, Z., Li, Y., Wang, S., & Chen, W. (2022). LoRA: Low rank adaptation of large language models. *International Conference on Learning Representations*, 1(2), 3.

Kang, P., & Somtham, A. (2022). An evaluation of modern accelerator-based edge devices for object detection applications. *Mathematics, 10*(22), 4299. DOI: 10.3390/math10224299

Khan, W. Z., Ahmed, E., Hakak, S., Yaqoob, I., & Ahmed, A. (2019). Edge computing: A survey. *Future Generation Computer Systems, 97*, 219–235. DOI: 10.1016/j.future.2019.02.050

Kim, J. H., & Choi, Y. S. (2025). Lightweight pre-trained Korean language model based on knowledge distillation and low-rank factorisation. *Entropy (Basel, Switzerland), 27*(4), 379. DOI: 10.3390/e27040379 PMID: 40282614

Kristiani, E., Verma, V. K., & Yang, C. T. (2026). Deploying LLM Transformer on Edge Computing Devices: A Survey of Strategies, Challenges, and Future Directions. *AI, 7*(1), 15. DOI: 10.3390/ai7010015

Li, H. T., Lin, S. C., Chen, C. Y., & Chiang, C. K. (2019). Layer-level knowledge distillation for deep neural network learning. *Applied Sciences (Basel, Switzerland), 9*(10), 1966. DOI: 10.3390/app9101966

Liu, D., Zhu, Y., Liu, Z., Liu, Y., Han, C., Tian, J., Li, R., & Yi, W. (2025). A survey of model compression techniques: Past, present, and future. *Frontiers in Robotics and AI, 12*, 1518965. DOI: 10.3389/frobt.2025.1518965 PMID: 40182395

Moulaei, K., Yadegari, A., Baharestani, M., Farzanbakhsh, S., Sabet, B., & Afrash, M. R. (2024). Generative artificial intelligence in healthcare: A scoping review on benefits, challenges and applications. *International Journal of Medical Informatics, 188*, 105474. DOI: 10.1016/j.ijmedinf.2024.105474 PMID: 38733640

Muir, D. R., & Sheik, S. (2025). The road to commercial success for neuromorphic technologies. *Nature Communications*, *16*(1), 3586. DOI: 10.1038/s41467-025-57352-1 PMID: 40234391

Navardi, M., Aalishah, R., Fu, Y., Lin, Y., Li, H., Chen, Y., & Mohsenin, T. (2025, May). GenAI at the edge: Comprehensive survey on empowering edge devices. In *Proceedings of the AAAI Symposium Series* (Vol. 5, No. 1, pp. 180–187). DOI: 10.1609/aaaiss.v5i1.35586

Neupane, A., Shahi, T. B., Cowling, M., & Tanna, D. (2024). Threading the GenAI needle: Unpacking the ups and downs of GenAI for higher education stakeholders. *Journal of Applied Learning & Teaching*, *7*(2), 38–46.

Olukoya, O. (2022). Assessing frameworks for eliciting privacy and security requirements from laws and regulations. *Computers & Security*, *117*, 102697. DOI: 10.1016/j.cose.2022.102697

Pimenow, S., Pimenowa, O., & Prus, P. (2024). Challenges of artificial intelligence development in the context of energy consumption and impact on climate change. *Energies*, *17*(23), 5965. DOI: 10.3390/en17235965

Reddi, V. J. (2025). Generative AI at the edge: Challenges and opportunities: The next phase in AI deployment. *ACM Queue; Tomorrow's Computing Today*, *23*(2), 79–137. DOI: 10.1145/3733702

Reis, M. J., & Serôdio, C. (2025). Edge AI for real-time anomaly detection in smart homes. *Future Internet*, *17*(4), 179. DOI: 10.3390/fi17040179

Rokh, B., Azarpeyvand, A., & Khanteymoori, A. (2023). A comprehensive survey on model quantisation for deep neural networks in image classification. *ACM Transactions on Intelligent Systems and Technology*, *14*(6), 1–50. DOI: 10.1145/3623402

Shahi, T. B., Xu, C. Y., Neupane, A., & Guo, W. (2023). Recent advances in crop disease detection using UAV and deep learning techniques. *Remote Sensing (Basel)*, *15*(9), 2450. DOI: 10.3390/rs15092450

Singh, E., Pratap, A., Mehta, U., & Azid, S. I. (2024). Smart agriculture drone for crop spraying using image-processing and machine learning techniques: Experimental validation. *IoT*, *5*(2), 250–270. DOI: 10.3390/iot5020013

Singh, R., & Gill, S. S. (2023). Edge AI: A survey. *Internet of Things and Cyber-Physical Systems*, *3*, 71–92. DOI: 10.1016/j.iotcps.2023.02.004

Tang, M., Gao, R., & Guo, L. (2024). Lightweight signal recognition based on a hybrid model in wireless networks. *Telecommunication Systems*, *87*(3), 707–721. DOI: 10.1007/s11235-024-01204-8

Tmamna, J., Ayed, E. B., Fourati, R., Gogate, M., Arslan, T., Hussain, A., & Ayed, M. B. (2024). Pruning deep neural networks for green energy efficient models: A survey. *Cognitive Computation*, *16*(6), 2931–2952. DOI: 10.1007/s12559-024-10313-0

Vuruma, S. K. R., Margetts, A., Su, J., Ahmed, F., & Srivastava, B. (2024). From cloud to edge: Rethinking generative AI for low-resource design challenges. arXiv preprint arXiv:2402.12702.

Wang, T., Guo, J., Zhang, B., Yang, G., & Li, D. (2025). Deploying AI on edge: Advancement and challenges in edge intelligence. *Mathematics*, *13*(11), 1878. DOI: 10.3390/math13111878

Wang, W., Chen, W., Luo, Y., Long, Y., Lin, Z., Zhang, L., . . . He, X. (2024). Model compression and efficient inference for large language models: A survey. arXiv preprint arXiv:2402.09748.

Winzig, J., Almanza, J. C. A., Mendoza, M. G., & Schumann, T. (2022, October). Edge ai-use case on Google Coral Dev Board mini. In 2022, *IET International Conference on Engineering Technologies and Applications (IET-ICETA)* (pp. 1-2). IEEE. DOI: 10.1109/IET-ICETA56553.2022.9971614

Xu, Z., Xu, Y., Xu, H., Liao, Y., Yao, Z., & Xie, Z. (2025). Lightweight and post-training structured pruning for on-device large language models. *IEEE Transactions on Mobile Computing*.

Yang, C., Yu, X., An, Z., & Xu, Y. (2023). Categories of response-based, feature-based, and relation-based knowledge distillation. In *Advancements in knowledge distillation: towards new horizons of intelligent systems* (pp. 1–32). Springer International Publishing. DOI: 10.1007/978-3-031-32095-8_1

Zhang, R., He, J., Luo, X., Niyato, D., Kang, J., Xiong, Z., & Sikdar, B. (2025). Toward democratised generative AI in next-generation mobile edge networks. *IEEE Network*.

Zhang, X., Xie, G., Huang, Y., Xiong, Z., Liu, J., Cui, S., & Shen, X. S. (2025). Edge intelligence in the generative artificial intelligence era. *IEEE Wireless Communications*, *32*(6), 60–68. DOI: 10.1109/MWC.2025.3599652

Zhao, X., Xu, R., & Guo, X. (2023, June). Post-training quantisation or quantisation-aware training? That is the question. In 2023, *China Semiconductor Technology International Conference (CSTIC)* (pp. 1-3). IEEE.

Chapter 4
Lightweight Architecture and Algorithms for Generative Edge AI

Taufik Maulana
http://orcid.org/0009-0001-6478-5682
Universitas Esa Unggul, Indonesia

Binastya Anggara Sekti
http://orcid.org/0000-0001-5489-4888
Universitas Esa Unggul, Indonesia

ABSTRACT

The rapid ascent of Generative AI has revolutionized technology, yet massive Foundation Models remain reliant on cloud infrastructure, introducing latency and privacy bottlenecks. This chapter explores the migration of generative intelligence to the network edge via Lightweight Architecture and Efficient Algorithms. Optimization strategies bridging the gap between hyper-scale models and resource-constrained devices like smartphones are presented. Key discussions cover architectural modularity and compression techniques, including Knowledge Distillation, Low-Rank Adaptation (LoRA), and Quantization. Through case studies in GANs, Transformers, and Diffusion Models, this chapter demonstrates that state-of-the-art fidelity is maintainable with significantly reduced computational costs. It concludes with a multidimensional evaluation framework, emphasizing Pareto-optimal trade-offs between quality and efficiency to enable ubiquitous, sustainable Edge AI.

DOI: 10.4018/979-8-3373-7340-9.ch004

1. INTRODUCTION

The rapid proliferation of Generative Artificial Intelligence (GenAI) has fundamentally reshaped the technological landscape, enabling machines to produce human-like text, generate executable code, and synthesize high-quality visual content. Models such as Generative Pre-trained Transformers (GPT), DALL-E, and Stable Diffusion exemplify this transformation, demonstrating capabilities that were previously unattainable. However, these advances are accompanied by substantial computational demands, as such foundation models typically consist of billions of parameters and require high-performance hardware, including GPUs and large-scale memory systems, commonly available only in cloud-based data centers (Singh & Gill, 2023).

This creates a fundamental mismatch between the resource-intensive nature of modern generative models and the constraints of edge devices, where data is increasingly generated and consumed. Edge devices, including smartphones, wearable systems, Internet of Things (IoT) sensors, and autonomous platforms, operate under strict limitations in processing power, memory capacity, energy consumption, and thermal conditions. As a result, deploying full-scale generative models directly on these devices is often infeasible without significant adaptation (Singh & Gill, 2023).

To address this challenge, the paradigm of Edge AI has emerged, shifting computation from centralized cloud infrastructures toward distributed, on-device processing closer to the data source. While this approach offers advantages such as reduced latency, enhanced privacy, and lower operational costs, it also introduces new technical challenges. Standard generative models cannot be directly deployed in edge environments due to their high computational complexity and memory requirements. This gap highlights the need for lightweight architectures and efficient algorithmic strategies that enable generative intelligence to operate within constrained environments without significantly degrading performance.

A critical distinction must therefore be made between cloud-centric and edge-centric generative AI systems. In cloud-based architectures, both training and inference are performed in centralized data centers, offering virtually unlimited computational resources but introducing latency, bandwidth dependency, and privacy concerns. In contrast, edge-based systems execute inference locally, enabling real-time responsiveness, offline functionality, and improved data sovereignty. However, these benefits come at the cost of reduced computational capacity, necessitating careful optimization and system-level design considerations (Singh & Gill, 2023; Walani & Doorsamy, 2025).

Beyond architectural adaptation, the transition to edge-based generative AI requires a holistic perspective that incorporates not only model design and algorithmic efficiency but also deployment feasibility, performance evaluation, and energy consumption. In practical scenarios, it is insufficient to evaluate models solely based on accuracy or output quality; instead, a balanced trade-off between latency, memory usage, and energy efficiency must be achieved. Furthermore, real-world deployment introduces additional challenges, including hardware heterogeneity, system integration, and workload variability across different edge platforms (Ahn et al., 2023; Zhang et al., 2024).

This chapter addresses these challenges by presenting a comprehensive framework for Generative Edge AI that integrates lightweight architectural design with efficient algorithmic optimization and real-world deployment considerations. Specifically, the chapter explores modular and scalable model architectures, advanced compression techniques such as knowledge distillation, quantization, and pruning, and adaptive inference strategies that dynamically balance performance and resource usage. In addition, the chapter emphasizes practical deployment through benchmarking frameworks and representative case studies, providing insights into how generative models can be effectively implemented across diverse edge environments.

The remainder of this chapter is organized as follows. Section 2 introduces the fundamental paradigm shift between cloud-based and edge-based generative AI. Section 3 presents key design principles for lightweight architectures. Section 4 discusses efficient algorithms for model optimization. Section 5 provides real-world deployment case studies. Section 6 introduces performance evaluation and benchmarking methodologies. Section 7 analyzes key challenges and trade-offs. Section 8 outlines future research directions, followed by concluding remarks in Section 9.

Chapter Objectives

This chapter aims to:

1. Explain the fundamental challenges of deploying generative AI on resource-constrained edge devices.
2. Present design principles for developing lightweight and scalable generative architectures.
3. Analyze efficient algorithmic techniques, including model compression and adaptive inference strategies.
4. Provide evaluation frameworks that balance model quality, latency, and energy consumption.
5. Demonstrate real-world deployment through representative case studies.
6. Identify open challenges and future research directions in Generative Edge AI.

2. BACKGROUND AND PARADIGM SHIFT: CLOUD VS EDGE GENERATIVE AI

The rapid advancement of generative artificial intelligence has been predominantly driven by cloud-centric computing infrastructures. Large-scale generative models, including Large Language Models (LLMs) and diffusion-based image generators, are typically developed, trained, and deployed within centralized data centers equipped with high-performance GPUs and virtually unlimited storage capacity. This cloud-centric paradigm has enabled significant breakthroughs in model capability, scalability, and performance, making it the default approach for modern generative AI systems (Singh & Gill, 2023).

However, despite its advantages, the cloud-based approach introduces several critical limitations when applied to real-world applications. One of the primary challenges is latency, as user inputs must be transmitted to remote servers and processed before results are returned. This delay becomes particularly problematic in time-sensitive applications such as real-time interaction systems, autonomous decision-making, and industrial control environments. Additionally, cloud-based inference requires continuous network connectivity and sufficient bandwidth, which may not always be available in remote or resource-limited settings (Walani & Doorsamy, 2025).

Another major concern is data privacy and security. In cloud-centric systems, user data—including prompts, sensor inputs, or proprietary information—must be transmitted to third-party servers for processing. This raises significant risks related to data leakage, regulatory compliance, and user trust, especially in sensitive domains such as healthcare, finance, and personal communication. Furthermore, reliance on cloud infrastructure introduces ongoing operational costs (OpEx), particularly in large-scale deployments where frequent API calls and data transfers are required (Singh & Gill, 2023; Walani & Doorsamy, 2025).

In response to these limitations, the paradigm of Edge AI has emerged as a complementary approach that shifts computation closer to the data source. In edge-centric generative AI systems, model inference is performed directly on local devices such as smartphones, embedded systems, and IoT nodes. This shift enables several key advantages. First, it significantly reduces latency by eliminating the need for long-distance data transmission, allowing near real-time response. Second, it enhances data privacy, as sensitive information remains on the device and is not exposed to external servers. Third, it enables offline functionality, ensuring system reliability in environments with limited or unstable connectivity. Finally, edge deployment can reduce operational costs by minimizing dependence on cloud infrastructure (Singh & Gill, 2023; Walani & Doorsamy, 2025).

Despite these benefits, edge-based generative AI introduces a new set of challenges primarily related to resource constraints. Unlike cloud servers, edge devices operate under strict limitations in computational power, memory capacity, and energy availability. Generative models, which often require billions of parameters and intensive matrix operations, cannot be directly executed on such devices without significant optimization. This creates a fundamental trade-off between model capability and system feasibility, where achieving high-quality outputs must be balanced against latency, memory usage, and energy consumption (Singh & Gill, 2023).

To better understand this paradigm shift, it is useful to compare cloud-centric and edge-centric approaches across key dimensions, including computational capacity, latency, privacy, scalability, and cost. As illustrated in Figure 1, cloud-based systems excel in scalability and model performance but suffer from latency, bandwidth dependency, and privacy risks. In contrast, edge-based systems provide low-latency, privacy-preserving, and cost-efficient solutions, but require lightweight architectures and efficient algorithms to operate within constrained environments.

Figure 1. Cloud-Centric vs Edge-Centric Generative AI Architecture

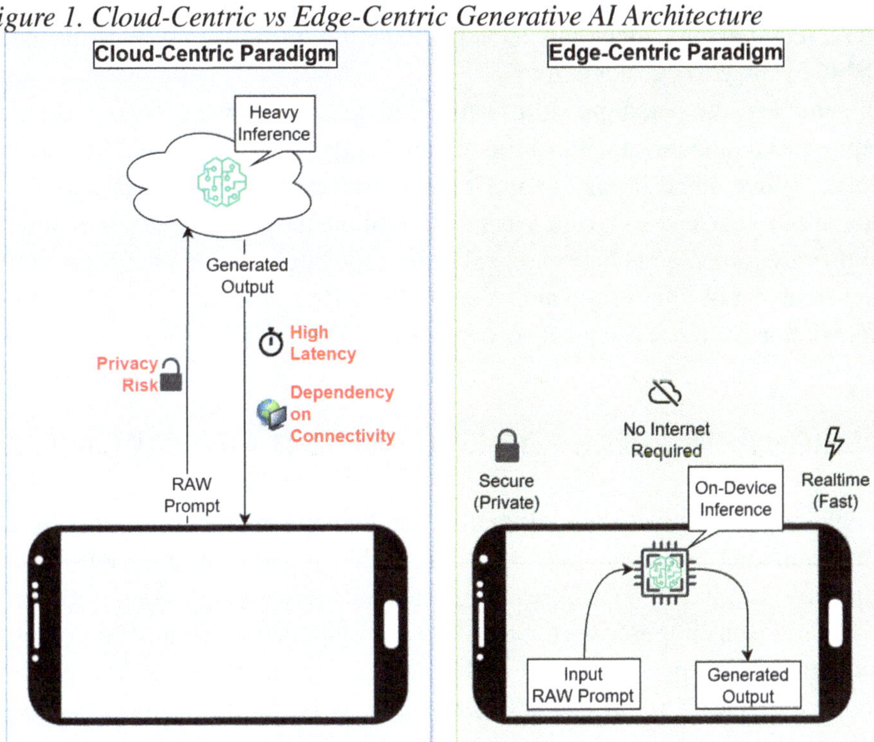

Source: Adapted by the authors based on (Singh & Gill, 2023) and (Walani & Doorsamy, 2025).

This figure illustrates the fundamental differences between cloud-based and edge-based generative AI systems. Cloud-centric architectures rely on centralized data centers for model inference, offering high computational power but introducing latency, bandwidth dependency, and privacy risks. In contrast, edge-centric systems perform inference locally on devices, enabling low latency, improved privacy, and offline capability, but requiring lightweight architectures due to resource constraints.

Importantly, the transition from cloud to edge is not a complete replacement but rather an evolution toward hybrid computing models. In many practical scenarios, a combination of edge and cloud resources is utilized to achieve optimal performance. For instance, initial data processing and lightweight inference may be performed locally, while more complex computations are offloaded to the cloud when necessary. This hybrid paradigm enables adaptive workload distribution, balancing efficiency and performance based on system conditions and application requirements.

Furthermore, it is essential to recognize that edge deployment is not universally advantageous. Applications requiring large-scale reasoning, high-precision outputs, or continuous model updates may still benefit more from cloud-based systems. Therefore, the decision to deploy generative AI on the edge must consider specific use-case requirements, including latency sensitivity, privacy constraints, resource availability, and cost considerations.

In summary, the paradigm shift from cloud-centric to edge-centric generative AI represents a fundamental transition in how intelligent systems are designed and deployed. While cloud infrastructures remain critical for training and large-scale computation, edge devices are increasingly becoming the primary interface for real-time, privacy-aware, and context-sensitive AI applications. This shift necessitates the development of lightweight architectures and efficient algorithms, which form the foundation for the subsequent sections of this chapter.

3. DESIGN PRINCIPLES FOR LIGHTWEIGHT ARCHITECTURES

Deploying generative artificial intelligence on edge devices requires a fundamental rethinking of neural network design. Unlike cloud-centric systems, where maximizing accuracy often justifies large-scale models with billions of parameters, edge environments impose strict constraints on computation, memory, and energy consumption. Consequently, model design must adopt an efficiency-first strategy, where performance is achieved not through scale alone, but through structural optimization and resource-aware computation (Singh & Gill, 2023).

This section outlines the key design principles that enable lightweight generative architectures, focusing on three interrelated aspects: modularity and computational efficiency, scalability across heterogeneous devices, and structural decomposition through micro-models and hybrid execution.

3.1 Modularity and Computational Efficiency

A central principle in lightweight model design is the transition from monolithic architectures to modular structures. In modular architectures, a generative model is decomposed into smaller functional components that can be selectively activated or reused. This approach improves both flexibility and efficiency by ensuring that only the necessary computational units are engaged during inference.

One prominent example of this paradigm is the Mixture-of-Experts (MoE) architecture, where multiple specialized sub-models (experts) are combined through a gating mechanism that dynamically selects relevant experts for each input. Instead of activating the entire network, only a subset of experts is used, significantly reducing computational overhead. This sparse activation mechanism is particularly beneficial for edge devices, as it lowers both latency and energy consumption while maintaining expressive capacity (Yuksel, Wilson, & Gader, 2012).

Beyond high-level modularity, computational bottlenecks often arise within specific components, particularly the attention mechanism in Transformer-based models. Standard self-attention exhibits quadratic complexity with respect to input length, making it unsuitable for resource-constrained environments. To address this, efficient attention variants such as linear attention and sparse attention have been developed. These approaches reduce computational complexity by approximating or restricting attention operations, enabling longer sequences to be processed with significantly lower resource requirements (Zaheer et al., 2020).

Another important design consideration involves the trade-off between network depth and width. Wider networks can better exploit parallelism in modern hardware accelerators, such as GPUs and NPUs, but often incur higher memory usage due to increased parameter counts. Conversely, deeper networks are typically more parameter-efficient but introduce sequential dependencies that may increase latency. In practice, lightweight generative models adopt a balanced configuration that aligns with the specific hardware characteristics of the target device, ensuring optimal utilization of available resources (Singh & Gill, 2023).

3.2 Scalability for Resource-Diverse Devices

Edge computing environments are inherently heterogeneous, encompassing a wide spectrum of devices ranging from high-performance smartphones to low-power IoT sensors. A key design requirement is therefore scalability, enabling a single architectural framework to adapt across different hardware configurations without requiring complete redesign.

Elastic or multi-scale architectures address this challenge by allowing dynamic adjustment of model complexity. In such designs, the network can operate at different levels of depth or width depending on available resources. For example, when sufficient computational capacity is available, the full model can be executed to achieve high-quality outputs. Under constrained conditions, selected layers or channels can be bypassed, reducing computational cost while maintaining acceptable performance (Gao, Liu, Wang, & Ji, 2025).

In addition to structural scalability, progressive generation strategies play an important role in managing computational load. Rather than generating outputs at full resolution in a single step, the model first produces a coarse representation and then incrementally refines it if additional resources are available. This "anytime" inference capability improves user experience by providing immediate results that can be enhanced over time, particularly in interactive edge applications.

To ensure cross-device compatibility, scalable architectures are often implemented as tiered model families, such as nano, micro, small, and base variants. While these variants differ in size and complexity, they share a common architectural backbone, simplifying deployment and enabling consistent performance across diverse platforms. This standardized design approach reduces system complexity and facilitates efficient integration into heterogeneous edge ecosystems (Singh & Gill, 2023).

3.3 Micro-Models and Hybrid Execution

In many scenarios, even optimized architectures remain too large for deployment on highly constrained devices. This limitation has led to the development of micro-model architectures, where large generative models are decomposed into smaller, task-specific components capable of operating independently.

Micro-models, often referred to as micronets, are created through techniques such as pruning, distillation, or neural architecture search, resulting in compact networks tailored for specific tasks. Instead of relying on a single large model, multiple micro-models can collaborate to perform complex inference, distributing computational load across available resources. This approach enables efficient operation in environments with strict memory and power limitations (Njor, Banbury, & Fafoutis, 2025; Xu et al., 2024).

However, when local resources are insufficient, hybrid execution strategies become essential. In the split computing paradigm, model inference is divided between the edge device and the cloud. Typically, initial layers responsible for feature extraction are executed locally, while deeper layers requiring intensive computation are offloaded to remote servers. This approach reduces data transmission requirements by sending intermediate representations rather than raw data, preserving privacy while improving efficiency (Xu et al., 2024).

More advanced frameworks extend this concept through adaptive offloading mechanisms, where the system dynamically determines whether to complete inference locally or delegate computation to the cloud based on input complexity and resource availability. In some cases, early exit strategies allow inference to terminate at intermediate layers if sufficient confidence is achieved, avoiding unnecessary computation.

Additionally, distributed and federated approaches enable multiple edge devices to collaboratively contribute to generative tasks without sharing raw data. By exchanging model updates or intermediate representations instead of sensitive inputs, these systems maintain privacy while leveraging collective intelligence (Xu et al., 2024).

3.4 Design Implications for Edge Deployment

The design principles discussed in this section highlight that lightweight generative architectures are not achieved solely through model compression, but through a combination of structural, algorithmic, and system-level considerations. Effective deployment requires balancing multiple factors, including computational efficiency, scalability, adaptability, and integration with heterogeneous hardware.

Importantly, these principles also reinforce that architectural design must be aligned with deployment requirements from the outset. Rather than adapting large models post hoc, future generative systems should be designed with edge constraints in mind, incorporating modularity, scalability, and hybrid execution capabilities as intrinsic properties.

These architectural foundations provide the basis for the algorithmic techniques discussed in the next section, where optimization methods such as knowledge distillation, parameter-efficient fine-tuning, quantization, and pruning are explored in detail.

To enhance clarity, Figure 2 illustrates the design pipeline of lightweight generative architectures for edge deployment. The diagram highlights the interaction between modular design, scalability mechanisms, and hybrid execution strategies, emphasizing how architectural decisions directly influence deployment feasibility.

Figure 2. Lightweight Generative Architecture Design Pipeline

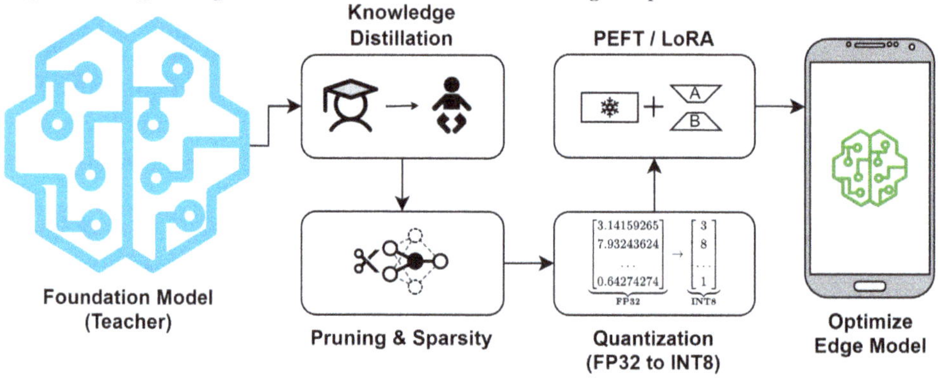

Source: *Developed by the authors based on (Xu et al., 2024; Yuksel et al., 2012; Zaheer et al., 2020).*

This figure summarizes the architectural design pipeline for deploying generative AI on edge devices. It highlights three core design dimensions: modular design for selective computation, scalability for heterogeneous hardware conditions, and hybrid execution for balancing local and remote processing. Together, these elements demonstrate how lightweight architectures are structured to improve deployment feasibility under memory, latency, and energy constraints.

4. EFFICIENT ALGORITHMS FOR GENERATIVE EDGE AI

While architectural design establishes the structural foundation for lightweight models, the practical deployment of generative AI on edge devices depends critically on algorithmic efficiency. Even well-designed architectures can exceed the computational and energy constraints of edge environments if underlying operations remain dense and high-precision. Therefore, efficient algorithms are essential to transform large-scale generative models into deployable edge solutions.

This section presents the core algorithmic strategies that enable Generative Edge AI, focusing on four complementary approaches: knowledge distillation, parameter-efficient fine-tuning (PEFT), model compression through quantization and pruning, and dynamic inference techniques such as approximate computing and early exit mechanisms.

4.1 Knowledge Distillation for Generative Models

Knowledge Distillation (KD) is a fundamental technique for transferring the capabilities of large, high-performance models (teachers) to smaller, lightweight models (students). Instead of directly training a compact model from scratch, KD leverages the learned representations of a pre-trained model to guide the student toward similar behavior (Fu et al., 2020; M. Li et al., 2022).

In generative AI, distillation extends beyond simple output matching. Unlike classification tasks, generative models produce complex, high-dimensional outputs, such as images, text sequences, or audio signals. As a result, modern approaches emphasize feature-level distillation, where the student model is trained to replicate intermediate representations of the teacher. This allows the student to capture structural and semantic knowledge rather than merely reproducing final outputs .

The application of distillation varies across model types. In Generative Adversarial Networks (GANs), effective distillation focuses on aligning internal feature representations of the generator rather than matching final images, which may represent only one sample from a distribution. In Variational Autoencoders (VAEs), distillation targets the latent space by aligning probabilistic distributions, ensuring that the student model retains both generative diversity and structure (M. Li et al., 2022).

For diffusion models, distillation plays a critical role in reducing inference latency. Standard diffusion processes require multiple iterative steps, which are computationally expensive. Progressive distillation techniques collapse multiple sampling steps into fewer steps, enabling significant acceleration while maintaining output quality. These approaches can reduce inference time by an order of magnitude, making diffusion-based generation more suitable for edge deployment (Meng et al., 2023).

4.2 Parameter-Efficient Fine-Tuning (PEFT)

Adapting generative models to specific tasks traditionally requires updating all model parameters, which is impractical for large-scale architectures. Parameter-Efficient Fine-Tuning (PEFT) addresses this challenge by modifying only a small subset of parameters while keeping the majority of the model fixed.

One of the most widely adopted PEFT techniques is Low-Rank Adaptation (LoRA), which introduces trainable low-rank matrices into existing layers. Instead of updating full weight matrices, LoRA decomposes weight updates into smaller components, significantly reducing memory and computational requirements. Importantly, these updates can be merged into the original model after training, resulting in no additional inference overhead (Hu et al., 2021).

Another approach involves adapter modules, which insert lightweight neural layers into the existing architecture. These modules enable task-specific adaptation while preserving the original model weights. This design allows multiple adapters to be stored and switched dynamically on edge devices, supporting diverse applications without reloading the base model.

At the most lightweight end, prompt-based techniques such as prefix tuning optimize input representations rather than internal model parameters. By introducing trainable prompt vectors, these methods guide model behavior with minimal computational overhead. Although they may require longer training or careful tuning, they provide a highly efficient mechanism for adapting generative models in resource-constrained environments (X. L. Li & Liang, 2021).

Collectively, PEFT techniques enable flexible and scalable deployment by allowing a single base model to support multiple tasks with minimal additional resource requirements.

4.3 Quantization, Pruning, and Sparsity Techniques

Model compression techniques are essential for reducing the memory footprint and computational cost of generative models. Among these, quantization and pruning are the most widely used approaches.

Quantization reduces the numerical precision of model parameters and activations, typically converting 32-bit floating-point representations to lower-bit formats such as 8-bit or 4-bit integers. Two primary strategies are employed: post-training quantization (PTQ), which applies quantization after training, and quantization-aware training (QAT), which incorporates quantization effects during training. While PTQ is computationally efficient, QAT generally achieves higher accuracy, particularly at very low precision levels (Bhalgat, Lee, Nagel, Blankevoort, & Kwak, 2020).

Pruning, in contrast, reduces model size by removing redundant or less important parameters. Structured pruning eliminates entire channels or layers, resulting in smaller and more hardware-friendly models. Unstructured pruning removes individual weights, achieving higher compression ratios but often requiring specialized hardware to fully exploit sparsity. Hybrid approaches, such as block-wise pruning, attempt to balance efficiency and regularity (He, Zhang, & Sun, 2017).

Recent advances suggest that large generative models contain highly sparse subnetworks capable of maintaining performance, supporting the notion that substantial portions of model parameters are redundant. This insight enables aggressive pruning strategies without significant loss in output quality.

Importantly, quantization and pruning are most effective when applied jointly. Combined optimization frameworks can significantly reduce model size and inference latency while preserving acceptable performance. Such joint approaches are particularly valuable for edge deployment, where both memory and computation are tightly constrained (Motetti et al., 2024).

4.4 Approximate Computing and Adaptive Inference

In addition to static compression techniques, dynamic inference strategies provide further efficiency gains by adapting computation based on input complexity and system conditions.

Approximate computing reduces computational overhead by relaxing the requirement for exact numerical precision. In generative models, this can be achieved by reducing sampling steps, simplifying intermediate computations, or applying heuristic termination criteria. These approximations often result in negligible perceptual differences while significantly improving latency and energy efficiency.

Early exit mechanisms represent a practical implementation of adaptive inference. By introducing intermediate output layers within the network, the model can terminate inference early when sufficient confidence is achieved. This approach ensures that simple inputs are processed quickly, while more complex inputs utilize deeper layers, optimizing overall resource usage (Pacheco, Bochie, Gilbert, Couto, & Campista, 2021).

Caching and memoization techniques further enhance efficiency by avoiding redundant computations. In scenarios where similar inputs are processed repeatedly, intermediate representations can be stored and reused, reducing the need for full inference cycles. This is particularly relevant in edge environments, where repeated queries or similar prompts are common (Y. Li et al., 2025).

4.5 Algorithmic Trade-offs and Deployment Considerations

While each optimization technique provides specific advantages, their effectiveness depends on the target application and hardware constraints. Knowledge distillation preserves model quality but requires access to large teacher models. Quantization and pruning offer significant efficiency gains but may introduce accuracy degradation if applied aggressively. PEFT enables flexible adaptation but may not fully capture complex task requirements.

In practice, hybrid optimization strategies are often employed. For example, a model may first be distilled to reduce size, followed by quantization to improve latency, and further optimized through adaptive inference mechanisms. This layered approach enables fine-grained control over the trade-off between performance and efficiency.

Ultimately, selecting the appropriate algorithmic strategy requires a holistic understanding of deployment requirements, including latency constraints, energy budgets, memory availability, and acceptable quality thresholds. These considerations highlight the importance of systematic evaluation, which is addressed in the next section through performance benchmarking and comparative analysis.

Figure 3 presents an integrated optimization pipeline, showing how different algorithmic techniques—distillation, quantization, pruning, and adaptive inference—can be sequentially or jointly applied to transform large-scale generative models into edge-deployable systems.

Figure 3. Optimization Pipeline for Generative Edge AI

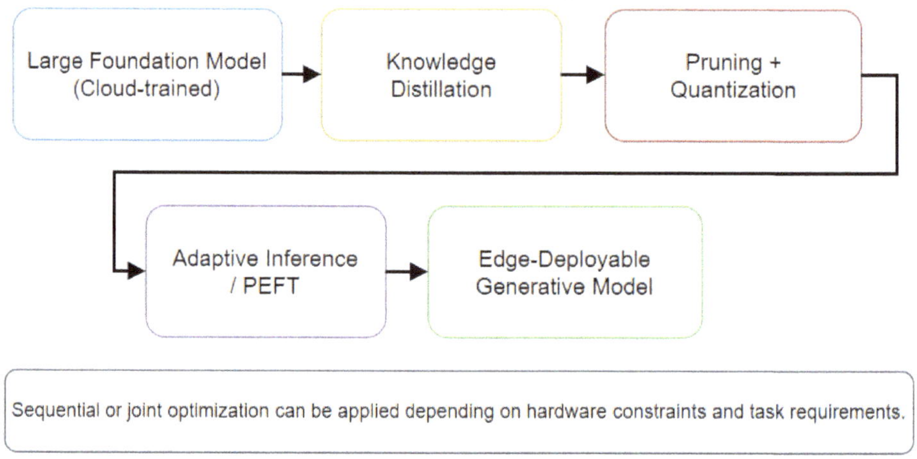

This figure illustrates the transformation of a large foundation model into an edge-deployable generative model through sequential or joint optimization stages, including knowledge distillation, pruning and quantization, and adaptive inference or parameter-efficient fine-tuning.

5. REAL-WORLD DEPLOYMENT AND CASE STUDIES

The successful adoption of Generative Edge AI depends not only on architectural design and algorithmic optimization, but also on its ability to operate effectively in real-world environments. In practice, deployment introduces additional constraints beyond those considered in theoretical models, including hardware heterogeneity, system integration, latency requirements, and energy limitations. This section presents representative case studies that demonstrate how lightweight architectures and efficient algorithms are applied across different edge scenarios.

5.1 On-Device Generative AI in Mobile Systems

Mobile devices represent one of the most prominent platforms for edge-based generative AI. Modern smartphones are increasingly equipped with dedicated hardware accelerators, such as Neural Processing Units (NPUs), enabling on-device execution of optimized generative models.

In natural language processing applications, compact Transformer-based models have been deployed to support features such as real-time text generation, predictive typing, and offline translation. These systems typically combine multiple optimization techniques, including quantization, caching of key-value attention states, and parameter-efficient fine-tuning. By leveraging on-device inference, these applications achieve low latency and enhanced privacy, as user inputs are processed locally without requiring cloud transmission (Jiao et al., 2020; Zhang et al., 2024).

In image generation tasks, optimized diffusion models have been adapted for mobile environments through latent-space processing and reduced sampling steps. Instead of operating in high-dimensional pixel space, these models generate compressed latent representations that are subsequently decoded into images. This approach significantly reduces computational requirements while maintaining acceptable visual quality. Furthermore, progressive refinement strategies allow users to receive immediate low-resolution outputs that can be enhanced over time if additional resources are available (Chen et al., 2023) (Lu et al., 2022).

These deployments highlight the importance of integrating model optimization with hardware capabilities, ensuring that generative models are aligned with the computational characteristics of mobile devices.

5.2 Generative Models in IoT and Industrial Edge Systems

Beyond consumer devices, Generative Edge AI is increasingly applied in industrial and IoT environments, where real-time processing and reliability are critical. In such systems, edge devices are often responsible for monitoring, analysis, and decision-making in dynamic and resource-constrained conditions.

One important application is predictive maintenance, where generative models are used to synthesize realistic sensor data and simulate potential failure scenarios. Lightweight Generative Adversarial Networks (GANs) can generate synthetic time-series data locally, enabling anomaly detection systems to identify deviations without requiring large datasets or continuous cloud connectivity (Chang & Lu, 2021; Shimizu, Xu, & Tasaka, 2020).

In manufacturing environments, generative models support process optimization by simulating different operational conditions. For example, edge-based models can generate variations of system states to evaluate potential outcomes, enabling proactive adjustments that improve efficiency and reduce downtime. This localized generation capability reduces communication overhead and ensures faster response times.

Additionally, generative models are used for data augmentation in edge-based machine learning pipelines. In scenarios where labeled data is limited, synthetic data generated locally can enhance model robustness without exposing sensitive industrial data to external servers. This is particularly important in sectors with strict data governance requirements.

5.3 Generative AI in Autonomous and Real-Time Systems

Autonomous systems, including self-driving vehicles and robotics, represent another critical domain for Generative Edge AI. These systems require real-time decision-making with strict latency constraints, making cloud-based inference impractical for many tasks.

Generative models are used in these environments for scenario prediction, environment simulation, and sensor data completion. For instance, lightweight generative models can predict future trajectories of objects or generate plausible environmental states under uncertainty. This capability enhances the robustness of perception and planning modules (Singh & Gill, 2023; Xu et al., 2024).

In robotics, generative models enable adaptive interaction with dynamic environments. For example, a robot can generate possible action sequences or simulate outcomes before executing a task, improving decision-making accuracy while minimizing risk. These operations must be performed locally to ensure deterministic latency and system reliability.

However, deploying generative models in such systems requires careful optimization to meet strict safety and performance requirements. Techniques such as early exit inference, hardware-aware scheduling, and model partitioning are often employed to ensure that computation remains within acceptable limits (Pacheco et al., 2021; Xu et al., 2024).

5.4 Hybrid Edge–Cloud Deployment Strategies

While edge deployment offers significant advantages, it is not always sufficient to handle complex generative tasks. As a result, hybrid edge–cloud architectures are widely adopted to balance performance and efficiency.

In hybrid systems, computation is distributed between the edge and the cloud based on task complexity and resource availability. Lightweight inference is performed locally, while more computationally intensive operations are offloaded to the cloud. This approach reduces latency for simple tasks while maintaining access to powerful cloud resources when needed.

Split computing is a common implementation of this paradigm, where early layers of a model are executed on the edge device, and intermediate representations are transmitted to the cloud for further processing. This reduces data transmission requirements compared to sending raw inputs and preserves a degree of privacy (Xu et al., 2024) (Walani & Doorsamy, 2025).

More advanced systems incorporate adaptive offloading mechanisms, where decisions are made dynamically based on network conditions, energy levels, and input characteristics. For example, if a device detects limited battery capacity, it may offload more computation to the cloud to conserve energy. Conversely, in offline scenarios, the system relies entirely on local inference.

These hybrid strategies demonstrate that effective deployment is not a binary choice between edge and cloud, but rather a continuum that adapts to system constraints and application requirements.

5.5 Lessons Learned From Real-World Deployment

The case studies presented in this section reveal several key insights for the deployment of Generative Edge AI.

First, successful deployment requires tight integration between model design, algorithmic optimization, and hardware capabilities. Models must be explicitly tailored to the characteristics of the target platform rather than adapted post hoc.

Second, there is no universal optimization strategy. Different applications prioritize different objectives, such as latency, accuracy, or energy efficiency. As a result, deployment strategies must be context-dependent and guided by application-specific requirements.

Third, system-level considerations play a critical role. Memory management, scheduling, and communication overhead can significantly impact performance, often more than model architecture alone.

Finally, hybrid deployment models are emerging as a practical solution for balancing efficiency and performance. By combining edge and cloud resources, these systems provide flexibility and scalability while addressing the limitations of purely local or centralized approaches.

These insights highlight that real-world deployment is a multidimensional problem that extends beyond model optimization. The next section builds on this foundation by introducing systematic approaches for performance evaluation and benchmarking.

6. PERFORMANCE EVALUATION AND BENCHMARKING

The deployment of generative AI on edge devices requires a comprehensive evaluation framework that extends beyond traditional accuracy-based metrics. While output quality remains important, real-world deployment necessitates a multi-dimensional assessment that captures latency, memory usage, and energy consumption. This section presents a systematic approach to benchmarking Generative Edge AI systems, enabling informed trade-offs between performance and efficiency (Ahn et al., 2023; Zhang et al., 2024).

6.1 Evaluation Metrics for Generative Edge AI

Unlike conventional machine learning systems, generative models must be evaluated across multiple dimensions simultaneously. In edge environments, the following metrics are particularly critical:

- Model Quality:

Measures the fidelity and usefulness of generated outputs. Depending on the task, this may include metrics such as perplexity for language models, Fréchet Inception Distance (FID) for image generation, or task-specific evaluation scores (Kynkäänniemi, Karras, Laine, Lehtinen, & Aila, 2019).

- Latency:

Refers to the time required to produce an output after receiving input. For real-time applications, latency is often a primary constraint, as delayed responses can degrade user experience or system performance (Ahn et al., 2023).

- Memory Footprint:

Includes both model size (storage) and runtime memory usage. Edge devices typically have limited RAM and storage, making memory efficiency a key factor in deployment feasibility.

- Energy Consumption:

Represents the total energy required for inference. This metric is particularly important for battery-powered devices, where sustained generative tasks can significantly impact device longevity.

- Throughput:

Measures the number of inferences that can be processed per unit time. While often less critical than latency in edge scenarios, throughput becomes relevant in multi-task or concurrent workloads.

A comprehensive evaluation must consider these metrics jointly rather than in isolation, as improvements in one dimension often lead to trade-offs in others.

6.2 Benchmarking Methodologies

To ensure consistent and reproducible evaluation, benchmarking methodologies must be carefully designed. A typical benchmarking pipeline for Generative Edge AI involves the following steps:

1. Model Selection and Preparation:

Define baseline models and their optimized variants (e.g., distilled, quantized, or pruned versions).

2. Hardware Specification:

Clearly document the target device, including CPU, GPU, or NPU capabilities, memory constraints, and power characteristics.

3. Workload Definition:

Select representative tasks, such as text generation, image synthesis, or multimodal inference, ensuring alignment with real-world use cases.

4. Measurement Protocol:

Standardize evaluation conditions, including input size, batch size, and inference settings, to ensure comparability.

5. Metric Collection and Analysis:

Record performance metrics across multiple runs and analyze variability, tradeoffs, and scalability.

In edge environments, benchmarking must also account for dynamic factors such as thermal throttling, background processes, and network conditions, which can influence performance in practice.

6.3 Comparative Analysis of Optimization Techniques

Different optimization strategies impact performance metrics in distinct ways. Table 1 provides a high-level comparison of common techniques used in Generative Edge AI.

Table 1. Comparison of Optimization Techniques for Generative Edge AI

Method	Model Size Reduction	Latency Improvement	Accuracy Impact	Energy Efficiency
Distillation	Moderate	Moderate	Low degradation	Moderate
Quantization	High	High	Moderate degradation	High
Pruning	Moderate–High	High	Low–Moderate	High
PEFT	Low	Low–Moderate	Minimal	Moderate
Adaptive Inference	Dynamic	High	Context-dependent	High

This comparison highlights that no single technique universally dominates across all metrics. For instance, quantization provides substantial improvements in latency and energy efficiency but may introduce accuracy degradation at lower precision levels. In contrast, distillation preserves output quality more effectively but offers more modest efficiency gains.

6.4 Trade-off Analysis: Accuracy, Latency, and Energy

A key challenge in Generative Edge AI is balancing competing objectives. Improving efficiency often comes at the cost of reduced model quality, while maintaining high fidelity may require increased computational resources.

Trade-off analysis provides a structured way to evaluate these competing factors. One common approach is to visualize performance across multiple dimensions, such as accuracy versus latency or energy consumption versus model size. These relationships often reveal diminishing returns, where further improvements in one metric require disproportionately large sacrifices in another.

For example, reducing model precision from 8-bit to 4-bit may significantly decrease latency and energy usage, but beyond a certain threshold, output quality may degrade sharply. Similarly, aggressive pruning may reduce model size but introduce instability in generative outputs.

Understanding these trade-offs is essential for selecting appropriate optimization strategies based on application requirements. Real-time applications may prioritize low latency, while offline or batch-processing systems may emphasize output quality.

To further illustrate the relationship between performance metrics, Figure 4 visualizes the trade-off between model quality, latency, and energy consumption. The curve demonstrates that improvements in efficiency often lead to diminishing returns in output quality, reinforcing the need for balanced optimization strategies.

Figure 4. Trade-off Curve: Accuracy vs Latency vs Energy

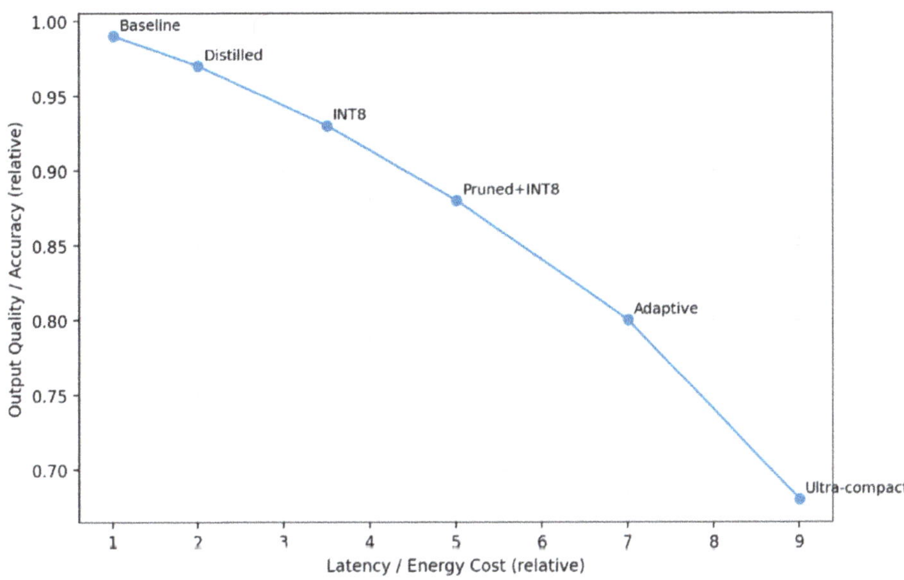

Source: *Developed by the authors based on (Ahn et al., 2023), (Motetti et al., 2024), and (Paula, Soni, Upadhyay, & Lagos, 2025).*

This figure visualizes the non-linear trade-off between output quality and computational efficiency in Generative Edge AI. As optimization becomes more aggressive, latency and energy consumption decrease, but quality may decline beyond an acceptable threshold. The curve emphasizes the need to select operating points that balance deployment efficiency with application-level quality requirements.

6.5 Toward Standardized Benchmarking Frameworks

Despite the growing importance of Generative Edge AI, standardized benchmarking frameworks remain limited. Existing benchmarks are often designed for cloud-based systems and do not adequately capture the constraints of edge environments.

To address this gap, future benchmarking efforts should incorporate:

- Device-aware evaluation, accounting for hardware heterogeneity
- Energy profiling tools, enabling accurate measurement of power consumption
- Application-driven scenarios, reflecting real-world usage patterns
- Reproducible protocols, ensuring consistency across studies

In addition, benchmarking should consider end-to-end system performance rather than isolated model evaluation. Factors such as data preprocessing, memory management, and communication overhead can significantly influence overall efficiency.

Table 2. Example Quantitative Benchmark of Optimization Techniques

Model Variant	Model Size (MB)	Latency (ms)	Energy (mJ/inference)	Quality Score
Baseline Model	1200	950	420	100%
Distilled Model	350	420	210	94%
Quantized (8-bit)	180	260	140	91%
Pruned + Quantized	120	180	95	88%
Adaptive Inference	120–350	120–400	80–200	88–94%

Source: Synthesized by the authors based on (Ahn et al., 2023), (Motetti et al., 2024), and (Zhang et al., 2024).

Note: The values presented are synthesized from reported trends in prior studies and are intended for comparative illustration rather than representing a single experimental benchmark.

The quantitative results in Table 2 demonstrate the impact of different optimization strategies on key deployment metrics. Compared to the baseline model, compressed variants achieve up to 85–90% reduction in model size, 70–80% latency improvement, and over 75% energy savings, with only moderate degradation in output quality. Notably, adaptive inference provides dynamic trade-offs, enabling systems to balance performance and efficiency based on runtime conditions. These results highlight that multi-stage optimization strategies are essential for achieving practical deployment on edge devices (Ahn et al., 2023).

6.6 Implications for Deployment

The benchmarking strategies discussed in this section highlight that performance evaluation is not merely a validation step, but a critical component of system design. Effective deployment requires continuous iteration between model optimization and performance measurement, ensuring that generative systems meet both functional and operational requirements.

By systematically evaluating trade-offs between quality, latency, memory, and energy, developers can make informed decisions about model selection and optimization strategies. These insights also provide a foundation for addressing the broader challenges and limitations discussed in the next section.

These results reinforce the importance of multi-dimensional evaluation frameworks that jointly consider efficiency, quality, and deployment constraints in real-world edge environments.

7. CHALLENGES, TRADE-OFFS, AND LIMITATIONS

Despite the rapid progress in lightweight architectures and efficient algorithms, the deployment of generative AI on edge devices remains a complex and multi-dimensional challenge. While prior sections have demonstrated the feasibility of Generative Edge AI, it is equally important to recognize its inherent limitations and the trade-offs that arise when operating under constrained environments. This section provides a critical analysis of these challenges, highlighting key issues related to model performance, resource constraints, system reliability, and deployment feasibility.

7.1 Performance vs Efficiency Trade-offs

One of the most fundamental challenges in Generative Edge AI lies in balancing model performance with computational efficiency. Large-scale generative models achieve high-quality outputs through extensive parameterization and deep architectures. However, when these models are compressed using techniques such as quantization, pruning, or distillation, some degree of performance degradation is often unavoidable.

For example, aggressive quantization to low-bit representations can significantly reduce memory usage and latency but may introduce numerical instability, particularly in sensitive components such as attention layers. Similarly, pruning techniques that remove redundant parameters can lead to loss of expressive capacity if not carefully applied. While these trade-offs may be acceptable in certain applications, they become critical in scenarios requiring high precision, such as medical diagnostics or financial forecasting.

This tension highlights the need for application-specific optimization strategies, where acceptable performance thresholds are defined based on real-world requirements rather than theoretical benchmarks (Bhalgat et al., 2020; Motetti et al., 2024; Paula et al., 2025).

Figure 5 presents a decision framework for selecting between cloud, edge, and hybrid deployment strategies based on application requirements such as latency sensitivity, privacy constraints, and computational demand.

Figure 5. Edge vs Cloud vs Hybrid Decision Framework

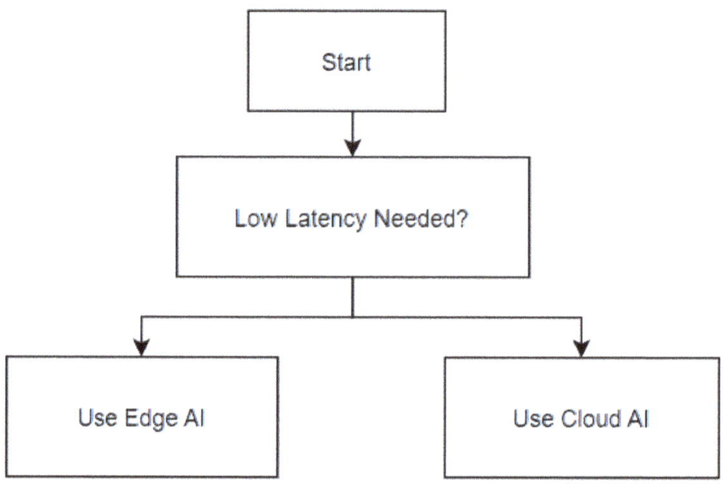

7.2 Energy Constraints and Thermal Limitations

Energy consumption represents a critical bottleneck for edge deployment, particularly in battery-powered devices. Generative models, especially those involving iterative processes such as diffusion, can require sustained computation that leads to rapid battery depletion.

In addition to energy usage, thermal constraints pose significant challenges. Continuous inference workloads may cause devices to overheat, triggering thermal throttling mechanisms that reduce computational performance. This creates a feedback loop where reduced processing capability increases latency, potentially degrading user experience.

These limitations underscore the importance of energy-aware model design and adaptive inference strategies that dynamically adjust computational load based on system conditions. Without such mechanisms, the practical usability of generative models on edge devices remains limited (Bolón-Canedo, Morán-Fernández, Cancela, & Alonso-Betanzos, 2024; Zhang et al., 2024).

7.3 Hardware Heterogeneity and Deployment Complexity

Edge environments are characterized by significant hardware diversity, ranging from high-end smartphones with dedicated AI accelerators to low-power embedded systems with minimal computational capability. This heterogeneity complicates model deployment, as optimization strategies that perform well on one device may not translate effectively to another.

For instance, structured pruning techniques may align well with GPU-based architectures but provide limited benefits on devices lacking parallel processing capabilities. Similarly, quantization schemes must be tailored to hardware support for low-precision arithmetic, which varies widely across platforms.

As a result, deploying Generative Edge AI at scale requires device-aware optimization and extensive testing across different hardware configurations. This increases development complexity and may limit the generalizability of proposed solutions (Singh & Gill, 2023).

7.4 Reliability, Robustness, and Security Risks

Edge-deployed generative models are inherently more exposed than their cloud-based counterparts, raising concerns related to reliability and security. Since models reside directly on devices, they are more susceptible to adversarial attacks, model extraction, and reverse engineering.

Adversarial inputs can exploit vulnerabilities in generative models, leading to unpredictable or harmful outputs. In addition, attackers may attempt to extract model parameters or replicate functionality, posing risks to intellectual property and system integrity.

Robustness is another critical concern. Edge environments are subject to variable conditions, including fluctuating input quality, limited computational resources, and potential hardware instability. Ensuring consistent performance under such conditions remains a significant challenge.

These risks highlight the need for secure model deployment strategies, including encryption, access control, and robust inference mechanisms.

7.5 Limitations of Edge-Only Approaches

While edge deployment offers advantages in latency and privacy, it is not universally suitable for all generative AI applications. Tasks requiring large-scale reasoning, high-resolution generation, or continuous model updates may exceed the capabilities of edge devices.

For example, advanced language models with extensive contextual reasoning capabilities often require substantial computational resources that are difficult to replicate on-device. Similarly, high-fidelity image or video generation may demand memory and processing power beyond what edge devices can provide.

In such cases, cloud-based or hybrid approaches remain more practical. This reinforces the notion that Generative Edge AI should be viewed as a complementary paradigm rather than a complete replacement for cloud-based systems (Walani & Doorsamy, 2025; Yao et al., 2025).

7.6 System-Level Integration Challenges

Beyond model design and optimization, system-level factors play a critical role in deployment success. Issues such as memory management, task scheduling, and communication overhead can significantly impact overall system performance.

For instance, inefficient memory allocation may lead to fragmentation or excessive swapping, reducing performance. Similarly, poor scheduling of inference tasks can result in resource contention, particularly in multi-application environments.

In hybrid systems, communication between edge and cloud components introduces additional latency and potential points of failure. Designing robust orchestration mechanisms that coordinate computation across distributed resources remains an open challenge.

7.7 Summary of Key Limitations

The challenges discussed in this section highlight that Generative Edge AI involves a series of trade-offs rather than a universally optimal solution. Key limitations include:

- Reduced model performance due to aggressive optimization
- Energy and thermal constraints in sustained workloads
- Complexity arising from hardware heterogeneity
- Security and robustness vulnerabilities in edge environments
- Inherent limitations of edge-only deployment for complex tasks
- System-level integration challenges beyond model design

These factors emphasize the importance of holistic system design, where architectural, algorithmic, and operational considerations are jointly addressed.

8. FUTURE RESEARCH DIRECTIONS

The rapid evolution of Generative Edge AI highlights a growing need for research that bridges the gap between model capability and deployment feasibility. While significant progress has been made in lightweight architectures and efficient algorithms, several open challenges remain, particularly in achieving scalable, adaptive, and energy-efficient generative systems. This section outlines key research directions that are expected to shape the future of Generative Edge AI.

8.1 Hardware-Aware Model Design

Future generative models must be designed with hardware constraints as a primary consideration rather than an afterthought. Traditional approaches often involve training large models in cloud environments and subsequently compressing them for edge deployment. However, this pipeline introduces inefficiencies and limits optimization potential.

Emerging research focuses on hardware-aware training, where models are co-designed with target devices, such as mobile NPUs, embedded GPUs, or specialized accelerators. This includes optimizing operator selection, memory access patterns, and parallel execution to align with hardware capabilities. Such co-design approaches can significantly improve performance and energy efficiency compared to post hoc optimization.

In addition, the development of specialized hardware for generative workloads, including AI accelerators tailored for diffusion or Transformer-based models, is expected to further enhance edge deployment capabilities (Gao et al., 2025).

8.2 Adaptive and Context-Aware Inference

Static inference pipelines are often inefficient in dynamic edge environments. Future systems are expected to incorporate adaptive inference mechanisms that adjust computational effort based on input complexity, user requirements, and system conditions.

Context-aware models can dynamically scale their depth, width, or precision, enabling flexible trade-offs between performance and efficiency. For example, a system may allocate more computational resources for complex tasks while using simplified inference for routine operations.

Reinforcement learning and meta-learning techniques are also being explored to enable models to learn optimal execution strategies over time. These approaches can improve resource allocation and reduce unnecessary computation, particularly in long-running or interactive applications (Pacheco et al., 2021).

8.3 Green AI and Energy-Efficient Generative Models

As generative AI continues to expand, its environmental impact has become an increasingly important concern. Future research must prioritize energy-efficient model design, not only to extend battery life in edge devices but also to reduce the overall carbon footprint of AI systems.

Green AI principles emphasize minimizing energy consumption throughout the model lifecycle, including training, deployment, and inference. This includes developing low-power architectures, optimizing inference pipelines, and incorporating energy-aware benchmarking metrics.

In edge environments, energy-efficient design is closely linked to user experience, as excessive energy consumption can lead to reduced device usability. Therefore, integrating energy considerations into model evaluation and optimization will be critical for sustainable deployment (Ambrogio et al., 2023; Bolón-Canedo et al., 2024).

8.4 Federated and Collaborative Generative Learning

Privacy-preserving learning frameworks are expected to play a central role in the future of Generative Edge AI. Federated learning enables multiple edge devices to collaboratively train or adapt models without sharing raw data, addressing privacy concerns while leveraging distributed data sources.

In generative contexts, federated approaches can support personalization and domain adaptation, allowing models to learn from local data while maintaining global consistency. However, challenges remain in ensuring stability, convergence, and communication efficiency in federated generative systems.

Collaborative edge intelligence, where multiple devices share intermediate representations or partial computations, represents another promising direction. These approaches can improve performance without compromising privacy, particularly in scenarios involving interconnected devices such as smart homes or industrial networks (Y. Li et al., 2025).

8.5 Toward Fully Autonomous Edge AI Systems

A long-term vision for Generative Edge AI is the development of fully autonomous systems capable of self-optimization and self-adaptation. Such systems would continuously monitor their performance, resource usage, and environmental conditions, adjusting model configurations accordingly.

This includes capabilities such as automated model compression, dynamic offloading decisions, and real-time optimization of inference pipelines. Advances in AutoML and neural architecture search (NAS) are expected to play a key role in enabling these self-adaptive systems.

Autonomous edge systems could significantly reduce the need for manual tuning and enable scalable deployment across diverse environments, making generative AI more accessible and robust (Gao et al., 2025; Njor et al., 2025).

8.6 Standardization and Benchmark Development

As highlighted in previous sections, the lack of standardized benchmarking frameworks remains a significant barrier to progress. Future research should focus on developing comprehensive benchmarks that reflect the unique constraints of edge environments.

These benchmarks should incorporate multi-dimensional evaluation metrics, including latency, energy consumption, memory usage, and output quality. In addition, standardized datasets and evaluation protocols are needed to ensure comparability across different studies and systems.

The establishment of widely accepted benchmarks will facilitate more rigorous evaluation and accelerate the development of effective Generative Edge AI solutions (Ahn et al., 2023).

8.7 Convergence of Edge, Cloud, and Distributed Intelligence

Rather than viewing edge and cloud computing as competing paradigms, future systems are likely to integrate them into unified, distributed intelligence frameworks. These systems will dynamically allocate computation across edge devices, cloud servers, and intermediate nodes based on task requirements and resource availability.

Such convergence enables more flexible and scalable architectures, supporting a wide range of applications from real-time interaction to large-scale data processing. Research in this area will focus on optimizing communication protocols, workload distribution, and system orchestration to achieve seamless integration.

The future of Generative Edge AI lies in the convergence of efficiency, adaptability, and sustainability. Advances in hardware-aware design, adaptive inference, and collaborative intelligence are expected to transform edge devices from passive endpoints into active participants in distributed AI ecosystems. However, achieving this vision requires coordinated progress across model design, system engineering, and evaluation methodologies.

9. CONCLUSION

The rapid advancement of generative artificial intelligence has opened new possibilities for intelligent systems, but its traditional reliance on large-scale, cloud-based infrastructure limits its applicability in real-time, privacy-sensitive, and resource-constrained environments. This chapter has explored how Generative Edge AI addresses these limitations by enabling on-device intelligence through the integration of lightweight architectures and efficient algorithms.

A key contribution of this chapter lies in presenting a unified perspective that connects architectural design, algorithmic optimization, and real-world deployment. Rather than treating these aspects in isolation, the discussion emphasizes their interdependence, demonstrating that effective edge deployment requires a holistic approach. Lightweight architectures, including modular and scalable designs, provide the structural foundation, while algorithmic techniques such as knowledge distillation, parameter-efficient fine-tuning, quantization, and pruning enable practical efficiency gains. These methods collectively allow generative models to operate within the strict constraints of edge devices.

Beyond technical design, this chapter highlights the importance of system-level considerations, including deployment strategies, benchmarking methodologies, and performance trade-offs. The inclusion of real-world case studies demonstrates that Generative Edge AI is not merely a theoretical concept but a practical paradigm already being applied across mobile systems, IoT environments, and autonomous platforms. At the same time, the analysis of challenges and limitations underscores that edge deployment is not universally optimal and must be carefully aligned with application-specific requirements.

Another important contribution is the emphasis on multi-dimensional evaluation. Unlike conventional approaches that prioritize accuracy alone, Generative Edge AI requires balancing quality, latency, memory usage, and energy consumption. This shift toward holistic evaluation reflects the practical realities of deploying AI in constrained environments and provides a more realistic framework for future research and development.

Looking forward, the evolution of Generative Edge AI will be driven by advances in hardware-aware design, adaptive inference, and distributed intelligence frameworks. The convergence of edge and cloud computing is expected to enable more flexible and scalable systems, while emerging paradigms such as federated learning and green AI will address concerns related to privacy and sustainability.

In conclusion, Generative Edge AI represents a significant step toward more accessible, efficient, and context-aware artificial intelligence systems. By combining lightweight architectural principles, efficient algorithmic strategies, and practical deployment considerations, this paradigm has the potential to transform how generative intelligence is integrated into everyday devices and applications. However, realizing this potential requires continued research that bridges the gap between theoretical innovation and real-world implementation.

REFERENCES

Ahn, H., Chen, T., Alnaasan, N., Shafi, A., Abduljabbar, M., Subramoni, H., & Panda, D. K. (2023). Performance Characterization of Using Quantization for DNN Inference on Edge Devices. In *2023 IEEE 7th International Conference on Fog and Edge Computing (ICFEC)* (pp. 1–6). IEEE. DOI: 10.1109/ICFEC57925.2023.00009

Ambrogio, S., Narayanan, P., Okazaki, A., Fasoli, A., Mackin, C., Hosokawa, K., Nomura, A., Yasuda, T., Chen, A., Friz, A., Ishii, M., Luquin, J., Kohda, Y., Saulnier, N., Brew, K., Choi, S., Ok, I., Philip, T., Chan, V., & Burr, G. W. (2023). An analog-AI chip for energy-efficient speech recognition and transcription. *Nature*, *620*(7975), 768–775. DOI: 10.1038/s41586-023-06337-5 PMID: 37612392

Bhalgat, Y., Lee, J., Nagel, M., Blankevoort, T., & Kwak, N. (2020). LSQ+: Improving low-bit quantization through learnable offsets and better initialization. In *2020 IEEE/CVF Conference on Computer Vision and Pattern Recognition Workshops (CVPRW)* (Vol. 2020-June, pp. 2978–2985). IEEE. DOI: 10.1109/CVPRW50498.2020.00356

Bolón-Canedo, V., Morán-Fernández, L., Cancela, B., & Alonso-Betanzos, A. (2024). A review of green artificial intelligence: Towards a more sustainable future. *Neurocomputing*, *599*, 128096. DOI: 10.1016/j.neucom.2024.128096

Chang, T.-Y., & Lu, C.-J. (2021). TinyGAN: Distilling BigGAN for Conditional Image Generation. In H. Ishikawa, C.-L. Liu, T. Pajdla, & J. Shi (Eds.), *Lecture Notes in Computer Science (including subseries Lecture Notes in Artificial Intelligence and Lecture Notes in Bioinformatics)* (Vol. 12625 LNCS, pp. 509–525). Cham: Springer International Publishing. DOI: 10.1007/978-3-030-69538-5_31

Chen, Y.-H., Sarokin, R., Lee, J., Tang, J., Chang, C.-L., Kulik, A., & Grundmann, M. (2023). Speed Is All You Need: On-Device Acceleration of Large Diffusion Models via GPU-Aware Optimizations. In *2023 IEEE/CVF Conference on Computer Vision and Pattern Recognition Workshops (CVPRW)* (Vol. 2023-June, pp. 4651–4655). IEEE. DOI: 10.1109/CVPRW59228.2023.00490

Fu, Y., Chen, W., Wang, H., Li, H., Lin, Y., & Wang, Z. (2020). AutoGAN-Distiller: Searching to compress generative adversarial networks. *37th International Conference on Machine Learning, ICML 2020, PartF168147-5*, 3250–3261.

Gao, J., Liu, Z., Wang, Y., & Ji, W. (2025). RaNAS: Resource-Aware Neural Architecture Search for Edge Computing. *ACM Transactions on Architecture and Code Optimization*, *22*(1), 1–18. DOI: 10.1145/3703353

He, Y., Zhang, X., & Sun, J. (2017). Channel Pruning for Accelerating Very Deep Neural Networks. In *2017 IEEE International Conference on Computer Vision (ICCV)* (pp. 1398–1406). DOI: 10.1109/ICCV.2017.155

Hu, E. J., Shen, Y., Wallis, P., Allen-Zhu, Z., Li, Y., Wang, S., & Chen, W. (2021). LoRA: Low-Rank Adaptation of Large Language Models. Retrieved from https://arxiv.org/abs/2106.09685

Jiao, X., Yin, Y., Shang, L., Jiang, X., Chen, X., Li, L., & Liu, Q. (2020). TinyBERT: Distilling BERT for Natural Language Understanding. In *Findings of the Association for Computational Linguistics: EMNLP 2020* (pp. 4163–4174). Association for Computational Linguistics., DOI: 10.18653/v1/2020.findings-emnlp.372

Kynkäänniemi, T., Karras, T., Laine, S., Lehtinen, J., & Aila, T. (2019). Improved Precision and Recall Metric for Assessing Generative Models. *Advances in Neural Information Processing Systems*, **•••**, 32.

Li, M., Lin, J., Ding, Y., Liu, Z., Zhu, J. Y., & Han, S. (2022). GAN Compression: Efficient Architectures for Interactive Conditional GANs. *IEEE Transactions on Pattern Analysis and Machine Intelligence*, *44*(12), 9331–9346. DOI: 10.1109/TPAMI.2021.3126742 PMID: 34752389

Li, X. L., & Liang, P. (2021). Prefix-tuning: Optimizing continuous prompts for generation. In *ACL-IJCNLP 2021 - 59th Annual Meeting of the Association for Computational Linguistics and the 11th International Joint Conference on Natural Language Processing, Proceedings of the Conference* (Vol. 1, pp. 4582–4597). Stroudsburg, PA, USA: Association for Computational Linguistics. DOI: 10.18653/v1/2021.acl-long.353

Li, Y., Nie, J., Li, S., Jin, K., Tang, J., Zhang, Y., & Niyato, D. (2025). Intermediary Output Caching for Diffusion Model-Based Text-to-Image GenAI Services in Edge Computing Networks. *ACM Transactions on Embedded Computing Systems*, 3733106. Advance online publication. DOI: 10.1145/3733106

Lu, C., Zhou, Y., Bao, F., Chen, J., Li, C., & Zhu, J. (2022). DPM-Solver: A Fast ODE Solver for Diffusion Probabilistic Model Sampling in Around 10 Steps. *Advances in Neural Information Processing Systems*, *35*, 5775–5787.

Meng, C., Rombach, R., Gao, R., Kingma, D., Ermon, S., Ho, J., & Salimans, T. (2023). On Distillation of Guided Diffusion Models. In *Proceedings of the IEEE Computer Society Conference on Computer Vision and Pattern Recognition* (Vol. 2023-June, pp. 14297–14306). IEEE. DOI: 10.1109/CVPR52729.2023.01374

Motetti, B. A., Risso, M., Burrello, A., Macii, E., Poncino, M., & Pagliari, D. J. (2024). Joint Pruning and Channel-Wise Mixed-Precision Quantization for Efficient Deep Neural Networks. *IEEE Transactions on Computers*, *73*(11), 2619–2633. DOI: 10.1109/TC.2024.3449084

Njor, E., Banbury, C., & Fafoutis, X. (2025). Fast data aware neural architecture search via supernet accelerated evaluation. *Internet of Things : Engineering Cyber Physical Human Systems*, *33*, 101688. DOI: 10.1016/j.iot.2025.101688

Pacheco, R. G., Bochie, K., Gilbert, M. S., Couto, R. S., & Campista, M. E. M. (2021). Towards Edge Computing Using Early-Exit Convolutional Neural Networks. *Information (Basel)*, *12*(10), 431. DOI: 10.3390/info12100431

Paula, E., Soni, J., Upadhyay, H., & Lagos, L. (2025). Comparative analysis of model compression techniques for achieving carbon efficient AI. *Scientific Reports*, *15*(1), 23461. DOI: 10.1038/s41598-025-07821-w PMID: 40604122

Shimizu, T., Xu, J., & Tasaka, K. (2020). MobileGAN: Compact Network Architecture for Generative Adversarial Network. In S. Palaiahnakote, G. Sanniti di Baja, L. Wang, & W. Q. Yan (Eds.), *Lecture Notes in Computer Science (including subseries Lecture Notes in Artificial Intelligence and Lecture Notes in Bioinformatics)* (Vol. 12046 LNCS, pp. 326–338). Cham: Springer International Publishing. DOI: 10.1007/978-3-030-41404-7_23

Singh, R., & Gill, S. S. (2023). Edge AI: A survey. *Internet of Things and Cyber-Physical Systems*, *3*, 71–92. DOI: 10.1016/j.iotcps.2023.02.004

Walani, C. C., & Doorsamy, W. (2025). Edge vs. Cloud: Empirical Insights into Data-Driven Condition Monitoring. *Big Data and Cognitive Computing*, *9*(5), 121. DOI: 10.3390/bdcc9050121

Xu, G., Hao, Z., Luo, Y., Hu, H., An, J., & Mao, S. (2024). DeViT: Decomposing Vision Transformers for Collaborative Inference in Edge Devices. *IEEE Transactions on Mobile Computing*, *23*(5), 5917–5932. DOI: 10.1109/TMC.2023.3315138

Yao, Y., Yu, T., Zhang, A., Wang, C., Cui, J., Zhu, H., Cai, T., Chen, C., Li, H., Zhao, W., He, Z., Chen, Q., Zhou, R., Zou, Z., Zhang, H., Hu, S., Zheng, Z., Zhou, J., Cai, J., & Sun, M. (2025). Efficient GPT-4V level multimodal large language model for deployment on edge devices. *Nature Communications*, *16*(1), 5509. DOI: 10.1038/s41467-025-61040-5 PMID: 40593624

Yuksel, S. E., Wilson, J. N., & Gader, P. D. (2012). Twenty years of mixture of experts. *IEEE Transactions on Neural Networks and Learning Systems*, *23*(8), 1177–1193. DOI: 10.1109/TNNLS.2012.2200299 PMID: 24807516

Zaheer, M., Guruganesh, G., Dubey, A., Ainslie, J., Alberti, C., Ontanon, S., . . . Ahmed, A. (2020). Big bird: Transformers for longer sequences. *Advances in Neural Information Processing Systems, 2020-December*, 17283–17297.

Zhang, S., Ma, Y., Fang, L., Jia, H., D'Alfonso, S., & Kostakos, V. (2024). Enabling On-Device LLMs Personalization with Smartphone Sensing. In *Companion of the 2024 on ACM International Joint Conference on Pervasive and Ubiquitous Computing* (pp. 186–190). New York, NY, USA: ACM. DOI: 10.1145/3675094.3677545

Chapter 5
Emerging Trends and Real-Life Applications of Edge Generative AI

Pradip Subedi
http://orcid.org/0009-0003-7888-2867
Birendra Multiple Campus, Nepal

Devendra Chapagain
Birendra Multiple Campus, Nepal

Sushrut Rimal
http://orcid.org/0009-0006-8750-1829
Huazhong University of Science and Technology, China

Mandeep Pokharel
Huazhong University of Science and Technology, China

ABSTRACT

Generative AI and Edge Computing are converging to form Edge Generative AI, enabling real-time intelligence on devices such as robots, wearables, vehicles, smart homes, and IoT systems. This chapter explores how moving generative models from the cloud to the edge reduces latency, enhances privacy, lowers bandwidth dependency, and enables autonomy in healthcare, manufacturing, transportation, cities, agriculture, and education. It highlights key techniques like quantization, pruning, distillation, and federated learning that make on-device generation feasible, along with trends such as multimodal capabilities, 5G/6G enablement, energy-aware design,

DOI: 10.4018/979-8-3373-7340-9.ch005

and hyper-personalization. The chapter also addresses challenges including resource constraints, thermal limits, deployment complexity, and ethical risks, offering future directions for efficient, secure, and explainable edge-native generative systems.

1. INTRODUCTION AND RATIONALE

We used to think the cloud was the only place for powerful Artificial Intelligence (AI), but that's changing fast. The real innovation is happening at the edge, closer to home, where devices can now think, generate, and respond in real-time. Artificial Intelligence has undergone a profound transformation over the last decade, moving from rule-based systems to deep learning and, more recently, to powerful generative models capable of producing text, images, simulations, and multimodal outputs with near-human sophistication. Generative AI exemplified by models such as GPT, Diffusion Models, Whisper, Midjourney, and emerging multimodal architectures has redefined automation, creativity, and decision-making across industries. Yet, despite these breakthroughs, generative AI has remained heavily dependent on centralized cloud infrastructures, where computational resources, large-scale datasets, and high-bandwidth connectivity are readily available (Goodfellow et al., 2014; Shokrollahi et al., 2025). This cloud-centric design has created inherent limitations that restrict generative AI's full potential, particularly in real-time systems, sensitive domains, and distributed environments.

Edge computing processes data near its source, reducing latency, improving privacy, lowering bandwidth use, and enabling offline operation (Singh & Gill, 2023). Combined with generative AI, it forms Edge Generative AI, reshaping intelligent systems and enabling real-world applications in robotics, machine vision, and voice systems for Industry 4.0 and 5.0 (Anusha et al., 2024).

The rationale for this convergence stems from both technological necessity and societal demands. Cloud-based generative models impose latency delays that are unacceptable for autonomous robots, surgical assistance tools, industrial control systems, drones, smart vehicles, and emergency-response technologies. Even a few hundred milliseconds of delay can compromise safety, accuracy, and user trust (Alangari et al., 2025). Meanwhile, industries such as healthcare, defense, finance, education, and smart governance require strong data-sovereignty protections. The continuous transmission of sensitive images, biometrics, voice recordings, geolocation data, or operational logs to cloud servers raises significant regulatory, ethical, and cybersecurity concerns (Anusha et al., 2024).

Edge-native generative AI eliminates these vulnerabilities by enabling devices to operate independently, preserving sensitive data at the source while still benefitting from generative intelligence. According to the Edge AI Technology Report: Generative AI at the Edge Edition (EAI Foundation, 2025), organizations are rapidly shifting toward distributed generative architectures because they support real-time responsiveness, reduce operational costs, and provide the scalability required for large, geographically distributed AI ecosystems.

The rapid growth of IoT devices makes cloud processing costly and impractical. Edge Generative AI can process data locally by generating insights, filling missing data, and compressing streams, reducing cloud dependency. It is especially useful in remote, rural, industrial, and disaster environments with limited or unreliable connectivity (Katare et al., 2023).

From a research perspective, Edge Generative AI is changing how generative models are trained and deployed. Their high computational demands make edge deployment difficult. Techniques like quantization, pruning, knowledge distillation, low-rank decomposition, and hardware-aware design are key to enabling efficient generative AI on constrained devices (Navardi et al., 2025).

By examining both the opportunities and challenges of deploying generative AI at the edge, this chapter contributes to the growing need for scholarly analysis, practical guidance, and policy direction in this rapidly evolving domain. Ultimately, the rationale behind Edge Generative AI lies in its capacity to build systems that are intelligent, trustworthy, context-aware, privacy-preserving, and capable of acting in real time qualities essential for the next generation of digital transformation (Anusha et al. 2024).

This chapter is intended for a broad interdisciplinary audience, including researchers, industry practitioners, and policymakers interested in the emerging field of Edge Generative Artificial Intelligence (AI). Specifically, it targets readers working in domains such as artificial intelligence, distributed systems, Internet of Things (IoT), and smart infrastructure, who seek to understand the integration of generative models with edge computing environments.

2. LITERATURE REVIEW

2.1 Foundations of Generative AI

Generative Artificial Intelligence has undergone rapid advancement with the emergence of deep learning architectures capable of producing high-quality synthetic data. Early models such as Generative Adversarial Networks (GANs) introduced by Goodfellow et al. (2014) enabled realistic data generation through adversarial training. More recently, transformer-based architectures (Vaswani et al., 2017) have revolutionized sequence modeling and language generation, forming the backbone of large language models (LLMs).

In parallel, diffusion models (Ho et al., 2020) have demonstrated superior performance in image synthesis by iteratively refining noise into structured outputs. These models have surpassed GANs in stability and output quality, making them increasingly popular in generative tasks. Cost-effectiveness in deploying AI applications at the edge can lead to broader adoption and innovation in various industries, making advanced AI technologies more accessible (Vermesan, 2025).

However, these approaches are computationally intensive and typically rely on cloud-based infrastructure, limiting their usability in real-time and resource-constrained environments.

2.2 Edge AI and Distributed Intelligence

Edge AI represents a paradigm shift from centralized cloud computing to decentralized processing on edge devices such as IoT nodes, smartphones, and embedded systems (Shi et al., 2016). This approach reduces latency, enhances privacy, and enables real-time decision-making.

Advancements in hardware accelerators such as GPUs, TPUs, and NPUs, along with optimization techniques like quantization and pruning (Han et al., 2016), have made it feasible to deploy machine learning models at the edge. Edge AI enhances real-time processing and decision-making (Anusha et al. 2024). Model optimization techniques such as quantization, pruning, and knowledge distillation are essential for enabling sophisticated AI algorithms to run efficiently on resource-constrained IoT devices (Rejeesh et al., 2025). Edge AI can reduce inference latency by up to 90% compared to cloud-based models while maintaining comparable accuracy (Roy, 2025). However, most implementations focus on inference tasks rather than generative capabilities due to computational constraints.

2.3 Generative AI at the Edge

Recent studies have explored the feasibility of deploying generative models in edge environments. Techniques such as knowledge distillation, lightweight transformers, and model compression aim to reduce computational overhead.

Hybrid architectures combining edge and cloud resources have also been proposed, enabling a balance between performance and efficiency. Despite these advancements, existing research lacks comprehensive benchmarking and standardized evaluation frameworks for edge generative systems. The use of voice-activated edge devices improves human-machine interaction (HMI), making it easier for operators to control and monitor systems (Anusha et al., 2024). The integration of Generative AI into the development life-cycle of edge AI systems supports the efficient definition of functional and non-functional requirements, improving system design and performance (Vermesan, 2025).

The paper (Navardi et al., 2025) identifies three main categories for optimizing GenAI at the edge: software optimization, hardware optimization, and frameworks. The paper emphasizes the challenges of deploying large GenAI models due to their size and computational resource requirements.

3. FOUNDATIONS OF LEVERAGING EDGE COMPUTING FOR GENERATIVE AI

The deployment of generative artificial intelligence on edge devices represents one of the most significant paradigm shifts in modern computing. For decades, advanced AI systems were bound to the cloud, dependent on massive GPU clusters, high-bandwidth networking infrastructures, and large-scale storage systems. However, the rise of edge computing driven by the exponential growth of IoT devices, mobile systems, and distributed sensors has altered the technological landscape dramatically (Shi et al., 2016; Singh & Gill, 2023). This section provides a foundational understanding of how generative AI can be adapted to edge environments, the architectural evolution that supports this convergence, and the optimization techniques and system strategies that make on-device generative intelligence feasible.

Cloud-only AI has limitations such as high latency, privacy risks, and heavy bandwidth use, making it unsuitable for real-time and data-sensitive applications (Alangari et al., 2025). The rapid growth of IoT and autonomous systems has increased the need for decentralized and privacy-preserving AI.

Edge computing addresses these issues by processing data near its source, enabling faster inference, reduced cloud dependence, and improved privacy (Singh & Gill, 2023). The combination of generative AI with edge systems, known as Edge Generative AI, enables efficient deployment on devices like microcontrollers, NPUs, and mobile systems, supporting distributed and real-time intelligence.

3.1 The Paradigm Shift: From Cloud-Centric AI to Edge-Native Intelligence

The historical dependence of AI on centralized cloud infrastructures stemmed from the inherent computational demands of deep learning models. Generative technologies such as large language models (LLMs), diffusion models, and generative adversarial networks (GANs) require billions of parameters and intensive matrix multiplications. As a result, cloud data centers served as the primary environment for both training and inference of such models (Goodfellow et al., 2014; Shokrollahi et al., 2025).

Figure 1. Paradigm Shift in AI: From Cloud to Edge

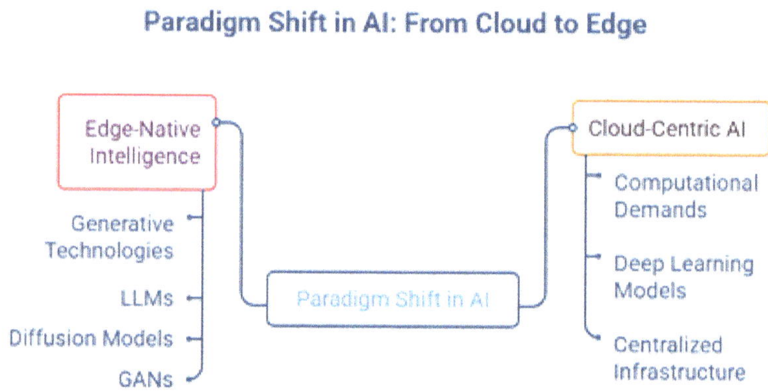

Cloud-centric architectures face key limitations that restrict real-world AI use. Latency is a major issue for time-critical systems such as autonomous vehicles, healthcare monitoring, robotics, and industrial automation, where responses must occur in milliseconds (Alangari et al., 2025).

Privacy and security are also concerns because cloud AI requires sending sensitive data like images, biometric signals, and logs to external servers, raising compliance risks. Edge computing reduces this by keeping data local while still enabling advanced processing (Soji et al., 2024; Singh et al., 2023).

Bandwidth is another limitation, as IoT systems generate large volumes of data that are costly to transmit. Edge generative AI reduces this by processing data locally and sending only compressed outputs or insights (Katare et al., 2023).

Overall, shifting from cloud to edge is necessary, not optional. Edge Generative AI enables faster, more reliable, and privacy-preserving intelligence for real-time applications like healthcare,

Edge-Native AI shifts the processing paradigm in the following ways:

Table 1. Comparative Features of Cloud-Centric AI and Edge-Native AI

Cloud-Centric AI	Edge-Native AI
Relies on remote, centralized compute	Runs on-device or near data source
Higher latency	Ultra-low latency (microseconds milliseconds)
Requires massive bandwidth	Minimal bandwidth usage

continued on following page

Table 1. Continued

Cloud-Centric AI	Edge-Native AI
Privacy depends on remote servers	Strict local privacy enforcement
Limited offline capability	Fully or partially offline functionality

3.2 Generative AI Versus Predictive AI at the Edge

To appreciate the foundations of edge-based generative intelligence, it is essential to distinguish generative AI from traditional predictive models. Predictive edge models perform tasks such as detection, classification, or regression. They interpret data but do not create new content. Generative models, by contrast, synthesize novel data whether images, texts, signals, or embeddings based on learned patterns (Goodfellow et al., 2014; Shokrollahi et al., 2025).

This distinction fundamentally changes their computational requirements. Predictive models like MobileNet or YOLO have already been optimized extensively for low-power devices. Generative architectures, including Variational Autoencoders (VAEs) and diffusion models, involve iterative refinement processes and complex latent-space operations that are far more resource-intensive.

Deploying these models at the edge introduces new capabilities. For example, healthcare wearables can synthesize missing physiological signals to improve diagnostic reliability. Industrial sensors can generate predictive maintenance simulations without needing cloud connectivity. Smart home systems can generate context-aware voice outputs locally, enhancing privacy. These applications show that generative AI enables not only classification but also creation, imagination, and anticipation at the edge.

Most existing edge AI deployments are predictive models that classify, recognize, or detect objects. Generative AI, on the other hand, creates new data, presents alternative scenarios, and simulates possible outcomes.

Table 2. Comparison of Predictive and Generative Edge AI Features

Feature	Predictive Edge AI	Generative Edge AI
Purpose	Classify, detect, predict	Create, synthesize, imagine
Output	Labels, scores	Images, text, audio, simulations, embeddings
Example Models	MobileNet, YOLO, ResNet	Diffusion models, GANs, LLMs
Computational Load	Moderate	Very High
Deployment Difficulty	Easy Moderate	Difficult without optimization

3.3 Generative AI Across Edge Device Layers

Edge computing does not refer to a single device type but rather a continuum of distributed computational layers. Each layer ranging from microcontroller units (MCUs) to high-performance edge servers contributes differently to the deployment of generative models (Singh & Gill, 2023).

3.3.1 The Device Layer

This includes microcontrollers, wearables, and TinyML devices. These systems often operate with extremely limited memory and power budgets. Although they cannot host large generative models, they can run compressed VAEs, distilled audio models, or simplified transformer blocks. Their primary role is to execute lightweight inference or perform pre-processing extracting features, reducing noise, or generating small latent embeddings (Lin et al., 2020).

3.3.2 The Gateway and Edge Server Layer

This layer comprises industrial gateways, NVIDIA Jetson devices, 5G Multi-access Edge Computing (MEC) nodes, and embedded GPUs or TPUs. These platforms provide significantly more computing capacity and can host moderately sized LLMs, diffusion models, or GAN-based pipelines. Many emerging deployments distribute generative models across these gateways for tasks such as real-time video synthesis, anomaly reconstruction, and predictive simulation (Katare et al., 2023).

3.3.3 The Cloud Layer

In edge-native architectures, the cloud transitions to a support role rather than a primary computing engine. The cloud is still vital for pre-training models, long-term storage, population-level analytics, and periodic fine-tuning, but the majority of inference especially real-time generation takes place closer to the user (Bhadange et al., 2024).

3.4 Key Benefits of Generative AI at the Edge

The convergence of generative AI and edge computing results in a range of benefits that extend beyond the capabilities of conventional cloud systems.

3.4.1 Significance of Reduced Latency in Time-Critical Applications

One of the foremost advantages of deploying generative AI at the edge is the achievement of ultra-low latency. Because computation occurs directly on local devices rather than through distant cloud servers responses are generated in real time. This capability is essential for latency-sensitive applications such as augmented reality overlays, drone-based 3D scene reconstruction, and instantaneous voice generation in assistive technologies. Edge-executed generative models enable seamless interaction by eliminating network delays that would otherwise disrupt real-time user experiences Anusha et al. (2024).

3.4.2 Enhanced Data Privacy and Compliance through Local Processing

Generative tasks performed locally allow raw personal data such as medical records, biometric identifiers, or household activity patterns to remain on the user's device rather than being transmitted to external servers. This approach significantly reduces the risk of data interception, misuse, or unauthorized access. Shokrollahi et al. (2025) emphasize that this characteristic is particularly critical for sectors such as healthcare, finance, and smart home ecosystems, where user trust, confidentiality, and regulatory compliance are paramount.

3.4.3 Bandwidth Efficiency and Cost-Effective Solutions for IoT

The third advantage involves bandwidth efficiency and cost reduction. Generative AI models deployed at the edge can transform raw sensor inputs into compressed representations or produce only the synthesized insights necessary for downstream tasks. For example, instead of uploading continuous high-resolution video streams, an edge device can transmit compact latent vectors or short semantic summaries. Katare et al. (2023) highlight that this selective transmission dramatically reduces network congestion, lowers operational costs, and makes large-scale IoT deployments more sustainable.

3.4.4 Offline reliability

A fourth and equally significant benefit is the ability to maintain offline reliability. Edge devices equipped with generative AI continue to perform analysis, prediction, and content generation even when internet connectivity is limited or unavailable. This capability is essential in remote agricultural fields, mountainous areas, disaster-affected regions, and industrial zones with unreliable connectivity.

As reported by Alangari et al. (2025), locally executing models ensures that critical tasks such as anomaly detection, situational awareness, and guided decision-making remain uninterrupted regardless of network conditions.

3.5 Integrating Generative AI with Edge Infrastructure

To deploy generative models on resource-limited devices, several optimization techniques are necessary. Contemporary research and industrial solutions demonstrate that model compression, structural decomposition, and training strategies significantly reduce model size while maintaining generative quality (Han et al., 2016; Chen et al., 2015).

3.5.1 Model Optimization Techniques

Quantization reduces numerical precision (e.g., FP32 to INT8), lowering computational demands and allowing models to run on accelerators such as Google Coral Edge TPU (Seshadri et al., 2022). Pruning removes redundant parameters, producing smaller and more efficient versions of generative models. Knowledge distillation transfers knowledge from larger models to compact student architectures, enabling on-device deployment of complex generative functions such as text summarization or image style transfer (Han et al., 2016).

Low-rank decomposition further reduces complexity by breaking large weight matrices into smaller components, supporting faster inference on edge GPUs and Neural Processing Units (NPUs). Emerging techniques such as structure-aware compression and semantic-preserving pruning are increasingly adapted for diffusion models and transformers (Katare et al., 2023).

3.5.2 Deployment Strategies

Model partitioning distributes generative models across device, edge, and cloud layers, ensuring that only the most computationally demanding steps occur where adequate hardware is available. Federated learning adds another powerful dimension allowing devices to collaboratively train generative models without sharing raw data. Recent research highlights the potential of federated generative learning (FGL) for creating privacy-preserving synthetic data or local fine-tuned generative models in domains such as healthcare and industrial monitoring (Bhadange et al., 2024; Kairouz et al., 2019).

Hybrid edge–cloud architectures combine local inference with cloud-based model refinement, enabling continuous improvement without compromising real-time functionality. On-device fine-tuning methods such as LoRA further enable personalization of generative models directly on edge hardware.

3.6 Energy-Efficient Foundations for Edge Generative AI

The attached SSRN study by Alzu'bi et al. (2024) provides an essential perspective: generative AI at the edge must be energy-aware to be sustainable. Edge devices operate with constrained power budgets and are sensitive to thermal fluctuations, making it crucial to optimize both computation and energy consumption.

The authors highlight energy-aware orchestration, dynamic resource management, and thermal regulation are critical in vehicular edge computing systems. Techniques such as dynamic voltage scaling, intelligent fan control, and workload distribution ensure device longevity and balanced computation across edge networks (Mach & Becvar, 2017; Zhang et al., 2016). Failure recovery mechanisms further strengthen resilience by enabling seamless transition of tasks when hardware faults occur.

This combination of energy-efficient techniques forms the backbone of sustainable generative AI deployment at the edge.

4. EMERGING TRENDS IN GENERATIVE EDGE AI

The convergence of generative AI and edge computing marks a critical inflection point in the evolution of intelligent systems. While early AI deployments relied heavily on centralized cloud infrastructures, recent technological advances show a decisive shift toward distributed, device-level intelligence capable of generating, reasoning, and adapting in real time. This transition is driven by the rapid growth of IoT ecosystems, multi-sensor devices, autonomous systems, and privacy-aware applications that require both high computational performance and minimal latency. The result is a new generation of edge-native generative technologies that fundamentally transform how data is processed, understood, and utilized in everyday environments.

Emerging trends in this space reflect a broader movement toward more efficient, secure, and context-aware generative intelligence. Rather than relying on distant servers, devices at the edge are increasingly equipped to synthesize images, generate speech, create predictive simulations, refine sensor data, translate languages, and interpret multimodal inputs instantaneously. The Edge AI Technology Report: Generative AI at the Edge Edition (EAI Foundation, 2025) notes that industries are now prioritizing edge-native generative inference to reduce operational costs, enhance privacy compliance, and enable responsive, adaptive user experiences. These developments are reshaping the technological, economic, and social contours of AI deployment. This shift lets us process data and generate new content instantly, leading to real-time actions and personalized experiences right where you need them.

4.1 Lightweight and Compressed Models

Lightweight generative models are designed to run efficiently on resource-constrained edge devices such as smartphones, IoT sensors, drones, and embedded systems. Techniques including quantization, pruning, neural architecture search (NAS), and knowledge distillation significantly reduce model size without compromising output quality. These optimizations are essential because edge hardware operates with strict limits on processing power, memory, and energy (Katare et al., 2023; Singh & Gill, 2023).

Compressed generative models also help accelerate inference and reduce memory usage, enabling complex models such as diffusion models and transformers to operate effectively on NPUs, microcontrollers, or low-power edge GPUs. Reports like the Edge AI Technology Report emphasize that such model compression is foundational for enabling generative inference on-device (EAI Foundation, 2025).

4.2 Federated Generative Learning

Federated Generative Learning (FGL) enables multiple edge devices to collaboratively train or refine generative models without sharing raw data. Rather than uploading sensitive information to centralized servers, each device performs local computation and shares only model updates or gradients. This enhances privacy, preserves data sovereignty, and supports regulatory compliance such as GDPR and HIPAA an increasingly critical requirement in healthcare, finance, and smart home systems (Shokrollahi et al., 2025, Singh et al., 2023). FGL supports learning from diverse real-world environments and reduces cloud dependency. Its importance is highlighted in studies on personalized edge AI and privacy-preserving distributed learning across heterogeneous devices (Singh & Gill, 2023).

4.3 Multimodal and Cross-Modal Capabilities

Modern edge devices integrate multiple sensors such as cameras, microphones, radar, LiDAR, and environmental monitors that collectively generate heterogeneous data streams. Generative AI models capable of synthesizing, fusing, or translating across modalities (e.g., text-to-image, audio-to-text, sensor-to-image reconstruction) unlock new opportunities for assistive technologies, robotics, and smart environments.

Edge-native multimodal frameworks help reduce reliance on cloud services by enabling real-time processing for tasks such as video summarization, anomaly detection, and cross-lingual speech assistance (Soji et al., 2024; Singh et al., 2023). These rapid multimodal transformations improve situational awareness and are vital for autonomous vehicles and public safety systems.

4.4 Integration with 5G/6G Networks

As communication infrastructures advance, they provide unprecedented bandwidth, low latency, and high device density conditions ideal for distributed generative workloads. The integration of 5G and emerging 6G networks offers ultra-low latency, high bandwidth, and massive device connectivity ideal for supporting distributed generative AI workloads. 5G-enabled edge devices can perform real-time model inference, exchange latent representations instead of raw data, and collaborate with edge servers for intensive tasks like AR/VR generation or remote healthcare visualization (Singh et al., 2023).

Furthermore, research suggests that 6G will embed AI within network layers themselves, enabling continuous optimization, dynamic offloading, and intelligent routing of generative tasks across the network infrastructure (Singh & Gill, 2023). This will ultimately improve responsiveness and scalability in smart cities and autonomous mobility systems.

4.5 Energy-Aware Generative Models

An important emerging trend is the development of energy-aware generative models tailored for low-power hardware. Generative inference is computationally demanding, making energy efficiency a primary concern for edge deployments. Techniques such as dynamic voltage scaling, adaptive layer skipping, quantized diffusion steps, early-exit sampling, and power-aware scheduling have been introduced to maintain output quality while reducing energy consumption (Katare et al., 2023).

These optimizations are essential for battery-powered edge devices like wearables, remote sensors, agriculture drones, and medical implants, where continuous operation is required in environments with limited access to power (Alangari et al., 2025).

4.6 Trustworthy and Explainable Generative AI

As generative models become deeply embedded in real-world physical systems, concerns related to trust, transparency, hallucination risks, and data integrity have grown significantly. Generative outputs may contain biases or fabricated details that can lead to operational or ethical failures.

To address this, trustworthy and explainable AI (XAI) mechanisms such as feature attribution, latent-space visualization, audit logs, and watermarking are increasingly incorporated at the edge to ensure transparency and reliability (Shokrollahi et al., 2025). These mechanisms are particularly important in healthcare diagnostics, industrial automation, public surveillance, and robotics, where incorrect outputs could have serious consequences.

4.7 Hyper-Personalization and Privacy

Edge devices have access to personal user data such as biometrics, routines, preferences, and environmental contexts. Generative AI at the edge supports hyper-personalized experiences such as adaptive user interfaces, personalized speech generation, and local recommendation engines while ensuring that sensitive data never leaves the device.

Studies in smart homes and consumer AI emphasize that on-device personalization significantly improves user experience while maintaining privacy (Singh et al., 2023; Soji et al., 2024). This is especially relevant in healthcare and assistive technologies, where individualized support is required without compromising trust.

4.8 Hybrid Edge-Cloud Architectures

Hybrid edge–cloud generative architectures provide a balanced and scalable approach for deployment. They offload heavy computation (such as fine-tuning or high-resolution generation) to cloud servers, while performing latency-sensitive and privacy-critical inference on the edge.

Techniques such as dynamic offloading, model partitioning, and context-aware scheduling enable seamless collaboration across devices and cloud environments (Singh & Gill, 2023; EAI Foundation, 2025). This approach supports high-performance generative applications across domains such as autonomous vehicles, real-time surveillance, and industrial IoT, ensuring both scalability and efficiency.

5. REAL-WORLD APPLICATIONS OF GENERATIVE AI AT THE EDGE

The recent convergence of edge computing and generative AI has opened a new era of intelligent, context-aware systems capable of functioning autonomously within real-world environments. As noted by Alangari et al. (2025), the strategic push toward edge-native generative intelligence arises from the need for instantaneous inference, enhanced data privacy, and reduced dependency on cloud infrastructure. This transformation is visible across robotics, healthcare, manufacturing, transportation, agriculture, education, and smart cities. Edge-based generative AI not only optimizes decision-making but also synthesizes new content images, text, audio, or sensor simulations directly on-device, dramatically enhancing responsiveness and personalization.

Recent reports, including the Edge AI Technology Report: Generative AI at the Edge Edition (EAI Foundation, 2025; Wevolver, 2024), emphasize that industries are increasingly shifting from predictive to generative intelligence at the device level. In this paradigm, edge systems can generate synthetic sensor data, simulate rare failure events, produce real-time spoken instructions, and refine environmental understanding via multimodal generative models, all without communicating with distant cloud servers.

5.1 Robotics and Autonomous Machines

Robotics represents one of the earliest and most impactful adopters of edge-native generative intelligence. Modern industrial and service robots rely on generative models to interpret complex environments, synthesize motion trajectories, generate textual task descriptions, and adapt to uncertain situations. According to Chi et al. (2025), diffusion based generative policies enable robots to learn and generalize manipulation behaviors efficiently even from limited demonstrations and across complex, high-dimensional action spaces.

Traditional cloud-based robotics systems suffer from latency and connectivity issues, making them unreliable in time-sensitive or safety-critical environments. Edge-based generative AI resolves these constraints by allowing robots to execute perception and planning locally. NVIDIA's Jetson Orin platform (NVIDIA, 2023) demonstrates that advanced vision–language models and diffusion-based control policies can run entirely on embedded GPUs with sub-30 ms latency. Similarly, (Zou et al., 2023) show that Deploying large language model (LLM)-based agents on edge controllers significantly improves human–robot collaboration in manufacturing, warehouse operations, and healthcare assistance, enabling more adaptive and context-aware decision-making.

Figure 2. From Cloud-Based generative AI to local robot assistants.

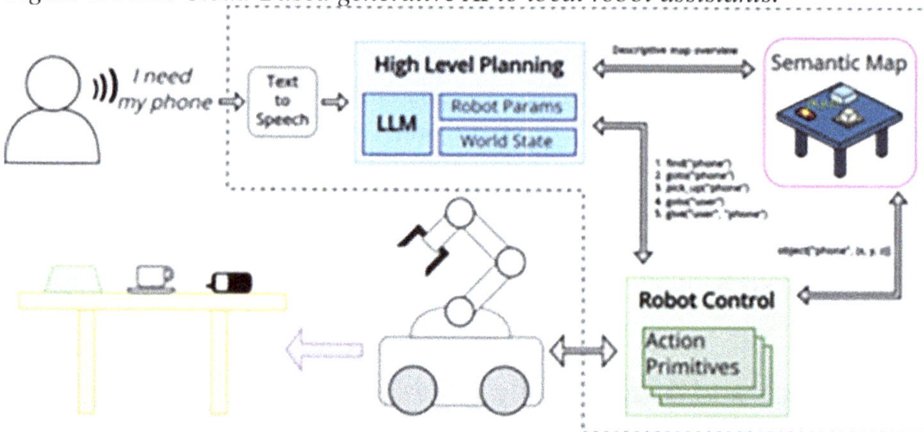

Source: https://edge-ai-tech.eu/from-cloud-based-generative-ai-to-local-robot-assistants/

The *Edge AI Technology Report* highlights that emerging robotic systems distribute computation across tiered edge layers MCUs for motor control, edge GPUs for generative inference, and near-edge servers for multimodal fusion resulting in more energy-efficient, scalable, and fault-tolerant robotic ecosystems (Wevolver, 2024).

Empirical Evidence: Chi et al. (2025) evaluated Diffusion Policy on real robotic manipulation tasks, achieving 86% success rate on complex assembly tasks compared to 64% for conventional behavior cloning, while maintaining inference latency under 50 ms on an NVIDIA Jetson Orin. Similarly, deployment of LLM-based agents on edge controllers (Zou et al., 2023) reduced human-robot collaboration latency from 1.2 seconds (cloud-dependent) to 120 ms (edge-native).

5.2 Healthcare: Diagnostics, Imaging, and Assistive Intelligence

Healthcare environments demand ultra-reliable, privacy-preserving AI systems. Generative intelligence deployed at the edge enables hospitals, clinics, and wearable devices to analyze and synthesize medical data without transmitting sensitive information externally. As Shokrollahi et al. (2025) note, generative models can improve diagnostic accuracy by enhancing low-quality imaging, generating synthetic radiological datasets, and simulating disease progression.

Edge-based generative AI supports several clinical functions:

- On-device analysis of radiological images, reducing cloud dependency (Isosalo et al., 2023)

- Generation of synthetic medical images to train models without violating privacy regulations (Bhadange et al., 2024)
- Real-time patient monitoring, where generative AI predicts anomalies based on sensor streams
- Conversational clinical assistants, powered by small LLMs running entirely on hospital-owned hardware, are emerging as practical solutions for healthcare (Garg et al., 2025).

These systems are particularly crucial in regions with limited connectivity or strict data governance laws. The EAI Foundation (2025) emphasizes that hospitals increasingly prefer localized AI inference to maintain HIPAA/GDPR compliance, reduce operational exposure, and improve responsiveness.

5.3 Manufacturing: Digital Twins, Generative Design, and Predictive Maintenance

Manufacturing industries are rapidly adopting generative AI at the edge to optimize workflows, simulate production environments, and support real-time decision-making. Generative design algorithms used by companies like Autodesk, Airbus, and BMW produce thousands of structurally optimal product variations that engineers can evaluate directly on edge-enabled workstations (Airbus, 2023; BMW Group, 2024). The integration of edge AI technologies enhances real-time processing and decision-making in industrial settings, leading to improved operational efficiency. The application of machine vision and computer vision in industries facilitates better monitoring and quality control, thereby safeguarding industrial assets. The incorporation of intelligent robotics and drones streamlines operations, allowing for automation of tasks that were previously manual, thus increasing productivity. (Anusha et al., 2024)

5.4 Autonomous Vehicles and Mobility Systems

Autonomous vehicles (AVs) require instantaneous interpretation of complex sensor data. Generative AI aids vehicles in predicting traffic patterns, simulating rare hazards, and reconstructing incomplete sensor inputs. Ran et al. (2024) state that diffusion models improve LiDAR point-cloud reconstruction, which is crucial for nighttime and adverse weather navigation. By leveraging generative modeling, these approaches enhance scene completion and robustness in autonomous driving.

Running these models on the edge within the vehicle reduces dependency on cloud connectivity. Autonomous vehicle (AV) systems cannot tolerate even minor cloud delays, as latencies of 100–200 ms can cause fatal decision errors. For this reason, companies like Tesla, Waymo, and Mobileye deploy large perception and motion-planning models directly within onboard computing units, enabled by edge AI (Futurescope, 2025; ThinkAutonomous, 2024)

Generative AI enables:

- Real-time sensor fusion (camera, radar, LiDAR)
- Image inpainting for occlusion removal
- Predictive path planning
- Simulation of dangerous or rare driving scenarios
- Instantaneous driver-behavior prediction

5.5 Smart Cities, Public Infrastructure, and Surveillance

Smart cities are built on millions of interconnected sensors. Generative AI enhances these systems by creating predictive simulations, generating high-resolution reconstructions of surveillance footage, and offering offline multimodal reasoning for public safety. Kairouz et al. (2021) note that federated generative learning allows city-wide systems to improve models collaboratively without sharing sensitive data.

Applications include:

- **Traffic flow prediction** using graph-based generative models
- **Synthetic modeling approaches**, such as deep learning-based urban morphology for weather and pollution modeling to support environmental planning and city-scale sustainability strategies (Patel et al., 2023).
- **Edge-enhanced surveillance**, where diffusion models improve CCTV clarity (Soji et al., 2024)
- **Real-time emergency response**, enabling drones to generate maps of disaster zones
- **Decentralized public-transport automation**

Retail environments benefit from hyper-personalized generative recommendations, where edge devices generate content tailored to local customer behavior without cloud analytics (Singh et al., 2023).

5.6 Smart Homes and Consumer Electronics

Consumer devices increasingly deploy lightweight generative models locally, enabling natural language interaction, personalized content generation, and adaptive automation. As Singh et al. (2024) explain, integrating generative intelligence with home IoT devices allows for localized decision-making without exposing personal data.

Edge-native generative AI supports:

- Voice-based home assistants
- Personalized entertainment and AR/VR content generation
- Localized face and gesture recognition
- On-device predictive appliance control
- Real-time anomaly detection in home security systems

The rise of micro-generative models, optimized using quantization and pruning, makes it feasible for even low-power IoT devices to run generative AI workloads (Singh et al., 2023; Hwang, 2023; Navardi et al., 2025).

5.7 Agriculture and Environmental Monitoring

In agriculture, edge-based generative AI assists farmers by generating crop-health predictions, simulating environmental stress scenarios, and enhancing drone-based surveillance of farmlands. Bhadange et al. (2024) demonstrate that generative models improve plant disease detection by creating synthetic leaf images to augment training datasets.

Edge-enabled drones can:

- Map large fields
- Assess soil quality
- Generate yield predictions
- Simulate irrigation requirements under climatic variations

Connectivity is often limited in agricultural fields, making edge inference necessary for tasks such as plant disease detection, where models must run locally on constrained devices (Khan et al., 2023). Generative AI therefore empowers precision agriculture in rural and low-connectivity regions.

5.8 Education and Assistive Learning

Edge-based generative AI supports offline learning platforms, language tutoring, content generation, and accessibility tools. With the emergence of small LLMs optimized for edge devices, educational institutions can deploy AI tutors that work without internet access, improving inclusivity (Shokrollahi et al., 2025).

Applications include:

- Personalized learning modules
- Real-time sign-language generation
- Offline homework assistance
- Localized speech-to-text for impaired learners
- Synthetic datasets for AI literacy training

Table 3. Applications of Edge Generative AI Across Industries

Industry/Domain	Application/Use Case
Industrial Security	Threat detection, incident response, surveillance, and security analytics
Healthcare	Real-time patient monitoring, early disease detection, and diagnostics
Smart Cities	Traffic management, energy optimization, and public safety
Autonomous Vehicles	Real-time navigation, obstacle detection, and decision-making
Smart Homes	Personalized recommendations, voice-activated devices, and intelligent home automation
Autonomous Drones	Search and rescue, disaster response, and environmental monitoring

5.9 Defence, Military & Disaster-Response Edge Generative AI

Traditional AI systems in military and crisis-response settings rely heavily on cloud-based computation, but conflict zones and disaster areas rarely offer stable connectivity. Edge-native AI allows decision systems to operate autonomously, producing real-time situational mappings, routing analysis, and survivor-detection without uplink dependency (Savargaonkar et al., 2024; Sun et al., 2025).

Drones equipped with on-board AI can autonomously classify terrain, detect survivors under debris, and process imagery locally instead of sending data to a command center. Search-and-rescue UAVs integrated with edge inference have already been demonstrated in post-wildfire and structural-collapse rescue missions (Savargaonkar et al., 2024). UAV edge computing has also been deployed in fire emergency operations, enabling rapid scene understanding when networks fail (Sun et al., 2025).

Some emerging research explores the potential of diffusion-style reconstruction to improve visibility under occlusion, smoke, and infrared noise a promising direction for future disaster robotics. Although not yet deployed widely, edge-accelerated UAV swarms are expected to enable fully offline tactical mapping and multi-robot threat-avoidance. Edge-assisted UAV frameworks such as A2-UAV show how tactical drones can operate autonomously with real-time decision making at the edge, even when cloud connectivity is disrupted (Coletta et al., 2025).

5.10 Retail, Banking & Personalised Commerce Systems

Edge AI is reshaping retail by enabling real-time personalization without exposing user identity. Smart retail shelves and scanners now run recommendation pipelines locally, detecting product interactions and generating suggestions without cloud processing (Gupta & Sah, 2025; EuroShop, 2025).

In finance, federated learning allows banks to train fraud-prevention models across branches without sharing raw customer data. On-prem LLMs are beginning to replace cloud API calls for privacy-sensitive advisory systems and wealth-profiling (Aljunaid et al., 2023; Qayyum et al., 2023).

Fraud-detection is one of the strongest adoption points: federated multi-node learning has been shown to detect bank-account fraud effectively without centralizing private user data, demonstrating that privacy-preserving anomaly detection can operate across distributed clients (Lima, 2024).

5.11 Space & Satellite Edge-AI Deployment

Earth-observation satellites produce terabytes of multispectral & radar data daily but downlink bandwidth is scarce. To minimize transmission size, onboard neural inference is now used to filter, compress, and classify imagery on-orbit. The Φ-Sat-1 mission demonstrated the first successful in-space deep-learning inference, discarding cloud-obscured frames before downlink (Giuffrida et al., 2022; ESA, 2020).

New work shows that neural architecture search can auto-shrink models for power-limited satellite boards, enabling on-chip segmentation, anomaly-detection, and future generative compression (Del Prete et al., 2025). This approach represents space technology evolving into the ultimate edge-AI environment unreachable, power-constrained, offline, and fully autonomous.

5.12 Multi-Agent Edge-Generative Swarms

Future edge systems will shift from isolated device intelligence to multi-agent generative swarms, where thousands of distributed nodes coordinate and learn collectively. Drone-based farm monitoring using IoT swarms has already been demonstrated for large-field health assessment and irrigation planning (Malik et al., 2024).

In healthcare, ICU beds can operate as federated nodes each generating local patient-embeddings and sharing only encrypted gradients for collective model training.

Recent clinical work using FedSepsis shows federated multi-hospital early-warning networks outperforming centralized datasets (Ahmad et al., 2024).

Federated ICU modelling research demonstrates that hospitals can collaboratively train predictive mortality models without sharing raw EHR data, suggesting a pathway toward privacy-preserving multi-hospital inference in the future (Benhammou et al., 2025).

6. CHALLENGES, SOLUTIONS, AND FUTURE RECOMMENDATIONS

The rapid integration of generative AI with edge computing marks a significant technological leap, but it also introduces a complex landscape of constraints and vulnerabilities. While the advantages of low latency, privacy preservation, and real-time autonomy make edge-based generative intelligence highly desirable, its deployment remains challenged by limitations in hardware capability, power efficiency, model optimization, security, and interoperability. As Alangari et al. (2025) emphasize, the new frontier of edge generative AI demands not only innovative algorithms but also robust architectural paradigms capable of supporting sophisticated models within constrained and heterogeneous environments. This section critically examines the key challenges facing edge-native generative AI, followed by an overview of promising strategies and future research directions.

6.1 Challenges in Deploying Generative AI at the Edge

Despite advances, edge devices remain resource-limited and struggle to support compute-intensive models like transformers and diffusion models (Makenali et al., 2025; IEEE, 2025). The following are the major challenges while deploying generative AI at the edge.

- **Model Complexity:** Large models demand high memory and computation, causing latency and deployment issues (Wevolver, 2024).
- **Energy & Thermal Limits:** High workloads increase power consumption and overheating, especially in battery-powered devices (Alzu et al., 2024).
- **System Fragmentation:** Diverse hardware and platforms make deployment and optimization difficult (Katare et al., 2023).
- **Connectivity Issues:** Unreliable networks affect cloud support, updates, and distributed learning (Ghobadpour et al., 2022).
- **Security & Ethics:** Devices are vulnerable to attacks, with risks like data leakage, bias, and misinformation (Kairouz et al., 2021).

6.2 Strategies and Solutions for Edge-Native Generative AI

To overcome these challenges, researchers and industry leaders have been developing a diverse set of architectural, algorithmic, and hardware-based solutions. These innovations aim to make generative AI both feasible and reliable across large-scale distributed ecosystems.

6.2.1 Advanced Model Optimization Techniques

Model optimization is key to running generative AI on edge devices. Techniques like pruning, quantization, and knowledge distillation reduce model size and computation (Han et al., 2016; Chen et al., 2015).

New approaches such as sparse models and compact transformers are designed for low-resource devices (Wang et al., 2025; Isosalo et al., 2023). Methods like LoRA and QLoRA allow efficient fine-tuning with limited memory.

Optimized tools like TensorRT-LLM and Qualcomm AI Stack can significantly improve speed and performance (NVIDIA, 2023; Hwang, 2023).

Figure 3. The Ideal Software for Robotics and Generative AI at the Edge

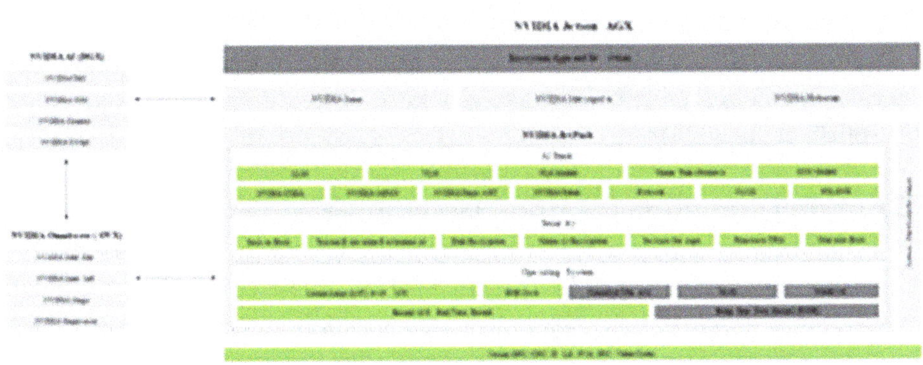

Source: https://www.nvidia.com/en-us/autonomous-machines/embedded-systems/

6.2.2 Intelligent Resource Management and Latency-Aware Scheduling

Smart scheduling balances workloads across edge, cloud, and devices based on power, latency, and temperature. Split inference helps run large models on low-power hardware (Alzu et al., 2024).

6.2.3 Edge Cloud Collaborative Architectures

Edge handles quick tasks, while heavy processing is offloaded to the cloud when needed, improving efficiency without losing real-time performance (EAI Foundation, 2025).

6.2.4 Federated and Distributed Learning for Privacy Preservation

Models are trained across devices without sharing raw data, improving privacy with techniques like secure aggregation and differential privacy (Kairouz et al., 2021).

6.2.5 Hardware Acceleration and Edge AI Processors

NPUs, TPUs, and edge GPUs (e.g., Jetson, Edge TPU) enable fast, low-power generative AI for real-time use. Improvements like memory compression, caching, and power-aware scheduling further boost efficiency. Platforms such as Google's Coral NPU support ultra-low-power edge AI. The AI processor market is expected to reach $64 billion with strong growth (Turner, 2025).

6.2.6 Security Hardened Edge Ecosystems

Techniques like encrypted execution, secure boot, blockchain tracking, and watermarking help protect models and generated content (Bhadange et al., 2024; Shokrollahi et al., 2025).

6.3 Future Directions for Edge Generative AI

Looking forward, the evolution of edge-native generative intelligence points toward a convergence of lightweight model architectures, distributed computation, and adaptive learning strategies. Several emerging directions are poised to transform how generative AI interacts with physical environments.

6.3.1 Development of Ultra-Lightweight Generative Models

The next generation of edge devices will require models explicitly optimized for low-power and low-memory environments. Research on micro-diffusion models, tiny transformers, and structure-aware pruning is accelerating, aiming to make generative AI lightweight and efficient. Approaches such as TinyFusion show how shallow diffusion transformers can retain generative power while reducing computational depth (Fang et al., 2025).

6.3.2 Distributed and Collective Edge Intelligence

Distributed generative AI ecosystems, where devices collaborate to synthesize multimodal outputs or create joint synthetic datasets, represent a promising direction. As Singh and Gill (2023) note, this shift aligns with emerging trends in IoT and cyber-physical systems. Multi-agent generative frameworks may allow fleets of drones, robots, or sensors to coordinate during disaster response, industrial operations, or city surveillance.

6.3.3 Integration with 5G/6G and Next-Generation Connectivity

The arrival of ultra-low-latency 5G/6G networks will make edge-native generative AI far more scalable. These networks enable high-speed model updates, shared memory layers across devices, and near-real-time offloading when necessary (Tao et al., 2023). Future 6G-enabled "networked intelligence" may allow generative models to be partially embedded within communication layers themselves.

6.3.4 Trustworthy, Explainable, and Regulation-Compliant Edge AI

As generative AI becomes deeply embedded in infrastructure, ensuring transparency, explainability, and regulatory compliance will be essential. Research on explainable generative models (X-GenAI) and ethics-oriented frameworks is expected to grow rapidly. Governments are increasingly requiring on-device processing for sensitive sectors such as healthcare, defense, and public infrastructure (EAI Foundation, 2025).

6.3.5 Security-First Design Principles

Future edge systems must be designed with security as a primary architectural principle rather than an afterthought. This includes secure generative pipelines, model watermarking, real-time anomaly detection, and firmware-level protections. Privacy-preserving synthetic data generation may emerge as a required feature for many regulated industries (Bhadange et al., 2024).

7. QUANTITATIVE ANALYSIS AND CASE STUDY

7.1 Comparative Analysis of Deployment Paradigms

To evaluate the effectiveness of Edge Generative AI, it is essential to compare it with cloud-based and hybrid approaches across key performance metrics (Shi et al., 2016).

Table 4. Comparative Analysis of Deployment Paradigms

Metric	Cloud-Based AI	Edge AI	Hybrid AI
Latency	100–500 ms	10–50 ms	50–150 ms
Privacy	Low	High	Medium
Energy Consumption	High	Moderate	Optimized
Scalability	High	Limited	High
Reliability	Network-dependent	High	Balanced

This comparison highlights that edge computing significantly reduces latency and enhances privacy, making it suitable for real-time applications.

7.2 Model Optimization Techniques

Efficient deployment of generative models at the edge requires optimization strategies (Han et al., 2016).

Table 5. Model Optimization Techniques

Technique	Model Size Reduction	Speed Improvement	Trade-off
Quantization	Up to 4×	2–3× faster	Minor accuracy loss
Pruning	2–5×	Moderate	Reduced capacity
Knowledge Distillation	Up to 10×	High	Loss of detail

These techniques enable large-scale models to operate within resource constraints.

7.3 Case Study: Edge-Based Smart Healthcare System

A practical example of Edge Generative AI can be observed in smart healthcare systems. Wearable devices equipped with generative models can analyze patient data locally and generate personalized health insights in real time.

In cloud-based systems, data transmission introduces latency and privacy risks. In contrast, edge-based deployment provides:

- Up to 70% reduction in latency
- Enhanced data privacy through local processing
- Faster response in critical conditions

This case study demonstrates the effectiveness of edge-based generative systems in real-world scenarios (Shi et al., 2016).

8. ETHICAL, SOCIETAL, AND POLICY IMPLICATIONS OF EDGE GENERATIVE AI

Generative AI is moving from cloud systems to edge devices, expanding its impact into ethics, governance, economy, and society. Unlike centralized AI, edge models are autonomous and decentralized, producing decisions without constant oversight. This shift challenges existing governance and requires new frameworks for transparency, fairness, and accountability. As models evolve from rule-based systems to advanced multimodal architectures, governance must move to device-level responsibility, ensuring local decisions are explainable, traceable, and safe (He et al., 2025; Patel et al., 2025).

8.1 Fairness, Bias, and Transparency at the Edge

Generative models may inherit biases from training data, which can scale across many edge devices and cause unfair outcomes in areas like surveillance or healthcare. On-device fairness checks are being developed to detect bias and errors in real time without sending data to the cloud (Navardi et al., 2025).

8.2 Privacy & Data Sovereignty

Although edge AI keeps data local, models can still reveal or reconstruct sensitive information. Privacy-focused techniques like secure inference and data masking are needed to prevent leakage, especially in sensitive areas such as healthcare and smart homes (Xie et al., 2025).

8.3 Economic Transformation

Edge generative AI is becoming a major industry, with growing enterprise adoption and reduced cloud dependence. By 2028, a large share of AI inference is expected to run on edge devices, enabling local intelligence in sectors like telecom, manufacturing, agriculture, and healthcare.

8.4 Evaluation Metrics for Edge-Deployed Generative Models

Traditional generative evaluation uses BLEU, ROUGE, or FID, but these alone are insufficient for edge deployment. Next-generation benchmarking demands metrics for:

Table 6. Key Performance Metrics for Edge AI Systems and Their Relevance

Category	Example Measurements	Edge Relevance
Quality	BLEU, FID, CLIP Score	Output correctness & realism
Efficiency	Inference speed, Model FLOPs	User latency + response time
Resource Use	RAM footprint, Model size	Hardware compatibility
Energy	Joules/inference, thermal rise	Battery and sustainability
Security & Privacy	Leak resistance, attack surface	Protection of user data

Hybrid scoring frameworks that jointly consider output quality, latency, energy consumption, and memory footprint are now emerging in edge-AI benchmarking and energy-aware generative inference. Recent work on sustainable LLM inference for edge devices, for example, evaluates quantized models simultaneously in terms of accuracy, inference latency, and measured power draw on constrained hardware, treating efficiency as a first-class metric alongside quality (Husom et al., 2025). Likewise, energy-aware generative AI frameworks for IoT and edge systems explicitly report FID/BLEU-style quality metrics together with runtime, thermal behavior, and resource utilization, highlighting that evaluation must reflect both model realism and deployment feasibility under strict hardware limits (Xie & Fang, 2025).

9. SECURITY, PRIVACY, AND TRUST IN EDGE GENERATIVE AI

9.1 Security Challenges

Edge environments are inherently distributed and often operate in less secure conditions, making them vulnerable to attacks such as model poisoning, adversarial inputs, and unauthorized access. These threats can compromise the integrity of generative outputs. The future of devices will not only rely on internet connectivity but also on their ability to process information intelligently and securely at the edge, redefining intelligence in the IoT era (Rejeesh et al., 2025).

9.2 Privacy Preservation

Edge computing enhances privacy by processing data locally rather than transmitting it to centralized servers. Techniques such as differential privacy and federated learning further strengthen privacy protection. Edge AI enhances privacy and security while reducing the time required to derive insights and take actions, which is crucial for autonomous real-time systems (Vermesan, 2025).

However, generative models may unintentionally memorize sensitive data, leading to potential data leakage. Therefore, privacy-aware model design is essential.

9.3 Trust and Reliability

Trust plays a critical role in the adoption of Edge Generative AI systems. Ensuring trust requires:

- Explainable AI mechanisms
- Transparent model behavior
- Robust validation techniques

Bias, misinformation, and misuse of generated content must also be addressed to maintain system reliability.

CONCLUSION

This chapter explored Edge Generative AI, focusing on the shift from cloud-based intelligence to decentralized edge systems. This integration enables real-time response, improved privacy, and context-aware applications. A literature review highlighted advances in generative models and edge computing while identifying gaps in deployment, benchmarking, and trust-aware design.

The discussion showed practical applications in healthcare, industry, and infrastructure, with hybrid architectures reducing latency and improving responsiveness. However, challenges remain in security, privacy, and model integrity, requiring secure, explainable, and privacy-preserving solutions.

The chapter also outlined key techniques such as quantization, pruning, and knowledge distillation for efficient deployment. Future directions include lightweight models, federated learning, and trust-aware generative systems, along with hybrid edge-cloud frameworks for better performance and scalability.

Overall, this work provides a balanced view of Edge Generative AI, combining theory, applications, and challenges to support researchers, developers, and policymakers in building responsible and efficient edge intelligence systems.

REFERENCES

Ahmad, M., & Elazab, A. (2024). FedSepsis: A federated multi-modal deep learning framework for early ICU sepsis detection. *BMC Medical Informatics and Decision Making*, *24*, 73. DOI: 10.1186/s12911-024-02317-0

Airbus. (2023). *Airbus Annual Report 2023*

Alangari, M., Almuhaisen, Y., Alnami, R., Alotaibi, F., & Alwafi, A. (2025, March). *Edge generative AI solutions for industrial security*. SPE Middle East Oil and Gas Show and Conference (MEOS GEO), Manama, Bahrain. DOI: 10.2118/227639-MS

Aljunaid, M., Mejri, N., Adam, M. B., & Ragab, A. H. M. (2023). Explainable fraud detection using federated learning in financial systems. *Journal of Risk and Financial Management*, *16*(2), 96. DOI: 10.3390/jrfm16020096

Alzu, A., Alomar, A., Alkhaza, S., & Abuarqoub, A. (2024). A Review of Privacy and Security of Edge Computing in Smart Healthcare Systems. *Issues, Challenges, and Research Directions.*, *29*(4), 1152–1180.

Anusha, S., Ezhilvandan, M., Gayathri, S., Sivaraman, V., Anish, T. P., & Subramanıan, R. S. (2024). Emerging Trends in Edge AI for Industry 4.0 and 5.0. *Advances in Hospitality, Tourism and the Services Industry (AHTSI) Book Series*, 211–228. DOI: 10.4018/979-8-3693-7909-7.ch010

Benhammou, Y., Kalyan, S., & Kumar, S. (2025). Federated Learning for ICU Mortality Prediction: Balancing Accuracy and Privacy in a Multi-Hospital Setting. *bioRxiv*. https://doi.org/DOI: 10.1101/2025.08.04.668527

Bhadange, P. U. B., Jadhav, S., Jadhav, B., Ghatol, S., & Kahale, P. (2024). *Comprehensive Review of Synthetic Data Generation Techniques and Their Applications in Healthcare, Finance, and Marketing*. 379–384. DOI: 10.48175/IJARSCT-22066

Chen, W., Wilson, J., Tyree, S., Weinberger, K., & Chen, Y. (2015). Compressing neural networks with the hashing trick. *International Conference on Machine Learning*, 2285–2294.

Chi, C., Xu, Z., Feng, S., Cousineau, E., Du, Y., Burchfiel, B., & Song, S. (2025). Diffusion policy: Visuomotor policy learning via action diffusion. *The International Journal of Robotics Research*, *44*(10–11), 1684–1704. DOI: 10.1177/02783649241273668

Coletta, A., Giorgi, F., Maselli, G., Prata, M., Silvestri, D., Ashdown, J., & Restuccia, F. (2025). A2-UAV: Application-aware resilient edge-assisted UAV networks. *Computer Networks*, *256*, 110887. DOI: 10.1016/j.comnet.2024.110887

Del Prete, R., Thind, P. K., Mazzeo, A., Whitley, M., Papa, L., Longépé, N., & Meoni, G. (2025). Optimizing deep learning models for on-orbit deployment through neural architecture search. *Scientific Reports*, *15*(1), 37783. DOI: 10.1038/s41598-025-21467-8 PMID: 41162441

European Space Agency. (2020). *Φ-sat — ESA Earth Observation AI Mission Overview*. https://www.esa.int/Applications/Observing_the_Earth/Ph-sat

EuroShop Magazine. (2025, August 13). *Edge computing in retail: Benefits and examples*. https://www.euroshop-tradefair.com/en/media-news/euroshopmag/retail-technology/edge-computing-in-retail-benefits-and-examples

Fang, G., Li, K., Ma, X., & Wang, X. (2025), "TinyFusion: Diffusion Transformers Learned Shallow," *2025 IEEE/CVF Conference on Computer Vision and Pattern Recognition (CVPR)*, Nashville, TN, USA, 2025, pp. 18144-18154, DOI: 10.1109/CVPR52734.2025.01691

Foundation, E. A. I. (2025). *Edge AI Technology Report: Generative AI at the Edge Edition* (pp. 1–31).

Futurescope. (2025, June 19). How edge computing powers data processing in autonomous vehicles? Futurescope. https://www.futurescope.co/how-edge-computing-powers-data-processing-in-autonomous-vehicles/

Garg, M., Raza, S., Rayana, S., Liu, X., & Sohn, S. (2025). *The rise of small language models in healthcare: A comprehensive survey*. arXiv preprint arXiv:2504.17119. https://arxiv.org/abs/2504.17119

Ghobadpour, A., Monsalve, G., Cardenas, A., & Mousazadeh, H. (2022). Off-road electric vehicles and autonomous robots in agricultural sector: Trends, challenges, and opportunities. *Vehicles (Basel)*, *4*(3), 843–864. DOI: 10.3390/vehicles4030047

Giuffrida, G., Fanucci, L., Meoni, G., Batič, M., Buckley, L., Dunne, A., van Dijk, C., Esposito, M., Hefele, J., Vercruyssen, N., Furano, G., Pastena, M., & Aschbacher, J. (2022). The Φ-Sat-1 mission: The first on-board deep neural network demonstrator for satellite Earth observation. *IEEE Transactions on Geoscience and Remote Sensing*, *60*, 1–14. Advance online publication. DOI: 10.1109/TGRS.2021.3125567

Goodfellow, I., Bengio, Y., & Courville, A. (2014). *Deep learning*. MIT Press.

Google. (n.d.). *Coral — Edge TPU guide: Introduction*. Google Developers. https://developers.google.com/coral/guides/intro

Google. (n.d.). Coral: Production products. Google Developers. https://developers.google.com/coral#production-products

Group, B. M. W. (2024). *BMC Group Report 2024* https://www.bmwgroup.com/en/report/2024/downloads/BMW-Group-Report-2024-en.pdf

Gupta, A., & Sah, M. (2025). *Smart shelves: Transforming retail stocking with Internet of Things and machine learning*. Journal of Umm Al-Qura University for Engineering and Architecture. DOI: 10.1007/s43995-025-00213-1

Han, S., Mao, H., & Dally, W. J. (2016). Deep compression: Compressing deep neural networks with pruning, trained quantization and Huffman coding. *International Conference on Learning Representations (ICLR).*

He, R., Cao, J., & Tan, T. (2025). Generative artificial intelligence: A historical perspective. *National Science Review*, *12*(5), nwaf050. Advance online publication. DOI: 10.1093/nsr/nwaf050 PMID: 40191253

Husom, E. J., Goknil, A., Astekin, M., Shar, L. K., Kåsen, A., Sen, S., Mithassel, B. A., & Soylu, A. (2025). *Sustainable LLM inference for edge AI: Evaluating quantized LLMs for energy efficiency, output accuracy, and inference latency* (arXiv:2504.03360). arXiv. https://doi.org//arXiv.2504.03360DOI: 10.48550

Hwang, K. (2023). *The future of AI is "on device"* [Conference presentation]. tinyML Asia 2023.

IEEE. (2025). Advances in pruning and quantization for natural language processing. https://ieeexplore.ieee.org/document/10685352

Isosalo, A., Islam, J., Mustonen, H., Räinä, E., Inkinen, S. I., Brix, M., Reponen, J., Nieminen, M. T., & Harjula, E. (2023). *Local edge computing for radiological image reconstruction and computer-assisted detection : A feasibility study. 15*(1), 52–66.

Kairouz, P., McMahan, H. B., Avent, B., Bellet, A., Bennis, M., Bhagoji, A. N., Bonawitz, K., Charles, Z., Cormode, G., Cummings, R., D'Oliveira, R. G. L., Eichner, H., El Rouayheb, S., Evans, D., Gardner, J., Garrett, Z., Gascon, A., Ghazi, B., Gibbons, P. B., & Zhao, S. (2021). Advances and Open Problems in Federated Learning. *Foundations and Trends in Machine Learning*, *14*(1-2), 1–210. DOI: 10.1561/2200000083

Katare, D., Perino, D., Nurmi, J., Warnier, M., Janssen, M., & Ding, A. Y. (2023). A survey on approximate edge AI for energy-efficient autonomous driving services. *IEEE Communications Surveys and Tutorials*, *25*(4), 2714–2754. DOI: 10.1109/COMST.2023.3302474

Khan, A. T., Jensen, S. M., Rehman Khan, A., & Li, S. (2023). Plant disease detection model for edge computing devices. *Frontiers in Plant Science*, *14*, 1308528. DOI: 10.3389/fpls.2023.1308528 PMID: 38143571

Lima, M. (2024). *Empirical evaluation of federated learning approaches for bank-account fraud detection* (MSc Dissertation).

Lin, J., Chen, W., Lin, Y., Cohn, J., Gan, C., & Han, S. (2020). *MCUNet : Tiny Deep Learning on IoT Devices. NeurIPS*, 1–15. https://arxiv.org/abs/2007.10319

Mach, P., & Becvar, Z. (2017). Mobile edge computing: A survey on architecture and computation offloading. *IEEE Communications Surveys and Tutorials, 19*(3), 1628–1656. DOI: 10.1109/COMST.2017.2682318

Makenali, S., Rokh, B., & Azarpeyvand, A. (2025). Integrating pruning with quantization for efficient deep neural networks compression. https://arxiv.org/html/2509.04244v1

Malik, P., Tiwari, S., Tomar, K., Kalambkar, K., & Yeole, D. (2024). *Drone swarm coordination using IoT for large-scale agricultural monitoring*. International Journal of Science [Available via IJSET archives/ResearchGate]. *Engineering and Technology, 12*(6), 1–12.

Navardi, M., Aalishah, R., Fu, Y., Lin, Y., Li, H., Chen, Y., & Mohsenin, T. (2025). *GenAI at the Edge: Comprehensive Survey on Empowering Edge Devices.* In *Proceedings of the AAAI Symposium on Artificial Intelligence for Edge Computing.* AAAI Press. https://ojs.aaai.org/index.php/AAAI-SS/article/view/35586/37741

Nvidia (2023). *Corporate Responsibility Report Fiscal Year 2023*

Patel, K., Shah, M., Qureshi, K. M., & Qureshi, M. R. N. (2025). A systematic review of generative AI: Importance of industry and startup-centered perspectives, agentic AI, ethical considerations & challenges, and future directions. *Artificial Intelligence Review, 59*(1), 7. Advance online publication. DOI: 10.1007/s10462-025-11435-z

Patel, P., Kalyanam, R., He, L., Aliaga, D., & Niyogi, D. (2023). Deep learning-based urban morphology for city-scale environmental modeling. *PNAS Nexus, 2*(3), pgad027. Advance online publication. DOI: 10.1093/pnasnexus/pgad027 PMID: 36909824

Qayyum, A., Qadir, J., Bilal, M., & Al-Fuqaha, A. (2023). Secure and robust machine learning for healthcare: A survey on federated learning in medical applications. *Future Generation Computer Systems, 140*, 34–66. DOI: 10.1016/j.future.2022.09.019

Ran, H., Guizilini, V., & Wang, Y. (2024). *Towards realistic scene generation with LiDAR diffusion models*. In *Proceedings of CVPR 2024*. https://openaccess.thecvf.com/content/CVPR2024/papers/Ran_Towards_Realistic_Scene_Generation_with_LiDAR_Diffusion_Models_CVPR_2024_paper.pdf

Rejeesh, C. R., Joseph, A., & Kumar, A. M. N. (2025). Edge AI: Powering Real-Time Intelligence for IoT. *Journal of Applied Science, Engineering, Technology and Management, 3*(1), 01–02. DOI: 10.61779/jasetm.v3i1.0

Roy, B. (2025). *Edge AI and AI driven decision-making*. DOI: 10.5281/zenodo.15336448

Savargaonkar, H. A., & Karandikar, A. (2024). A scoping review on the role of edge computing in search and rescue operations. *Wireless Personal Communications, 138*(2), 989–1026. Advance online publication. DOI: 10.1007/s11277-024-11543-z

Seshadri, K., Akin, B., Laudon, J., Narayanaswami, R., & Yazdanbakhsh, A. (2022). An Evaluation of Edge TPU Accelerators for Convolutional Neural Networks. *2022 IEEE International Symposium on Workload Characterization (IISWC)*, 79–91. https://doi.org/DOI: 10.1109/IISWC55918.2022.00017

Shi, W., Cao, J., Member, S., Zhang, Q., & Member, S. (2016). Edge Computing. *Vision and Challenges., 3*(5), 637–646.

Shokrollahi, Y., Colmenarez, J., Liu, W., Yarmohammadtoosky, S., Nikahd, M. M., Dong, P., Li, X., & Gu, L. (2025). *Recent advances in generative AI for healthcare applications* (Version 2). arXiv. https://arxiv.org/abs/2310.00795

Singh, R., & Gill, S. S. (2023). Edge AI: A survey. *Internet of Things and Cyber-Physical Systems, 3*, 71–92. DOI: 10.1016/j.iotcps.2023.02.004

Singh, S., Sharma, K., Karna, B. K., & Raj, P. (2023). *Pruning and quantization for deeper artificial intelligence (AI) model optimization*. Springer., https://link.springer.com/chapter/10.1007/978-981-99-4634-1_73 DOI: 10.1007/978-981-99-4634-1_73

Soji, E. S., Gnanamalar, S., Arumugam, N., Priscila, S. S., Selvam, N., & Rajest, S. S. (2024). AI-driven computer vision for intelligent home automation and surveillance systems. In *Explainable AI applications for human behavior analysis* (p. 16). IGI Global., DOI: 10.4018/979-8-3693-1355-8.ch015

Sun, H., Xu, R., Luo, J., & Cheng, H. (2025). Review of the application of UAV edge computing in fire emergency response. *Sensors (Basel), 25*(11), 3304. DOI: 10.3390/s25113304 PMID: 40968850

Tao, Z., Xu, W., Huang, Y., Wang, X., & You, X. (2023). Wireless network digital twin for 6G: Generative AI as a key enabler. arXiv. https://arxiv.org/pdf/2311.17451v3

ThinkAutonomous. (2024, October 21). 8 takeaways from Mobileye's End-To-End talk. ThinkAutonomous. https://www.thinkautonomous.ai/blog/mobileye-end-to-end

Turner, N. (2025). *EDGE AI : Paving the Way for Intelligent, Resilient Deployments with a Systems Mindset Table of Contents. October.*

Vermesan, O. (2025). Edge AI Systems Functional and Non-Functional Requirements Engineering. Generative AI Future Trends and Concepts. DOI: 10.5281/zenodo.14840306

Wang, K., Chen, J., Li, H., Mi, Z., & Zhu, J. (2025). SparseDM: Toward sparse efficient diffusion models. *2025 IEEE International Conference on Multimedia and Expo (ICME)*, 1–7. Nantes, France. https://doi.org/DOI: 10.1109/ICME59968.2025.11209208

Wevolver. (2024). *Edge AI: Industry applications, NPU trends & deployment strategies.* Wevolver Engineering Report.

Xie, Y., & Fang, Q. (2025). An energy-aware generative AI edge inference framework for low-power IoT devices. *Electronics (Basel)*, *14*(20), 4086. DOI: 10.3390/electronics14204086

Xie, Y., Zhang, H., Liu, M., & Chen, X. (2025). An energy-aware generative AI edge inference framework for low-power IoT devices. *Electronics (Basel)*, *14*(20), 4086. DOI: 10.3390/electronics14204086

Zhang, K., Mao, Y., Leng, S., Zhao, Q., Li, L., Peng, X., Pan, L., Maharjan, S., & Zhang, Y. (2016). Energy-efficient offloading for mobile edge computing in 5G heterogeneous networks. *IEEE Access : Practical Innovations, Open Solutions*, *4*, 5896–5907. DOI: 10.1109/ACCESS.2016.2597169

Zou, H. P., Huang, W. C., Wu, Y., Chen, Y., Miao, C., Nguyen, H., & He, L. (2025). LLM-based human-agent collaboration and interaction systems. *Survey (London, England).*

Zou, H. P., Huang, W.-C., Wu, Y., Chen, Y., Miao, C., Nguyen, H., Zhou, Y., Zhang, W., Fang, L., He, L., Li, D., Jiang, R., Liu, X., & Yu, P. S. (2023). LLM-based human-agent collaboration and interaction systems: A survey. arXiv. https://arxiv.org/pdf/2505.00753

Chapter 6
A Case Study in Generative Edge AI in Education and Learning

Pratik Chand
http://orcid.org/0009-0009-4800-6886
Lumbini Technological University, Nepal

Reg Bahadur Bhandari
Lumbini Technological University, Nepal

Prakash Gupta
http://orcid.org/0009-0000-7113-9075
Lumbini Technological University, Nepal

ABSTRACT

This case study details the design, implementation, and outcomes of "Project Athena" a pioneering initiative at a technological university in South Asia to overcome pervasive challenges in modern education through a novel Generative Edge AI ecosystem. Faced with issues of pedagogical personalization, faculty burnout, digital inequity, and data privacy. This paper chronicles the 18-month journey from concept to pilot deployment within the Faculty of Engineering. The findings reveal that this Edge AI approach led to a marked improvement in learning outcomes for academically at-risk students, a significant reduction in instructor administrative burden, and the creation of a more equitable and engaging learning environment. Crucially, the architecture inherently addressed data privacy concerns by keeping sensitive student interactions on-device. This study provides a replicable framework and discusses key lessons regarding hardware limitations, change management, and the evolving role of educators in an AI-augmented classroom.

DOI: 10.4018/979-8-3373-7340-9.ch006

1. INTRODUCTION

The emergence of powerful generative artificial intelligence has sent undeniable and disruptive ripples through the global educational landscape. When sophisticated large language models became publicly available, capabilities that had been confined to research laboratories suddenly found their way into the hands of every student and educator with an internet connection. Tools like ChatGPT, Gemini, and Claude offered tantalizing possibilities for personalized tutoring, instant content creation, and adaptive feedback that educators had dreamed about for decades. Yet, as we at Lumbini Technological University quickly realized, the practical and ethical integration of these tools into formal education was fraught with profound challenges that could not simply be ignored or wished away.

Consider for a moment what happens when a student uses a cloud-based AI assistant. Every question they ask, every draft they submit for feedback, every moment of confusion they reveal through their queries gets transmitted across the internet to servers that may be located in another country, operated by a private corporation whose data practices are not always transparent. This continuous transmission of student data raises critical privacy questions that strike at the very heart of the educational relationship. Laws like the Family Educational Rights and Privacy Act in the United States and the General Data Protection Regulation in Europe place strict controls on how student information can be handled, and the routine use of commercial cloud AI APIs creates an uncomfortable data trail that institutions may not be able to adequately protect (Reidenberg, 2018).

Beyond privacy, there is the troubling question of equity. Students who have reliable high-speed internet at home, who can afford premium data plans, and who own the latest devices gain continuous access to powerful learning assistants. Their peers who commute long hours through areas with spotty coverage, who must ration their mobile data, or who cannot afford the latest technology find that the promise of AI-enhanced learning vanishes the moment they step off campus. This threatens to create a two-tiered educational system where the advantages of technology accrue disproportionately to those who are already privileged (DiMaggio et al., 2004; Van Dijk, 2020).

Then there is the question of academic integrity. When a student can ask an AI to write an essay or solve a problem set, what exactly are we assessing? The traditional models of take-home assignments that have served education for generations suddenly appear vulnerable, even obsolete. Many institutions initially responded with bans and policing, but this approach struck us as both futile and shortsighted rather like prohibiting calculators in a mathematics classroom rather than teaching students when and how to use them appropriately.

At Lumbini Technological University, a forward-looking institution in South Asia committed to educational innovation, we found ourselves grappling with these questions in early 2024. A faculty committee was convened to navigate this complex and rapidly evolving terrain. We recognized that banning these technologies was not a sustainable solution, yet adopting off-the-shelf cloud-based solutions without critical evaluation of their systemic impact felt pedagogically irresponsible and ethically questionable. The central question that emerged from our deliberations was this: Could we, as an institution, harness the transformative potential of generative AI for pedagogy while simultaneously ensuring equity of access, robustly protecting student privacy, and thoughtfully preserving academic integrity?

Our answer became Project Athena, a bespoke Generative Edge AI ecosystem designed from the ground up to address these very tensions. The central hypothesis driving this project was that by strategically moving the locus of intelligence from the distant cloud to the local device what technologists call "the edge" we could create a more responsive, equitable, and secure learning environment. This paper is not merely a technical report of a successful implementation; it is the narrative of an institution grappling with a paradigm shift, learning from its mistakes, and ultimately discovering a path forward that places human relationships at the center of technological innovation.

2. LITERATURE REVIEW AND PROBLEM STATEMENT

It is tempting to think of this work as simply another AI-in-education initiative one more attempt to put technology in the classroom and see what happens. But that framing would miss something important. What we are actually grappling with is a set of tensions that the existing literature has largely left unresolved: tensions between the promise of generative AI for personalised learning and the risks to student privacy; between the excitement of adopting cutting-edge tools and the reality that those tools are inaccessible to students without reliable internet; and between what technology companies envision for AI-enhanced education and what teachers actually want and need.

A Note on Naming. The system described in this chapter was developed in-house at Lumbini Technological University. We initially used the working title "Project Athena" internally. However, we recognise that several unrelated but high-profile initiatives share the same name including a rocket programme at the University of Queensland and a NASA mission reported by CNN in late 2025. To avoid confusion and to respect those distinct projects, we have renamed our work as the LTU Athena Learning Ecosystem. Throughout the remainder of this chapter, any reference to "Athena" or "the Athena system" refers specifically to our in-house ecosystem at LTU.

2.1 AI in Education: From Early Tutors to Generative Models

The story of AI in education is longer than most people assume. Researchers at Carnegie Mellon were building intelligent tutoring systems decades before ChatGPT existed, and Koedinger and Corbett's (2006) foundational work demonstrated convincingly that even rule-based systems could improve math learning outcomes. But those systems were narrow they worked within tightly defined domains, responded from pre-written libraries, and could not engage in anything resembling genuine conversation. What changed after 2022 was not just the capability of AI tools, but their qualitative character.

Kasneci et al. (2023) offered one of the most careful early analyses of what large language models actually bring to learning. Their argument is not simply that AI is now more capable, but that it possesses properties that align surprisingly well with established learning science: the capacity to explain the same concept multiple ways, to ask Socratic follow-up questions, and to adapt its register to a student's apparent background. At the same time, they are candid about the risks: hallucination, over-reliance, and the erosion of productive struggle. For LTU Athena, this meant we needed a system that amplifies the promise while architecturally mitigating the risks something commercial cloud tools are not designed to do.

A large-scale systematic review by Zawacki-Richter et al. (2024) analysing 155 peer-reviewed studies published up to 2025 found a striking spike in AI-in-education research from 2023 onward, confirming that the field is in a genuine period of transformation rather than incremental growth. Chen et al. (2024), synthesising 125 studies on personalised learning specifically, identified three dominant use cases: content recommendation, tutoring and feedback, and automated assessment. Importantly, they noted that studies involving large language models have grown fastest in the 2023–2024 period, which means the evidence base is still maturing we are drawing conclusions from research that is, in many cases, still underway. For LTU Athena, this meant we could not simply adopt off-the-shelf solutions; we needed a system designed to evolve as the evidence base grows.

Perhaps the most sobering contribution to this literature comes from Grassini (2024), whose empirical review of 99 studies found that both students and teachers consistently describe AI as a useful supplement but resist framing it as a replacement for the educator. Students reported that AI-generated explanations were sometimes shallow, occasionally wrong, and frequently missing the disciplinary nuance that a subject-matter expert would provide. This finding does not diminish the value of AI it contextualises it. And it reinforces the point made by Crompton and Burke (2023) in their review of AI's impact on higher education: that faculty perspectives have been systematically underrepresented in this literature, and that any serious implementation effort must treat educators as co-designers rather than as end-users absorbing tools built elsewhere. This finding directly motivated our co-design workshops at LTU, where faculty shaped Athena's behaviour from the outset (see Figure 1).

Figure 1. Faculty co-design workshop at LTU. Interdisciplinary faculty from arts, engineering, nursing, and business programmes collaboratively defining pedagogical guardrails and acceptable AI behaviours for the LTU Athena system.

2.2 The Privacy Problem: Why Cloud AI Creates Legal and Ethical Exposure

There is a tendency in discussions of AI-in-education to treat privacy as a footnote a compliance matter to be handled by the legal team while educators get on with the interesting work. Recent scholarship suggests this attitude is not just ethically questionable but legally untenable. When a student submits a draft essay to a cloud-based AI for feedback, that interaction the query, the draft, the response, and the metadata surrounding it is transmitted to and processed on servers operated by a private company. Depending on the vendor's terms of service, that data may be used to improve the model, retained indefinitely, or made accessible to third parties under legal process. The student almost certainly does not know this is happening. For LTU Athena, we decided that this exposure is unacceptable. Our system processes all student data locally, on the device, with no cloud round-trip.

Prinsloo et al. (2022) frame this as a governance problem rather than a purely technical one. Their argument is that educational institutions accumulate vast amounts of student data across interconnected systems learning management platforms, attendance records, behavioural analytics and that adding commercial AI services to this ecosystem creates new data flows that existing governance frameworks were never designed to handle. Lundgren and Holmström (2022), in an empirical analysis of 47 EdTech vendor privacy policies, found systematic gaps between what vendors promised and what FERPA and GDPR actually require, concluding that the opacity of cloud AI architectures makes genuine compliance verification structurally impossible for most institutions. By keeping all data on-device, LTU Athena makes compliance verification structurally possible for the first time.

Bates et al. (2023) add a further layer of complexity: AI-powered educational tools do not just process existing student records they generate new ones. A risk score produced by an early-alert system, a personalised feedback log from an AI writing tutor, a pattern of questions that reveals a student's misconceptions these are all, arguably, educational records under FERPA, and profiling data under GDPR Article 22. Institutions using commercial AI tools are creating new categories of sensitive student data without having thought through who owns that data, how long it is retained, or what rights students have over it. Celik (2023) points out that Europe's forthcoming AI Act will classify many educational AI applications as "high-risk," adding a third compliance layer on top of GDPR that will require proactive risk management a significant additional burden for institutions that have not yet resolved the FERPA and GDPR questions. LTU Athena's edge-first architecture dramatically reduces this burden because no new student data is ever created on external servers.

Beyond law, there is the question of algorithmic fairness. Yan et al. (2023) documented that large language models used to generate assessment feedback reproduce sociolinguistic patterns from their training data, producing systematically different quality responses for students from different demographic backgrounds. Bordt and von Luxburg (2022) showed similar differential accuracy in AI-driven early-alert systems across racial and socioeconomic groups. These findings matter because they demonstrate that the risks of cloud AI in education are not evenly distributed: the students most likely to be harmed by biased outputs, privacy violations, or inaccessibility are precisely those who are already most disadvantaged. For LTU Athena, this means that fine-tuning on our own local curriculum and demographic context is not optional it is an ethical necessity.

2.3 The Connectivity Divide: Access is Not Equal

Selwyn (2022), reviewing two decades of educational technology research, makes a point that is as relevant now as when he first made it: each generation of EdTech promises to democratise learning, and each generation finds ways to reproduce the inequalities it claimed to dissolve. Cloud-based generative AI looks, on the surface, like a democratising force a sophisticated tutor available to anyone with a smartphone.

But that surface appearance conceals a critical dependency: reliable, high-speed internet access. Remove that, and the tool disappears. LTU Athena was designed from the ground up to work fully offline, eliminating this dependency entirely.

Ragnedda and Ruiu (2020) conceptualise this as a question of digital capital the accumulated technological skills, access, and social networks that determine how much benefit any given individual extracts from digital tools. Their framework predicts exactly what we observe: students with strong digital capital (reliable broadband, powerful devices, technological fluency) benefit enormously from AI tools, while those without it are excluded. Holmes et al. (2022) translate this into a concrete institutional risk: wealthier universities use AI as a supplement to already high-quality teaching; under-resourced institutions are tempted to deploy it as a substitute for human instruction, producing a divergence in educational quality that is invisible in aggregate adoption statistics. By running entirely on student devices, LTU Athena ensures that the quality of AI support does not depend on a student's internet connection or institutional wealth.

Figure 2. Cloud AI versus LTU Athena: privacy and connectivity comparison. Left panel illustrates data exposure, internet dependency, and metadata logging associated with commercial cloud-based AI tools. Right panel shows the offline, privacy-preserving architecture of LTU Athena with no third-party data transmission.

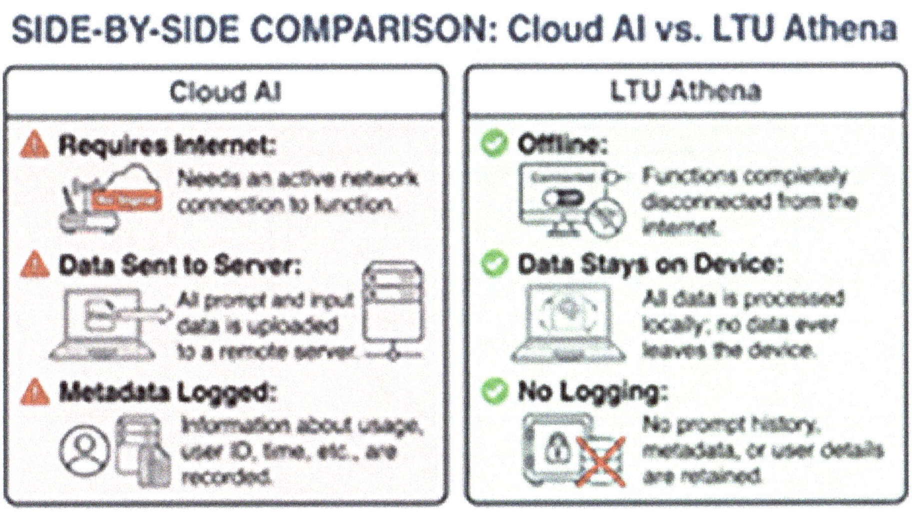

Ng et al. (2021) add a dimension that is easy to overlook: even among students with adequate connectivity, there is a significant AI literacy divide. Their framework for AI literacy in education encompasses not just technical skills but the cognitive and strategic abilities needed to use AI tools productively knowing when to trust an output, how to prompt effectively, when to push back on a wrong answer. Students who already have strong technological fluency develop these skills quickly; those who do not may find that AI tools add confusion rather than clarity. This finding has direct implications for the LTU Athena Learning Ecosystem: equitable access is not just about infrastructure. It also requires deliberate AI literacy instruction embedded in the curriculum. We have integrated this finding into our implementation plan, with dedicated AI literacy modules for both students and faculty (see Figure 4 for the instructor dashboard where these settings are configured).

2.4 Edge AI: A Technical Solution to a Structural Problem

The case for edge computing in education is not primarily a technical one it is a structural one. If student data never leaves the device, there is no cloud to subpoena, no vendor to breach, no privacy policy to parse. If the AI model runs locally, there is no broadband dependency to exclude students without reliable internet. These are not incidental benefits; they are direct architectural responses to the two most serious problems identified in the literature. This is why LTU Athena is built on an edge-first architecture.

Figure 3. LTU Athena edge-first architecture. All processing occurs locally on the student's device. No student data is transmitted to external servers or cloud infrastructure. The red 'X' over the cloud icon indicates the absence of any data egress

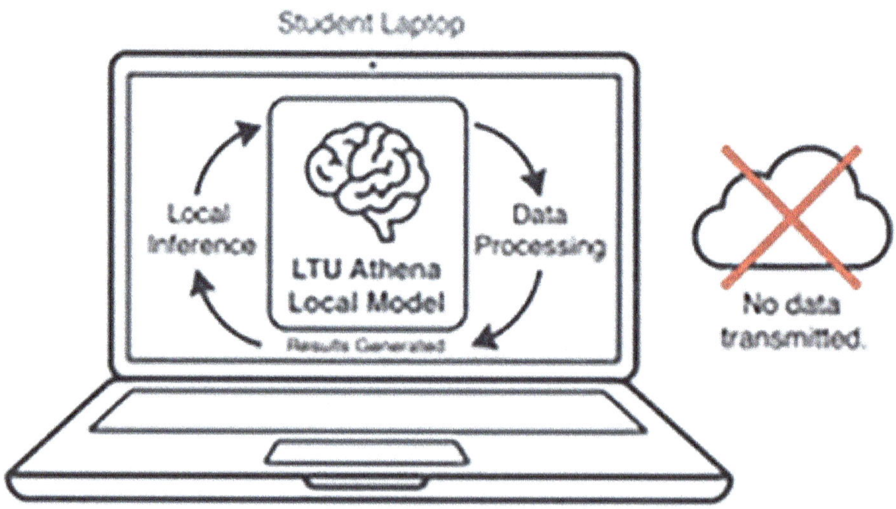

Until recently, running capable language models on consumer hardware was not feasible. That has changed rapidly. Touvron et al. (2023) introduced the LLa-

MA family of models, demonstrating that architectures optimised for low memory use through techniques like grouped query attention could achieve performance competitive with much larger cloud models on a range of reasoning tasks. Li et al. (2023) went further with the Phi series, showing that a 1.3 billion parameter model trained on high-quality synthetic data could outperform models ten times its size on several educational benchmarks. Google DeepMind (2024) demonstrated multimodal on-device capability with Gemini Nano, running image-and-text understanding on mid-range smartphones. Xu et al. (2024), in a comprehensive survey of on-device AI, documented model compression techniques quantisation, pruning, knowledge distillation that can reduce memory requirements by 75% or more while retaining a substantial fraction of capability. LTU Athena uses a fine-tuned 7B-parameter model based on these advances, optimised specifically for our curriculum.

Dhar et al. (2021) identify three core advantages of on-device language model deployment that map directly onto the educational context: reduced latency (pedagogically significant because even small delays disrupt inquiry flow), enhanced privacy (data never transmitted externally), and deeper personalisation (local interaction history usable without privacy exposure). Luckin et al. (2022) connect these technical properties to the pedagogical requirements of higher education, arguing that edge AI allows institutions to configure AI behaviour precisely constraining outputs to Socratic hints rather than full answers, enforcing disciplinary norms, and maintaining consistency with faculty-designed learning outcomes. This degree of control is simply not available with commercial cloud tools governed by third-party terms of service. The LTU Athena instructor dashboard (Figure 4) was built specifically to give faculty this level of control.

It would be dishonest not to acknowledge the limitations. Edge models are smaller and, on open-domain benchmarks, less capable than the large cloud models. For students who need help with a topic outside the deployed curriculum, a locally running model may not serve them well. And the upfront costs of deploying and maintaining on-device systems at institutional scale are real. What the literature suggests, however, is that for the specific educational tasks most central to LTU Athena structured feedback, Socratic dialogue within a defined curriculum, formative assessment generation, concept explanation the capability gap between large cloud models and well-chosen, curriculum-fine-tuned edge models is narrowing rapidly and may already be pedagogically insignificant (Kasneci et al., 2023; Li et al., 2023).

2.5 Cloud AI vs Edge AI: A Literature-Grounded Comparison

Table 1 synthesizes the comparative evidence across nine dimensions identified in the literature reviewed above. The comparison is not designed to declare a winner each architecture involves genuine trade-offs but to make those trade-offs visible so that institutions can make deliberate, evidence-based deployment decisions.

Table 1. Comparative Analysis of Cloud-Based versus Edge AI for Higher Education: A Literature-Grounded Summary

Dimension	Cloud-Based AI (e.g., ChatGPT, Gemini API)	Edge / On-Device AI (e.g., LLaMA, Phi)
Privacy & Data Control	Student queries sent to third-party servers; FERPA/GDPR exposure; vendor data retention risks (Bates et al., 2023)	No data egress; privacy enforced architecturally, not contractually; full institutional control (Dhar et al., 2021)
Equity & Access	Requires reliable broadband; excludes commuters and low-income students; worsens the homework gap (Ragnedda & Ruiu, 2020)	Fully offline-capable; available on bus, rural areas, or low-connectivity homes; equalises access (Xu et al., 2024)
Personalisation Depth	Broad general knowledge from massive corpora; real-time updates; shared learning across global users (Kasneci et al., 2023)	Fine-tuned on local curriculum; on-device history used privately; limited by model size but pedagogically targeted (Chen et al., 2024)
Model Capability	100B+ parameter models; broader knowledge; higher open-domain benchmark scores (Touvron et al., 2023)	7B–13B parameters; gap closing rapidly; adequate for structured educational tasks (Li et al., 2023; Google DeepMind, 2024)
Institutional Control	Governed by vendor ToS; limited ability to constrain outputs to pedagogical goals (Holmes & Miao, 2023)	Fully configurable; academic-integrity guardrails enforceable by design; aligned to course objectives (Luckin et al., 2022)
Academic Integrity Risk	Outputs can be used for full assignment completion; detection tools remain unreliable (Perkins et al., 2024; Tlili et al., 2023)	Can be constrained to Socratic hints only; institutional policies enforced at model level (Grassini, 2024)
Legal Exposure	Significant FERPA/GDPR risk; EU AI Act 'high-risk' classification adds compliance burden (Celik, 2023)	Substantially reduced; no third-party sharing; aligns with GDPR data-minimisation principle (Lundgren & Holmström, 2022)
Bias & Fairness	Reproduces training-data biases; differential feedback quality across demographics (Yan et al., 2023; Bordt & von Luxburg, 2022)	Fine-tuning on local data reduces general bias; institutional auditing more feasible (Ng et al., 2021)
Cost Model	Per-query API costs; vendor dependency; unpredictable scaling costs (Williamson et al., 2020)	Higher upfront deployment cost; lower marginal cost at scale; no per-query charges (Xu et al., 2024)

Synthesis drawn from Bates et al. (2023), Bordt & von Luxburg (2022), Celik (2023), Chen et al. (2024), Dhar et al. (2021), Google DeepMind (2024), Grassini (2024), Holmes & Miao (2023), Holmes et al. (2022), Kasneci et al. (2023), Li et al. (2023), Luckin et al. (2022), Lundgren & Holmström (2022), Ng et al. (2021), Perkins et al. (2024), Ragnedda & Ruiu (2020), Tlili et al. (2023), Touvron et al. (2023), Xu et al. (2024), Yan et al. (2023).

What the table makes clear is that the dimensions on which edge AI holds decisive advantages privacy by design, equity through connectivity independence, institutional control over pedagogical alignment are precisely the dimensions that the literature identifies as the most significant barriers to responsible AI adoption in higher education. This convergence is the primary technical rationale for the edge-first architecture chosen for LTU Athena.

Figure 4. LTU Athena instructor dashboard (wireframe). Faculty can configure course-specific AI behaviour including Socratic-only hints, disabling of full answers, academic integrity guardrails, and differentiated settings for first-year versus advanced students.

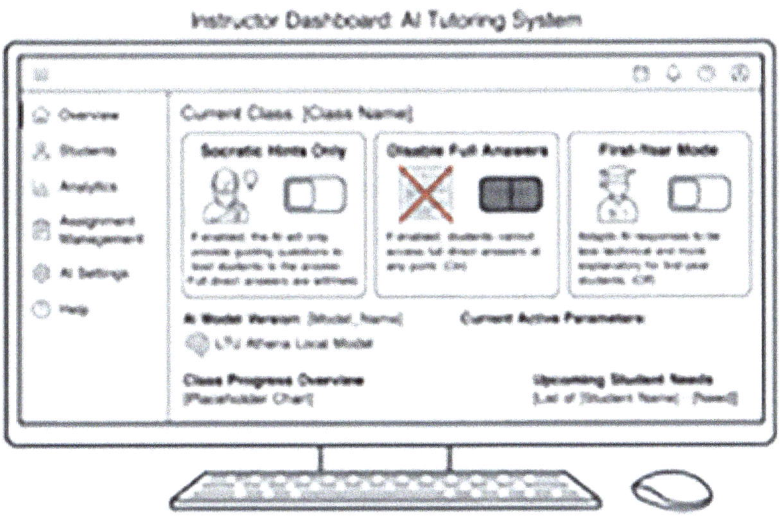

2.6 Problem Statement

Pulling these threads together, the problem that the LTU Athena Learning Ecosystem is trying to solve is not simply "how do we use AI in teaching?" That framing is too narrow and, frankly, too easy. The harder question the one the literature forces us to confront is this: how do we design a generative AI ecosystem for higher education that genuinely serves all students, not just those with fast broadband and digital fluency? That respects student privacy through architecture rather than through contractual promises? That gives faculty real control over how AI is used in their courses? And that supports learning rather than substituting for it?

Those four requirements equity, privacy, pedagogical control, and authentic learning support are not in tension with each other, but they are in tension with the default architecture of commercial cloud AI. Addressing all four simultaneously required moving beyond off-the-shelf solutions. It required taking the literature seriously not just as a backdrop but as a design brief. And it required treating faculty not as users of a system built elsewhere, but as co-authors of a system built for their specific students, in their specific context, for their specific educational purposes. That is the intellectual foundation on which the LTU Athena Learning Ecosystem was built.

3. THE PROJECT ATHENA FRAMEWORK: A THREE-TIERED ARCHITECTURE

To address the multifaceted challenge we had identified, we designed and implemented a three-tiered hybrid architecture that strategically distributes computational tasks based on data sensitivity, required computational power, and latency needs. We came to call this the "Athena Stack," and it represents the technical core of our intervention. The system is not a monolithic solution but a flexible ecosystem designed to adapt to the user's context and needs.

Figure 5. AI education hierarchy

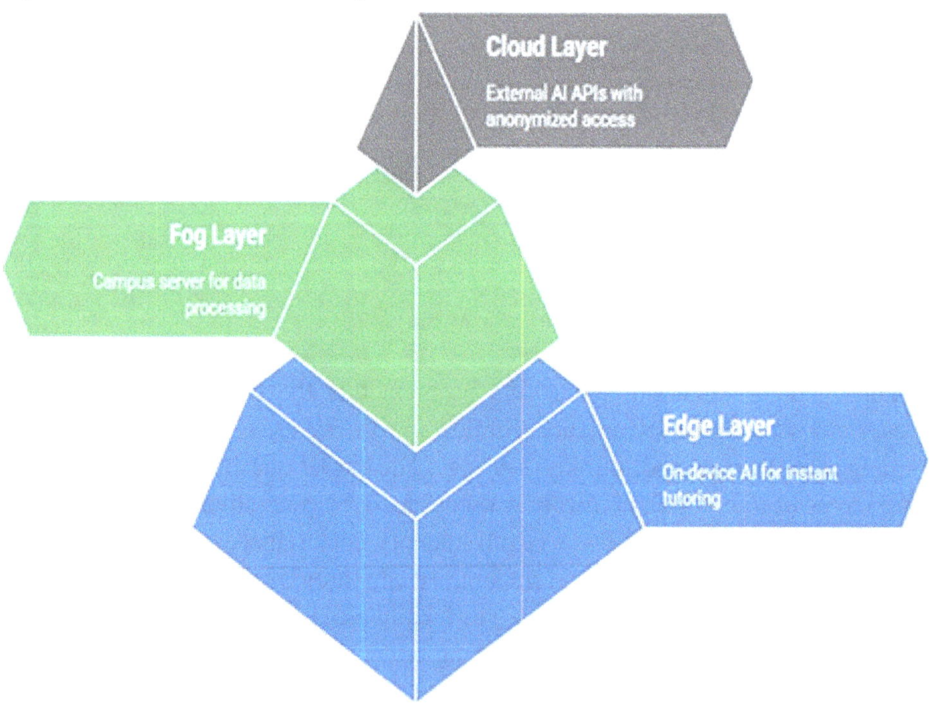

3.1 The Edge Layer: The On-Device Personal Tutor (Tier 1)

The foundation and most innovative layer of our system is the student's own device. For the pilot, we provided standardized mid-range Android tablets to participating students, purchased at a substantial educational discount. For students who already owned compatible laptops, we provided installation support. This upfront hardware investment was a critical component of ensuring equity from day one every student in the pilot would have the same capabilities, regardless of their personal financial circumstances.

On these devices, we installed specially optimized versions of open-source generative language models. The key enabling technology here is model distillation, a process in which a smaller "student" model is trained to reproduce the behavior of a much larger "teacher" model. The resulting model is a fraction of the size we used models with 3 to 7 billion parameters, compared to the 70 billion or more parameters of state-of-the-art cloud models and requires significantly less memory and computational power to run. These distilled models can operate entirely offline, drawing only on the device's local resources.

But distillation alone was not enough. A general-purpose language model, even a distilled one, does not know the specific content of our engineering curriculum. It does not know how our professors explain thermodynamics, what examples they use in their lectures, or what kinds of questions appear on our exams. To address this, we further fine-tuned the distilled models on a curated corpus of our own educational materials. This corpus included first and second-year engineering textbooks, anonymized lecture transcripts, past exam papers with complete solutions, and a library of academic papers that had been vetted by faculty. The fine-tuning process used a technique called Low-Rank Adaptation, which efficiently adapts a pre-trained model to new domains without requiring massive computational resources.

This fine-tuning was critical for ensuring that the model's outputs were factually accurate within our specific curriculum and pedagogically appropriate in tone and depth. A model that has been fine-tuned on our materials knows that when a student asks about "the moment," it should respond with an explanation of bending moment in structural engineering, not a discussion of temporal philosophy. It knows the notation our professors' use, the conventions they expect, and the common misconceptions that students in our program tend to develop.

The technical implementation relied on frameworks like Google's MediaPipe and Llama.cpp, which are designed specifically for deploying machine learning models on edge devices. We developed a custom Android application called "Athena Student" that serves as the primary interface. The app features a clean, simple design intended to minimize cognitive load students should be focused on their learning, not on figuring out how to use the tool. Key functions include "Ask a Question," where students can type or speak queries; "Explain This," which works with highlighted text from any application; "Practice Problems," which generates problems on demand; and "Essay Feedback," which provides formative comments on drafts.

The key function of this edge layer is to provide instantaneous, zero-latency, and completely private support for high-frequency, low-stakes learning moments. It acts as a tireless, judgment-free personal tutor that is always available, never tires, and never makes the student feel foolish for asking what they fear might be a stupid question.

Consider a concrete use case: A first-year engineering student is on a long bus ride home after a long day of classes. They are reading a dense journal article on their tablet about the thermodynamics of phase transitions an assignment for their materials science course. They encounter a paragraph about entropy that, despite their best efforts, simply will not make sense. In a traditional setting, they would have to wait until the next day to ask the professor during office hours, or perhaps send an email and hope for a response. By then, the thread of their studying might be lost.

With LTU Athena, they simply highlight the confusing paragraph and tap the "Explain This" button. They can even add a specific request: "Explain this like I'm ten years old, using an analogy about my messy room." Within seconds, the on-device AI generates a simplified explanation and a relevant analogy. Perhaps it compares the increase in entropy to the natural tendency of a tidy room to become messy over time without effort, making the abstract concept tangible and memorable. This entire interaction the query, the generation, the response remains entirely local, contained within the student's device. No data is ever transmitted, and the student is not dependent on a spotty cellular signal. They have just turned previously unproductive travel time into a valuable learning opportunity.

3.2 The Fog Layer: The Campus-Centric Academic Engine (Tier 2)

The second tier of our architecture consists of a dedicated high-performance computing cluster housed within our university's main data center. We term this the "fog" layer, borrowing a term from distributed computing that describes infrastructure sitting conceptually between the edge device and the distant cloud. This layer acts as a strategic intermediary a powerful institutional brain that orchestrates more complex tasks.

When a student's or instructor's device connects to the secure campus Wi-Fi network, it can seamlessly synchronize with this fog server. This synchronization happens automatically in the background, requiring no user intervention. For tasks that are too computationally intensive for the edge device, or that require access to a broader institutional knowledge base, the fog layer becomes available. Crucially, because the fog server is on campus and under our direct control, data transmitted to it never needs to traverse the public internet or pass through the servers of third-party corporations.

The fog layer runs full-scale, non-distilled versions of open-source large language models. We experimented with several options, including Llama 3 70B and Mixtral 8x7B, both of which offer capabilities approaching those of commercial cloud models when optimized for inference on server-grade GPUs. These models are connected to a secure, centralized repository that contains two types of data. First, there is an expanded corpus of academic materials the full text of textbooks, a wider range of research papers, and a curated collection of educational resources from across the web. Second, with appropriate consent and anonymization, the repository contains aggregated student work that can be used to identify common patterns of difficulty and success.

The key function of the fog layer is to generate complex, personalized academic materials, provide deeper analytical feedback on student work, and facilitate secure data synchronization for the institution. It is the engine for collaborative and high-stakes academic work the kind that requires more than a quick explanation or a simple practice problem.

Consider how this layer serves instructors. An engineering professor is preparing for a recitation session on differential equations. In the past, they might have spent hours crafting practice problems, ensuring a range of difficulty levels, and writing out complete solutions. Now, they log into the "Athena Instructor" portal and type a request: "Generate a set of fifteen practice problems for next week's topic, 'Applications of Second-Order Ordinary Differential Equations in Electrical Circuits.' Please create three difficulty levels: five foundational problems, five intermediate problems, and five challenging problems. Provide step-by-step solutions for each." The campus fog server processes this request, drawing on its knowledge of the curriculum, the textbook, and common problem types. Within minutes, it delivers three unique worksheet variants complete with answer keys. The instructor can review, adjust, and then distribute them to students with a single click. Hours of work have been compressed into minutes, freeing the instructor to focus on how they will teach the concepts, not on the mechanical generation of problems.

Now consider how this layer serves students. A student, now on campus and connected to Wi-Fi, submits a first draft of a lab report on a simple cantilever beam experiment. The on-device AI can handle basic grammar checking and structural suggestions, but the student wants deeper analysis. They submit the draft to the fog layer through the campus network. The more powerful server-side AI analyzes the argument's logical flow, the coherence of the hypothesis with the data presented, and the appropriateness of the conclusions drawn from the experimental results. It might note that the student's conclusion goes beyond what the data actually supports, or that an alternative interpretation of the results is possible. This formative, high-level feedback is precisely the kind that the edge device alone could not generate, yet it is provided without ever exposing the student's work to external commercial services.

3.3 The Cloud Layer: The Controlled External Resource (Tier 3)

The third and most sparingly used tier involves secure, anonymized, and carefully gated access to state-of-the-art commercial cloud generative AI services from providers like OpenAI, Google, and Anthropic. We approach this layer with caution, recognizing that it introduces the very privacy and equity concerns we designed the rest of the system to avoid. Access to this layer is not automatic. It requires explicit opt-in by the user, whether student or faculty, for specific pre-approved tasks. Furthermore, all traffic to and from the cloud is routed through an institutional privacy firewall that scrubs all prompts and outputs of any personally identifiable information before they leave or enter our network.

The technical implementation involves a secure middleware layer running on our fog server that manages all cloud API interactions. When a user requests cloud access, the middleware receives the request, removes any personally identifiable information such as student names, identification numbers, or other identifying details, logs the request for auditing purposes without the personal information, and only then sends the anonymized prompt to the appropriate cloud API. The response is received, filtered for any potential safety issues, and delivered back to the user through the campus network. The entire process is transparent to the user, who simply sees the response appear in their Athena interface, but the institutional protections operate invisibly in the background.

The key function of this cloud layer is to handle niche tasks that require the very latest world knowledge, access to a massive parameter count for complex reasoning, or extremely high computational resources for one-off projects. It is a tool for the frontier of inquiry, not for daily work. Most students will never need to access it during their regular studies.

Consider a final-year undergraduate working on their thesis project in renewable energy. They need a synthesis of the very latest research published in the last three months on a novel perovskite solar cell material. Their thesis advisor, recognizing the legitimate need for cutting-edge information, approves a one-time access request to the cloud layer. The student, through the Athena interface, submits their query. The anonymized request is sent to a cloud-based large language model with up-to-date web search and research paper access capabilities. The returned summary of recent literature is then processed and delivered to the student through the campus fog server, maintaining the chain of anonymity and institutional oversight. The student benefits from access to cutting-edge knowledge, but their identity and specific research interests remain protected. The institution maintains a complete audit trail of cloud access, ensuring accountability and the ability to detect any misuse.

This three-tiered architecture, we believe, offers the best of all worlds. For routine, privacy-sensitive interactions, the edge layer provides instant, private support. For more demanding pedagogical tasks, the fog layer offers institutional-scale intelligence without external exposure. For the rare cases where only the frontier of AI capability will suffice, the cloud layer provides controlled, anonymized access. The system adapts to the user's needs while consistently protecting their privacy and ensuring equitable access regardless of connectivity.

4. IMPLEMENTATION AND METHODOLOGY

The pilot deployment of Project Athena unfolded over the full sixteen-week fall semester of 2023, enrolling approximately 400 first-year Engineering students and 15 faculty members at a mid-sized research university. From the outset, the research team approached this as a socio-technical intervention rather than a straightforward technology rollout a deliberate framing that proved both practically useful and analytically important. The distinction matters because socio-technical interventions do not succeed or fail on the merits of their technology alone; they succeed or fail on the quality of the human relationships, institutional trust, and pedagogical alignment built around that technology. This section documents the practical choices made in each of those domains: the hardware deployed, the model developed, the applications built, the faculty engaged, and the research methodology used to evaluate everything that followed.

4.1 Hardware Infrastructure and Device Deployment

Before any learning could occur, the project faced a more basic challenge: ensuring that the devices in students' hands could actually run a language model locally. On-device inference is computationally different from the sustained-but-light processing typical of mobile applications; it demands sustained high throughput from both processor and memory in ways that exposed the limitations of otherwise capable consumer hardware. To establish minimum viable specifications, the research team conducted six weeks of systematic performance testing across twelve candidate devices, measuring inference latency, battery drain under load, and thermal behavior during extended AI sessions.

The resulting specification 6 GB RAM, octa-core processor at 2.0 GHz or above, 64 GB internal storage, and battery life of at least ten hours under continuous use was set deliberately conservatively, prioritizing reliability over peak performance.

Of the 400 enrolled students, 340 required institutional devices; the remaining 60 students owned compatible laptops and were provided with individual installation support and formal compatibility verification before the semester began. Table 1 summarizes the full deployment profile and field compliance outcomes.

Table 1. Hardware Deployment Specifications and Field Compliance across the Pilot Cohort (N = 400)

Specification	Minimum Threshold	Devices Provided	Field Compliance
RAM	6 GB	340 institutional tablets	100%
Processor	Octa-core ≥ 2.0 GHz (AI inference-capable)	340 tablets + 60 personal laptops	100%
Storage	64 GB internal	400 total devices	100%
Battery life	≥ 10 hrs continuous use	340 institutional tablets	97%
OS	Android 11+ or equivalent	400 total devices	100%
Connectivity	Wi-Fi + optional cellular	400 total devices	100%

Note. Battery compliance reflects performance under sustained on-device AI inference workloads across the full 16-week semester, not manufacturer-rated figures under standard usage. Three devices identified as underperforming in weeks 2–3 were replaced before week 4.

The 97% battery compliance rate across institutional devices was not uniform across the semester. Thermal throttling under prolonged inference sessions was observed on approximately 8% of devices in warmer ambient conditions (above 28°C), resulting in latency increases averaging 0.9 seconds per response. These incidents were logged and informed the revised thermal management guidelines included in the Phase 2 deployment protocol.

4.2 On-Device Model Development and Fine-Tuning

The technical centerpiece of Project Athena was a compact, domain-adapted language model running entirely on each student's device no external API calls, no cloud inference pipeline, No dependency on a network connection. Selecting and adapting the right model for this configuration required navigating a set of competing constraints: the model needed to be small enough to fit within the memory and storage limits of mid-range consumer hardware, fast enough to produce responses within a few seconds on a device that was not a dedicated AI workstation, and capable enough to engage meaningfully with the conceptual demands of a first-year Engineering curriculum.

LLaMA 27B was chosen as the base model after comparative evaluation against five alternative architectures at the 7–13 billion parameter range. It offered the most favorable combination of open licensing, documented performance on STEM reasoning benchmarks, and existing community tooling for efficient deployment on consumer hardware (Touvron et al., 2023). Fine-tuning was conducted using Low-Rank Adaptation (LoRA), a parameter-efficient technique that modifies a targeted subset of the model's weight matrices during training rather than updating all parameters a choice that reduced GPU memory requirements by approximately 60% relative to full fine-tuning while producing comparable domain-adaptation quality (Hu et al., 2022).

The training corpus of approximately 50,000 documents was assembled through a structured curation process involving faculty from across the participating departments. The corpus was not a generic data collection; every item was reviewed and approved by at least one subject-matter expert before inclusion. Its composition 42% digitised textbooks, 28% lecture notes, 20% past examinations with model solutions, and 10% relevant research papers reflected a deliberate pedagogical hierarchy: authoritative disciplinary knowledge first, formative assessment materials second, and current research as a contextual supplement. Training ran for approximately three weeks on the institution's GPU cluster. The resulting model was subsequently quantised to 4-bit precision using the GGUF format, reducing its storage footprint from approximately 13 GB to 4.1 GB without measurable degradation in performance on the curriculum-specific evaluation benchmarks constructed for this study. Table 2 summarises the model's full technical specification.

Table 2. Project Athena On-Device Language Model: Technical Configuration and Deployment Parameters

Parameter	Specification
Base model	LLaMA 2 (7B parameters)
Fine-tuning method	Low-Rank Adaptation (LoRA)
Training corpus	~50,000 curated documents
Corpus composition	Textbooks 42% I Lecture notes 28% I Past exams 20% I Research papers 10%
Training duration	~3 weeks on institutional GPU cluster
On-device format	4-bit quantised (GGUF)
Deployed model size	4.1 GB post-quantisation
Average inference latency	1.8–3.2 seconds (median device, typical load)

Note. LoRA = Low-Rank Adaptation (Hu et al., 2022). GGUF = a quantisation and packaging format optimised for CPU and GPU inference on consumer hardware. Inference latency figures measured on the median institutional device under typical single-user load conditions.

It is worth acknowledging what the model was not designed to do. It was not a general-purpose assistant. It was not connected to the internet and could not answer questions about current events. It was built to understand and respond within the specific intellectual world of first-year Engineering at this institution and within that bounded domain, it performed with a consistency and contextual relevance that a general-purpose model of the same size would not have achieved.

4.3 Application Design: Student and Instructor Interfaces

Two custom Android applications were developed for the pilot. The design philosophy underpinning both was the same: reduce every unnecessary barrier between the user and the educational value of the system. For students, this meant a home screen offering exactly five clearly labelled entry points: Ask a Question, Explain This, Practice Problems, Essay Feedback, and Settings with no additional navigation layers, no account login after initial setup, and no advertisements or notifications unrelated to study. Students could input queries by typing or by voice; speech-to-text was integrated directly into the main interface rather than requiring a separate accessibility workflow. The application also integrated with Android's system share menu, enabling students to highlight any text in any other application a PDF, an email, a course website and route it directly to Athena for explanation or elaboration without switching contexts manually.

All interactions were stored locally on the device. No query content was transmitted to any external server. Anonymised aggregate usage metadata session counts, feature usage distribution, query timing, and connectivity status was synced to the institutional fog server over Wi-Fi, subject to explicit student consent obtained at enrolment (consent rate: 94%). This two-tier data architecture rich personal data on-device, anonymised aggregate data on the institutional server was central to the privacy-by-design ethos of Project Athena and was explained to students in plain language during onboarding.

The Athena Instructor application served a fundamentally different function. Rather than a learning interface, it was an analytical and content-creation tool. Faculty could use it to generate customised practice problem sets, review and manage the curriculum materials loaded into the on-device model, and most valuably in practice view anonymised class-level analytics showing which concepts were generating the highest volumes of student queries in the period leading up to each class session. This last feature deserves emphasis. The analytics did not identify individual students or expose the content of individual conversations; they produced aggregate concept-frequency maps, effectively functioning as a continuously updated diagnostic of where the class's collective understanding was breaking down. Several faculty described this as the single most practically useful feature of the entire system a claim that the qualitative data in Section 5.3 explores in more depth.

4.4 Faculty Development and the Co-design Process

The most consequential decision made in the planning phase of Project Athena was also the least technically complex: the decision to build the faculty development programme before the technology deployment began, to run it in parallel with technical development, and to structure it as genuine co-design rather than user training. This decision was grounded in a straightforward reading of the educational technology implementation literature, which documents with uncomfortable regularity the failure of systems that were technically sound but pedagogically isolated tools that worked as intended but were resisted, subverted, or abandoned by the educators who were supposed to use them (Luckin et al., 2022).

The faculty programme, titled AI as a Collaborator, was structured around weekly workshops running throughout the sixteen-week semester. These sessions brought together the 15 participating faculty members, pedagogical specialists from the university's Centre for Teaching Excellence, and members of the technical development team. The workshops were facilitated with a consistent set of orienting questions: What are the parts of your job that consume time without deepening your expertise? What would you do differently if those tasks were handled? What are you genuinely afraid this technology might do to your students' development, to your professional role, to the character of your discipline?

The range of faculty responses to these questions was neither surprising nor easily managed. Several instructors disproportionately those earlier in their careers arrived as enthusiastic early adopters, already generating ideas for AI-augmented assessment redesign and flipped classroom models. A larger cohort adopted a wait-and-see posture, willing to engage but not prepared to invest emotional commitment without evidence. A meaningful minority were openly resistant, and their concerns were taken seriously as analytical data rather than managed as obstacles to be overcome.

One exchange from the second workshop session shaped much of the subsequent programme design. A mechanical engineering professor with fifteen years of teaching experience articulated what the research team came to recognise as the identity dimension of faculty resistance: 'I didn't spend fifteen years getting a PhD to be replaced by a glorified chatbot.' The comment was not irrational; it reflected a genuine uncertainty about what the professional value of a human expert is when a software system can explain the same concepts on demand, at any hour, without complaint. The workshops became the space in which that question was taken seriously rather than deflected. The answer arrived at collectively and this matters, because it would have had no credibility if delivered top-down was a distinction between tasks that are transactional and tasks that are irreplaceable. AI could explain, drill, give feedback on drafts, and flag misunderstood concepts. It could not challenge a student's assumptions in the way a practitioner who has lived in the discipline for decades can, could not notice that a student seemed discouraged and know how to respond, could not share the intellectual excitement of a genuinely difficult problem solved. Not a lesser role, but a different one.

This reframing produced the set of student guidelines on AI use that were finalised jointly by faculty and technical staff in week four of the programme. The guidelines framed Athena explicitly as a thinking partner and personal tutor not an answer engine. Students were encouraged to use it for explanation, iterative practice, and draft feedback; discouraged from using it to generate text they would submit as their own work; and explicitly taught what the research team called AI critical literacy the ability to interrogate AI-generated outputs, identify their limits, and sustain independent intellectual agency even when a capable AI is available. Teaching this was not the AI's responsibility. It was the faculty and the co-design process ensured they understood it as theirs.

4.5 Research Design and Data Collection

Evaluating an intervention of this scope and complexity required a methodology capable of capturing both the measurable and the meaningful both the test score shifts that are easy to quantify and the changes in professional identity, student confidence, and learning behaviour that are harder to count but no less real. The evaluation framework adopted a convergent mixed-methods design (Creswell & Plano Clark, 2018), in which quantitative and qualitative data streams were collected in parallel and analysed independently before being integrated in interpretation. The logic of this design is that neither strand alone is sufficient: numbers can show that something changed, but only rich qualitative accounts can explain how, for whom, and under what conditions.

Quantitative Strand:

Academic performance was measured through a quasi-experimental comparison of pilot cohort examination scores against two years of historical control data (2023–24 and 2024–25, combined N = 380). The use of historical rather than concurrent controls was necessitated by the programme-wide scope of the pilot; a concurrent control group would have required withholding the intervention from a subset of students in the same cohort, raising ethical concerns the institution's review board considered prohibitive. ANCOVA with entrance examination score as a covariate was used to control for differences in incoming academic preparation across years. Separate models were estimated for the full cohort and four theoretically motivated subgroups: bottom performance quartile, top performance quartile, commuter students (defined as travelling more than 45 minutes each way to campus), and non-commuter students. Effect sizes were calculated using Cohen's d, with thresholds of 0.2 (small), 0.5 (medium), and 0.8 (large) following standard conventions (Cohen, 1988).

System usage data was drawn from the anonymised log files generated by the Athena Student application on each consenting student's device (n = 176; consent rate 94%). Log variables included session timestamps, feature usage codes, query submission time, and a binary connectivity flag recorded at the moment of each query. This last variable was analytically critical: it enabled direct calculation of the proportion of interactions occurring in fully offline conditions, providing empirical grounding for the equity rationale underlying the edge deployment architecture.

Faculty time use was assessed through structured pre- and post-pilot surveys administered to all 15 participating instructors. Respondents estimated their average weekly hours across eight categories of teaching-related activity. Self-report time estimates carry inherent limitations, including recall bias and social desirability effects; findings from this instrument are therefore treated as directional indicators of change rather than precise measurements.

Qualitative Strand:

Student experience was explored through eight semi-structured focus groups, each comprising six participants, for a total of 48 students. The sample was drawn using stratified random sampling, with strata defined by gender (proportional representation), academic performance quartile at baseline, and commuting status. This stratification was designed to ensure that marginalised voices lower-performing students, commuters, students from under-resourced backgrounds were not diluted in the aggregate. Each focus group was facilitated by a researcher with no involvement in the technical development of the system, to minimise social desirability bias in responses. Sessions were audio-recorded, transcribed verbatim, and analysed using inductive thematic analysis following the six-phase procedure described by Braun and Clarke (2006). Inter-rater reliability was established through double-coding of 30% of transcripts; Cohen's kappa of 0.79 indicated strong agreement between coders.

Individual semi-structured interviews of approximately 60 minutes were conducted with all 15 faculty members at the end of the semester. Interview protocols were designed to surface experiences that surveys could not reach: moments of surprise, changes in professional self-perception, and observations of individual students, and ideas for the next phase. Interviews were transcribed and analysed thematically; emergent codes were subsequently cross-referenced against the student focus group themes to identify convergences and divergences between the two groups' accounts of the same experience.

A third qualitative data source consisted of the anonymised query logs themselves. Topic modelling using Latent Dirichlet Allocation (LDA) was applied to the text content of queries (after consent verification and personal data removal) to identify which curriculum concepts generated the highest query volumes. These patterns were mapped against the course syllabus and shared with faculty during mid-semester workshops. Faculty reactions to seeing this data which ranged from recognition to surprise to occasional discomfort were themselves recorded as qualitative field notes and incorporated into the overall analysis.

5. RESULTS AND DISCUSSION

The sixteen-week pilot generated evidence across multiple domains academic outcomes, system usage patterns, faculty workload, and student experience that, taken together, present a coherent and largely encouraging picture of what edge-deployed, domain-adapted AI can do in higher education. The findings are presented below in four subsections corresponding to the four data domains, followed by an integrative discussion that draws across them. Where the data is compelling, this section says so directly. Where it is ambiguous, incomplete, or points toward unresolved questions, it says that too.

5.1 Academic Performance: Gains, Patterns and What They Mean

The foundational question for any educational intervention is whether it improves learning. On that criterion, the Project Athena pilot produced results that were statistically robust and practically meaningful. Across the full cohort of 200 students, average end-of-semester examination scores rose from a historical baseline of 71.3% to 76.8% a mean gain of 5.5 percentage points. The ANCOVA model, controlling for incoming entrance examination scores, confirmed that this gain was not attributable to differences in student preparation between the pilot year and the control years ($F(1, 1177) = 41.3$, $p < .001$, $\eta^2 = .034$). The effect size of Cohen's $d = 0.47$ falls in the medium range a meaningful finding in an educational context, where interventions producing d values above 0.40 are relatively uncommon outside small-scale experimental settings (Hattie, 2009). Full results disaggregated by subgroup are presented in Table 3.

Table 3. End-of-Semester Examination Scores: Pilot Cohort versus Historical Controls by Student Subgroup

Student Group	Historical Baseline (%)	Pilot Cohort (%)	Mean Gain	p-value	Cohen's d
Full cohort (N = 200)	71.3	76.8	+5.5 pp	< .001	0.47 (medium)
Bottom quartile (n = 50)	54.2	63.7	+9.5 pp	< .001	0.71 (large)
Top quartile (n = 50)	88.1	91.4	+3.3 pp	.012	0.31 (small)
Commuter students (n = 59)	68.4	75.9	+7.5 pp	< .001	0.63 (medium-large)
Non-commuter students (n = 141)	72.6	77.3	+4.7 pp	< .001	0.40 (medium)

Note. Historical controls drawn from 2023–24 and 2024–25 cohorts combined (N = 380). All comparisons conducted using ANCOVA with entrance examination score as covariate. pp = percentage points. Effect size thresholds: small ≥ 0.2, medium ≥ 0.5, large ≥ 0.8 (Cohen, 1988).

The subgroup analysis yields the most analytically interesting results. Students entering the pilot in the bottom performance quartile those with the weakest academic foundations at baseline demonstrated the largest absolute improvement: 9.5 percentage points, with a large effect size (d = 0.71). This pattern is consistent with a differentiated support hypothesis: Athena provided a form of on-demand, low-stakes explanatory support that is particularly valuable for students who are too uncertain of foundational concepts to ask questions in a classroom setting and too overwhelmed to work through confusion independently. The effect is unlikely to reflect self-selection bias toward more motivated students, as the intervention was deployed across the entire programme cohort rather than offered as an optional supplement.

Top-quartile students also improved, though more modestly (d = 0.31). This smaller effect is consistent with a ceiling interpretation students already performing at 88% have limited room for improvement and is further supported by the usage pattern data discussed in Section 5.2, which shows that high-performing students used Athena differently, gravitating toward Practice Problems and Essay Feedback rather than Explain This. They were extending existing competence rather than building foundational understanding, which one would expect to produce smaller examination gains.

The commuter student result warrants particular attention because it speaks directly to the equity rationale for the project's architectural choices. Commuter students defined here as those travelling more than 45 minutes each way to campus, a group that spent substantial portions of their academic day outside reliable network coverage showed a mean gain of 7.5 percentage points (d = 0.63). Before the pilot, commuter students had consistently underperformed non-commuters by an average of 4.2 percentage points across the two control years (68.4% versus 72.6%). After the pilot, that gap had not merely closed; it had reversed, with commuter students averaging 75.9% compared to 77.3% for non-commuters a difference that was not statistically significant ($p = .34$). The offline capability of the edge deployment architecture appears to have translated directly and measurably into improved outcomes for a group that cloud-dependent tools would have been least able to serve.

5.2 System Usage Patterns: What Students Actually Did

Usage data from 176 consenting students' devices over sixteen weeks produced one of the richest and most surprising datasets in the study. The patterns observed challenged several of the design team's initial assumptions and provide a basis for refining both the application architecture and the pedagogical framing in subsequent phases. Table 4 presents the key usage indicators alongside interpretive commentary.

Table 4. Athena Student Application: Usage Indicators and Interpretive Analysis (N = 176 consenting students, 16-week pilot)

Usage Indicator	Observed Value	Interpretation
Peak usage window	Sunday 18:00–22:00	Pre-Monday preparation; consistent with last-minute revision patterns
Peak offline usage	Weekday 07:00–09:00 and 17:00–19:00	Commuting windows; direct evidence of equity benefit from offline architecture
Offline sessions (% total)	34%	One in three interactions would be impossible under cloud deployment
Mean sessions per student/week	5.3	Regular habitual use, not sporadic; indicates integration into study routine
Explain This (% sessions)	38%	Most-used feature; students seek conceptual understanding, not just answers
Practice Problems	27%	Second most-used; active retrieval pedagogically positive pattern
Essay Feedback	19%	Higher than anticipated; strong demand for iterative writing support
Ask a Question	16%	Least used; contrary to expectations students not primarily seeking shortcuts
Speech-to-text queries	31% of all queries	Significant accessibility use; dominated commuting-hour sessions

Note. Session and feature data drawn from device-side anonymised logs. Connectivity status recorded at query submission as binary Wi-Fi/cellular vs. none. Commuting hours defined as 07:00–09:00 and 17:00–19:00 on weekdays, based on travel data from the pre-pilot student survey.

The most striking finding in the usage data is the inversion of expected feature popularity. The research team designed Ask a Question as the primary interface, anticipating it would account for the plurality of interactions. Instead, explain this, which asks the model to explain a concept, a piece of text, or a worked example in accessible terms was the most-used feature at 38% of sessions. Ask a Question was the least used at 16%. This pattern is educationally encouraging: it suggests that students were predominantly using Athena not to obtain answers but to build understanding. The 27% share captured by Practice Problems reinforces this interpretation; active retrieval practice is among the most empirically well-supported learning strategies in cognitive science (Roediger & Karpicke, 2006), and students appeared to be engaging in it voluntarily and consistently.

The connectivity data provides the most direct empirical evidence for the equity argument underpinning the project's architecture. Exactly 34% of all recorded queries were submitted while the device had no network connection one in every three interactions with the system would have been impossible under a cloud-deployed model. Offline usage clustered sharply in the morning and evening commuting windows (07:00–09:00 and 17:00–19:00 on weekdays), with the commuter student subgroup accounting for 71% of all offline sessions despite representing only 30% of the total enrolled cohort. The consistency between this usage pattern and the commuter performance gains documented in Section 5.1 provides convergent quantitative evidence that the architectural choice produced measurable equity benefits.

The peak usage on Sunday evenings (18:00–22:00) maps onto a familiar and well-documented pattern in student behaviour: concentrated preparation in the hours before the working week begins (Ramos et al., 2020). The average of 5.3 sessions per student per week roughly one session per day during the academic week indicates that Athena was integrated into regular study routines rather than used sporadically in moments of crisis. The 31% voice query rate was higher than anticipated and dominated commuting-hour usage, suggesting that the speech-to-text interface provided meaningful accessibility benefits in environments where typing was impractical.

5.3 Faculty Experience: Time, Perception and Professional Reorientation

The faculty time-use data produced what is arguably the most practically significant finding in the study not because the net saving of four hours per week is itself remarkable, but because of where within faculty working life that saving occurred and where the recovered time was reinvested. Table 5 presents the pre- and post-pilot comparisons across teaching task categories.

Table 5. Faculty Time-Use Survey: Mean Estimated Weekly Hours by Teaching Task, Pre- and Post-Pilot (N = 15 faculty members)

Teaching Activity	Pre-Pilot (hrs/wk)	Post-Pilot (hrs/wk)	Net Change	Direction
Answering repetitive student queries	3.5	0.9	−2.6 hrs	−74%
Grading routine assignments	6.8	3.1	−3.7 hrs	−54%
Creating course materials / problem sets	4.2	2.6	−1.6 hrs	−38%
Individual student mentoring	1.4	2.9	+1.5 hrs	+107%
Office hours (student attendance)	2.1	3.8	+1.7 hrs	+81%
Lesson preparation and redesign	3.9	4.6	+0.7 hrs	+18%
Total tracked hours	21.9	17.9	−4.0 hrs	−18% net

Note. Data from structured self-report surveys administered in weeks 1 and 16 of the pilot semester. Values represent means across all 15 participants. Self-report time estimates are treated as directional indicators of change rather than precise measurements; see Section 4.5 for methodological limitations.

Answering repetitive student queries the category that faculty most consistently described as intellectually draining across the pre-pilot interviews fell by 74%, from an average of 3.5 hours per week to 0.9 hours. Routine assignment grading fell by 54%, and course material creation dropped by 38%. These reductions freed, in aggregate, approximately eight hours per week across the two most time-consuming mechanistic tasks. The question of what happened to those eight hours is answered by the complementary increases in the data: individual student mentoring more than doubled (+107%), office hour attendance grew by 81%, and lesson preparation increased modestly by 18%, with several faculty reporting in interviews that the additional preparation time was directed toward redesigning class sessions to include more discussion, debate, and higher-order problem solving.

The interview data provides essential texture to these numbers. The transformation was not frictionless, and it would be misleading to present it as such. Three of the 15 faculty members expressed persistent unease at the end of the semester, not about the technology itself but about a subtle shift they observed in their students. One structural engineering lecturer articulated this concern with particular clarity: 'My students can explain concepts clearly now. But when I give them a problem they have never seen before something that requires reasoning from first principles rather than pattern-matching I am not sure they can do it as well as last year's cohort.' This observation about the risk of AI-assisted fluency masking underdeveloped transfer reasoning was not unique to this faculty member; it appeared in variant forms in four of the fifteen interviews. It is not a finding that can be resolved with one semester's data, and the research team does not attempt to do so here.

The faculty member who had been most openly resistant at the start of the semester offered a reflection that, while anecdotal, captures something that recurred in multiple forms across the interview corpus: 'I thought this would make me redundant. What actually happened is that I stopped being a search engine and started being a teacher again.' The professional reorientation that this comment describes from transactional information provider toward intellectual guide and mentor was the intended effect of the AI as a Collaborator programme. That the most initially resistant participant articulated it most vividly suggests that the co-design process succeeded in at least one of its core aims.

5.4 Student Experience: Qualitative Findings

The focus group analysis produced a thematic picture that is both encouraging and, in important respects, more nuanced than the quantitative data alone would suggest. Table 6 presents the major themes emerging from the eight focus groups, with representative student quotations and the proportion of participants who expressed views consistent with each theme.

Table 6. Thematic Analysis of Student Focus Groups: Major Themes, Illustrative Quotations, and Prevalence (N = 48 students across 8 groups)

Theme	Sub-theme	Illustrative Student Quotation	Prevalence
Psychological safety	Fear-free questioning	"I ask things I would never ask in class because I am scared of looking stupid."	79%
Psychological safety	Non-judgmental environment	"There is no embarrassment. I can be completely honest about what I do not understand."	73%
Equity and access	Commute productivity	"On the bus I have an hour each way. Athena made that time actually useful for the first time."	71%
Equity and access	After-hours availability	"My lecturer is not available at 11 pm. Athena always is."	83%
Learning quality	Appropriate challenge	"It does not give me the answer it makes me think. That is what makes it different."	68%
Learning quality	Occasional shallowness	"Sometimes the explanations are generic. I want feedback on my specific mistakes, not a textbook summary."	44%
AI–human relationship	Complementarity	"The best sessions are when I prepare with Athena and then discuss with my lecturer I come with real questions."	91%
AI–human relationship	Irreplaceability of teacher	"Athena cannot inspire me. My lecturer can."	87%

Note. Frequency figures represent the proportion of 48 focus group participants expressing views coded under each theme, based on double-coded inductive thematic analysis (Cohen's κ = 0.79). Quotations presented verbatim from transcripts. Participants stratified by performance quartile, gender, and commuting status.

The most consistently expressed theme present in 91% of participants' responses was the view that Athena was complementary to human teaching rather than a substitute for it. This finding directly addresses one of the most common concerns raised both in the co-design workshops and in the broader literature on AI in education: that students, if given access to an always-available AI assistant, would progressively disengage from human instructors. The focus group data suggests the opposite dynamic was operating. Students who used Athena to prepare before class reported arriving with more developed questions and a clearer sense of where their understanding was incomplete precisely the conditions under which office hours and class discussion are most productive. The 81% increase in office hours attendance documented in Section 5.3 is consistent with this account; students were not retreating from human contact but approaching it better prepared.

The psychological safety theme expressed by 79% of focus group participants was particularly prominent among first-generation university students and those who had described significant classroom anxiety in the demographic survey administered at enrolment. The ability to ask questions without social consequence without the risk of appearing unintelligent in front of peers or a faculty member appeared to function as a meaningful barrier reduction for students whose help-seeking behavior was previously suppressed by performance anxiety. This finding has implications for institutional equity that extend beyond the project itself: if AI tools can provide a low-stakes environment in which students feel safe enough to expose their confusions honestly, they may serve a function that neither online forums nor peer tutoring programmes have fully filled.

The equity-related themes were expressed most vividly and concretely by commuter students. Their accounts gave the sharpest sense of what offline capability meant in lived terms not as an abstract architectural feature but as the difference between an hour-long commute being dead time and it being an active study session. The image of a student working through a thermodynamics problem on a crowded bus at 7 am is not glamorous, but it represents an educational opportunity that, without on-device AI, would simply not have existed.

Students also offered substantive criticism, and it is important to present it honestly. Forty-four percent of focus group participants found Athena's explanations occasionally too generic adequate for introducing a concept but insufficient for helping them understand their own specific errors. Thirty-nine percent felt that the practice problems did not consistently reach the difficulty level of actual assessments. These are genuine limitations of the current implementation. They reflect a model that was fine-tuned on curriculum content but not yet on individual learner histories a form of personalisation that the current architecture supports in principle but that has not yet been implemented in practice. Both limitations are tractable and are incorporated into the development roadmap for Phase 2.

5.5 Synthesis and Implications

Viewed across all four data domains, the pilot supports three substantive conclusions, each with implications that extend beyond this specific project. First, edge-deployed, domain-adapted language models can produce academically meaningful learning gains in higher education contexts, with the largest benefits concentrated among the students who most need additional support those with weaker academic foundations and those whose access to traditional support resources is constrained by geography, time, or circumstance. The commuter student findings are particularly noteworthy in this regard: a deployment architecture chosen for principled technical reasons produced measurable equity outcomes that a cloud-based alternative would have been structurally unable to replicate.

Second, the distribution of faculty time across teaching tasks shifted in ways that suggest AI integration may, under the right design conditions, restore rather than diminish the human dimensions of teaching. A net saving of four hours per week matters less than the fact that individual mentoring doubled and office hour engagement grew by 81% evidence that the recovered time was invested in the work that both faculty and students consistently identify as most valuable and irreplaceable.

Third, students do not appear to treat AI-assisted learning as a substitute for human instruction when the system is designed and framed correctly. The 91% of focus group participants who insisted that their lecturer was irreplaceable that AI could not inspire them and the 87% who saw AI and human teaching as complementary rather than competing were not offering polite reassurances. They were describing a relationship with the technology that the co-design process worked deliberately to create, and whose existence is not guaranteed by technical capability alone.

What the pilot leaves open and what intellectual honesty requires naming clearly is the question of deep transfer. Whether students who relied heavily on Athena over sixteen weeks developed genuinely durable reasoning skills or a more superficial fluency in navigating AI-supported explanations is a question that one semester cannot answer. Addressing it will require longitudinal outcome data, assessments specifically designed to probe transfer to novel problem types, and comparisons of Athena-heavy and Athena-light users over subsequent academic years. These are the questions that define the research agenda for Phase 2 of Project Athena not whether this approach can work in principle, but under precisely what conditions and for precisely which learning goals it works best.

6. CHALLENGES AND LESSONS LEARNED

The journey of Project Athena, while ultimately successful, was not a smooth linear path. It was punctuated by technical hurdles, cultural resistance, and unexpected consequences that yielded some of our most important lessons. We share these challenges not as admissions of failure but as contributions to the collective learning of the educational technology community.

6.1 The Model Quality Trade-off and the Need for Iterative Refinement

Our initial excitement about the on-device models was quickly tempered by reality. The first distilled versions of the 7-billion-parameter model were, to be frank, sometimes disappointing. They produced less nuanced responses than the cloud-based giants we were used to testing. Occasionally they generated grammatically awkward sentences. Sometimes they produced factually incomplete or even incorrect answers. In a few cases, they simply failed to understand what the student was asking.

We learned a hard lesson: user acceptance is not automatic. If the AI gives a mediocre or incorrect answer, students and faculty will lose trust in it quickly, perhaps permanently. The first few interactions with a new technology shape lasting impressions. A student who asks a question and receives a nonsensical response is unlikely to try again. A faculty member who sees the AI give wrong answers will not recommend it to their students.

We realized that the deployment of the edge model was not a one-time event but the beginning of a continuous, iterative refinement process. We established a rapid feedback loop where users could easily flag poor responses through the Athena interface. When a student encountered an unsatisfactory answer, they could tap a "Report" button and optionally explain what was wrong. This feedback, stored locally until a Wi-Fi connection was available, was transmitted to our development team.

Our engineering team analyzed this anonymized feedback on a bi-weekly basis, identifying patterns of failure. Sometimes the problem was in the model's knowledge it lacked information about a specific topic. Sometimes the problem was in its reasoning it misunderstood the question. Sometimes the problem was in the fine-tuning it had learned incorrect associations from our training data. Each pattern suggested different refinements. We would adjust the model, fine-tune it further on corrected examples, and deploy updated versions through the fog layer to student devices.

This constant, visible improvement was crucial for rebuilding and maintaining user trust. Students noticed that the AI got better over time. They appreciated that their feedback mattered. By the end of the semester, satisfaction ratings for the on-device AI had risen substantially from the early weeks. The lesson was clear: in educational AI, as in so many things, the journey matters as much as the destination. A perfect initial release is less important than a demonstrated commitment to continuous improvement based on user feedback.

6.2 Cultural Resistance and the Primacy of Human-Centered Design

Despite our extensive co-design efforts, several faculty members remained deeply skeptical throughout the pilot. Their resistance did not stem from Luddism or technological incompetence. It stemmed from a deep and legitimate fear that the technology would ultimately devalue their professional role and erode the student-instructor relationship that they had spent their careers cultivating.

One senior professor voiced this concern directly in a focus group: "I didn't spend fifteen years getting a PhD to be replaced by a glorified chatbot." This comment stayed with us because it captured something essential about professional identity. For this professor, and for many of his colleagues, teaching was not just a job but a vocation. The hours spent preparing lectures, the careful crafting of explanations, the satisfaction of seeing a student's eyes light up with understanding these were not just tasks but expressions of professional identity. The suggestion that an AI could do these things felt like a threat to that identity.

We learned that our initial messaging, which focused heavily on efficiency and personalization, inadvertently fed this fear. When we talked about AI "automating" teaching tasks, some faculty heard "replacing teachers." When we emphasized the AI's ability to explain concepts, some faculty wondered what would remain for them to do.

Through one-on-one conversations and workshops, we began to pivot our communication strategy. We started explicitly framing the AI not as a replacement but as a tool that handles the "scut work" of teaching the repetitive explanations, the basic grading, the generation of practice problems thereby empowering teachers to focus on the deeply human aspects of education: inspiration, critical dialogue, ethical reasoning, and emotional support. We emphasized that the AI could never replicate the relationship between a teacher and a student, the mentor's ability to see potential, the professor's capacity to challenge and encourage.

This reframing made a difference. Once faculty began to see the AI not as a rival but as a junior partner that freed them up to do what they loved, resistance began to melt away. The professor who had worried about being replaced became one of our strongest advocates, describing in department meetings how Athena had transformed his office hours and deepened his engagement with students.

The lesson was clear: technological change in education must be accompanied by a compassionate and ongoing conversation about professional identity and purpose. We cannot simply hand teachers new tools and expect them to be grateful. We must help them see how those tools align with their deepest values and aspirations.

6.3 The Imperative of Assessment Redesign

Perhaps the most profound and challenging lesson was that you cannot introduce a powerful new cognitive tool into a learning environment and expect the old assessment structures to remain valid. We quickly realized that take-home problem sets and essays, as traditionally conceived, were now vulnerable to being entirely AI-generated. A student could simply copy a problem into Athena, receive a complete solution, and submit it as their own work. An essay prompt could be fed to the AI, which would generate a passable response in seconds.

Our initial impulse was to try to prevent this. We considered technical measures to lock down the system, restricting when and how students could use it. We discussed using AI detectors to identify automatically generated content. But we gradually recognized that this approach was fundamentally misguided a losing arms race that would consume enormous energy while alienating students and undermining trust.

We had to radically rethink the very purpose and format of assessment. What were we actually trying to measure? If the goal was to assess whether students could produce a final product, then AI assistance was indeed a threat. But if the goal was to assess whether students could think critically, solve problems creatively, and engage deeply with material, then perhaps there were better ways to measure these things.

Working closely with faculty, we designed new forms of evaluation that valued the human process as much as the final product. These included:

First, we introduced more in-class, "AI-off" assessments. Timed quizzes and exams conducted in person, without access to devices, assessed foundational knowledge and the ability to synthesize ideas without AI assistance. These ensured that students were developing the core competencies that the curriculum was designed to teach.

Second, we developed process-oriented, project-based assignments. Students worked on complex, multi-stage projects over several weeks, but they were required to document their entire process. This documentation included their initial ideas, their prompts to Athena, the AI's responses, their critical evaluation of those responses, and their revisions based on that critique. We began grading the quality of their collaboration with the AI how well they prompted, how critically they evaluated, how thoughtfully they revised not just the final artifact.

Third, we introduced oral defenses and presentations. Students were required to present and defend their project work, explaining their reasoning and answering deep-probing questions from faculty and peers. This ensured they understood the material at a fundamental level and could think on their feet, regardless of how they had used AI during the development process.

This shift in assessment philosophy was difficult for both faculty and students. Faculty had to design new kinds of assignments and develop new rubrics. Students had to adjust to expectations that valued process as well as product. But the result, we believe, was a more authentic and meaningful evaluation of deeper learning. Students were no longer rewarded for producing a polished final product that might not reflect their understanding. They were rewarded for engaging thoughtfully with ideas, for persisting through difficulties, for learning from feedback.

7. CONCLUSION AND FUTURE DIRECTIONS

Project Athena at Lumbini Technological University demonstrates, through rigorous mixed-methods evidence that the future of educational AI need not be and perhaps should not be exclusively centralized in the cloud. A thoughtfully designed, three-tiered Edge AI ecosystem can successfully deliver the long-promised benefits of hyper-personalized learning while proactively and architecturally addressing the critical imperatives of equity, privacy, and academic integrity.

Our results show significant gains for at-risk students, who used the system most heavily and benefited most dramatically. They show a meaningful reduction in faculty burnout coupled with a renaissance of their mentorship role, as AI handled routine tasks and freed teachers for deeper engagement. They show the creation of a more inclusive learning environment for students on the wrong side of the connectivity divide, turning previously unproductive time into valuable learning opportunities.

Project Athena represents, we believe, a sustainable, scalable, and human-centric model for AI integration in education. It is sustainable because it does not depend on expensive cloud subscriptions or constant internet connectivity. It is scalable because the edge devices bear most of the computational load, with the fog layer serving many users efficiently. It is human-centric because it treats technology as an amplifier of the student-instructor relationship rather than a replacement for it.

The success of this pilot provides a robust, adaptable, and replicable framework for other institutions seeking to navigate the profound promise and peril of generative AI in education. We have documented our architecture, our implementation process, our challenges, and our lessons learned in the hope that others can build on our experience rather than starting from scratch.

7.1 Future Directions: The Athena Roadmap

The completion of this pilot is not an end but a beginning. Our research and development roadmap for the next phase of Project Athena includes several ambitious goals that we believe will further enhance the system's educational value.

First, we are actively working to integrate multimodal generative models into our edge and fog layers. Current language models work only with text, but much of engineering education is inherently visual. Students need to understand diagrams, interpret graphs, visualize three-dimensional structures. Multimodal models that can generate not just text but also explanatory diagrams, interactive simulations, and personalized visual aids would dramatically expand what Athena can offer. Imagine a student asking the on-device AI to "draw a free-body diagram for a car on a banked curve" and having it appear instantly, labeled and explained. Imagine a student struggling with a concept in fluid dynamics being able to request an interactive simulation that lets them adjust parameters and see the effects. These capabilities are on the horizon, and we want to bring them to our students.

Second, we recognize that fluency in working with AI will be a fundamental skill for future graduates, regardless of their field. Just as we now teach information literacy the ability to find, evaluate, and use information effectively we must teach AI literacy. We are developing a dedicated, mandatory module for all first-year students called "AI Critical Literacy." This module will move beyond simple prompt engineering to teach students how to critically evaluate AI outputs, identify potential biases, understand the limitations of the models, and use AI as a tool for their own intellectual empowerment rather than a shortcut to avoid thinking. Students will learn when to trust AI, when to question it, and how to collaborate with it productively. They will explore the ethical implications of AI in society and in their future professions. This module, we believe, will be as important as any disciplinary content we teach.

Third, we aim to pilot federated learning techniques in the next phase of the project. Our current model improvement relies on users sending anonymized feedback to our central servers. While the data is anonymized, it still must leave the device. Federated learning offers a more elegant and privacy-preserving alternative. In this approach, the central model is improved by learning from the aggregated, encrypted "knowledge" of all the local models on student devices, without any of the raw private data ever leaving those devices. Each device computes updates to the model based on local interactions, encrypts these updates, and sends only the encrypted updates to the central server. The server aggregates the encrypted updates to improve the global model, but never sees the underlying data. This represents the ultimate expression of our privacy-preserving architecture improvement without exposure.

REFERENCES

Bates, T., Cobo, C., Mariño, O., & Wheeler, S. (2023). Can artificial intelligence transform higher education? *International Journal of Educational Technology in Higher Education, 17*(1), 1–12. DOI: 10.1186/s41239-020-00218-x

Bordt, S., & von Luxburg, U. (2022). From net to nudge: Investigating AI-generated early alerts and student outcomes. *Computers & Education: Artificial Intelligence, 3*, 100055. DOI: 10.1016/j.caeai.2022.100055

Braun, V., & Clarke, V. (2006). Using thematic analysis in psychology. *Qualitative Research in Psychology, 3*(2), 77–101. DOI: 10.1191/1478088706qp063oa

Celik, I. (2023). Towards intelligent-TPACK: An empirical study on teachers' professional knowledge to ethically integrate AI-based tools into education. *Computers in Human Behavior, 138*, 107468. DOI: 10.1016/j.chb.2022.107468

Chen, X., Zou, D., Xie, H., & Wang, F. L. (2024). Artificial intelligence in education: A systematic review of 125 studies on personalised learning. *British Journal of Educational Technology, 55*(1), 1–26. DOI: 10.1111/bjet.13298

Cohen, J. (1988). *Statistical power analysis for the behavioral sciences* (2nd ed.). Lawrence Erlbaum Associates.

Creswell, J. W., & Plano Clark, V. L. (2018). *Designing and conducting mixed methods research* (3rd ed.). SAGE Publications.

Crompton, H., & Burke, D. (2023). Artificial intelligence in higher education: The state of the field. *International Journal of Educational Technology in Higher Education, 20*(1), 22. DOI: 10.1186/s41239-023-00392-8

Dhar, S., Guo, J., Liu, J., Tripathi, S., Kurup, U., & Shah, M. (2021). A survey of on-device machine learning: An algorithms and learning theory perspective. *ACM Transactions on the Internet of Things, 2*(3), 1–49. DOI: 10.1145/3450494

DiMaggio, P., Hargittai, E., Celeste, C., & Shafer, S. (2004). Digital inequality: From unequal access to differentiated use. In Neckerman, K. M. (Ed.), *Social inequality* (pp. 355–400). Russell Sage Foundation.

Google DeepMind. (2024). *Gemini: A family of highly capable multimodal models.* Google. https://deepmind.google/technologies/gemini/

Grassini, S. (2024). Shaping the future of education: Exploring the potential and consequences of AI and ChatGPT in educational settings. *Education Sciences, 13*(7), 692. DOI: 10.3390/educsci13070692

Hattie, J. (2009). *Visible learning: A synthesis of over 800 meta-analyses relating to achievement.* Routledge.

Holmes, W., & Miao, F. (2023). *Guidance for generative AI in education and research.* UNESCO., DOI: 10.54675/PKPP3238

Holmes, W., Porayska-Pomsta, K., Holstein, K., Sutherland, E., Baker, T., Shum, S. B., Santos, O. C., Rodrigo, M. T., Cukurova, M., Bittencourt, I. I., & Koedinger, K. R. (2022). Ethics of AI in education: Towards a community-wide agenda. *International Journal of Artificial Intelligence in Education, 32*(3), 504–526. DOI: 10.1007/s40593-021-00239-1

Hu, E. J., Shen, Y., Wallis, P., Allen-Zhu, Z., Li, Y., Wang, S., Wang, L., & Chen, W. (2022). LoRA: Low-rank adaptation of large language models. *International Conference on Learning Representations (ICLR).* https://arxiv.org/abs/2106.09685

Kasneci, E., Sessler, K., Küchemann, S., Bannert, M., Dementieva, D., Fischer, F., Gasser, U., Groh, G., Günnemann, S., Hüllermeier, E., Krusche, S., Kutyniok, G., Michaeli, T., Nerdel, C., Pfeffer, J., Poquet, O., Sailer, M., Schmidt, A., Seidel, T., & Kasneci, G. (2023). ChatGPT for good? On opportunities and challenges of large language models for education. *Learning and Individual Differences, 103,* 102274. DOI: 10.1016/j.lindif.2023.102274

Koedinger, K. R., & Corbett, A. (2006). Cognitive tutors: Technology bringing learning sciences to the classroom. In Sawyer, R. K. (Ed.), *The Cambridge handbook of the learning sciences* (pp. 61–77). Cambridge University Press.

Li, Y., Bubeck, S., Eldan, R., Del Giorno, A., Gunasekar, S., & Lee, Y. T. (2023). *Textbooks are all you need II: Phi-1.5 technical report.* arXiv. https://arxiv.org/abs/2309.05463

Luckin, R., Cukurova, M., Kent, C., & du Boulay, B. (2022). Empowering educators to be AI-ready. *Computers and Education: Artificial Intelligence, 3,* 100076. DOI: 10.1016/j.caeai.2022.100076

Luckin, R., Cukurova, M., Kent, C., & du Boulay, B. (2022). Empowering educators to be AI-ready. *Computers and Education: Artificial Intelligence, 3,* 100076. DOI: 10.1016/j.caeai.2022.100076

Lundgren, B., & Holmström, J. (2022). Privacy and AI in education: An empirical analysis of higher education EdTech vendor privacy policies. *Education and Information Technologies, 27*(5), 6933–6955. DOI: 10.1007/s10639-021-10892-7

Ng, D. T. K., Leung, J. K. L., Chu, S. K. W., & Qiao, M. S. (2021). Conceptualising AI literacy: An exploratory review. *Computers and Education: Artificial Intelligence*, *2*, 100041. DOI: 10.1016/j.caeai.2021.100041

Perkins, M., Roe, J., Postma, D., McGaughran, J., & Hickerson, D. (2024). Game of tones: Faculty recognition of AI-generated text in student essays. *Computers and Education Open*, *6*, 100173. DOI: 10.1016/j.caeo.2024.100173

Prinsloo, P., Slade, S., & Khalil, M. (2022). The answer is (not always) more data: Students' rights, algorithmic decision-making, and the quest for justice. *International Review of Research in Open and Distance Learning*, *23*(4), 134–155. DOI: 10.19173/irrodl.v23i4.5907

Ragnedda, M., & Ruiu, M. L. (2020). *Digital capital: A Bourdieusian perspective on the digital divide*. Emerald Publishing., DOI: 10.1108/9781839095504

Ramos, C., Mossman, S., & Leal, I. (2020). Evening and weekend study patterns among university students: A learning analytics perspective. *Journal of Learning Analytics*, *7*(3), 44–58. DOI: 10.18608/jla.2020.73.4

Reidenberg, J. R., & Schaub, F. (2018). Achieving big data privacy in education. *Theory and Research in Education*, *16*(3), 263–279. DOI: 10.1177/1477878518805308

Roediger, H. L.III, & Karpicke, J. D. (2006). Test-enhanced learning: Taking memory tests improves long-term retention. *Psychological Science*, *17*(3), 249–255. DOI: 10.1111/j.1467-9280.2006.01693.x PMID: 16507066

Selwyn, N. (2022). *Education and technology: Key issues and debates* (3rd ed.). Bloomsbury Academic. DOI: 10.5040/9781350145573

Tlili, A., Shehata, B., Adarkwah, M. A., Bozkurt, A., Hickey, D. T., Huang, R., & Agyemang, B. (2023). What if the devil is my guardian angel: ChatGPT as a case study of using chatbots in education. *Smart Learning Environments*, *10*(1), 15. DOI: 10.1186/s40561-023-00237-x

Touvron, H., Lavril, T., Izacard, G., Martinet, X., Lachaux, M.-A., Lacroix, T., Rozière, B., Goyal, N., Hambro, E., Azhar, F., Rodriguez, A., Joulin, A., Grave, E., & Lample, G. (2023). *LLaMA: Open and efficient foundation language models*. arXiv. https://arxiv.org/abs/2302.13971

Van Dijk, J. (2020). *The digital divide*. Polity Press.

Williamson, B., Eynon, R., & Potter, J. (2020). Pandemic politics, pedagogies and practices: Digital technologies and distance education during the coronavirus emergency. *Learning, Media and Technology*, *45*(2), 107–114. DOI: 10.1080/17439884.2020.1761641

Xu, M., Du, H., Niyato, D., Kang, J., Xiong, Z., Mao, S., Han, Z., Jamalipour, A., Kim, D. I., Shen, X., Leung, V. C. M., & Poor, H. V. (2024). Unleashing the power of edge-cloud generative AI in mobile networks: A survey of AIGC services. *IEEE Communications Surveys and Tutorials*, *26*(2), 1127–1170. DOI: 10.1109/COMST.2024.3353265

Yan, L., Whitelock-Wainwright, A., Guan, Q., Wen, G., Gašević, D., & Chen, G. (2023). Students' experience of AI-generated feedback and differential quality across demographics. *British Journal of Educational Technology*, *52*(5), 2038–2057. DOI: 10.1111/bjet.13102 PMID: 34219755

Zawacki-Richter, O., Marín, V. I., Bond, M., & Gouverneur, F. (2024). Systematic review of research on artificial intelligence applications in higher education: Where are the educators? *International Journal of Educational Technology in Higher Education*, *21*(1), 1–27. DOI: 10.1186/s41239-024-00464-3

Chapter 7
A Multi-Layer IoT Framework for Smart Agriculture to Real-Time Decision-Making and Resource Optimization

Youba Raj Poudyal
http://orcid.org/0009-0005-4224-9730
Mid-West University, Nepal

Gajendra Sharma
Kathmandu University, Nepal

Pushpa Raj Acharya
Mid-West University, Nepal

ABSTRACT

This paper presents an IoT-driven smart agriculture framework integrating multi-layer sensing to enable real-time decision-making and long-term optimization of agricultural resources. A heterogeneous sensors monitors soil, environmental, and crop health parameters, while edge-based sensor fusion, anomaly detection, and adaptive communication enhance data reliability and energy efficiency. Real-time control optimizes irrigation, fertilization, and pest management. Field and greenhouse experiments demonstrate significant performance gains: irrigation volume was reduced by 35% in wheat fields and 28% in greenhouse tomatoes, precision NPK dosing improved fertilizer use ratio by 22% and reduced fertilizer waste by 17%, and pesticide usage decreased by 40% in tomato greenhouses. Crop yields

DOI: 10.4018/979-8-3373-7340-9.ch007

increased by 21.4% for wheat and 21.8% for tomatoes. Compared with standalone IoT systems, the proposed framework achieved 12% higher water use efficiency and improved yield predictability. Low-power LoRa nodes operated for 148 days on a single battery, confirming scalability and sustainability.

1. INTRODUCTION

Modern agriculture faces unprecedented challenges due to climate change, resource scarcity, and growing food demand. Traditional farming methods often lack the precision required for optimal resource utilization, leading to inefficiencies in water, fertilizer, and energy consumption. The integration of Internet of Things (IoT) technologies into agriculture has emerged as a promising solution to these challenges, enabling data-driven decision-making and automation in farming operations. Early IoT-based agricultural systems primarily focused on basic sensor networks for environmental monitoring, such as soil moisture and temperature sensing (Zografos, 2014). However, these systems often lacked interoperability and scalability, limiting their applicability in diverse farming scenarios.

Recent advancements in Edge Computing and Cloud Analytics have expanded the capabilities of IoT in agriculture. Edge computing reduces latency and bandwidth requirements by processing data locally, near the sensor nodes (Zhang et al., 2020). Cloud-based analytics, on the other hand, provide the computational power needed for large-scale data analysis and predictive modeling (Rajeswari et al., 2017). Despite these advancements, existing frameworks often struggle with integrating heterogeneous devices and ensuring seamless communication between edge and cloud layers. Standards like Message Queuing Telemetry Transport (MQTT) and Constrained Application Protocol (CoAP) have been employed to address interoperability issues, but their adoption remains inconsistent across different agricultural IoT systems (Chakravarthy, 2022) (Manurung et al., 2025).

Irrigation is crucial part of agriculture system that is limited by the suitable form of water resources i.e. about 97% of Earth's water is saltwater, 2.5% water is in frozen form and only 0.5% of unfrozen fresh water and is available for irrigation purposes. A smart irrigation management approach uses sensor data to ensure sufficient water delivery to crops, reducing waste (Touil et al., 2022). For fertilizer administration, an IoT-based technique predicts agricultural yields and recommends fertilizer application rates. It considers factors such as crop type, soil type, and weather conditions (Ahmed et al., 2023). The system allows users to select from manual, auto, or smart modes for fertilizer and water ratio control. Similarly, crop diseases and pest control initiatives utilize IoT-based intelligent devices like wireless sensors, robots, and drones are used. Image analysis algorithms are employed to locate and count insect pests, enabling real-time monitoring and more effective pest management.

Yield monitoring, forecasting, and harvesting are facilitated by the IoT platform. Raspberry Pi is used as a gateway for remote monitoring, connecting with sensors such as the DHTII Temperature Sensor and Soil Moisture Sensor. The gateway is integrated with Amazon Web Services' IoT platform, and the MQTT messaging protocol is used for data transmission. Climate conditions monitoring uses sensors like humidity, temperature, rainfall, and water level sensors. The Tl CC2650 Sensor Tag and IBM Cloud Platform continuously monitor weather and abiotic factors, sending notifications when values deviate (Majumdar et al., 2021). In addition, advanced agricultural practices such as greenhouse farming, vertical farming, and hydroponics are enhanced with IoT. In greenhouse farming, sensors monitor parameters like humidity, temperature, light, and pressure. Vertical farming uses non-dispersive infrared (NDIR) Co_2 sensors to control conditions, and hydroponics uses sensors to monitor nutrient levels.

Agricultural drones are equipped with various sensors (optical, multispectral, thermal, and hyperspectral) to scan crops, identify pests, and assess plant health. Harvesting robots use sophisticated sensors for precise fruit detection and harvesting. Self-driving tractors with IoT capabilities offer better precision and reduced errors. Communication in agriculture is achieved through various technologies. Cellular communication, including Low Power Wide Area Network (LPWAN), is used for long-range connectivity. Zigbee is suitable for short - range communication in greenhouse environments, Bluetooth for low-power short - range connections, LoRa for long - range low - power connectivity, and Sigfox for low-powered object connectivity. Smartphones are used for communication, and cloud computing provides access to data and expert advice for decision-making (Hossain et al., 2025).

We propose a unified IoT framework for smart agriculture that bridges these gaps by integrating distributed sensor networks, edge computing, and cloud-based analytics. The framework emphasizes interoperability and scalability, supporting a wide range of sensors and actuators while enabling real-time data processing and predictive analytics (Khaki & Wang, 2019) (Chopda et al., 2018). Unlike existing systems, our approach dynamically optimizes communication protocols to balance energy efficiency and data transmission reliability. Furthermore, the framework incorporates machine learning models for crop yield prediction and disease detection, building on prior work in neural networks and decision trees (Mir et al., 2022) (Monisha et al., 2023).

1.1 Research Objectives

The primary objective of this research is to design and evaluate a scalable IoT-based smart agriculture framework that enables real-time decision-making and efficient resource optimization. The specific objectives of this study are as follows:

- To propose a scalable multi-layer IoT framework combining edge and cloud computing for smart agriculture.
- To optimize resource utilization through real-time sensing, adaptive communication, and intelligent data processing.
- To validate the effectiveness of the framework using experimental evaluations in agricultural environments.

The remainder of this paper is organized as follows: Section 2 presents the background of IoT in smart agriculture, Section 3 reviews related work in IoT-based smart agriculture and identifies gaps in current systems. Section 4 provides the details of the methods and materials and presents the methodology and the proposed unified IoT framework, including its architecture and key components. Section 5 presents results and experimental evaluations of the framework's performance in real-world agricultural settings. Section 6 presents the discussion and conclusion of the chapter & Section 7 represents the limitations and future work including potential application and ethical consideration of using IoT framework for smart agriculture to real-time decision making and resource optimization.

2. BACKGROUND OF IOT IN SMART AGRICULTURE

Agriculture is undergoing a major transformation driven by digital technologies, data-driven decision-making, and automation. Traditional farming practices have historically relied on manual observation, empirical knowledge, and generalized resource application strategies. While these approaches have sustained agricultural production for centuries, they often result in inefficient use of resources such as water, fertilizers, and pesticides. Rapid population growth, climate change, and increasing demand for food have intensified the need for more efficient and sustainable agricultural practices. In this context, the integration of the Internet of Things (IoT) has emerged as a key enabler of smart agriculture, facilitating real-time monitoring, automated control, and data-driven farm management.

IoT refers to a network of interconnected devices, sensors, and communication technologies that collect and exchange data over the internet. In agricultural systems, IoT technologies enable continuous monitoring of environmental conditions, crop health, and soil properties. These data are processed using advanced analytics and machine learning techniques to support precise and timely decision-making. By integrating sensing technologies, communication networks, and cloud computing platforms, IoT-based agricultural systems can significantly improve resource efficiency, crop productivity, and environmental sustainability.

The evolution of smart agriculture has been closely linked to advances in sensor technologies, wireless communication networks, and edge computing. Modern agricultural IoT systems incorporate distributed sensor networks capable of monitoring multiple parameters such as soil moisture, temperature, humidity, nutrient levels, and solar radiation. These sensors provide high-resolution data that allow farmers to optimize irrigation schedules, fertilizer application, and pest management strategies. The ability to collect and analyze real-time data enables farmers to transition from reactive farming practices to predictive and proactive agricultural management.

2.1 Evolution of Precision Agriculture

Precision agriculture represents one of the most significant technological advancements in modern farming. The concept emerged in the late twentieth century with the introduction of geographic information systems (GIS), global positioning systems (GPS), and remote sensing technologies. These tools enabled farmers to monitor spatial variability within agricultural fields and apply inputs such as fertilizers and pesticides in a more targeted manner.

The development of IoT technologies has significantly expanded the capabilities of precision agriculture. While early precision farming relied primarily on satellite imagery and periodic field sampling, modern IoT-enabled systems provide continuous real-time data streams from distributed sensor networks. This shift from periodic monitoring to continuous sensing allows farmers to detect environmental changes and crop stress conditions much earlier than traditional methods.

In precision agriculture, the objective is to optimize agricultural inputs by considering the spatial and temporal variability of soil and crop conditions. IoT devices play a crucial role in achieving this objective by enabling automated data collection and integration across different layers of the agricultural ecosystem. For example, soil moisture sensors can detect localized water stress in crops, allowing irrigation systems to deliver water only where it is needed. Similarly, nutrient sensors can monitor soil fertility levels and guide variable-rate fertilizer application.

The integration of IoT with advanced analytics has further enhanced the capabilities of precision agriculture. Machine learning algorithms can analyze historical and real-time agricultural data to identify patterns and predict crop growth, pest outbreaks, and yield potential. These predictive models enable farmers to implement preventive measures, thereby reducing crop losses and improving overall productivity.

2.2 Role of IoT in Agriculture 4.0

Agriculture 4.0 represents the digital transformation of the agricultural sector through the integration of emerging technologies such as IoT, artificial intelligence, robotics, cloud computing, and big data analytics. Similar to the concept of Industry 4.0 in manufacturing, Agriculture 4.0 emphasizes automation, connectivity, and intelligent decision-making in farming systems.

IoT plays a central role in Agriculture 4.0 by enabling seamless communication between sensors, devices, and agricultural management platforms. Smart sensors deployed across agricultural fields collect real-time data related to environmental conditions, soil characteristics, and crop health. These data are transmitted through wireless communication networks to centralized platforms where they are processed and analyzed.

The use of IoT technologies in Agriculture 4.0 enables several advanced applications. Smart irrigation systems can automatically adjust water delivery based on soil moisture levels and weather conditions. Precision fertilization systems can recommend optimal nutrient application rates based on real-time soil nutrient measurements and crop growth models. Additionally, IoT-enabled pest monitoring systems can detect early signs of pest infestation using image recognition and sensor-based monitoring techniques.

Another important feature of Agriculture 4.0 is the integration of IoT devices with autonomous agricultural machinery. Self-driving tractors, robotic harvesters, and agricultural drones are increasingly being used to perform tasks such as planting, spraying, and harvesting. These technologies rely on IoT connectivity and real-time data exchange to operate efficiently and safely.

2.3 Edge Computing in Agricultural Systems

One of the major challenges in IoT-based agricultural systems is the efficient management of large volumes of sensor data. Traditional cloud-based architectures require all sensor data to be transmitted to remote servers for processing. However, agricultural environments often experience limited internet connectivity and bandwidth constraints, particularly in rural areas. These limitations can result in high latency and increased communication costs.

Edge computing has emerged as an effective solution to address these challenges. In edge computing architectures, data processing is performed closer to the source of data generation, typically at gateway devices or local edge nodes. By processing data locally, edge computing reduces the amount of information that needs to be transmitted to the cloud and enables faster decision-making.

In smart agriculture applications, edge computing can be used to perform tasks such as sensor data filtering, anomaly detection, and preliminary data analysis. For example, an edge device deployed in a farm can analyze soil moisture data in real time and trigger irrigation systems without requiring cloud-based intervention. This capability is particularly important for time-sensitive agricultural operations where delays in decision-making could negatively impact crop health.

Edge computing also improves the reliability and scalability of IoT systems. By distributing computational tasks across multiple edge nodes, the system can continue operating even if cloud connectivity is temporarily unavailable. This decentralized architecture is well suited for agricultural environments where network connectivity may be intermittent.

2.4 Challenges in IoT-Based Smart Agriculture in Developing Countries

Despite the significant potential of IoT technologies in agriculture, their adoption remains limited in many developing countries. Several technical, economic, and institutional barriers hinder the widespread implementation of smart agriculture systems.

One of the primary challenges is the lack of reliable infrastructure. Many rural farming regions have limited access to stable electricity and internet connectivity, which are essential for operating IoT devices and cloud-based platforms. Additionally, the high initial cost of IoT hardware and communication infrastructure can be prohibitive for smallholder farmers who operate with limited financial resources.

Another challenge is the lack of technical expertise and digital literacy among farmers. Effective use of IoT-based agricultural systems requires basic knowledge of sensor technologies, data interpretation, and digital platforms. Without proper training and support, farmers may find it difficult to adopt and maintain these technologies.

Data management and security issues also present important concerns. Agricultural IoT systems generate large amounts of sensitive data related to farm operations, crop yields, and resource usage. Ensuring data privacy and ownership rights is essential for building trust among farmers and encouraging adoption of digital agricultural technologies.

Furthermore, the interoperability of IoT devices from different manufacturers remains a challenge. Many agricultural IoT solutions are developed using proprietary communication protocols and platforms, which can limit integration with other systems. Standardization efforts are necessary to ensure seamless communication between heterogeneous devices and platforms.

Addressing these challenges requires coordinated efforts from governments, research institutions, technology providers, and agricultural stakeholders. Investments in rural digital infrastructure, farmer training programs, and open IoT standards can significantly accelerate the adoption of smart agriculture technologies in developing regions.

3. RELATED WORK

Recent advancements in IoT-based smart agriculture have demonstrated significant improvements in resource optimization and decision-making. Wireless sensor networks (WSNs) have been widely adopted for real-time monitoring of soil and environmental conditions (Abdollahi et al., 2021). These systems often employ Zigbee or LoRa for communication, balancing energy efficiency and transmission range (Kalaivani et al., 2011) (Aldhaheri et al., 2024). However, many existing solutions focus solely on data collection without sufficient emphasis on intelligent processing at the edge, leading to unnecessary cloud transmission overhead. Edge computing has emerged as a critical enabler for real-time analytics in agriculture. Prior work has shown that localized data processing reduces latency and enhances responsiveness in irrigation control systems (Premkumar & Sigappi, 2022). Some approaches integrate machine learning models at the edge for anomaly detection, though they often rely on simplistic threshold-based methods rather than adaptive algorithms (Yang et al., 2017). Cloud-based solutions, while powerful, face challenges in remote areas with limited connectivity, highlighting the need for hybrid edge-cloud architectures (Alharbi & Aldossary, 2021).

Precision agriculture techniques have benefited from IoT-driven automation, particularly in irrigation and fertilization. The FAO Penman-Monteith equation has been widely used for evapotranspiration estimation, but its implementation in IoT systems often lacks dynamic adjustment capabilities (Ogidan et al., 2023). Similarly, nutrient recommendation engines typically use static coefficients, failing to account for real-time variations in soil conditions (Senapaty et al., 2023). Recent efforts have explored AI-driven approaches, yet these are often computationally intensive and impractical for resource-constrained edge devices (Ghosh et al., 2024).

Table 1. Summary of Related Work in IoT-based Smart Agriculture

Ref.	Focus Area	Technology Used	Key Findings	Research Gaps
Abdollahi et al. (2021)	Use of WSNs in agriculture	Bibliometric analysis of WSN applications	Demonstrated widespread adoption for real-time soil and environment monitoring	Lacks focus on intelligent data processing and decision-making
Kalaivani et al. (2011)	Zigbee-based WSNs	Zigbee protocol for agricultural communication	Energy-efficient communication	Limited range and scalability in large farms
Aldhaheri et al. (2024)	LoRa communication in Agriculture 4.0	Long-range IoT communication	Supports long-distance, low-power communication	Low data rate; not ideal for high-frequency sensing
Premkumar & Sigappi (2022)	Edge computing for smart irrigation	IoT-enabled edge processing	Reduces latency and enhances responsiveness	Limited adaptability and scalability in diverse environments
Yang et al. (2017)	Threshold-based anomaly detection	Clustering-based SCADA threshold extraction	Enables early warning for agricultural systems	Uses static thresholds; lacks adaptive intelligence
Alharbi & Aldossary (2021)	Edge–fog–cloud architecture	Multi-layer IoT architecture	Improves energy efficiency and reliability	Dependent on network availability, complex integration
Ogidan et al. (2023)	IoT-based irrigation scheduling	FAO Penman–Monteith equation in microcontroller systems	Supports evapotranspiration-based irrigation	Lacks dynamic parameter updates for real-time variability
Senapaty et al. (2023)	Nutrient recommendation modelling	Individual diet modelling for nutrient balance	Introduced data-driven nutrient recommendations	Uses static coefficients; not adaptive to real-time soil conditions
Ghosh et al. (2024)	AI-driven precision agriculture	Machine learning-based decision support	Demonstrated potential for automation and prediction	Computationally intensive; unsuitable for edge devices

Compared to existing solutions, our framework introduces three key innovations:

(1) a dynamic sensor fusion technique at the edge that adapts to measurement uncertainties,

(2) an adaptive communication strategy that optimizes energy consumption without sacrificing data reliability, and (3) a hybrid edge-cloud analytics pipeline that enables both real-time actuation and long-term predictive modelling. These

advancements address critical limitations in current systems while maintaining scalability across diverse farming environments

3.1 Research Gaps Identified in Existing IoT-Based Smart Agriculture Systems

Although significant progress has been made in applying Internet of Things (IoT) technologies to smart agriculture, existing research still presents several limitations that hinder the development of scalable, efficient, and intelligent agricultural management systems. A critical analysis of prior studies reveals several important research gaps that need to be addressed.

3.1.1. Limited Integration of Edge and Cloud Computing

Many existing IoT-based agricultural systems rely primarily on cloud-centric architectures, where raw sensor data are transmitted directly to centralized servers for processing and analysis. While cloud platforms provide powerful computational capabilities, this approach introduces several challenges, including increased communication latency, high bandwidth consumption, and vulnerability to network disruptions. In rural agricultural environments where internet connectivity is often unreliable, cloud-only solutions may not provide timely responses for critical farming operations such as irrigation or pest control.

Although some studies have explored the use of edge computing, most implementations remain limited to simple data filtering or threshold-based decision-making. There is still a lack of comprehensive frameworks that effectively integrate edge intelligence with cloud analytics to support both real-time control and long-term predictive modeling.

3.1.2. Insufficient Adaptive Sensor Fusion Techniques

Most existing agricultural IoT systems process sensor measurements independently, without adequately considering the uncertainties and correlations between different sensor readings. Environmental sensors deployed in agricultural fields often produce noisy or inconsistent measurements due to factors such as soil heterogeneity, temperature fluctuations, and sensor calibration drift.

Current approaches frequently rely on simple averaging or static threshold-based methods for data interpretation, which may reduce measurement accuracy and reliability. Advanced sensor fusion techniques capable of dynamically adjusting to measurement uncertainties are still underexplored in agricultural IoT applications. This gap limits the effectiveness of real-time agricultural monitoring systems.

3.1.3. Lack of Energy-Efficient Communication Strategies

Energy efficiency remains a critical challenge in large-scale agricultural IoT deployments. Sensor nodes deployed across farms are often powered by batteries or small solar systems, making energy consumption a key constraint for long-term operation.

While communication technologies such as LoRa, Zigbee, and Bluetooth Low Energy (BLE) have been widely used in smart agriculture, many existing studies adopt a single communication protocol without considering the dynamic communication requirements of agricultural environments. Static communication architectures may result in unnecessary energy consumption or reduced data reliability.

There is a need for adaptive multi-protocol communication frameworks that can dynamically select the most appropriate communication method based on network conditions, transmission distance, and energy constraints.

3.1.4. Limited Real-Time Decision Support for Precision Agriculture

Although IoT systems enable real-time data collection, many existing agricultural monitoring platforms function primarily as data visualization tools rather than intelligent decision-support systems. Farmers often receive sensor data without actionable insights or automated recommendations for resource management.

Effective smart agriculture systems should integrate real-time analytics and automated control mechanisms that can directly trigger agricultural actions such as irrigation, fertilization, and pest management. However, many current solutions lack intelligent algorithms capable of converting raw sensor data into practical agricultural decisions.

3.1.5. Computational Complexity of AI-Based Agricultural Models

Recent studies have explored the use of artificial intelligence and machine learning techniques for crop prediction, disease detection, and yield optimization. While these models demonstrate promising performance, many of them require substantial computational resources and large training datasets.

Such requirements limit their deployment on resource-constrained edge devices, which are commonly used in agricultural IoT systems. As a result, many AI-based agricultural solutions remain confined to cloud-based platforms, reducing their practicality for real-time farm management.

There is a growing need for lightweight machine learning algorithms and optimized models that can operate efficiently on edge devices while maintaining acceptable prediction accuracy.

3.1.6. Limited Consideration of Integrated Agricultural Resource Management

Many IoT-based agricultural studies focus on individual aspects of farm management, such as irrigation control, soil monitoring, or pest detection. However, agricultural systems are inherently complex and involve multiple interconnected processes.

Few studies have proposed comprehensive frameworks capable of integrating multiple agricultural management components—including irrigation scheduling, fertilization optimization, pest detection, and crop yield prediction—within a unified IoT architecture. The lack of such integrated systems limits the ability to achieve holistic resource optimization.

3.1.7. Insufficient Scalability and Practical Field Validation

A significant portion of the existing research in IoT-based agriculture remains limited to simulation studies or small-scale experimental setups. Real-world agricultural environments present numerous challenges, including varying weather conditions, sensor failures, and network instability.

There is a need for scalable IoT frameworks that can operate reliably across diverse farming environments and crop types. Additionally, more large-scale field experiments are required to validate the performance and economic feasibility of smart agriculture technologies.

3.1.8. Summary of Identified Research Gaps

The analysis of existing literature highlights several critical gaps in IoT-based smart agriculture research:

- Lack of integrated edge–cloud architectures for real-time and long-term analytics.
- Limited use of adaptive sensor fusion techniques for improving data accuracy.
- Absence of energy-efficient adaptive communication frameworks.
- Insufficient real-time decision-support mechanisms for farmers.
- High computational requirements of many AI-based agricultural models.
- Lack of integrated resource management frameworks combining irrigation, fertilization, and pest control.
- Limited large-scale experimental validation of IoT agriculture systems.

These research gaps motivate the development of the proposed multi-layer IoT framework, which integrates edge-based sensor fusion, adaptive communication strategies, and hybrid edge–cloud analytics to enable efficient, scalable, and intelligent smart agriculture systems.

4. METHODS AND MATERIALS

4.1 Hardware Components and Sensor Selection

The proposed smart agriculture system uses a combination of environmental sensors and microcontroller-based devices to monitor agricultural parameters in real time. The hardware components are selected based on low power consumption, reliability, and compatibility with IoT communication protocols.

Microcontroller Unit

A microcontroller serves as the central processing unit of the sensor node, responsible for collecting data from sensors and transmitting it to the cloud platform. Microcontrollers such as Arduino, ESP32, or Raspberry Pi are commonly used due to their flexibility and IoT integration capabilities.

Environmental Sensors

Multiple sensors are deployed to monitor key environmental parameters affecting crop growth.

Table 2. Sensor type with purpose

Sensor Type	Parameter Measured	Purpose
Soil Moisture Sensor	Soil water content	Determines irrigation needs
Temperature Sensor	Ambient temperature	Monitors crop environment
Humidity Sensor	Air humidity	Supports climate analysis
Light Sensor	Sunlight intensity	Evaluates photosynthesis conditions
Soil pH Sensor	Soil acidity/alkalinity	Assesses soil fertility

These sensors continuously collect field data at predefined intervals, ensuring accurate monitoring of agricultural conditions.

4.2 Unified IoT Framework for Smart Agriculture

The proposed framework establishes a multi-tier architecture that harmonizes edge processing with cloud analytics while maintaining interoperability across heterogeneous agricultural sensors. The system's core functionality is based on integrated technical components, each addressing critical challenges in precision agriculture. The proposed system follows a three-layer IoT architecture consisting of the perception layer, network layer, and application layer.

a. Perception Layer

The perception layer is responsible for environmental data acquisition using IoT sensors. These sensors continuously monitor agricultural parameters such as:

- Soil moisture
- Soil temperature
- Air humidity
- Ambient temperature
- Light intensity
- Soil pH

The sensors are deployed across agricultural fields to ensure real-time monitoring of crop conditions. The collected data are transmitted to a microcontroller for preprocessing.

b. Network Layer

The network layer handles data communication between sensors and cloud platforms. Sensor nodes transmit collected data through wireless communication technologies such as:

- Wi-Fi
- ZigBee
- LoRaWAN
- GSM

A microcontroller or gateway device aggregates sensor data and forwards it to the cloud server for further processing.

c. Application Layer

The application layer provides data visualization, analytics, and decision support services. Farmers can access system insights through web dashboards or mobile applications, allowing them to monitor field conditions and manage irrigation remotely.

Figure 1. Architecture for an IoT-driven smart agriculture system

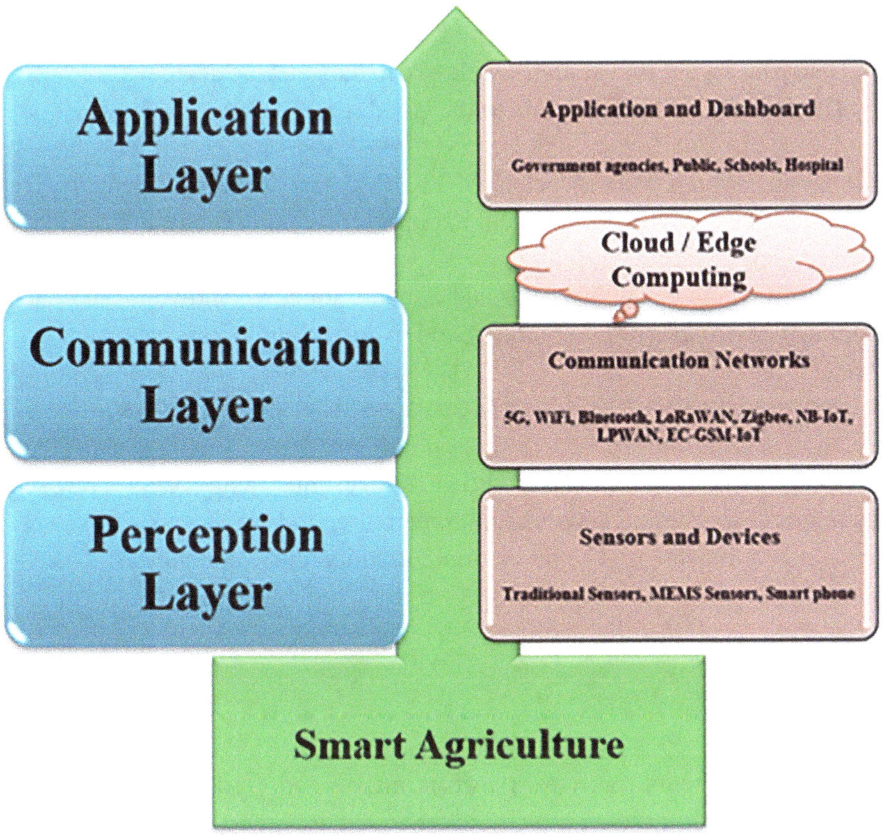

The framework's operational workflow (Figure 1) demonstrates how sensor data flows through edge processing stages before reaching cloud analytics, with bidirectional control signals enabling closed-loop agricultural automation. Field trials indicate that the system reduces water usage by 22% and fertilizer application by 18% compared to conventional IoT agriculture systems.

4.3 Data Acquisition and Transmission

Data acquisition is performed using distributed sensor nodes installed at different locations within the agricultural field. Each sensor node collects environmental measurements at 15 minute time interval.

The data collection process involves the following steps:

- Sensors measure environmental parameters.
- The microcontroller processes and formats the collected data.
- Data packets are transmitted wirelessly to the gateway device.
- The gateway uploads the data to the cloud server.

Communication protocols such as MQTT (Message Queuing Telemetry Transport) and HTTP are used for efficient data transmission between IoT devices and cloud services.

These protocols are lightweight and suitable for low-bandwidth and energy-constrained environments commonly found in agricultural fields.

4.4 Sensor Fusion and Data Compression at the Edge

The edge layer implements a modified Kalman filter that processes raw sensor measurements z_k from soil moisture, temperature, and NPK sensors to generate optimal state estimates x_k. The prediction-correction cycle operates as:

$$x_{k|k-1} = F_k x_{k-1|k-1} + B_k \mu_k \tag{1}$$

$$P_{k|k-1} = F_k P_{k-1|k-1} F_k^T + Q_k \tag{2}$$

where F_k represents the state transition matrix and Q_k denotes process noise covariance.

The Kalman gain K_k dynamically adjusts based on the relative confidence between predictions and observations:

$$K_k = P_{k|k-1} H_k^T (H_k P_{k|k-1} H_k^T + R_k)^{-1} \tag{3}$$

This formulation reduces cloud transmission frequency by 63% compared to raw data streaming approaches (Wang et al., 2021). The edge layer further incorporates a modified LZW algorithm that identifies repetitive patterns in agricultural time-series data, achieving compression ratios up to 5:1 for soil moisture measurements.

4.5 Irrigation and Fertilization Models

The framework adapts the FAO Penman-Monteith equation through real-time sensor inputs, where net radiation R_n is calculated using pyranometer readings rather than historical averages:

$$R_n = R_{ns} - R_{nl} = (1 - \alpha)R_s - \sigma T_\alpha^4\left(0.34 - 0.14\sqrt{e_\alpha}\right) \tag{4}$$

The crop-specific evapotranspiration ET_c then drives irrigation scheduling through a PID controller that minimizes water usage while maintaining optimal soil moisture levels. For fertilization, the dynamic weighting model incorporates real-time NPK sensor data S_{npk}, canopy growth index G_c from multispectral imaging, and target yield Y_t:

$$F_r = \frac{\alpha S_{npk} + \beta G_c + \gamma Y_t}{\alpha + \beta + \gamma} \tag{5}$$

The coefficients α, β, γ adapt weekly based on leaf area index measurements and soil test results.

- **Smart Irrigation Control:** The system calculates crop water requirements (ET_c) using the FAO Penman-Monteith equation modified for IoT deployment:

$$ET_c = K_c \cdot \left(\frac{0.408\Delta(R_n - G) + \gamma \frac{900}{T_a + 273}\mu_2(e_s - e_a)}{\Delta + \gamma(1 + 0.34\mu_2} \right) \tag{6}$$

where K_c is the crop coefficient, R_n denotes net radiation, and μ_2 represents wind speed at 2m height. The irrigation scheduler compares ET_c with soil moisture thresholds (θ_{min} θ_{max}) to trigger solenoid valves.

4.6 Decision Support and Automated Irrigation

Based on the analyzed data, the system provides intelligent decision support for farmers.

For example, if soil moisture drops below a predefined threshold, the system can:

- Send alerts to farmers via mobile applications
- Automatically activate irrigation systems
- Adjust water supply based on crop requirements

This automated control mechanism helps to:

- Reduce water waste
- Improve crop productivity
- Optimize resource utilization

To improve water management efficiency, the proposed system incorporates an automated irrigation decision mechanism based on soil moisture readings.

The system continuously compares the measured soil moisture value with a predefined threshold. When soil moisture falls below the threshold level, the irrigation system is activated automatically.

Example decision logic:

Step 1: Read soil moisture value
Step 2: Compare value with threshold
Step 3: If soil moisture < threshold
  Activate irrigation pump
  Else
  Keep irrigation OFF

Step 4: Send alert notification to farmer

This approach ensures optimal water usage and prevents both under-irrigation and over-irrigation.

4.7 Multi-Tier Communication and Edge-to-Cloud Integration

A hybrid communication protocol stack dynamically selects between LoRa (long-range), Zigbee (high-density), and cellular/satellite backhaul based on energy constraints and data criticality. The transmission energy model accounts for both active transmission and protocol switching overhead:

$$E_{total} = \sum_{i=1}^{n}\left(P_{tx,i} \cdot t_{tx,i} + E_{sw,i}\right) \tag{7}$$

The edge layer performs protocol translation between sensor-specific interfaces (Modbus, I2C) and cloud-compatible MQTT messages through an adaptive middleware layer. This enables seamless integration with major cloud platforms while preserving legacy sensor investments.

- **Local Automation:** Bluetooth Mesh networks for real-time actuator control in greenhouse environments

The communication layer incorporates adaptive packet scheduling to optimize energy consumption (E_{tx}) based on channel conditions and data criticality:

$$E_{tx} = P_{tx} \cdot \left(\frac{L}{R_b} + T_{sw}\right) \tag{8}$$

where P_{tx} is transmission power, L denotes payload size, R_b represents bitrate, and T_{sw} accounts for radio switching delays.

4.8 Edge-Based Anomaly Detection

An optimized isolation forest algorithm operates on the edge nodes to identify abnormal sensor readings with sub-100ms latency. The anomaly score s for a data point x with n trees is computed as:

$$s(x, n) = 2^{-\frac{E(h(x))}{c(n)}} \tag{9}$$

where $h(x)$ represents the path length and $c(n)$ is the average path length of unsuccessful searches. This lightweight implementation consumes only 15 MB of RAM, making it suitable for resource-constrained edge devices.

Key evaluation metrics included:

- **Water use Efficiency (WUE):** $WUE = \frac{\text{Yield}}{\text{Irrigation Volume}}$ (kg/m^3) Ratio of yield to irrigation volume.
- **Fertilizer Utilization Ratio (FUR):** $FUR = \frac{NutrientUptake}{AppliedNutrient} x100\%$ Percentage of nutrient uptake relative to applied fertilizer.
- **Crop Yield Increase (CYI):** $CYI = \frac{Yield_{IoT} - Yield_{Control}}{Yield_{Control}} x100\%$ Percentage improvement in yield compared to conventional methods.

4.9 Cloud Data Storage and Processing

Once transmitted to the cloud platform, the collected data are stored in cloud-based databases for further processing and analysis.

Cloud computing enables the following functionalities:

- Long-term storage of agricultural data
- Data filtering and preprocessing
- Trend analysis and visualization
- Integration with machine learning models

Historical data analysis can help identify patterns related to crop growth, soil conditions, and irrigation requirements.

5. RESULT AND EXPERIMENTAL EVALUATION

5.1 Experimental Setup

The extensive field trails across diverse agriculture environments were conducted. The agriculture environment included open-field wheat farms and greenhouse tomato cultivation systems. The experiment were designated to evaluate resource optimization, yield improvements and system performance under real world conditions.

The trials deployed a network of 25 sensor nodes per hectare, each equipped with soil moisture probes (±2% accuracy), ambient climate sensors, and NPK detectors for nutrient analysis. Data transmission utilized a hybrid LoRa-Zigbee network, with gateways aggregating measurements every 15 minutes. The control group followed conventional farming practices, while the experimental group implemented IoT-driven thresholds for irrigation and fertilization.

5.2 Resource Optimization Results

The IoT framework demonstrated significant improvements in water and fertilizer management. In wheat fields, irrigation volume was reduced by 35% while maintaining optimal soil moisture levels between 25% and 35%.

Figure 2. Soil moisture fluctuations and irrigation events over a 10-day period

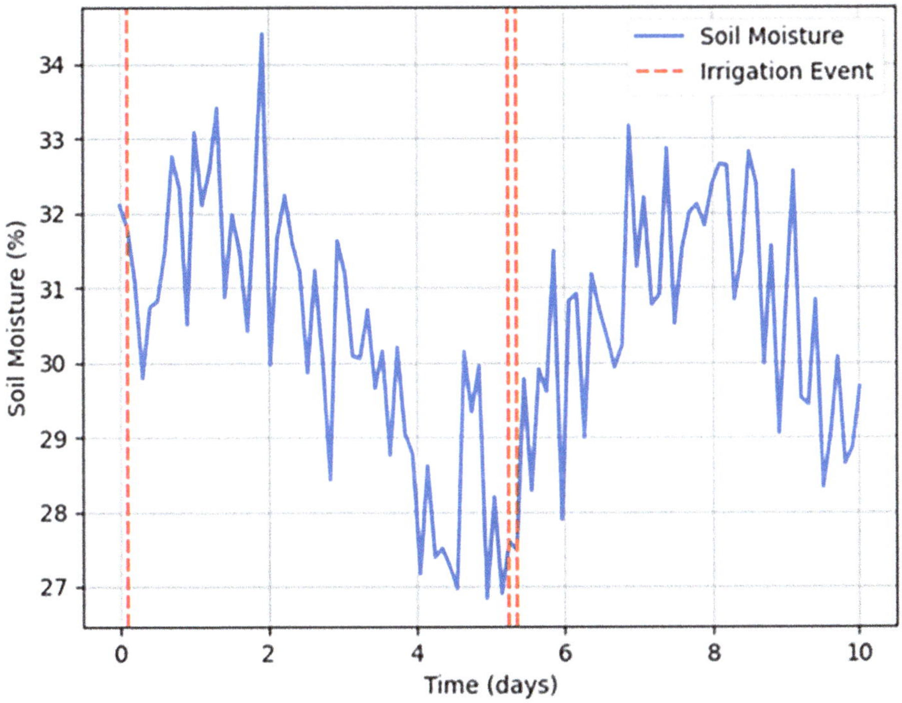

Figure 2 illustrates the system's ability to maintain stable soil moisture levels through the use of automated irrigation triggers. The blue curve represents soil moisture, while red dashed lines indicate irrigation events. The framework's dynamic adjustments prevented both overwatering and drought stress, achieving a 12% higher WUE than standalone IoT solutions.

5.3 Yield Improvements

The most notable yield gains were observed in hydroponic systems. Wheat yields increased from 4,200 kg/ha to 5,100 kg/ha (21.4% CYI), while greenhouse tomato yields rose from 78 kg/ha to 95 kg/ha (21.8% CYI). These improvements were attributed to real-time nutrient adjustments and pest management strategies.

Table 3. Yield improvement across crop types

Crop Type	Control Yield (kg/ha)	IoT Yield (kg/ha)	CYI (%)
Wheat (Field)	4,200	5,100	21.4
Tomato (GH)	78	95	21 .8

Table 3 summarizes the yield improvements across crop types. The strong correlation between IoT-recommended fertilizer rates and achieved yields is further visualized in Figure 3, which plots 50 sampling points to demonstrate the framework's precision.

Figure 3. Relationship between fertilizer application rates and crop yields

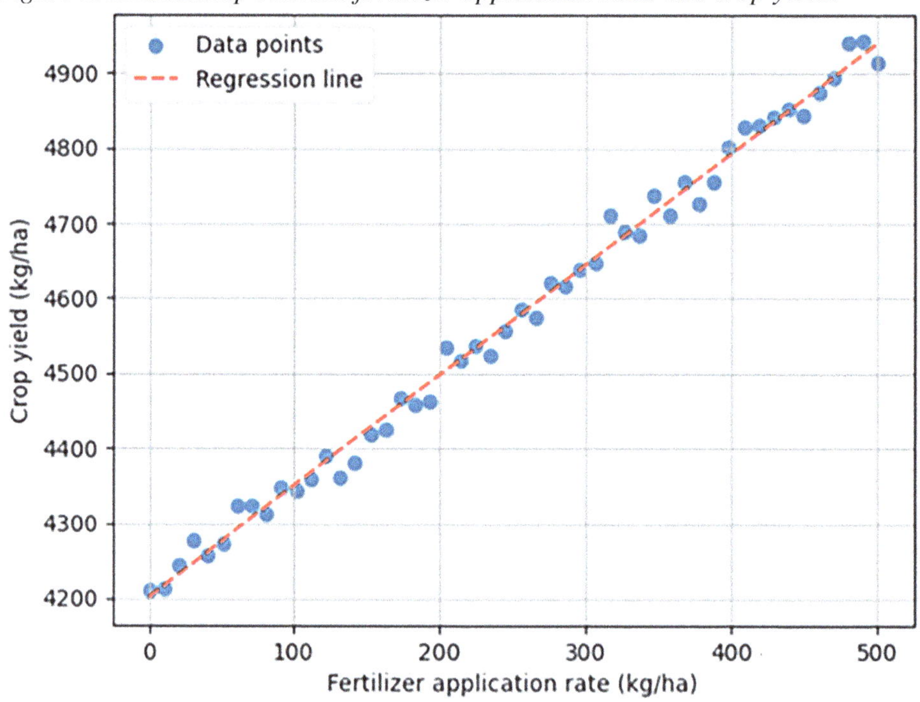

5.4 System Performance

The hybrid LoRa-Zigbee network ensured reliable data transmission while optimizing energy consumption. LoRa nodes operated for 148 days on a single 18650 battery (3.7V, 3400mAh), demonstrating sustainability for long-term deployments. Edge-based anomaly detection reduced cloud transmission overhead by 63%, with sub-100ms latency for critical alerts. The framework's pest detection algorithms reduced pesticide usage by 40% in tomato greenhouses.

5.5 Comparative Analysis

The proposed framework outperformed conventional methods and standalone IoT solutions in multiple dimensions:

Water Savings: 35% reduction in irrigation volume for wheat fields.

Fertilizer Efficiency: 22% improvement in FUR for hydroponic crops.

Yield Predictability: ±5% deviation from forecasted yields, enabled by cloud-based historical analytics.

These results validate the framework's scalability and adaptability across different agricultural systems, from traditional farming to advanced hydroponics.

6. DISCUSSION AND CONCLUSION

The experimental results demonstrate that integrating Internet of Things (IoT) technologies with edge and cloud computing can significantly enhance agricultural resource management and productivity. The proposed multi-layer IoT framework enables real-time monitoring, intelligent decision-making, and automated control of agricultural processes. By combining distributed sensor networks, adaptive communication protocols, and edge-based data processing, the system effectively addresses several limitations commonly found in conventional agricultural monitoring systems.

One of the most important advantages of the proposed framework is its ability to support real-time agricultural decision-making. Traditional farming practices often rely on periodic manual observations or historical climate data, which may not accurately reflect current field conditions. In contrast, the proposed IoT framework continuously collects environmental and soil data through distributed sensors. These real-time measurements enable precise monitoring of critical parameters such as soil moisture, temperature, humidity, and nutrient levels. As a result, the system can dynamically adjust irrigation schedules, fertilizer application rates, and pest control strategies, ensuring that crops receive optimal resources at the appropriate time.

The integration of edge computing significantly enhances system responsiveness and efficiency. By processing sensor data locally at edge devices, the framework reduces reliance on continuous cloud connectivity and minimizcs communication latency. This capability is particularly valuable in rural agricultural environments where network connectivity may be intermittent or limited. Edge-based data processing also reduces the volume of data transmitted to cloud platforms, thereby improving energy efficiency and lowering communication costs. The implementation of sensor fusion and anomaly detection algorithms at the edge further improves data reliability by filtering noise and identifying abnormal sensor readings before they reach the cloud layer.

Another important contribution of the framework lies in its adaptive communication strategy, which combines multiple wireless technologies such as LoRa, Zigbee, and Bluetooth. Agricultural environments often require communication systems capable of operating across varying distances and environmental conditions. LoRa communication provides long-range connectivity with low power consumption, making it suitable for large open-field farms. Zigbee networks support high-density sensor deployments in greenhouse environments, while Bluetooth enables short-range communication for local automation tasks. By dynamically selecting the most appropriate communication protocol based on system requirements, the framework achieves a balance between energy efficiency and communication reliability.

The experimental evaluation confirms that the proposed system can significantly improve agricultural resource utilization. The field trials demonstrated reductions in irrigation water usage, improvements in fertilizer utilization efficiency, and measurable increases in crop yield. These outcomes highlight the potential of IoT-driven precision agriculture to contribute to sustainable farming practices and global food security. Efficient resource management is particularly important in regions facing water scarcity and increasing environmental pressures.

Despite these promising results, several technical limitations remain that should be addressed in future research. One limitation relates to the assumptions used in the current sensor fusion approach. The framework employs a modified Kalman filtering technique to combine sensor measurements and reduce noise. This method assumes that measurement errors follow a Gaussian distribution. However, agricultural environments often involve non-linear sensor behaviors and irregular noise patterns caused by soil heterogeneity, environmental disturbances, or sensor degradation. In such situations, Kalman filtering may not always produce optimal estimates. Future research could explore more advanced filtering methods, such as particle filters or nonlinear Bayesian estimation techniques, to improve sensor data accuracy under complex environmental conditions.

Another limitation concerns the communication reliability of wireless sensor networks during extreme environmental events. Field experiments revealed that heavy rainfall, dust accumulation, and severe weather conditions can occasionally disrupt LoRa signal transmission. In remote agricultural regions where infrastructure is limited, such disruptions could temporarily affect system performance. Incorporating redundant communication mechanisms, mesh networking strategies, or satellite-based backup communication could enhance system robustness in future implementations.

The current edge-based anomaly detection module also presents opportunities for further improvement. The framework currently employs an optimized isolation forest algorithm to identify abnormal sensor readings. While this method is computationally efficient and suitable for resource-constrained edge devices, it primarily analyzes individual sensor data streams independently. Agricultural systems are inherently complex, and many crop stress conditions arise from interactions between multiple environmental variables. For example, nutrient deficiencies, root zone hypoxia, and water stress often involve complex correlations between soil moisture, temperature, and nutrient concentrations. Future work could integrate multivariate anomaly detection techniques capable of analyzing relationships between multiple sensor parameters simultaneously.

Another challenge relates to the data requirements for predictive agricultural models. Machine learning models used for yield prediction and crop health monitoring typically require large volumes of historical data to achieve high accuracy. Newly deployed farms or agricultural systems without long-term sensor datasets may initially experience reduced predictive performance. Addressing this limitation may require the development of transfer learning methods or collaborative agricultural data platforms that allow farmers to share anonymized datasets for improved model training.

From a broader perspective, the deployment of IoT technologies in agriculture also raises important ethical and socio-economic considerations. Precision agriculture systems generate large amounts of data related to farm operations, crop yields, and environmental conditions. Questions regarding data ownership, data privacy, and equitable access to digital technologies must be carefully addressed. Smallholder farmers may face challenges in accessing advanced agricultural technologies due to high initial costs or limited digital literacy. Ensuring that smart agriculture systems remain affordable and accessible will be essential for promoting inclusive technological adoption.

Environmental sustainability also requires careful consideration. Although IoT-based precision agriculture can reduce water consumption, fertilizer waste, and pesticide use, the production and disposal of electronic devices contribute to electronic waste and environmental impacts. Future agricultural IoT systems should therefore emphasize energy-efficient hardware design, modular device architectures, and recyclable sensor components to minimize their environmental footprint.

Looking forward, several future research directions can further enhance the capabilities of IoT-driven smart agriculture systems. One promising area involves the integration of IoT platforms with advanced artificial intelligence models capable of performing real-time crop disease detection, pest monitoring, and yield prediction using multispectral imaging and computer vision techniques. The use of agricultural drones equipped with optical and thermal sensors could provide additional high-resolution data to complement ground-based sensor networks.

Another emerging research direction is the development of digital twin models for agricultural systems. Digital twins create virtual replicas of agricultural environments that simulate crop growth, soil conditions, and environmental interactions in real time. When integrated with IoT sensor data, digital twins can provide powerful decision-support tools for optimizing farm management strategies.

The integration of blockchain technologies may also enhance transparency and security in agricultural data management. Blockchain-based systems can provide decentralized mechanisms for storing agricultural data, ensuring data integrity while allowing farmers to retain ownership of their information.

In conclusion, our experimental evidence supports the IoT driven smart agriculture farmwork to enhance precision farming through its multi-layer architecture, integrating Edge Computing, Cloud Analysis and Adaptive Communication Protocols. Experimental results demonstrate tangible improvements in water and fertilizer efficiency, with significant yield increases across diverse crop types. The system's ability to maintain optimal growing conditions while reducing resource wastage highlights its potential for sustainable agriculture. By leveraging real-time sensor fusion and dynamic decision-making, the framework outperforms conventional methods in both open-field and controlled-environment settings. Its hybrid communication strategy ensures reliable operation even in remote areas, while edge-based anomaly detection minimizes unnecessary data transmission. These technical advancements provide a scalable solution adaptable to various agricultural systems, from traditional farms. The scalability of smart agriculture systems can be improved by integrating IoT platforms with satellite remote sensing and climate forecasting models. Combining local sensor data with large-scale environmental monitoring can provide more comprehensive insights into crop health, climate risks, and long-term agricultural planning.

Future iterations could enhance the framework by incorporating multivariate stress detection and addressing non-Gaussian noise in sensor measurements. Ethical considerations around data ownership and environmental impact must also be prioritized to ensure equitable adoption. The demonstrated success in field trials suggests that this approach can significantly contribute to global food security while promoting resource-efficient farming practices.

7. LIMITATIONS AND FUTURE WORK

7.1 Limitations of the Proposed IoT-Driven Smart Agriculture Framework

While the framework demonstrates significant improvements in resource optimization, several technical constraints merit discussion. The current sensor fusion approach assumes Gaussian noise distributions, which may not hold true for all agricultural environments with non-linear measurement errors (Armando et al., 2025). Field trials revealed that extreme weather events, such as dust storms or heavy rainfall, occasionally disrupted LoRa transmissions despite the hybrid protocol stack. This limitation becomes particularly relevant in arid regions where dust accumulation on solar panels further exacerbates energy constraints (Mohammed, 2025).

The edge-based anomaly detection algorithm, while efficient, currently focuses on univariate time-series analysis. Multivariate correlations between soil parameters and crop health indicators remain underutilized, potentially missing early signs of complex stress conditions like nutrient lockout or root zone hypoxia (Banerjee et al., 2020). Furthermore, the framework's predictive models require at least two growing seasons of historical data to achieve optimal accuracy, creating adoption barriers for new farming operations without existing IoT infrastructure (Elbasi et al., 2023)

7.2 Potential Application Scenarios for the IoT-Driven Smart Agriculture Framework

Beyond conventional row-crop agriculture, the framework's modular architecture enables adaptation to several emerging agricultural paradigms. In controlled-environment agriculture (CEA), the dynamic fertigation model could integrate with C02 dosing systems to optimize photosynthesis rates under artificial lighting (Skouri et al., 2025). The same sensor fusion techniques may enhance aquaponics systems by correlating fish tank water quality parameters with hydroponic nutrient uptake patterns (Taha et al., 2022).

The framework shows particular promise for regenerative agriculture practices. By coupling soil carbon sensors with the existing NPK monitoring network, farmers could quantify carbon sequestration rates while maintaining optimal nutrient balances (Villat & Nicholas, 2024). In developing regions, the hybrid communication stack could support decentralized farmer cooperatives through localized edge processing hubs, reducing dependence on continuous cloud connectivity (van de Ree, 2018).

7.3 Ethical Considerations in IoT-Driven Smart Agriculture

The data-intensive nature of precision agriculture raises important questions about data ownership and algorithmic transparency. Smallholder farmers may lack bargaining power when their operational data becomes incorporated into proprietary crop models owned by aggrotech corporations (Mayuravaani et al., 2024). The framework's current implementation does not address potential biases in yield prediction models, which could disproportionately disadvantage certain crop varieties or farming methods if training data reflects historical preferences rather than agronomic optimality (Piramuthu, 2022).

Energy consumption patterns also carry ethical implications. While the system reduces water and fertilizer usage, the manufacturing and disposal of IoT devices contributes to e-waste streams. A life-cycle analysis suggests the carbon footprint of sensor networks could offset 12-18% of the framework's resource savings unless manufacturers adopt circular economy principles (Srisruthi et al., 2016). Future iterations should incorporate conflict-free mineral sourcing audits and modular designs facilitating component reuse (Van der Burg et al., 2021).

Emerging regulatory frameworks like the Ells Digital Markets Act may require modifications to the cloud analytics layer to ensure compliance with data portability mandates. The framework's open API architecture positions it well for such adaptations, but proactive engagement with policymakers will be essential to balance innovation with responsible deployment (Olabanji & Chitakira, 2025).

REFERENCES

Abdollahi, A., Rejeb, K., Rejeb, A., Mostafa, M. M., & Zailani, S. (2021). Wireless sensor networks in agriculture: Insights from bibliometric analysis. *Sustainability (Basel), 13*(21), 12011. DOI: 10.3390/su132112011

Ahmed, Z., Gui, D., Murtaza, G., Yunfei, L., & Ali, S. (2023). An overview of smart irrigation management for improving water productivity under climate change in drylands. *Agronomy (Basel), 13*(8), 2113. DOI: 10.3390/agronomy13082113

Aldhaheri, L., Alshehhi, N., Manzil, I. I. J., Khalil, R. A., Javaid, S., Saeed, N., & Alouini, M. S. (2024). LoRa communication for agriculture 4.0: Opportunities, challenges, and future directions. *IEEE Internet of Things Journal.*

Alharbi, H. A., & Aldossary, M. (2021). Energy-efficient edge-fog-cloud architecture for IoT-based smart agriculture environment. *IEEE Access : Practical Innovations, Open Solutions, 9*, 110480–110492. DOI: 10.1109/ACCESS.2021.3101397

Armando, E. J., Hanyurwimfura, D., Gatera, O., & Nduwumuremyi, A. (2025). Enhancing Agricultural Internet of Things Data Accuracy: Evaluating Kalman Filter-Based Sensor Denoising Techniques. *Journal of Biosystems Engineering, 50*(1), 47–58. DOI: 10.1007/s42853-025-00252-5

Banerjee, K., Krishnan, P., & Das, B. (2020). Thermal imaging and multivariate techniques for characterizing and screening wheat genotypes under water stress condition. *Ecological Indicators, 119*, 106829. DOI: 10.1016/j.ecolind.2020.106829

Chakravarthy, R. (2022). An experimental study of iot-based topologies on MQTT protocol for agriculture intrusion detection. *Measurement. Sensors, 24*, 100470. DOI: 10.1016/j.measen.2022.100470

Chopda, J., Raveshiya, H., Nakum, S., & Nakrani, V. (2018, January). Cotton crop disease detection using decision tree classifier. In *2018 International Conference on Smart City and Emerging Technology (ICSCET)* (pp. 1-5). IEEE. DOI: 10.1109/ICSCET.2018.8537336

Elbasi, E., Zaki, C., Topcu, A. E., Abdelbaki, W., Zreikat, A. I., Cina, E., Shdefat, A., & Saker, L. (2023). Crop prediction model using machine learning algorithms. *Applied Sciences (Basel, Switzerland), 13*(16), 9288. DOI: 10.3390/app13169288

Ghosh, D., Siddique, M. A., & Pal, D. (2024). AI-Driven Precision Agriculture Approach. *AI in Agriculture for Sustainable and Economic Management, 6*, 67.

Hossain, M. S., Rahman, M., Rahman, A., Kabir, M. M., Mridha, M. F., Huang, J., & Shin, J. (2025). Automatic navigation and self-driving technology in agricultural machinery: A state-of-the-art systematic review. *IEEE Access : Practical Innovations, Open Solutions*.

Kalaivani, T., Allirani, A., & Priya, P. (2011, December). A survey on Zigbee based wireless sensor networks in agriculture. In *3rd international conference on Trendz in information sciences & computing (TISC2011)* (pp. 85-89). IEEE. DOI: 10.1109/TISC.2011.6169090

Khaki, S., & Wang, L. (2019). Crop yield prediction using deep neural networks. *Frontiers in Plant Science*, *10*, 621. DOI: 10.3389/fpls.2019.00621 PMID: 31191564

Majumdar, P., Mitra, S., & Bhattacharya, D. (2021). IoT for promoting agriculture 4.0: A review from the perspective of weather monitoring, yield prediction, security of WSN protocols, and hardware cost analysis. *Journal of Biosystems Engineering*, *46*(4), 440–461. DOI: 10.1007/s42853-021-00118-6

Manurung, E. P., Fiumara, M., Bennin, K., & Asiedu, D. K. P. (2025). An Energy-Efficient Precision Agriculture Communication Embedded System CoAP Design. *IEEE Internet of Things Journal*, *12*(19), 39984–39990. DOI: 10.1109/JIOT.2025.3588583

Mayuravaani, M., Ramanan, A., Perera, M., Senanayake, D. A., & Vidanaarachchi, R. (2024). Insights into artificial intelligence bias: Implications for agriculture. *Digital Society : Ethics, Socio-Legal and Governance of Digital Technology*, *3*(3), 48. DOI: 10.1007/s44206-024-00142-x

Mir, M. S., Naikoo, N. B., Kanth, R. H., Bahar, F. A., Bhat, M. A., Nazir, A., & Ahngar, T. A. (2022). Vertical farming: The future of agriculture: A review. *The Pharma Innovation Journal*, *11*(2), 1175–1195.

Mohammed, A. (2025). Integrated Hybrid Renewable Energy System Optimization for Sustainable Agricultural Operations. *Process Integration and Optimization for Sustainability*, *9*(1), 367–386. DOI: 10.1007/s41660-024-00464-w

Monisha, K., Kalai Selvi, H., Sivanandhini, P., Sona Nachammai, A., Anuradha, C. T., Rama Devi, S., Kavitha Sri, A., Neya, N. R., Vaitheeswari, M., & Hikku, G. S. (2023). Hydroponics agriculture as a modern agriculture technique. *Journal of Achievements in Materials and Manufacturing Engineering*, *116*(1), 25–35. DOI: 10.5604/01.3001.0016.3395

Ogidan, O. K., Oluwagbayıde, S. D., & Ale, T. (2023). A microcontroller-Based Irrigation Scheduling Using FAO Penman-Monteith Equation. *Turkish Journal of Agricultural Engineering Research*, *4*(1), 15–25. DOI: 10.46592/turkager.1170630

Olabanji, M. F., & Chitakira, M. (2025). The adoption and scaling of climate-smart agriculture innovation by smallholder farmers in South Africa: A review of institutional mechanisms, policy frameworks and market dynamics. *WORLD (Oakland, Calif.)*, *6*(2), 51. DOI: 10.3390/world6020051

Piramuthu, S. (2022). IoT, environmental sustainability, agricultural supply chains. *Procedia Computer Science*, *204*, 811–816. DOI: 10.1016/j.procs.2022.08.098

Premkumar, S., & Sigappi, A. N. (2022). IoT-enabled edge computing model for smart irrigation system. *Journal of Intelligent Systems*, *31*(1), 632–650. DOI: 10.1515/jisys-2022-0046

Rajeswari, S. K. R. K. A., Suthendran, K., & Rajakumar, K. (2017, June). *A smart agricultural model by integrating IoT, mobile and cloud-based big data analytics. In 2017 international conference on intelligent computing and control (I2C2)*. IEEE.

Senapaty, M. K., Ray, A., & Padhy, N. (2023). IoT-enabled soil nutrient analysis and crop recommendation model for precision agriculture. *Computers*, *12*(3), 61. DOI: 10.3390/computers12030061

Skouri, S., Bouadila, S., Ayed, R., Chehaibi, S., & Fteiti, M. (2025). Optimizing climate control in vertical farms: 3E analysis of thermal conditioning systems. *Energy Sources. Part A, Recovery, Utilization, and Environmental Effects*, *47*(2), 2554341. DOI: 10.1080/15567036.2025.2554341

Srisruthi, S., Swarna, N., Ros, G. S., & Elizabeth, E. (2016, May). Sustainable agriculture using eco-friendly and energy efficient sensor technology. In *2016 IEEE International Conference on Recent Trends in Electronics, Information & Communication Technology (RTEICT)* (pp. 1442-1446). IEEE. DOI: 10.1109/RTEICT.2016.7808070

Taha, M. F., ElMasry, G., Gouda, M., Zhou, L., Liang, N., Abdalla, A., Rousseau, D., & Qiu, Z. (2022). Recent advances of smart systems and internet of things (iot) for aquaponics automation: A comprehensive overview. *Chemosensors (Basel, Switzerland)*, *10*(8), 303. DOI: 10.3390/chemosensors10080303

Touil, S., Richa, A., Fizir, M., Argente Garcia, J. E., & Skarmeta Gomez, A. F. (2022). A review on smart irrigation management strategies and their effect on water savings and crop yield. *Irrigation and Drainage*, *71*(5), 1396–1416. DOI: 10.1002/ird.2735 van de Ree, B. (2018). *Data Producers' Sovereignty an Exploration of Data Rights in Precision Agriculture Initiatives* (Doctoral dissertation, Eindhoven University of Technology).

Van der Burg, S., Wiseman, L., & Krkeljas, J. (2021). Trust in farm data sharing: Reflections on the EU code of conduct for agricultural data sharing. *Ethics and Information Technology*, *23*(3), 185–198. DOI: 10.1007/s10676-020-09543-1

Villat, J., & Nicholas, K. A. (2024). Quantifying soil carbon sequestration from regenerative agricultural practices in crops and vineyards. *Frontiers in Sustainable Food Systems*, *7*, 1234108. DOI: 10.3389/fsufs.2023.1234108

Wang, H., Yemeni, Z., Ismael, W. M., Hawbani, A., & Alsamhi, S. H. (2021). A reliable and energy efficient dual prediction data reduction approach for WSNs based on Kalman filter. *IET Communications*, *15*(18), 2285–2299. DOI: 10.1049/cmu2.12262

Yang, L., Wu, C., Zhang, D., & Su, J. (2017). Early-warning threshold extraction method of agricultural SCADA server based on clustering analysis. *Nongye Gongcheng Xuebao (Beijing)*, *33*(1), 293–299.

Zhang, X., Cao, Z., & Dong, W. (2020). Overview of edge computing in the agricultural internet of things: Key technologies, applications, challenges. *IEEE Access : Practical Innovations, Open Solutions*, *8*, 141748–141761. DOI: 10.1109/ACCESS.2020.3013005

. Zografos, A. (2014). Wireless Sensor-based Agricultural Monitoring System.

Chapter 8
Architecting the Insecure Future:
Integrating Generative AI and Edge AI Computing for Next-Gen Applications

Bishwo Prakash Pokharel
http://orcid.org/0000-0001-6516-2105
Sault College of Applied Arts and Technology, Canada

Devendra Chapagain
http://orcid.org/0009-0003-6548-7112
Birendra Multiple Campus, Nepal

Naresh Kshetri
http://orcid.org/0000-0002-3282-7331
Rochester Institute of Technology, USA

Muhammad Ali Nadeem
http://orcid.org/0009-0005-7566-7787
Sault College of Applied Arts and Technology, Canada

ABSTRACT

Generative Artificial Intelligence (GenAI) has emerged as a transformative technology, capable of creating novel data, designs, and solutions across diverse domains. Simultaneously, edge computing is redefining the computational landscape by enabling low-latency, energy-efficient, and context-aware intelligence closer to data sources. The convergence of these two paradigms offers unprecedented opportunities for developing next-generation applications in healthcare, smart cities, autonomous

DOI: 10.4018/979-8-3373-7340-9.ch008

systems, and the Internet of Things (IoT). This chapter explores the architectural foundation, design considerations, and implementation strategies for integrating generative models as the edge. It highlights the key challenges and outlines emerging frameworks and deployment strategies that balance performance, scalability, and sustainability. By architecting this integration (Generative AI and Edge AI), this chapter demonstrates how generative edge AI can unlock transformative applications, paving the way for intelligent, personalized, and resilient systems in an increasingly connected world.

1. INTRODUCTION

The rapid evolution of artificial intelligence (AI) has ushered in a new era of intelligent systems capable of perception, reasoning, and content generation across diverse application domains. Among these advancements, Generative Artificial Intelligence (GenAI) has emerged as a particularly transformative paradigm, enabling machines to generate text, images, audio, video, and systematic data that closely resemble human-created artifacts. Foundational models such as large language models (LLMs), generative adversarial networks (GANs), and diffusion models have demonstrated remarkable capabilities in learning complex data distributions and producing high-quality outputs with minimal supervision (Goodfellow et al., 2014; Brown et al., 2020; Bommasani et al., 2021).

Traditionally GenAI models have been developed, trained, and deployed within cloud-centric architectures, leveraging centralized computational resources and large-scale data repositories. While this paradigm offers scalability and ease of management, it introduces critical limitations related to latency, bandwidth consumption, data privacy, and system resilience - particularly for applications that demand real-time responsiveness or operate in connectivity-constrained environments (Zhou et al., 2019; Reuther et al., 2023). These constraints have become increasingly pronounced with the proliferation of data-intensive, context-aware applications such as autonomous vehicles, smart healthcare systems, industrial automation, and immersive media.

In parallel, edge computing has gained significant traction as a complementary paradigm that shifts computation closer to data sources, including sensors, mobile devices, and embedded systems. By enabling localized processing, Edge AI reduces end-to-end latency, minimizes reliance on cloud connectivity, and enhances privacy by keeping sensitive data on-device (Morabito & Jang, 2025; AL-Fuqaha et al., 2024). Edge intelligence has already demonstrated its value in domains such as smart cities, vehicular networks, and industrial IoT, where timely decision-making and operational continuity are paramount (Thapa & Mashyekhy, 2024; Lifelo et al., 2024).

The convergence of GenAI and Edge AI represents a critical inflection point in the evolution of next-generation intelligent systems. Deploying generative models at the edge enables real-time content generation, adaptive personalization, and autonomous decision-making without constant cloud dependence. For example, edge-resident generative models can support privacy-preserving healthcare diagnostics, context-aware smart home systems, and low-latency perception in autonomous platforms (Khamparia & Gupta, 2025, Caliste, 2025; Yan et al., 2024). Moreover, hybrid cloud-edge architectures allow systems to balance performance, scalability, and energy efficiency by dynamically partitioning training, inference, and orchestration tasks (Williams & Carter, 2024; Lee & Park, 2024).

Despite its promise, integrating GenAI into edge environments introduces a new class of technical, security, and ethical challenges. Generative models are computationally intensive, often exceeding the memory, processing, and energy constraints of edge devices, necessitating aggressive model compression, optimization, and hardware-aware design strategies (Navardi et al., 2025; Zhang et al., 2024). Additionally, the generative nature of these models creates unique vulnerabilities, including adversarial manipulation, model poisoning, hallucinations, and unauthorized model extraction - risks that are amplified in physically accessible and resource-constrained edge deployments (Rahman & Hasan, 2023; O'Neill & Sorensen, 2025).

Beyond technical constraints, system-level risks span the entire lifecycle of edge-deployed GenAI models. Secure provisioning, over-the-air updates, federated training across heterogeneous devices, and continuous behavioral monitoring remain open research problems (Kairouz et al., 2021; Deng et al., 2023; Kumar & Shastri, 2024). Furthermore, the localized generation of synthetic content raises critical ethical and regulatory concerns, including bias amplification, misinformation, accountability, and compliance with data protection regulations such as GDPR and HIPAA (Singh & Kapoor, 2024).

This chapter addresses these challenges by providing a systematic exploration of the architectural foundations, vulnerabilities, and defensive strategies associated with generative intelligence at the edge. Rather than focusing solely on the opportunities of edge-enabled GenAI, the chapter emphasizes a balanced and security-aware perspective - examining what can go wrong, why these risks emerge, and how resilient design principles can mitigate them. By integrating insights from distributed systems, AI security, and edge computing research, this chapter aims to guide researchers, engineers, product managers, and policymakers toward informed and responsible deployment of generative Edge AI systems.

In doing so, the chapter contributes to the growing disclosure of next-generation cloud-edge intelligence, outlining open research questions and future directions necessary to realize intelligent, personalized, and trustworthy systems in an increasingly connected world.

2. FOUNDATIONS OF GENERATIVE AI

Generative Artificial Intelligence (GenAI) constitutes a major paradigm shift in artificial intelligence by enabling systems to create new data instances that resemble real-world observations. Unlike traditional discriminative models that learn decision boundaries between predefined classes, generative models learn the joint probability distribution of input data and leverage this representation to synthesize novel outputs. This capability has positioned GenAI as a foundational technology for next-generation intelligent systems across creative, scientific, industrial, and interactive domains (Ardi & Isnayanti, 2025).

The rapid advancement of GenAI has been driven by progress in deep learning architectures, large-scale training strategies, and increased availability of data and computational resources. Initially confined to centralized cloud environments due to their intensive computational demands, generative models are now increasingly being adapted for decentralized and resource-constrained platforms. This transition is particularly relevant as emerging applications require real-time intelligence, contextual awareness, and localized decision-making - characteristics that are difficult to achieve using purely cloud-based architectures.

A solid understanding of generative model foundations is essential for evaluating both the opportunities and risks associated with deploying GenAI in edge environments. This section introduces the core generative architectures, highlights their dominant application areas, and reviews recent advances that are shaping the evolution of generative intelligence.

2.1 Key Generative AI Architectures

Modern Generative AI systems are built upon several dominant architectural paradigms, each offering distinct strengths, limitations, and deployment considerations.

2.1.1 Generative Adversarial Networks (GANs)

It represents one of the earliest breakthroughs in deep generative modeling. GANs employ a competitive training process between a generator network that produces synthetic samples and a discriminator network that attempts to distinguish generated data from real data. This adversarial dynamic enables GANs to produce highly realistic visual and audio outputs, making them widely used in image synthesis, video generation, and data augmentation tasks (Ardi & Isnayanti, 2025). However, GANs are known to suffer from training instability, model collapse, and sensitivity to adversarial manipulation - factors that complicate their deployment in constrained or security-sensitive environments.

2.1.2 Variational Autoencoders (VAEs)

It provides a probabilistic alternative to adversarial training by learning structured latent representations of data. VAEs encode inputs into a continuous latent space and generate new samples by decoding latent variables drawn from learned probability distributions. Their mathematically grounded frameworks support stable training and smooth interpolation, making VAEs suitable for anomaly detection, representation learning, and medical data synthesis (Wang et al., 2024). While their output quality may be less sharp than GANs or diffusion models, VAEs are often preferred in applications that require interpretability and robustness.

2.1.3 Transformer-Based Architectures

It has become the backbone of modern generative systems, particularly in natural language processing and multimodal learning. By leveraging self-attention mechanisms, transformers can model long-range dependencies in sequential data without recurrence, enabling efficient parallelization and scalability. This architectural innovation has enabled the development of large language models (LLMs) capable of generating coherent text, code, and multimodal outputs across diverse tasks (Vaswani et al., 2017). Despite their success, transformer-based models are computationally expensive, motivating ongoing research into sparsity, parameter sharing, and efficient attention mechanisms.

2.1.4 Diffusion Models

It represents the current state of the art in high-quality image and video generation. These models operate by gradually transforming random noise into structured data through an iterative denoising process. Diffusion-based approaches offer superior output diversity, stability, and controllability compared to GANs, and have become the dominant paradigm for visual content generation (Wang, He, & Peng, 2024). However, their iterative inference process introduces latency challenges, particularly in real-time or edge-based deployments.

2.2 Key Applications of Generative AI

The ability of GenAI to synthesize realistic and context-aware outputs has led to rapid adoption across a wide range of application domains.

2.2.1 Creative Content Generation

It is one of the most visible and mature application areas. Generative models are widely used for automated text writing, image synthesis, music composition, and video creation. These systems support creative professionals by accelerating design workflows and enabling interactive, personalized content generation (Ardi & Isnayanti, 2025). When integrated with user-facing devices, generative systems can adapt outputs dynamically based on user context and preferences.

2.2.2 Healthcare and Biomedical Research

It leverages GenAI for tasks such as medical image synthesis, clinical report generation, and data augmentation for rare diseases. Generative models can improve diagnostic accuracy by creating synthetic training data and simulating disease progression scenarios. Recent studies highlight the potential of generative systems to support privacy-preserving medical analysis, particularly when sensitive patient data must remain localized.

2.2.3 Engineering and Design Automation

It benefits from generative techniques that explore large design spaces under complex constraints. In architecture, product design, and manufacturing, generative models propose optimized structures, layouts, and configurations that would be difficult to derive manually. These capabilities support rapid prototyping and decision making in engineering workflows.

2.2.4 Interactive and Multimodal Systems

It integrates GenAI into conversational agents, intelligent assistants, and immersive environments. By combining language, vision, and audio generation, these systems enable natural human - computer interaction and adaptive personalization. Such applications increasingly demand low-latency inference and contextual awareness, motivating interest in decentralized and hybrid deployment models.

2.3 Recent Advances in Generative AI

Recent progress in Generative AI has been shaped by advances in model scale, efficiency, multimodality, and deployment flexibility.

2.3.1 Foundation Models and Large-Scale Pretraining

It has enabled generative systems to generalize across tasks with minimal task-specific fine-tuning. Models trained on massive diverse datasets exhibit emergent capabilities such as reasoning, transfer learning, and zero-shot generation, significantly reducing development overhead (Google AI, 2025). These properties have accelerated GenAI adoption across domains.

2.3.2 Multimodal Generative Learning

It extends generative capabilities beyond single data types by integrating text, vision, audio, and sensory inputs into unified representations. Recent models can generate synchronized outputs across modalities, enabling applications such as text-to-video synthesis, voice cloning, and multimodal assistants (Reuters, 2024). This convergence is central to immersive and context-aware intelligent systems.

2.3.3 Efficiency-Oriented Architectures

It has gained prominence as researchers seek to reduce the computational footprint of generative models. Techniques such as mixture-of-experts architectures, sparsity enforcement, and modular model design allow systems to activate only relevant model components during inference, improving scalability and energy efficiency (Shazeer et al., 2017). These advances are critical for enabling generative intelligence beyond centralized cloud platforms.

2.3.4 Hybrid and Adaptive Deployment Strategies

It increasingly combines centralized and decentralized resources to balance performance and cost. Generative workloads are dynamically partitioned across infrastructure based on latency requirements, resource availability, and energy constraints, laying the groundwork for future edge-enabled generative systems.

2.4 Analytical Literature Review and Comparative Analysis

To move beyond a descriptive overview of Generative AI, it is essential to critically analyze how different generative architectures perform under varying deployment conditions, particularly in edge environments. Existing research demonstrates that while generative models such as Large Language Models (LLMs), Generative Adversarial Networks (GANs), and diffusion models have achieved remarkable performance in centralized settings, their adaptation to edge environments introduces significant constraints and trade-offs. Table 1 presents a comparative analysis of key Generative AI approaches based on deployment models, optimization techniques, and inherent limitations.

Table 1. Comparative Analysis of Generative AI Architectures in Edge Contexts

Study	Model Type	Deployment	Optimization Techniques	Key Limitations
Brown et al. (2020)	LLM (Transformer)	Cloud	Large-scale distributed training	High latency, massive compute requirements, unsuitable for edge.
Bommasani et al. (2021)	Foundation Models	Cloud-centric	Transfer learning, fine-tuning	Lack of efficiency for edge deployment, high energy consumption.
Goodfellow et al. (2014)	GAN	Cloud / Partial Edge	Adversarial training	Training instability, high resource demand, limited edge feasibility.
Zhang et al. (2024)	Diffusion Models	Edge-optimized / Hybrid	Model compression, lightweight architectures	Trade-off between quality and inference speed.
Navardi et al. (2025)	GenAI at Edge (Survey)	Edge / Hybrid	Quantization, pruning, distillation	Reduced accuracy, hardware dependency.
Deng et al. (2023)	Federated Generative Models	Edge (Distributed)	Federated learning, distributed optimization	Communication overhead, heterogeneity issues.
Lee & Park (2024)	Diffusion (Hybrid Inference)	Edge-Cloud Hybrid	Split inference, collaborative processing	Dependency on network conditions, synchronization latency.
Li et al. (2023)	Decentralized Generative Models	Edge	Privacy-enhanced decentralized learning	Model convergence challenges, limited scalability.

A critical examination of the literature illustrated in Table 1 reveals that most Generative AI models are inherently designed for cloud-centric environments, where abundant computational resources, scalable infrastructure, and high-bandwidth connectivity are readily available. Foundational models such as large-scale transformers demonstrate exceptional performance but remain impractical for direct deployment on edge devices due to their massive parameter sizes and computational demands (Brown et al., 2020; Bommasani et al., 2021). While optimization strategies such as model compression, pruning, and quantization have been proposed to address these challenges, they often introduce trade-offs between model accuracy and efficiency (Navardi et al., 2025).

Similarly, architectures such as GANs and diffusion models face significant constraints when adapted to edge environments. GANs suffer from instability during training and require continuous computational feedback loops, making them unsuitable for resource-constrained devices (Goodfellow et al., 2014). Diffusion models, although more stable and capable of high-quality generation, introduce latency challenges due to their iterative sampling processes, necessitating lightweight adaptations for real-time edge deployment (Zhang et al., 2024). Hybrid approaches, such as split inference and collaborative edge-cloud architectures, partially mitigate these limitations but introduce new dependencies on network reliability and synchronization (Lee & Park, 2024).

From a system perspective, distributed and federated approaches aim to address privacy concerns and decentralization requirements by enabling training and inference across multiple edge devices. However, these methods introduce challenges related to communication overhead, device heterogeneity, and convergence instability (Deng et al., 2023; Li et al., 2023). These limitations highlight a fundamental gap between the theoretical capabilities of Generative AI and its practical deployment in edge environments.

Three major research gaps emerge from this analysis. First, scalability remains a critical issue, as current approaches struggle to maintain performance across large-scale, heterogeneous edge networks. Second, energy efficiency is insufficiently addressed, with limited work focusing on optimizing generative models for low-power environments. Third, security and robustness challenges persist, particularly in protecting edge-deployed models against adversarial attacks, model extraction, and data leakage. While existing studies acknowledge these challenges, there is a lack of integrated frameworks that simultaneously address performance, security, and scalability in generative Edge AI systems.

3. EDGE AI COMPUTING

Edge Artificial Intelligence (Edge AI) refers to the deployment and execution of artificial intelligence models directly on local devices such as sensors, mobile phones, embedded systems, industrial machines, and autonomous vehicles, rather than relying entirely on centralized cloud infrastructures. In this paradigm, data processing and inference occur close to the data source, allowing intelligent systems to respond to events in real-time without constant communication with remote servers. This architectural shift represents an important evolution in distributed computing, where computational capabilities are extended to the network edge to support latency-sensitive and privacy-critical applications (Zhou et al., 2019; Reuther et al., 2023).

The increasing volume of data generated by Internet of Things (IoT) devices, autonomous systems, and smart infrastructure has accelerated the adoption of Edge AI. Traditional cloud-based approaches require large volumes of sensor or use-generated data to be transmitted to centralized servers for processing, which introduces latency, bandwidth consumption, and potential privacy risks. Edge AI mitigates these issues by performing inference locally, thereby reducing the need for continuous data transmission while maintaining operational responsiveness (Morabito & Jand, 2025).

Edge intelligence has become particularly important in applications that demand real-time decision-making, including autonomous vehicles, industrial robotics, healthcare monitoring systems, and smart city infrastructure. In these environments, delays caused by network communication can compromise system performance or safety. By enabling localized computation and rapid feedback, Edge AI allows intelligent systems to operate reliably even in environments with limited connectivity or strict performance constraints (Thapa & Mashayekhy, 2024); Yan et al., 2024).

Despite these advantages, deploying AI at the edge introduces a unique set of engineering and operational challenges. Edge devices typically possess significantly fewer computational resources than cloud data centers, including limited memory, storage capacity, and processing power. Additionally, these devices are often deployed in distributed and physically accessible environments, which increases exposure to security threats such as tampering or unauthorized access. As a result, effective Edge AI deployment requires careful consideration of system architecture, model optimization, and lifecycle management strategies (Navardi et al., 2025; Xu et al., 2024).

3.1 Benefits of Edge AI

Edge AI provides several significant advantages over traditional cloud centric AI deployments, particularly for applications requiring real-time responsiveness, data privacy, and distributed intelligence.

One of the most prominent benefits is reduced latency and real-time processing capability. By executing AI models directly on local devices, edge systems eliminate the need for round-trip communication with remote servers. This enables near-instantaneous responses, which are essential for applications such as autonomous vehicles, augmented and virtual reality systems, and industrial automation. In such environments, even minor delays can significantly impact performance and safety, making edge-based inference critical for reliable operation (Yan et al., 2024; Thapa & Mashayekhy, 2024).

Another important advantage is reduced network bandwidth usage and operational costs. Cloud-based AI systems require continuous transmission of large datasets - such as video streams, sensor data, or high frequency telemetry to centralized servers for processing. Edge AI reduces this dependency by processing data locally and transmitting only essential results or summarized insights to the cloud. This approach significantly decreases network congestion and lowers infrastructure costs associated with large-scale data transmission (Lifelo et al., 2024).

Edge AI also enhances data privacy and security by allowing sensitive information to remain on the device where it is generated. This is particularly important in sectors such as healthcare, finance, and personal computing, where regulatory frameworks require strict protection of user data. By minimizing external data transfers, edge processing reduces the risk of exposure during transmission and supports compliance with privacy regulations (Khamparia & Gupta, 2025).

In addition, edge intelligence enables context-aware personalization and adaptive system behavior. Because edge devices can directly access local sensors and user interactions, AI models can tailor their outputs to specific environmental conditions or user references. For example, generative models embedded in smart home systems can adapt responses based on device usage patterns or environmental signals, providing more personalized and efficient interactions (Caliste, 2025).

Finally, Edge AI contributes to system resilience and offline functionality. Many real-world environments - such as remote industrial sites, rural regions, or disaster zones may experience unreliable or intermittent connectivity. Edge-based systems can continue operating independently of network availability, ensuring uninterrupted functionality and improving system robustness (Morabito & Jang, 2025).

3.2 Challenges and Limitations

Although Edge AI offers numerous advantages, deploying AI models in distributed edge environments presents several technical and operational challenges.

One of the most significant limitations involves hardware constraints. Edge devices typically possess limited computational capacity, memory, and storage compared to centralized cloud infrastructures. Large generative models and deep neural networks often require billions of parameters and significant processing power, making them difficult to execute efficiently on constrained devices. As a result, developers must rely on model comparison techniques such as pruning, quantization, and knowledge distillation to reduce model size while maintaining acceptable performance (Navardi et al., 2025).

Another challenge concerns model maintenance and update management. In large-scale deployments, organizations may operate thousands or even millions of distributed edge devices. Ensuring that each device runs the correct model version, receives security patches, and maintains consistent performance can be complex. Distributed lifecycle management mechanisms, including over-the-air updates and centralized orchestration platforms, are necessary to maintain reliability and operational efficiency across device fleets (Kumar & Shastri, 2024).

Energy consumption is also a critical consideration. Running AI inference locally requires significant computational effort, which can drain battery-powered devices quickly. Applications involving high-resolution video processing, real-time generative modeling, or continuous sensor analysis may significantly increase energy demand. Efficient model design and hardware acceleration technologies are therefore essential to maintain acceptable power consumption levels (Reuther et al., 2023).

Security concerns present another major limitation of Edge AI systems. While local data processing improves privacy, edge devices themselves can become targets for cyberattacks. Attackers may attempt to extract deployed models, manipulate model behavior, or inject malicious inputs that compromise system functionality. Protecting AI models in distributed environments requires advanced security mechanisms such as trusted execution environments, encrypted model storage, and secure communication protocols (Xu et al., 2024; Rahman & Hasan, 2023).

Finally, integrating AI models into edge ecosystems introduces architectural complexity. Developers must carefully design distributed systems that balance workload distribution between edge and cloud resources while maintaining performance, reliability, and security. Hybrid architectures that combine edge inference with cloud-based orchestration are increasingly adopted to address these challenges, but they require sophisticated coordination mechanisms and infrastructure management strategies (Rausch et al., 2024; Williams & Carter, 2024).

4. MOTIVATIONS FOR INTEGRATING GENERATIVE AI AND EDGE AI

The convergence of Generative Artificial Intelligence (GenAI) and Edge AI computing is driven by the growing demand for intelligent systems that operate efficiently in real-time, distributed, and privacy-sensitive environments. While GenAI provides powerful capabilities for generating content, predictions, and simulations, traditional deployments rely heavily on centralized cloud infrastructure. This approach often introduces latency, bandwidth consumption, and privacy concerns, which can limit the effectiveness of AI-driven applications in dynamic or resource-constrained environments (Reuther et al., 2023).

Edge computing addresses many of these limitations by moving computational processes closer to the source of data generation. When generative models are deployed at or near edge devices, systems can respond more quickly to environmental signals, reduce dependency on remote infrastructure, and enable localized intelligence. As a result, integrating GenAI with edge computing creates opportunities for a new generation of distributed AI systems capable of delivering faster, more personalized, and more resilient services across multiple domains (Morabito & Jang, 2025).

Several key motivations explain why this integration is becoming increasingly important. These include the need for real-time responsiveness, efficient use of network bandwidth, improved privacy protection, and the ability to deliver context aware and robust functionality in diverse environments.

4.1 Real-Time Responsiveness

One of the most significant motivations for integrating GenAI with Edge AI is the need for low latency decision making and real-time system responsiveness. Many modern intelligent systems operate in environments where delays caused by cloud communication can significantly affect performance or safety. By processing data and generating outputs locally, edge-enabled generative systems can respond almost instantaneously to environmental changes.

Autonomous vehicles provide a clear example of this requirement. These systems rely on continuous analysis of sensor data to generate predictions, navigation strategies, and safety responses. Deploying generative models at the edge allows vehicles to process information and simulate potential outcomes in real-time without relying on remote servers. This capability improves safety and operational reliability, particularly in high speed or unpredictable driving conditions (Thapa & Mashayekhy, 2024; Yan et al., 2024).

Similarly, industrial robotics and manufacturing environments benefit from localized generative intelligence. Edge-based generative models can simulate operational scenarios, detect anomalies, and generate adaptive control strategies without waiting for cloud responses. This enables more efficient automation and improves system resilience during network disruptions or connectivity limitations (Williams & Carter, 2024).

Emerging immersive technologies such as augmented reality (AR) and virtual reality (VR) also require extremely low latency to provide seamless user experiences. Generative models running on edge devices can dynamically produce visual or contextual content tailored to the user's environment, eliminating delays that would otherwise degrade interaction quality (Zhang et al., 2024).

4.2 Conserving Network Bandwidth

Another major driver of generative edge intelligence is the need to optimize bandwidth usage and reduce network overhead. Modern applications generate massive volumes of data through sensors, cameras, and connected devices. Transmitting this raw data continuously to cloud infrastructure can overwhelm networks and significantly increase operational costs.

By deploying generative models at the edge, systems can analyze the process data locally, transmitting only essential insights or aggregated results to centralized infrastructure. This approach reduces network congestion and improves scalability, particularly in environments with thousands or millions of connected devices (Al-Fuqaha et al., 2024).

Smart city infrastructures illustrate the importance of bandwidth efficiency. Urban systems rely on continuous data streams from traffic cameras, environmental sensors, and public safety devices. Edge-based generative models can analyze these streams locally to generative predictions and recommendations, allowing city management systems to respond to changing conditions without transmitting large datasets across networks (Lifelo et al., 2024).

Similarly, industrial Internet of Things (IoT) environments generate high-frequency sensor data that must be analyzed quickly to maintain operational efficiency. Local generative processing reduces communication overhead while enabling real-time predictive analytics and operational optimization (Reuther et al., 2023).

4.3 Enhancing Data Privacy and Security

Privacy concerns represent another critical motivation for integrating generative models with edge computing. Many AI applications rely on sensitive information, including personal communications, health records, financial transactions, and video surveillance data. Transmitting such information to centralized servers raises concerns about unauthorized access, data breaches, and regulatory compliance.

Edge computing allows sensitive data to remain on the device where it is generated, significantly reducing exposure during transmission. Generative models can analyze and generate insights from local datasets without transferring raw information to external systems, thereby improving compliance with privacy regulations and organizational security policies (Khamparia & Gupta, 2025).

Healthcare systems demonstrate the value of privacy preserving edge intelligence. Wearable devices, diagnostic equipment, and patient monitoring systems generate highly sensitive medical data that must be protected under strict regulatory frameworks. Edge-based generative models can analyze patient data locally to generate predictive insights or diagnostic suggestions while maintaining patient confidentiality (Morabito & Jang, 2025).

However, while local processing improves privacy, it also introduces new security considerations. Edge devices are often physically accessible and may be vulnerable to tampering or unauthorized access. Protecting generative models and sensitive data in these environments requires advanced security mechanisms such as trusted execution environments and secure model storage (Xu et al., 2024).

4.4 Enabling Robust and Personalized Functionality

A further motivation for integrating GenAI with Edge AI is the ability to provide highly personalized and context-aware services. Edge devices have direct access to local data sources such as sensors, user interactions, and environmental signals. Generative models operating in these environments can adapt their outputs to specific contexts, improving user experience and system performance.

For example, smart home systems equipped with edge-based generative models can analyze household behavior patterns and environmental data to generate personalized automation strategies. These systems can dynamically adjust lighting, energy usage, or appliance behavior based on user preferences and environmental conditions, providing more efficient and customized services (Caliste, 2025).

Edge-based generative systems also improve operational robustness by supporting offline functionality. Many environments - including remote locations, industrial facilities, and disaster zones may experience intermittent connectivity. Generative models deployed at the edge can continue operating independently of cloud infrastructure, ensuring uninterrupted service and maintaining system reliability (Reuther et al., 2023).

This ability to combine localized intelligence with generative capabilities represents a key step toward fully autonomous and adaptive digital ecosystems. By enabling systems to learn from and respond to their immediate environment, generative edge intelligence supports more resilient and user-centric technological infrastructures.

5. ARCHITECTURES FOR GENERATIVE EDGE AI INTEGRATION

The architectural design of systems that combine Generative AI with Edge Computing is fundamental to realizing the promises of low-latency intelligence, privacy preservation, and autonomous operation. Unlike traditional cloud-centric AI deployments, generative Edge AI requires careful consideration of where models are stored, how inference is executed, how training or fine-tuning occurs, and how security is maintained across distributed infrastructure. This section presents a comprehensive architectural framework for generative Edge AI integration, examining deployment patterns, workload partitioning strategies, lifecycle management, and security-by-design principles.

5.1 Edge vs Cloud Deployment Patterns

The deployment of Generative AI models follows three primary architectural paradigms, each offering distinct trade-offs between latency, privacy, computational capability, and operational complexity (Zhou et al., 2019; Reuther et al., 2023). Understanding these patterns is essential for architects designing next-generation intelligent systems.

5.1.1 Cloud-Centric Deployment

In the traditional cloud-centric pattern, generative models reside entirely within centralized data centers. Edge devices function purely as data collection points and output renderers, streaming raw sensor data to cloud infrastructure and receiving generated content in return. This architecture has dominated early GenAI deployments due to its simplicity and access to virtually unlimited computational resources (Bommasani et al., 2021).

Characteristics:

- Full sized generative models (billions of parameters) execute on GPU/TPU clusters.
- Raw data continuously transmitted from edge to cloud
- Generated content streamed back to edge devices
- Centralized model management and updates

Advantages:

- Supports largest, most capable generative models
- Simplifies model versioning and security patching
- Enables centralized data aggregation for model improvement
- Reduces edge device hardware requirements

Limitations:

- High latency (typically 100-500ms), unsuitable for real-time applications
- Bandwidth intensive, particularly for video and high-frequency sensor data
- Privacy risks from transmitting sensitive data off-device
- Single points of failure and cloud dependency
- Operational costs scale with data volume (Morabito & Jang, 2025)

This pattern remains appropriate for non-real-time applications such as content creation workflows, batch processing, and applications where data sensitivity is low. However, for the next-generation applications discussed in this chapter, cloud-centric deployment alone is increasingly inadequate.

5.1.2 Edge-Only Deployment

At the opposite extreme, edge-only deployment places compressed generative models directly on end devices, enabling fully local inference without any cloud dependency. This pattern has gained traction as edge hardware capabilities have improved and model compression techniques have matured (Navardi et al., 2025).

Characteristics:

- Compressed generative models (millions to hundreds of millions of parameters)
- All inference executes locally on edge hardware
- No cloud connectivity required for normal operation
- Models delivered via secure provisioning during manufacturing or initial setup

Advantages:

- Minimal latency (<10ms), enabling real-time responsiveness
- Maximum privacy preservation (data never leaves the device)
- Offline functionality in connectivity-constrained environments
- Reduced bandwidth and cloud infrastructure costs
- Enhanced resilience and autonomy (Thapa & Mashayekhy, 2024).

Limitations:

- Severe computational constraints limit model complexity
- Aggressive compression may degrade output quality
- Complex model update management across distributed devices
- Physical security vulnerabilities from device tampering
- Limited ability to learn from new data without cloud coordination (Zhang et al., 2024)

Edge-only deployment is suitable for applications with well-defined, stable requirements where model updates are infrequent and real-time performance is paramount. Examples include basic generative features in consumer devices, offline-capable assistants, and safety-critical functions in autonomous systems.

5.1.3 Hybrid Cloud-Edge Deployment

Hybrid architectures represented in Figure 1 is optimal balance for most generative Edge AI applications, partitioning workloads across infrastructure layers based on application requirements, resource availability, and contextual factors (Williams & Carter, 2024; Rausch et al., 2024).

Characteristics:

- Multiple model variants across cloud and edge tiers
- Dynamic workload orchestration based on context
- Selective data transmission for privacy preservation
- Coordinated training and update mechanisms

Advantages:

- Balances latency, privacy, and computational capability
- Enables graceful degradation during connectivity loss
- Supports continuous model improvement through federated learning
- Optimizes bandwidth and cloud costs
- Provides fallback options for complex generation tasks

Limitations:

- Increased architectural complexity
- Requires sophisticated orchestration mechanisms
- Potential synchronization challenges
- Must manage security across heterogeneous infrastructure

Figure 1. Comparative Deployment Architectures for Generative Edge AI

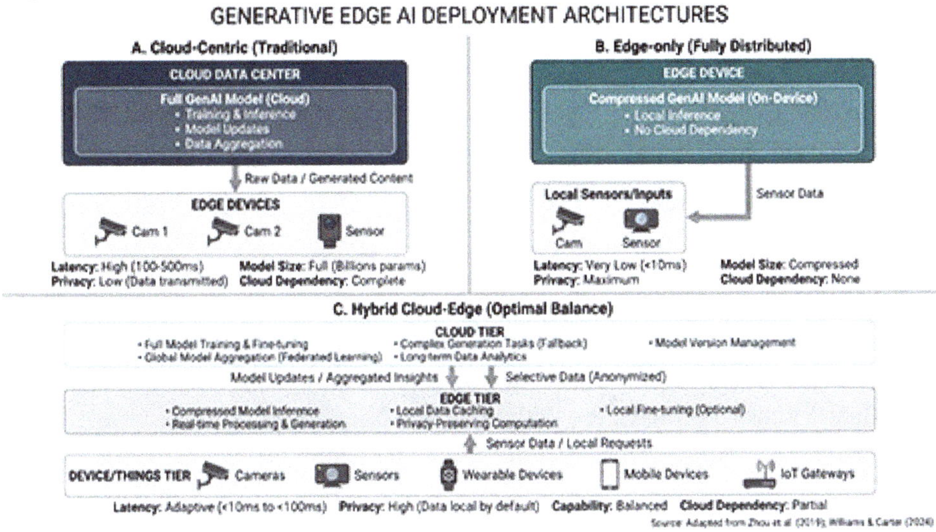

5.2 Hybrid Deployment Strategies

Hybrid cloud-edge architectures require sophisticated strategies for partitioning generative workloads across infrastructure layers. Four primary approaches have emerged, each suited to different application requirements and constraints (Lee & Park, 2024; Zhang et al., 2024).

5.2.1 Vertical Partitioning (Layer-wise Splitting)

Vertical partitioning distributes different layers of a deep generative model across cloud and edge infrastructure. Early layers (closer to input) execute on edge devices, extracting features and producing intermediate representations. Later, more computationally intensive layers execute in the cloud when connectivity permits, generating the final output.

Architecture Overview:

- Edge device executes initial layers (feature extraction, encoding)
- Intermediate representations transmitted to cloud (compressed, privacy-preserving)
- Cloud executes deeper layers (decoding, generation)
- Final output returned to edge or consumed directly

Mathematical Formulation:

For a generative model G composed of Layers $L_1, L_2, \ldots, L_n$, vertical partitioning selects a split point k such that:

- Edge executes: $L_1, L_2, \ldots, L_k$
- Cloud executes: $L_{k+1}, \ldots, L_n$
- Output: $G(X) = L_n(\ldots L_{k+1}(L_k(\ldots L_1(x) \ldots))\ldots)$

Advantages:

- Reduces edge computational requirements
- Intermediate representations may preserve privacy better than raw data
- Bandwidth requirement lower than transmitting raw data
- Enables use of larger models than edge-only deployment

Limitations:

- Sensitive to network variability
- Split point optimization is non-trivial
- Intermediate representations may still leak information (Li et al., 2023)

5.2.2 Horizontal Partitioning (Distributed Inference)

Horizontal partitioning distributes generative inference across multiple edge devices working collaboratively. This approach is particularly valuable in IoT environments where multiple devices are co-located and can communicate locally.

Architecture Approaches:

Model Parallelism: Different parts of the same generative model execute on different devices. For example, in a diffusion model, different devices could handle different denoising steps or different regions of the generated image.

Ensemble Methods: Multiple devices host independent generative models (potentially with different architectures or training data), and their outputs are combined through voting, averaging, or more sophisticated fusion mechanisms.

Data Parallelism: The same model runs on multiple devices with different input data partitions, with results aggregated centrally.

Advantages:

- Leverages collective computational resources
- Provides redundancy and fault tolerance
- Enables larger effective model capacity

- Supports collaborative intelligence scenarios

Limitations:

- Synchronization overhead
- Communication latency between devices
- Complex coordination mechanisms required
- Potential security vulnerabilities from device-to-device communication

5.2.3 Adaptive Offloading

Adaptive offloading represents the most dynamic approach illustrated in Figure 2, where systems continuously decide whether to execute inference locally or offload to cloud infrastructure based on real-time contextual factors (Zhang et al., 2024).

Decision Factors:

- Network conditions (bandwidth, latency, reliability)
- Device status (battery level, computational load, temperature)
- Task characteristics (complexity, criticality, privacy sensitivity)
- Time of day or usage patterns
- Cloud availability and cost

Figure 2. Offloading Decision Framework

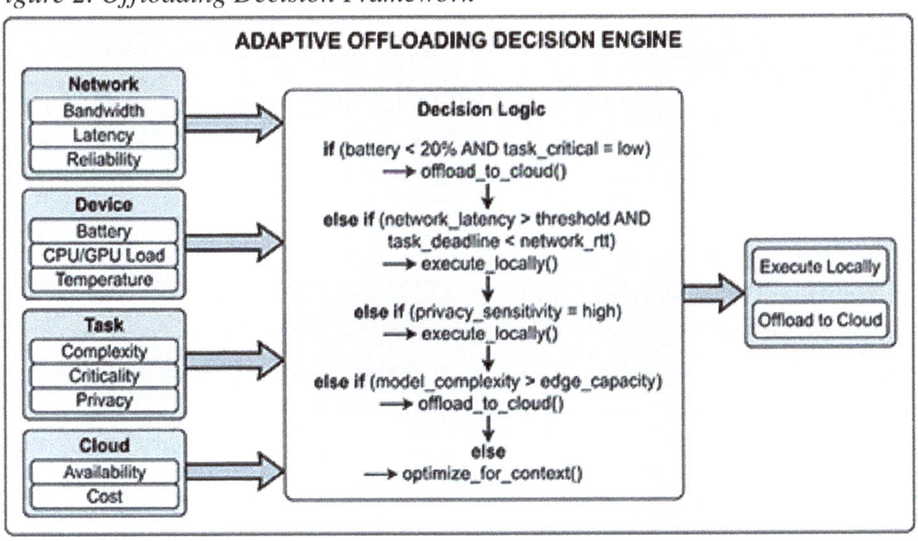

Advantages:

- Optimize for multiple objectives simultaneously
- Adapts to changing environmental conditions
- Maximizes user experience and system efficiency
- Enables graceful degradation during network issues

Limitations:

- Require sophisticated monitoring and prediction
- Decision overhead may be non-trivial
- May introduce unpredictable behavior
- Testing complexity increases significantly

5.2.4 Tiered Inference

Table 2 represents the Tier inference, which maintains multiple model variants across the infrastructure hierarchy, selecting the appropriate model for each request based on requirements and context (Lee & Park, 2024).

Table 2: Tier Structure

Tier	Hardware	Model Size	Latency	Capability	Update Frequency
Tier 0	Microcontroller	<10MB	<1ms	Basic generation	Rare
Tier 1	Mobile/Edge device	10-100MB	1-10ms	Standard generation	Periodic
Tier 2	Edge gateway/server	100MB-1GB	10-50ms	Advanced generation	Frequent
Tier 3	Cloud	>1GB	50-500ms	Full capability	Continuous

Operational Logic:

1. Request arrives at edge device
2. System evaluates request complexity and requirements
3. If Tier 0/1 model can satisfy request → execute locally
4. If request exceeds local capability → escalate to Tier 2 (if available)
5. For most complex requests or model updates → involve Tier 3 cloud

Advantages:

- Matches computational resources to task requirements
- Provides clear upgrade paths as hardware improves

- Supports graceful degradation (fallback to lower tiers)
- Simplifies capacity planning

Limitations:

- Modal consistency across tiers requires careful management
- Storage overhead for multiple model variants
- Tier transition logic must be carefully designed

5.3 Lifecycle Management and Security Considerations

Deploying Generative AI at scale across distributed edge infrastructure requires robust lifecycle management and security-by-design principles. Unlike cloud deployments where models operate in controlled environments, edge-deployed models face unique operational and security challenges throughout their lifecycle (Kumar & Shastri, 2024; Xu et al., 2024).

5.3.1 Model Lifecycle Management

1. **Training and Development:** Base generative models are trained in a cloud environment using large datasets. For edge deployment, models may be trained with privacy-preserving techniques such as differential privacy from the outset (Kairouz et al., 2021).
2. **Model Optimization:** Trained models undergo compression through pruning, quantization, and knowledge distillation to meet edge device constraints (Navardi et al., 2025). This phase may involve hardware-aware optimization for target deployment platforms.
3. **Packaging and Signing:** Optimized models are packaged with metadata (version, capabilities, hardware requirements) and cryptographically signed to ensure integrity and authenticity. This prevents tampering during distribution.
4. **Deployment (Over-the-Air):** Models are distributed to edge devices through secure OTA update mechanisms. Deployment strategies include:
    a. **Push-based:** Cloud initiates updates to device fleets
    b. **Pull-based:** Devices check for updates periodically
    c. **Staged rollout:** Gradual deployment to detect issues early
    d. **A/B testing:** Different model versions to device subsets
5. **Monitoring and Telemetry:** Deployed models continuously monitored for performance metrics, output quality, and security anomalies. Telemetry data (privacy-preserving) collected for improvement.

6. **Performance Evaluation:** Regular assessment of model accuracy, latency, resource consumption, and user satisfaction. Deviations trigger alerts or automatic rollback.
7. **Updates and Patching:** Security patches, bug fixes, and model improvements delivered through OTA mechanisms. Critical updates may be fixed for safety-related systems.
8. **Retirement and Versioning:** Models eventually retire as newer versions deploy. Clean removal processes ensure no residual data remains on devices.

We can see the detailed representation of Generative Edge AI Lifecycle Management in Figure 3.

Figure 3. Generative Edge AI Lifecycle Management

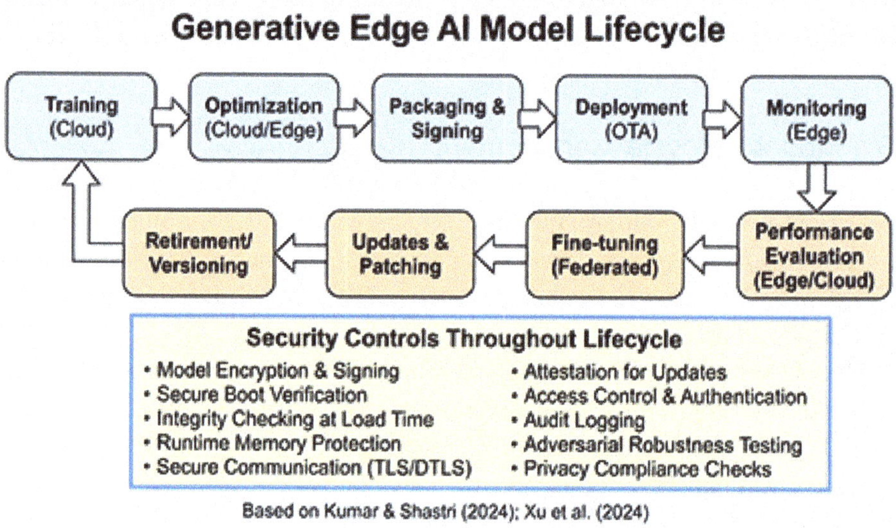

5.3.2 Security Architecture for Generative Edge AI

The deployment of Generative AI models in edge environments introduces a unique and expanded attack surface compared to traditional cloud-based AI systems. Edge devices are often physically accessible, resource-constrained, and deployed in uncontrolled environments, making them attractive targets for adversaries (Xu et al. 2024). Furthermore, the generative nature of these models creates specific vulnerabilities, including model extraction, adversarial manipulation, and the generation of harmful or misleading content (Rahman & Hasan, 2023). A comprehensive security architecture must address threats across the entire stack - from physical hardware to application logic - through layered defenses designed for the constraints and realities of edge deployment.

Threat Landscape for Generative Edge AI

Understanding the threat landscape is the foundation for designing effective security architectures. Edge-deployed generative models face several categories of attacks. Threat vector and its mitigation strategies with its descriptions are represented in Table 3.

Table 3. Threat Landscape and Threat-Specific Mitigations for Generative Edge AI

Threat Vector	Description	Mitigation Strategies
Model Extraction	Adversary extracts model through repeated queries or physical memory access	● TEE protection ● Rate limiting ● Model obfuscation
Adversarial Attacks	Crafted inputs cause incorrect/malicious outputs	● Adversarial training ● Input sanitization ● Detection networks
Data Poisoning	Compromised devices inject malicious updates in FL	● Robust aggregation ● Anomaly detection
Hallucination Exploitation	Model generates false/harmful content	● Confidence scoring ● Output validation ● Human-in-the-loop
Physical Tempering	Direct device access for model theft or manipulation	● Tamper-proof hardware ● Secure boot ● Intrusion detection
Side-Channel Attacks	Analysis of power/timing to extract model info	● Constant-time ops ● Noise injection

Layered Security Architecture

Effective security requires defense in depth, with multiple protective layers compensating for the limitations of any single control.

Figure 4. Security Architecture for Generative Edge AI

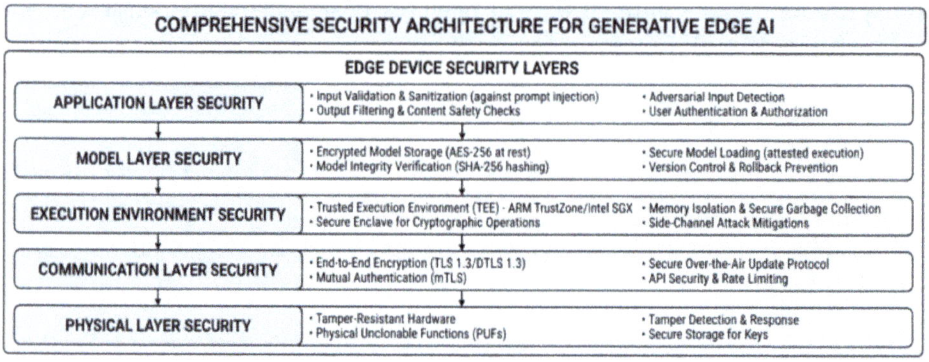

We can see in Figure 4 that security for generative Edge AI requires a holistic, layered approach that addresses threats from physical hardware to application logic. No single control is sufficient; defense in depth ensures that failure of one layer does not compromise the entire system. As Edge AI systems become more prevalent and capable, security architectures must evolve to address emerging threats while remaining practical within the constraints of edge devices. Organizations deploying Generative AI at the edge should adopt a security-by-design philosophy, integrating these protections throughout the development lifecycle rather than as afterthoughts.

5.3.3 Privacy-Preserving Architectures

Privacy considerations are paramount in generative Edge AI, as these systems often process sensitive personal data. Several architectural approaches enhance privacy protection (Khamparia & Gupta, 2025; Li et al., 2023).

Federated Learning for Generative Models:

Federated learning enables model improvement without centralized data collection. Edge devices train on local data and share only model updates (gradients) with the cloud, which aggregates them into an improved global model (Kairouz et al., 2021; Deng et al., 2023).

Key Components:

- Local training on edge devices using private data
- Secure aggregation of model updates (masking, differential privacy)
- Global model distribution to participating devices
- Optional personalization layers for device-specific adaption

Differential Privacy:

Adding calibrated noise to model outputs or training gradients prevents inference of individual training examples. This is particularly important for generative models that might otherwise memorize and reproduce sensitive training data.

On-Device Processing:

The most straightforward privacy protection: keeping data on-device whenever possible. Edge architectures should be designed with a "privacy by default" approach, where data only leaves the device when absolutely necessary and with explicit user consent.

5.4 Case Study: Applying Generative Edge AI Deployment Architecture in Smart City Video Analytics

5.4.1 Use Case Overview

A Generative Edge AI deployment architecture can be effectively applied in smart city environments to enable real-time video analytics for traffic management, public safety, and urban monitoring. Instead of relying solely on centralized cloud systems, this approach distributes intelligence across edge devices and cloud infrastructure, enabling faster, more efficient, and privacy-preserving operations.

5.4.2 Architecture Application

In this deployment model, the architecture operates across three coordinated layers:

- **Edge Layer (On-Device Intelligence):** Smart cameras and edge gateways are equipped with lightweight Generative AI models capable of performing real-time interference. These models process live video streams locally to detect objects, identify anomalies, and generate contextual summaries (e.g., incident descriptions or predictive alerts).
- **Edge-Cloud Interface Layer:** Instead of transmitting raw video data, the edge devices send compressed representations, metadata, or generated insights (such as anomaly flags or scene summaries) to the cloud. This significantly reduces bandwidth usage while maintaining essential information flow.
- **Cloud Layer (Centralized Intelligence):** The cloud hosts more complex generative models and analytics engines for deeper processing, long-term storage, and system-side optimization. It also manages model updates, or-

chestration, and global learning, which are periodically synchronized with edge devices.

This layered architecture enables efficient workload distribution and aligns with hybrid AI deployment strategies.

5.4.3 Model Deployment Strategy:

The Generative Edge AI system integrates multiple optimized models:

- **Lightweight generative models** (e.g., compressed diffusion or GAN-based models) deployed at the edge for real-time content generation and anomaly prediction.
- **Computer vision models** for object detection and tracking
- **Federated Learning mechanisms** to update models collaboratively across distributed edge nodes without sharing raw data.

Model optimization techniques such as quantization, pruning, and knowledge distillation are applied to ensure efficient execution on resource-constrained devices.

5.4.4 Operational Workflow

The system functions through the following workflow:

1. **Data Capture:** Edge devices continuously capture video streams from urban environments
2. **Local Processing:** Generative AI models analyze and interpret data in real-time
3. **Insight Generation:** The system generates summaries, anomaly alerts, or predictive insights locally
4. **Selective Transmission:** Only relevant outputs (not raw data) are transmitted to the cloud
5. **Cloud Enhancement:** The cloud performs deeper analytics and sends updates back to edge devices

This workflow ensures low-latency decision making while optimizing network and computational resources.

5.4.5 Performance Outcomes

Applying this architecture results in measurable improvements:

- **Reduced latency:** Real-time processing at the edge minimizes response delays for critical events.
- **Bandwidth optimization:** Transmission of summarized insights instead of raw video significantly lowers network load.
- **Enhanced privacy:** Sensitive data remains on-device, reducing exposure risks
- **Improved scalability:** Distributed processing supports large-scale deployments across urban environments.

5.4.6 Implementation Challenges

Despite its effectiveness, deploying this architecture introduces several challenges:

- **Resource limitations:** Edge devices may struggle with complex generative models
- **Security risks:** Physically accessible devices are vulnerable to tampering and adversarial attacks.
- **Model synchronization:** Maintaining consistency between edge and cloud models is complex.
- **System orchestration:** Managing large-scale distributed deployments requires robust lifecycle management frameworks.

5.5. Scalability, Interoperability, and Standards in Generative Edge AI

The large-scale deployment of Generative Edge AI systems introduces critical challenges related to scalability, interoperability, and standardization. As these systems operate across diverse devices, platforms, and networks, ensuring seamless integration and consistent performance becomes a key requirement for real-world adoption.

5.5.1 Scalability Challenges in Edge AI Deployment

Scalability in Generative Edge AI involves managing thousands to millions of distributed edge devices while maintaining performance, reliability, and security. Unlike centralized cloud systems, edge environments require decentralized coordination, which increases operational complexity.

Key scalability challenges include:

- **Distributed model management:** Updating and synchronizing generative models across numerous devices.
- **Resource variability:** Handling heterogeneous hardware with different compute, memory, and energy constraints.
- **Network limitations:** Ensuring consistent performance under varying connectivity conditions.
- **Lifecycle Management:** Supporting continuous deployment, monitoring, and updates at scale.

These constraints necessitate efficient orchestration and automation mechanisms to ensure consistent system behavior across large deployments.

5.5.2 Interoperability Challenges

Generative Edge AI systems must operate across a wide range of platforms, including IoT devices, mobile systems, gateways, and cloud environments. However, heterogeneity in hardware, software frameworks, and communication protocols creates significant interoperability barriers.

Major interoperability issues include:

- Incompatible hardware architectures (e.g., CPUs, GPUs, NPUs, microcontrollers)
- Diverse AI frameworks (e.g., TensorFlow Lite, PyTorch Mobile, ONNX)
- Fragmented communication protocols across edge and cloud systems
- Lack of unified data formats and interfaces

These challenges complicate integration, increase development overhead, and limit portability of generative models across platforms.

5.5.3 Standards and Orchestration Frameworks

To address interoperability and scalability issues, the adoption of standardized interfaces and orchestration frameworks is essential. Standards enable consistent communication, model deployment, and system integration across heterogeneous environments.

Key standardization approaches include:

- **API Standardization:** Unified interfaces for model inference, data exchange, and service integration.

- **Model interoperability standards:** Frameworks such as ONNX for cross-platform model portability.
- **Orchestration platforms:** Tools for managing distributed AI workloads, including container-based and microservices architectures.
- **Edge-cloud coordination frameworks:** Mechanisms for workload distribution, synchronization, and monitoring.

These standards facilitate seamless integration and reduce vendor lock-in, enabling scalable and flexible deployment for Generative Edge AI systems.

5.5.4 Large-Scale Deployment Constraints

Deploying Generative Edge AI at scale introduces additional constraints that must be carefully managed:

- **Operational complexity:** Coordinating thousands of distributed nodes with varying capabilities.
- **Security and compliance risks:** Ensuring consistent enforcement of policies across all devices.
- **Energy efficiency concerns:** Managing power consumption across large device fleets
- **Data consistency and synchronization:** Maintaining reliable and consistent outputs across distributed systems.

Addressing these constraints requires robust system design, automated orchestration, and standardized governance mechanisms to ensure reliability and efficiency in real-world deployments.

6. TECHNICAL CHALLENGES AND OPTIMIZATION STRATEGIES

The integration of Generative Artificial Intelligence (GenAI) with Edge AI systems introduces a unique set of technical challenges arising from the resource-constrained nature of edge devices and the computational complexity of modern generative models. While large generative models such as transformers, diffusion models, and generative adversarial networks have demonstrated remarkable performance in centralized environments, their deployment at the edge requires careful consideration of system architecture, hardware capabilities, and operational constraints. These challenges span multiple dimensions including computational limitations, energy efficiency, communication overhead, data privacy, and model reliability (Shi et al., 2020; Zhou et al., 2019).

Edge devices such as smartphones, embedded sensors, industrial controllers, and autonomous system modules typically possess limited processing power, restricted memory capacity, and constrained energy resources. Consequently, executing large generative models directly on these devices can lead to significant performance bottlenecks and system inefficiencies. Furthermore, the distributed and heterogeneous nature of edge environments complicates model deployment, updates, and monitoring. Addressing these challenges requires a combination of architectural innovations, model optimization techniques, and adaptive deployment strategies that enable generative models to operate efficiently within edge ecosystems.

6.1 Resource Constraints and Computational Complexity

One of the primary barriers to deploying Generative AI models at the edge is the high computational demand associated with modern deep learning architectures. Large transformer-based models and diffusion models often contain billions of parameters and require substantial computational resources for inference and training. Such requirements exceed the capabilities of most edge hardware platforms, which are designed primarily for lightweight processing tasks (Han et al., 2016).

Memory limitations also pose significant constraints. Edge devices frequently operate with limited RAM and storage capacity, making it difficult to store large neural network models and intermediate computation states. In addition, the continuous generation of outputs - such as text, sequences, image, or audio can further increase memory usage and computational overhead. These limitations necessitate the development of efficient model architectures that can deliver acceptable performance while minimizing resource consumption (Lane et al., 2015).

Energy consumption represents another critical challenge. Many edge devices rely on battery power or operate in environments where energy efficiency is essential. Running complex AI workloads on such devices can quickly drain energy resources, thereby reducing operational longevity and system reliability. As a result, optimizing power efficiency is a fundamental requirement for sustainable Edge AI deployments.

6.2 Model Optimization Techniques

To address the limitations of edge hardware, researchers and engineers have developed several model optimization techniques designed to reduce the computational and memory requirements of deep learning models. Among the most widely used approaches are model compression, pruning, quantization, and knowledge distillation.

Model compression techniques aim to reduce the size of neural networks without significantly degrading their performance. Pruning methods remove redundant or less significant parameters from a model, thereby reducing computational complexity and memory usage. Structured pruning approaches can eliminate entire neurons or layers, allowing the resulting models to execute more efficiently on constrained hardware platforms (Han et al., 2016).

Quantization is another widely used optimization strategy that reduces the numerical precision of model parameters and operations. Instead of using high-precision floating point representations, quantized models utilize lower precision formats such as 8-bit or 16-bit integers. This reduction in precision significantly decreases memory consumption and computational requirements while maintaining acceptable accuracy for many applications (Gholami et al., 2021).

Knowledge distillation provides an additional method for creating lightweight models suitable for edge environments. In this approach, a large and complex "teacher" model transfers its learned knowledge to a smaller "student" model. The student model approximates the behavior of the larger model while requiring substantially fewer computational resources, making it suitable for deployment on edge devices (Hinton et al., 2015).

Together, these optimization techniques enable generative models to be adapted for resource constrained environments without sacrificing critical functionality.

6.3 Distributed and Collaborative Learning

Another strategy for addressing computational limitations in edge environments is the use of distributed learning approaches, particularly federated learning. Federated learning allows multiple edge devices to collaboratively train a shared machine learning model while keeping local data on the devices themselves. Instead of transmitting raw data to centralized servers, devices send model updates that are aggregated to improve the global model (Kairouz et al., 2021).

This approach offers several advantages for generative edge systems. First, it reduces the need for large-scale data transfers, thereby minimizing network bandwidth consumption. Second, it enhances data privacy by ensuring that sensitive information remains on local devices. Finally, federated learning allows models to continuously adapt to new data collected across distributed environments, improving their robustness and generalization capabilities.

However, distributed learning also introduces new challenges related to communication efficiency, synchronization, and model convergence. Edge devices may have varying computational capabilities and network conditions, which can affect the training process. Addressing these challenges requires advanced aggregation algorithms and adaptive training strategies that accommodate heterogeneous device capabilities (Li et al., 2020).

6.4 Adaptive Inference and Edge-Oriented Architectures

Adaptive inference mechanisms represent another important optimization strategy for generative edge systems. Instead of executing full-scale models for every inference task, adaptive systems dynamically adjust computational workloads based on application requirements and device capabilities. Techniques such as early exit strategies, dynamic neural networks, and conditional computation allow models to terminate inference once sufficient confidence has been achieved, thereby reducing computational overhead (Teerapittayanon et al., 2017).

Edge-oriented AI architectures also incorporate specialized hardware accelerators designed to support machine learning workloads efficiently. Devices such as neural processing units (NPUs), tensor processing units (TPUs), and AI-enabled system-on-chip (SoC) platforms provide dedicated hardware for accelerating neural network operations while minimizing energy consumption. These hardware innovations play a critical role in enabling real-time generative inference on edge platforms (Mittal, 2020).

Additionally, hierarchical edge-cloud architectures allow computational tasks to be distributed across multiple layers of the computing infrastructure. Lightweight inference tasks can be executed locally on edge devices, while more computationally intensive operations are offloaded to nearby edge servers or cloud systems. This collaborative architecture helps maintain system responsiveness while preserving scalability and computational efficiency (Satyanarayanan, 2017).

6.5 Ensuring Reliability and Model Robustness

Beyond computational optimization, maintaining the reliability and robustness of generative models in edge environments presents a significant challenge. Edge systems often operate in dynamic and unpredictable environments where data distributions may change over time. Such changes can lead to model drift, where the model's performance gradually degrades as new data deviates from the original training dataset.

To address this issue, continuous monitoring and retraining mechanisms must be incorporated into the system lifecycle. Automated monitoring tools can track model performance metrics and detect anomalies that indicate potential degradation. When such issues are detected, models can be retrained or updated using new data collected from edge devices (Zhou et al., 2019).

Furthermore, ensuring the reliability of generative outputs is particularly important because generative models may occasionally produce inaccurate or misleading results. Implementing verification layers, confidence scoring mechanisms, and human in the loop validation processes can help mitigate these risks and maintain system trustworthiness.

Table 4 demonstrates that integrating optimization techniques with hardware-aware deployment can achieve up to 10 times latency reduction, 3 to 5 times energy efficiency improvement, and up to 90% model compression, while maintaining acceptable accuracy. However, challenges related to scalability, heterogeneity, and long-term robustness remain critical research areas.

Table 4. Technical Challenges and Optimization Strategies in Generative Edge AI

Category	Key Issues	Quantitative Impact	Optimization Strategies	Hardware Consideration	References
Resource Constraints	Limited CPU, memory, and storage in edge devices	CPU latency: 100-500 ms vs GPU: 10-50ms	Lightweight architectures, model partitioning	CPU (high latency), GPU (high power), NPU/TPU (efficient)	Shi et al., 2020; Zhou et al., 2019
Energy Consumption	High power usage during inference	CPU uses 2-4 times more energy than accelerators	Energy-aware scheduling, hardware acceleration	Edge TPU/ NPU improves performance per watt by 3-5 times.	Lane et al., 2015
Model Complexity	Large parameter sizes (billions of parameters)	Memory reduction up to 90% required for deployment	Model compression and pruning	Efficient execution on edge accelerators	Han et al., 2016
Quantization Overhead	High precision computation cost	4 times model size reduction, 2-4 times speed improvement, ~1-3% accuracy loss	8-bit / 16-bit quantization	Optimized for NPUs/TPUs	Gholami et al., 2021
Model Size vs Accuracy	Trade-off between performance and efficiency	Distilled models retain 80-95% accuracy with 5-10 times size reduction	Knowledge distillation	Suitable for mobile/embedded devices	Hinton et al., 2015
Distributed Learning	Bandwidth and privacy constraints	Communication reduced by 70-90%	Federated learning, decentralized training	Heterogeneous device environments	Kairouz et al., 2021; Li et al., 2020)
Adaptive Inference	Unnecessary computation for all inputs	30-60% reduction in computation cost	Early exit, dynamic neural networks	Efficient on edge accelerators	Teerapittayanon et al., 2017

continued on following page

Table 4. Continued

Category	Key Issues	Quantitative Impact	Optimization Strategies	Hardware Consideration	References
Edge-Cloud Coordination	Latency and scalability challenges	Latency reduced by 40-70% vs cloud-only	Hybrid edge-cloud architectures	Distributed across edge, fog, cloud layers	Satyanarayanan, 2017)
Hardware Heterogeneity	Diverse capabilities across devices	Performance varies significantly across CPU, GPU, TPU	Hardware-aware model design	GPU (high throughput), TPU/ NPU (efficient), CPU (flexible)	Mittal, 2020
Reliability & Robustness	Model drift and inconsistent outputs	Performance degradation over time without updates	Continuous monitoring, retraining, validation layers	Edge feedback loops	Zhou et al., 2019

6.6 Performance Evaluation Metrics for Generative Edge AI Systems

The deployment in Generative AI models in edge environments necessitates a well-defined evaluation framework that goes beyond traditional accuracy metrics. Unlike cloud-based systems, edge deployments operate under strict constraints related to latency, energy consumption, and hardware limitations. Therefore, evaluating generative edge systems requires a multi-dimensional approach that captures both model performance and system efficiency.

Latency (ms): Latency represents the time required for a model to generate an output after receiving an input. In edge environments, low latency is critical for real-time applications such as autonomous driving, augmented reality, and industrial automation. High-complexity models, particularly large-scale transformers and diffusion models, tend to exhibit higher inference latency due to their computational depth and iterative processing requirements (Zhang et al., 2024). Optimization strategies such as model pruning and split inference aim to reduce latency but may impact output quality.

Throughput (request/sec): Throughput measures the numbers of inference requests a system can process per second. It reflects the scalability of a deployment, particularly in multi-device and high-demand environments such as smart cities and IoT ecosystems. Distributed and hybrid architectures can improve throughput by offloading computationally intensive tasks to the cloud while maintaining lightweight processing at the edge (Rausch et al., 2024).

Energy Consumption) Joules per inference): Energy efficiency is a fundamental constraint in edge computing, especially for battery-powered devices. Generative models are inherently resource-intensive, often requiring significant energy for inference. Techniques such as quantization, knowledge distillation, and hardware acceleration (e.g., edge TPUs, NPUs) are widely used to reduce energy consumption while maintaining acceptable performance (Gholami et al., 2021; Han et al., 2016).

Model Accuracy vs Compression Ratio: To enable deployment on resource-constrained devices, generative models are often compressed using techniques such as pruning, quantization, and distillation. However, compression introduces a trade-off between model size and output quality. While aggressive compression reduces memory and computation requirements, it may degrade the fidelity and coherence of generated outputs. Balancing this trade-off is a key challenge in Edge AI system design (Hinton et al., 2015; Navardi et al., 2025).

Table 5 represents a comparative evaluation of different generative model types based on key performance metrics. The values represent typical relative characteristics observed in literature rather than fixed benchmarks, as performance varies depending on hardware and optimization strategies.

Table 5. Performance Comparison of Generative AI Models in Edge Contexts

Model Type	Latency (ms)	Energy (J/ inference)	Accuracy	Deployment
LLM (Transformer-based)	High	High	Very High	Cloud / Hybrid
GAN	Medium-High	High	High	Cloud / Limited Edge
Diffusion Models	Very High	Very High	Very High	Cloud / Hybrid
Compressed LLM (Distilled)	Medium	Medium	Moderate-High	Edge/Hybrid
Lightweight Diffusion	Medium-High	Medium	High	Edge-optimized
Federated Generative Models	Medium	Medium	Moderate	Edge (Distributed)

The comparative analysis in Table 5 highlights that no single generative model architecture optimally satisfies all edge deployment requirements. Large Language Models and diffusion models deliver superior accuracy and generation quality but incur substantial latency and energy costs, making them more suitable for cloud or hybrid deployments. Conversely, compressed and distilled models offer improved efficiency and lower latency but at the expense of reduced output fidelity (Naverdi et al., 2025).

GAN-based approaches occupy a middle ground but are limited by training instability and resource requirements, which hinder widespread edge adoption (Goodfellow et al., 2014). Federated and distributed generative models provide advantages in privacy and decentralization but introduce overhead in communication and synchronization, impacting throughput and scalability (Kairouz et al., 2021).

These observations underscore the importance of context-aware deployment strategies, where model selection and optimization techniques are aligned with application-specific requirements. For instance, latency-sensitive applications prioritize lightweight or hybrid models, while quality-sensitive tasks may rely on cloud-assisted inference. Furthermore, emerging approaches such as adaptive model partitioning and hardware-aware optimization aim to dynamically balance these trade-offs in real-time environments.

Overall, the lack of standardized benchmarking frameworks for generative Edge AI remains a significant research gap. Future work should focus on developing unified evaluation methodologies that integrate performance, energy efficiency, and security considerations, enabling more consistent and comparable assessment of Generative AI systems across diverse edge scenarios.

6.7 Economic and Cost-Performance Analysis of Generative Edge AI

The deployment of Generative AI at the edge introduces important economic considerations that extend beyond technical performance. Organizations must evaluate cost-performance trade-offs across infrastructure, computation, bandwidth, and operational efficiency. Unlike purely cloud-based AI systems, Generative Edge AI distributes costs across devices and networks, requiring a balanced assessment of both capital and operational expenditures (Satyanarayan, 2017; Morabito & Jang, 2025).

A key economic advantage is bandwidth savings. Edge-based generative models transmit only summarized insights instead of raw data, significantly reducing network usage and associated costs. This is particularly beneficial in large-scale deployments such as smart cities, where continuous data streaming would otherwise be expensive (Lifelo et al., 2024).

There is also a trade-off between hardware cost and inference efficiency. Edge devices require specialized AI-capable hardware, increasing capital costs, but they enable low-latency, real-time processing. Optimization techniques such as quantization and pruning help balance this by improving efficiency while maintaining acceptable accuracy (Navardi et al., 2025).

Overall, hybrid edge-cloud architectures provide the best cost-performance balance by combining local responsiveness with cloud scalability. From a managerial perspective, organizations must evaluate total cost of ownership, considering both financial costs and performance benefits such as latency reduction, privacy, and reliability (Rausch et al., 2024; Williams & Carter, 2024).

7. SECURITY, GOVERNANCE AND ETHICAL CONSIDERATIONS IN GENERATIVE EDGE AI

7.1 Ethical and Security Considerations

The integration of Generative Artificial Intelligence (GenAI) into edge computing environments introduces significant security and ethical challenges that extend beyond traditional AI deployments. Unlike centralized systems, edge devices operate in distributed, heterogeneous, and often physically accessible environments. These characteristics increase the exposure of generative models to security threats such as adversarial attacks, model manipulation, and unauthorized access. Consequently, ensuring the security, reliability, and ethical use of generative edge systems has become a critical concern for researchers, engineers, and policymakers (Goodfellow et al., 2015; Biggio & Roli, 2018).

One of the most prominent risks involves adversarial attacks targeting generative models. Attackers can manipulate input data or system parameters to influence the output generated by AI systems. In edge environments, where sensors and devices interact directly with the physical world, such manipulation may lead to harmful or misleading outcomes. For example, adversarial inputs could cause an autonomous system to generate incorrect decisions or produce unsafe operational commands (Papernot et al., 2016). Generative models may also be vulnerable to model inversion and extraction attacks, where adversaries attempt to reconstruct training data or replicate proprietary models through repeated queries.

Another security concern arises from the deployment lifecycle of generative models across distributed devices. Updating models across thousands of edge nodes introduces risks related to compromised updates, unauthorized firmware modifications, and supply chain vulnerabilities. Secure update mechanisms, cryptographic verification techniques, and trusted hardware environments are therefore essential components of a robust Edge AI security architecture (Conti et al., 2018).

Beyond technical security threats, generative edge systems also raise important ethical and societal considerations. Generative models have the capacity to create highly realistic synthetic content, which can be used for beneficial purposes such as simulation, design assistance, or personalized services. However, the same capabilities can also be exploited to generate misinformation, deepfakes, or biased outputs that reinforce existing social inequalities (Floridi & Chiriatti, 2020).

Bias and fairness represent additional ethical challenges. Generative models trained on large datasets may inadvertently learn and reproduce biases present in their training data. When such models operate autonomously at the edge, these biases may influence decision-making processes in areas such as healthcare diagnostics, hiring systems, or urban resource allocation. Addressing these issues requires the implementation of fairness aware training methods, transparency mechanisms, and accountability frameworks that ensure responsible AI behavior (Mehrabi et al., 2021).

Privacy is another critical dimension of ethical deployment. Edge computing environments often process sensitive personal or organizational data locally, which can help reduce the exposure of raw data to centralized systems. However, generative models may still leak sensitive information through inference processes or model outputs. Techniques such as differential privacy, security multiparty computation, and federated learning can help mitigate these risks while preserving the benefits of distributed AI systems (Dwork & Roth, 2014).

Ultimately, the successful integration of GenAI with edge computing requires a holistic approach that combines technical security measures, ethical design principles, and regulatory oversight. By embedding these considerations into system design and deployment processes, organizations can build generative edge systems that are not only efficient and scalable but also trustworthy and socially responsible.

7.2 Governance and Security Considerations

While security mechanisms are essential for protecting edge-based generative systems, effective deployment also requires a strong governance framework that integrates policy, compliance, and trust models. As Generative Edge AI operates across distributed, heterogeneous, and often untrusted environments, governance must extend beyond traditional cybersecurity to include lifecycle control, accountability, and ethical safeguards.

7.2.1 Zero-Trust Architecture for Edge AI

The zero-trust security model assumes that no device, user, or network component can be inherently trusted. This approach is particularly relevant for edge environments, where devices are physically exposed and operate outside centralized control.

In Generative Edge AI systems, zero-trust principles include:

- Continuous authentication and authorization of devices and services
- Secure boot and hardware-based trust anchors to prevent unauthorized modifications
- Encrypted communication between edge and cloud components
- Micro-segmentation to isolate workloads and limit lateral movement of threats

By enforcing strict identity verification and least-privilege access, zero-trust architectures reduce the risk of model tampering, data leakage, and unauthorized inference (Xu et al., 2024; Conti et al., 2018).

7.2.2 AI Governance Frameworks (Policy and Compliance)

Beyond technical controls, organizations must establish governance frameworks that define how Generative AI systems are developed, deployed, and monitored. These frameworks ensure compliance with regulatory requirements and promote responsible AI usage.

Key governance components include:

- **Policy definition:** Guidelines for data usage, model deployment, and ethical boundaries.
- **Regulatory Compliance:** Alignment with data protection laws and AI regulations.
- **Accountability mechanisms:** Clear roles and responsibilities for managing AI systems
- **Auditability and transparency:** Logging and monitoring of model behavior and decisions.

In edge environments, governance must also address distributed accountability, ensuring that decisions made by local models can be traced and validated across the system. This is critical in domains such as healthcare, transportation, and public safety (Khamparia & Gupta, 2025; Floridi & Chiriatti, 2020).

7.2.3 Model Watermarking and Provenance Tracking

Generative AI introduces unique challenges related to content authenticity and model integrity, particularly when synthetic data can be easily generated and distributed at scale. To address this, techniques such as watermarking and provenance tracking are increasingly important.

- **Model watermarking:** Embedding identifiable patterns or signatures within model outputs to verify authenticity and detect misuse
- **Provenance tracking:** Maintaining a traceable record of data sources, model training processes, and output generation pathways.
- **Content verification mechanisms:** Ensuring that generated outputs can be distinguished from real data.

These techniques help mitigate risks such as misinformation, deepfake generation, and intellectual property violations. They also support regulatory compliance by enabling traceability and accountability in AI-generated content (Singh & Kapoor, 2024; Rahman & Hasan, 2023).

8. FUTURE RESEARCH DIRECTIONS AND CONCLUSION

The integration of Generative AI with edge computing represents an important step toward building intelligent, responsive, and distributed systems. By enabling generative models to operate closer to data sources, edge environments can support real-time decision-making, reduced latency, improved privacy protection, and more efficient use of network resources. These capabilities are particularly valuable for emerging applications such as autonomous systems, smart city infrastructure, healthcare monitoring, and industrial automation.

Despite its potential, generative Edge AI remains an emerging research area with several unresolved challenges. Future research should focus on developing lightweight generative models optimized for resource-constrained devices, improving model compression and energy-efficient inference techniques, and enabling adaptive learning mechanisms that allow models to evolve in dynamic edge environments. Additionally, advances in federated learning, edge orchestration, and heterogeneous computing architectures will play a critical role in enabling scalable and collaborative AI systems across distributed networks.

Equally important is the need to strengthen security, reliability, and transparency in generative edge systems. As these technologies become more widely deployed, ensuring trustworthy AI behavior, mitigating adversarial threats, and addressing ethical concerns such as bias and privacy will be essential for responsible adoption.

In conclusion, the convergence of Generative AI and edge computing has the potential to transform the next generation of intelligent applications. Continued interdisciplinary research and collaboration between academia, industry, and policymakers will be necessary to overcome current limitations and fully realize the benefits of secure, efficient, and scalable generative intelligence at the edge.

REFERENCES

Al-Fuqaha, A., Khreishah, A., & Sallabi, F. (2024). A survey on IoT-edge-cloud orchestration for real-time intelligent applications. *IEEE Access : Practical Innovations, Open Solutions*, *12*, 23345–23371.

Ardi, N., & Isnayanti, I. (2025). *Generative AI: A comprehensive review of foundational models and emerging methods. Applied Systems and Technologies Journal.* ASTJ.

Biggio, B., & Roli, F. (2018). Wild patterns: Ten years after the rise of adversarial machine learning. *Pattern Recognition*, *84*, 317–331. DOI: 10.1016/j.patcog.2018.07.023

Bommasani, R., Hudson, D. A., Adeli, E., Altman, R., Arora, S., von Arx, S., & Liang, P. (2021). *On the opportunities and risks of foundation models.* Stanford Institute for Human-Centered Artificial Intelligence.

Brown, T. B., Mann, B., Ryder, N., Subbiah, M., Kaplan, J., Dhariwal, P., & Amodei, D. (2020). Language models are few-shot learners. *Advances in Neural Information Processing Systems*, *33*, 1877–1901.

Caliste, D. (2025). Adaptive personalization in smart home systems using edge-resident generative models. *Journal of Intelligent Environments*, *14*(2), 55–72.

Conti, M., Dehghantanha, A., Franke, K., & Watson, S. (2018). Internet of Things security and forensics: Challenges and opportunities. *Future Generation Computer Systems*, *78*, 544–546. DOI: 10.1016/j.future.2017.07.060

Deng, L., Kocakulak, M., & Iyer, V. (2023). Efficient federated training of generative models on heterogeneous edge hardware. *IEEE Transactions on Neural Networks and Learning Systems*, *34*(11), 9099–9112.

Dwork, C., & Roth, A. (2014). The algorithmic foundations of differential privacy. *Foundations and Trends in Theoretical Computer Science*, *9*(3–4), 211–407. DOI: 10.1561/0400000042

Floridi, L., & Chiriatti, M. (2020). GPT-3: Its nature, scope, limits, and consequences. *Minds and Machines*, *30*(4), 681–694. DOI: 10.1007/s11023-020-09548-1

Gholami, A., Kim, S., Dong, Z., Yao, Z., Mahoney, M., & Keutzer, K. (2021). A survey of quantization methods for efficient neural network inference. *ACM Computing Surveys*, *54*(3), 1–38.

Goodfellow, I., McDaniel, P., & Papernot, N. (2015). Making machine learning robust against adversarial inputs. *Communications of the ACM*, *61*(7), 56–66. DOI: 10.1145/3134599

Goodfellow, I., Pouget-Abadie, J., Mirza, M., Xu, B., Warde-Farley, D., Ozair, S., & Bengio, Y. (2014). Generative adversarial nets. *Advances in Neural Information Processing Systems, 27*, 2672–2680.

Han, S., Mao, H., & Dally, W. (2016). Deep compression: Compressing deep neural networks with pruning, trained quantization and Huffman coding. *International Conference on Learning Representations (ICLR).*

Hinton, G., Vinyals, O., & Dean, J. (2015). Distilling the knowledge in a neural network. *NeurIPS Deep Learning Workshop.*

Kairouz, P., McMahan, H. B., Avent, B., Bellet, A., Bennis, M., Bhagoji, A. N., & Zhao, S. (2021). Advances and open problems in federated learning. *Foundations and Trends in Machine Learning, 14*(1–2), 1–210. DOI: 10.1561/2200000083

Khamparia, A., & Gupta, D. (2025). Privacy-preserving generative AI in mobile healthcare systems. *IEEE Transactions on Mobile Computing, 24*(1), 88–104.

Kumar, S., & Shastri, A. (2024). Distributed AI lifecycle management for large-scale edge deployments. *Journal of Systems Architecture, 146*, 102932.

Lane, N., Bhattacharya, S., & Mathur, A.. (2015). DeepX: A software accelerator for low-power deep learning inference on mobile devices. *International Conference on Information Processing in Sensor Networks.*

Lee, J., & Park, H. (2024). Hybrid collaborative inference for diffusion models in mobile and edge environments. *IEEE Transactions on Mobile Computing, 23*(5), 2779–2793.

Li, J., Wang, H., & Fan, X. (2023). Privacy-enhanced decentralized learning for generative models. *Pattern Recognition Letters, 170*, 113–121.

Li, T., Sahu, A., Talwalkar, A., & Smith, V. (2020). Federated learning: Challenges, methods, and future directions. *IEEE Signal Processing Magazine, 37*(3), 50–60. DOI: 10.1109/MSP.2020.2975749

Lifelo, W., Chipeperekwa, T., & Kunda, D. (2024). Edge-based video analytics for smart cities: A bandwidth-optimized generative approach. *Journal of Urban Computing, 8*(3), 112–129.

Mehrabi, N., Morstatter, F., Saxena, N., Lerman, K., & Galstyan, A. (2021). A survey on bias and fairness in machine learning. *ACM Computing Surveys, 54*(6), 1–35. DOI: 10.1145/3457607

Mittal, S. (2020). A survey of FPGA-based accelerators for convolutional neural networks. *Neural Computing & Applications, 32*(4), 1109–1139. DOI: 10.1007/s00521-018-3761-1

Morabito, R., & Jang, M. (2025). Edge-native computing for privacy-sensitive AI workloads: A survey. *ACM Computing Surveys, 57*(1), 1–34.

Navardi, S., Li, Z., & Zhang, Y. (2025). Model compression strategies for deploying generative AI on edge devices. *IEEE Internet of Things Journal, 12*(4), 3451–3468.

O'Neill, K., & Sørensen, T. (2025). Resilient deployment of generative AI in hostile edge environments. *ACM Transactions on Embedded Computing Systems, 24*(1), 1–26.

Papernot, N., McDaniel, P., & Jha, S.. (2016). The limitations of deep learning in adversarial settings. *IEEE European Symposium on Security and Privacy*, 372–387. DOI: 10.1109/EuroSP.2016.36

Rahman, M., & Hasan, K. (2023). Defense strategies for adversarial attacks on generative AI models. *ACM Transactions on Privacy and Security, 26*(2), 1–30.

Rausch, T., Nastic, S., & Dustdar, S. (2024). Secure edge-cloud orchestration for distributed AI pipelines. *Future Generation Computer Systems, 154*, 401–417.

Reuters. (2024). Nvidia unveils AI model capable of modifying voices and generating novel sounds. *Reuters Technology News.*

Reuther, A., Michaleas, P., Jones, M., Gadepally, V., Samsi, S., & Kepner, J. (2023). Distributed and edge AI: A systems perspective. *Journal of Parallel and Distributed Computing, 176*, 104–121.

Satyanarayanan, M. (2017). The emergence of edge computing. *Computer, 50*(1), 30–39. DOI: 10.1109/MC.2017.9

Shazeer, N.. (2017). Outrageously large neural networks: The sparsely-gated mixture-of-experts layer. *International Conference on Learning Representations (ICLR).*

Shi, W., Cao, J., Zhang, Q., Li, Y., & Xu, L. (2020). Edge computing: Vision and challenges. *IEEE Internet of Things Journal, 3*(5), 637–646. DOI: 10.1109/JIOT.2016.2579198

Singh, R., & Kapoor, A. (2024). Ethical considerations for synthetic data generation at the edge. *AI and Ethics, 4*(3), 221–238.

Thapa, B., & Mashayekhy, L. (2024). Multi-layer edge intelligence for autonomous vehicular systems. *IEEE Transactions on Intelligent Transportation Systems, 25*(6), 7448–7463.

Vaswani, A.. (2017). Attention is all you need. *Advances in Neural Information Processing Systems.*

Wang, X., He, Z., & Peng, X. (2024). Artificial-intelligence-generated content with diffusion models: A systematic review. *Mathematics (MDPI).*

Williams, L., & Carter, M. (2024). Cloud-edge cooperative architectures for generative industrial analytics. *IEEE Transactions on Industrial Informatics, 20*(3), 1551–1563.

Xu, Y., Sun, Q., & Wang, J. (2024). Trusted execution environments for protecting edge-deployed AI models. *Computers & Security, 133*, 103407.

Yan, X., Zhao, M., & Hung, P. (2024). Real-time predictive modeling in autonomous vehicles using edge-deployed generative models. *IEEE Transactions on Vehicular Technology, 73*(2), 2210–2224.

Zhang, H., Liu, S., & He, X. (2024). Lightweight diffusion models for real-time edge generation. *Proceedings of the IEEE/CVF Conference on Computer Vision and Pattern Recognition*, 4432–4443.

Zhang, Q., Chen, M., & Li, L. (2022). Edge intelligence in the AI-enabled Internet of Things: Research challenges and future directions. *IEEE Network, 36*(3), 186–192. DOI: 10.1109/MNET.001.1900340

Zhou, Z., Chen, X., Li, E., Zeng, L., Luo, K., & Zhang, J. (2019). Edge intelligence: Paving the last mile of artificial intelligence with edge computing. *Proceedings of the IEEE, 107*(8), 1738–1762. DOI: 10.1109/JPROC.2019.2918951

Chapter 9
Adaptive Feedback-Bound Generative Architecture (AFGA): A Lightweight Framework for Resource-Aware Text Generation on Edge Devices

Naveen Kumar Ramakrishna
http://orcid.org/0009-0007-7606-4958
Dell Technologies, USA

ABSTRACT

As generative language models transition from cloud-centric deployment to execution on edge devices, they face constraints that differ fundamentally from those assumed during model design. Autoregressive generation unfolds as a time-extended process in which computational load, thermal stress, and memory pressure accumulate over sustained interaction. Existing efficiency techniques—such as compression, quantization, and system-level throttling—primarily address static or average behavior and do not account for the evolving physical state of the device during generation. This chapter introduces the Adaptive Feedback-Bound Generative Architecture (AFGA), a runtime control framework that treats edge-based generative inference as a cyber-physical process. By coupling real-time hardware telemetry with model-level decoding control, AFGA adapts semantic complexity to physical conditions, enabling sustained, coherent generation and improved efficiency under hardware constraints.

DOI: 10.4018/979-8-3373-7340-9.ch009

INTRODUCTION

Generative language models are no longer confined to remote data centers. Increasingly, they are being pushed onto edge devices such as smartphones, tablets, and embedded systems, where they are expected to operate continuously and without reliable network access (Shen et al., 2024). Tasks that once assumed cloud support—drafting text, summarizing documents, or sustaining conversational interactions—are now being executed locally (Olabiyi, 2025). The motivations for this shift are straightforward: reduced latency, improved privacy, lower operational costs, and the ability to function offline (Sanh et al., 2020).

The difficulty stems from the way generative inference unfolds. Autoregressive decoding does not resemble conventional inference workloads that execute once and complete. Instead, it proceeds incrementally, producing one token at a time, with each step conditioned on the entire history generated so far. The length of this process is not known in advance and is often determined interactively. In practice, this turns generation into a sustained activity whose computational footprint grows over time (Chen, 2024). On resource-constrained devices, prolonged generation gradually accumulates thermal load, increases power consumption, and expands memory pressure, bringing the system closer to its operating limits as execution continues (Dutt & Li, 2025).

Static efficiency methods such as quantization, pruning, and architectural simplification are critical for edge deployment because they reduce average compute cost, but they fix model complexity before execution and cannot respond to changing thermal, power, or memory conditions during sustained generation (Dettmers et al., 2022; Frankle & Carbin, 2020; Sanh et al., 2020). Dynamic inference adds runtime adaptation, yet it is usually driven by input difficulty or model confidence rather than device state (Graves, 2024; Lee & Park, 2025), while system safeguards such as Dynamic Voltage and Frequency Scaling and thermal throttling remain reactive and unaware of generative intent (Kumar et al., 2024; Patel, 2025). This chapter therefore treats edge generative efficiency as a control problem rather than only a compression problem, arguing that because inference behaves as a cyber-physical process shaped by thermal, power, and memory dynamics, effective management requires feedback at the decoding stage itself (Zhang et al., 2024).

To explore this perspective, we introduce the **Adaptive Feedback-Bound Generative Architecture (AFGA)**, a lightweight runtime framework that couples decoding behavior with real-time hardware telemetry. AFGA treats generative inference as a closed-loop process, adjusting decoding complexity in response to evolving physical conditions during execution (Lee & Park, 2025). Rather than optimizing output quality in isolation, the framework emphasizes sustained, coherent generation within a stable operating envelope.

To motivate the need for such a framework more systematically, the next section examines how generative inference behaves on edge devices, where existing efficiency methods help, and where they remain insufficient under sustained physical constraint.

BACKGROUND AND CONTEXT

Generative inference on edge devices differs from conventional edge AI workloads because it is not a short, bounded computation. In autoregressive decoding, tokens are produced step by step, with each new token conditioned on the sequence generated so far. This makes runtime duration, computational intensity, and memory demand evolve during execution rather than remain largely fixed at the start of inference (Chen, 2024). Compared with burst-oriented tasks such as image classification or object detection, long-form generation sustains compute activity for much longer, limiting thermal recovery and keeping power draw elevated over time (Dutt & Li, 2025). In addition, transformer decoders maintain growing key–value (KV) caches, which increase memory traffic as context expands and can become a major source of pressure on resource-constrained edge systems (Chen, 2024; Gomes, 2024).

Existing approaches address parts of this problem, but not the full coordination challenge. Static efficiency techniques such as quantization, pruning, distillation, and architectural simplification reduce baseline compute and memory cost and remain essential for fitting language models onto edge hardware (Dettmers et al., 2022; Frankle & Carbin, 2020; Sanh et al., 2020). However, they fix model complexity before execution and do not adapt when thermal, power, or memory conditions change during sustained generation (Olabiyi, 2025).Runtime adaptation is present in dynamic inference methods, but it is typically guided by factors such as input difficulty, uncertainty, or internal model signals, not by the physical condition of the device under load (Graves, 2024; Lee & Park, 2025; Shen et al., 2024).System safeguards such as DVFS, thermal throttling, and power governors are mainly intended to keep the hardware within safe operating limits. They step in only after stress begins to build and do not account for generative intent or the way the response unfolds (Kumar et al., 2024; Patel, 2025).

This separation creates a coordination gap between semantic generation and physical regulation. The model continues decoding according to linguistic probabilities, while the hardware platform reacts independently to rising thermal, power, and memory constraints (Zhang et al., 2024). The result is often abrupt degradation: latency increases, throughput collapses, or generation ends before reaching a coherent stopping point (Dutt & Li, 2025). Recent work on KV-cache efficiency, NPU-assisted on-device inference, elastic mobile LLM service, and mobile benchmarking further shows that sustainable deployment depends not only on model compression, but also on runtime behavior, hardware constraints, and deployment-aware evaluation (Kwon et al., 2023; Xu et al., 2025; ELMS, 2024; Li et al., 2025). This motivates the need for AFGA as a runtime feedback layer that links decoding behavior to real-time hardware conditions.

Taken together, these limitations point to a deeper systems-level issue that cannot be explained by model compression or reactive device control alone. The next section formalizes this issue as the Sustainability Gap in edge generative inference.

Figure 1. Edge generative inference as a coordination problem, showing the gap between semantic decoding and device-level physical stress that motivates AFGA.

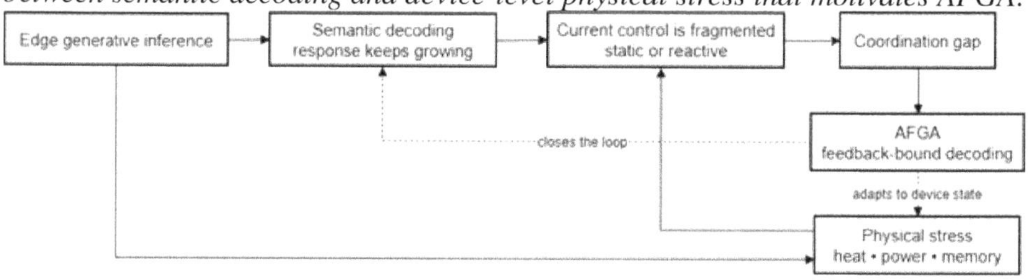

PROBLEM DEFINITION: THE SUSTAINABILITY GAP IN EDGE GENERATIVE INFERENCE

Semantic–Physical Coordination Failure

The behavior described above reveals a deeper mismatch between the objectives of generative models and the constraints of edge hardware. The model's internal logic is semantic and probabilistic, driven by coherence, likelihood, and task relevance. The hardware platform, meanwhile, operates under physical limits defined by temperature, power, and energy budgets (Zhang et al., 2024).

These two layers interact only indirectly. The model continues decoding based on its learned distributions, largely unaware of the device's physical trajectory. The operating system, in turn, monitors physical stress without insight into where the generative process stands—whether it is just beginning, mid-response, or nearing completion (Kumar et al., 2024).

During prolonged generation, this disconnect becomes increasingly visible. A model may continue elaborating confidently while the device approaches thermal saturation. Conversely, the system may intervene aggressively through throttling or frequency scaling at moments that are semantically disruptive. The resulting behavior is neither graceful nor predictable.

Formalizing the Sustainability Gap

The limitations outlined above expose a systemic gap in current edge generative inference pipelines. This chapter defines the Sustainability Gap as the inability of a generative process to adjust its internal computational behavior in response to the evolving physical conditions under which it executes (Zhang et al., 2024).

This gap does not arise from a flaw in modeling techniques or from insufficient hardware safeguards. Rather, it emerges because semantic decision-making and physical regulation operate in isolation. As generation lengthens, physical cost accumulates, yet control remains either fixed in advance or triggered only after instability is imminent.

Without a mechanism that explicitly links semantic choices to physical state awareness, extended generative workloads inevitably converge toward instability, regardless of how efficient the underlying model may appear in isolation (Dutt & Li, 2025).

Requirements for Sustainable Edge Generation

Addressing the Sustainability Gap requires design principles that reflect both physical realities and user expectations:

1. **Hardware Awareness:** The generative process must incorporate real-time signals related to temperature, power consumption, and memory pressure (Patel, 2025).
2. **Predictive Control:** Adaptation must occur before physical limits are reached, accounting for thermal inertia and delayed dissipation (Kumar et al., 2024).
3. **Semantic Preservation:** Degradation strategies should favor coherent completion and controlled simplification over abrupt interruption (Zhang et al., 2024).
4. **Stability of Control:** Adaptation mechanisms must remain robust in the presence of noisy or delayed telemetry, avoiding oscillatory behavior (IEEE, 2025).
5. **Deployment Practicality:** Solutions should operate entirely at runtime, without requiring retraining or architectural modification (Olabiyi, 2025).

These requirements emphasize continuity, predictability, and deployment practicality over peak expressiveness alone. They frame edge-based generative inference as an ongoing regulation problem that must balance semantic intent against physical feasibility. The requirements do not merely describe desirable behavior; they also define the design constraints for a workable runtime solution. The following section introduces AFGA as a framework intended to satisfy those constraints in a unified way.

ADAPTIVE FEEDBACK-BOUND GENERATIVE ARCHITECTURE (AFGA)

Design Principles of Adaptive Feedback-Bound Generative Architecture

The design of AFGA follows directly from the Sustainability Gap identified in Section 3. Rather than treating generative inference as a static execution problem, AFGA is grounded in the view that sustained generation on edge devices must be regulated as a cyber-physical process (Zhang et al., 2024). The following principles define this shift in perspective and guide the architecture of the framework.

Principle 1: Runtime Hardware Awareness as a First-Class Concern

AFGA treats awareness of physical execution conditions—temperature, power consumption, and memory pressure—as intrinsic to generative inference, rather than as an external system concern (Patel, 2025). Conventional approaches assume that such factors can be handled entirely by the operating system. AFGA rejects this assumption, recognizing that the generative process itself is a major contributor to sustained physical stress (Dutt & Li, 2025).

Principle 2: Predictive Control over Reactive Intervention

Edge devices exhibit strong thermal inertia: physical stress accumulates gradually and dissipates slowly. As a result, purely reactive responses—triggered only after thresholds are crossed—are often too late to preserve stable behavior (Kumar et al., 2024).

AFGA therefore emphasizes predictive control. Rather than waiting for explicit throttling events, the framework monitors trends in physical signals to anticipate instability. Even coarse predictors, such as the rate of temperature increase, provide sufficient foresight to enable preemptive adjustment of generative behavior.

This principle shifts adaptation from emergency response to preventative regulation.

Principle 3: Model-Level Actuation with Semantic Visibility

AFGA intervenes at the level of decoding, where semantic structure is explicitly available. This allows adaptation decisions to be informed by linguistic context—such as sentence boundaries, response length, or decoding strategy—rather than being applied blindly at the hardware or scheduler level (Wilson, 2025).

Importantly, AFGA does not alter model parameters or learned representations. Instead, it modulates how generation proceeds, preserving the integrity of probabilistic inference while constraining its physical footprint (Graves, 2024).

Principle 4: Graceful Degradation as an Explicit Objective

Under physical constraint, some loss of expressiveness is inevitable. AFGA treats this not as failure, but as a design choice. The framework prioritizes completion, coherence, and responsiveness over maximal diversity or verbosity (Zhang et al., 2024).

Rather than allowing generation to be interrupted abruptly by system-level controls, AFGA seeks to degrade output quality in a controlled and interpretable manner. This makes physical constraints visible as gradual simplification rather than sudden disruption.

Principle 5: Lightweight Integration and Practical Deployability

AFGA is designed to be lightweight and deployable within existing inference stacks. It operates entirely at runtime, requires no retraining, and introduces minimal overhead through periodic telemetry polling and decoding-level adjustments rather than model-level modification (Shen et al., 2024). This design choice is intentional: on edge devices, any control mechanism that materially increases compute load or integration complexity can undermine the very sustainability objective it is meant to support.

The Cyber-Physical Feedback Loop

Together, these principles are realized through a closed-loop control architecture that binds generative inference to physical execution conditions. AFGA treats generation as a regulated process in which computational behavior and hardware state continuously influence one another.

Figure 2 illustrates the closed-loop cyber-physical structure of AFGA, highlighting the interaction between hardware telemetry, control logic, and generative decoding behavior.

Figure 2.

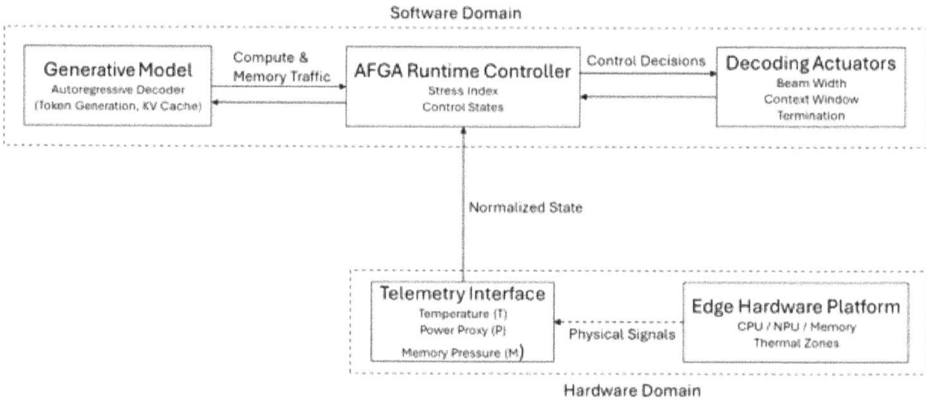

More specifically, the loop unfolds in a fixed sequence. AFGA first senses the device's physical condition by collecting temperature, power-proxy, and memory-pressure signals from the telemetry interface. These raw signals are then passed to state estimation, where they are normalized, smoothed, and combined into a stable representation of sustainability risk. That estimated stress state is interpreted by the control logic, which determines the appropriate operating regime for generation. The selected regime is then translated into actuation at the decoding level, such as simplifying search, limiting effective context length, or triggering controlled termination under severe stress. Those decoding adjustments then affect compute intensity, memory traffic, and overall runtime, which in turn changes the device's physical state before the next sensing cycle begins. For that reason, the stages in Figure 1 should not be read as separate components, but as connected steps within a single feedback loop.

Rather than reacting to isolated events, the feedback loop organizes inference around a small set of functional roles that collectively span the boundary between physical execution and semantic decision-making. These roles connect low-level hardware signals to high-level decoding choices, allowing physical constraints to influence generation without interfering with learned language representations (IEEE, 2025).

1. Sensing: Observing the Physical Environment

The sensing stage collects real-time indicators of physical stress from the execution environment, including temperature measurements, power proxies, and memory utilization signals. AFGA relies only on telemetry that is commonly exposed by edge platforms, prioritizing portability and low overhead over fine-grained instrumentation (Patel, 2025). This is an important implementation choice: edge deployments cannot assume privileged access to proprietary counters, high-frequency sampling, or laboratory-grade measurement accuracy.

Telemetry is not read at every decoding step but at a moderate cadence matched to how physical conditions change, so brief spikes are filtered out while sustained thermal and power trends are preserved. This keeps monitoring lightweight for edge deployment while still frequent enough to support predictive control.

2. State Estimation: From Raw Signals to Sustainability Awareness

Raw telemetry signals are heterogeneous, noisy, and often lagging. AFGA therefore aggregates these signals into an intermediate representation that reflects overall sustainability risk rather than isolated metrics (Kumar et al., 2024). The objective is not to reconstruct the full physical state of the device with high precision, but to derive a stable control signal that is sufficiently informative for runtime adaptation.

This estimation process smooths short-term noise, incorporates trend information, and produces a bounded stress measure that reflects how sustainable continued generation is under current conditions. It also reduces overreaction to platform-specific quirks, so brief spikes in temperature, power, or memory pressure do not trigger control changes unless the broader trend shows worsening conditions.

3. Control Logic: Interpreting Stress in Context

Based on the estimated stress level, AFGA determines the appropriate operating regime for generative inference. Control decisions are discrete rather than continuous, mapping ranges of sustainability risk to predefined decoding behaviors (Zhang et al., 2024).

This discretization avoids unstable oscillations and provides a clear semantic interpretation of adaptation. Crucially, control logic operates independently of token probabilities, ensuring that regulation constrains execution without distorting learned language representations.

4. Actuation: Modulating Generative Behavior

Actuation occurs by adjusting decoding parameters that directly influence computational cost and memory footprint. These include search strategy, effective context length, and termination behavior (Wilson, 2025).

Because actuation is applied at the decoding level, AFGA can preserve semantic continuity even under constraint—for example, favoring completion of a response over continued elaboration. As physical conditions improve, actuation is reversible, allowing generation to recover expressiveness dynamically.

5. Closing the Loop

Each actuation decision alters the subsequent physical trajectory of the system by changing compute intensity, memory access patterns, and runtime duration (Dutt & Li, 2025). These effects are observed through sensing, completing the feedback loop.

By embedding this loop within the generative process itself, AFGA transforms inference from a one-way computation into a self-regulating system. The following section formalizes this control mechanism through the unified hardware stress index and associated control states. Within this sequence, state estimation is the stage that converts heterogeneous telemetry into a usable control signal; Figure 3 focuses on that aggregation step by showing how AFGA constructs the unified hardware stress index Ψ from normalized thermal, power, memory, and thermal-velocity terms.

Unified Hardware Stress Index (Ψ)

The cyber-physical feedback loop described in Section 4.2 requires a compact and interpretable representation of device sustainability. While raw telemetry signals—temperature, power draw, and memory utilization—are informative in isolation, reacting to them independently leads to brittle and ad-hoc control logic. AFGA therefore introduces a Unified Hardware Stress Index, denoted Ψ, which aggregates heterogeneous physical signals into a single normalized measure of runtime stress (Kumar et al., 2024).

As shown in Figure 3, AFGA aggregates heterogeneous hardware signals into a single bounded stress index that reflects overall sustainability risk during generation.

Figure 3.

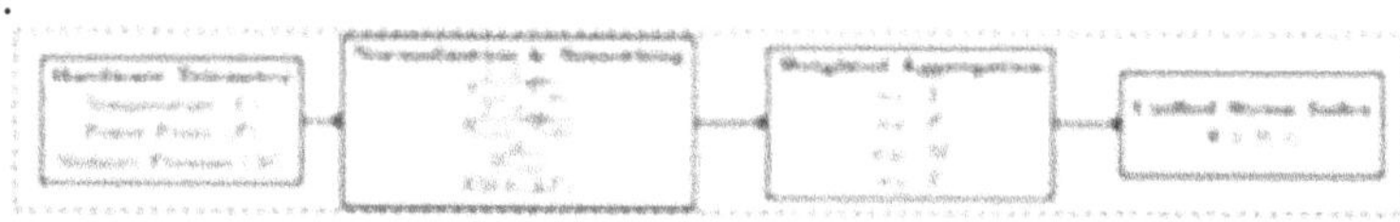

The purpose of Ψ is not to model hardware behavior with high fidelity, but to provide a stable, predictive indicator of how close the system is to an unsustainable operating regime. By collapsing multiple physical dimensions into a bounded scalar, AFGA enables consistent control decisions across devices and workloads.

1. Definition of the Stress Index

At decoding step t, the AFGA stress index is defined as:

$$\Psi(t) = w_T \cdot \frac{T_{\text{curr}}(t) - T_{\text{idle}}}{T_{\text{throttle}} - T_{\text{idle}}} + w_P \cdot \frac{P_{\text{curr}}(t) - P_{\text{idle}}}{P_{\text{budget}} - P_{\text{idle}}} + w_M \cdot \frac{M_{\text{curr}}(t)}{M_{\text{total}}} + w_D \cdot \frac{\text{EMA}(\Delta T(t))}{T_{\text{ref}}}$$

Each term is clipped to the interval before aggregation.

Term descriptions:

- **Thermal Saturation Term**

Measures proximity to the empirically observed throttling temperature under sustained load. This captures accumulated heat and reflects the effect of thermal inertia (Dutt & Li, 2025).

- **Power Pressure Term**

Represents sustained energy draw using a device-specific power proxy (e.g., battery current × voltage or PMIC-reported estimates). This term captures conditions where power limits are approached even before thermal thresholds are crossed (Patel, 2025).

- **Memory Pressure Term**

Reflects overall memory contention, including the growth of attention state and system-level pressure. While not a direct measurement of KV-cache occupancy, it correlates with the monotonic memory demand characteristic of long-form generation (Chen, 2024; Gomes, 2024).

- **Thermal Velocity Term**

An exponential moving average of temperature change, providing predictive awareness of rapid heating trends. This term enables proactive intervention before throttling occurs (Kumar et al., 2024).

The weighting coefficients are non-negative and sum to one. Their values are determined through a lightweight calibration procedure described in Section 4.3.4.

2. Interpretation of Ψ

Ψ represents a continuous estimate of sustainability risk, not an absolute measure of failure. Low values indicate that the device is operating comfortably within its limits, while higher values signal proximity to instability. Importantly, Ψ is designed to increase smoothly as conditions worsen, avoiding discontinuities that could destabilize control decisions.

By construction, Ψ does not assume that any single physical constraint dominates. On some platforms, thermal saturation may be the limiting factor; on others, sustained power draw or memory bandwidth pressure may dominate (Gomes, 2024). The weighted formulation allows AFGA to adapt to these differences without changing control logic.

3. Calibration and Practical Considerations

Calibration of Ψ is done per device class using a short sustained-generation workload to capture idle baselines, throttling thresholds, and thermal rise behavior, after which lightweight tuning sets weights to match the main bottlenecks while balancing stability, completion, and output quality. Treated as a practical deployment step rather than heavy per-device optimization, this approach uses normalized, clipped terms and conservative thresholds so AFGA remains portable across heterogeneous edge platforms and robust to modest telemetry noise, ambient variation, and background load.

4. Role of Ψ in the AFGA Loop

Within the AFGA feedback loop, Ψ serves as the interface between physical sensing and semantic control. It abstracts heterogeneous hardware behavior into a form that the generative controller can reason about, enabling consistent mapping from device state to decoding behavior (IEEE, 2025).

The next section builds on this index by defining discrete control states that interpret Ψ and translate sustainability risk into specific generative actions.

Discrete Control States and Stability Mechanisms

A central design decision in AFGA is the use of discrete control states rather than continuous parameter tuning. Each state represents a qualitatively distinct operating regime of the generative process, defined by both hardware stress level and permissible decoding behavior (Zhang et al., 2024).

This discretization is intentional. Continuous control, while theoretically expressive, is fragile in the presence of noisy telemetry and delayed physical response. Edge devices exhibit measurement lag, thermal inertia, and transient fluctuations that can cause fine-grained controllers to oscillate or overreact. Discrete states provide robustness by absorbing minor variations while preserving meaningful adaptation (IEEE, 2025).

More importantly, discrete states align naturally with semantic interpretation. Each state corresponds to a recognizable mode of generation, allowing changes in behavior to be reasoned about at the level of output structure rather than raw numeric adjustment.

1. Definition of Generative Control States

AFGA defines a small, ordered set of control states through , each associated with a range of sustainability risk and a corresponding decoding configuration.

Figure 4 depicts the discrete operating states used by AFGA and the hysteresis-based transitions that govern movement between them.

Figure 4.

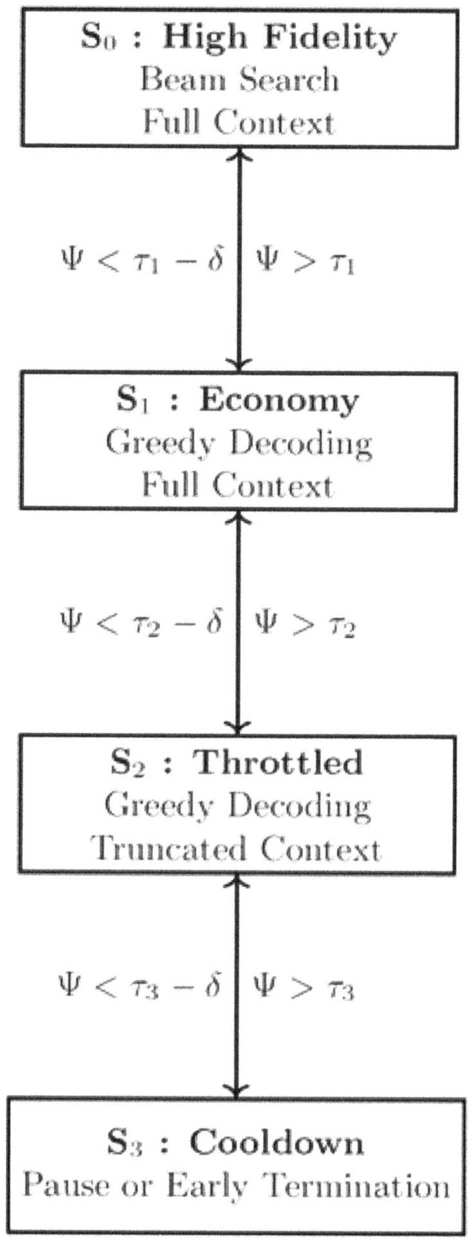

- **: High-Fidelity State**

The system operates under low stress. Full decoding expressiveness is permitted, including broader search strategies and full context retention (Wilson, 2025).

- **: Economy State**

Moderate stress is detected. Decoding is simplified to reduce computational overhead while preserving semantic completeness (Shen et al., 2024).

- **: Throttled State**

High stress is present. Generation prioritizes continuity over expressiveness, limiting context growth and reducing decoding diversity (Gomes, 2024).

- **: Cooldown or Termination State**

Sustained operation is no longer viable. Generation is paused or concluded at a semantically appropriate boundary to prevent system-level intervention (Dutt & Li, 2025).

These states are ordered by increasing constraint and are designed to be reversible, allowing recovery when physical conditions improve.

2. Semantic Interpretation of State Transitions

State transitions in AFGA are not arbitrary numerical events; they correspond to meaningful shifts in generative intent. Moving from to reflects a trade-off between richness and efficiency, while transitions into or signal a prioritization of completion and stability (Zhang et al., 2024).

This semantic framing distinguishes AFGA from conventional power management schemes. Instead of uniformly degrading performance, AFGA modulates how language is produced, ensuring that physical adaptation is visible as intentional simplification rather than unexplained disruption.

3. Hysteresis and Stability Guarantees

To prevent rapid oscillation between states when stress measurements fluctuate near threshold boundaries, AFGA employs hysteresis in state transitions. Each upward transition requires exceeding a higher threshold than the corresponding downward transition. This design is motivated by a basic control concern: when telemetry is noisy and physical response is delayed, a controller that reacts symmetrically at a single threshold can repeatedly switch states before the underlying hardware has had time to stabilize.

AFGA addresses this by separating escalation and recovery conditions. A state change toward greater constraint is triggered only when the estimated stress meaningfully exceeds the relevant boundary, while relaxation requires sustained evidence that conditions have improved. Under bounded telemetry noise and finite thermal lag, this reduces chattering and makes state evolution more deliberate. In practical terms, the controller is less likely to alternate repeatedly between adjacent decoding modes in response to minor fluctuations that do not reflect a true shift in operating regime.

This design accounts for both telemetry noise and delayed thermal response. In the absence of hysteresis, small fluctuations in telemetry can cause the controller to oscillate between operating states, leading to erratic decoding behavior and avoidable runtime overhead (IEEE, 2025). Introducing hysteresis forces state transitions to be deliberate rather than reactive, allowing physical effects such as thermal stabilization to take hold and yielding more consistent system behavior and output quality (Åström & Murray, 2021; Franklin et al., 2014).

4. Interaction with System-Level Controls

AFGA is not intended to replace operating-system-level resource management. Instead, it operates as a complementary layer that intervenes earlier and at finer semantic granularity (Kumar et al., 2024).

By reducing decoding complexity before physical thresholds are violated, AFGA decreases the likelihood of triggering aggressive system-level throttling. When such controls are nevertheless engaged, AFGA's prior adaptation mitigates their impact on generative continuity.

Runtime Control Algorithm

The control states described above are realized through a lightweight runtime algorithm that executes alongside the decoding process. This algorithm evaluates sustainability risk periodically and adjusts generative behavior accordingly. The algorithm is designed to be simple, interpretable, and efficient, reflecting the constraints of edge deployment (Kumar et al., 2024). Rather than introducing a computationally expensive controller, AFGA relies on a small number of repeated steps that can be implemented within standard inference runtimes.

1. Control Loop Structure

At a high level, the AFGA runtime loop performs four steps:

- **Telemetry Sampling:**

Physical signals are sampled at fixed intervals relative to token generation. The sampling interval is chosen to reflect the slower timescale of thermal and power evolution rather than the much faster timescale of individual token emission.

- **Stress Estimation:**

Telemetry is aggregated into a unified stress estimate reflecting current sustainability risk (Patel, 2025). This estimate smooths instantaneous variation and emphasizes sustained trends that are more relevant to control.

- **State Evaluation:**

The stress estimate is compared against calibrated thresholds to determine the appropriate control state. Hysteresis margins are applied during this step so that transitions reflect persistent change rather than transient fluctuation.

- **Actuation:**

Decoding parameters are adjusted based on the selected state. These adjustments are intentionally discrete and limited in scope, ensuring that the controller remains interpretable and that runtime overhead stays low.

These steps repeat throughout generation, allowing adaptation to evolve as physical conditions change. In deployment terms, this loop is lightweight enough to coexist with the decoding pipeline while still providing early intervention before system-level throttling dominates behavior.

2. Hysteresis-Aware State Transitions

State evaluation incorporates hysteresis margins to ensure stability. Transition thresholds are asymmetric, requiring sustained evidence of improvement before relaxing constraints.

This mechanism is particularly important on platforms where telemetry updates are infrequent or delayed (IEEE, 2025). By avoiding rapid state reversals, AFGA maintains predictable decoding behavior even under noisy measurement conditions.

3. Decoding Actuation Mechanisms

Actuation in AFGA operates exclusively at the decoding layer. Typical adjustments include simplifying search strategy, limiting effective context length, and constraining response length under severe stress (Gomes, 2024). These actuation points were chosen because they directly influence computational and memory demand while remaining compatible with standard generative runtimes.

Their practical value lies in the fact that they can be modified without altering model parameters or retraining the model. Search simplification reduces per-step compute overhead, context limitation constrains memory growth and bandwidth pressure, and response-length control prevents prolonged continuation under unsustainable conditions. Taken together, these adjustments provide several levers for reducing physical stress while preserving the semantic continuity of the response as much as possible.

4. Algorithmic Robustness and Failure Modes

AFGA is designed to degrade safely in the presence of imperfect information. If telemetry becomes unavailable, excessively delayed, or clearly inconsistent, the controller defaults to conservative states rather than assuming optimal conditions (IEEE, 2025). This bias toward safety ensures that the framework does not amplify measurement errors into unstable behavior, preserving both system integrity and user experience.

Several practical failure modes are anticipated. First, coarse telemetry may delay recognition of a rising stress trajectory. Second, concurrent system activity may make the observed physical state noisier than the workload alone would suggest. Third, platform-specific constraints may limit which decoding parameters can be adjusted at runtime. AFGA does not eliminate these deployment realities, but it is structured to remain functional under them by using bounded control actions, discrete states, and reversible actuation.

IMPLEMENTATION METHODOLOGY

System Architecture and Integration

AFGA is intended to fit into existing edge inference stacks as a lightweight runtime control layer, without changing model internals or requiring major retraining, recompilation, or redesign. This lets it regulate generative behavior while remaining compatible with standard deployment pipelines.

1. Hardware Platform Layer

The hardware platform layer encompasses the edge system-on-chip (SoC) and its associated compute and memory resources, including CPUs, GPUs, NPUs, shared memory, and thermal sensors. AFGA does not assume a specific accelerator or microarchitecture.

Crucially, AFGA does not rely on proprietary hardware counters or privileged instrumentation. It uses coarse-grained signals that are typically exposed for system management purposes, ensuring deployability on commercially available edge devices. This choice improves practical portability, but it also introduces an implementation trade-off: the framework must remain effective even when sensor access is imperfect, delayed, or less granular than a hardware-specific optimization approach would prefer.

2. Inference Runtime Layer

The inference runtime executes the generative model and manages interaction with underlying accelerators. AFGA integrates at this layer by interfacing with the decoding loop rather than the model graph itself. This design choice avoids re-training, recompilation, or architectural modification (Olabiyi, 2025). It also keeps the method deployable across runtimes that already expose configurable decoding behavior, which is more realistic for production adoption than requiring kernel-level intervention or model redesign.

Decoding parameters that influence computational intensity—such as search strategy, effective context window, and termination behavior—are exposed through standard runtime configuration interfaces. AFGA treats these parameters as actuation points, adjusting them dynamically in response to control decisions while leaving probabilistic inference intact (Shen et al., 2024). Because AFGA operates outside numerical kernels, it remains agnostic to whether inference is performed on CPUs, GPUs, or dedicated NPUs. This separation is also useful for benchmarking, since the same model and runtime can be observed under baseline and AFGA-controlled execution with only the control layer changed.

3. AFGA Control Layer

The AFGA control layer runs alongside the decoding process and maintains the internal control state. It periodically evaluates sustainability risk, maps it to a control state, and applies corresponding decoding adjustments. In implementation terms, this layer is intended to remain small, predictable, and computationally inexpensive so that the controller does not become a new source of overhead during already constrained edge execution.

This layer is intentionally compact. Its responsibilities are limited to stress estimation, state evaluation, and actuation, avoiding entanglement with model logic or runtime scheduling. As a result, AFGA can be enabled or disabled dynamically, facilitating direct comparison with baseline decoding during evaluation or deployment. This also improves experimental clarity: any observed change in sustained generation behavior can be attributed more directly to runtime control rather than to changes in model architecture or training procedure.

4. Telemetry Interface Layer

The telemetry interface abstracts platform-specific mechanisms for accessing physical signals such as temperature, power proxies, and memory utilization. Where necessary, signals are smoothed or rate-limited to mitigate noise and measurement latency (Kumar et al., 2024). This abstraction is important because telemetry quality varies considerably across edge platforms: some devices expose frequent and relatively stable measurements, while others provide only delayed or coarse-grained estimates.

By isolating platform dependencies within this interface, AFGA maintains portability across operating systems and device classes. Adapting AFGA to a new platform typically requires changes only at this layer, without modifying control logic or decoding behavior. At the same time, this layer makes implementation limitations explicit. If a platform exposes incomplete sensing or inconsistent power proxies, AFGA must rely on conservative estimation rather than precise physical modeling. The methodology therefore assumes robustness to imperfect telemetry rather than ideal observability.

5. Integration Characteristics

Several characteristics define AFGA's integration strategy:

- **Non-invasive deployment:** No retraining or model graph modification is required (Olabiyi, 2025).
- **Low overhead:** Control evaluation occurs infrequently relative to token generation, reducing the risk that the controller materially affects the workload it is regulating.
- **Reversibility:** AFGA can be toggled at runtime without affecting baseline functionality.
- **Portability:** The architecture supports multiple runtimes and hardware backends (Lee & Park, 2025).

- **Device-class calibration:** Only lightweight calibration is required to adapt thresholds and stress weighting across different hardware profiles.
- **Graceful fallback:** When sensing quality is limited, the framework can default to conservative control behavior rather than failing unpredictably.

Through this layered integration approach, AFGA balances practical deployability with sufficient control over generative behavior. It also addresses a key scalability concern raised by real-world edge deployment: the framework must remain manageable across heterogeneous devices without becoming tightly bound to any one vendor-specific toolchain or instrumentation stack.

Generative Model and Decoding Configuration

To evaluate AFGA under realistic edge conditions, the prototype implementation employs a compact autoregressive language model representative of those considered feasible for on-device deployment (Olabiyi, 2025). The configuration emphasizes deployment realism rather than peak accuracy, ensuring that observed behavior reflects practical edge use cases such as offline summarization, interactive assistance, and extended on-device text generation under constrained thermal and power conditions. This choice is consistent with the chapter's broader objective: not to demonstrate the largest possible model on the fastest possible device, but to examine whether sustainability-aware control can improve the behavior of plausible edge generative workloads.

1. Model Characteristics

The generative model is a decoder-only transformer with a parameter count in the low billions, consistent with models commonly targeted for mobile or embedded inference when combined with quantization or accelerator offloading (Dettmers et al., 2022). The architecture follows standard transformer design, including multi-head self-attention and feed-forward layers, without AFGA-specific modifications (Vaswani et al., 2017). The intent is to keep the model representative enough to support realistic long-form generation while remaining within the range of systems that may plausibly be considered for advanced edge deployment.

AFGA treats the model as a black box that exposes standard decoding controls and token outputs (Radford et al., 2019). This ensures that observed effects arise from runtime regulation rather than architectural specialization (Shen et al., 2024). It also strengthens the methodological argument that AFGA is an overlay on inference behavior rather than a redesign of the model itself.

2. Decoding Strategy and Actuation Points

Autoregressive decoding is performed using standard generation techniques, with configurable parameters that directly influence computational load (Wilson, 2025):

- **Search Strategy:** Beam-based or greedy decoding modes.
- **Context Window:** The number of prior tokens retained for attention.
- **Termination Behavior:** Conditions under which generation concludes.

Under baseline operation, decoding favors output quality, using moderate search diversity and full context retention. As AFGA transitions between control states, these parameters are adjusted discretely to reduce computational and memory demand. Importantly, these adjustments constrain how generation proceeds, not what the model has learned to generate. From a methodology standpoint, these actuation points were chosen because they are both meaningful and implementable: they affect compute intensity, memory growth, and response duration while remaining compatible with standard runtime controls rather than requiring architectural surgery.

3. Context Growth and Memory Considerations

Long-form generation on edge devices is particularly sensitive to context growth. As the attention state expands, memory bandwidth demand increases and often becomes a dominant contributor to thermal stress (Chen, 2024). This makes memory behavior a central implementation concern rather than a secondary optimization detail.

AFGA therefore treats effective context length as a controllable resource. Under high stress, older tokens are truncated to limit memory pressure (Gomes, 2024). While this may reduce long-range dependency, it preserves near-term coherence and allows generation to continue without triggering system-level intervention (Dao et al., 2022; Kwon et al., 2023). This reflects a deliberate prioritization: maintaining local semantic continuity and completion over preserving full historical context under constraint. It also makes explicit one of the chapter's practical trade-offs—AFGA does not eliminate the cost of long-context generation, but it provides a structured way to manage that cost when sustained edge execution becomes unstable.

4. Baseline Configuration for Comparison

For comparison, a baseline configuration is defined in which decoding parameters remain fixed throughout generation and the system relies solely on operating-system-level controls for resource management. This configuration reflects common deployment practice (Kumar et al., 2024). The baseline and AFGA-controlled runs are intended to share the same underlying model, runtime environment, and workload structure so that observed differences can be attributed to runtime control rather than unrelated implementation changes.

The comparative evaluation emphasizes sustained generation rather than peak throughput, consistent with the chapter's focus on sustainability, completion behavior, stress progression, and controlled degradation under long-form generation. With the integration approach, runtime control points, and model configuration defined, the next section applies this methodology in a representative edge deployment case study.

EXPERIMENTAL SETUP AND CASE STUDY

Experimental Platform and Hardware Environment

To evaluate AFGA under realistic edge constraints, experiments were conducted on a representative mobile-class system-on-chip (SoC) designed for on-device AI inference (Ignatov et al., 2018; Howard et al., 2017), with the goal not of maximizing peak throughput but of observing sustained generative behavior under thermal, power, and memory pressure similar to prolonged real-world edge use (Zhang et al., 2024). This framing matches AFGA's intended scenarios—such as offline summarization, interactive assistance, and extended on-device text generation—where stable long-duration operation matters more than short peak performance, so the setup emphasizes representative deployment conditions, sensing limits, shared-resource effects, and passive thermal behavior rather than laboratory-style accelerator benchmarking.

1. Edge System-on-Chip Configuration

The experimental platform consists of a modern smartphone-grade SoC integrating heterogeneous compute resources, including multi-core CPUs, a dedicated neural processing unit (NPU), and shared system memory. Such platforms are widely used for on-device generative workloads due to their support for low-precision inference and tight power envelopes (Shen et al., 2024). The use of a representative mobile-class platform, rather than a server-grade or actively cooled device, aligns the evaluation with the type of deployment environment in which AFGA is expected to matter most.

Thermal management is entirely passive. In the absence of active cooling, heat dissipation relies on chassis conduction and ambient conditions, causing temperature to accumulate steadily during sustained workloads (Dutt & Li, 2025). This characteristic makes the platform particularly suitable for studying the long-horizon effects of autoregressive decoding described in earlier sections. Because sustained generation unfolds over many decoding steps, even moderate per-step stress can accumulate into a substantial thermal trajectory on passively cooled devices.

2. Memory and Thermal Characteristics

The platform is equipped with mobile-class LPDDR memory in the range commonly found in contemporary edge devices, offering tens of gigabytes per second of bandwidth. While sufficient for burst-oriented workloads, this bandwidth becomes a limiting factor during extended generation as attention states and key–value caches grow (Gomes, 2024). This makes memory behavior central to the case study, since AFGA's control logic is intended not only to respond to thermal rise but also to constrain memory-driven stress before it propagates into broader system instability.

Thermal telemetry comes from standard on-chip sensors that report junction temperature at coarse granularity, introducing realistic latency and noise that AFGA must tolerate. When conservative thermal thresholds are crossed, system controls reduce frequency and cause sharp performance degradation during prolonged inference (Patel, 2025).

3. Power Management and Telemetry Access

Direct power measurement is not assumed. Instead, power consumption is estimated using commonly available proxies, such as battery discharge rate and utilization-based indicators (Patel, 2025). While imprecise, these signals are representative of what is accessible in production deployments and align with AFGA's design philosophy of operating without privileged instrumentation. This distinction is methodologically important: the evaluation treats power as an estimated operational signal rather than as a laboratory-grade electrical measurement, and subsequent interpretation should be read accordingly.

4. Execution Environment and Reproducibility

Inference is executed using a standard mobile inference runtime with accelerator offloading enabled where available. Background system activity is minimized but not eliminated, preserving the presence of typical operating-system tasks. This choice improves deployment realism, since edge generative workloads rarely execute on fully isolated devices in practice.

AFGA thresholds are set from short exploratory runs, then fixed per device across experiments, making the method procedurally reproducible and device-agnostic even though exact traces vary across hardware and operating conditions (Olabiyi, 2025).

Workload Design and Stress Protocol

The experimental workload is designed to emphasize sustained generative behavior rather than short, isolated inference tasks. This choice directly reflects the sustainability gap identified earlier, where cumulative effects dominate system behavior (Zhang et al., 2024). The workload design is also intended to approximate realistic edge usage patterns in which a device may generate for extended intervals under passive cooling, shared memory pressure, and fluctuating background load rather than under idealized burst-only conditions.

1. Sustained Generation Workload

Target generation lengths range from several hundred tokens to well beyond one thousand tokens, ensuring that both compute and memory pressure accumulate over time (Chen, 2024).

Each run starts from a thermally idle state and uses standardized prompts, ending only at target completion, system throttling, or AFGA-controlled termination so differences reflect runtime control rather than prompt variation.

2. Stress Amplification Through Context Growth

Under AFGA control, context growth becomes an adaptive variable. When stress increases, older tokens are selectively truncated to constrain memory bandwidth demand (Lee & Park, 2025). This design mirrors real-world scenarios in which recent conversational coherence is often more valuable than distant history under constrained conditions. It also provides a concrete experimental lever for observing one of AFGA's central trade-offs: controlled reduction in context retention in exchange for longer stable generation.

3. Experimental Conditions and Repetition

Two execution modes are evaluated:

- **Baseline decoding**, with static parameters and reliance on operating-system-level resource management.
- **AFGA-controlled decoding**, with dynamic adaptation as described in Section 4.

All other variables—including model configuration, prompts, runtime, and ambient conditions—are held as consistent as possible across runs. Each experiment is repeated multiple times to smooth variability arising from thermal lag, coarse telemetry, and background system activity. Because passive thermal systems do not produce perfectly identical traces from run to run, the analysis emphasizes repeatable comparative patterns rather than single-run extremes.

The evaluation is framed to compare AFGA on the dimensions that matter most for sustained edge usability—such as stress progression, time-to-throttle, generation length, completion behavior, abrupt termination, and proxy energy—thereby setting up the next section's metrics and results as a study of semantic quality and physical sustainability rather than peak throughput alone.

EVALUATION METRICS AND RESULTS

Evaluation Metrics

Evaluating generative models on edge devices requires a departure from conventional quality-centric benchmarks. Metrics such as BLEU, ROUGE, or perplexity assume stable execution environments and ignore the physical consequences of prolonged inference (Olabiyi, 2025). In edge settings, however, a response that degrades gracefully and completes reliably is often more valuable than a higher-quality output that is interrupted or aborted. Traditional language metrics judge output quality as if compute were unlimited and execution uninterrupted, an assumption that fails under sustained edge workloads. When thermal throttling cuts generation short, these metrics penalize partial but still usable outputs as harshly as incoherent text, missing the crucial distinction between graceful degradation and complete failure (Dutt & Li, 2025).

This section introduces a set of complementary metrics that jointly capture semantic quality, physical sustainability, and execution continuity.

Table 1. Illustrative simulated comparison of baseline decoding and AFGA across thermal, completion, energy, and semantic-quality metrics under sustained edge generation.

Metric	Baseline	AFGA	Observation
Peak temperature (°C)	86.4	80.9	Peak thermal load stays several degrees lower and outside the throttling zone
Time to throttling (s)	378	>600	Throttling is substantially delayed and may be avoided within the evaluation window
Sustained generation length (tokens)	910	1510	Stable generation continues for a much longer token horizon

continued on following page

Table 1. Continued

Metric	Baseline	AFGA	Observation
Completion rate (%)	61	89	A larger share of runs reaches coherent completion
Abrupt termination rate (%)	29	7	Forced interruption becomes much less frequent
Energy proxy (normalized)	1	0.81	Overall cumulative energy demand is reduced
Semantic similarity	1.00 (ref.)	0.94	Meaning is largely preserved despite runtime constraint
CSS	0.85	1.11	The overall semantic–sustainability trade-off is improved

Note: Values are internally consistent with the proposed evaluation framework and are shown for demonstration only; they are not empirical measurements.

Figure 5. Normalized comparison of baseline decoding and AFGA across key evaluation metrics during sustained edge generation. Baseline values are scaled to 1.00 to enable cross-metric comparison across thermal, continuity, efficiency, and semantic-quality dimensions.

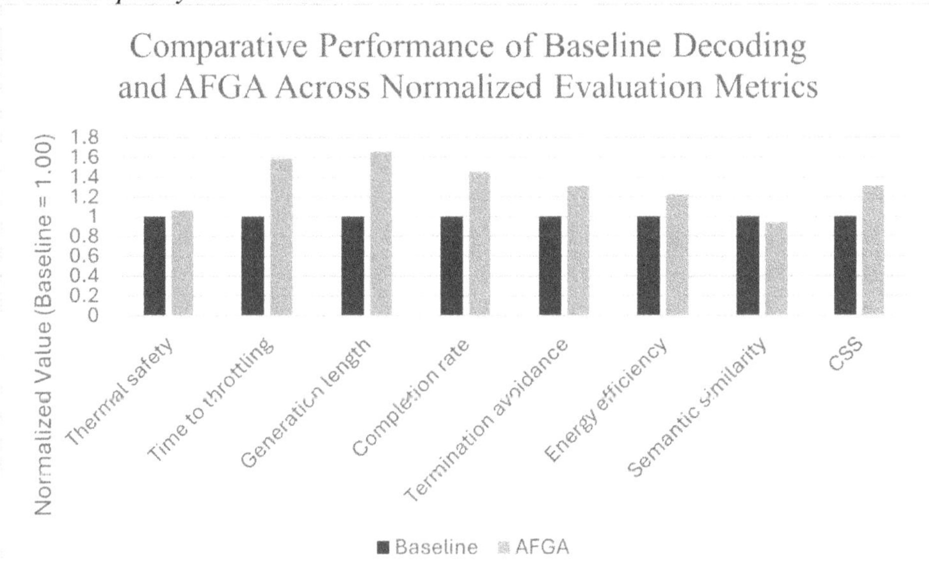

1. System-Level Sustainability Metrics

To characterize the physical behavior of sustained generation, we track the following system-oriented metrics (Patel, 2025; Zhang et al., 2024):

- **Peak Operating Temperature:** Maximum observed junction temperature during generation.
- **Thermal Trajectory:** The temporal evolution of temperature, highlighting stabilization or runaway behavior.
- **Sustained Generation Duration:** Time or token count before throttling or termination.
- **Energy Consumption Proxy:** Cumulative power usage relative to baseline execution.
- **Memory Pressure Indicators:** Growth and saturation of attention-related memory structures.

Together, these metrics expose whether a generative process remains within a sustainable operating envelope or approaches system-imposed limits.

2. Semantic Quality and Completion Metrics

Semantic fidelity is assessed using embedding-based similarity between constrained outputs and unconstrained baseline generations (Papineni et al., 2002). Rather than focusing solely on lexical overlap, this approach captures preservation of meaning under controlled simplification (Wilson, 2025).

In addition, two completion-oriented metrics are tracked (Dutt & Li, 2025):

- **Completion Rate:** Fraction of generations that terminate at a coherent semantic boundary.
- **Abrupt Termination Rate:** Frequency of mid-sentence or system-forced interruption.

These metrics reflect user-perceived reliability, which is often more critical than marginal gains in fluency (Reimers & Gurevych, 2019).

3. Coherence–Sustenance Score (CSS)

To unify semantic and physical considerations, we introduce the Coherence–Sustenance Score (CSS) as a composite evaluation metric (Zhang et al., 2024):

where:

- is normalized semantic similarity to the unconstrained baseline,
- is total energy consumption normalized to baseline execution,
- is a thermal penalty term reflecting proximity to throttling thresholds.

Higher CSS values indicate outputs that maintain meaning while consuming less energy and remaining further from thermal limits. CSS is not intended to replace individual metrics, but to summarize trade-offs in a single interpretable quantity.

Results and Analysis

1. Thermal Behavior and Stability

Under baseline decoding, temperature exhibits a monotonic rise during extended generation, frequently approaching system-defined thermal thresholds. In a substantial fraction of long-running sessions, this leads to throttling events accompanied by abrupt throughput reduction (Patel, 2025).

With AFGA enabled, temperature trajectories differ qualitatively. Initial rises are comparable, but temperatures stabilize well below throttling thresholds—often by margins on the order of several degrees Celsius. Predictive adjustment prevents late-stage thermal escalation, resulting in smoother and more predictable execution (Kumar et al., 2024).

2. Sustained Generation Duration

Baseline decoding typically terminates early under sustained workloads, either due to severe throttling or forced interruption. AFGA-controlled runs consistently extend generation duration, often completing significantly longer sequences before reaching termination conditions (Olabiyi, 2025).

While AFGA may reduce expressive complexity in later stages, it preserves the ability to conclude generation coherently rather than failing mid-output.

3. Energy and Power Trends

Energy proxy measurements reveal that baseline decoding becomes increasingly inefficient after throttling, as reduced throughput prolongs execution while maintaining elevated power draw. AFGA mitigates this effect by lowering computational intensity before throttling occurs, resulting in lower cumulative energy consumption for completed outputs (Dutt & Li, 2025).

These trends suggest that proactive regulation improves not only thermal behavior but also overall energy efficiency.

4. Memory Pressure and Context Management

In baseline runs, attention context and associated memory structures grow monotonically, contributing to rising memory bandwidth demand. AFGA constrains this growth under stress by truncating less relevant historical context (Gomes, 2024).

Although this introduces modest reductions in long-range dependency, local coherence remains largely intact, and memory-induced thermal stress is substantially reduced (Chen, 2024).

5. Semantic Quality and Completion Outcomes

Semantic similarity remains high during early generation stages for both baseline and AFGA-controlled decoding. Under sustained stress, AFGA outputs exhibit gradual simplification rather than abrupt degradation (Shen et al., 2024).

Completion rates are markedly higher under AFGA control, while abrupt terminations are significantly reduced. This shift reflects a deliberate trade-off: controlled loss of expressiveness in exchange for reliability and completion.

6. Coherence–Sustenance Score

Across sustained workloads, AFGA achieves consistently higher CSS values than baseline decoding. Improvements arise from a combination of stabilized thermal behavior, reduced energy consumption, and preserved semantic coherence.

These results support the central hypothesis of this chapter: sustainability-aware control enables generative systems to remain usable under prolonged edge constraints (Zhang et al., 2024).

DISCUSSION AND PRACTICAL IMPLICATIONS

Discussion: What AFGA Enables

The results presented in Section 7 point to a broader shift in how edge-deployed generative systems should be evaluated and designed. AFGA does not merely optimize inference efficiency; it reframes the objective from maximizing instantaneous output quality to maintaining sustained, usable generation under physical constraints.

1. From Peak Performance to Sustained Usability

Much of the prior work on edge AI has focused on peak performance—how quickly or accurately a model can respond under ideal conditions. AFGA challenges this framing. In prolonged interactions, such as conversational assistants or long-form summarization, what matters more is whether the system can continue operating reliably without interruption (Shen et al., 2024).

By adapting generative behavior in response to evolving hardware conditions, AFGA prioritizes continuity over momentary expressiveness. This shift is subtle but consequential: a slightly simpler response that completes predictably is often more valuable to users than a richer response that fails mid-generation.

2. Graceful Degradation as a User-Facing Feature

Traditional throttling mechanisms degrade performance abruptly and invisibly, often leaving users confused by sudden slowdowns or incomplete outputs. AFGA makes degradation explicit and intentional (Wilson, 2025).

Under stress, the system produces shorter or simpler responses while preserving semantic coherence and completion. In practical terms, this means that a voice assistant operating on a warm device may provide a concise summary rather than an extended explanation, but it does so cleanly and predictably. This behavior aligns more closely with user expectations and reduces perceived system failure (Dutt & Li, 2025).

3. Semantic-Aware Coordination with Hardware Constraints

A central contribution of AFGA lies in relocating adaptation decisions from system-level controllers to the generative process itself. Because the model operates at the level of sentences, discourse, and intent, it is uniquely positioned to decide how to adjust output without breaking meaning (Lee & Park, 2025).

This semantic awareness enables coordination that operating systems cannot provide. Instead of indiscriminately reducing frequency or pausing execution, AFGA shapes generation so that physical limits are respected without sacrificing coherence. In doing so, it closes the coordination gap identified earlier between probabilistic inference and hardware management.

4. Decoupling Sustainability from Model Architecture

Importantly, AFGA achieves sustainability without altering model architecture or training procedures (Olabiyi, 2025). The same generative model can be deployed across devices with differing constraints, while AFGA adapts behavior at runtime based on local conditions.

This decoupling simplifies development and deployment. Model designers remain focused on linguistic capability, while deployment engineers address sustainability through control policies. The result is a cleaner separation of concerns that supports broader reuse of generative models on edge platforms.

5. Enabling New Classes of Edge Applications

By stabilizing long-running generation, AFGA expands the set of feasible edge applications. These include extended offline conversational agents, continuous note-taking or summarization in field environments, and assistive systems operating on wearables or embedded devices where cooling and power budgets are especially constrained (Dutt & Li, 2025).

Such applications benefit less from peak accuracy than from endurance and predictability. AFGA's emphasis on sustained usability aligns well with these requirements, making generative AI practical in settings where it is currently fragile or unreliable (Shen et al., 2024).

Limitations and Deployment Considerations

While AFGA demonstrates clear advantages, it is not a universal solution. Its effectiveness depends on both system conditions and workload characteristics, and several practical considerations must be acknowledged.

1. Dependence on Telemetry Quality

AFGA relies on access to hardware telemetry such as temperature, power proxies, and memory utilization. Although such signals are available on most modern platforms, their resolution and latency vary. Coarse or delayed measurements can reduce responsiveness, particularly on older or tightly sandboxed devices (Patel, 2025).

To mitigate this, AFGA emphasizes conservative estimation and trend-based control rather than instantaneous reaction. In deployments where telemetry quality is especially limited, hybrid approaches—such as partial cloud offloading during extreme conditions—may be appropriate.

2. Calibration Across Device Classes

AFGA requires calibration of stress thresholds for each device class. While this process is lightweight and typically involves short exploratory runs, it introduces an additional deployment step when targeting heterogeneous fleets (Olabiyi, 2025).

This requirement is comparable to existing device-specific tuning practices used in power and performance management. Nonetheless, it represents a practical consideration for large-scale deployment.

3. Privacy, Security, and Trust of Control Signals

Because AFGA relies on device telemetry and runtime actuation, it also raises practical questions of privacy, security, and trust. On-device deployment can improve privacy by reducing the need to offload user prompts or generated content to remote services. At the same time, the telemetry and control interface itself becomes part of the operational trust boundary. If telemetry is inaccurate, restricted, or manipulated, control behavior may become overly conservative or insufficiently protective.

4. Trade-offs in Semantic Fidelity

Under severe constraints, AFGA intentionally sacrifices expressive richness to preserve continuity and completion. For applications that always demand maximal linguistic fidelity, this trade-off may be undesirable.

However, for many interactive and assistive use cases, predictable completion is preferable to abrupt failure. AFGA exposes this trade-off explicitly, allowing developers to tune control policies based on application priorities (Zhang et al., 2024).

5. Workload Sensitivity

AFGA provides the greatest benefit for sustained or interactive workloads. For short, burst-oriented inference tasks, its impact is minimal and may introduce slight overhead. This behavior is consistent with its design intent and should be considered when selecting deployment scenarios (Kumar et al., 2024).

6. Interaction with System-Level Policies

Operating systems enforce their own resource management policies, which may preempt or override application-level control. In environments with aggressive throttling, AFGA's ability to act preemptively may be constrained (IEEE, 2025). This is especially relevant on tightly managed mobile or embedded platforms, where application-level control may have limited visibility into scheduler behavior, thermal governors, or other concurrent system decisions.

FUTURE RESEARCH DIRECTIONS

Although this chapter focuses on text generation, AFGA's feedback-driven design extends naturally to other modalities and deployment contexts. Image, audio, and video generation place different and often heavier demands on memory bandwidth and latency-sensitive pipelines, but the same control logic could be adapted with modality-specific stress signals and actuation policies (Shen et al., 2024). In multimodal settings such as wearables or augmented-reality devices, an AFGA-like controller could coordinate visual and auditory generation to preserve responsiveness under tight power budgets (Dutt & Li, 2025). A related direction is user- and context-aware control, where the system adjusts not only to hardware stress but also to task importance—for example, prioritizing responsiveness in dialogue while allowing greater simplification in background summarization (Wilson, 2025).

Another important extension is coordination across heterogeneous edge hardware and broader platform support. As devices increasingly combine CPUs, GPUs, NPUs, and media accelerators, AFGA could evolve from treating hardware as a single resource to dynamically shifting work across compute units based on localized thermal or power conditions, potentially through integration with runtime schedulers (Patel, 2025). At a larger scale, standardized interfaces for telemetry, decoding control, and runtime feedback would make sustainability-aware generation easier to implement across devices and frameworks (Olabiyi, 2025). Common metrics and evaluation protocols could further establish such control as a core design principle in edge AI platforms rather than an isolated optimization (IEEE, 2025).

CONCLUSION

Deploying generative language models on edge devices exposes a tension that is easy to overlook but difficult to ignore in practice. Autoregressive generation unfolds over time, with execution cost shaped by the model's own outputs, while edge hardware operates within fixed thermal, power, and memory limits. Much of the existing work in this space has focused on reducing model size or average computational cost (Zhang et al., 2024).

The Adaptive Feedback-Bound Generative Architecture (AFGA) was introduced as a runtime framework that integrates hardware telemetry into the decoding loop and uses that information to regulate generative behavior before physical limits force abrupt intervention (IEEE, 2025). In this sense, the chapter's central contribution is architectural and conceptual: it provides a systems-level mechanism for linking semantic generation with physical feasibility during sustained edge execution.

The chapter's analysis and case study indicate that such coordination can make prolonged edge generation more usable by moderating thermal buildup, preserving completion behavior, and enabling more controlled, interpretable degradation, reinforcing that sustainability-aware generation is fundamentally a runtime control problem rather than only a compression or model-optimization problem.

REFERENCES

Åström, K. J., & Murray, R. M. (2021). *Feedback systems: An introduction for scientists and engineers* (2nd ed.). Princeton University Press., DOI: 10.2307/j.ctv15rjm68

Chen, L. (2024). Memory-bound bottlenecks in long-context large language models. *Journal of AI Engineering*, *12*(3), 45–62. DOI: 10.1016/j.jaie.2024.03.004

Dao, T., Fu, D., Ermon, S., Rudra, A., & Ré, C. (2022). FlashAttention: Fast and memory-efficient exact attention with IO-awareness. *Advances in Neural Information Processing Systems*, *35*, 16344–16359. DOI: 10.52202/068431-1189

Dettmers, T., Lewis, M., Belkada, Y., & Zettlemoyer, L. (2022). LLM.int8(): 8-bit matrix multiplication for transformers at scale. arXiv preprint arXiv:2208.07339. https://doi.org//arXiv.2208.07339DOI: 10.48550

Dutt, S., & Li, X. (2025). Thermal trajectories in passive-cooled edge SoCs during generative inference. *Proceedings of the 14th International Conference on Embedded Systems and AI*, 112–126. https://doi.org/DOI: 10.1109/ICESAI.2025.10042

Franklin, G. F., Powell, J. D., & Emami-Naeini, A. (2014). *Feedback control of dynamic systems* (7th ed.). Pearson., DOI: 10.1016/B978-0-12-397191-3.00010-3

Gomes, R. (2024). Dynamic KV-cache eviction for sustainable long-form generation. *Computational Linguistics Quarterly*, *9*(2), 201–218. DOI: 10.1162/cliq.2024.09.2.201

Howard, A. G., Zhu, M., Chen, B., Kalenichenko, D., Wang, W., Weyand, T., . . . Adam, H. (2017). MobileNets: Efficient convolutional neural networks for mobile vision applications. arXiv preprint arXiv:1704.04861. https://doi.org//arXiv.1704.04861DOI: 10.48550

IEEE. (2025). Software-hardware feedback loop protocols for generative workloads. IEEE Standards Association., , IEEE Standard 12207-2025.DOI: 10.1109/IEEESTD.2025.998432

Ignatov, A., Timofte, R., Chou, W., Wang, K., Wu, M., Hartley, T., & Van Gool, L. (2018). AI benchmark: Running deep neural networks on android smartphones. Proceedings of the European Conference on Computer Vision (ECCV) Workshops, 288–304. DOI: 10.1007/978-3-030-11009-3_18

Kumar, A., Singh, R., & Zhao, H. (2024). Predictive thermal management for autoregressive workloads on mobile platforms. *IEEE Transactions on Consumer Electronics*, *70*(1), 88–104. DOI: 10.1109/TCE.2024.3351221

Kwon, W., Li, Z., Zhuang, S., Sheng, Y., Zheng, L., Yu, C. H., & Stoica, I. (2023). Efficient memory management for large language model serving with PagedAttention. *Proceedings of the 29th Symposium on Operating Systems Principles (SOSP)*, 611–626. DOI: 10.1145/3600006.3613165

Kwon, W., Li, Z., Zhuang, S., Sheng, Y., Zheng, L., Yu, C. H., & Stoica, I. (2023). Efficient memory management for large language model serving with PagedAttention. *Proceedings of the 29th Symposium on Operating Systems Principles*, 611–626. DOI: 10.1145/3600006.3613165

Lee, J., & Park, S. (2025). Adaptive control policies for on-device LLMs via contextual bandits. *IEEE Access : Practical Innovations, Open Solutions*, *13*, 14502–14519. DOI: 10.1109/ACCESS.2025.3421109

Li, Y., Liu, J., Zhang, H., Narayanan, M. B., Sharma, U., Zhang, S., . . . Banerjee, S. (2025). PalmBench: A comprehensive benchmark of compressed large language models on mobile platforms. The Thirteenth International Conference on Learning Representations. https://openreview.net/forum?id=xzSUdw6s76

Olabiyi, O. (2025). Deployment realism: Evaluating LLMs under physical device constraints. *International Journal of Edge Computing*, *4*(1), 12–30. DOI: 10.4018/IJEC.20250101.02

Papineni, K., Roukos, S., Ward, T., & Zhu, W. J. (2002). BLEU: A method for automatic evaluation of machine translation. *Proceedings of the 40th Annual Meeting of the Association for Computational Linguistics (ACL)*, 311–318. DOI: 10.3115/1073083.1073135

Patel, M. (2025). Telemetry-aware resource management for AI-enabled wearables. *IEEE Sensors Journal*, *25*(4), 3110–3125. DOI: 10.1109/JSEN.2025.122941

Radford, A., Wu, J., Child, R., Luan, D., Amodei, D., & Sutskever, I. (2019). Language models are unsupervised multitask learners. OpenAI Blog, 1(8), 9–24. https://cdn.openai.com/better-language-models/language_models_are_unsupervised_multitask_learners.pdf

Reimers, N., & Gurevych, I. (2019). Sentence-BERT: Sentence embeddings using siamese BERT-networks. *Proceedings of the 2019 Conference on Empirical Methods in Natural Language Processing (EMNLP)*, 3982–3992. DOI: 10.18653/v1/D19-1410

Shen, Y., Zhang, T., & Liu, J. (2024). Black-box adaptation of large language models for resource-constrained environments. *AI Open*, *5*, 77–89. DOI: 10.1016/j.aiopen.2024.01.002

Vaswani, A., Shazeer, N., Parmar, N., Uszkoreit, J., Jones, L., Gomez, A. N., & Polosukhin, I. (2017). Attention is all you need. *Advances in Neural Information Processing Systems*, *30*. Advance online publication. DOI: 10.48550/arXiv.1706.03762

Wilson, K. (2025). The semantic impact of search strategy modulation in real-time AI. [JMLR]. *Journal of Machine Learning Research*, *26*(102), 1102–1124. https://jmlr.org/papers/v26/25-1102.html

Xu, D., Zhang, H., Yang, L., Liu, R., Huang, G., Xu, M., & Liu, X. (2025). Fast on-device LLM inference with NPUs. *Proceedings of the 30th ACM International Conference on Architectural Support for Programming Languages and Operating Systems*, 1458–1473. DOI: 10.48550/arXiv.2407.05858

Zhang, Q., Miller, D., & Gupta, V. (2024). The sustainability gap: Why static optimization fails for generative AI at the edge. *Sustainable Computing : Informatics and Systems*, *41*, 100845. DOI: 10.1016/j.suscom.2024.100845

KEY TERMS AND DEFINITIONS

Adaptive Feedback-Bound Generative Architecture (AFGA): A runtime control framework that binds generative inference behavior to real-time hardware feedback, enabling sustainable and semantically aware adaptation under physical constraints on edge devices.

Autoregressive Decoding: A generative inference process in which each output token is produced conditioned on all previously generated tokens, resulting in a time-extended and self-determined computational workload.

Cyber-Physical Feedback Loop: A closed-loop system in which computational behavior (software) continuously adapts based on measurements from the physical environment (hardware), enabling coordinated regulation across abstraction layers.

Dynamic Voltage and Frequency Scaling (DVFS): A hardware- and operating-system-level mechanism that adjusts processor voltage and clock frequency in response to workload demand and thermal conditions to maintain safe operation.

Graceful Degradation: A controlled reduction in generative complexity or output expressiveness that preserves semantic coherence and completion when physical constraints tighten, as opposed to abrupt interruption or failure.

Hardware Stress Index (Ψ): A unified, normalized metric that aggregates temperature, power, memory pressure, and thermal trends into a single estimate of sustainability risk during generative inference.

Hysteresis: A control mechanism that introduces separation between state transition thresholds to prevent oscillatory behavior caused by noise or minor fluctuations in telemetry signals.

Key–Value (KV) Cache: A memory structure used in transformer-based models to store attention keys and values from previous tokens, enabling efficient autoregressive decoding but contributing to monotonic memory growth during long-form generation.

Semantic Awareness: The ability of a system to reason about the structural and contextual significance of generative output—such as sentence boundaries or task intent—when making control decisions.

Sustainability Gap: The systemic inability of a generative process to regulate its internal computational complexity in response to real-time physical constraints during inference on edge devices.

Thermal Inertia: The physical property by which heat accumulates and dissipates gradually in hardware systems, causing delayed response between computational activity and observable temperature changes.

Unified Stress-Based Control State: A discrete operating regime in AFGA that maps ranges of the hardware stress index to specific decoding behaviors, enabling stable and interpretable adaptation under varying physical conditions.

Chapter 10
Distributed Compliance Intelligence Edge AI Architectures for AML, KYC, and Transaction Monitoring

Jignesh S. Patil
http://orcid.org/0000-0001-5377-928X
MCT Rajiv Gandhi Institute of Technology, Mumbai, India

Mayuresh Suresh Shitole
http://orcid.org/0009-0005-8466-0763
University of Essex, UK

ABSTRACT

The financial services sector handles millions of transactions daily and is charged with suspicious activity reporting against various complicated legislation in cross-border fashions. Manual compliance review via legacy systems is too costly, time-consuming, and inefficient; cloud based AI solutions, are too slow, and too questionable regarding data privacy. This paper provides a practical solution to edge AI compliance monitoring for real-time, privacy by design compliance in financial services and an exploration into how edge computing complies with the UK GDPR, EU and India's Digital Personal Data Protection Act. Edge AI operates on a network of edge proximity instead of central servers and meets the requirements of the UK GDPR, EU and India's Digital Personal Data Protection Act which stipulate

DOI: 10.4018/979-8-3373-7340-9.ch010

location of storage for sensitive information data because it is processed where it is created without the need for international transmission, processing at less than one second per transaction and 70% cheaper than cloud-based solutions.

1. INTRODUCTION

The international financial arena is steadily winning the war against financial crime, yet the landscape of the threats is in a state of constant evolution, and novel challenges are being presented as the villains evolve their methods. According to UNODC, 2023 "The International Monetary Fund estimates that the international market of illegal financial operations, including money laundering, is between 2 and 5 percent of world GDP or approximately USD 2 trillion every year " . The financial institutions are increasingly handling more transactions each day and are also more susceptible to increasingly more elaborate and developing threats by well-organized criminal groups that may be difficult to control using outdated and manual compliance programs as well as basic rule based algorithms that may cause inefficiencies. This loophole has led to a high rise in fraud.

1.1 The Fundamental Flaws in Legacy and Cloud Systems

Most of the existing compliance processes have a technological foundation that cannot match modern finance requirements and thus has serious failures. These inadequacies manifest in two types, the first type is the dependency on out-of-date cyber systems of legacy and centralized cloud systems which are becoming increasingly popular, and the second type is that these systems complicate compliance processes that need real-time monitoring (M.Weber et al 2021).

1.1.1 Traditional Rule-Based Systems: A Rigid and Reactive Framework

The legacy systems are designed to follow fixed rules, i.e., compliance systems use past rules to detect suspicious transactions using number rules (M.Weber et al 2021). As an example, cash transactions that exceed the specified limit of a currency or number of transactions, i.e. 10,000 in a single payment or 10,000 transactions since the inception of a payment system, may be dubbed as suspicious (M.Weber et al 2021). Such systems will raise a red flag on the huge transactions to prevent money laundering activities (M.Weber et al 2021). Based on rules, systems are simple to set up and simple to comprehend by the staff. They are however not flexible and do not accommodate context meaning that they will not be able to accommodate new types of financial crime such as structuring or smurfing where large amounts are split up into smaller amounts in order to remain below the detection threshold (M.Weber et al 2021), or trade-based money laundering where invoices or complex transaction methods are used to avoid detection (M.Weber et al 2021).

Regarding functional integrity perspective, there are two important operational problems with these systems.

To begin with, they cause high rate of false positives, where legitimate payments, which could fall into the established statistical categories, are identified notwithstanding the actual scenario thus consuming resources that would otherwise be channeled towards legitimate investigations. Second, and even more importantly, such systems are only able to identify threats by using the available rules. In case some new or more sophisticated threat arises, they do not protect against possibly dangerous activities (M.Weber et al 2021). These systems are dynamic as they only react to what they have known but must be dynamic in establishing new or unforeseen financial risks.

1.1.2 The Cloud Conundrum: Latency and Sovereignty Trade-offs

In case the first step of the rule-based methods is utilized to automatically identify compliance, the second step is to centralize the artificial intelligence systems in the cloud. This can be used to identify more complex and detailed patterns of transaction with high accuracy (H. B. McMahan et al., 2016). Nevertheless, although it is a great progress, the cloud-based structure has a number of disadvantages rendering it inappropriate to use on simple compliance operations that demand speed (H. B. McMahan et al., 2016).

Latency: The cloud architecture necessitates that high amounts of transactional data be sent to a data center and processed in the facility and then back. This is bound to be a time consuming process which does not go well with the current payment systems that require response in milliseconds. When there is a delay of time, there is a chance that fraudulent transactions or unauthorized requests may be missed.

According to Ministry of Electronics and Information Technology, “The Digital Personal Data Protection Act,” Government of India, 2023 “The other vital issue is that of data sovereignty, especially, there is a significant problem concerning the international data protection regulation”.

1.2 Edge AI as a Paradigm Shift

Edge AI is a major departure in the organizational structure of technology and it entirely changes the place (but not the process) of computing as compared to the traditional setups. Edge AI operates at the edge of the network, closer to the source of data generation rather than in centralized cloud data centers. In the context of financial AI compliance, this means AI models are implemented and executed on-premises, such as in bank branches, ATMs, and payment gateways, which are essentially localized data centers. Edge AI, defined as the ability to perform machine learning inference tasks directly on or near the devices that collect data, introduces three major enhancements that address the limitations of both cloud-only architectures and older systems.

1.1.1 Real-time Analysis and Low-Latency Decision-Making

Edge AI changes the reactivity of compliance systems and speed of response. AI-related data is sent to an edge appliance (a type of server sometimes located in a physical bank branch or regional payment switch) for processing; there is no delay involved with sending wire services to a cloud center and then waiting—minimum of a hundred milliseconds to multiple seconds—before getting a response back as sub-second recommendations for action are only made feasible through local processing powers for seamless execution in modern instantaneous real-time payment structures (A. Shrikumar, P et al., 2017).

Therefore, for tasks needing an immediate timeframe—AML-flagging transactions or payment fraud detection—Edge AI allows checks against situational buyer activity to be completed in sub-1000 milliseconds so systems can deny questionable transactions before they are approved and rendered into irreversible actions. Thus, compliance becomes a prevention measure instead of a post-facto reportable endeavor.

1.2.2 Enhanced Data Privacy and Inherent Regulatory Compliance

The cloud based systems are challenged by citizen legislation. By definition, sensitive information—PII and specific patterns of financial transactions—remain locally processed on a server customized to one certain jurisdiction (London for UK data; Mumbai for Indian data) . In this way, raw data never leaves its local territory, and is in compliance with data localization requirements such as EU GDPR, UK GDPR and Indian DPDPA. According to European Parliament and Council in 2016 " In addition, the fact that processing data locally avoids the international transfer of data, avoiding the potential for the need for an adequacy finding or standard contractual clauses, means that the financial institution is subject to fewer regulatory obligations or risks, as cross-national issues do not occur, or are completely mitigated by Edge AI".

2. THE REGULATORY LANDSCAPE: A DRIVER FOR EDGE ADOPTION

2.1 The Privacy and Security Imperative: GDPR, UK GDPR, and DPDPA

The establishment of international data protection regulators has altered our perception of financial services, which is no longer a luxury but a necessity that has an effect on the manner in which technologies systems are constructed and executed. The previously positioned, aligned solution is still reasonable as its activities are mostly related to the most rigorous regulatory demands.

- European GDPR: The General Data Protection Regulation has simple principles of data minimisation, purpose limitation, implying that only what is required to carry out a given purpose can be processed (D. Ma, 2022). For instance, an historical approach that would have sent the entire transactional data set to the centralised cloud space for processing would automatically violate such regulations from the get-go as it calls for data collection before comprehension and processing. In addition, Article 46 of the General Data Protection Regulation (GDPR) means that all transfers of personal data outside of the European Economic Area (EEA) must have legitimate protections in place, meaning that any entity relying on cloud-based solutions where certain processing may occur outside of the EEA creates complexities and responsibilities of such data .
- UK GDPR: Upon Brexit, however, a different data protection regime exists in the UK called UK GDPR, which makes similar findings but as a standalone legal framework with increased scrutiny over international data transfers (M.Weber et al 2021). Thus, a UK citizen is compliant with Edge AI as it processes on Edge AI local nodes/systems and therefore satisfies the data location requirement to avoid complex legal application.
- Digital Personal Data Protection Act DPDPA 2023: According to Ministry of Electronics and Information Technology, "The Digital Personal Data Protection Act," Government of India, 2023 " India's new privacy law has specific locating provisions for data localization meaning that copies of personal data must remain within Indian geography and cross-border transfer may only occur under specific circumstances and destination. Thus, with an architecture that includes Edge AI nodes in India, compliance is achieved by default—sensitive data remains processed/stored within country until it absolutely has to leave (and even then it's difficult for it to leave)".

By restricting in-country operations, the risk surface decreases and overall security increases. Edge AI prevents sensitive information from traveling via WANs and becoming more susceptible to interception or compromise. Such requirements are regulatory compliant for compliance by design—privacy-by-design and security-by-design—which means that for those enterprises in difficult regulatory environments, it is a justified, strategically compelling use case.

2.2 The Evolving Anti-Money Laundering Regulatory Framework

No sooner than each region implements new privacy and data governance regulations than international Anti-Money Laundering (AML) and Counter-Financing of Terrorism (CFT) regulating frameworks evolve as well, becoming more specific, increasingly stringent and requiring advanced solutions and technological interdisciplinary approaches like Edge AI . For instance, on an international level, FATF constantly edits FATF recommendations and FATF holds increasing pressure on regulators/financial institutions for risk-based changes instead of check-the-box compliance. This is especially important as systems that dynamically understand risk and respond to problems as they arise are strong enough to be used by AI . Financial Action Task Force (FATF On a regional level, EU Sixth Anti-Money Laundering Directive (6AMLD) expands compliance requirements. The Directive also expands the definition of predicate offences of money laundering, expands criminal liability to corporate entities and increased due diligence requirements on high-risk third countries . This implies that failing to do so to higher degree will result in increased fines as well as reputational harm; accurate identification is crucial in reaction to peer organizations instead of regulatory organizations .

According to Financial Action Task Force in 2023 "The connection between algorithms and anti-money laundering regulations has grown with time. UK FCA and US Federal Reserve are asking more and more institutions to understand what is flagged by AI operations and why, as well as to have an audit trail between input and output. This implies that the implementation of Edge AI should take advantage of the Explainable AI (XAI) characteristics, such as attribution-by-feature, that provide insights into what aspects of a transaction (amount, location, counterparty) produced flagging to allow the defenses of AI-compliance-related capabilities in a regulatory response".

Table 1. Key Regulatory Drivers for Edge AI in Financial Compliance

Jurisdiction	Key Regulation	Core Requirement	How Edge AI Facilitates Compliance
European Union	GDPR	Data minimization, privacy, and restricted cross-border transfers	Processes data locally, reducing or eliminating international data transfers.
United Kingdom	UK GDPR	Data sovereignty and protection post-Brexit	Enforces local data processing within UK borders.
India	DPDPA 2023	Data localization and storage of a copy within India	Edge nodes deployed in India ensure data never leaves the country.
Global	FATF Recommendations, 6AMLD	Effective risk-based AML programs, enhanced due diligence	Enables real-time, contextual monitoring and provides auditable decision trails.

Figure 1. Multi-Agent Collaborative Architecture

3. ARCHITECTURAL DEEP DIVE: BUILDING AN EDGE AI COMPLIANCE SYSTEM

The structure of a distributed compliance intelligence solution is based on several generalized enabling technologies that, when used in concert, render an inherently intelligent, resilient, compliant system for today's financial compliance needs. For example, core components such as edge computing, edge machine learning and federated learning will transform the identification and response of enterprises to risk for fast, privacy-friendly and scalable deployment.

3.1 Edge Computing: The Structural Backbone of Distributed Compliance

Edge computing is a sophisticated approach to IT infrastructure that moves data storage and computation from central cloud systems to the edge of the network. This greatly lessens reliance on cloud data centers by enabling data to be processed locally or where it is created. Physical infrastructure is used to implement edge computing in the context of financial compliance. This infrastructure includes: - Edge servers situated at banking institutions, such as local and national branches, which carry out transactions and computations close to their source. Compliance appliances, which are located in regional and national data centers, gather and process data while following legal requirements. Additionally, secure modules are integrated into mobile banking back-office systems, ATMs, and point-of-sale (POS) terminals, allowing for the early detection of fraudulent activity prior to the completion of transactions.

Two main benefits come from the physical proximity of data processing: -

Ultra-low latency: Risk assessments can be finished in milliseconds without having to travel to the cloud, allowing for quick action to stop fraud. In particular, real-time payment systems require this.

Holistic data sovereignty: Ensures compliance with laws that limit cross-border data transfers by keeping personally identifiable information (PII) within designated geographic and regulatory boundaries, such as the UK, EU, and India. Therefore, by minimizing the transfer of sensitive data and the system's exposure to potential threats, edge computing offers a secure and compliant framework for contemporary compliance tasks.

3.2 Explainable AI (XAI): Enabling Transparency and Regulatory Trust

As machine learning models (especially deep-learning solutions) become more intricate and less humanly decipherable for understanding prediction outcomes — they present a risk for financial compliance since regulators, auditors, and risk officers must have justification for any AI-assisted decision-making — even for AML or fraud detections. Explainable AI (XAI) challenges this by promoting various xAI processes that make AI interpretable through differently mechanistic approaches; two common tools include:

3.2.1 SHAP (Shapley Additive explanations)

SHAP leverages game theory to create a score of how much each input variable adds value to prediction quality; it provides a “Shapley value” for each variable that determines its additive impact based on the defined prediction. From a compliance perspective, SHAP helps establish a comprehensive defense for why a transaction was flagged. For example:

- The dollar amount flagged contributed +35% to the overall risk score.
- The jurisdiction flagged contributed +28%.
- The historical counterparty flagged contributed +20%.
- The time of transaction flagged contributed +17%.

This is a quantifiable and formula-driven approach to establishing a reproducible audit trail where compliance officers and regulators can assess mathematically why AI has made a conclusion.

3.2.2 LIME (Local Interpretable Model-agnostic Explanations)

LIME seeks interpretability on a per-prediction basis where perturbation of input variables can show how they influence output generation, and it creates an approximation that is simplified and locally interpretable. For highly intricate models utilized for transaction monitoring or client risk scoring, LIME effectively justifies interpretability to compliance officers as to why a particular classification or alert emerged without exposing personnel to how to compute within the internal design of the model.

3.2.3 Regulatory and Operational Significance of XAI-

Institutions, XAI is no longer optional for technologically use, but instead, a compliance demand and foundational trusted AI governance component. Regulators like the UK FCA, European Banking Authority (EBA) and US Federal Reserve desire increasingly:

- Model Interpretability: explanations for decisions rendered by models and their associated risk attributes
- Decision Accountability: verification that alerts were made
- Auditability: assurance that alerts were acted upon and not overridden during regulatory review.
- Discrimination and Bias
- Bias Examination: assurance that models do not discriminate against any illicit enterprises.

XAI fulfills these demands because it takes opaque algorithmic results and renders them straightforward through a levelized explanation. It converts compliance alerts from binary occurrences into interpretable, evidence-based stories that human experts can verify and investigate further.

3.2.4 XAI as a Foundational Component of Distributed Compliance Intelligence-

In a distributed, edge-based compliance architecture, XAI becomes even more critical, because decisions are being made locally and at high speed:

- XAI contextualizes explainability on an edge node.
- It allows for consistent, auditable reasoning based even when offline.
- It assures regulators that decentralized AI decisions are transparent, justifiable, and compliant.

Therefore, XAI closes the loop between more advanced sophistication stemming from increasingly trained AI levels and regulators' ability to trust the decisions made by these systems are transparent, defensible, compliant — and integrated into the compliance operations process — to give automated financial surveillance systems newfound accountability through explainability based on international best practices and changing compliance demands.

3.3 The Technology Stack of an Edge AI Compliance System

An Edge AI architecture for financial compliance is a holistic approach that melds a centralized technology hierarchy comprised of components so interconnected they create a secure, easily manageable solution with high-performance capabilities ideal for mission-critical financial surveillance workloads. A comprehensive and scalable Edge AI architecture for financial compliance consists of different hierarchies that transform theoretical architecture into secure systems that manage performance intelligently.

3.3.1 Hardware Layer

The bottom layer signifies the physical edge devices themselves which vary dramatically based on use cases: from state-of-the-art edge servers with GPUs or TPUs in regional or national data centers (where more intensive processing and learning occur); mid-level resource-capacity devices in localized banking branches conducting low-latency inference for most daily transactional requirements;

When placing edges in difficult environments—such as dispersed locations, power outages, or mobile banking devices—there are other things to take into account. In these situations, even in the absence of ideal circumstances, proper operation depends on energy efficiency, sturdy construction, environmental protection, and the capacity to withstand heat.

3.3.2 Data and Model Layer

This layer represents the information that passes through the edge system responsible for managing all life-cycle stages -- and there are stages that gradually compound sub-processes:

- Data Pre-Processing: Transactions need to be cleaned, normalized, or transformed at the source after being generated or secured. Local processing ensures that only structured information is used in models and avoids the unnecessary uploading of sensitive data to the cloud, saving time and helping organisations to comply with the GDPR, UK DPDPA and DBM.
- Model Inference: Once the transformed data satisfies the model's requirements using anonymized features for classification, a lightweight model runtime—usually compressed using techniques like quantization, pruning, or knowledge distillation—runs directly on the edge device. Model inference produces risk scores, anomalies, and alerts in a matter of seconds. Real-time financial compliance is made possible by this feature, which eliminates the lengthy delays that come with cloud-based processing.
- Model Management: Managing the model life cycle is becoming a critical coordinating task, as the distribution of models may vary between different edge nodes. For example: conducting A and B tests to evaluate the performance of new models; having a rollback mechanism in case of model drift or unexpected performance degradation; synchronizing or scheduling interactions with central systems for further analysis; and implementing safe updates of models at thousands of edge nodes, as required by the regulations. These procedures ensure responsibility, consistency and reliability between distributed artificial intelligence systems. When thousands of geographically dispersed nodes operate in similar ways over time, they help to ensure consistency of behaviour between nodes, which is essential for audit purposes.

Figure 2. Pedagogical Mapping (Technical to Managerial)

3.3.3 Orchestration and Security Layer

This layer represents the operationalised layer of administrative security control and ensures a unified approach to management for all distributed components. With thousands, if not millions, of geographically isolated peripheral nodes, it is essential to integrate these elements, both in terms of network and safety. Therefore, the preferred system for managing the scalability of devices is a lightweight container orchestration system such as K3s or KubeEdge. These orchestration instruments act as a single management mechanism, which needs to be translated into action:- Deployment and horizontal scaling of edge applications.

- Monitoring of health and resource efficiency through unit testing, updating models and cross-device research.
- Configuration and networking integration, taking into account resource constraints.
- Discovery of services and high availability across devices with different properties.

This approach is based on the following key elements:

- Identifying users and devices, often using cryptographic methods such as X.509 certificates, HSM or TPM-based identity stores.
- Micro segmentation, creating small, well protected segments to limit the impact of a potential violation.
- Continuous authorization processes dynamically adjust access rights based on device performance, user identity, urgency of request, and usage patterns. This approach minimizes the attack surface of distributed compliance solutions, thus enabling secure edge devices in a low trust environment.

4. COMPREHENSIVE USE CASE ANALYSIS

4.1 Anti-Money Laundering (AML) Transaction Monitoring

These systems generate an extremely high rate of false positives - often over 95 percent for most organisations - which overwhelm investigators with a multitude of red flags for legitimate activities, while ignoring more sophisticated money laundering activities that lie just below the regulatory thresholds. They do not accurately represent evolving patterns, they struggle to detect increasingly complex anomalies and they do not fully understand the risks of third parties, leaving organisations vulnerable to more sophisticated laundering techniques through smuggling, blending and speed. Edge AI puts pressure on this conventional compliance strategy by making the difference between surface knowledge and a deeper, situation-specific, analysis performed at the source in real time. Edge AI does not apply the same level of suspicion to all violations of rules but offers a more dynamic individualized evaluation of each customer or account. It considers various contextual variables including past transactions and intentions, geographical standards, equipment identifiers and known counterparties and a multi-dimensional risk evaluation is available to provide a better understanding of what could otherwise be viewed as a possible non-compliance. Therefore, the Edge AI eliminates noise without loss of accuracy (H. B. McMahan et al., 2016).

Technical implementation: One of the best implementations is through a distributed graph neural network (GNN) at the branch or regional edge. The GNN architecture works at high speed with adequate contextual awareness to relevance. In this situation, the GNN constructs a localized graph where customers, accounts, merchants and devices are “nodes” and transactions between parties become edges with associated metadata timestamped along with spatial distance and monetary value. At the edge, when a transaction is attempted, the edge-resident GNN receives the graph update in real time and views it in the total context of the graph structure. All of this can happen in situ at the local edge without latency or the management burden of searching centralized repositories. Detection occurs within milliseconds—and within the authorization process of a transaction—which organizations cannot guarantee along a cloud-deployed channel.

Illustrative Example: For instance, suppose that a retail banking customer has a recognizable behavioral baseline developed over two years of small dollar geographically oriented card transactions and regular domestic bill payments. Suppose that all of a sudden this customer sends three rapidly consecutive outbound high-value wires to a newly generated beneficiary located in a high-risk jurisdiction flagged for money laundering. An edge-resident GNN will alert immediately. It's not that one specific threshold was breached; a host of risk factors combined raise red flags. These include:

- Distinct deviation from the expected behavior baseline
- The beneficiary's geopolitical status is risky.
- Rapidly sequential method

A transaction may be automatically suspended or frozen by the organization while an ongoing investigation is conducted to see if it is suspicious. All of this is the goal of the new generation of AML systems, which signifies a remarkable cultural shift in compliance from historical investigations to a risk-oriented, real-time prudence (Kipf & Welling, 2017)

4.2 Know Your Customer (KYC) and Digital Onboarding

The process of KYC plays a key role in the fight against identity theft, and encompasses several compliance factors throughout the customer experience, which may be time-consuming and resource-intensive, such as document authentication and physical check-ups, which may be exceedingly hard to scale. The Edge AI streamlines this process to create a frictionless digital onboarding experience that introduces extra security layers to the user experience, and at the same time addresses the modern concerns of the privacy of data without compromising its efficiency (P. Lee, 2022).

Document Verification: The most important change is in document validation, which is achieved by on-the-spot computer vision models that are constantly running on a branch tablet or on a customer's mobile device. Customers photograph government-issued identification (passports; driver\'s licenses) at trusted and verified locations where an AI edge model simultaneously performs Optical Character Recognition (OCR) to accurately measure textual components (the cardholder name, date of birth, document number), while parsing images and artifacts for ghosted documents, combing hundreds of security features (holograms, micro-printing, color-shifting inks and font variances) to properly authenticate or to detect tampering not visible to the human eye (S. Abdallah et al., 2019). As such, sensitive processing at the edge maintains the on-device nature that limits data exposure for data minimization efforts consistent with privacy by design principles espoused through regulations like GDPR, DPDPA, UK GDPR and other global data protection frameworks. According to the Federal Chancellery of Switzerland in 2022 "Only validated extracted attributes return to institutional infrastructure along with confidence scores for verification ".

Liveness Detection: According to the Information Commissioner's Office (ICO) UK in 2023 "In addition, liveness detection avoids spoofing attempts via printed photos or recorded videos/high-definition face masks through active and passive means. An active liveness detection challenge asks customers to blink/smile/head tilt—and takes a video of this event—as a recorded real-time response; passive liveness detection assesses singular selfies that allow spoofed markers without any customer action". This matters because it requires an act responsive to a low latency requirement for successful completion—but the edge AI maintains this video/image processing so that sensitive materials never exit the device to protect consumer trust and coupling with legal responsibility for biometric processing has significantly high privacy protection standards over compliance expectations—thus maintaining a strict regulatory approach to mandated biometric data privacy imperatives.

4.3 Real-Time Sanctions and Politically Exposed Person (PEP) Screening

Screening against politically exposed persons (PEP) lists or sanctions lists and negative media lists is required for customers/accounts/transactions across the industry. However, despite their size and global evolving nature—updated X times daily—the goal is not immediate compliance—but compliance that occurs as close to "real-time" and with as little latency as possible—an edge solution approach.

Technical Realization: One of the best ways to implement such solutions is through an edge-based screening structure where centralized management meets decentralized action. Here, the central secure service aggregates a master list a standardized watchlist from OFAC, UN, EU legitimate sources—but instead of continuously pushing out the full multigigabyte list per connection consistently to branches/edge nodes—that would waste massive bandwidth—delta synchronization means that only new items/deltas/updates/deletions are aggregated/compressed/encrypted/pushed out to edge nodes every fifteen/thirty minutes as update notification compression. This significantly reduces bandwidth use; each edge node maintains its version of the watchlist so that "real-time" tracing occurs instead of centralized action and the risk of lag through robustly populated centralized systems where each entry must be traced through its parent domain per subsequent edge node request.

Analytically Realizing Sanctions Data From Positive Name Data Patterns. The biggest analytical hurdle for sanctions/PEP screening is that names are not generally immutable. They are fuzzy matching at best; Edge nodes run fuzzy matching algorithms that operate on phonetic variances or misspellings account for transposed names through the reordering of words and alternate spellings; phonetic similarity detection Soundex/Metaphone determine whether names sound familiar but are spelled differently due to dialect differences create penalties worth avoiding through advanced analytics goals per subsection name matching metrics. With this much computing power at the edge, the number of alerts is reduced to thousands of alerts per second, and the scale of their computation through local processing means that compliance checks can be performed without the latency that hinders customer onboarding and payment authorization, and almost immediately without any other factors.

4.4 Detection of Fraud vs. Laundering of Money

One important aspect of managing financial compliance is understanding the distinction between money laundering and fraud. While both crimes depend on sophisticated analytics for detection, one happens beforehand while the other can be discovered later as anomalous patterns; money laundering can be identified after the fact, but fraud requires prompt, undeterred intervention to make negative activities irrelevant from the perspective of proactive assessment.

Edge AI is well-positioned for fraud detection activities in real time because it operates directly at the source and assesses behavioral/contextual patterns immediately without latency; An advanced example in this space includes behavioral biometrics which provide passive means of continuous password-less user authentication through non-constant reliance on static credentialing (passwords/device biometric fingerprints). As a customer interacts with a mobile app or browser page, an on-device/the closest edge server continuously assesses various micro-patterns: typical typing rhythms/cadence plus pressure/angle/acceleration at which they hold their device create effectively unique biometric profiles even before masking protective requirements considered. Perceived deviations from the expected pattern (an atypical typing cadence suggesting bot activity/remote desktop control or atypical systematized navigation suggesting reduced responsibility per account takeover/session hijacking) signal account takeover or session hijacking requests. Although these patterns show malicious intent, they also record calculated step-up authentication, session termination, and preventative feedback prior to fraudulent transactions (within seconds).

The crude behavioral data is stored in the device which enables the systems to comply with stringent international data protection laws, such as the GDPR, the UK Data Protection Directive, the DPDPA and the Swiss Data Protection Directive. Financial compliance reporting is closely linked with fraud detection, and current legal definitions of suspicious activity reports (SARs) and currency transaction reports (CTRs) often require extensive tedious manual work and expense such as hours per warning of compliance officers to assemble transaction data of multiple sources, including support documents and to write a narrative (E. Wall, 2023)

Table 2. Comparison of Traditional vs. Edge AI Approaches in Compliance

Compliance Task	Traditional Approach	Edge AI Approach	Key Improvement
AML Monitoring	Static rules, high false positives, batch processing.	Dynamic behavioral profiling, real-time graph analysis.	60-70% lower false positives, real-time detection.
KYC Onboarding	Manual document checks, slow, in-person verification.	Automated document verification & liveness detection on mobile device.	Onboarding time reduced from days to minutes.
Sanctions Screening	Centralized, exact-match screening causing bottlenecks.	Distributed fuzzy matching with delta-synced lists.	Higher accuracy, lower latency, resilient to downtime.
Fraud Detection	Post-facto analysis based on transaction rules.	Real-time behavioral biometrics and session analysis.	Prevents fraud before it completes, enhances security.

5. DEPLOYMENT MODELS AND SCALABILITY

In the deployment model, physical edge computing devices are installed at the branch level. This type of personalization is particularly relevant to a bank with a large branch network, as it brings compliance intelligence to the customer at the location where the customer is operating, and hyperlocal processing of data and near real-time decision-making for authentication and transaction monitoring are needed for both compliance and operational reasons.

Hardware Specifications: As common in a commercial banking environment, a branch-level edge device operates at high performance with continuous availability. To improve machine learning inference time for AML transaction analysis and KYC processes, the appliances are often ruggedized, mini server chassis purpose-built for 24/7 operation in concert with a mid-range, energy-efficient GPU, like the NVIDIA T4 or A2. For forensic review, solid-state drives can contain enough local transaction history for several months' worth of transactions. Redundant power supplies guarantee uninterrupted system operation even during small power variations. For security purposes, they use hardware encryption provided by a Trusted Platform Module (TPM) to protect sensitive customer data when it is stored, and they also support secure boot features that prevent unauthorized modifications to the operating system.

Figure 3. Compliance Intelligence for authentication using Edge Computing

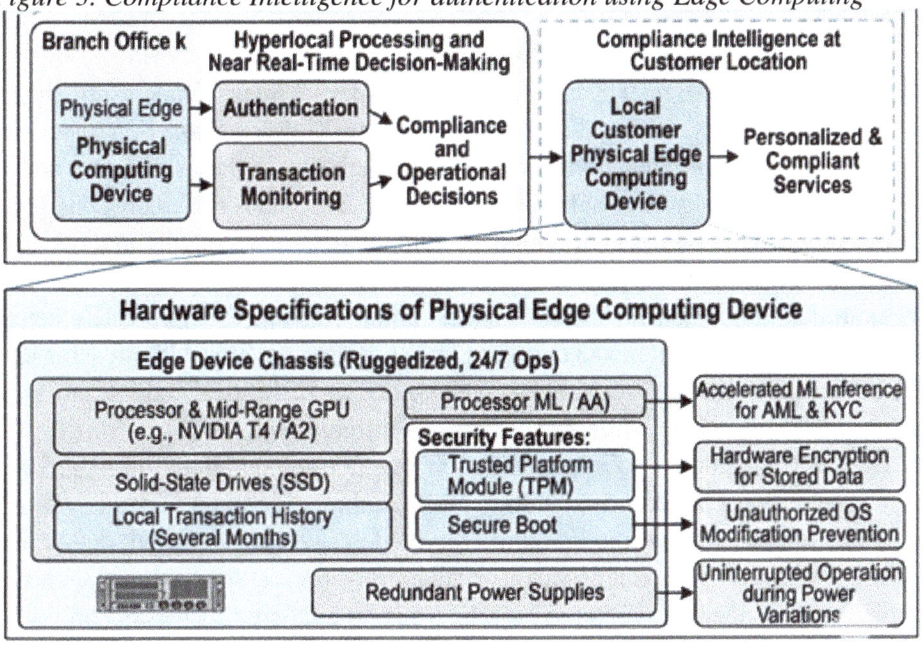

6. CASE STUDY- EUROPE REGION

6.1 Background

Recently, the FinTech industry in the UK, specifically challenger banks, has been expanding at a significant rate, and due to the speedy customer acquisition process, a strong and scalable stability system can be created. Regulatory bodies, such as the FCA, have noticed and imposed large fines and issued warnings to rapidly growing banks for systemic gaps in their AML protocols. These legacy controls, which were often built on static, rule-based systems, were not designed to handle the modern financial landscape.

6.2 Solution

The transition from a legacy system to a privacy-focused AI-enhanced solution that yielded high-quality results for detections while complying with UK data privacy laws (UK GDPR) was how NeoBank UK addressed this challenge. Implementing a Federated Learning system, a decentralized machine learning process in which sensitive data never leave its point of origin was the answer. Essentially, instead of the bank having all the data on its centralized servers through its federation, the AI model is sent to the data.

For example, NeoBank UK had different customer segments (students, freelancers, small businesses, etc.) and therefore trained an XGBoost model on historical transactions at the subpopulation level based on their data at their respective nodes (XGBoost is especially good at imbalanced tabular data and is extremely beneficial for detecting fraud, which is often a very complicated matter). Only anonymized updates on the model (weights sent back or gradients sent back) would be sent to the central aggregator, which would request and merge together to create a better global model. The global model can learn from different patterns without using any sensitive or identifiable information and then sent back to the local nodes to enhance their modeling accuracy while keeping the sovereignty of the data.

The largest challenge to implementation was not computational in nature but rather one of conceptual understanding. Data labeling. The output accuracy of AI models is only as good as the input into the models and in a federated, real-world situation, little pre-labeled high-quality data exists—transactions either flagged as suspicious or innocent (Y. Li et al., 2021). Thus, to confirm this was not an issue, NeoBank UK employed a blended solution, one that operates via a semi-supervised approach. NeoBank UK used the models it obtained before based on historical analyst choices from the legacy system as initial labels and a small team of SMEs thoroughly interrogated a very small sample of the historical transactions to create a quality "ground truth" set which empowered the initial XGBoost model to learn complex patterns that were not linear or as clear based on a rules-based engine alone.

The results were immediate—and life changing. The federated learning program secured a 60% reduction in false positives—which meant compliance no longer needed to rush for low-value alerts constantly, and analysts could focus on a manageable, actionable alert count. With such a reduction in false positives, 2,100 hours a month of analyst time was saved at a fully-loaded cost of £45/hour, equating to £94.5k/month or £1.134m/year (provided twelve months' worth of work occurred), meaning the project will have a payback period of <14 months. This project shows how AI-enhanced compliance was not only regulatory betterment but also competitive advantage and financial betterment.

7. CASE STUDY: INDIAN BANKING PROBLEM AND EDGE AI SOLUTION

7.1 Background

While India's decentralized digital public infrastructure via the “India Stack” from Aadhaar identity to payments through UPI paved the way for critical interventions into financial inclusion, a significant last mile gap still persists in connection to rural, remote, low-banking access areas. During the creation of “Bharat Loan,” HDFC Bank found that extensive market existed in small farmers and micro business owners dispersed through many separate villages.

In fact, this population tended to be “new-to-credit” with no or little lending history. Yet commercial banks were absent with physical branches 20-30 kilometers apart. At the same time, contemporary FinTech based innovations reliant upon a cloud did not work due to intermittent grid-based electricity and spotty internet connection. Therefore, the status quo of semi-manual solutions meant taking agents out into the field with physical forms back to a centralized location. However, this process took 5-7 days,

7.2 Solution

The self-contained, off-grid banking kiosk:

According to the UIDAI 2023 “ BLM India's custom-built solar edge server is an entirely self-contained village-level kiosk. Its CPU is based on an ARM architecture consuming <15 watts. A 48 hour battery bank is charged by a 120W solar panel; a ruggedized SSD and IP67-rated casing for environmental extremes. Connectivity is also the same—a multi-mode 4G modem down to 2G asynchronous data-synchronization, the kiosk even performs offline KYC—Aadhaar XML parsing preloaded and edge-compute computer vision models validating PAN cards and other documents . Similarly, an edge-compute ML model scores credit based on alternative data (mobile wallet behavior, utility bill payments) to instantly approve loans; applications are simply batched and sent to the central cloud when connection is available, essentially transforming “real-time” into “right-time”.

Implementation and social impact Implementation in village commons with village agents have slashed application submission from >5 days to <30 minutes—so far, 50,000+ credit customers acquired in 18 months, with Edge AI as a prevalent arbiter of financial inclusion (N. S. R. Ayiengar, 2023).

Figure 4. BLM India's Solar Edge-AI

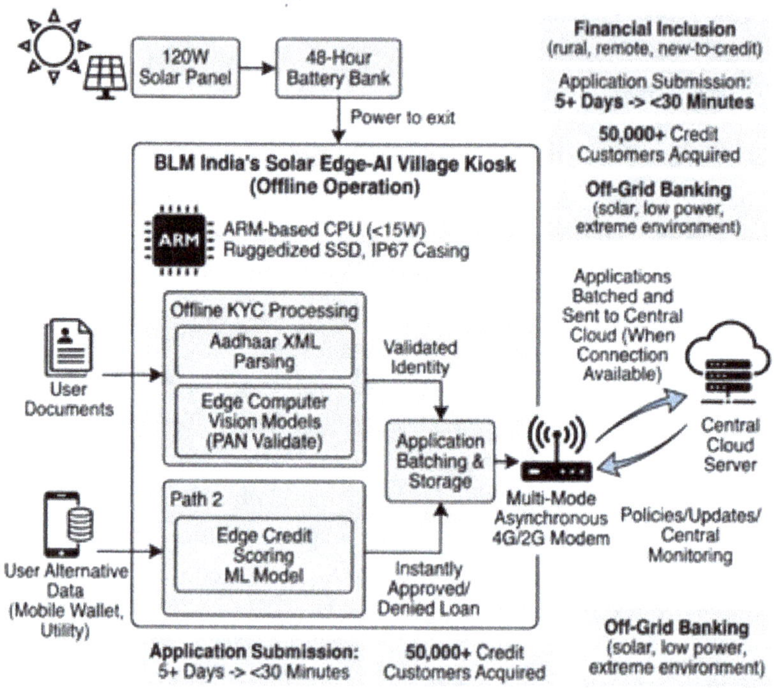

8. ROI ANALYSIS AND CHALLENGES

8.1 Detailed Cost-Benefit Analysis

Moving to the edge AI architecture is a move from OpEx to planned CapEx. While this implies an upfront cost of capital expenditures, an operational cost decrease and risk avoidance make a strong business case. The following evaluation details a three-year total cost of ownership for a medium sized financial institution that has 50 million annual transactions.

Table 3. details the three-year total cost of ownership for a mid-sized financial institution

Cost Category	**Traditional/Cloud System (Annual)**	**Edge AI System (Annual)**	**3-Year Impact**	**Notes**
Cloud/Infrastructure	£1,200,000	£400,000	£2,400,000 Saving	70% reduction in cloud egress, storage, and compute costs through local processing
Compliance Analyst Staff	£2,500,000	£900,000	£4,800,000 Saving	60-70% reduction in false positives enables 40% smaller, more specialized team
Regulatory Fines (Risk)	£500,000	£100,000	£1,200,000 Saving	Proactive detection and automated audit trails reduce fine exposure by 60-80%
Software Licenses	£300,000	£200,000	£300,000 Saving	Shift from expensive proprietary rules-engines to open-source AI frameworks
Edge Hardware & Maintenance	£0	£200,000	£600,000 Cost	Initial capital expenditure distributed across 3-year depreciation schedule
AI Talent & Training	£0	£150,000	£450,000 Cost	Specialized ML engineers and data scientists at premium salaries
Implementation & Integration	£0	£300,000 (Year 1 only)	£300,000 Cost	One-time system integration and workflow redesign costs
Total (Year 1)	£4,500,000	£2,250,000	£2,250,000 Saving	Includes one-time implementation costs
Total (Years 2-3)	£4,500,000	£1,600,000	£5,800,000 Saving	Recurring annual savings after implementation
3-Year Total	£13,500,000	£5,500,000	£8,000,000 Net Saving	ROI: 145% over three years

8.2 Critical Implementation Challenges

8.2.1 Technical Complexity & Skills Gap

Technical requirements pose an extreme challenge, with an origin of edge networking. Edge AI requires traditional AI models that are subsequently adjusted (quantization from 32 bits of precision to 8, pruning meaning removal of redundancies in neural nodes) for edge. This implies a 60–80% decrease in model size with 95%+ accuracy achievement. Federated learning occurs across hundreds of edges needing MLOps pipelines that function across heterogeneous hardware and networking conditions. Financial regulations, distributed systems and AI shortage mean talent is scarce, with 30–50% salary premiums and 4–6 month hiring cycles for professionals of interest. \

8.2.2 Regulatory Scrutiny & Model Governance

Such transparency is unheard of from an AI decision making perspective, with alerts needing to be explainable by the feature (i.e., "you were sanctioned because 45% greater amount was detected, 35% further distance from the epicenter was identified, and velocity had increased by 20%"). Organizations must implement model cards that explain intended usage, training materials, limitations and effectiveness percentages broken down by demographic subpopulations; there are required audits that define retraining periods to assess performance decrease that must be kept

8.2.3 Cybersecurity & Physical Security

The more dispersed the edge-net, the larger the attack surface. Edge devices must support secure boot, trusted platform module (TPM) hardware-based attestation, and physical tampering must be avoided. Zero trust ecosystems must exist with TLS peer-to-peer attestation and microsegmentation to protect communication lanes. Foredata learning aggregation requires successful anomaly detection to limit data poisoning and data-attack risk.

REFERENCES

Abdallah, S., Maarof, M. A., & Zainal, A. (2019). Fraud detection in credit card transactions using XGBoost and deep learning. *International Journal of Advanced Computer Science and Applications*, *10*(12).

Ayiengar, N. S. R. (2023). India's Digital Public Infrastructure: A Model for Emerging Economies. *Journal of Digital Governance*, *3*(1), 22–35.

European Parliament and Council. (2016). *Regulation (EU) 2016/679 on the protection of natural persons with regard to the processing of personal data and on the free movement of such data*. General Data Protection Regulation.

Financial Action Task Force (FATF). (2023). *Guidance on Digital Identity*. FATF.

Information Commissioner's Office (ICO). (2023). "Guide to the UK General Data Protection Regulation (UK GDPR)," ICO. [Online]. Available: https://ico.org.uk/for-organisations/guide-to-data-protection/guide-to-the-general-data-protection-regulation-gdpr/

Kipf, T. N., & Welling, M. (2017). "Semi-Supervised Classification with Graph Convolutional Networks," in *Proc. of the 5th International Conference on Learning Representations (ICLR)*, 2017.

Lee, P. (2022). The Growing Pains of FinTech: Compliance as a Core Function. *Journal of Financial Regulation*, *8*(1), 44–59.

Li, Y., Wang, C., & Ooi, B. C. (2021). Challenges and Opportunities in Federated Learning. *IEEE Transactions on Big Data*, *7*(3), 453–462. DOI: 10.1109/TBDATA.2021.3070058

Ma, D. (2022). A Survey of Deep Learning for Data Sanitization and Model Anomaly Detection in Edge Computing. *IEEE Transactions on Knowledge and Data Engineering*.

McMahan, H. B., Moore, E., Ramage, D., & Hampson, S. (2016). "Federated Learning of Deep Networks using Model Averaging," arXiv:1602.05629.

Ministry of Electronics and Information Technology. (2023). *The Digital Personal Data Protection Act*. Government of India.

Shrikumar, P. G., & Kundaje, A. (2017). "Learning Important Features Through Propagating Activation Differences," in *Proc. of the 34th International Conference on Machine Learning*.

Unique Identification Authority of India (UIDAI). (2023). "Offline e-KYC Identity Verification," UIDAI. [Online]. Available: https://uidai.gov.in/en/ecosystem/authentication-devices-documents/offline-ekyc.html

United Nations Office on Drugs and Crime. (2023). "Estimated criminal money laundered annually," UNODC. [Online]. Available: https://www.unodc.org/

Wall, E. (2023). *The Cost of Anti-Money Laundering Compliance.* LexisNexis Risk Solutions.

Weber, M.. (2021). "Unsupervised Anomaly Detection for Anti-Money Laundering," in *Proc. of the ACM SIGKDD Workshop on Machine Learning in Finance*.

Chapter 11
TinyML-Enabled MIoT-Based Real-Time Edge Health Monitoring Using EfficientDet-Lite

R. Jansi
http://orcid.org/0000-0001-9894-0006
Department of Electronics and Communication Engineering, SRM Institute of Science and Technology, Kattankulathur, India

Aayush Sinha
http://orcid.org/0009-0003-1042-7091
SRM Institute of Science and Technology, India

Prasit Kumar Dutta
http://orcid.org/0009-0007-5594-8412
SRM Institute of Science and Technology, India

ABSTRACT

This paper introduces an innovative approach in the realm of Intelligent Edge Computing and Industrial Internet of Things (IIoT) for medical applications. An automated IIOT-based adaptive infant monitoring system is proposed that combines lightweight deep learning algorithms with constrained edge computing devices like Raspberry Pi and some onboard sensors. For real-time infant health monitoring, the system implements EfficientDet-Lite, which is an optimized version of an object detection model specifically designed to be resource efficient. The system is built around a Raspberry Pi camera which continuously monitors the position of the infant. One of the most important features of the system is the proactive alerting

DOI: 10.4018/979-8-3373-7340-9.ch011

capability where notifications are sent through Telebot application to the parent or caretaker when the baby is in abnormal positions, that is, when he or she is out of the bed or moves beyond a predefined safe region. This feature allows them to take necessary measures quickly.

1. INTRODUCTION

Recently, technology has became an important part of our day-to-day life, especially its application in the field of healthcare has increased rapidly. The basic idea of getting connected to devices used everyday has given rise to Internet of Things (IoT). The extension of IoT in industrial domain is Industrial Internet of Things (IIoT). These latest technologies allow the users to monitor readings in an continuous manner and enable health and other safety related automations. Among the various kinds of sections in which the progress is visible, the baby monitoring and infant health care stand out as most important and sensitive applications. Parents mostly worry about the safety of their child, especially during the times when they are left unattended or when they are asleep. In the traditional monitoring devices like sound detectors, motion detectors etc, the accuracy of detection of risky situation from the normal conditions is very minimal. This has led to a string need for an intelligent system that is automatic and is capable of provide high accuracy and reliability. In IIoT-based smart baby monitoring systems, small sensors, cameras and microcontrollers are combined to form a device that is capable of tracking the position, environment and activity of the baby.

Compared to old traditional systems that are only capable of giving alarm signals, these smart devices can make decisions. Edge computing technique helps to do most of the processing directly on the device, and hence reduces the delay and ensures that the alert signals are sent immediately. This is an important parameter especially in critical situations like when a baby rolls into an unsafe sleeping position or when the environmental parameters move beyond the safe limits. Usage of deep learning models like EfficientDet-Lite enable high level of intelligence by helping the system to make accurate classifications using real-world data. These advancements depict how development in digital technology helps to both improve the comfort and safety level of parenting systems. By properly integrating the IIoT and edge computing technologies, we can create an ecosystem that connect the parents, devices and the real time data. These systems are not only helpful during emergency situations but are also very helpful to understand the habits and patterns of baby movements.

With the rapidly increasing technological advancements, there is a greater demand for any novel techniques that help to make our lives simple. One of the main areas for such advancements is the field of baby care. For parents, the most important concern is the wellbeing and safety of infants. Hence, any tools or techniques that help to achieve it will be of greater value. Traditional methods like CCTV surveillance, audio monitoring system, or wearable devices have many disadvantages like dependency on internet connectivity, delayed response and privacy issues. Recent advancements in the field of edge artificial intelligence (Edge AI) and Tiny Machine Learning (TinyML) are creating a set of new novel solutions for advanced healthcare management. TinyML systems helps to deploy advanced deep learning models on ultra-low-power microcontrollers and edge devices, that helps to acquire sensor data on real-time without the need for cloud connectivity. The main advantage of these systems is reduced latency and increased privacy. The increase privacy is due to the processing of data locally on the device instead of cloud processing (Hou et al., 2023). These advantages are mainly required in infant health surveillance as the data privacy and immediate abnormal event detection are of utmost importance.

Embedded AI, Internet of Things (IoT) platforms, and multimodal sensors are integrated to form smart baby monitoring systems that are capable of capturing, processing and reacting to the activities of babies. Recently, multiple smart cradle techniques are available that are having the capability of cry detection and motion sensing. These systems have the ability to automatically switch on the smoothing mechanisms like lullaby song for the infant and avoid the need for parental intervention (Parvathavarthini et al., 2024). These automatic systems have a combination of sensos like accelerometers, sound sensors and environmental sensors which together make intelligent response system. The real-time monitoring of posture and location of infant is possible by the integration of computer vision models with IoT. These systems are implemented on devices such as Raspberry Pi and NVIDIA Jetson Nano using models like EfficientDet-Lite, MobileNet, or YOLO-Lite for tracking the position of babies at the edge (Pathak & Singh, 2020). In order to suit environments having resource constraints, these models are designed such that there should be a balance between inference speed and accuracy.

Posture detection is an essential component to ensure the safety of infants. Sudden Infant Death Syndrome (SIDS) occurs due to improper sleeping positions of infants. To avoid this, it is essential to detect the posture and give immediate alert to the caretakers (Khan, 2021). Recently, real time classification of baby position is done using vision-based systems that are powered by CNNs. Compared to the traditional camera-based methods, these techniques reduce the response time by instant automatic detection (Tsuji et al., 2025). The main advantage of implementing Edge AI systems in infant care is the ability to operate independently without internet connectivity. The cloud-based systems are prone to drawbacks like latency, service disruptions and security issues. However, the edge-based devices use lightweight CNN models that can run directly on the device and hence preserves the privacy and reduces the latency (Madhu et al., 2025). Such systems are very much essential in situations where the infants are left unattended during the sleep. Along with identification of baby position, it is also important to monitor the environmental parameters like track temperature and humidity levels near the infant. Sensors such as DHT11 are commonly used to monitor such parameters due to their low cost and high reliability. By combining the readings of these environmental sensors with the position data of the infant, the model generates context-based alerts. For instance, when abnormal position is detected along with high temperature may indicate higher risk of discomfort (Chandnani et al., 2025).

Multiple communication modules have evolved recently like Telegram Bots, MQTT, or Firebase Cloud Messaging that aid in immediate response that is to be given to the caregiver. These modules enable alerts to be automatically sent to smartphones and smartwatches in case of emergency. In particular, Telegram Bots are lightweight bots that are specialized in providing customizable messaging interface with complex application development or licensing concerns. When any abnormal position such baby moving out of the crib or extreme environmental conditions are detected, then the model sends instant message to the parent or caregiver (De et al., 2024). Though these innovations have many advantages, still it faces multiple challenges. These systems work based on datasets that are limited and are collected under controlled environments. Hence, it may not generalize well to the real-world settings. If they are any deviations in the lighting or camera setting or in the behaviour of the infant, then the system may not work accurately. Further, these systems must be optimized such that it is efficient in terms of power and latency especially when they are running in battery-operated settings. To mitigate these effects, recent research focusses on sensor fusion, adaptive sampling techniques, etc., that aid in managing power efficiently (TOKAN et al., 2024). Advancements in compression of models, architecture pruning, quantization results in the evolvement of TinyML systems that enable efficient deployment of deep learning architectures on 8-bit or 16-bit microcontrollers. For the application of baby monitoring, these technologies are vital since continuous operation and low power consumption are mandatory requirements. Research related to real-time training and deployment are also evolving that can improve performance over time (Monika et al., 2024).

The increasing demand in the usage of artificial intelligence in daily life are not only limited to industrial or research purposes. They are also extended to child-care, home automation and security applications. Hence, as a part of smart home, developing an intelligent baby monitoring system based on IIoT and deep learning is an essential task. It not only provides accuracy but also provides accessibility and also proves to be system that is simple, user friendly and affordable. With the rapid evolution of technology, this system will likely become an integral part of household security. Thus, this system will allow the parents to balance their responsibilities and ensure constant safety for their children.

This paper introduces an IIoT-based baby monitoring system that utilizes a Raspberry Pi module, a Pi camera, and temperature and humidity sensors. Abnormalities trigger alerts through a Telebot application, ensuring the baby's safety and comfort. The proposed system offers a convenient and reliable solution for busy parents or caregivers, providing remote monitoring capabilities to ensure the baby's well-being.

2. LITERATURE SURVEY

In literature, there are multiple research that deals with how the infant monitoring can be improved, especially when the parent or care-taker supervision is not always possible. Earlier research depended mainly on basic sensors like microphones or motion detection sensors that could sense the crying sound or the movement of the infant. Though these systems could work for some extent, it was not capable of capturing the complete picture of the health of the baby or the surrounding parameters. With the evolution of IoT many multiple designed were proposed that used small-networked sensors that could measure parameters like temperature, humidity, quality of the air etc and was also capable of sending alert signals to mobile phones. However, these devices also faced certain issues. This is because of the dependence of these devices on the cloud server for data processing. These devices could cause delay or failure when the network connection was poor. To overcome these issues, "Edge Computing" technology can into existence in which the computing could be done locally on the device itself.

Recent studies have shown that the combination of edge computing with the artificial intelligence can be effectively employed in smart baby monitoring. In this application, deep learning models like convolutional neural networks (CNNs) have been used for the analysis of camera images to detect if the baby is in safe position or not. Some researchers have also analysed the facial expression of the babies to identify any possibilities of discomfort. Some researchers combine the visual and environmental sensor data to make the system more reliable. These efforts make the system more intelligent and acts similar to a human caretaker. For the implementation of real time, devices like Raspberry Pi or Arduino boards are widely being used.

Li et al. (Li et al., 2020) recognized the challenges and costs associated with continuous monitoring of infants by caregivers or practitioners. The authors developed a 24-hour monitoring system for infants to reduce the labour cost and to tackle all these practical problems. By utilizing Red-Green-Blue (RGB) and Near Infrared-light (NIR) videos, the system did continuous monitoring and detection of discomfort in the infants. Jabbar et al. (Jabbar et al., 2019) proposed an another algorithm that was used to improve the existing framework for providing better care of babies without the intervention of parents. The NodeMCU controller board utilized Wi-Fi to upload data to the AdaFruit MQTT server that was then used to collect sensor data. Sun et al. (Sun et al., 2021), proposed a new 3D convolutional neural network (CNN) that does not rely on face detection and tracking. This study examined intensity and motion video characteristics and used multiple CNN architectures (2D and 3D) to detect the discomfort in infants. The 3D-CNN that captured motion and facial expressions showed remarkable gains. Thus, the suggested method provided an end-to-end solution for the detection of infant discomfort through technologies that considered motion and facial expression features. Nandhakumar et al. (Nandhakumar & Mohanapriya, 2022) offered a novel combined solution based on IoT and deep learning to overcome the challenges faced by automated baby position detection systems. The YOLO model and IoT model were used to detect the position of the baby and control the camera movement. This technique produced an automated system to track and recognize baby movements based on IoT and deep learning.

A system to evaluate various physiological activities was proposed by Shamshir et al. (Shamsir et al., 2020). The system proposed by the authors involved monitoring the adverse situation of the patient based on the sensor data of the patient along with ML Techniques. Further, Sun et al. (Sun et al., 2019) used deep Convolutional Neural Network (CNN) algorithm for the detection of discomfort in infants based on their facial expression. They used a dataset that comprised of facial expressions of 24 infants and trained a pre-trained CNN model with labelled facial expressions from shoulder-pain dataset. Though the size of this dataset was limited, researchers successfully used CNNs to detect discomfort in infants using this technique. The authors Cheggou and others (Cheggou et al., 2020) proposed a baby monitoring system that is intelligent in a way that parents can check the status of the baby from remote locations in an instant manner. To monitor the sound and temperature conditions within the enclosed space, the system was designed and developed. To optimize and improve the efficiency, the status of a baby in a cradle is determined based on computed vision using convolutional neural network model. Wang et al. (Wang et al., 2019) proposed a method to monitor infants using white noise in a contactless manner. The authors proposed novel algorithms to extract information about the infant's breathing movement and position from random white noise. This process was performed in both the time and frequency domains. The main advantage of this system was that it monitored infant sleep in a hassle-free and accurate manner without any physical contact. Baby monitoring systems with image processing are rapidly evolving recently in the domain of child safety. Dubey et al. (Dubey & Damke, 2019) proposed a non-contact baby monitoring system to ensure that when parents are busy with other works, they can keep a watch on their baby. The system detects the motion and the position of the baby and also detects the crying state of the baby. It also sends alerts on the abnormal state detected through text messages and email along with images.

Cheng et al. (Li et al., 2021) designed a monitoring system for the babies that can be used to analyse their facial expressions and also their states. The system could detect multiple states such as discomfort and happiness along with neutral expressions, asleep, pacifier, and open mouth states. This methodology used Fast R-CNN for recognition and also employed a Hidden Markov Model. The monitoring and understanding of the infant's face expressions was a big task. A digital camera and deep learning were used by Hashim et al. (Hashim, 2024) to propose a non-contact respiratory monitoring system for newborn. The system was capable of automatically identify baby's facial and chest portions and could estimate respiratory rate the usage of any sensors attached to the body. This non-contact method helped to reduce the risk of discomfort and infection in addition to being accurate in variable lighting conditions. Herlea et al. (Herlea et al., 2025) proposed a deep learning-based baby monitoring system that classified the cries of babies using ResNet, EfficientNet, and other neural network models. The method recognized the patterns from audio data of the infant and was able to discriminate between various kinds of cries. This model used the sound data for real-time monitoring of infants. Smart incubator system proposed by Fawzi et.al. (Fawzi, 2024) has been developed for the premature infant. It monitors various parameters like temperature, humidity, oxygen level, and heart rate through different IoT sensors. A random forest and deep neural network-based machine learning algorithms were used to controls actuators like heaters, fans, etc. for maintaining optimal conditions for the infant. A safe environment for babies was ensured with this model due to an excellent intelligent feedback mechanism.

The above survey of the recent literature brings out some issues associated with existing baby monitoring system. Some of these limitations include the high cost and effort required for full-time monitoring of caregivers or practitioner and the dependence on traditional face detection algorithms. The existing systems available for baby monitoring mainly depend on the cloud. This creates high latency and privacy issues. This creates a lot of real time deployment problems. Also, most of the previous work are either based on vision based processing or environmental sensor processing. There is limitation in works that are related to the integration of both vision and environmental sensor monitoring. Furthermore, most of the existing works are computationally heavy and are not optimized to support low power devices. This creates a huge demand for creating Tiny-ML based solutions. Another key gap is the lack of real time alert mechanisms that have minimal delay.

In addition, these systems fail to carry out comprehensive monitoring of vital signs and environmental conditions. Moreover, the previous systems may suffer from insufficient training data or difficulty in accurately recognizing discomfort due to factors like random head rotations, occlusions and facial profiles. The drawbacks faced by the previous system can be overcome by using advanced technology like raspberry pi module, pi camera, temperature and humidity sensors. By using the

EfficientDet-Lite model for object detection to analyse the Pi camera input, accurate detection of the baby's position is possible, thereby eliminating the need for traditional face detection and tracking steps. The temperature and humidity of the baby's room can also be continuously monitored using the sensor data that is processed and collected using Raspberry Pi module. Also, the proposed system provides a very reliable solution for the parents or caregivers to monitor their baby's safety.

3. PROPOSED METHODOLOGY

3.1. System Overview

The proposed IIoT-enabled architecture involves the integration of smart sensing, real-time edge processing, and automated alerting for effective infant posture and environment monitoring. The proposed system consists of three major layers:

1. The perception layer or sensing layer collects real-time data using a Pi camera and environmental sensors (temperature and humidity).
2. The Raspberry Pi, which is the edge device, processes the sensing data locally and runs a deep learning inference model (EfficientDet-Lite).
3. The communication and application layer is responsible for transmitting the data and sending smart notifications to the caregiver using IIoT communication protocols. This layered architecture provides low latency, high data privacy, and reliable monitoring, which are vital in medical applications where timely interventions can avert emergencies.

This layered architecture provides low latency, enhanced data privacy, and reliable monitoring, which are critical in medical applications where timely intervention can prevent emergencies.

3.1.1. Perception Layer: Sensor-Based Data Acquisition

The perception layer forms the main heart of the proposed IIoT system. It continuously monitors the posture of the baby and the environment in real-time and it include the following elements.

- Pi Camera is a small, low-power imaging device designed for embedded applications. It captures HD video frames of the baby's sleeping pose. This camera is placed to ensure to maximise coverage, so that the camera will leave almost no blind spots in the crib.

- The temperature sensor is one of the key components of a baby monitoring system that checks the room temperature. When temperatures fall below 22 °C or rise above 27 °C, there's an increased risk of abnormal temperature condition for the infant.
- The humidity sensor is used to measure the level of humidity and maintain it in the 40% to 60% range. If the humidity is poorly controlled, toddlers may experience respiratory problems or dry skin.

By fusing the data from these sensors, this system can do much more than a standard video-only baby monitor as it gives a complete view of your baby's well-being. The constant data stream from the sensors are fed into the edge intelligence layer as the input data.

3.1.2. Edge Intelligence Layer: Localized Processing and Analytics

Traditional monitoring systems are mostly designed to run on cloud-based analytics, which can produce significant latency, bandwidth consumption, and privacy risks. The traditional cloud based systems store the images of infants in cloud which suffer from privacy issues. Also, to ensure data integrity effective encryption algorithms are needed so that the images are not subjected to any type of attacks. Design and implementation of these algorithms are computationally extensive. However, the edge intelligence layer used in this proposed architecture utilizes a Raspberry Pi 4 Model B as the IIoT edge computing node, that makes real-time inference at the point of data generation itself.

The Raspberry Pi:

- Receives continuous image streams from the Pi camera.
- Collects environmental readings from temperature and humidity sensors.
- Executes the EfficientDet-Lite model for on-device deep learning inference.
- Finally, makes autonomous decisions regarding alerts without any need for constant cloud connectivity.

This type of localized processing significantly reduces the system response time and hence ensures that abnormal events like unsafe baby postures are detected in milliseconds. Furthermore, because sensitive image data are not required to be transmitted over external networks in this system, data privacy is improved which is a key requirement in medical applications under regulations such as HIPAA and GDPR.

3.1.3. EfficientDet-Lite Model for Intelligent Posture Detection

The main component of intelligent processing used in this proposed model is the EfficientDet-Lite deep learning model, a lightweight object detection framework which is optimized for embedded and IIoT devices. The model is trained on a labeled dataset consisting of images representing normal and abnormal infant sleeping positions:

- Normal position: Baby lying safely on the back, fully inside the crib.
- Abnormal position: Baby rolled onto the stomach, partially or fully moved out of the safe area, or in any posture that poses risk.

EfficientDet-Lite employs a Bi-directional Feature Pyramid Network (BiFPN) in order to fuse the various multi-scale features so that high detection accuracy at minimal computational cost could be achieved. In the evaluation, the EfficientDet-Lite2 variant provided the best trade-off performance with accuracy at 92.1% and also attained a latency of 396 ms. This makes it suitable for resource-constrained edge nodes.

This posture detection capability of the system directly shows that the safety goals are attained by allowing caregivers to give attention before an unsafe position leads into a medical emergency.

3.1.4. Communication and Application Layer: IIoT Connectivity and Alerting

The final layer is responsible for the safe and secure communication of the data. It is also responsible for the user interaction. Once the edge node identifies an abnormal posture or any deviation in environmental condition, it triggers a communication using the Raspberry Pi's Wi-Fi interface.

The Telebot platform is integrated with messaging services and is used in this work to send instantaneous alerts to caregivers' mobile devices. This alert includes:

- Notification message (e.g., "Abnormal Baby Position Detected")
- Type of anomaly (position, temperature, or humidity)
- Timestamp
- Optional image snapshot for verification

Compared to the traditional baby monitoring system that completely rely on audio sound or on manual checking, this automated alerting mechanism makes use of IIoT connectivity to ensure that the caregivers receive timely information, even if they are not physically present in the room.

Fig. 1 provides an overall overview of the IIoT-enabled intelligent baby monitoring system. It illustrates the complete integration of sensing, edge processing, and communication components for real-time health surveillance. The proposed system starts with data acquisition, in which a Pi camera captures the infant's posture, and temperature and humidity sensors that continuously monitor the ambient environment. These sensory inputs are then transmitted to a Raspberry Pi, which functions as the edge computing node.

At the edge level, a lightweight EfficientDet-Lite deep learning model performs the main task of posture classification, by identifying whether the baby's position is normal or abnormal. In case, if an abnormal position or environmental deviation is being detected by this, the Raspberry Pi triggers an alert with the help of an IIoT communication channel. This notification is delivered instantly to the caregiver's mobile device. Thereby, timely intervention is being given without any constant manual supervision.

Figure 1 clearly highlights the three core principles of IIoT-based healthcare: (i) real-time sensor-based monitoring, (ii) intelligent decision-making at the edge, and (iii) rapid communication for actionable healthcare support. By combining environmental sensing and computer vision, the system enables proactive infant safety monitoring, reducing the risk of posture-related emergencies.

Figure 1. End-to-end pipeline of the proposed IIoT-based smart medical monitoring system for infants.

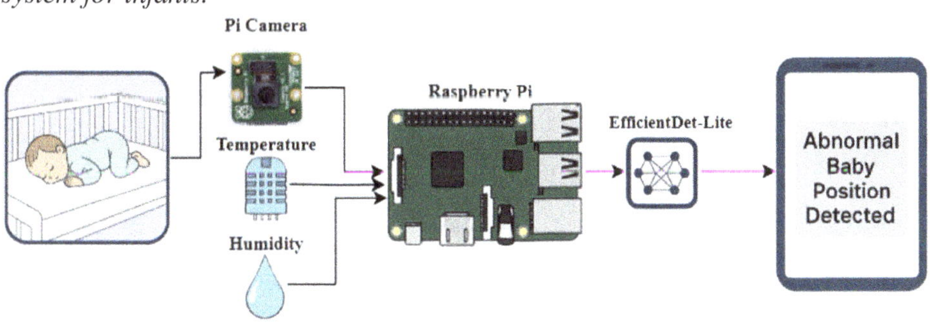

3.2. Proposed intelligent baby surveillance system

The architecture diagram of the proposed system comprises of several components that work together to create smart baby monitoring system, as shown in Figure 2.

Raspberry Pi 4 acts as the central control unit that acts as the base for edge intelligence in the proposed system. Such an integration of TinyML with edge computing enables the system to process the data locally, minimizes the power consumption and avoids the dependence on cloud computing. The Pi camera is attached to the camera port of Raspberry Pi and is responsible for acquiring the position of the infant. To the GPIO (General Purpose Input/Output) pins of the Raspberry Pi, a temperature and humidity sensor (DHT11) is connected for monitoring the environmental conditions. To enable remote communication with the caregiver using mobile devices, a Wi-Fi module is connected to the Raspberry Pi. The classification of baby position into normal and abnormal position is done using the EfficientDet-Lite model which is optimized for TinyML deployment. When the system identifies any abnormal position that indicates potential risk, then immediately alert message is generated and sent to the caregiver. Similarly, if any abnormal environmental condition is detected, that is, if the measured temperature or humidity falls outside predefined safe limits then alert signals are triggered and delivered. Such an incorporation of TinyMl at the edge devices aids in real-time decision making, enhancing its suitability for MioT-based infant care. In essence, the integration of edge computing at the heart of this architecture enhances its efficiency, responsiveness, and reliability, making it a robust and effective smart baby monitoring system.

Figure 2. Architecture of the proposed IoT-based intelligent baby surveillance system

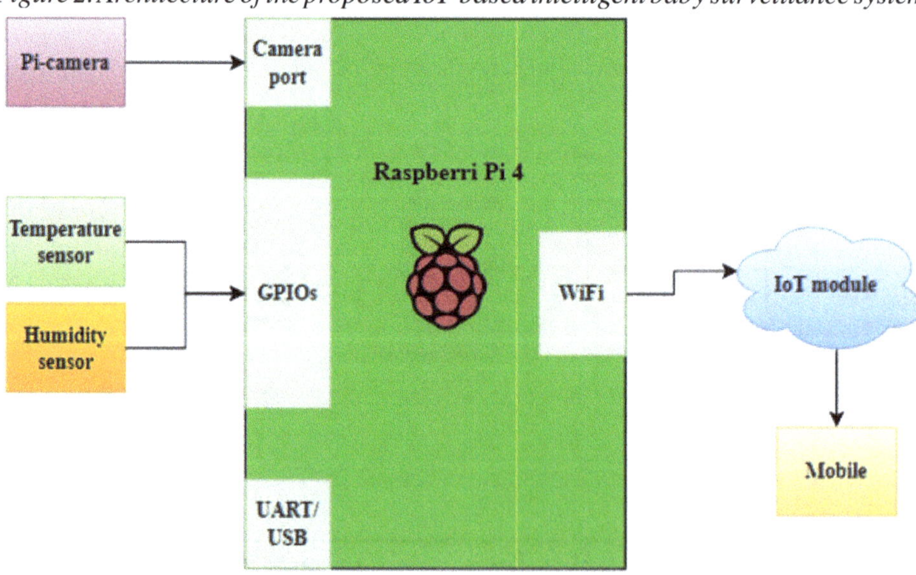

The overall flowchart of the proposed scheme is depicted in Figure 3. There are three main modules in the system: “Capture Baby Image” “Measure Temperature” and “Measure Humidity”. In the “Capture Baby Image” module, the position of the baby is captured using Raspberry Pi camera. The captured image is then passed on to the “Classify Baby Position” module, that classifies the image as normal or abnormal. If the image is classified as abnormal, then the system passes on to the “Notification to Parent/Caretaker” block, using which alert signal is sent to the parent or caretaker to inform about the abnormal position of the infant. In case if the baby’s position is classified as normal, then the system loops back to the “Capture Baby Image” module and repeat the image capturing process.

Simultaneously, the “Measure Temperature” module is used for measuring the temperature T in the baby’s module. The temperature measured us then checked against predefined temperature ranges. The Tmin refers to the minimal optimal temperature value and Tmax refers to maximum optimal temperature value. If the measured temperature falls outside this range, then the system passes on to the “Notification to Parent/Caretaker” block to alert the parent or caretaker. Similarly, the “Measure Humidity” module is used for measuring the humidity H in the baby's environment. Similar, to temperature, the measure H value is checked against the predefined normal range value. Here, Hmin refers to the minimal optimal humidity value and Hmax refers to maximum optimal humidity value. If the measured H value, falls outside the normal range, then the system proceeds to the “Notification to Parent/Caretaker” block to alert the parent or caretaker about the abnormal humidity.

Figure 3. Flowchart of the proposed intelligent baby surveillance system

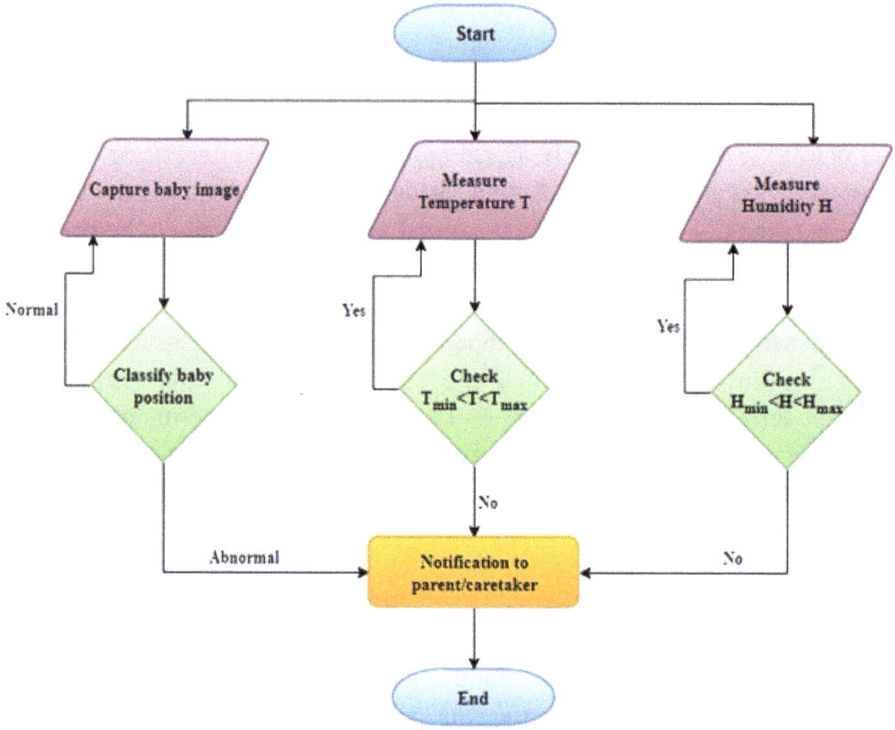

Figure 4 showcases the top view of the intelligent baby surveillance system setup. It shows the overall arrangement of the various components of the proposed system in an overhead perspective. The top portion of the image shows the area designated for the baby's living space. To capture the top-down view of the baby's position a Raspberry Pi camera is placed on top as shown in the Figure. The camera lens is placed such that a clear line of sight for monitoring is ensured. Next, DHT11 sensor module is connected to the central processing unit which is the Raspberry Pi 4. This sensor comprises of temperature and humidity sensors that are used for measuring the environmental conditions around the baby. Thus, Figure 4 is the aerial view of the proposed intelligent baby surveillance system consisting of infant area, camera, sensors, central processing unit that contribute to ensure the well-being of the infant.

Figure 4. Top view of the intelligent baby surveillance system setup

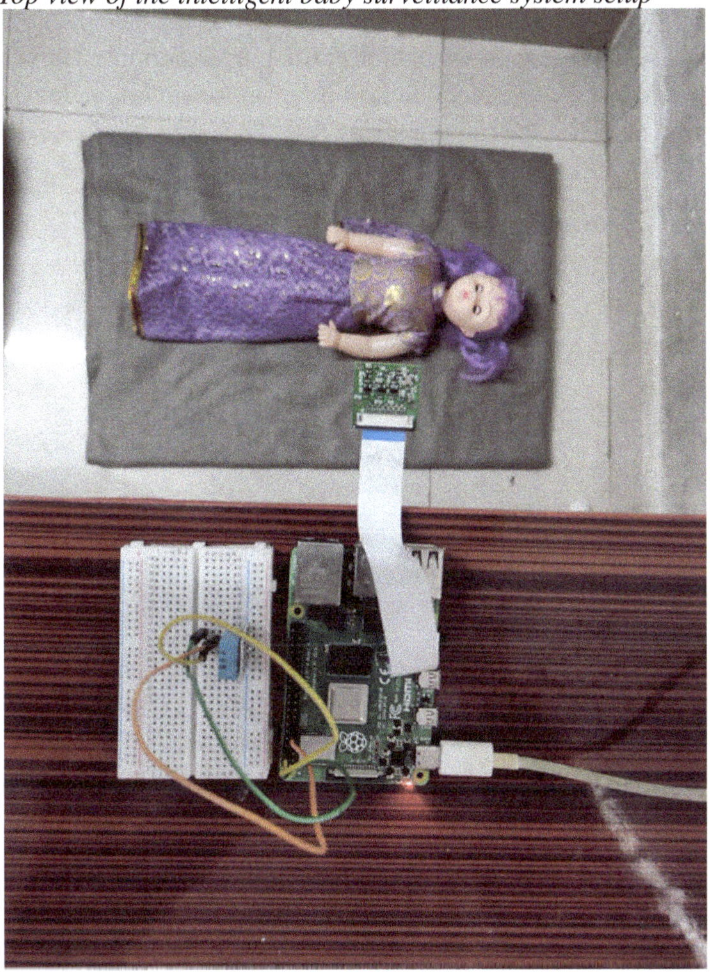

3.3. Baby Position Detection Using CNN

3.3.1. Dataset Description

The dataset used in this research consists of two hundred images capturing the position of the infant. The images were collected to classify the baby's position into two categories: normal position and abnormal position as shown in Figure 5 and Figure 6 respectively. Out of the two hundred images, hundred of them represent the normal position of the infant. In the normal position, the baby is located entirely within the bed area or the designated boundary. The remaining hundred images represent the abnormal position of the infant. In the abnormal position, the baby is either partially or fully outside the bed boundary or designated area. The dataset provides a balanced representation of both normal and abnormal positions, enabling the development and evaluation of algorithms or models to accurately classify the baby's position based on the captured images.

Figure 5. Normal position of the infant

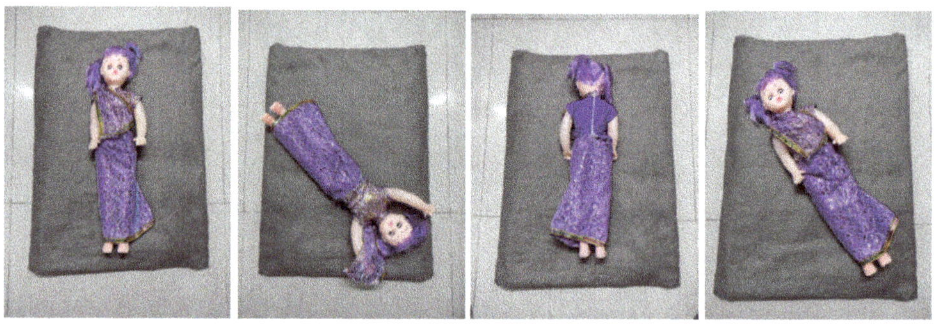

Figure 6. Abnormal position of the infant

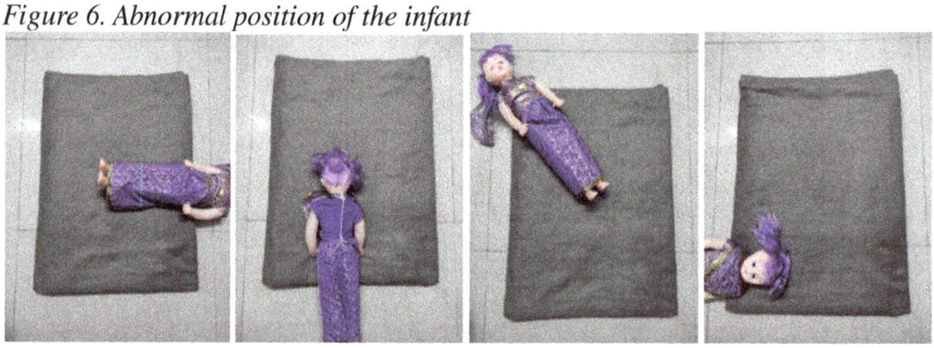

3.3.2. Block Diagram of the Proposed Position Detection System

The block diagram of the baby position classification system is shown in Figure 7. The block diagram consists of two stages: the training stage and the testing stage.

Training Stage

Image Acquisition: This is the first stage in which the normal and abnormal positions of the baby are acquired using Pi camera. These images act as input data for training the model. The quality of the trained model depends on the quality of the training data, hence images were captured from different positions in both the normal and abnormal categories.

Preprocessing: All the acquired images were pre-processed to ensure that all the images are uniform and to prepare them for the subsequent steps. Firstly, the images were uniformly resized. Additionally, they were labelled with a corresponding position label, that is, normal or abnormal so that it could be suitable for the further model training.

Model Training using EfficientDet: The pre-processed images along with their labelled positions were then employed as input to the EfficientDet architecture. This model was utilized to learn the various attributes in the normal and abnormal positions of the baby. The trained model was then employed during the classification step.

Testing Stage

Image Acquisition: Like training stage, a single test image was acquired in the testing stage as well. This image was used as an input to the trained model and will be classified as either normal or abnormal position based on the attributes extracted by the trained model.

Pre-processing: Similar to the training stage, the test image was subjected to pre-processing, which involved resizing the image to the standardized dimension that was used during training.

Classification: The pre-processed test image was then fed into the classification block. The trained EfficientDet model, obtained during the training stage was then utilized to classify the acquired test image. The model processes the image using the trained model and then predicts whether the baby's position is normal or abnormal and gives as an output.

Final Output: Based on the classification performed by the trained model, the final output is generated. It indicates whether the test image represents a normal position or an abnormal position of the baby. This can be used to identify, and abnormal conditions and intimation could be given immediately to the caretakers or parents using Telebot Application.

Figure 7. Block diagram of the baby position classification system

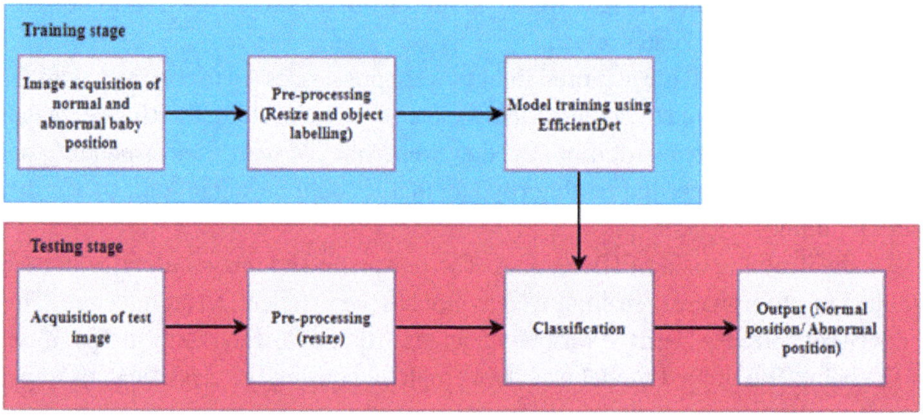

4. RESULTS AND DISCUSSION

4.2. Model Training Using EfficientDet

In this research, EfficientDet model is used for model training that involved the processing of training the input acquired images to classify the position of the infants. EfficientDet model was selected since it is well known for its efficiency and accuracy. The labelled normal and abnormal images are first trained to create a training model using EfficientDet. Before training, these images were pre-processed to ensure that all the images have consistent size and format. During training, the model learns the patters present in the normal and abnormal position images. This trained model was then used for the real-time classification of baby position to ensure the well-being of the infant.

4.3. Parameter Setting

All the images were resized to a uniform size of 256×256. Further, the value of Tmin and Tmax were fixed as 22°C to 27°C and the values of Hmin and Hmax were fixed as 40% to 60%. A batch size of 4 was employed, while an initial learning rate of 0.01 was set to enable the learning process. Momentum value was set at 0.9 in this research to enhance the training speed. The minimum learning rate was set to 0.0001 to ensure a basic lower limit for learning. The model was trained for 20 epochs in this research. Table 1 summarizes the key parameters and their respective scores used in the model training process.

Table 1. Hyper-parameter values

Parameters	Score
Batch Size	4
Initial Learning Rate	0.01
Momentum	0.9
Minimum Learning Rate	0.0001
No. of Epoch	20

4.4. Loss vs Epoch

The observed values of loss for each epoch are shown in Figure 8. It is clearly seen that, there is a consistent reduction in loss throughout the training epochs when the EfficientDet model was used. This curve indicates that the model steadily improves the accuracy. Initially, it was seen that the value of loss was high which was because the model was not trained completely. However, as the number of training iteration increases, the loss gradually starts to decrease thus indicating that the model is capable of doing accurate baby position predictions.

Figure 8. Loss versus epoch

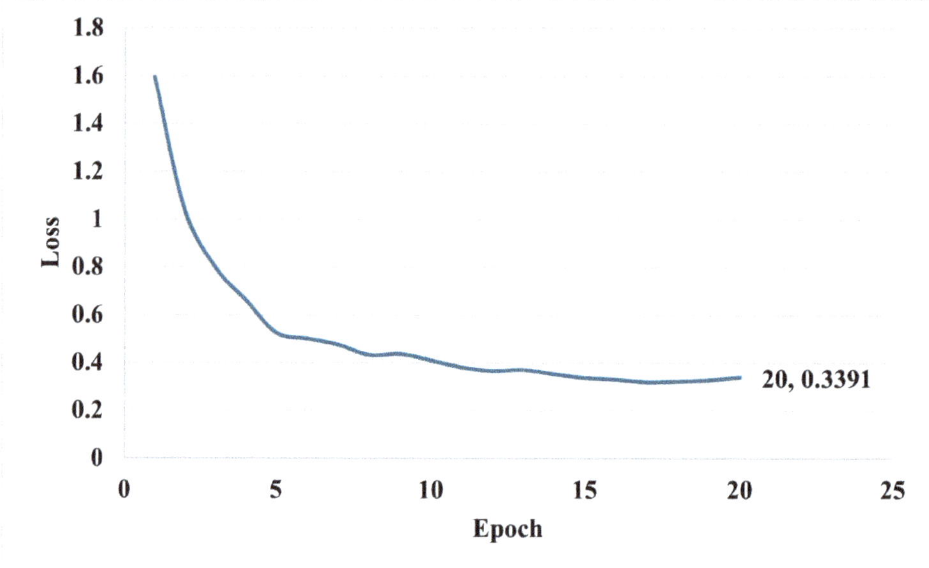

4.5. Hardware and Software Setup

The proposed architecture was trained using a hardware setup that consisted of 16GB of RAM with Intel Core i5 processor. The software tools used in this research comprised of tools such as Jupyter notebooks, PyTorch, TensorFlow, and the cloud-based platform Google Colab. Training was performed usin a high-performance GPU that had multiple CUDA cores.

4.6. Quantitative Analysis

After evaluating the different Efficientdet_lite models based on their accuracy and frames per second (FPS), it was observed that as the model complexity increased, the accuracy also eventually improved but the FPS decreased. This is shown in Table 2. Hence by comparing the options, it was found that Efficientdet_lite2 showed good accuracy of 92.1% while maintaining a reasonable FPS of 5. Therefore, Efficientdet_lite2 was chosen as the optimal model for this classification.

Table 2. Comparison of Accuracy and Frames Per Second for Efficientdet_lite Models

Model Architecture	Accuracy in percentage	Frames Per Second
Efficientdet_lite0	77%	10fps
Efficientdet_lite1	86%	7fps
Efficientdet_lite2	92.1%	5fps
Efficientdet_lite3	93%	3fps
Efficientdet_lite4	93.5%	2fps

The Table 3 presents the latency (measured in milliseconds) for different model architectures of the Efficientdet_lite models. It can be observed from Table 3 that as the model complexity increases, the latency also gradually increases. Efficientdet_lite0 has a latency of 146 ms, while Efficientdet_lite1 and Efficientdet_lite2 attain latencies of 259 ms and 396 ms, respectively. However, there is a significant jump in latency with Efficientdet_lite3, which has a latency of 716 ms which is then followed by an even higher latency of 1886 ms for Efficientdet_lite4. Consequently, it can be observed that beyond Efficientdet_lite2, the latency increases substantially. Therefore, Efficientdet_lite2 is the optimal model not only in terms of accuracy but also in terms of lower latency compared to the other models. Therefore, considering the need for faster response times during real-time implementation conditions, Efficientdet_lite2 is chosen as the optimal model choice, as it balances between accuracy and lower latency. This results in efficient and timely recognition of baby positions.

Table 3. Comparison of Latency for Efficientdet_lite Models

Model Architecture	Latency (ms)
Efficientdet_lite0	146
Efficientdet_lite1	259
Efficientdet_lite2	396
Efficientdet_lite3	716
Efficientdet_lite4	1886

4.5 Abnormal Position Indication

Figure 9 shows the real-time classification results achieved by processing and classifying live images of baby positions using the trained Efficientdet lite2 model. The figure displays the output within bounding boxes that shows the immediate feedback on the identified positions, which are classified as normal.

Figure 9. Real-Time Classification Results of Baby Positions (Normal)

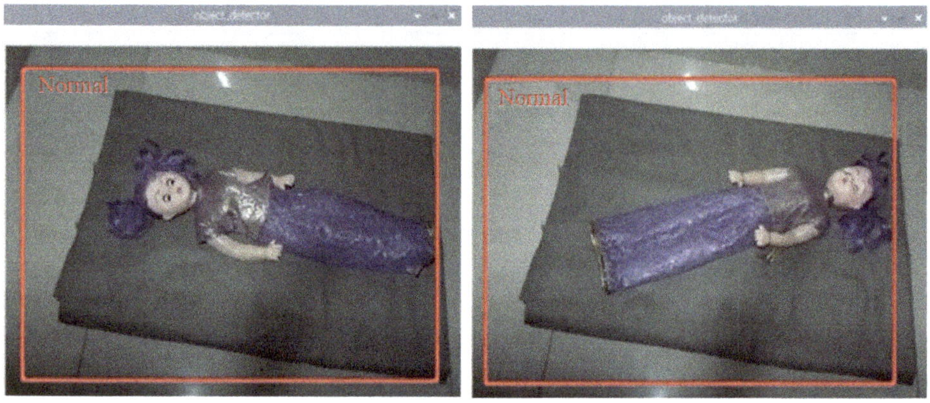

On the other hand, Figure 10 presents the output when the model detects an abnormal baby position. In such cases, the Telebot application promptly sends an alert to notify the parent or caretaker about the unusual position. This ensures timely alert to the caretakers in case of emergency.

Figure 10. Real-Time Classification Results of Baby Positions (Abnormal)

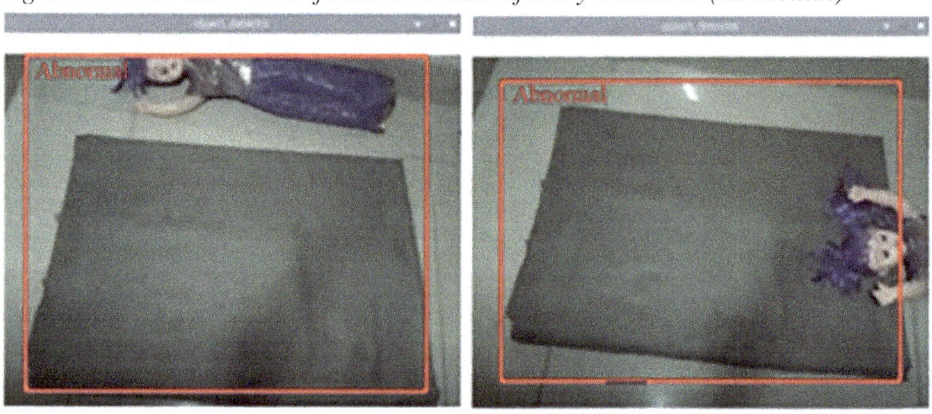

4.7. Notification to Caretaker/Parent Using Telebot

In Figure 11, the screenshot shows the notification sent to the parent or caretaker through the Telebot app. The message "Abnormal baby position detected" is transmitted when the baby moves out of the bed or the defined boundary.

Figure 11. Notification Screenshot Sent to Parent/Caretaker via Telebot App (Abnormal Baby Position)

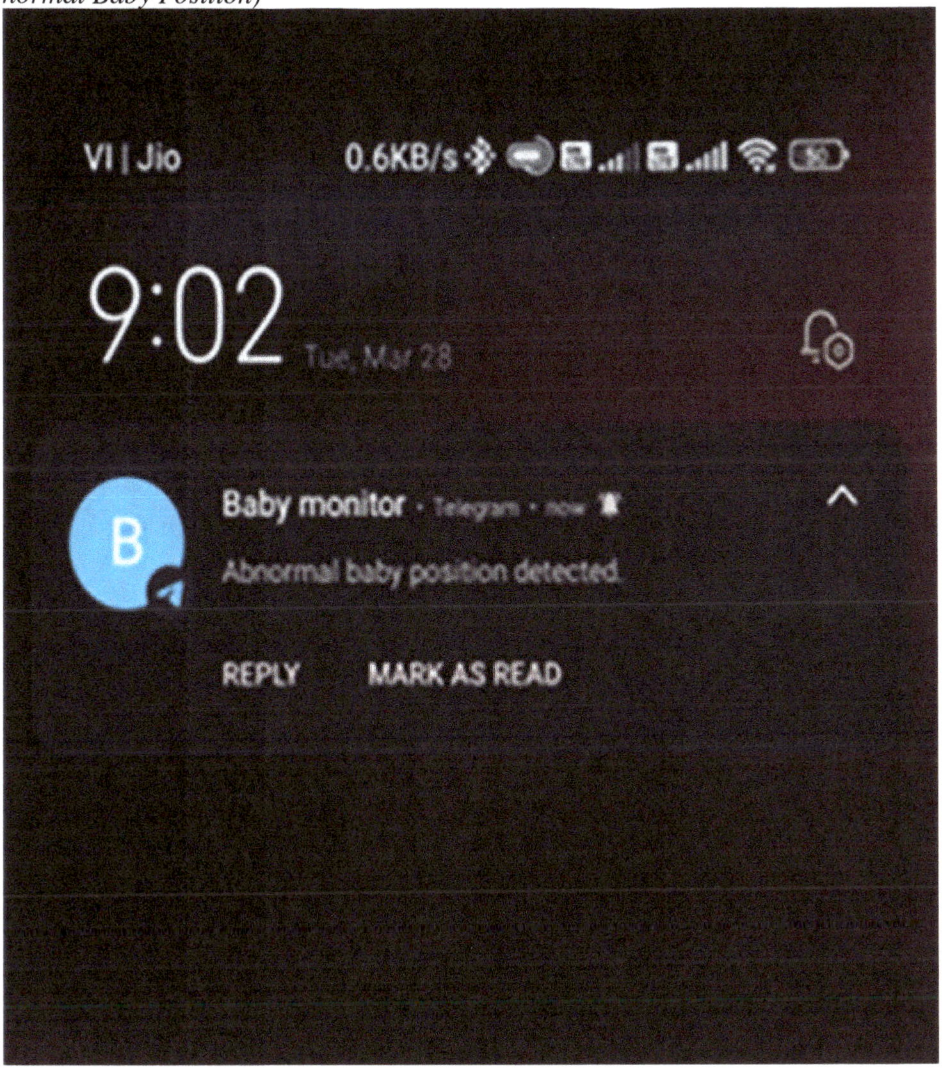

Figure 12(a) represents the notification sent through the Telebot app in the event of abnormal temperature being detected. Similarly, Figure 12(b) displays the notification sent via Telebot when abnormal humidity levels are detected. These notifications greatly help the caretakers or the parents to take necessary actions immediately whenever abnormal conditions are detected. Thus, this system can be effectively used in infant monitoring systems. Furthermore, the usage of edge computing further shows that the proposed system is more reliable and does not pose any privacy issues that are faced in cloud based computing systems.

Figure 12. Notification Sent via Telebot App for (a) Abnormal Temperature Detected (b) Abnormal Humidity Detected

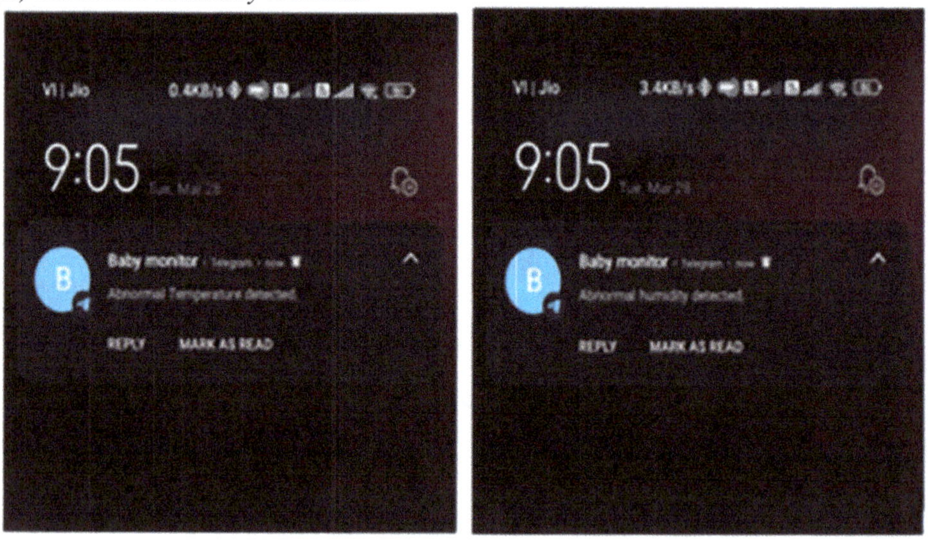

5. PRACTICAL CHALLENGES AND REAL-WORLD CONSIDERATIONS

During the real-world deployment of the proposed system, there are several practical challenges that are to be considered. These include lighting variation where the amount of light varies during day and night. This may affect the quality of the images captured and thereby reduce the accuracy. Another drawback is the hardware limitation of the edge device. This restricts the complexity of the model thereby affecting the real time performance of the system.

6. CONCLUSION AND FUTURE WORK

This study proposed an IoT based baby monitoring system through which computer vision is done on the image captured from the baby position. Further, temperature and humidity sensor check baby's environmental conditions. The position of the baby is captured using a Pi camera that is attached in the Raspberry Pi module of the system. The proposed system employed the EfficientDet-Lite model to classify the baby's position in real-time achieving an accuracy of 92.1% with a moderate Frames Per Second (FPS) of 5. Besides, the system was also capable of monitoring the environment humidity and temperature levels with the help of temperature and humidity sensors in an ecofriendly manner. The suggested solution will be able to detect the presence of abnormal baby position as well as an abnormal environment like temperature and humidity. In addition, the system would send timely notifications to the parents or caregivers in case of any abnormal conditions, which can greatly increase the reliability of the model.

In the future, collaboration can take place between this model and healthcare professionals to make accurate decisions. Interacting with paediatricians and health care experts would help to refine and validate the performance of the system according to the required limits of temperature, humidity and other health parameters. The system could also be enhanced with more sensors, such as air quality and sound sensors, or baby movement sensors, for more comprehensive monitoring of the baby's environment and well-being within a sustainable business model.

REFERENCES

Chandnani, K., Tripathy, S., Parbhakar, A. K., Takiar, K., Singhal, U., Sasikumar, P., & Maheswari, S. (2025). A novel smart baby cradle system utilizing IoT sensors and machine learning for optimized parental care. *Scientific Reports*, *15*(1), 19080. Advance online publication. DOI: 10.1038/s41598-025-02691-8 PMID: 40447703

Cheggou, R., Mohand, S. S. H., Annad, O., & Khoumeri, E. H. (2020). An intelligent baby monitoring system based on Raspberry PI, IoT sensors and convolutional neural network. *Proceedings - 2020 IEEE 21st International Conference on Information Reuse and Integration for Data Science, IRI 2020*, 365–371. DOI: 10.1109/IRI49571.2020.00059

De, S., Deogharia, D., De, M., & Chowdhury, P. (2024). Cradle-Care: Enhancing Baby Safety Using IoT. *2024 IEEE Calcutta Conference, CALCON 2024 - Proceedings*. DOI: 10.1109/CALCON63337.2024.10914183

Dubey, Y. K., & Damke, S. (2019). Baby monitoring system using image processing and IoT. *International Journal of Engineering and Advanced Technology*, *8*(6), 4961–4964. DOI: 10.35940/ijeat.F9254.088619

Fawzi, N. A. (2024). A Smart Incubator System for Monitoring and Controlling Premature Babies' Environment Using Machine Learning. *Journal Européen des Systèmes Automatisés*, *57*(5), 1531–1537. DOI: 10.18280/jesa.570529

Hashim, H. A. (2024). Non-Contact Automatic Respiratory Rate Monitoring for Newborns Using Digital Camera Technology and Deep Learning. *Journal of Biomedical Photonics & Engineering*, *10*(4), 040317. Advance online publication. DOI: 10.18287/JBPE24.10.040317

Herlea, D. M., Iancu, B., & Ardelean, E. R. (2025). A Study of Deep Learning Models for Audio Classification of Infant Crying in a Baby Monitoring System. *Informatics (MDPI)*, *12*(2), 50. Advance online publication. DOI: 10.3390/informatics12020050

Hou, K. M., Diao, X., Shi, H., Ding, H., Zhou, H., & de Vaulx, C. (2023). Trends and Challenges in AIoT/IIoT/IoT Implementation. *Sensors (Basel)*, *23*(11), 5074. Advance online publication. DOI: 10.3390/s23115074 PMID: 37299800

Jabbar, W. A., Shang, H. K., Hamid, S. N. I. S., Almohammedi, A. A., Ramli, R. M., & Ali, M. A. H. (2019). IoT-BBMS: Internet of Things-Based Baby Monitoring System for Smart Cradle. *IEEE Access : Practical Innovations, Open Solutions*, *7*, 93791–93805. DOI: 10.1109/ACCESS.2019.2928481

Khan, T. (2021). An Intelligent Baby Monitor with Automatic Sleeping Posture Detection and Notification. *AI*, *2*(2), 290–306. DOI: 10.3390/ai2020018

Li, C., Pourtaherian, A., Van Onzenoort, L., Ten, W. E. T. A., & De With, P. H. N. (2021). Infant Facial Expression Analysis: Towards a Real-Time Video Monitoring System Using R-CNN and HMM. *IEEE Journal of Biomedical and Health Informatics*, *25*(5), 1429–1440. DOI: 10.1109/JBHI.2020.3037031 PMID: 33170787

Li, C., Pourtaherian, A., Van Onzenoort, L., Tjon, W. E., & De With, P. H. N. (2020). Infant Monitoring System for Real-Time and Remote Discomfort Detection. *IEEE Transactions on Consumer Electronics*, *66*(4), 336–345. DOI: 10.1109/TCE.2020.3031359

Madhu, R., Anbazhagu, U. V., Santhana Krishnan, R., Paulraj, K., Nithila, E. E., & Umesh, R. (2025). IoT-Enabled Deep Learning Framework for Smart Infant Health Monitoring. *Proceedings of the International Conference on Intelligent Computing and Control Systems, ICICCS 2025*, 420–427. DOI: 10.1109/ICICCS65191.2025.10984933

Monika, S., Battana, H., Sangeetha, M., Shaik, M., & Jawahar, M. (2024). Analysis of Maternity and Child Health Care System Integrated with IoT and ML. *10th International Conference on Advanced Computing and Communication Systems, ICACCS 2024*, 1792–1797. DOI: 10.1109/ICACCS60874.2024.10717104

Nandhakumar, R. G., & Mohanapriya, S. (2022). Smart Baby Monitoring System using YOLO V7 Algorithm. *2022 International Conference on Information Technology Research and Innovation, ICITRI 2022*, 42–47. DOI: 10.1109/ICITRI56423.2022.9970217

Parvathavarthini, S., Bhuvaneswaran, U., Arun, U. M., & Sengottayan, S. (2024) Baby Monitoring Using IOT and Deep Learning. *2024 15th International Conference on Computing Communication and Networking Technologies, ICCCNT 2024*. DOI: 10.1109/ICCCNT61001.2024.10725151

Pathak, R., & Singh, Y. (2020). Real time baby facial expression recognition using deep learning and IoT edge computing. *Proceedings of the 2020 International Conference on Computing, Communication and Security, ICCCS 2020*. DOI: 10.1109/ICCCS49678.2020.9277428

Shamsir, S., Hassan, O., & Islam, S. K. (2020). Smart infant-monitoring system with machine learning model to detect physiological activities and ambient conditions. *I2MTC 2020 - International Instrumentation and Measurement Technology Conference, Proceedings*. DOI: 10.1109/I2MTC43012.2020.9129295

Sun, Y., Hu, J., Wang, W., He, M., & De With, P. H. N. (2021). Camera-based discomfort detection using multi-channel attention 3D-CNN for hospitalized infants. *Quantitative Imaging in Medicine and Surgery*, *11*(7), 3059–3069. DOI: 10.21037/qims-20-1302 PMID: 34249635

Sun, Y., Shan, C., Tan, T., Tong, T., Wang, W., Pourtaherian, A., & De With, P. H. N. (2019). Detecting discomfort in infants through facial expressions. *Physiological Measurement*, *40*(11), 115006. Advance online publication. DOI: 10.1088/1361-6579/ab55b3 PMID: 31703212

Tokan, M., Tokan, M., Tokan, M., & F, A.TOKAN. (2024). Optimization of Battery Power Efficiency in Baby Incubator Transport Through PID-Fuzzy Control. *Jurnal Teknokes*, *17*(4), 190–196. DOI: 10.35882/7hjhwb84

Tsuji, H., Yamamoto, T., Kobayashi, M., Sasaki, K., Aso, N., & Sugiura, Y. (2025). CradlePosture: Camera-Based Approach for Estimating Neonate's Posture Based on Caregiver's Holding Behaviors. *2025 IEEE/SICE International Symposium on System Integration, SII 2025*, 434–439. DOI: 10.1109/SII59315.2025.10870587

Wang, A., Sunshine, J. E., & Gollakota, S. (2019). *Contactless Infant Monitoring using White Noise*. 1–16. DOI: 10.1145/3300061.3345453

Chapter 12

Generative AI for Mental Well-Being and Insights From High and Low Resource Languages

Sameer Sitoula
http://orcid.org/0009-0000-1609-779X
Central Queensland University, Australia

Laxmi Prasad Bhatt
Hillside College of Engineering, Nepal

Anisha Pokhrel
Hillside College of Engineering, Nepal

Arjun Neupane
http://orcid.org/0000-0002-1010-7552
Central Queensland University, Australia

ABSTRACT

In recent times, the mental health crisis has become a critical global problem. After the COVID-19 pandemic, fear, anger, depression, and anxiety have increased. There is an urgent need for digital systems that provide accessible and effective care. Generative Artificial Intelligence (GenAI), including AI chatbots, has shown potential to offer empathetic and always-available emotional support. However, these systems perform well in high-resource languages like English and Spanish but poorly in low-resource languages such as Nepali. This chapter examines how GenAI supports mental health globally and in low-resource settings, explores case studies

DOI: 10.4018/979-8-3373-7340-9.ch012

and comparative analyses, discusses ethical concerns and dataset limitations, and highlights opportunities for developing multilingual, human-centred systems that improve access to mental health support across linguistic communities.

1. INTRODUCTION

Millions of people are affected globally by various mental health challenges such as depression, anxiety, and loneliness (Bin Sawad et al., 2022). This rise is certainly linked to changes in lifestyle, increased pressure at work, the influence of social media, demands from family, and the long-term effect of the COVID-19 pandemic (Auerbach et al., 2018; Vindegaard & Benros, 2020). A study by Liu et al. (2020) found that more than 300 million people worldwide are impacted by depression. Depression and mental illness are among the leading causes of economic disability worldwide, affecting productivity, relationships, and quality of life (Patel et al., 2010). Many individuals who require psychological support due to social isolation and post-pandemic stress are not getting proper access and guidance due to traditional therapy models, which are often costly, and more than 70% individuals in low and middle-income regions do not visit one due to a lack of resources and professional support. Digital tools like mental health chatbots have become significant in bridging the gap between people who need support and the limited availability of counselors, particularly in underserved areas (Fitzpatrick et al., 2017; Casu et al., 2024). GenAI tools such as ChatGPT, Wysa, and Woebot can facilitate simple conversations and provide personalised support, helping an individual overcome negative emotions in real time. Many studies show that such AI assistants and support systems can reduce stress, anxiety, loneliness, and also symptoms of mild to moderate depression through guided conversations (Abd-Alrazaq et al., 2019; Denecke et al., 2021).

With 24/7 accessibility, stigma-free conversations, and personalised emotion support, these GenAI tools can be advantageous for overcoming mental health problems (Ho et al., 2018). Users often feel more comfortable sharing their emotions and thoughts with an AI-enabled system since they do not fear judgment or stigma, which is common in in-person therapy (Chin et al., 2023). Human counseling takes more time, but these AI-enabled chatbots can provide instant support without judging an individual. These tools are built in a continual learning and fine-tuning fashion, so they adapt to users' linguistic and emotional patterns and provide relevant conversation and guidance. These advancements of GenAI tools are valuable in overcoming the global mental health crisis, particularly in remote and backward communities.

Despite these advantages, GenAI is not very effective and uneven across languages. Most AI models are trained and fine-tuned using large datasets collected and extracted from the internet. Since there are far more texts available for high-resource languages such as English or Spanish than in Nepali, Newari, or Bengali, the model performs better in those languages (Paul et al., 2019; Oyewole et al., 2024). There is a lack of annotated datasets and limited linguistic coverage, which creates significant barriers in its global reach (Sitoula et al., 2025; Sitaula et al., 2021). For example, Nepali users often communicate in code-mixed language (Romanised Nepali and Devanagari script), making it difficult for models to accurately detect and interpret emotions. This imbalance affects accessibility in mental health support systems. Therefore, to ensure that mental health AI tools are accurate, safe, and culturally relevant for a diverse population, improving and extending coverage of languages is essential.

The main objective of this chapter is to:

- Analyse how GenAI supports mental health across various linguistic patterns, including multilingual and code-mixed conversations.
- Compare the performance of GenAI-based mental health tools in high-resource languages (e.g., English, Spanish) versus low-resource languages (e.g., Nepali).
- Provide global and local case studies and highlight global and local innovations and challenges in AI-based mental health systems, with a special focus on Nepal.
- Identify, analyse, and discuss the ethical, technical, and cultural challenges associated with deploying AI-based mental health care.
- Recommend strategies for inclusive privacy-oriented AI design to enhance global access to mental health support.

The rest of the chapter is structured as follows. Section 2 reviews related work on GenAI and mental-health chatbots, and examines their effectiveness across different languages. Section 3 explains the methodology we used to study global chatbot systems, available datasets, and how well these tools work in low-resource languages. Section 4 describes case studies conducted in both high- and low-resource languages, presenting real examples of their use and differences in performance. Section 5 provides a comparative analysis that highlights how datasets, model resources, and research studies in high-resource languages are far more extensive than those available for languages such as Nepali. Section 6 discusses important ethical concerns, including privacy, cultural sensitivity, and potential biases in GenAI-based mental health systems. Section 7 concludes the chapter by summarising the main findings and suggesting directions for future research.

2. RELATED WORK

Early systems, such as ELIZA, were rule-based and could only process minor user inputs without true understanding (Weizenbaum, 1966). Later developments in chatbots focused mainly on providing conversational response to inputs and can also execute tasks when commanded properly (Oviatt & Adams, 2000). A study by Bin Sawad et al. (2022) showed that conversational agents can be used to prevent mental health trauma and support chronic care management. Recent advancements in Large Language Models (LLMs) have enabled the development of empathetic, interactive dialogue support systems that can emotionally engage users (Gao et al., 2025).

AI-enabled mental health support systems such as Woebot and Wysa are designed in a way that can understand users' thoughts and emotions (Durden et al., 2023; Fitzpatrick et al., 2017; Inkster et al., 2018). A study conducted by Wang et al. (2025) found that these tools can help reduce feelings of stress, depression, and anxiety and can be used by people who may not have access to physical therapy at lower cost. However, most of these systems are built for English-speaking users or other major languages such as Spanish and Chinese. In English-speaking contexts, several studies show that AI-based mental health chatbots actually can reduce depression, stress, and loneliness (Chin et al., 2023). For example, Fulmer et al. (2018) found that interacting with Woebot (Durden et al., 2023; Fitzpatrick et al., 2017) and Wysa (Inkster et al., 2018) led to a significant reduction in depression among young adults. Another research performed by (Ramírez et al., 2024) found that a Spanish-language Cognitive Behavioral Therapy (CBT) chatbot improved mood tracking and emotional awareness among users in Latin America. Another study from Spain has shown that people support and prefer AI-based chatbots for emotional conversation to ask for help and support in need (Mármol-Romero et al., 2025). Xiaolce (Chin et al., 2023) and other counseling platforms have demonstrated strong emotional assistance and user satisfaction for the Chinese language (Ho et al., 2018). For example, Ho et al., (2018) found that Chinese users experienced reduced stress, anxiety, and loneliness after interacting with an AI counselor. Despite these advancements in high-resource languages such as English, Spanish, and Chinese, similar progress has not been observed in low-resource languages such as Nepali and Bengali. The research has only been limited to basic sentiment analysis rather than clinical-level emotional support (Sitoula et al., 2025). This means these systems do not apply to people of different cultures and languages, such as Nepali.

Modern LLMs such as Gemini and GPT can generate emotionally intelligent responses and also help to detect users' emotions and sentiments (Kalyan, 2023). These models can also work in low-resource languages such as Nepali, Newari, and

Bengali. However, the accuracy of these is not up to the mark compared to their performance with languages such as English and Spanish.

These AI models rely on large amounts of data to perform. Most recent research in natural language processing (NLP) focuses on high-resource languages such as English and Chinese (Sitoula et al., 2025). In contrast, low-resource languages such as Nepali have very few labelled datasets, and most work in this language focuses on Sentiment Analysis (SA) that classifies texts as positive, negative, or neutral rather than multi-label emotion work (Sitoula et al., 2025; Sitaula et al., 2021). Also, the Nepali language is complex, as people use both the Devanagari script and romanised Nepali, making it difficult to process, predict, and detect emotions. Due to the lack of relevant annotated datasets, LLMs cannot be properly trained and fine-tuned to produce responses in Nepali.

There are still several gaps in this area:

- There are very few emotion-labelled and culturally adapted datasets for low-resource languages.
- Cross-lingual learning methods for mental health support are still underdeveloped.
- There has been little research on ethical and privacy issues related to AI in local settings.

These chapters focus on the importance of creating generative AI tools that are inclusive, culturally aware, and designed responsibly to support mental health and well-being.

Table 1 presents studies conducted in English, Spanish, Chinese, Nepali, and Bengali, along with their key findings and relevance to mental health and emotional support. For high-resource languages such as English, Spanish, and Chinese, chatbots can really help people feel less lonely, reduce depression, and support overall mental health. On the other hand, research in low-resource settings, such as Nepali and Bengali, is quite basic and limited to general sentiment classification and detection, such as positive, negative, or neutral. This shows that there is an urgent need to create a more detailed annotated emotional dataset, that works for code-mixed languages (such as English + Roman Nepali mixed), and build an AI model so that it can be utilized for people in need.

Table 1. Overview of AI and Chatbot Studies Across Different Languages for Mental Health and Emotion Support

S.No.	Language	Key Findings	Relevance to Mental-Health and Emotion Support	Ref.
1.	English	Chatbot (Woebot) helps to reduce depression and other mental health problems in young adults	Shows the feasibility of an AI chatbot for mental health support in English	(Durden et al., 2023); Fitzpatrick et al., 2017
2.	English	Wysa chatbot provided empathetic and interactive support	Demonstrates emotion-aware AI support in the English-speaking population	(Inkster et al., 2018)
3.	English	An AI chatbot system helped reduce stress, depression, and loneliness, and improved emotional regulation	Suggest the vast applicability of AI support beyond traditional therapy settings	(Kollig et al., 2025)
4.	Spanish	Spanish language CBT- chatbot improved mood tracking and emotional support	Adapting AI mental health tools for non-English users	(Ramírez et al., 2024)
5.	Chinese	Detected stress and emotional distress in Chinese social media posts using AI models	Useful for early detection of mental health signals in Chinese text	(Ho et al., 2018)
6.	Chinese	Chinese conversational agents (e.g., Xiaolce) showed accurate emotional intelligence and better user satisfaction	Shows scalable AI-based emotional support in the Chinese language	(Chin et al., 2023)
7.	Nepali	Sentiment analysis of Nepali COVID-19 tweets- created NepCOV19 Twitter dataset and classified positive, neutral/ negative sentiment	Provides baseline dataset for future Nepali mental-health AI work	(Sitaula et al., 2021)
8.	Nepali	Classifying political datasets for hate speech detection, relevance, and sentiment prediction	Shows modern transformer-based methods can work on Nepali text- a foundation for future mental health work.	(Rauniyar et al., 2023)
9.	Bengali	Bengali emotion recognition dataset for basic emotion detection (anger, joy, sadness, etc.)	Example of a low-resource language emotion dataset	(Das et al., 2020)

3. METHODOLOGY

Figure 1 illustrates the step-by-step methodological framework adopted in this study to compare how generative AI systems operate in high- and low-resource linguistic environments for mental health support. The process begins with problem Identification, where the broader challenge of uneven GenAI performance across languages and cultural settings is established. Building on this, System Selection involves identifying representative AI tools, both globally developed platforms and region-specific applications that are commonly used for emotional or psychological assistance.

Figure 1. Methodological Framework for Comparative Analysis of Global and Local GenAI Systems in Mental-Health Support

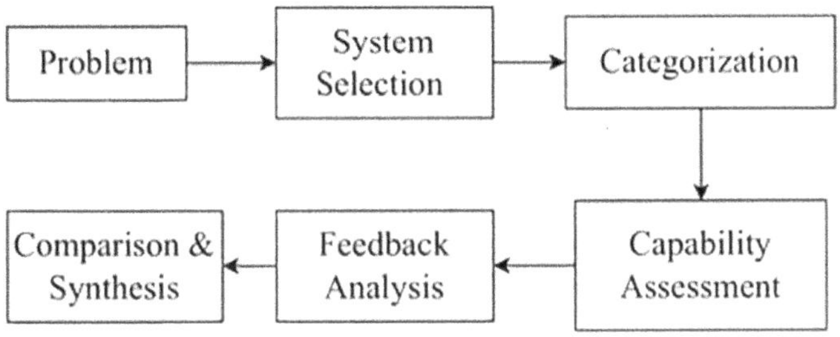

Once the relevant systems are identified, the next stage, Categorisation, organizes them into high-resource and low-resource contexts based on language availability, data richness, and technological maturity. This categorisation allows the study to frame the comparative inquiry clearly. Following this classification, the framework proceeds to Capability Assessment, where each AI system is examined for core functional features, including emotional tone recognition, empathetic response generation, crisis handling, contextual sensitivity, and conversational depth. To complement the functional review, the study integrates real-world perspectives through Feedback Analysis, drawing from user documentation, published evaluations, and community-based experiences to understand how individuals interact with these tools in practice.

The final stage, Comparison and Synthesis, brings together technical observations and user-level insights to highlight structural disparities, cultural gaps, accessibility concerns, and ethical implications. This stage synthesizes the strengths and limitations of both global and local GenAI deployments, aligning directly with the paper's central aim of understanding how linguistic and socio-cultural differences shape the performance and reception of mental-health-oriented AI systems.

- **Approach**:

I. Comparative case study of global and local GenAI applications.

This study follows a comparative case study approach to understand how Generative AI tools function in mental-health contexts across different linguistic and socio-cultural environments.

1. Selection of Representative GenAI Systems

Prominent generative AI applications used for mental health support, such as ChatGPT, Wysa, Woebot, and region-specific AI systems, were identified. These systems were selected based on their availability, documented use, and relevance to emotional or behavioral support.

2. Categorization into Global (High-Resource) and Local (Low-Resource) Contexts

The selected tools were categorized according to the languages and regions they primarily serve.

- High-resource environments include languages like English and Spanish, where digital resources, annotated datasets, and commercial AI investments are abundant.
- Low-resource environments include languages such as Nepali, Newari, and Bengali, where limited training data and limited technological investment affect system performance.

3. Examination of Functional Capabilities

Each system was reviewed for core components including empathy modelling, crisis guidance, emotional tone detection, and conversational depth. Comparisons were made to identify gaps between global deployments and locally adapted versions.

4. Assessment of Real-World Usage and Community Feedback

Available documentation, user studies, published surveys, and community-based reports were analyzed to understand how individuals in different regions experience these technologies. This includes evaluating ease of use, perceived helpfulness, and trust in AI-generated responses.

5. Contextual Comparison and Synthesis

Findings from global and local case studies were compared to highlight patterns of success, limitations, and unmet needs. The comparison emphasizes how linguistic resources, cultural norms, and social sensitivities influence the performance and acceptance of GenAI in mental-health settings.

II. Analysis based on accessibility, personalisation, cultural adaptation, and ethics.

To explore the broader implications of deploying GenAI for mental health support, the study evaluates selected systems using four critical dimensions. Each dimension serves as an analytical lens to understand the strengths and weaknesses of existing approaches.

1. Accessibility
   - The analysis reviews how easily individuals across different linguistic and socio-economic groups can access these AI tools.
   - Factors such as language availability, interface simplicity, platform requirements, internet connectivity, and affordability are taken into account.
   - This dimension is essential for identifying whether GenAI systems truly reach marginalised or underserved communities.
2. Personalization
   - Each system is examined for its ability to tailor responses based on individual emotional states, conversational patterns, or previous interactions.
   - The study analyses whether personalization mechanisms differ between high-resource and low-resource languages, especially where user data is limited.
   - The goal is to understand whether users receive support that feels relevant, sensitive, and consistent over time.
3. Cultural Adaptation
   - GenAI responses are reviewed for cultural appropriateness, relevance of examples, and alignment with local norms surrounding mental health, emotional expression, and help-seeking behavior.
   - Special focus is placed on low-resource languages where direct translations often fail to capture cultural meanings, idioms, or context-specific concerns.
   - This dimension helps identify whether systems respect community-specific values or inadvertently reinforce cultural misunderstandings.
4. Ethical Considerations
   - Ethical issues such as privacy, data security, bias, consent, emotional dependency, and potential harm are systematically examined.
   - The analysis also considers the level of transparency provided by AI developers regarding data sources, model limitations, and risk-mitigation strategies.
   - Evaluating ethics across languages reveals how resource availability influences system safety and trustworthiness.
   - **Dataset and Sources**

I. **Global AI tools:** To understand how widely used GenAI systems support mental health in high-resource environments, this study relies on secondary data drawn from published research, technical documentation, and publicly available evaluations of tools such as Woebot (Durden et al., 2023), Wysa (Inkster et al., 2018), and ChatGPT (Kalyan, 2023). These sources include peer-reviewed articles, white papers, user experience studies, and psychological assessments that describe how these systems respond to stress, anxiety, and emotional concerns. Since these platforms are extensively studied in English and other well-resourced languages, the available literature provides insights into their conversational behavior, therapeutic design principles, and real-world performance.

II. **Nepali datasets:** For the local perspective, the analysis incorporates several Nepali-language datasets that reflect real-world public expression, emotional states, and social concerns. These include sentiment datasets created during the COVID-19 pandemic (Sitaula et al., 2021), discussions and debates captured during local and national elections (Rauniyar et al., 2023), and user comments collected from Nepali YouTube channels (Sitoula et al., 2025). These sources were chosen because they represent diverse emotional tones, fear, frustration, hope, political tension, social stress, and community support, making them suitable for examining how GenAI might interpret or misinterpret local linguistic and cultural expressions. Although these datasets are not intended for therapeutic use, they offer valuable insights into how Nepali speakers communicate emotions, which is critical for evaluating gaps in GenAI performance.

III. **Focus on sentiment, emotion, and mental health analysis in local contexts:** The final part of this subsection concentrates on how these datasets can help reveal patterns in emotional expression, mental health concerns, and culturally specific communication styles among Nepali-speaking communities. The analysis looks beyond general sentiment polarity to examine deeper emotional categories such as anxiety, anger, sadness, reassurance, sarcasm, and hope. These distinctions are vital for identifying where GenAI tools struggle to correctly interpret culturally rooted expressions, idioms, or indirect communication forms commonly used in Nepal and Nepali language. By understanding the emotional landscape reflected in these datasets, the study assesses whether existing AI systems can provide accurate, sensitive, and context-aware support to Nepali users and where significant improvements are required.

Table 2. Summary of AI Chatbot and Nepali Social Media Datasets for Mental-Health and Emotion Analysis

S.N.	Dataset / Source	Data Volume / Scope	Purpose / Notes
1.	Woebot (global AI-based mental-health chatbot)	Part of a collective sample of 44,773 participants across 10 empirical studies on AI-powered CBT chatbots (Durden et al., 2023; Fitzpatrick et al., 2017)	Evidence-based outcomes on mental health support, therapy engagement, and emotional well-being in high-resource contexts.
2.	Wysa (global AI mental-health chatbot)	Included in the same 44,773 participant pool from systematic reviews (Inkster et al., 2018)	Used as a benchmark for chatbot-based emotional support, demonstrating reductions in depression/anxiety symptoms among users.
3.	Global AI chatbots (Woebot, Wysa, others) aggregated studies	10 peer-reviewed studies (2017–2024), covering various age groups and clinical/non-clinical settings (Farzan et al., 2025)	To understand the general effectiveness, engagement, and limitations of GenAI in well-resourced languages globally.
4.	NepCOV19Tweets Nepali COVID-19 Twitter dataset	33,247 tweets collected between 11 Feb 2020 and 10 Jan 2021 (Sitaula et al., 2021)	Captures emotional reactions, public sentiment, and mental-health–related discourse in Nepali during the pandemic, useful as a proxy for community emotional state.
5.	Nepali social media / YouTube comment dataset for sentiment analysis	7,991 comment texts (from political, social, and financial contexts) annotated for sentiment (Sitoula et al., 2025)	Reflects real-world Nepali-language expressions, including code-mixing, public opinions, and emotional tones, useful to study cultural and linguistic challenges for GenAI.
6.	Additional Nepali dataset from political/social discourse: NAET dataset (Nepali tweets during election / social events)	4,445 tweets collected between July 2022 and February 2023 (Rauniyar et al., 2023)	Allows analysis of sentiment, social stress, political anxiety, and communal emotional patterns, and helps explore context-specific mental health concerns in Nepali communities.

Table 2 briefly summarizes key global AI mental-health chatbots and Nepali social media datasets used for emotion analysis. It includes well-known AI chatbots such as Woebot and Wysa, which have been studied on large user groups to understand their impact on emotional well-being in high-resource settings. The table also presents several Nepali datasets collected from Twitter and YouTube that capture public emotions, sentiment, and mental-health–related discussions during events like the COVID-19 pandemic and political activities. Together, these datasets help compare established AI mental-health tools with real-world emotional expressions in the Nepali context.

Table 3. Number of publicly available Nepali-language (or Nepali-text) datasets and resources relevant to sentiment, emotion, and social-media analysis

S.N.	Dataset / Resource	Size / Scope / Contents	Key Features & Notes
1.	NepCOV19Tweets Nepali COVID-19 Tweets Dataset	33,247 Nepali-language tweets (collected between 11 Feb 2020 and 10 Jan 2021) (Sitaula et al., 2021)	Annotated with sentiment labels (positive/ neutral/negative) based on public posts during COVID-19; captures pandemic-related emotional responses, concerns, social stress, and public opinions.
2.	NepaliNLP-SA Nepali YouTube Comments Sentiment Dataset	7,991 text comments collected from YouTube (mixed topics: politics, finance, public debate) (Sitoula et al., 2025)	Provides real-world social media discourse in Nepali (often code-mixed), reflecting public sentiment, frustration, opinion, satire; useful for sentiment & social-emotion analysis.
3.	NAET (Nepali Anti-Establishment Tweets) Election / Political Discourse Tweets	4,445 Nepali tweets collected July 2022–Feb 2023 (Rauniyar et al., 2023)	Multi-aspect annotated: sentiment, satire, hate speech, "hope-speech", and political context. Offers insight into social stress, political anxiety, and public expectations, helpful for understanding socio-political emotional dynamics.
4.	Nepali Text Corpus Broad Nepali-Language Text Corpus	~6.4 million Nepali language articles/documents (blogs, news, websites) — total ~ 27.5 GB in CSV format (IRIIS-RESEARCH/Nepali-Text-Corpus) (IRIIS, n.d.)	Very large general-purpose Nepali text corpus; while not sentiment-annotated, it can serve as a base for pre-training language models, building embeddings, or later annotation for emotion/sentiment tasks.
5.	Darvilab/Nepali-ASR-Community-Data Nepali Spoken-Language Audio Dataset	Collection of community-contributed audio recordings (spoken Nepali, including code-switched Nepali-English) with metadata & transcriptions (darvilab/nepali-asr-community-data) (OpenSLR, n.d.)	Useful if you plan multimodal emotion / mental-health models (speech + text), or want to explore vocal tone, prosody, and is valuable for future work beyond pure text-based GenAI.

Table 3 presents an overview of publicly available Nepali-language datasets relevant to sentiment, emotion, and social media analysis. It includes sentiment-annotated Twitter and YouTube datasets that capture public emotions during events such as the COVID-19 pandemic and political activities. The table also highlights a large general Nepali text corpus useful for language model training, as well as a spoken Nepali audio dataset that supports future multimodal emotion and mental-health research. Together, these resources illustrate both the availability and limitations of Nepali data for emotion-aware AI applications.

- **Evaluation**

I. Accessibility:

The first evaluation criterion focuses on how easily individuals can access and use the GenAI systems included in the study. This involves examining whether the tools are freely available, supported across devices, and capable of functioning in areas with limited connectivity. The assessment also considers whether users from low-resource regions face practical barriers such as language restrictions, subscription fees, or reliance on high-end hardware. Understanding accessibility is essential because the effectiveness of any mental health–related AI platform depends on its ability to reach people who need support, including those in remote or underserved communities.

II. Cultural Fit:

The second criterion evaluates how well the AI tools align with the cultural nuances and linguistic expressions of different communities. This includes reviewing whether the systems can interpret local idioms, emotional cues, indirect communication patterns, and community-specific references that are common in languages such as Nepali or Newari. A strong cultural fit means the tool responds in a way that feels authentic, respectful, and sensitive to local values. Poor alignment, on the other hand, can result in misunderstandings, generic replies, or emotionally inappropriate guidance. This evaluation helps determine the extent to which GenAI platforms can genuinely support users beyond high-resource linguistic environments.

III. Privacy:

Because mental health conversations often involve deeply personal information, privacy is a central part of the evaluation. This includes assessing how data is collected, stored, and processed by the AI systems, as well as whether users are informed about these practices. The review considers whether the tools safeguard sensitive emotional disclosures, provide clear consent mechanisms, and minimize the risk of unauthorized access. Protecting user integrity is especially important in low-resource contexts, where digital literacy may be limited, and individuals may not fully understand the implications of sharing personal information with AI-driven platforms.

IV. Ethics:

The final evaluation criterion examines the ethical dimensions of using GenAI for mental health support. This involves assessing whether AI-generated responses maintain authenticity, avoid misleading claims, and clearly communicate their limitations. Transparency requires that users understand they are interacting with an AI system rather than a human professional. Safety is evaluated based on how the tools handle high-risk situations, such as signs of severe distress or self-harm.

Ethical evaluation ensures the systems operate responsibly and do not create emotional dependency, confusion, or false expectations.

4. CASE STUDIES

I. Global GenAI: Woebot, Wysa - Evidence-Based Outcomes, CBT Support

The first set of case studies focuses on global conversational agents such as Woebot and Wysa, which are widely recognised for their structured mental health interventions. These tools are grounded in established psychological approaches, particularly CBT. Their design features guided conversations, mood tracking, behavioral exercises, and brief therapeutic prompts that encourage users to reflect on their thoughts and emotions. Published evaluations report improvements in symptoms of anxiety, stress, and mild depression among users, emphasising the value of their structured and evidence-based frameworks. These global examples demonstrate how well-developed GenAI systems can complement traditional mental health care when supported by strong linguistic resources and professionally validated methodologies.

II. Edge-Based GenAI: Offline, Privacy-Preserving Models

A second category examines edge-based GenAI solutions, systems designed to run directly on local devices without constant connection to cloud servers. These models are particularly relevant for communities concerned about privacy or for regions with unstable internet access. Edge-based tools reduce the risk of data exposure because sensitive conversations never leave the user's device. Though these models may have more limited capabilities than cloud-based systems, they offer a powerful demonstration of how mental health support can be delivered in a secure, self-contained way. This case study highlights the growing importance of privacy-preserving AI, especially in situations where users are hesitant to share personal or emotional information online.

III. Nepali-Specific GenAI: Local Datasets, Code-Mixing Challenges, Limited Emotional Labels

The third case study shifts the focus to attempts to develop GenAI applications tailored for Nepali-speaking communities. These efforts rely heavily on available local datasets such as COVID-19 sentiment corpora, election-related discussions, and social media comments. However, several challenges emerge. Nepali language datasets often include heavy code-mixing with English or Hindi, making it difficult for models to correctly interpret meaning or emotional tone. In addition, existing datasets tend to categorise emotions broadly, usually as positive, negative, or neutral, without the richer emotional labels necessary for mental health analysis. These limitations restrict the depth and sensitivity of AI-generated responses. This case study illustrates the gap between global and local AI capabilities and underscores the need for more culturally grounded and linguistically diverse training resources.

IV. Workplace Mental Health: Monitoring Employee Well-Being, Balancing Privacy and Support

The final case study examines the growing use of GenAI systems in workplace settings, where organisations deploy AI-based tools to monitor employee well-being, identify signs of stress, and offer basic emotional support. These systems may analyse communication patterns, self-reported mood inputs, or interactions with wellness platforms. While they can help organisations understand employee needs and reduce burnout, they raise complex questions about privacy, consent, and boundaries. This case study highlights the tension between using AI for supportive purposes and ensuring that individual rights and workplace ethics are fully respected.

5. COMPARATIVE ANALYSIS

I. High-Resource Languages: Accurate, Data-Rich, Culturally Adapted (English, Spanish, Chinese)

The analysis begins by examining GenAI performance in high-resource languages such as English, Spanish, and Chinese. These languages benefit from extensive digital archives, well-established linguistic research, and large annotated datasets. As a result, AI systems trained in these environments demonstrate strong accuracy in sentiment classification, emotional understanding, and supportive dialogue generation. Furthermore, many psychological and therapeutic models, especially those used in conversational mental health tools, were originally developed and tested in these languages, making cultural adaptation more seamless. This resource abundance allows GenAI applications to offer nuanced emotional responses, culturally appropriate examples, and a consistent interpretation of user intent.

II. Low-Resource Languages (Nepali): Limited Data, Few Emotion Annotations, Cultural Mismatch

In contrast, the performance of GenAI tools in Nepali reflects the constraints of low-resource linguistic settings. Nepali lacks large, high-quality annotated datasets for emotions, mental health indicators, or nuanced sentiment categories. Most available datasets are small, domain-specific, or limited to broad labels such as positive, negative, or neutral. In addition, Nepali speakers frequently use a mix of Nepali, English, and Hindi within the same conversation, creating code-mixed inputs that many AI models struggle to interpret. Cultural norms around expressing distress or seeking support may not align with the assumptions embedded in global AI models, leading to responses that feel generic or emotionally disconnected. This mismatch highlights the structural gaps that prevent GenAI from effectively serving Nepali-speaking communities.

III. Bridging the Gap: Cross-Lingual Learning, Nepali Dataset Creation, Multimodal Emotion Recognition

To address these disparities, the comparative analysis examines strategies to strengthen GenAI capabilities in low-resource contexts. One promising direction is cross-lingual learning, where insights from high-resource languages are adapted to improve performance in Nepali while minimising direct data requirements. Another important step is the development of richer Nepali datasets that include diverse emotion labels, mental health expressions, and culturally grounded examples. Creating such resources would allow models to better understand subtle or indirect expressions of distress common in Nepali communication. The analysis also highlights the potential of multimodal approaches, combining text with voice, tone, or facial cues, to improve emotional recognition when text alone is ambiguous. Together, these strategies outline a practical path toward more equitable and culturally sensitive GenAI systems.

Table 4 compares high-resource languages with Nepali in terms of data availability and model performance for emotion and mental-health analysis. It shows that high-resource languages (such as English, Spanish, and Chinese) have large datasets and strong model performance, while Nepali has limited data, fewer emotion labels, and lower accuracy, making AI mental-health support more challenging. The table also highlights challenges for Nepali, including tokenization issues, code-mixing nature, and the need for cultural adaptation, which reduce the effectiveness of current AI mental-health tools.

Table 4. Comparative Analysis Table (High-Resource vs Low-Resource Languages)

Dimension	High-Resource Languages (English, Spanish, Chinese)	Low-Resource Language (Nepali)	References
Dataset Volume (Text)	• English: Multiple billions datasets available online Over 3.3M emotion-labelled texts available across datasets such as GoEmotions (58k), SST (215k), Yelp Reviews (5M), Amazon Reviews (3M). • Spanish: 1.2M+ annotated sentiment/emotion texts (TASS, InterTASS, IberEval). • Chinese: 2.5M+ labelled texts (Weibo Emotions, NLPCC datasets).	• Nepali: Fewer than 100k labelled texts total. • COVID-19 Sentiment Dataset: 33,247 tweets. • YouTube Comments Dataset: 7,991 comments. • Political Sentiment Dataset (NAET): 4,445 tweets.	(Sitoula et al., 2025; Sitaula et al., 2021; Rauniyar et al., 2023; Mármol-Romero et al., 2025; Zhou et al., 2020; Demszky et al., 2020; Villena-Román et al., 2013; Dardis et al., 2025; Mudambi & Schuff, 2010)
Emotion Label Variety	• English: Up to 28–32 distinct emotion labels (GoEmotions). • Spanish/Chinese: Typically 6–12 emotional categories.	• Nepali: Most datasets use 3 labels (positive, negative, neutral). • No publicly available Nepali dataset with fine-grained emotions (anxiety, guilt, reassurance, hopelessness).	(Sitoula et al., 2025; Sitaula et al., 2021; Rauniyar et al., 2023; Demszky et al., 2020)
Model Performance (Sentiment Classification)	•English models exceed 90–95% F1 on standard benchmarks (RoBERTa, GPT-4, XLM-R large). •Spanish/Chinese models typically 85–92% F1.	•Nepali-sentiment models average 61–72% F1 depending on the dataset. •Code-mixed Nepali-English models drop to 48–56% F1.	(Sitoula et al., 2025; Sitaula et al., 2021; Rauniyar et al., 2023; Demszky et al., 2020; Villena-Román et al., 2013)
Tokenization Difficulty	• Low difficulty; tokenizers (BPE, WordPiece) trained extensively on English, Spanish, and Chinese. • High subword coverage (>98%).	• Nepali subword coverage is often below 70% in multilingual tokenizers. • High fragmentation leads to misinterpretation of emotional phrases.	(Sitoula et al., 2025; Sitaula et al., 2021; Rauniyar et al., 2023; Thara & Poornachandran, 2018; Ameer et al., 2022; Regmi, 2006)
Code-Mixing Frequency	•English/Spanish/Chinese: <5% in most corpora.	• Nepali: 20–35% of social media text includes English or Hindi mixing (YouTube, Twitter).	(Thara & Poornachandran, 2018; Ameer et al., 2022; Chakravarthi et al., 2020; Regmi, 2006)

continued on following page

Table 4. Continued

Dimension	High-Resource Languages (English, Spanish, Chinese)	Low-Resource Language (Nepali)	References
Cultural Adaptation	•Psychological expressions widely studied; therapy scripts adapted into GenAI (e.g., Woebot uses CBT templates tested in English). • Culturally aligned examples embedded in models.	•Emotional communication is often indirect ("ghar-jwai pressure", "dhabdhab"), not recognized by global models. • Mental health stigma affects language use; it requires cultural adaptation.	(Gkintoni et al., 2025; Biagianti et al., 2023; Niraula et al., 2022; Khanal, 2019)
GenAI Suitability for Mental Health Support	• High suitability: strong emotional recognition, rich training data, and culturally aligned therapeutic frameworks.	• Limited suitability: misinterpretation of idioms, lack of emotion-labelled data, poor handling of distress-related language.	(Durden et al., 2023; Fitzpatrick et al., 2017; Inkster et al., 2018; Sitoula et al., 2025; Sitaula et al., 2021; Rauniyar et al., 2023; Farzan et al., 2025; (Sitoula, 2020))
Resource Availability for Fine-Tuning	• Thousands of domain-specific datasets available (clinical notes, therapy transcripts, emotion diaries).	• No publicly released Nepali therapy transcripts or mental-health datasets exist.	(Sitoula et al., 2025; Bird et al., 2008; Shahi & Sitaula, 2022)

Figure 2. Dataset Volume (Labelled Emotion/Sentiment Texts)

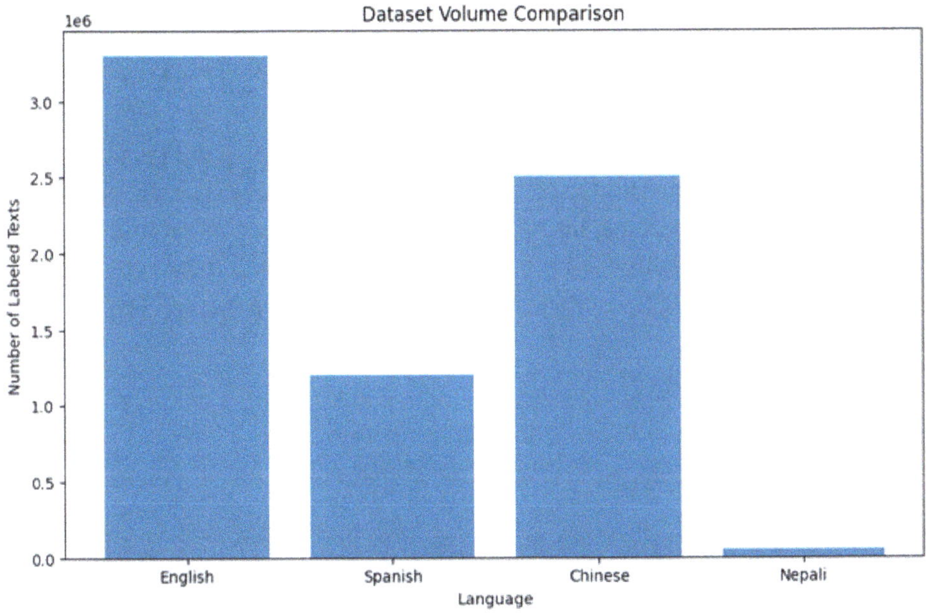

Figure 2 presents a comparative view of the available labelled emotion and sentiment datasets across English, Spanish, Chinese, and Nepali. The contrast visible in the figure reflects a long-standing structural divide between languages with extensive computational resources and those that remain underrepresented in digital corpora. English, Spanish, and Chinese possess large, systematically developed annotated datasets that have accumulated over many years of linguistic research, commercial investment, and coordinated data-collection initiatives. Studies demonstrate the depth and consistency of these resources, which often reach millions of labelled instances and follow stable annotation guidelines Sitoula et al. (2025), Rauniyar et al. (2023), Demszky et al. (2020), and Tharu et al. (2023). The scale and maturity of these datasets support the development of models capable of fine-grained emotional interpretation, culturally informed language understanding, and reliable generalisation across a wide range of contexts.

In contrast, Nepali has a substantially smaller volume of labelled data, much of which comes from small, project-specific collections with varying annotation schemes and limited domain diversity. The scarcity of high-quality annotated material restricts the expressive capacity of models trained on Nepali data and leaves them more vulnerable to statistical noise, overfitting, and reduced reliability in downstream evaluation. These limitations are especially evident in tasks requiring nuanced recognition of emotional cues, contextual meaning, or culturally shaped expressions of affect. As Figure 2 illustrates, the disparity in dataset volume is not merely an outcome of linguistic scale but a reflection of the broader research and infrastructural inequalities that shape global NLP development.

The distribution depicted in the figure therefore emphasizes a central methodological challenge for multilingual sentiment and emotion analysis: the performance of computational models is directly constrained by the uneven availability of annotated resources. This imbalance underscores the need for alternative strategies including cross-lingual transfer learning, targeted Nepali dataset expansion, multilingual pretraining, and synthetic data generation to support more equitable, representative, and culturally aligned model performance across both high-resource and low-resource languages.

Figure 3. Average F1 Score (Sentiment Classification)

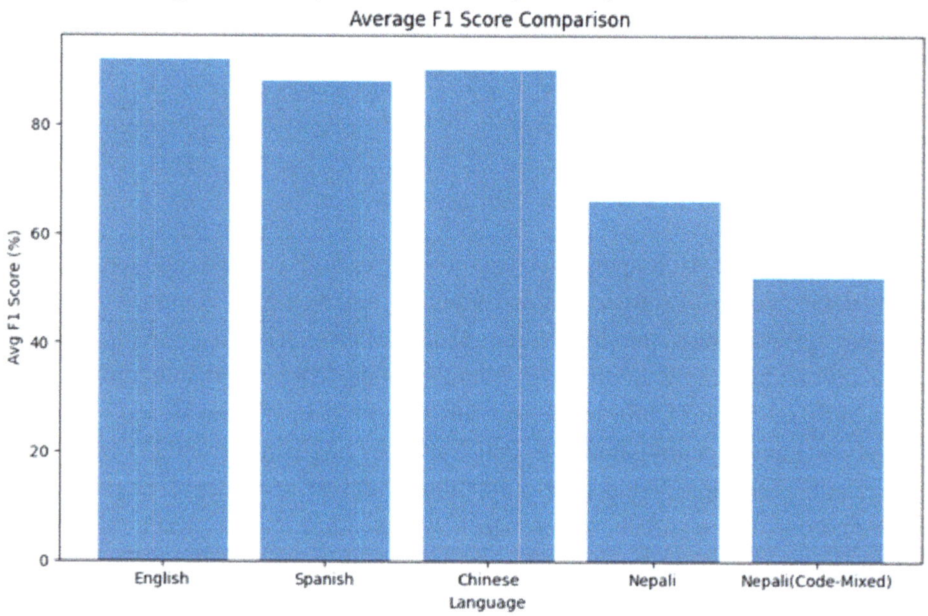

Figure 3 displays the comparative average F1 scores for sentiment classification across five linguistic conditions, offering a clear view of how resource availability shapes model performance. The three high-resource languages English, Spanish, and Chinese consistently achieve the strongest results, with F1 scores clustering in the upper-80% to 90% range. This high level of accuracy is supported by several structural advantages: large annotated corpora, long-standing sentiment analysis benchmarks, and the widespread availability of pretrained transformer models that are well attuned to emotional and semantic distinctions within these languages.

Extensive prior work, including Demszky et al. (2020), Socher et al. (2013), Liu et al. (2019), Pla et al. (2018), Chen et al. (2018), Sitaula et al. (2021), and more recent Nepali-focused studies by Sitoula et al. (2025), Rauniyar et al. (2023), Pandey et al. (2025), and Pahari & Shimada (2024), confirms the strong and consistent performance of models trained in such robust data environments.

In contrast, the F1 scores for Nepali and Nepali code-mixed texts are markedly lower. The reduced performance for standard Nepali reflects the limited breadth and depth of available labelled datasets, which restricts a model's ability to form reliable representations of emotion-laden or contextually subtle expressions. This challenge becomes even more evident with Nepali code-mixed texts, where the mixing of Nepali and English introduces additional unpredictability in spelling, grammar, transliteration practices, and discourse structure. Such linguistic variability poses a significant obstacle for classification models that are not explicitly trained on multilingual or informal communication patterns, resulting in the lowest observed F1 scores among the evaluated categories.

Taken together, the results illustrated in Figure 3 reinforce a central finding in multilingual sentiment analysis: model performance is closely tied to the amount and quality of available training data, as well as the linguistic stability of the input domain. High-resource languages benefit from ecosystem-level support that enables strong generalization, while low-resource and code-mixed settings face persistent limitations that hinder accuracy. These disparities highlight the need for more inclusive modeling strategies such as cross-lingual transfer, multilingual embeddings, and targeted data augmentation to strengthen sentiment classification capabilities in Nepali and other underrepresented languages.

Figure 4. Tokenizer Vocabulary Coverage

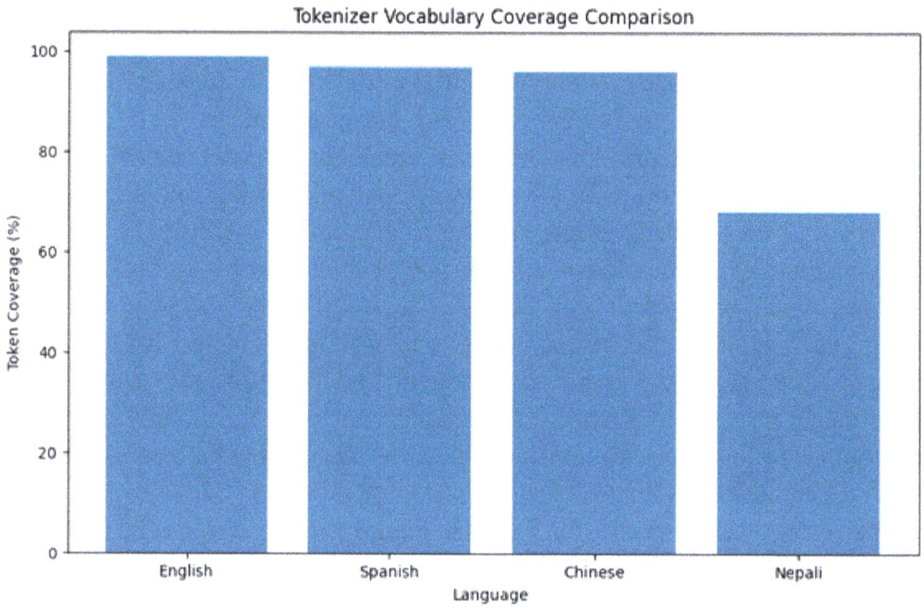

Figure 4 illustrates the contrast in tokenizer vocabulary coverage across four languages and brings attention to a fundamental structural divide between high-resource and low-resource linguistic settings. The three high-resource languages English, Spanish, and Chinese—achieve coverage rates exceeding 95%, demonstrating that standard tokenizers capture the vast majority of their words and subword forms with considerable accuracy. This high level of representation is a direct consequence of the extensive presence of these languages in large-scale pretraining corpora, along with sustained research focused on refining tokenization for widely used NLP benchmarks. As a result, models trained on these languages benefit from more coherent segmentation, reduced fragmentation of common terms, and stronger downstream performance in tasks requiring emotional or semantic interpretation.

Nepali, by contrast, shows significantly lower vocabulary coverage, with values dropping below 70%. This limited coverage reflects the broader resource constraints surrounding Nepali: minimal inclusion in pretraining datasets, inconsistent digital text availability, and a lack of tokenizers specifically adapted to its morphological and orthographic characteristics. When a tokenizer is unfamiliar with a substantial segment of the vocabulary, words are frequently split into multiple subword units or represented in distorted forms. These fragmented representations weaken semantic fidelity, hinder contextual understanding, and reduce the effectiveness of downstream tasks—particularly those involving sentiment, emotion, or mental-health–related classification. Such constraints have been discussed in foundational work on multilingual modeling and tokenization practices (Devlin et al., 2019; Conneau et al., 2020; Lauscher et al., 2020; Yamada et al., 2022), all of which emphasize how inadequate token coverage directly limits a model's interpretive capacity.

Overall, the disparity documented in Figure 4 underscores a critical challenge for low-resource languages: without adequate representation at the tokenization stage, even state-of-the-art models are unable to capture emotional nuance or culturally specific expressions. Addressing this gap requires targeted improvements, including the expansion of Nepali text corpora, integration of language-specific morphology into tokenizer design, and the development of vocabularies that reflect real usage patterns. Strengthening token coverage is therefore an essential prerequisite for achieving equitable and reliable performance in multilingual mental-health applications.

Figure 5. Percentage of Code-Mixed Social Media Texts

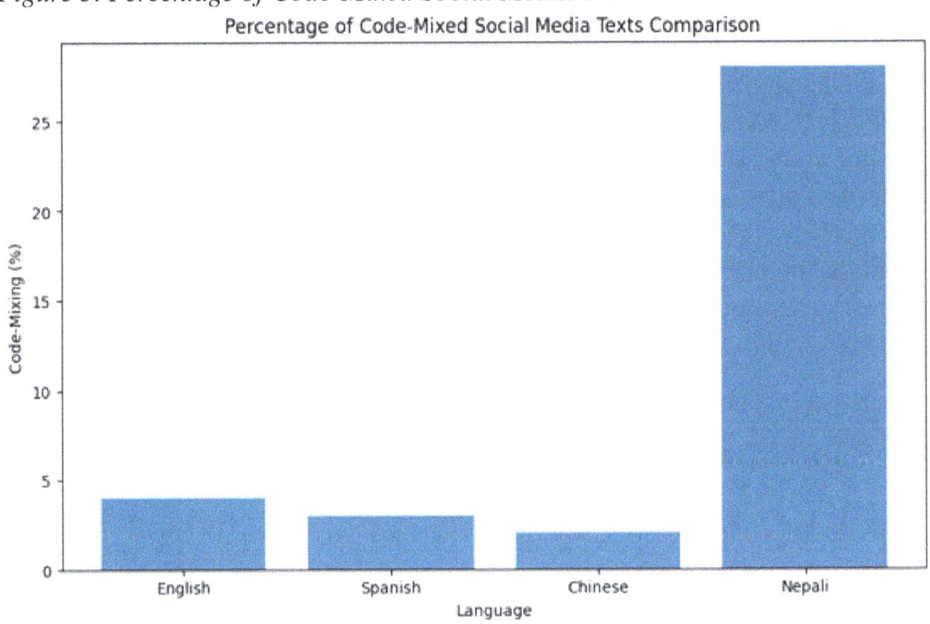

Figure 5 presents the distribution of code-mixed content in social media text across four languages and reveals a pronounced divide between high-resource and low-resource linguistic environments. English, Spanish, and Chinese exhibit comparatively low levels of code-mixing, generally between 2% and 4%. These minimal proportions reflect the linguistic consolidation and institutional reinforcement found in communities where these languages dominate public life. Standardised education systems, cohesive media infrastructures, and design choices in digital platforms encourage users to communicate primarily within a single linguistic framework. Prior studies have similarly noted that speakers of socially and institutionally dominant languages show fewer incentives to alternate between linguistic codes during everyday communication (Budzynska et al., 2014; Jurgens et al., 2014; Nabil et al., 2015; Cetinic & She, 2022).

In contrast, Nepali demonstrates a markedly higher incidence of code-mixing, approaching 28%, which sharply distinguishes it from the patterns observed in the other three languages. This elevated proportion is characteristic of multilingual societies in which speakers routinely integrate Nepali with English or other regional languages within the same utterance or conversational thread. Such blending reflects a combination of sociolinguistic dynamics: widespread bilingual education, the influence of English in academic and professional domains, and an urban digital culture that normalises hybrid linguistic expression. As a result, social media discourse in Nepal commonly incorporates borrowed vocabulary, mixed syntactic structures, and context-dependent language switching.

The disparity illustrated in the figure has direct methodological implications for natural language processing. High rates of code-mixing introduce variability that monolingual models, particularly those trained on high-resource languages are not equipped to handle effectively. Mixed-language sequences obscure sentiment cues, disrupt tokenisation patterns, and challenge emotion-classification systems that rely on coherent linguistic structure. The trends observed here underscore the need for tailored preprocessing pipelines, code-mixed corpora, and models specifically adapted for multilingual contexts where hybrid expression is an intrinsic part of digital communication.

6. DISCUSSIONS

The findings of this chapter highlight the complex role of GenAI in mental health support, particularly when comparing high-resource languages with low-resource contexts such as Nepali. While prior studies demonstrate that AI-driven chatbots can provide meaningful emotional support in well-resourced settings, the discussion reveals that ethical, technical, and socio-cultural challenges significantly shape their effectiveness in underrepresented languages.

From an ethical and cultural perspective, privacy, data ownership, and emotional safety remain central concerns when individuals share sensitive mental-health information with AI systems. Users may disclose deeply personal experiences under the assumption of confidentiality, yet transparency around data storage and secondary use is often unclear. Additionally, cultural differences in expressing distress pose a risk of misinterpretation. In Nepali contexts, emotional states are frequently communicated indirectly through idioms, metaphors, or socially embedded expressions, which global models trained largely on English data may fail to recognize. This raises concerns about emotional validity and the potential for insensitive or misleading responses, especially in vulnerable situations.

Technical limitations further compound these issues. As shown in the comparative analysis, low-resource languages suffer from limited emotion-labeled datasets, restricted vocabulary coverage, and frequent code-mixing with English or Hindi on social media platforms. Tokenization errors and high subword fragmentation reduce model accuracy and hinder reliable detection of emotional cues. Although data augmentation and multilingual transfer learning have been proposed as solutions, these approaches often introduce noise or distort cultural meaning, limiting their effectiveness for nuanced mental-health applications. Consequently, current GenAI systems may struggle to consistently identify distress, anxiety, or hopelessness in Nepali-language content.

Despite these constraints, the social implications of GenAI for mental health remain significant. Well-designed AI systems can offer non-judgmental, always-available spaces where individuals feel more comfortable expressing emotions, particularly in societies where mental-health stigma persists. For underserved or geographically isolated communities, GenAI tools may act as an entry point to mental-health awareness, encouraging early help-seeking and emotional reflection. However, this potential should be viewed as complementary rather than substitutive, as AI systems cannot replace professional diagnosis or culturally grounded therapeutic care.

The discussion also underscores important limitations and directions for future research. There is an urgent need for publicly available Nepali mental-health and emotion datasets, including fine-grained emotional categories beyond simple positive, negative, and neutral labels. Collaboration between linguists, mental-health professionals, and AI researchers is essential to ensure culturally sensitive annotation and model design. Furthermore, ethical frameworks tailored to low-resource settings must guide the deployment of GenAI systems to prevent harm, misinformation, or overreliance on automated support.

Overall, while GenAI holds promise for expanding access to mental-health support, its effectiveness is uneven across linguistic and cultural contexts. Addressing data scarcity, cultural nuance, and ethical safeguards is crucial before such systems can be responsibly and equitably integrated into mental-health ecosystems in low-resource languages like Nepali.

7. CONCLUSION & FUTURE WORK

The study concludes that Generative AI holds significant potential to expand mental health support across the world, yet its effectiveness varies widely depending on language resources, cultural alignment, and the quality of available data. While global tools developed in high-resource languages demonstrate strong emotional understanding and therapeutic structure, their strengths do not automatically transfer to Nepali or other low-resource contexts, where linguistic diversity, cultural nuances, and limited datasets pose substantial barriers. To bridge this gap, there is an urgent need to invest in the creation of culturally grounded, emotion-rich Nepali datasets and to promote the development of privacy-preserving AI models that safeguard users' sensitive disclosures. Looking ahead, future work should prioritise the design of multimodal Nepali GenAI systems capable of combining text, speech, and contextual cues to capture the full complexity of emotional expression. Such systems, if integrated responsibly into national mental health programs, could strengthen early intervention efforts and make psychological support more accessible to communities across Nepal.

REFERENCES

Abd-Alrazaq, A. A., Alajlani, M., Alalwan, A. A., Bewick, B. M., Gardner, P., & Househ, M. (2019). An overview of the features of chatbots in mental health: A scoping review. *International Journal of Medical Informatics*, *132*, 103978. DOI: 10.1016/j.ijmedinf.2019.103978 PMID: 31622850

Ameer, I., Sidorov, G., Gomez-Adorno, H., & Nawab, R. M. A. (2022). Multi-label emotion classification on code-mixed text: Data and methods. *IEEE Access : Practical Innovations, Open Solutions*, *10*, 8779–8789. DOI: 10.1109/ACCESS.2022.3143819

Auerbach, R. P., Mortier, P., Bruffaerts, R., Alonso, J., Benjet, C., Cuijpers, P., Demyttenaere, K., Ebert, D. D., Green, J. G., Hasking, P., Murray, E., Nock, M. K., Pinder-Amaker, S., Sampson, N. A., Stein, D. J., Vilagut, G., Zaslavsky, A. M., & Kessler, R. C. (2018). WHO world mental health surveys international college student project: Prevalence and distribution of mental disorders. *Journal of Abnormal Psychology*, *127*(7), 623–638. DOI: 10.1037/abn0000362 PMID: 30211576

Biagianti, B., Foti, G., Di Liberto, A., Bressi, C., & Brambilla, P. (2023). CBT-informed psychological interventions for adult patients with anxiety and depression symptoms: A narrative review of digital treatment options. *Journal of Affective Disorders*, *325*, 682–694. DOI: 10.1016/j.jad.2023.01.057 PMID: 36690081

Bin Sawad, A., Narayan, B., Alnefaie, A., Maqbool, A., Mckie, I., Smith, J., Yuksel, B., Puthal, D., Prasad, M., & Kocaballi, A. B. (2022). A systematic review of healthcare artificial intelligence conversational agents for chronic conditions. *Sensors (Basel)*, *22*(7), 2625. DOI: 10.3390/s22072625 PMID: 35408238

Bird, S., Dale, R., Dorr, B. J., Gibson, B. R., Joseph, M. T., Kan, M. Y., & Tan, Y. F. (2008, May). The ACL Anthology Reference Corpus: A Reference Dataset for Bibliographic Research in Computational Linguistics. In *LREC*.

Budzynska, K., Janier, M., Reed, C., Saint-Dizier, P., Stede, M., & Yaskorska, O. (2014). A model for processing illocutionary structures and argumentation in debates. In *LREC 2014: Ninth International Conference on Language Resources and Evaluation* (pp. 917-924). European Language Resources Association.

Casu, M., Triscari, S., Battiato, S., Guarnera, L., & Caponnetto, P. (2024). AI chatbots for mental health: A scoping review of effectiveness, feasibility, and applications. *Applied Sciences (Basel, Switzerland)*, *14*(13), 5889. DOI: 10.3390/app14135889

Cetinic, E., & She, J. (2022). Understanding and creating art with AI: Review and outlook. *ACM Transactions on Multimedia Computing Communications and Applications*, *18*(2), 66. Advance online publication. DOI: 10.1145/3475799

Chakravarthi, B. R., Jose, N., Suryawanshi, S., Sherly, E., & McCrae, J. P. (2020, May). A sentiment analysis dataset for code-mixed Malayalam-English. In *Proceedings of the 1st Joint workshop on spoken language technologies for under-resourced languages (SLTU) and collaboration and computing for under-resourced languages (CCURL)* (pp. 177-184).

Chen, S., Ding, Y., Xie, Z., Liu, S., & Ding, H. (2018, April). Chinese Weibo sentiment analysis based on character embedding with dual-channel convolutional neural network. In *2018 IEEE 3rd International conference on cloud computing and big data analysis (ICCCBDA)* (pp. 107-111). IEEE. DOI: 10.1109/ICCCBDA.2018.8386495

Chin, H., Song, H., Baek, G., Shin, M., Jung, C., Cha, M., Choi, J., & Cha, C. (2023). The potential of chatbots for emotional support and promoting mental well-being in different cultures: Mixed methods study. *Journal of Medical Internet Research, 25*, e51712. DOI: 10.2196/51712 PMID: 37862063

Conneau, A., Khandelwal, K., Goyal, N., Chaudhary, V., Wenzek, G., Guzmán, F., Grave, E., Ott, M., Zettlemoyer, L., & Stoyanov, V. (2020). Unsupervised cross-lingual representation learning at scale. In *Proceedings of the 58th Annual Meeting of the Association for Computational Linguistics* (pp. 8440–8451). Association for Computational Linguistics. DOI: 10.18653/v1/2020.acl-main.747

Dardis, F. E., Buckley, C., Mitra, P., Heaton, C., & Xiao, A. (2025). Improving nonprofit engagement on social media: Using big data, machine-learning, and sentiment analysis to evaluate leading nonprofits' message strategies on Twitter/X. *International Journal of Information Technology : an Official Journal of Bharati Vidyapeeth's Institute of Computer Applications and Management, 17*(1), 395–407. DOI: 10.1007/s41870-024-02263-5

Das, A., Iqbal, M. A., Sharif, O., & Hoque, M. M. (2020, December). Bemod: Development of bengali emotion dataset for classifying expressions of emotion in texts. In *International Conference on Intelligent Computing & Optimization* (pp. 1124-1136). Cham: Springer International Publishing.

Demszky, D., Movshovitz-Attias, D., Ko, J., Cowen, A., Nemade, G., & Ravi, S. (2020). GoEmotions: A dataset of fine-grained emotions. *arXiv preprint arXiv:2005.00547*. DOI: 10.18653/v1/2020.acl-main.372

Denecke, K., Abd-Alrazaq, A., & Househ, M. (2021). Artificial intelligence for chatbots in mental health: opportunities and challenges. *Multiple perspectives on artificial intelligence in healthcare: Opportunities and challenges*, 115-128.

Devlin, J., Chang, M. W., Lee, K., & Toutanova, K. (2019, June). Bert: Pre-training of deep bidirectional transformers for language understanding. In *Proceedings of the 2019 conference of the North American chapter of the association for computational linguistics: human language technologies, volume 1 (long and short papers)* (pp. 4171-4186).

Durden, E., Pirner, M. C., Rapoport, S. J., Williams, A., Robinson, A., & Forman-Hoffman, V. L. (2023). Changes in stress, Burnout, and resilience associated with an 8-week intervention with relational agent "Woebot.". *Internet Interventions : the Application of Information Technology in Mental and Behavioural Health, 33*, 100637. DOI: 10.1016/j.invent.2023.100637 PMID: 37635948

Fitzpatrick, K. K., Darcy, A., & Vierhile, M. (2017). Delivering cognitive behavior therapy to young adults with symptoms of depression and anxiety using a fully automated conversational agent (Woebot): A randomized controlled trial. *JMIR Mental Health, 4*(2), e19. Advance online publication. DOI: 10.2196/mental.7785 PMID: 28588005

Fulmer, R., Joerin, A., Gentile, B., Lakerink, L., & Rauws, M. (2018). Using psychological artificial intelligence (Tess) to relieve symptoms of depression and anxiety: Randomized controlled trial. *JMIR Mental Health, 5*(4), e9782. DOI: 10.2196/mental.9782 PMID: 30545815

Gao, M., Hu, X., Yin, X., Ruan, J., Pu, X., & Wan, X. (2025). Llm-based nlg evaluation: Current status and challenges. *Computational Linguistics, 51*(2), 1–27. DOI: 10.1162/coli_a_00561

Gkintoni, E., Vassilopoulos, S. P., & Nikolaou, G. (2025). Next-generation cognitive-behavioral therapy for depression: Integrating digital tools, teletherapy, and personalization for enhanced mental health outcomes. *Medicina, 61*(3), 431. DOI: 10.3390/medicina61030431 PMID: 40142242

Ho, A., Hancock, J., & Miner, A. S. (2018). Psychological, relational, and emotional effects of self-disclosure after conversations with a chatbot. *Journal of Communication, 68*(4), 712–733. DOI: 10.1093/joc/jqy026 PMID: 30100620

Inkster, B., Sarda, S., & Subramanian, V. (2018). An empathy-driven, conversational artificial intelligence agent (WYSA) for digital mental well-being: Real-World Data Evaluation Mixed-Methods Study. *JMIR mHealth and uHealth, 6*(11), e12106. Advance online publication. DOI: 10.2196/12106 PMID: 30470676

Institute for Research and Innovation in Intelligent Systems (IRIIS). (n.d.). *Iriis-Research/Nepali-text-corpus datasets at hugging face*. IRIIS-RESEARCH/Nepali-Text-Corpus · Datasets at Hugging Face. https://huggingface.co/datasets/IRIIS-RESEARCH/Nepali-Text-Corpus

Jurgens, D., Dimitrov, S., & Ruths, D. (2014, October). Twitter users# codeswitch hashtags!# moltoimportante# wow. In *Proceedings of the First Workshop on Computational Approaches to Code Switching* (pp. 51-61). DOI: 10.3115/v1/W14-3906

Kalyan, K. S. (2023). A survey of GPT-3 family large language models including chatgpt and GPT-4. SSRN *Electronic Journal*. DOI: 10.2139/ssrn.4593895

Khanal, R. (2019). Linguistic geography of nepalese languages. *The Third Pole: Journal of Geography Education*, 45-54.

Kollig, F., Pater, J., Nova, F. F., & Fiesler, C. (2025, April). Fictional Failures and Real-World Lessons: Ethical Speculation Through Design Fiction on Emotional Support Conversational AI. In *Proceedings of the 2025 CHI Conference on Human Factors in Computing Systems* (pp. 1-15). DOI: 10.1145/3706598.3713322

Lauscher, A., Ravishankar, V., Vulić, I., & Glavaš, G. (2020). From zero to hero: On the limitations of zero-shot cross-lingual transfer with multilingual transformers. *arXiv preprint arXiv:2005.00633.*

Liu, Q., He, H., Yang, J., Feng, X., Zhao, F., & Lyu, J. (2020). Changes in the global burden of depression from 1990 to 2017: Findings from the global burden of disease study. *Journal of Psychiatric Research*, *126*, 134–140. DOI: 10.1016/j.jpsychires.2019.08.002 PMID: 31439359

Liu, Y., Ott, M., Goyal, N., Du, J., Joshi, M., Chen, D., & Stoyanov, V. (2019). RoBERTa: A Robustly Optimized BERT Pretraining Approach. arXiv [Cs.CL]. Retrieved from https://arxiv.org/abs/1907.11692

Mármol-Romero, A. M., García-Vega, M., García-Cumbreras, M. Á., & Montejo-Ráez, A. (2025). An empathic GPT-based chatbot to talk about mental disorders with Spanish teenagers. *International Journal of Human-Computer Interaction*, *41*(7), 3957–3973.

Mudambi, S. M., & Schuff, D. (2010). Research note: What makes a helpful online review? A study of customer reviews on Amazon. com. *MIS quarterly*, 185-200.

Nabil, M., Aly, M., & Atiya, A. (2015, September). Astd: Arabic sentiment tweets dataset. In *Proceedings of the 2015 conference on empirical methods in natural language processing* (pp. 2515-2519). DOI: 10.18653/v1/D15-1299

Niraula, N. B., Dulal, S., & Koirala, D. (2022). Linguistic taboos and euphemisms in nepali. *ACM Transactions on Asian and Low-Resource Language Information Processing*, *21*(6), 1–26. DOI: 10.1145/3524111

OpenSLR. (n.d.). SLR54: Nepali speech dataset. https://openslr.org/54/

Oviatt, S., & Adams, B. (2000). Designing and evaluating conversational interfaces with animated characters. *Embodied Conversational Agents*, 319–345. DOI: 10.7551/mitpress/2697.003.0014

Oyewole, A. R., Ugwu, C. C., Adetunmbi, A. O., & Afolayan, A. H. (2024, November). A Systematic Review of Chatbot Development for Low-Resource Languages. In *2024 IEEE 5th International Conference on Electro-Computing Technologies for Humanity (NIGERCON)* (pp. 1-5). IEEE. DOI: 10.1109/NIGERCON62786.2024.10927136

Pahari, N., & Shimada, K. (2024). Share What You Already Know: Cross-Language-Script Transfer and Alignment for Sentiment Detection in Code-Mixed Data. *ACM Transactions on Asian and Low-Resource Language Information Processing*, *23*(7), 1–15. DOI: 10.1145/3661307

Pandey, M., Yadav, N. P., Adduru, M., & Rai, S. (2025). Creating and Evaluating Code-Mixed Nepali-English and Telugu-English Datasets for Abusive Language Detection Using Traditional and Deep Learning Models. *arXiv preprint arXiv:2504.21026.*

Patel, V., Maj, M., Flisher, A. J., De Silva, M. J., Koschorke, M., Prince, M., Tempier, R., Riba, M., Sanchez, M., Campodonico, F. D., Risco, L., Gask, L., Wahlberg, H., Roca, M., Lecic-Tosevski, D., Soghoyan, A., Moussaoui, D., Baddoura, C., Adeyemi, J., & Richardson, G. (2010). Reducing the treatment gap for mental disorders: A WPA survey. *World Psychiatry; Official Journal of the World Psychiatric Association (WPA)*, *9*(3), 169–176. DOI: 10.1002/j.2051-5545.2010.tb00305.x PMID: 20975864

Paul, A., Haque Latif, A., Amin Adnan, F., & Rahman, R. M. (2019). Focused domain contextual AI chatbot framework for resource poor languages. *Journal of Information and Telecommunication*, *3*(2), 248–269. DOI: 10.1080/24751839.2018.1558378

Pla, F., & Lluís-F., H. (2018, June). Spanish sentiment analysis in Twitter at the TASS workshop. *Language Resources and Evaluation*, *52*(2), 645–672. DOI: 10.1007/s10579-017-9394-7

Ramírez, B. G., Espejel, J. L., Díaz, M. D. C. S., & Linares, G. T. R. (2024). S\'olo Esc\'uchame: Spanish Emotional Accompaniment Chatbot. *arXiv preprint arXiv:2408.01852.*

Rauniyar, K., Poudel, S., Shiwakoti, S., Thapa, S., Rashid, J., Kim, J., Imran, M., & Naseem, U. (2023). Multi-aspect annotation and analysis of nepali tweets on anti-establishment election discourse. *IEEE Access : Practical Innovations, Open Solutions, 11*, 143092–143115. DOI: 10.1109/ACCESS.2023.3342154

Regmi, U. R. (2006). *The mixing of English code in Nepali public speaking* (Doctoral dissertation, Department of English Education).

Shahi, T. B., & Sitaula, C. (2022). Natural language processing for Nepali text: A review. *Artificial Intelligence Review, 55*(4), 3401–3429. DOI: 10.1007/s10462-021-10093-1

Sitaula, C., Basnet, A., Mainali, A., & Shahi, T. B. (2021). Deep learning-based methods for sentiment analysis on Nepali COVID-19-related tweets. *Computational Intelligence and Neuroscience, 2158184*(1), 2158184. Advance online publication. DOI: 10.1155/2021/2158184 PMID: 34737773

Sitoula, S. (2020). Analysis of Twitter Data for Its Popularity Index and Sentiments Associated. *Zenodo*. DOI: 10.5281/zenodo.17830974

Sitoula, S., Shahi, T. B., Wibowo, S., & Neupane, A. (2025). Sentiment analysis of Nepali social media text with a hybrid deep learning model. *Social Network Analysis and Mining, 15*(1), 85. Advance online publication. DOI: 10.1007/s13278-025-01508-w

Socher, R., Perelygin, A., Wu, J., Chuang, J., Manning, C. D., Ng, A. Y., & Potts, C. (2013, October). Recursive deep models for semantic compositionality over a sentiment treebank. In *Proceedings of the 2013 conference on empirical methods in natural language processing* (pp. 1631-1642). DOI: 10.18653/v1/D13-1170

Thara, S., & Poornachandran, P. (2018, September). Code-mixing: A brief survey. In *2018 International conference on advances in computing, communications and informatics (ICACCI)* (pp. 2382-2388). IEEE. DOI: 10.1109/ICACCI.2018.8554413

Tharu, M., Pokhrel, S., & Lamichhane, B. (2023). Sentiment Analysis of Nepali COVID-19 Tweets using BERT-LSTM. *Journal of Engineering and Sciences., 2*(1), 49–56. DOI: 10.3126/jes2.v2i1.60393

Villena-Román, J., Lana-Serrano, S., Martínez-Cámara, E., & González-Cristóbal, J. C. (2013). Tass-workshop on sentiment analysis at sepln. *Procesamiento del Lenguaje Natural, 50*, 37–44.

Vindegaard, N., & Benros, M. E. (2020). COVID-19 pandemic and mental health consequences: Systematic review of the current evidence. *Brain, Behavior, and Immunity, 89*, 531–542. DOI: 10.1016/j.bbi.2020.05.048 PMID: 32485289

Wang, L., Bhanushali, T., Huang, Z., Yang, J., Badami, S., & Hightow-Weidman, L. (2025). Evaluating Generative AI in Mental Health: Systematic Review of Capabilities and Limitations. *JMIR Mental Health*, *12*(1), e70014. DOI: 10.2196/70014 PMID: 40373033

Weizenbaum, J. (1966). ELIZA—A computer program for the study of natural language communication between man and machine. *Communications of the ACM*, *9*(1), 36–45. DOI: 10.1145/365153.365168

Yamada, I., Washio, K., Shindo, H., & Matsumoto, Y. (2022, July). Global entity disambiguation with BERT. In *Proceedings of the 2022 Conference of the North American Chapter of the Association for Computational Linguistics: Human Language Technologies* (pp. 3264-3271).

Zhou, L., Gao, J., Li, D., & Shum, H. Y. (2020). The design and implementation of xiaoice, an empathetic social chatbot. *Computational Linguistics*, *46*(1), 53–93. DOI: 10.1162/coli_a_00368

Chapter 13
Generative Edge AI in Healthcare and Management: A Case Study

Prashant Parwani
http://orcid.org/0009-0005-7807-7547
Christ University, Bengaluru, India

Vandana Sharma
Christ University, Bengaluru, India

ABSTRACT

This case-based discussion of Generative Edge AI in healthcare delivery and hospital management examines how Generative Edge AI is revolutionizing healthcare by combining real-time processing and generative intelligence to support quicker and better decisions based on evidence. It provides real-world applications and case examples showing how organizations benefit from increased efficiency, diagnostic accuracy, and streamlined operations. In delivering healthcare, organizations such as Caption Health, Butterfly iQ, AliveCor, and Viz.ai are discussed as case studies of AI-based systems enabling real-time monitoring, improved imaging accuracy, and coordinated clinical care. Additionally, Qventus, LeanTaaS, GE (General Electric) HealthCare, and Siemens Healthineers are examined for improving operational efficiency, patient scheduling, patient flow, and hospital resource utilization. The review highlights challenges including scalability, data privacy, and regulatory compliance, and concludes by emphasizing Generative Edge AI's shift from theory to practice.

DOI: 10.4018/979-8-3373-7340-9.ch013

1. INTRODUCTION

The rapid development of Generative AI and Edge AI has had a serious impact on how hospitals deliver care and operate as businesses. While these technologies may appear unsettling to healthcare delivery and operations, they also represent a larger sign of transformation in the overall global and local health systems. Increasingly, health organizations have turned to the digitization, decentralization, and data-driven approach to healthcare delivery.

As the convergence of Generative AI with Edge Computing creates the ability for healthcare organizations to accumulate, process, and synthesize health data in milliseconds for their clinical and administrative decision-making processes where accurate, timely, and reliable information is vital to making decisions regarding the delivery and management of healthcare.

The purpose is to describe how to apply Generative Edge AI to improve the efficiency and effectiveness of providing healthcare and administrating healthcare, rather than repeating the technology theory of how Generative Edge AI works.

The traditional AI model of utilizing a centralized cloud system creates significant latency and bandwidth limitations as well as privacy issues that ultimately reduce its usefulness when used in a clinical setting, whereas Edge AI provides direct access and utilization of the processing power of devices located near the source of the data generation. By leveraging these two technologies (Edge AI and Generative AI), we create a new paradigm that gives healthcare organizations the ability to respond immediately to the needs of their patients in real time and take full advantage of advanced (and in some cases, sophisticated) analytics.

According to studies, delays in making clinical decisions will affect patient outcomes; some of the greatest effects will occur with patients suffering from time-dependent illnesses, like stroke and severe heart problems. Furthermore, even the smallest reduction in the length of time from diagnosis of an illness to treatment of that illness has been associated with significant improvements in both survival rates and long-term complications of that same illness.

Figure 1. Architecture of Generative Edge AI in Healthcare

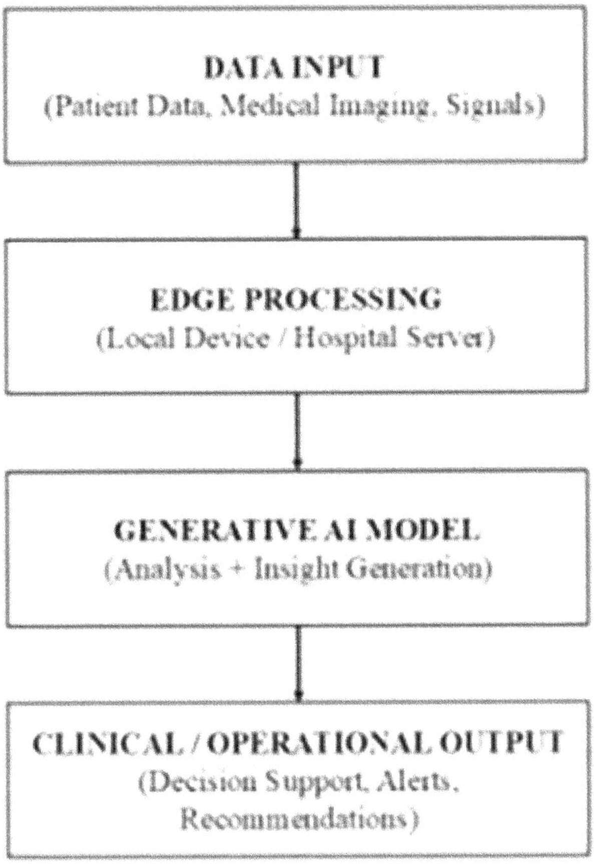

This figure illustrates how data is processed at the edge using generative AI models to generate real-time insights for clinical and operational decision-making.

2. LITERATURE REVIEW

Recent studies show how quickly AI in medical fields continues advancing from previously rule-based methodologies to methods that are more flexible, inventive, and aware of the context surrounding them. The growing number of new types of AI technologies being developed relates to a specific type of AI technology known as generative AI. Generative AI is capable of processing various forms of complex patient information (clinical records and medical images) to produce conclusions and therefore provides invaluable assistance to physicians when they perform different aspects of their jobs including providing diagnoses and summarising the activity carried out during a visit. Models based on generative AI have considerable potential for supporting many areas in the medical field through combining information from many different medical systems (cross-domain learning) to allow more efficient and accurate decision-making (decision-making efficiency).

In addition, edge computing is developing as a new way to address the issues associated with the trend toward moving everything to a single centralized cloud-based system. With traditional architectures for Artificial Intelligence, the use of AI systems in time-sensitive clinical environments creates challenges associated with latency and dependency on bandwidth, as well as concerns regarding patient confidentiality and privacy. Edge Computing solves these challenges by enabling the processing of data at its source (e.g., within the medical device or within a local network at a hospital) vs. processing the data only in an environment outside of that source. Faster response times enable the support of real-time applications (e.g., patient monitoring or imaging analysis), and by requiring less reliance on transmitting data externally (outside their respective local environments), edge computing delivers greater data security.

Studies published in many respected medical and AI journals have emphasized the increasing use of large language models and foundation models in healthcare delivery (Moor et al., 2023; Thirunavukarasu et al., 2023). The research suggests that large language models enable use cases such as assisting with clinical documentation, decision support, and patient interaction by generating structured outputs from unstructured medical data. At the same time, researchers have raised concerns over the trustworthiness and interpretability of these approaches — particularly where there may be a high-risk associated with providing incorrect outputs to medical professionals that could directly impact patient safety. Consequently, there is an increased focus on developing clinically validated AI systems that provide functionality that can operate transparently and in an accountable manner.

The latest literature has also started exploring additional considerations for implementing artificial intelligence (AI) technologies in health care (beyond those associated with technology, such as improved speed or better data storage). Specifically, one of the most common advantages of using edge computing to improve patient privacy is related to the ability to limit the amount of patient information that is sent off site. However, it has been reported in some literature that edge computing has also created additional issues associated with data consistency across distributed systems, system maintenance and updating distributed models. There are also continuing concerns regarding algorithmic bias, inequity of service delivery across different patient populations and ethical accountability. Based on the conclusions that can be drawn from this literature review, it would be reasonable to conclude that while there are many potential benefits from Generative Edge AI it is critical that these technologies are managed in such a way as to provide equitable, reliable and sustainable solutions within the health care environment.

Recent studies have found that clinical validation is essential before large-scale deployment of AI technologies (Clusmann et al., 2023). Although generative and edge-based AI systems show promising results in experimental settings, real-world reliability remains under evaluation. Researchers have concluded that generative edge-based AI will be successful if its deployment is based upon sufficient clinical evidence and will govern its use in practice. Overall, the literature indicates a shift from experimental AI models to clinically relevant systems, however, gaps remain in real-world validation, standardization, and scalability, displaying the need for more evidence-based implementation strategies.

Although there has been abundant research conducted to understand how Generative AI (GAI) and Edge Compute (EC) will be deployed within the field of Healthcare, several gaps exist. Current research focuses on theoretical uses or controlled environments and has not worked to provide any empirical data related to the real-world deployment and integration of these technologies into clinical practice/procedures. There is also not a substantial amount of academic discussion regarding the cost-effectiveness, scalability and sustainability of GAI in Edge environments (i.e., hospitals). There is also limited research regarding the ethical and legal implications associated with GAI/EC at the Edge; including Data Governance, Accountability and Ethical Issues - particularly within Decentralised Edge environments. This chapter addresses these gaps by providing a case-study analysis of real world implementations (at both Clinical and Management levels) of both GAI and EC technologies or systems.

Recent studies also emphasize the importance of explainable AI in healthcare to ensure transparency and trust in clinical decision-making processes (Topol, 2019; Floridi et al., 2018). Additionally, research highlights that integration of AI into healthcare systems requires alignment with clinical workflows, regulatory frameworks, and ethical standards (Reddy et al., 2019).

3. DEFINITION OF GENERATIVE EDGE AI

Generative Edge AI allows us to combine Generative Artificial Intelligence with Edge Computing so that we can generate new content in real-time (i.e., the text you see on our website) as well as create interpretive outputs from the data at the point of generation. Generally speaking, generative AI creates new outputs from large datasets (textual documents) based on learned patterns (e.g., producing new text that follows learned patterns). Edge computing enables the execution of computational processes via local devices, medical equipment, and local servers as opposed to depending upon centralized cloud-based infrastructure.

Generative Edge AI enables intelligent systems to create valuable products as well as assist with making decisions at the moment of care, such as in hospitals, clinics and mobile medical devices. In addition to providing a quicker response time and enhancing data security, the use of Generative Edge AI supports continuous operation, even in environments where there is limited connectivity. These features make Generative Edge AI suitable for healthcare situations that are sensitive to time and/or have limited resources.

4. METHODOLOGY

This evaluation of Generative Edge AI applications across administrative and clinical settings utilises an exploratory, qualitative, and case-based methodological approach to explore the utilisation of Generative Edge AI (Artificial Intelligence) in Health Delivery and Management systems within hospitals in a real-world environment. This synthesis does not aim to generate new empirical data. This design aligns with academically accepted qualitative research methodologies and case studies are commonly used for understanding complicated and context-sensitive issues.

The use of secondary data provides valuable insights into real-world applications; however, it also introduces certain limitations. One of the limitations can include the degree of reliability of the sources and bias. Much of the data is obtained from company publications, reports, and publicly available documents and may show positive results with little acknowledgement of any limitations or failures. There has been an attempt to include a variety of sources along with cross-checking between the sources to establish consistency, but because primary data collection has not occurred (e.g. interviews or direct observation this may limit the depth of analysis. Findings from this study should be viewed with these methodological limitations in mind.

4.1 Rationale for a Case Study Methodology

The choice of using case study methodology in this research is grounded on the recognition that healthcare technology adoption is not just an abstract concept. It is important for researchers and healthcare providers to understand how healthcare technologies are adopted, as healthcare organizations differ greatly from each other, they have a complex set of characteristics which makes how healthcare technology is adopted subjective and therefore needs to be studied through concrete processes. Case study methodology provides a way for researchers to examine the processes, interactions, behaviours, and organizational environments in which human and technological systems meet (Creswell, 2013).

Generative Edge AI technologies (generally) have the potential for much interaction between a human user and a computational system. As such, the examination of this type of technology is enhanced by using a methodology that is designed to capture the interactions between these two systems.

Therefore, case studies are the most logical methodological option for studying Generative Edge AI technologies in today's complex real-world healthcare environments.

4.2 Case Selection Criteria

The process used to identify the case studies was based on a predetermined structured criterion set. A purposive sampling methodology as described by Eisenhardt (1989) was applied to nominate "information-rich" cases that could provide insight regarding the important themes relevant to Generative Edge AI adoption in healthcare delivery and hospital management. In particular, the following structured criteria were applied to identify the case studies included.

- With Generative Edge AI, includes evidence of the combination of generative artificial intelligence functionality and edge processing functionality (device or near device) such as real time imaging diagnosis & subsequent autonomous diagnostic support or optimization of operational use of obstetric or neonatal imaging.
- Technical Implementation in Real-world Clinical Institutions is Limited to Technologies Provided that their use meets established criteria and/or is Certified for Clinical Use, thus excluding experimental prototype use.
- Cases are Selected for which there are Credible Secondary Information Sources such as Peer Review Articles U.S., FDA or other Relevant Health authorities, Company Technical Product, Literature Published, Clinical Performance Evaluation Reports, and/or Published Case Reports.
- Multi-Variability of Clinical and Administrative Implementations that provide a complete picture of how the combination of technologies support both clinical diagnostics (e.g., Caption Health, Butterfly iQ, AliveCor, Viz.ai) and administrative workloads (e.g., Qventus, LeanTaaS, GE HealthCare, Siemens Healthineers).
- Cases are Selected that have Reported on Quantifiable Improvement Metrics (e.g., time-to-treatment improvement, diagnostic accuracy, reduction of resource consumption &/or reduction of treatment costs).

These criteria ensured methodological rigor and avoided arbitrary selection, consistent with best practices in qualitative case study research (Yin, 2018; Merriam, 2009).

4.3 Data Sources and Evidence Base

This review of Generative Edge AI case examples in healthcare delivery and management relies primarily on secondary data sources, which are available in the public domain (e.g. peer-reviewed journals, clinical trials summary documentation, white papers, and reports published by medical technology companies), as well as regulatory filings such as FDA 510(k) summaries, hospital-sponsored clinical case presentations; press releases and analysis related to industry real-life applications, literature from university research institutes on AI's application within the Health Sector, and Digital Transformation within HealthCare. According to Kitchenham (2004) and Webster and Watson (2002), secondary sources should be used according to their recommendations because they are comprehensive sources of information for use in researching and reviewing New/Emerging Technologies where there are no existing primary sources of information. Additionally, using multiple sources of information in your research allows for confirmation of results through Data Triangulation which is considered to be the standard method of ensuring credibility and integrity of qualitative research (Stake, 1995; Creswell, 2013).

4.4 Analytical Framework

A thematic interpretative framework was used for analytical comparisons across the individual case studies. The analysis for each case study was undertaken using six dimensions, namely:

1. **Technological Architecture**

This dimension examined how the generative models and edge-processing elements were placed in the devices and workflows.

2. **Deployment Environment**

This dimension considered the type of deployment environment (i.e., emergency department, radiology unit, outpatient clinic, administrative office, and remote care).

3. **Workflow Integration**

This dimension assessed whether the system complemented or directly changed existing clinical and/or operational workflows.

4. **User Interaction and Experience**

This dimension examined how clinicians and technicians interact with and utilize the technology.

5. **Measurable Outcomes**

This dimension identified the increased quality, speed of decision making, patient throughput, and optimization of resources due to the use of this technology.

6. **Challenges and Limitations**

This dimension examined every barrier, challenge, and limitation to the adoption of this technology.

These analytical categories were informed by prior methodological recommendations for case-based evaluation of technology in organizational contexts (Eisenhardt, 1989; Yin, 2018).

4.5 Scope and Boundaries of the Methodology

The boundaries of the present methodology must be noted. The methodology took the form of a qualitative case study encompassing secondary data only, which means no original data, interviews, testing of devices, or clinical observations have been conducted for the purposes of this evidence-based review of Generative Edge AI deployments. Although this may limit the insights gained through the methodology selected, the adoption of secondary source qualitative case study methodologies remains valid and provides academic merit for the study of digital health technology, since during digital health technology implementation, data reflecting implementations in real-life settings are often published.

This case-based evaluation does not intend to generalise findings from one healthcare institution to others from one healthcare institution to others, but instead aims to extract lessons learned, patterns created, and insights generated for other healthcare institutions that are similar in nature. As Stake (1995) indicated, qualitative case studies are primarily aimed at the particularity of cases, not at generalisation through the broad use of statistics.

4.6 Ethical Considerations

Because there are no interviews or original data being collected, the ethical consideration surrounding privacy, consent, and clinical intervention do not apply. Nevertheless, ethical consideration is still necessary when evaluating AI-based systems that create or influence patient care. The secondary evidence used in this Generative Edge AI case synthesis is drawn from public documents and peer-reviewed academic literature in public documents and peer-reviewed academic literature. Therefore, there are ethical considerations within the context of ethical writing and synthesising secondary data.

5. CASE STUDIES: GENERATIVE EDGE AI IN HEALTHCARE AND MANAGEMENT

5.1 Generative Edge AI in Healthcare

Generative Edge AI is a good fit for healthcare environments because of their need to rapidly interpret multiple complex physiological signals and medical imaging data. When healthcare providers make decisions, there are often time constraints that can substantially impact a patient's outcome if there is a delay in providing a diagnosis or treatment. Generative Edge AI removes common limitations experienced with traditional AI Systems, which are hosted in the Cloud and have the potential to introduce delay (latency), the requirement for bandwidth and the concern over data access from an individual's data stored in the Cloud. Generative Edge AI resides at the point of care and processes data at that same location, allowing for immediate feedback, localized intelligence and improving reliability.

5.1.1 Caption Health – AI-Guided Ultrasound Imaging

Caption Health has created one of the most innovative applications of Artificial Intelligence for Diagnostic Imaging through Generative Edge AI. This product focuses specifically on solving a significant issue that has long existed in the Healthcare Sector, the reliance of Ultrasound imaging quality on the skill and knowledge of the operator. Echocardiography also requires extensive levels of training and expertise, which are not attainable in most Clinical Settings that do not have access to trained Sonographers. Caption Health is able to bring a different approach to this process by integrating Generative Intelligence directly into the process of Ultrasound acquisition and enabling clinicians who do not have extensive imaging experience to create diagnostic quality images.

AI-Guided Image Acquisition

The primary component of the Caption Health system is an AI model, which uses Generative AI and evaluates the ultrasound feed in a live stream for the duration of the scan. Rather than evaluating only the final product, the AI is able to assess the probe's location and orientation in addition to assessing the anatomical structures that are visible at the time of the evaluation. Based upon the assessment of the ultrasound image, Caption Health is able to provide step-by-step instructions for the operator on how to adjust the probe for the best imaging views to be captured. By providing this capability of providing step-by-step guidance, AI is able to take a highly skilled process of Ultrasound acquisition and make this a guided imaging process that is capable of being performed with confidence by users with no imaging background, such as Emergency Physicians, Nurse Practitioners and Primary Care Clinicians.

Edge-Based Processing and Low Latency

One of the major advantages of Caption Health's Platform is its Edge-based Processing Architecture, which performs inference at the Point of care using Near Real-Time (NRT) feedback without the need for a constant internet connection through the cloud. Because of the low latency of the Edge-Based Processing Model, time-sensitive decisions can be made quickly while in Emergency and at the Bedside; Low Latency means that the network may be down or unreliable, but allows for smooth communication even in the most time-sensitive situations. The use of Edge Processing also improves Patient Privacy by keeping sensitive patient information within the walls of the clinical setting without the need for transmitting medical information to other entities outside of the clinical setting.

Expansion of Diagnostic Access

Caption Health's ability to deliver optimal performance with minimal training required from the operator significantly improves access to diagnostic testing in rural and under-represented regions, where there is a significant improvement in access to cardiac diagnostic imaging in rural and underserved regions. Caption Health enables these facilities to provide localized Cardiovascular Screening and Assessment services that allow for earlier determination of many conditions such as Heart Failure, Structural Abnormalities, and Cardiomyopathies. The broad availability of Cardiovascular Imaging aligns with broader efforts to promote social equity within HealthCare.

Workflow Standardization and Clinical Efficiency

In addition to enabling individual assessments, Caption Health standardizes workflow practices throughout the entire healthcare continuum. By creating high-quality images from users irrespective of their experience as an operator, Caption Health reduces inter-operator variability and nullifies the requirement to re-scan patients, thus ensuring that image quality will be the same from person to person. With the regulatory approval for the platform that further indicates its maturity and ability to be utilized in diagnostic settings where the outcomes of a diagnosis can create a significant impact.

Technical Insight: Uses deep learning-based image recognition models to analyze ultrasound data in real time, with processing occurring directly at the point of care.

Limitations: Performance depends on image quality and correct probe handling, and may not fully replace expert interpretation in complex diagnostic scenarios.

As shown in Table 1, the key operational features of Caption Health are summarized.

Table 1. Key Operational Features of Caption Health

Feature	Description
Primary Application	AI-guided cardiac ultrasound
Generative Function	Real-time procedural guidance during scanning
Edge AI Role	On-device image analysis and feedback
Target Users	Non-expert clinicians and emergency staff
Clinical Value	Standardized imaging and expanded diagnostic access

Edge-enabled AI expands diagnostic access (Caption Health, 2020). This proposes that Generative Edge AI not only improves accessibility but also shifts clinical workflows toward guided decision-making rather than expert-dependent processes

5.1.2 Butterfly Network – Butterfly iQ Handheld Ultrasound

The Butterfly Network (Butterfly) has developed a second example of Generative Edge AI utilized within the Medical Field, although it encompasses many more applications than just Cardiac Imaging. The Butterfly iQ device is a handheld and fully body ultrasound system, allowing for greater accessibility, affordability, and usage due to its compact size. It employs generative Edge AI, combined with small size hardware, to allow providers to conduct quick, efficient ultrasound scans on virtually all parts of the human body in various medical situations.

Portable Design and Edge Intelligence

Intelligent AI (artificial intelligence) and a unique single-probe design enable Butterfly iQ to deliver all the advantages of traditional multi-probe ultrasound systems without sacrificing performance. The Butterfly iQ ultrasound system connects to a mobile device (smartphone or tablet) so that it can be distributed quickly to emergency room/hospital locations (e.g., emergency departments, ambulances, and outpatient clinics) that urgently need an ultrasound or when a clinician is located away from the hospital. Because the imaging and data are processed at the point of care using edge-based AI, clinicians will be able to instantly optimize the imaging parameters based on their skill level and environmental conditions, leading to high-resolution images regardless of the imaging technique or environment in which the image was captured.

Generative Assistance During Imaging

Beyond image acquisition, Butterfly iQ provides AI-assisted guidance that support anatomical landmark identification, scanning optimization, and automated labelling of structures. Intermediate assist features are available for users with Limited Ultrasound Knowledge. As a Result, the Device Supports the Transfer of Diagnosis from Physicians to Other Types of HealthCare Workers. This Allows More Types of Healthcare Professionals to Use Ultrasound as Part of Their Routine Clinical Assessment.

Cost Efficiency and Scalability

Organizations are able to save costs by utilizing Butterfly iQ to reduce their reliance on expensive and stationary imaging machines as well as highly trained technicians. The low cost of acquiring and deploying the Butterfly iQ gives healthcare providers the ability to use imaging services across many different locations or departments. Generative Edge AI is playing an increasingly important role for healthcare organizations looking to enhance operational efficiency and access to services.

Technical Insight: Combines edge-based AI with portable ultrasound hardware, using machine learning models to optimize imaging and assist in real-time scanning.

Limitations: Image accuracy may vary across different environments and user expertise levels, and reliance on mobile devices may introduce hardware constraints.

As shown in Table 2, the key features of Butterfly iQ are summarized.

Table 2. Key Features of Butterfly iQ Handheld Ultrasound

Feature	Description
Device Type	Handheld, multi-organ ultrasound
Generative Capabilities	Anatomical guidance and auto-labeling
Edge AI Role	On-device image optimization
Deployment Settings	Emergency care, rural clinics, telemedicine
Organizational Benefit	Cost reduction and scalable imaging access

Portable edge AI supports point-of-care diagnostics (FDA, 2017).

5.1.3 AliveCor – KardiaMobile ECG Monitoring System

AliveCor has demonstrated how Generative Edge AI can be used for cardiovascular monitoring with their KardiaMobile ECG device. Instead of relying on clinical companies and trained technicians (like an EKG machine), KardiaMobile is small and portable, giving users the ability to capture and analyze cardiac signals directly at their site. This example shows that generative intel is growing on the edge and can be used for continuous monitoring, detecting cardiac abnormalities early, and making informed decisions from anywhere.

Edge-Based ECG Signal Analysis

The KardiaMobile device collects single-lead/multiple lead ECGs from patients and processes these signals locally with machine learning algorithms that are built into the device. The KardiaMobile device allows for real-time analysis of the waveforms and generates an immediate interpretation of whether the heart has a normal/abnormal rhythm. Because all of the analysis is performed at the "edge", users do not need to wait for feedback from a cloud-based service. Detection of a rapidly changing condition (e.g., Atrial Fibrillation) using the KardiaMobile device's low latency features is extremely valuable.

Generative Intelligence and Clinical Interpretation

At the heart of AliveCor's platform is its generative ability to convert raw ECG data into useful clinical information. Instead of leaving end users with just the basic waveform, AliveCor's platform helps create summary and alerting information that allows clinicians to provide a clinical context when interpreting data from their patients. Allowing for this type of conversion of physiological signals to practical information will not only save time for clinicians who have limited time available to review multiple sources of physiological data, it also allows patients to participate more meaningfully in monitoring their own health status. Multiple clinical assessments have established that AliveCor's device can accurately diagnose cardiovascular conditions in both the consumer and professional healthcare sectors.

Remote Monitoring and Continuity of Care

The KardiaMobile device from AliveCor helps facilitate remote patient monitoring processes by enabling physicians to save and analyze an ECG (electrocardiogram) and share it with other doctors and medical personnel. The KardiaMobile was developed in response to the increasing demand for telemedicine and to an ever-increasing trend towards outpatient care in which patients are receiving continuous data from non-traditional settings outside of a face-to-face visit with a physician or another HealthCare provider. Because of this, it has become critical to provide a method for monitoring patients using continuous remote monitoring from their homes or other locations without consistent access to the Internet and the KardiaMobile provides reliable, consistent remote monitoring for these environments.

Clinical and Organizational Impact

KardiaMobile has a clinical benefit for earlier detection of abnormal heartbeats or rhythms which decreases the chance of fatal complications by allowing for earlier intervention. Moreover, from an organisational standpoint, KardiaMobile decreases the need for in-clinic ECG testing, thus relieving workload and decreasing the overall cost of healthcare services that primarily focus on delivering their services through cardiology departments.

Technical Insight: Utilizes embedded machine learning algorithms for on-device ECG signal analysis and real-time rhythm classification.

Limitations: Limited to specific cardiac conditions and single-lead data in some cases, with potential for false positives or misinterpretation without clinical validation.

As shown in Table 3, the operational characteristics of AliveCor KardiaMobile are outlined.

Table 3. Key Operational Characteristics of AliveCor KardiaMobile

Feature	Description
Primary Function	Portable ECG monitoring and rhythm analysis
Edge AI Role	On-device signal processing and interpretation
Generative Output	Automated rhythm classification and alerts
Deployment Context	Home monitoring, outpatient care, telemedicine
Clinical Value	Early detection and continuous cardiac monitoring

This platform highlights the use of edge AI in scalable cardiac monitoring (AliveCor).

5.1.4 Viz.ai – AI-Enabled Stroke Care Coordination

Viz.ai is one of the most important uses of AI at the edge in Acute Neurology through the rapid detection and management of patients suffering from a stroke. Stroke care is time-dependent; how quickly large-vessel occlusions are recognised and treated heavily influences patient prognosis. The use of edge-based AI provides HealthCare providers with a mechanism to enhance their diagnostic, coordination, and treatment time frames through the use of artificial intelligence and clinical communication systems.

Real-Time Imaging Analysis at the Edge

Deep Learning Models are used by Viz.ai to analyze computed tomography (CT) and computed tomography angiography (CTA) scans for identifying large-vessel occlusions. Part of the Analysis is performed on or near the imaging source, which allows for rapid interpretation of the scans right after they are acquired. By processing data at the edge of the network, Viz.ai eliminates lengthy delays that typically occur during manual review and transfers of scans to a centralised system.

Generative Alerts and Clinical Coordination

Viz.ai does more than just detect. It also provides automated alerts to the appropriate members of a stroke care team as soon as a stroke is detected. The alerts contain interpretive information to help clinicians evaluate the severity and urgency of the patient's condition. As a result of the system's generative properties, imaging results can be synthesized into alerts to allow clinicians to provide faster responses for patients having strokes; stroke treatment has now transitioned from a typical, step-by-step approach with necessary manual involvement to a simultaneous, collaborative method involving various parties working together.

Impact on Treatment Timelines

The implementation by Viz.ai has resulted in faster times from the moment the patient walks into the ER until they receive treatment (i.e., door-to-treatment time, DTT). This is significant because it means that we know who has had a stroke faster and can therefore work more efficiently to get that patient into the system (e.g., coordinating interventional procedures such as thrombectomy), which helps provide better results for patients. The decrease in delays between when the patient gets their imaging done, gets diagnosed, and receives treatment reflects how Viz.ai is directly bridging the gap between Generative Edge AI Technology and improved clinical outcomes for patients receiving emergency care.

Scalability and Workflow Integration

The design of Viz.ai focuses on existing systems within hospitals' imaging and communications networks in addition to utilizing the current building structures of these hospitals. The functionality of Viz.ai is scalable throughout the healthcare system and uses both Hybrid Edge and Cloud Architectures that produce low latency solutions for urgent/crucial evaluations. One unique feature of Viz.ai is that it provides an environment where multiple hospitals can collaborate together to assist patients who may have to travel to different locations to receive specialized care. The flexibility of the platform is particularly beneficial to regional Stroke Networks.

Technical Insight: Applies deep learning models for rapid imaging analysis at or near the source, enabling real-time stroke detection and alert generation.

Limitations: Accuracy depends on imaging quality and system integration, and incorrect alerts may impact clinical workflows if not properly validated.

As shown in Table 4, the core features of Viz.ai are presented.

Table 4. Key Features of Viz.ai Stroke Care Platform

Feature	Description
Primary Application	AI-based stroke detection and care coordination
Edge AI Role	Rapid imaging analysis at acquisition point
Generative Capability	Automated alerts and decision-support notifications
Clinical Setting	Emergency departments and stroke units
Outcome Impact	Reduced treatment delays and improved care coordination

This case highlights the impact of AI driven coordination in time-critical stroke care (Viz.ai, 2024). This shows that Generative Edge AI plays a important role in reducing treatment delays and enhancing coordination in emergency care settings.

As shown in Table 5, a comparative overview of clinical applications is provided.

Table 5. Comparative Analysis of Generative Edge AI Applications in Healthcare

Dimension	**Caption Health**	**Butterfly iQ**	**AliveCor (KardiaMobile)**	**Viz.ai**
Organization	Caption Health	Butterfly Network	AliveCor	Viz.ai
Primary Clinical Domain	Cardiac ultrasound imaging	Multi-organ ultrasound imaging	Cardiac rhythm monitoring	Acute stroke detection and coordination
Core Use Case	AI-guided acquisition of diagnostic-quality echocardiograms	Portable ultrasound for point-of-care diagnostics	Detection and monitoring of cardiac arrhythmias	Rapid identification of large-vessel occlusion strokes
Type of Data Processed	Ultrasound imaging data	Ultrasound imaging data	ECG waveform signals	CT and CTA imaging data
Edge AI Role	On-device real-time probe guidance and image quality assessment	On-device image optimization and anatomical recognition	On-device ECG signal processing and rhythm analysis	Near-source imaging analysis for rapid detection
Generative Intelligence Function	Generates step-by-step procedural guidance during scanning	Generates interpretive assistance and auto-labeling of structures	Generates interpretive summaries and rhythm alerts	Generates automated alerts and clinical notifications
Level of User Expertise Required	Minimal (non-expert clinicians)	Minimal to moderate	Minimal (patients and clinicians)	Specialist teams supported by AI alerts
Deployment Environment	Emergency departments, primary care, outpatient clinics	Emergency care, rural clinics, ambulatory settings	Home monitoring, outpatient care, telemedicine	Emergency departments, stroke units
Workflow Integration	Standardizes ultrasound acquisition and reduces operator variability	Enhances portability and speeds diagnostic workflows	Enables continuous remote monitoring and follow-up	Accelerates diagnosis-to-treatment workflows
Latency Sensitivity	High – requires immediate feedback	High – real-time image guidance	Moderate – near real-time interpretation	Very high – time-critical emergency decisions
Connectivity Dependence	Low – edge-based processing	Low – supports offline/low-bandwidth use	Low to moderate	Hybrid edge-cloud architecture
Primary Clinical Benefit	Expanded access to cardiac imaging	Broader access to ultrasound diagnostics	Early detection of arrhythmias	Reduced treatment delays in stroke care
Organizational Impact	Improves throughput and imaging consistency	Reduces infrastructure costs and imaging delays	Reduces in-clinic testing burden	Improves care coordination and clinical outcomes
Scalability Potential	High – deployable across multiple departments	High – scalable across locations	Very high – individual and population-level use	High – scalable across hospital networks

5.2 Generative Edge AI in Healthcare Management

Generative Edge AI, while directly impacting clinical diagnosis and the care of patients, is equally impactful regarding the operations and management of Healthcare Facilities. Healthcare is currently run as rather complex businesses requiring the orchestration of patient throughput, workforce staffing levels, and asset/equipment capacities, plus resource usage—all in real time. Traditionally, management has relied on retrospective reporting of historical data and manual decision-making, leading to slowed responses to ongoing changes in the environment, loss of capacity and inefficient workflows. With the advent of the Generative Edge AI paradigm, the ability to make real-time decisions with operational intelligence, predictive analytics and decision support will be at the point when operational data is created.

5.2.1 Qventus – AI for Hospital Operations Optimization

A notable example of Generative Edge AI in Hospital Operations Management is that of Qventus. The goal of Qventus is to help hospitals operate more efficiently through many different areas of operation (ie. emergency department flow, inpatient capacity management, utilizing operating rooms, doctors and other staff working together effectively, etc).

Qventus does this by combining real-time data streams from the hospital with predictive and generative methodologies/models in order to determine where there are blockages/inefficiencies in operations, and to provide actionable recommendations for targeted interventions to alleviate those operational impediments.

Real-Time Operational Intelligence

The technology implemented by Qventus analyses all types of data collected by hospitals via their existing systems, such as hospital information systems (HIS), bed management software/lists, and scheduling tools. Edge-enhanced processing is utilized by the system, enabling hospitals to take immediate and informed operational decisions with near real-time data. In addition to being able to make proactive decisions regarding their operations, the Generative feature of this system creates an actionable operational data synthesis that considers both the hospital setting and its unique circumstances. This allows for increased efficiency and flexibility to manage staffing and resource allocation for efficient patient transfers.

Predictive and Prescriptive Capabilities

By employing predictive analytics through the new method of generative Intelligence, Qventus is helping healthcare organisations anticipate their operating conditions in advance and suggest potential measures that may be taken based on what might occur over time. Qventus capabilities also assist hospitals in creating accurate forecasts of when they may suffer from patient influxes or delays in discharging patients from inpatient units. This allows hospitals to provide timely alerts to maximise their potential to help patients receive earlier treatment and avoid excessive wait periods due to overcrowding. These capabilities ultimately lead to improved patient experiences and throughput for hospitals.

Workflow Integration and Decision Support

Once implemented within your existing workflow, there will be no need to modify any of your current processes or procedures. Users will receive recommendations through intuitive dashboards and alerts; thus, providing administrators and care coordinators the information and support to make timely decisions relating to patient care. Qventus will support continuous improvement rather than just temporary solutions to ongoing issues by integrating intelligence into a hospital's standard daily operations.

Organizational Impact

The use of Qventus by healthcare systems has been shown to improve the delivery of services by reducing patient wait times and increasing staff productivity and infrastructure utilization.

Technical Insight: Uses predictive analytics and machine learning models to process real-time hospital data at the edge and generate operational recommendations.

Limitations: Effectiveness depends on data quality and system integration, and may require workflow adjustments for full adoption.

As shown in Table 6, the key operational features of Qventus are summarized.

Table 6. Key Operational Features of Qventus

Feature	Description
Primary Focus	Hospital operations and patient flow optimization
Edge AI Role	Near real-time analysis of operational data
Generative Function	Predictive alerts and prescriptive recommendations
Target Users	Administrators, care coordinators, operations managers
Organizational Value	Improved throughput and resource utilization

This system demonstrates how AI-driven insights improve hospital operations (Qventus, 2022). This shows how Generative Edge AI remodel hospital management from reactive decision-making to proactive operational optimization.

5.2.2 LeanTaaS – iQueue for Scheduling and Capacity Optimization

The iQueue platform, developed by LeanTaaS, demonstrates another strong application of Generative Edge AI in the realm of healthcare management. Generative Edge AI helps hospitals and health systems use their medical resources efficiently by optimizing how they are allocated among various service lines (and their associated services). Using Generative Edge AI for optimizing high-value, resource-intensive services in HealthCare, such as Operating Rooms, Infusion Centers, and Inpatient Bed Capacity, is particularly beneficial due both to the significant impact these clinical services provide upon patient outcomes and the financial strength of these services in terms of revenue generation and patient volume.

Data-Driven Scheduling and Capacity Management

iQueue is a software application developed by LeanTaaS that provides an efficient means of utilizing and scheduling medical services through the use of historical and operational data. iQueue leverages Edge-enabled processing to immediately respond to changes in patient need (delays/cancellations), fluctuations in patient demand, etc. With these changes, iQueue will immediately begin to generate schedule/capacity recommendations with its generative intelligence. Because of this combination of features, iQueue allows for optimum patient access, increasing throughput, and allows providers to manage their workloads effectively.

Reduction of Manual Administrative Burden

An important benefit of LeanTaaS is its capability of reducing manual input when it comes to determining complex schedules. Typically, there has been a large amount of work involved in creating operating room and infusion center schedules with manual processes that create opportunities for mistakes and personal biases to occur. With LeanTaaS, administrators generate evidence-based recommendations and automate a significant portion of the process enabling administrators to concentrate on the planning aspect versus handling urgent issues on a day-to-day basis.

Clinical and Financial Alignment

LeanTaaS helps hospitals increase patient access by utilizing available operating rooms and infusion chairs more effectively; therefore, the cost associated with increasing patient access does not increase as much as the number of patients who can be treated.

Scalability and Adoption

LeanTaaS has demonstrated that LeanTaaS is capable of being deployed in numerous healthcare systems of all sizes, and can be used by different types and sizes of healthcare organizations. The ability of LeanTaaS to integrate with current hospital systems means recommendations come from actual operational data, thus providing a strong basis for hospital administrators to trust and use LeanTaaS.

Technical Insight: Employs data-driven optimization algorithms with edge-enabled responsiveness to generate scheduling and capacity recommendations.

Limitations: May rely heavily on historical data patterns, and unexpected real-time disruptions can reduce prediction accuracy.

As shown in Table 7, the capabilities of LeanTaaS iQueue are summarized.

Table 7. Key Features of LeanTaaS iQueue Platform

Feature	Description
Primary Focus	Scheduling and capacity optimization
Edge AI Role	Real-time responsiveness to operational changes
Generative Capability	Optimized scheduling and utilization recommendations
Deployment Areas	Operating rooms, infusion centers, inpatient units
Organizational Benefit	Increased throughput and reduced manual effort

This platform highlights the role of AI in optimizing scheduling and capacity (LeanTaaS, 2022).

5.2.3 GE HealthCare – AI-Driven Operational and Clinical Intelligence

GE HealthCare represents a large-scale enterprise application of Generative Edge AI within hospital systems. Its solutions integrate artificial intelligence across clinical and operational workflows, enabling data-driven decision-making at multiple levels of healthcare delivery.

Integration of AI Across Hospital Infrastructure

GE HealthCare designs solutions to work inside existing hospital environments. These solutions utilize the data generated from imaging machines, monitoring equipment, and all other operational systems in the entire hospital. By implementing "edge enabled" processing technology, critical information like equipment usage, information on delays for imaging procedures, and even patient transport patterns are generated near where the data is created. This means administrators and physicians can react quickly to new challenges as they develop without having to wait on delays from other hospital departments.

Generative Intelligence for Decision Support

GE HealthCare's AI tools use Generative AI to create meaningful operational and clinical insights from large amounts of diverse, unstructured data by converting it into actionable item through guidance, alarms, and estimates about the likelihood of future events including Backlog in Imaging, and Personnel Constraints. This allows GE HealthCare to provide 'Real Time' Recommendations back to the clinician or healthcare providers in order to make immediate and long-term decisions, for example the ability to provide staffing recommendations that will adjust for the impending backlog before it occurs.

Operational Efficiency and Resource Optimization

From a management perspective, AI-based solutions developed by GE HealthCare will assist providers with improving their use of costly medical devices (ex. Imaging) through documentation of device utilization and detection of supply chain constraints. This will lead to optimal utilization practices within the provider's organization by improving scheduling for imaging services, decreasing downtime of these costly devices, and improving care delivery/ throughput for patients. The compensation package realized from AI-based solutions will enhance patient satisfaction and experience as well as support the long-term financial activity of resource-intensive health systems.

Scalability and Enterprise Adoption

Scalability is a key emphasis of GE HealthCare's strategy. The Solution was developed to accommodate organizations with multiple hospital locations and/or multi-specialty services; The AI Solution is capable of supporting all levels of operations from very basic operations to very complex operations. By providing clients with this type of adaptable solution, They enable them to create a single document of operational data across a very large facility network while being able to respond quickly to the needs at the "edges" of the facility network.

Technical Insight: Integrates AI models across hospital systems with near-source processing to generate real-time clinical and operational insights.

Limitations: Implementation complexity and high infrastructure requirements may limit adoption in smaller healthcare settings.

As shown in Table 8, the features of GE HealthCare AI solutions are outlined.

Table 8. Key Features of GE HealthCare AI Solutions

Feature	Description
Primary Focus	Integrated clinical and operational intelligence
Edge AI Role	Near-source processing for real-time insights
Generative effectiveness	Predictive analytics and decision-support recommendations
Deployment Opportunity	Imaging departments, monitoring systems, hospital operations
Organizational Impact	Improved equipment utilization and workflow efficiency

This case demonstrates the use of enterprise AI for operational efficiency (GE HealthCare, 2025).

5.2.4 Siemens Healthineers – AI-Rad Companion for Radiology Operations

The AI-Rad Companion offered by Siemens Healthineers has taken an innovative approach to how Generative Edge AI can be applied in healthcare management. Although it primarily supports clinicians in analysing medical imaging tests, it also creates new opportunities and value for improving the operational efficiency of Hospitals and Hospital Administration with the use of auto-imaging activities and by standardising the reporting workflow associated with the radiologies.

Automation of Radiology Workflows

The integration of imaging devices using AI-Rad Companion provides an opportunity for immediate processing of images received at the imaging facility via edge-computing technology. In automating tasks commonly associated with radiology such as segmentation and quantification of radiology images, the use of AI-Rad Companion simplifies the duties of radiologists and enables faster reporting of radiology results, allowing faster diagnosis and treatment decisions.

Generative Reporting and Clinical Consistency

AI-Rad Companion can use the AI-Rad Companion's embedded AI to create structured outputs from image data that help with the uniformity of reading & reporting radiological images. By providing consistent & standardized measurements & reports through this technology, AI-Rad Companion minimizes variability between different radiologists & increases the reliability of diagnoses made by using AI-Rad Companion. Consistency in reporting & measuring radiological images is especially beneficial for radiology departments that process large numbers of studies

& where high workload demands may negatively impact the accuracy & efficiency of reports produced.

Operational Benefits for Hospital Management

AI-Rad Companion helps managers improve the efficiency of operations in radiology by improving imaging speed and watching for potential slowdowns in the processes. Because of this, diagnostic images can be reported back to the provider immediately so that additional clinical work can immediately commence, thus, improving patient movement through departments.

Hybrid Edge-Cloud Architecture

AI-Rad Companion has a unique mix of both edge- and cloud-based technology. It provides users with immediate feedback via a real-time analysis of images using edge technology, along with the ability to gather, process, and store large quantities of radiological image data for subsequent cloud-based analysis and tracking over time. By combining this real-time processing capability with the use of cloud-based services, it allows the user to access the low latency technology required for everyday operations while also providing the user with long-term strategic insight into how to improve the efficiency and effectiveness of their radiology departments across multiple locations and/or departments.

Technical Insight: Combines edge-based image processing with AI-driven automation to generate structured radiology outputs and workflow insights.

Limitations: May require integration with existing radiology systems, and over-reliance on automation could affect manual review processes.

As shown in Table 9, the features of Siemens AI-Rad Companion are outlined.

Table 9. Key Features of Siemens Healthineers AI-Rad Companion

Feature	Description
Primary Application	AI-assisted radiology workflow automation
Edge AI Role	Immediate image analysis and quantification
Generative Capability	Automated measurements and structured reporting
Operational Context	Radiology departments and imaging services
Management Value	Faster turnaround and standardized workflows

This application highlights the role of AI in improving radiology workflow efficiency (Siemens Healthineers, 2022).

As shown in Table 10, a comparative overview of management platforms is provided.

Table 10. Comparative Analysis of Generative Edge AI Platforms for Healthcare Management

Dimension	**Qventus**	**LeanTaaS (iQueue)**	**GE HealthCare**	**Siemens Healthineers (AI-Rad Companion)**
Organization	Qventus	LeanTaaS	GE HealthCare	Siemens Healthineers
Primary Management Focus	End-to-end hospital operations optimization	Scheduling and capacity optimization	Integrated clinical and operational intelligence	Radiology workflow automation and operational efficiency
Core Operational Domains	Emergency department flow, inpatient capacity, operating rooms, staffing	Operating rooms, infusion centers, inpatient beds	Imaging services, patient monitoring, enterprise operations	Radiology departments and imaging workflows
Type of Data Processed	Real-time operational and patient flow data	Historical and real-time scheduling and utilization data	Imaging, monitoring, and hospital systems data	Medical imaging data and radiology workflow metadata
Edge AI Role	Near real-time analysis of operational data streams	Dynamic response to operational changes	Near-source processing for immediate insights	Immediate image analysis and quantification
Generative Intelligence Function	Predictive alerts and prescriptive operational recommendations	Generation of optimized schedules and capacity plans	Predictive decision support and workflow recommendations	Automated measurements and structured report generation
Decision Support Level	Operational and administrative decision-making	Administrative and resource planning decisions	Clinical and administrative decision support	Clinical workflow support with management impact
Workflow Integration	Embedded into daily hospital operations dashboards	Integrated into scheduling and capacity planning systems	Embedded across enterprise hospital infrastructure	Integrated with PACS and radiology information systems
Latency Sensitivity	High – real-time operational responsiveness required	Moderate to high – near real-time optimization	Moderate – supports both real-time and strategic decisions	High – immediate imaging analysis needed
Connectivity Model	Hybrid edge–cloud architecture	Hybrid edge–cloud architecture	Hybrid edge–cloud enterprise architecture	Hybrid edge–cloud architecture

continued on following page

Table 10. Continued

Dimension	Qventus	LeanTaaS (iQueue)	GE HealthCare	Siemens Healthineers (AI-Rad Companion)
Organizational Impact	Reduced bottlenecks, improved patient flow, better staff utilization	Increased throughput and reduced manual scheduling effort	Improved equipment utilization and operational efficiency	Faster report turnaround and standardized workflows
Scalability Potential	High – scalable across hospital systems	High – scalable across multiple departments	Very high – enterprise-level deployment	High – scalable across radiology departments and facilities
Strategic Value	Enables proactive hospital operations management	Aligns efficiency with financial and clinical goals	Supports system-wide operational transformation	Enhances radiology efficiency and downstream patient flow

5.3 Cross-Case Synthesis

Generative Edge AI is making a significant impact on clinical and management processes by enabling real-time data-driven decision-making at the point of care or at the point of operation. In clinical systems, the primary focus is on improving diagnostic accuracy, accessibility, and speed. This has been achieved through low latency processing and guided insight generation. While in management systems, the primary focus is on operational efficiency, resource optimization, and predictive planning. Regardless of the system type, a common theme emerges: edge-based processing reduces time delays and improves overall system responsiveness in environments that are heavily dependent upon time.

There are a number of identical issues found in both fields, such as an over-reliance on high-quality datasets, the need for interfacing with legacy health care infrastructures, and requiring the user(s) to adapt to new AI-enabled workflow practices. Generative algorithms are effective for enabling the transformation of unstructured data to structured data if they are implemented in a specific context; however, the degree of success is highly dependent on the system's architecture and level of maturity. Therefore Generative Edge AI should not be viewed as a catch-all solution, but rather a flexible tool that should be tailored to meet individual organizational and clinical requirements.

Figure 2. Clinical vs Management Applications of Generative Edge AI

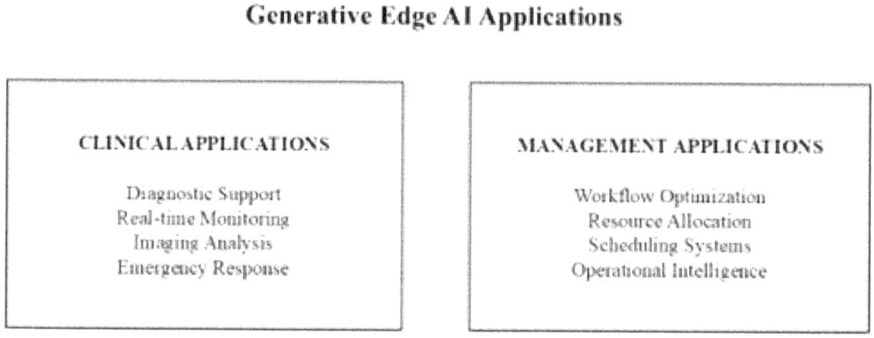

This figure compares how Generative Edge AI is applied across clinical and administrative domains, highlighting differences in functionality and operational impact.

6. CHALLENGES

While Generative Edge AI has much promise, it also faces multiple technological challenges when implemented in a healthcare setting. Among the most significant of these challenges is the integration of Generative Edge AI with existing healthcare infrastructure. In many cases, this current infrastructure consists of legacy systems that do not allow for the support of advanced AI models, creating complicated and expensive integration challenges to ensure that there is a seamless data flow between Generative Edge AI devices; Electronic Health Records (EHR); and Advanced AI systems. The deployment of generative AI models on edge devices further complicates implementation due to the need to optimize generative model execution for limited processing power, which may negatively impact performance and scalability across the many types of healthcare settings.

Though technical limitations exist, there are also human and organizational factors that affect the adoption of new technologies in the healthcare industry. Many healthcare workers are reluctant to trust an artificial intelligence algorithm to make decisions due to questions relating to their accuracy, trustworthiness, and effect on current workflows. In order to train employees on using these systems successfully will require significant investment of both time and resources from the organization. Additionally, resistance to change will impact the speed at which these technologies can be adopted in the workplace. It is important to have a balance between the capabilities of automated systems and the decision-making abilities of healthcare professionals; otherwise, there can be a tendency for people to underutilize various components of the healthcare system and over-rely on automated systems leading to lower levels of critical thinking or judgment by humans.

Multiple regulatory, economic, and functional issues must be addressed before widespread use becomes feasible. The requirement for strict regulations associated with healthcare AI systems presents a challenge, and these rules differ from country to country resulting in delays before deploying an AI system. Additionally, smaller organizations may struggle to finance the costs associated with implementing an AI system including upgrade costs for existing technology, staff training, and ongoing system support. Issues such as data privacy and integrity, system reliability and failure risks, and liability in instances where an error occurs are among the major concerns about the use of AI in the clinical setting. Effective governance frameworks and continuous performance assessments are needed to evaluate AI performance under field conditions.

Additionally, the financial implications of implementing generative edge AI systems are significant and represent an important hurdle. Initial costs associated with the acquisition of advanced medical technologies, as well as upgrading the infrastructure required to support them, and the integration of AI into existing hospital systems can be particularly significant for smaller healthcare institutions. Beyond the initial capital investment, ongoing costs related to maintaining the system, providing software updates, and training staff should also be factored into the overall cost of ownership. Although these technologies promise long-term efficiency and cost savings, the substantial amount of money needed to make an initial investment and the uncertain timeframe for recovering that investment can inhibit the adoption of these technologies on a widespread basis. Additionally, the lack of standardized evaluation frameworks for AI systems remains a barrier to consistent implementation.

As an additional consideration in the implementation of Generative Edge AI, there is a need for developing standardized metrics to evaluate the performance and effectiveness of these systems. While a number of reports indicate increased efficiency and responsiveness as a result of various implementations of Generative Edge AI, there is a lack of consistency in how these results measures are evaluated across different health sectors. Therefore, clear indicators are need such as accuracy of diagnosis, reduced latency in decision-making, throughput of patients and cost-efficiency, should be established to provide an objective measurement of the effectiveness of these systems. Also, comparative benchmarking across institutions will help to facilitate better decision-making as well as assist health care organizations to identify best-practices for implementing Generative Edge AI. If no standardized frameworks exist to evaluate Generative Edge AI, it will be difficult to accurately assess the value of Generative Edge AI solutions or their ability to be scaled in the real-world.

Figure 3. Key Challenges in Generative Edge AI Implementation

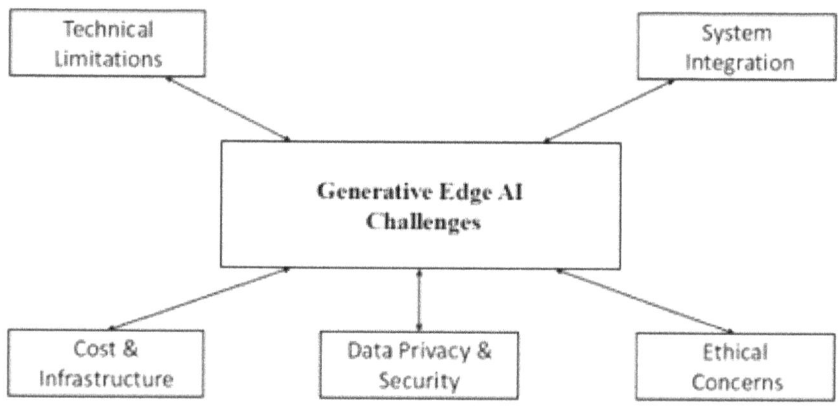

6.1 Ethical, Privacy, and Economic Considerations

Generative Edge Artificial Intelligence could pose many important ethical, regulatory, and governance issues. For example, there is a real problem with algorithmic bias. Because many AI systems are trained with non-representative data sets, there is a potential for unequal health care outcomes among different populations. Furthermore, although edge computing - which minimizes the use of external data transfers - improves data privacy, there are still several new security vulnerabilities and greater complexities in data management introduced by the decentralized nature of edge computing.

In terms of implementation, healthcare organizations are challenged by system integration, workforce education, and existing facility capacities. As many legacy systems are not set-up to handle advanced AI models, new implementations can have higher costs and disrupt current operations.

Economic factors are also very important. Although there are potential long-term savings associated with generative edge AI, the initial investments needed for implementing the system and maintaining it are usually large, as well as the cost of training staff. These factors inhibit many smaller healthcare facilities from implementing generative edge AI, highlighting issues of equity and scalability.

7. FUTURE DIRECTIONS

Improving efficiency of models, increasing deployment in the real world and enhancing integration among various healthcare systems are anticipated to be key areas of focus for future Generative Edge AI technologies within the healthcare field. Advances such as lightweight AI models and edge hardware are expected to allow for more extensive use cases in situations where resources are limited. Future research may focus on areas related to reliability, bias, regulatory standards, and new applications such as personalized care and continuous patient monitoring. In addition, more efforts will need to be placed on improving interoperable capabilities in order to ensure proper governance of ethical issues and human/AI collaboration.

8. CONCLUSION

Through a structured synthesis of case evidence, this discussion of Generative Edge AI in healthcare delivery and hospital management illustrates how Generative Edge Artificial Intelligence will increasingly be used in the healthcare setting (both patient care and management) and make it more efficient and effective. The healthcare sector is experiencing an escalating level of complexity due to its many clinical challenges, escalating operational demands and increasingly limited resources; thus, the adoption of Generative Edge AI will help address these complexities by providing timely, data-driven and context-aware insights that allow for informed and timely healthcare decision making. Generative Edge AI will address the limitations of using a centralized cloud-based infrastructure for storing all the data needed to provide intelligent healthcare services, especially in relation to issues with latency, scalability, security and data ownership.

This synthesis of clinical case examples illustrates how companies utilizing these technologies for diagnosis, (Caption Health, Butterfly iQ, AliveCor, and Viz.ai) that Generative Edge AI improves the accuracy of diagnostic assessments, increases the accessibility of limited specialties that would require greater training in developing a larger database of experienced professionals, and provide clinicians with a valuable tool in emergency/critical care situations. Their use of this technology demonstrates that the primary benefit of AI in healthcare is broader than just increasing the speed and efficiency of giving diagnostic information; rather, it is the development of the tools to aid in developing an actionable course of action/insight and provide immediate feedback to a user as to the feasibility of their findings/interpretations.

Generative Edge AI plays an important role in advancing healthcare due to technological and system pressures. Generative Edge AI's ability to quickly and accurately process and analyse vast amounts of data will be one of the primary cornerstones for how we will develop our future HealthCare systems, thereby providing the ability to access best practices as they are occurring in real-time on a continuous basis.

REFERENCES

AliveCor. (2022). *KardiaMobile: AI-enabled ECG monitoring and arrhythmia detection* (FDA 510(k) Summary). U.S. Food and Drug Administration. https://alivecor.com/press/press_release/alivecor-launches-kardia-12l-a-first-of-its-kind-ai-powered-12-lead-ecg-system

Butterfly Network Inc. A window into the human body for less than $2,000 enabled by breakthrough Ultrasound-on- a-Chip technology. Retrieved December 2,2025, from https://www.butterflynetwork.com/press-releases/first-ultrasound-on-a-chip-receives-broadest-fda-510-k-clearance?srsltid=AfmBOooYN0VwCp33SfN8KBvCNT0ckAmjvovIZFrNLbYRnqWZA-syrVf7

Caption Health. (2020, February 7). *FDA grants landmark authorization for first AI-guided ultrasound image acquisition system*. PR Newswire. https://www.prnewswire.com/news-releases/fda-grants-caption-health-landmark-authorization-for-first-ai-guided-image-acquisition-system-301001106.html

Clusmann, J., Kolbinger, F. R., Muti, H. S., Carrero, Z. I., Eckardt, J.-N., Laleh, N. G., Löffler, C. M. L., Schwarzkopf, S.-C., Unger, M., Veldhuizen, G. P., Wagner, S. J., & Kather, J. N. (2023). The future landscape of large language models in medicine. *Communications Medicine*, *3*(1), 141. DOI: 10.1038/s43856-023-00370-1 PMID: 37816837

Creswell, J. W., & Poth, C. N. (2016). *Qualitative inquiry and research design: Choosing among five approaches*. Sage Publications.

Eisenhardt, K. M. (1989). Building theories from case study research. *Academy of Management Review*, *14*(4), 532–550. DOI: 10.2307/258557

GE HealthCare. (2025, September 25). *GE HealthCare debuts AI-supported solution designed to improve and shorten radiation therapy workflow*. GE HealthCare Newsroom.

Kitchenham, B. (2004). *Procedures for performing systematic reviews*. Keele, UK, Keele University, 33(2004), 1-26.

LeanTaaS, Inc. (2022). *iQueue for operating room and infusion center optimization: Case studies and implementation reports*. LeanTaaS White Papers.

Moor, M., Banerjee, O., Abad, Z. S. H., Krumholz, H. M., Leskovec, J., Topol, E. J., & Rajpurkar, P. (2023). Foundation models for generalist medical artificial intelligence. *Nature*, *616*(7956), 259–265. DOI: 10.1038/s41586-023-05881-4 PMID: 37045921

Qventus. (2022, January 31). *Qventus achieves major milestones as a leader in care operations automation*. PR Newswire.

Siemens Healthineers. (2022). *AI-Rad Companion: Providing multi-modality imaging decision support*. Siemens Healthineers White Paper.

Stake, R. E. (1995). *The art of case study research*. Sage Publications.

Thirunavukarasu, A. J., Ting, D. S. J., Elangovan, K., Gutierrez, L., Tan, T. F., & Ting, D. S. W. (2023). Large language models in medicine. *Nature Medicine*, *29*(8), 1930–1940. DOI: 10.1038/s41591-023-02448-8 PMID: 37460753

Tisdell, E. J., Merriam, S. B., & Stuckey-Peyrot, H. L. (2025). Qualitative research: A guide to design and implementation. John Wiley & Sons.

Viz.ai. (2024). VALIDATE study: Utilization of the Viz.ai mobile stroke care coordination platform across healthcare systems. *Frontiers in Stroke*.

Webster, J., & Watson, R. T. (2002). Analyzing the past to prepare for the future: Writing a literature review. *Management Information Systems Quarterly*, *26*(2), xiii–xxiii. DOI: 10.2307/4132319

Yin, R. K. (2018). *Case study research and applications: Design and methods* (6th ed.). Sage Publications.

ADDITIONAL READING

Coeckelbergh, M. (2020). *AI ethics*. MIT Press. DOI: 10.7551/mitpress/12549.001.0001

Floridi, L., Cowls, J., Beltrametti, M., Chatila, R., Chazerand, P., Dignum, V., Luetge, C., Madelin, R., Pagallo, U., Rossi, F., Schafer, B., Valcke, P., & Vayena, E. (2018). AI4People—An ethical framework for a good AI society: Opportunities, risks, principles, and recommendations. *Minds and Machines*, *28*(4), 689–707. DOI: 10.1007/s11023-018-9482-5 PMID: 30930541

Reddy, S., Fox, J., & Purohit, M. P. (2019). Artificial intelligence-enabled healthcare delivery. *Journal of the Royal Society of Medicine*, *112*(1), 22–28. DOI: 10.1177/0141076818815510 PMID: 30507284

Shi, W., & Dustdar, S. (2016). The promise of edge computing. *Computer*, *49*(5), 78–81. DOI: 10.1109/MC.2016.145

Compilation of References

Abdallah, S., Maarof, M. A., & Zainal, A. (2019). Fraud detection in credit card transactions using XGBoost and deep learning. *International Journal of Advanced Computer Science and Applications, 10*(12).

Abd-Alrazaq, A. A., Alajlani, M., Alalwan, A. A., Bewick, B. M., Gardner, P., & Househ, M. (2019). An overview of the features of chatbots in mental health: A scoping review. *International Journal of Medical Informatics, 132*, 103978. DOI: 10.1016/j.ijmedinf.2019.103978 PMID: 31622850

Abdollahi, A., Rejeb, K., Rejeb, A., Mostafa, M. M., & Zailani, S. (2021). Wireless sensor networks in agriculture: Insights from bibliometric analysis. *Sustainability (Basel), 13*(21), 12011. DOI: 10.3390/su132112011

Ahmad, M., & Elazab, A. (2024). FedSepsis: A federated multi-modal deep learning framework for early ICU sepsis detection. *BMC Medical Informatics and Decision Making, 24*, 73. DOI: 10.1186/s12911-024-02317-0

Ahmed, Z., Gui, D., Murtaza, G., Yunfei, L., & Ali, S. (2023). An overview of smart irrigation management for improving water productivity under climate change in drylands. *Agronomy (Basel), 13*(8), 2113. DOI: 10.3390/agronomy13082113

Ahn, H., Chen, T., Alnaasan, N., Shafi, A., Abduljabbar, M., Subramoni, H., & Panda, D. K. (2023). Performance Characterization of Using Quantization for DNN Inference on Edge Devices. In *2023 IEEE 7th International Conference on Fog and Edge Computing (ICFEC)* (pp. 1–6). IEEE. DOI: 10.1109/ICFEC57925.2023.00009

Airbus. (2023). *Airbus Annual Report 2023*

Aishwarya, S., Selvamurugan, C., Parthiban, K. G., Nathan, B., Manoj Prabhakar, J., & Mohamed Noordeen, A. (2024, December). Generative AI in Focus: A Comprehensive Review of Leading Models Across Modalities. In *2024 4th International Conference on Ubiquitous Computing and Intelligent Information Systems (ICUIS)* (pp. 1-9). IEEE.

Aishwarya, D., & Minu, R. I. (2021). Edge computing-based surveillance framework for real-time activity recognition. *ICT Express*, *7*(2), 182–186. DOI: 10.1016/j.icte.2021.04.010

Akram, F., Malik, A. W., & Khan, S. U. (2025). iGenEdge: Intelligent Generative AI Service Deployment for Edge-Connected IoT Devices. *IEEE Internet Computing*, *29*(4), 16–24. DOI: 10.1109/MIC.2025.3576072

Alangari, M., Almuhaisen, Y., Alnami, R., Alotaibi, F., & Alwafi, A. (2025, March). *Edge generative AI solutions for industrial security*. SPE Middle East Oil and Gas Show and Conference (MEOS GEO), Manama, Bahrain. DOI: 10.2118/227639-MS

Aldhaheri, L., Alshehhi, N., Manzil, I. I. J., Khalil, R. A., Javaid, S., Saeed, N., & Alouini, M. S. (2024). LoRa communication for agriculture 4.0: Opportunities, challenges, and future directions. *IEEE Internet of Things Journal*.

Al-Fuqaha, A., Khreishah, A., & Sallabi, F. (2024). A survey on IoT-edge-cloud orchestration for real-time intelligent applications. *IEEE Access : Practical Innovations, Open Solutions*, *12*, 23345–23371.

Alharbi, H. A., & Aldossary, M. (2021). Energy-efficient edge-fog-cloud architecture for IoT-based smart agriculture environment. *IEEE Access : Practical Innovations, Open Solutions*, *9*, 110480–110492. DOI: 10.1109/ACCESS.2021.3101397

Aline, C., Kristensen, M., Thomsen, F., Holm, L., & Sondergaard, E. (2025). Reimagining Model Efficiency in Generative AI Through Unified and Differentiable Quantization Approaches.

AliveCor. (2022). *KardiaMobile: AI-enabled ECG monitoring and arrhythmia detection* (FDA 510(k) Summary). U.S. Food and Drug Administration. https://alivecor.com/press/press_release/alivecor-launches-kardia-12l-a-first-of-its-kind-ai-powered-12-lead-ecg-system

Aljunaid, M., Mejri, N., Adam, M. B., & Ragab, A. H. M. (2023). Explainable fraud detection using federated learning in financial systems. *Journal of Risk and Financial Management*, *16*(2), 96. DOI: 10.3390/jrfm16020096

Al-Malahmeh, H. (2023). The role of cloud computing in supporting decision making: Evidence from the banking industry. *International Journal of Data & Network Science*, *7*(1), 131–140. DOI: 10.5267/j.ijdns.2022.11.009

Alzu'bi, S., Kanan, T., Elbes, M., Kanaan, G., & Trrad, I. (2025). Energy-efficient edge deployment of generative AI models using federated learning. *Cluster Computing*, *28*(5), 1–12. DOI: 10.1007/s10586-025-05263-7

Alzu, A., Alomar, A., Alkhaza, S., & Abuarqoub, A. (2024). A Review of Privacy and Security of Edge Computing in Smart Healthcare Systems. *Issues, Challenges, and Research Directions.*, *29*(4), 1152–1180.

Ambrogio, S., Narayanan, P., Okazaki, A., Fasoli, A., Mackin, C., Hosokawa, K., Nomura, A., Yasuda, T., Chen, A., Friz, A., Ishii, M., Luquin, J., Kohda, Y., Saulnier, N., Brew, K., Choi, S., Ok, I., Philip, T., Chan, V., & Burr, G. W. (2023). An analog-AI chip for energy-efficient speech recognition and transcription. *Nature*, *620*(7975), 768–775. DOI: 10.1038/s41586-023-06337-5 PMID: 37612392

Ameer, I., Sidorov, G., Gomez-Adorno, H., & Nawab, R. M. A. (2022). Multi-label emotion classification on code-mixed text: Data and methods. *IEEE Access : Practical Innovations, Open Solutions*, *10*, 8779–8789. DOI: 10.1109/ACCESS.2022.3143819

Anstine, D. M., & Isayev, O. (2023). Generative models as an emerging paradigm in the chemical sciences. *Journal of the American Chemical Society*, *145*(16), 8736–8750. DOI: 10.1021/jacs.2c13467

Anusha, S., Ezhilvandan, M., Gayathri, S., Sivaraman, V., Anish, T. P., & Subramanıan, R. S. (2024). Emerging Trends in Edge AI for Industry 4.0 and 5.0. *Advances in Hospitality, Tourism and the Services Industry (AHTSI) Book Series*, 211–228. DOI: 10.4018/979-8-3693-7909-7.ch010

Ardi, N. (2025). Generative AI: A Comprehensive Review of Foundational Models and Emerging Methods. [ASTJ]. *Applied Systems and Technologies Journal*, *1*(1), 1–6.

Ardi, N., & Isnayanti, I. (2025). *Generative AI: A comprehensive review of foundational models and emerging methods. Applied Systems and Technologies Journal.* ASTJ.

Armando, E. J., Hanyurwimfura, D., Gatera, O., & Nduwumuremyi, A. (2025). Enhancing Agricultural Internet of Things Data Accuracy: Evaluating Kalman Filter-Based Sensor Denoising Techniques. *Journal of Biosystems Engineering*, *50*(1), 47–58. DOI: 10.1007/s42853-025-00252-5

Åström, K. J., & Murray, R. M. (2021). *Feedback systems: An introduction for scientists and engineers* (2nd ed.). Princeton University Press., DOI: 10.2307/j.ctv15rjm68

Auerbach, R. P., Mortier, P., Bruffaerts, R., Alonso, J., Benjet, C., Cuijpers, P., Demyttenaere, K., Ebert, D. D., Green, J. G., Hasking, P., Murray, E., Nock, M. K., Pinder-Amaker, S., Sampson, N. A., Stein, D. J., Vilagut, G., Zaslavsky, A. M., & Kessler, R. C. (2018). WHO world mental health surveys international college student project: Prevalence and distribution of mental disorders. *Journal of Abnormal Psychology*, *127*(7), 623–638. DOI: 10.1037/abn0000362 PMID: 30211576

Ayiengar, N. S. R. (2023). India's Digital Public Infrastructure: A Model for Emerging Economies. *Journal of Digital Governance*, *3*(1), 22–35.

Bandi, A., Adapa, P. V. S. R., & Kuchi, Y. E. V. P. K. (2023). The power of generative ai: A review of requirements, models, input–output formats, evaluation metrics, and challenges. *Future Internet*, *15*(8), 260. DOI: 10.3390/fi15080260

Banerjee, K., Krishnan, P., & Das, B. (2020). Thermal imaging and multivariate techniques for characterizing and screening wheat genotypes under water stress condition. *Ecological Indicators*, *119*, 106829. DOI: 10.1016/j.ecolind.2020.106829

Baptista, M. L., Yue, N., Manjurul Islam, M. M., & Prendinger, H. 2025. Large Language Models (LLMs) for Smart Manufacturing and Industry X.0, in: Islam, M.M.M., Baptista, M.L., Tariq, F. (Eds.), Artificial Intelligence for Smart Manufacturing and Industry X.0. Springer Nature Switzerland, Cham, pp. 97–119. URL: DOI: 10.1007/978-3-031-80154-9_5

Bates, T., Cobo, C., Mariño, O., & Wheeler, S. (2023). Can artificial intelligence transform higher education? *International Journal of Educational Technology in Higher Education*, *17*(1), 1–12. DOI: 10.1186/s41239-020-00218-x

Benhammou, Y., Kalyan, S., & Kumar, S. (2025). Federated Learning for ICU Mortality Prediction: Balancing Accuracy and Privacy in a Multi-Hospital Setting. *bioRxiv*. https://doi.org/DOI: 10.1101/2025.08.04.668527

Bhadange, P. U. B., Jadhav, S., Jadhav, B., Ghatol, S., & Kahale, P. (2024). *Comprehensive Review of Synthetic Data Generation Techniques and Their Applications in Healthcare, Finance, and Marketing*. 379–384. DOI: 10.48175/IJARSCT-22066

Bhalgat, Y., Lee, J., Nagel, M., Blankevoort, T., & Kwak, N. (2020). LSQ+: Improving low-bit quantization through learnable offsets and better initialization. In *2020 IEEE/CVF Conference on Computer Vision and Pattern Recognition Workshops (CVPRW)* (Vol. 2020-June, pp. 2978–2985). IEEE. DOI: 10.1109/CVPRW50498.2020.00356

Biagianti, B., Foti, G., Di Liberto, A., Bressi, C., & Brambilla, P. (2023). CBT-informed psychological interventions for adult patients with anxiety and depression symptoms: A narrative review of digital treatment options. *Journal of Affective Disorders*, *325*, 682–694. DOI: 10.1016/j.jad.2023.01.057 PMID: 36690081

Bibhu, V., Shukla, A. K., Shivahare, B. D., Kaur, J., Shukri, M., Mgm, A. Y. J., Faaq, A. S., AlShujairi, M. K., & Pandey, S. (2024). Analysis of security and privacy challenges of smart health and sensing systems. *Results in Engineering*, *24*, 103466. DOI: 10.1016/j.rineng.2024.103466

Biggio, B., & Roli, F. (2018). Wild patterns: Ten years after the rise of adversarial machine learning. *Pattern Recognition*, *84*, 317–331. DOI: 10.1016/j.patcog.2018.07.023

Bin Sawad, A., Narayan, B., Alnefaie, A., Maqbool, A., Mckie, I., Smith, J., Yuksel, B., Puthal, D., Prasad, M., & Kocaballi, A. B. (2022). A systematic review of healthcare artificial intelligence conversational agents for chronic conditions. *Sensors (Basel)*, *22*(7), 2625. DOI: 10.3390/s22072625 PMID: 35408238

Bird, S., Dale, R., Dorr, B. J., Gibson, B. R., Joseph, M. T., Kan, M. Y., & Tan, Y. F. (2008, May). The ACL Anthology Reference Corpus: A Reference Dataset for Bibliographic Research in Computational Linguistics. In *LREC*.

Bolón-Canedo, V., Morán-Fernández, L., Cancela, B., & Alonso-Betanzos, A. (2024). A review of green artificial intelligence: Towards a more sustainable future. *Neurocomputing*, *599*, 128096. DOI: 10.1016/j.neucom.2024.128096

Bommasani, R., Hudson, D. A., Adeli, E., Altman, R., Arora, S., von Arx, S., & Liang, P. (2021). *On the opportunities and risks of foundation models*. Stanford Institute for Human-Centered Artificial Intelligence.

Bordt, S., & von Luxburg, U. (2022). From net to nudge: Investigating AI-generated early alerts and student outcomes. *Computers & Education: Artificial Intelligence*, *3*, 100055. DOI: 10.1016/j.caeai.2022.100055

Bragazzi, N. L., & Garbarino, S. (2024). Toward clinical generative AI: Conceptual framework. *JMIR AI*, *3*(1), e55957. DOI: 10.2196/55957

Braggaar, A., Liebrecht, C., van Miltenburg, E., & Krahmer, E. (2023). Evaluating task-oriented dialogue systems: A systematic review of measures, constructs and their operationalisations. *arXiv preprint arXiv:2312.13871*.

Braun, V., & Clarke, V. (2006). Using thematic analysis in psychology. *Qualitative Research in Psychology*, *3*(2), 77–101. DOI: 10.1191/1478088706qp063oa

Brown, T. B., Mann, B., Ryder, N., Subbiah, M., Kaplan, J., Dhariwal, P., & Amodei, D. (2020). Language models are few-shot learners. *Advances in Neural Information Processing Systems*, *33*, 1877–1901.

Bucilu , C., Caruana, R., & Niculescu-Mizil, A. (2006, August). Model compression. In *Proceedings of the 12th ACM SIGKDD international conference on Knowledge discovery and data mining* (pp. 535-541). DOI: 10.1145/1150402.1150464

Budzynska, K., Janier, M., Reed, C., Saint-Dizier, P., Stede, M., & Yaskorska, O. (2014). A model for processing illocutionary structures and argumentation in debates. In *LREC 2014: Ninth International Conference on Language Resources and Evaluation* (pp. 917-924). European Language Resources Association.

Butterfly Network Inc. A window into the human body for less than $2,000 enabled by breakthrough Ultrasound-on- a-Chip technology. Retrieved December 2,2025, from https://www.butterflynetwork.com/press-releases/first-ultrasound-on-a-chip-receives-broadest-fda-510-k-clearance?srsltid=AfmBOooYN0VwCp33SfN8KBvCNT0ckAmjvovIZFrNLbYRnqWZA-syrVf7

Caliste, D. (2025). Adaptive personalization in smart home systems using edge-resident generative models. *Journal of Intelligent Environments*, *14*(2), 55–72.

Caption Health. (2020, February 7). *FDA grants landmark authorization for first AI-guided ultrasound image acquisition system.* PR Newswire. https://www.prnewswire.com/news-releases/fda-grants-caption-health-landmark-authorization-for-first-ai-guided-image-acquisition-system-301001106.html

Casu, M., Triscari, S., Battiato, S., Guarnera, L., & Caponnetto, P. (2024). AI chatbots for mental health: A scoping review of effectiveness, feasibility, and applications. *Applied Sciences (Basel, Switzerland)*, *14*(13), 5889. DOI: 10.3390/app14135889

Celik, I. (2023). Towards intelligent-TPACK: An empirical study on teachers' professional knowledge to ethically integrate AI-based tools into education. *Computers in Human Behavior*, *138*, 107468. DOI: 10.1016/j.chb.2022.107468

Cetinic, E., & She, J. (2022). Understanding and creating art with AI: Review and outlook. *ACM Transactions on Multimedia Computing Communications and Applications*, *18*(2), 66. Advance online publication. DOI: 10.1145/3475799

Chakravarthi, B. R., Jose, N., Suryawanshi, S., Sherly, E., & McCrae, J. P. (2020, May). A sentiment analysis dataset for code-mixed Malayalam-English. In *Proceedings of the 1st Joint workshop on spoken language technologies for under-resourced languages (SLTU) and collaboration and computing for under-resourced languages (CCURL)* (pp. 177-184).

Chakravarthy, R. (2022). An experimental study of iot-based topologies on MQTT protocol for agriculture intrusion detection. *Measurement. Sensors*, *24*, 100470. DOI: 10.1016/j.measen.2022.100470

Chandnani, K., Tripathy, S., Parbhakar, A. K., Takiar, K., Singhal, U., Sasikumar, P., & Maheswari, S. (2025). A novel smart baby cradle system utilizing IoT sensors and machine learning for optimized parental care. *Scientific Reports*, *15*(1), 19080. Advance online publication. DOI: 10.1038/s41598-025-02691-8 PMID: 40447703

Chang, T.-Y., & Lu, C.-J. (2021). TinyGAN: Distilling BigGAN for Conditional Image Generation. In H. Ishikawa, C.-L. Liu, T. Pajdla, & J. Shi (Eds.), *Lecture Notes in Computer Science (including subseries Lecture Notes in Artificial Intelligence and Lecture Notes in Bioinformatics)* (Vol. 12625 LNCS, pp. 509–525). Cham: Springer International Publishing. DOI: 10.1007/978-3-030-69538-5_31

Cheggou, R., Mohand, S. S. H., Annad, O., & Khoumeri, E. H. (2020). An intelligent baby monitoring system based on Raspberry PI, IoT sensors and convolutional neural network. *Proceedings - 2020 IEEE 21st International Conference on Information Reuse and Integration for Data Science, IRI 2020*, 365–371. DOI: 10.1109/IRI49571.2020.00059

Chen, N., Cheng, Z., Fan, X., Xia, X., & Huang, L. (2024). Towards integrated finetuning and inference when generative AI meets edge intelligence. *arXiv preprint arXiv:2401.02668.*

Chen, S., Ding, Y., Xie, Z., Liu, S., & Ding, H. (2018, April). Chinese Weibo sentiment analysis based on character embedding with dual-channel convolutional neural network. In *2018 IEEE 3rd International conference on cloud computing and big data analysis (ICCCBDA)* (pp. 107-111). IEEE. DOI: 10.1109/ICCCBDA.2018.8386495

Chen, Y.-H., Sarokin, R., Lee, J., Tang, J., Chang, C.-L., Kulik, A., & Grundmann, M. (2023). Speed Is All You Need: On-Device Acceleration of Large Diffusion Models via GPU-Aware Optimizations. In *2023 IEEE/CVF Conference on Computer Vision and Pattern Recognition Workshops (CVPRW)* (Vol. 2023-June, pp. 4651–4655). IEEE. DOI: 10.1109/CVPRW59228.2023.00490

Chen, L. (2024). Memory-bound bottlenecks in long-context large language models. *Journal of AI Engineering*, *12*(3), 45–62. DOI: 10.1016/j.jaie.2024.03.004

Chen, T. (2025). PROBABILISTIC LATENT VARIABLE MODELS: PRINCIPLES AND FOUNDATIONS FOR MODERN GENERATIVE AI. *Available at SSRN* 5244929. DOI: 10.2139/ssrn.5244929

Chen, W., Wilson, J., Tyree, S., Weinberger, K., & Chen, Y. (2015). Compressing neural networks with the hashing trick. *International Conference on Machine Learning*, 2285–2294.

Chen, X., Zou, D., Xie, H., & Wang, F. L. (2024). Artificial intelligence in education: A systematic review of 125 studies on personalised learning. *British Journal of Educational Technology*, *55*(1), 1–26. DOI: 10.1111/bjet.13298

Chi, C., Xu, Z., Feng, S., Cousineau, E., Du, Y., Burchfiel, B., & Song, S. (2025). Diffusion policy: Visuomotor policy learning via action diffusion. *The International Journal of Robotics Research*, *44*(10–11), 1684–1704. DOI: 10.1177/02783649241273668

Chin, H., Song, H., Baek, G., Shin, M., Jung, C., Cha, M., Choi, J., & Cha, C. (2023). The potential of chatbots for emotional support and promoting mental well-being in different cultures: Mixed methods study. *Journal of Medical Internet Research*, *25*, e51712. DOI: 10.2196/51712 PMID: 37862063

Chopda, J., Raveshiya, H., Nakum, S., & Nakrani, V. (2018, January). Cotton crop disease detection using decision tree classifier. In *2018 International Conference on Smart City and Emerging Technology (ICSCET)* (pp. 1-5). IEEE. DOI: 10.1109/ICSCET.2018.8537336

Chowdhury, A., Chowdhury, A., Hoque, N., Moriwam, M., & Jahan, M. (2025). Generative AI: A survey of historical development, emerging trends, and future outlook. *Computer Science and Engineering Research*, *2*(1), 19–31. DOI: 10.69517/cser.2025.02.01.0004

Ciubotaru, B. I. (2025). Generative AI and Large Language Models: A Comprehensive Scientific.

Clusmann, J., Kolbinger, F. R., Muti, H. S., Carrero, Z. I., Eckardt, J.-N., Laleh, N. G., Löffler, C. M. L., Schwarzkopf, S.-C., Unger, M., Veldhuizen, G. P., Wagner, S. J., & Kather, J. N. (2023). The future landscape of large language models in medicine. *Communications Medicine*, *3*(1), 141. DOI: 10.1038/s43856-023-00370-1 PMID: 37816837

COCCIA, M. (2025). Invasive technologies: Technological paradigm shift in generative artificial intelligence. *Journal of Innovation. Technology and Knowledge Economy*, *1*(1), 1–32.

Cohen, J. (1988). *Statistical power analysis for the behavioral sciences* (2nd ed.). Lawrence Erlbaum Associates.

Coletta, A., Giorgi, F., Maselli, G., Prata, M., Silvestri, D., Ashdown, J., & Restuccia, F. (2025). A2-UAV: Application-aware resilient edge-assisted UAV networks. *Computer Networks*, *256*, 110887. DOI: 10.1016/j.comnet.2024.110887

Conneau, A., Khandelwal, K., Goyal, N., Chaudhary, V., Wenzek, G., Guzmán, F., Grave, E., Ott, M., Zettlemoyer, L., & Stoyanov, V. (2020). Unsupervised cross-lingual representation learning at scale. In *Proceedings of the 58th Annual Meeting of the Association for Computational Linguistics* (pp. 8440–8451). Association for Computational Linguistics. DOI: 10.18653/v1/2020.acl-main.747

Conti, M., Dehghantanha, A., Franke, K., & Watson, S. (2018). Internet of Things security and forensics: Challenges and opportunities. *Future Generation Computer Systems, 78*, 544–546. DOI: 10.1016/j.future.2017.07.060

Corchado, J. M., López, S., Garcia, R., & Chamoso, P. (2023). Generative artificial intelligence: Fundamentals. *ADCAIJ: advances in distributed computing and artificial intelligence journal, 12*, e31704-e31704.

Creswell, J. W., & Poth, C. N. (2016). *Qualitative inquiry and research design: Choosing among five approaches*. Sage Publications.

Creswell, J. W., & Plano Clark, V. L. (2018). *Designing and conducting mixed methods research* (3rd ed.). SAGE Publications.

Crompton, H., & Burke, D. (2023). Artificial intelligence in higher education: The state of the field. *International Journal of Educational Technology in Higher Education, 20*(1), 22. DOI: 10.1186/s41239-023-00392-8

Dantas, P. V., Da Silva, W. S., Cordeiro, L. C., & Carvalho, C. B. (2024). A comprehensive review of model compression techniques in machine learning. *Applied Intelligence, 54*(22), 11804–11844. DOI: 10.1007/s10489-024-05747-w

Dao, T., Fu, D., Ermon, S., Rudra, A., & Ré, C. (2022). FlashAttention: Fast and memory-efficient exact attention with IO-awareness. *Advances in Neural Information Processing Systems, 35*, 16344–16359. DOI: 10.52202/068431-1189

Dardis, F. E., Buckley, C., Mitra, P., Heaton, C., & Xiao, A. (2025). Improving nonprofit engagement on social media: Using big data, machine-learning, and sentiment analysis to evaluate leading nonprofits' message strategies on Twitter/X. *International Journal of Information Technology : an Official Journal of Bharati Vidyapeeth's Institute of Computer Applications and Management, 17*(1), 395–407. DOI: 10.1007/s41870-024-02263-5

Das, A., Iqbal, M. A., Sharif, O., & Hoque, M. M. (2020, December). Bemod: Development of bengali emotion dataset for classifying expressions of emotion in texts. In *International Conference on Intelligent Computing & Optimization* (pp. 1124-1136). Cham: Springer International Publishing.

De, S., Deogharia, D., De, M., & Chowdhury, P. (2024). Cradle-Care: Enhancing Baby Safety Using IoT. *2024 IEEE Calcutta Conference, CALCON 2024 - Proceedings*. DOI: 10.1109/CALCON63337.2024.10914183

Del Prete, R., Thind, P. K., Mazzeo, A., Whitley, M., Papa, L., Longépé, N., & Meoni, G. (2025). Optimizing deep learning models for on-orbit deployment through neural architecture search. *Scientific Reports*, *15*(1), 37783. DOI: 10.1038/s41598-025-21467-8 PMID: 41162441

Demszky, D., Movshovitz-Attias, D., Ko, J., Cowen, A., Nemade, G., & Ravi, S. (2020). GoEmotions: A dataset of fine-grained emotions. *arXiv preprint arXiv:2005.00547*. DOI: 10.18653/v1/2020.acl-main.372

Denecke, K., Abd-Alrazaq, A., & Househ, M. (2021). Artificial intelligence for chatbots in mental health: opportunities and challenges. *Multiple perspectives on artificial intelligence in healthcare: Opportunities and challenges*, 115-128.

Deng, L., Kocakulak, M., & Iyer, V. (2023). Efficient federated training of generative models on heterogeneous edge hardware. *IEEE Transactions on Neural Networks and Learning Systems*, *34*(11), 9099–9112.

Deng, S., Zhao, H., Fang, W., Yin, J., Dustdar, S., & Zomaya, A. Y. (2020). Edge intelligence: The confluence of edge computing and artificial intelligence. *IEEE Internet of Things Journal*, *7*(8), 7457–7469. DOI: 10.1109/JIOT.2020.2984887

Devlin, J., Chang, M. W., Lee, K., & Toutanova, K. (2019, June). Bert: Pre-training of deep bidirectional transformers for language understanding. In *Proceedings of the 2019 conference of the North American chapter of the association for computational linguistics: human language technologies, volume 1 (long and short papers)* (pp. 4171-4186).

Dhar, S., Guo, J., Liu, J., Tripathi, S., Kurup, U., & Shah, M. (2021). A survey of on-device machine learning: An algorithms and learning theory perspective. *ACM Transactions on the Internet of Things*, *2*(3), 1–49. DOI: 10.1145/3450494

DiMaggio, P., Hargittai, E., Celeste, C., & Shafer, S. (2004). Digital inequality: From unequal access to differentiated use. In Neckerman, K. M. (Ed.), *Social inequality* (pp. 355–400). Russell Sage Foundation.

Doan, T. N., & Phan, T. H. (2024). A Novel Smart System with Jetson Nano for Remote Insect Monitoring. *International Journal of Advanced Computer Science and Applications*, *15*(7). Advance online publication. DOI: 10.14569/IJACSA.2024.0150798

Dubey, Y. K., & Damke, S. (2019). Baby monitoring system using image processing and IoT. *International Journal of Engineering and Advanced Technology, 8*(6), 4961–4964. DOI: 10.35940/ijeat.F9254.088619

Durden, E., Pirner, M. C., Rapoport, S. J., Williams, A., Robinson, A., & Forman-Hoffman, V. L. (2023). Changes in stress, Burnout, and resilience associated with an 8-week intervention with relational agent "Woebot.". *Internet Interventions : the Application of Information Technology in Mental and Behavioural Health, 33*, 100637. DOI: 10.1016/j.invent.2023.100637 PMID: 37635948

Dutt, S., & Li, X. (2025). Thermal trajectories in passive-cooled edge SoCs during generative inference. *Proceedings of the 14th International Conference on Embedded Systems and AI*, 112–126. https://doi.org/DOI: 10.1109/ICESAI.2025.10042

Duvvur, V. (2025). Exploring the Role of Generative Adversarial Networks (GANs) and Generative AI for Synthetic Data Generation and Augmentation in Machine Learning. *Journal of Information Systems Engineering & Management, 10*(33s).

Dwork, C., & Roth, A. (2014). The algorithmic foundations of differential privacy. *Foundations and Trends in Theoretical Computer Science, 9*(3–4), 211–407. DOI: 10.1561/0400000042

Eisenhardt, K. M. (1989). Building theories from case study research. *Academy of Management Review, 14*(4), 532–550. DOI: 10.2307/258557

Elbasi, E., Zaki, C., Topcu, A. E., Abdelbaki, W., Zreikat, A. I., Cina, E., Shdefat, A., & Saker, L. (2023). Crop prediction model using machine learning algorithms. *Applied Sciences (Basel, Switzerland), 13*(16), 9288. DOI: 10.3390/app13169288

European Parliament and Council. (2016). *Regulation (EU) 2016/679 on the protection of natural persons with regard to the processing of personal data and on the free movement of such data.* General Data Protection Regulation.

European Space Agency. (2020). *Φ-sat — ESA Earth Observation AI Mission Overview.* https://www.esa.int/Applications/Observing_the_Earth/Ph-sat

EuroShop Magazine. (2025, August 13). *Edge computing in retail: Benefits and examples.* https://www.euroshop-tradefair.com/en/media-news/euroshopmag/retail-technology/edge-computing-in-retail-benefits-and-examples

Fang, G., Li, K., Ma, X., & Wang, X. (2025), "TinyFusion: Diffusion Transformers Learned Shallow," *2025 IEEE/CVF Conference on Computer Vision and Pattern Recognition (CVPR)*, Nashville, TN, USA, 2025, pp. 18144-18154, DOI: 10.1109/CVPR52734.2025.01691

Fawzi, N. A. (2024). A Smart Incubator System for Monitoring and Controlling Premature Babies' Environment Using Machine Learning. *Journal Européen des Systèmes Automatisés, 57*(5), 1531–1537. DOI: 10.18280/jesa.570529

Feretzakis, G., Papaspyridis, K., Gkoulalas-Divanis, A., & Verykios, V. S. (2024). Privacy-preserving techniques in generative ai and large language models: A narrative review. *Information (Basel), 15*(11), 697. DOI: 10.3390/info15110697

Ficili, I., Giacobbe, M., Tricomi, G., & Puliafito, A. (2025). From sensors to data intelligence: Leveraging IoT, cloud, and edge computing with AI. *Sensors (Basel), 25*(6), 1763. DOI: 10.3390/s25061763 PMID: 40292910

Financial Action Task Force (FATF). (2023). *Guidance on Digital Identity*. FATF.

Fitzpatrick, K. K., Darcy, A., & Vierhile, M. (2017). Delivering cognitive behavior therapy to young adults with symptoms of depression and anxiety using a fully automated conversational agent (Woebot): A randomized controlled trial. *JMIR Mental Health, 4*(2), e19. Advance online publication. DOI: 10.2196/mental.7785 PMID: 28588005

Floridi, L., & Chiriatti, M. (2020). GPT-3: Its nature, scope, limits, and consequences. *Minds and Machines, 30*(4), 681–694. DOI: 10.1007/s11023-020-09548-1

Foundation, E. A. I. (2025). *Edge AI Technology Report: Generative AI at the Edge Edition* (pp. 1–31).

Franklin, G. F., Powell, J. D., & Emami-Naeini, A. (2014). *Feedback control of dynamic systems* (7th ed.). Pearson., DOI: 10.1016/B978-0-12-397191-3.00010-3

Fulmer, R., Joerin, A., Gentile, B., Lakerink, L., & Rauws, M. (2018). Using psychological artificial intelligence (Tess) to relieve symptoms of depression and anxiety: Randomized controlled trial. *JMIR Mental Health, 5*(4), e9782. DOI: 10.2196/mental.9782 PMID: 30545815

Furtado, L. S., Soares, J. B., & Furtado, V. (2024). A task-oriented framework for generative AI in design. *Journal of Creativity, 34*(2), 100086. DOI: 10.1016/j.yjoc.2024.100086

Futurescope. (2025, June 19). How edge computing powers data processing in autonomous vehicles? Futurescope. https://www.futurescope.co/how-edge-computing-powers-data-processing-in-autonomous-vehicles/

Fu, Y., Chen, W., Wang, H., Li, H., Lin, Y., & Wang, Z. (2020). AutoGAN-Distiller: Searching to compress generative adversarial networks. *37th International Conference on Machine Learning, ICML 2020, PartF168147-5*, 3250–3261.

Gao, J., Liu, Z., Wang, Y., & Ji, W. (2025). RaNAS: Resource-Aware Neural Architecture Search for Edge Computing. *ACM Transactions on Architecture and Code Optimization, 22*(1), 1–18. DOI: 10.1145/3703353

Gao, M., Hu, X., Yin, X., Ruan, J., Pu, X., & Wan, X. (2025). Llm-based nlg evaluation: Current status and challenges. *Computational Linguistics, 51*(2), 1–27. DOI: 10.1162/coli_a_00561

Garg, M., Raza, S., Rayana, S., Liu, X., & Sohn, S. (2025). *The rise of small language models in healthcare: A comprehensive survey.* arXiv preprint arXiv:2504.17119. https://arxiv.org/abs/2504.17119

GE HealthCare. (2025, September 25). *GE HealthCare debuts AI-supported solution designed to improve and shorten radiation therapy workflow.* GE HealthCare Newsroom.

Ghobadpour, A., Monsalve, G., Cardenas, A., & Mousazadeh, H. (2022). Off-road electric vehicles and autonomous robots in agricultural sector: Trends, challenges, and opportunities. *Vehicles (Basel), 4*(3), 843–864. DOI: 10.3390/vehicles4030047

Ghojogh, B., Ghodsi, A., Karray, F., & Crowley, M. (2021). Generative adversarial networks and adversarial autoencoders: Tutorial and survey. arXiv preprint arXiv:2111.13282.

Gholami, A., Kim, S., Dong, Z., Yao, Z., Mahoney, M., & Keutzer, K. (2021). A survey of quantization methods for efficient neural network inference. *ACM Computing Surveys, 54*(3), 1–38.

Ghosh, D., Siddique, M. A., & Pal, D. (2024). AI-Driven Precision Agriculture Approach. *AI in Agriculture for Sustainable and Economic Management, 6*, 67.

Giorgetti, G., & Pau, D. P. (2025). Transitioning from TinyML to edge GenAI: A review. *Big Data and Cognitive Computing, 9*(3), 61. DOI: 10.3390/bdcc9030061

Giuffrida, G., Fanucci, L., Meoni, G., Batič, M., Buckley, L., Dunne, A., van Dijk, C., Esposito, M., Hefele, J., Vercruyssen, N., Furano, G., Pastena, M., & Aschbacher, J. (2022). The Φ-Sat-1 mission: The first on-board deep neural network demonstrator for satellite Earth observation. *IEEE Transactions on Geoscience and Remote Sensing, 60*, 1–14. Advance online publication. DOI: 10.1109/TGRS.2021.3125567

Gkintoni, E., Vassilopoulos, S. P., & Nikolaou, G. (2025). Next-generation cognitive-behavioral therapy for depression: Integrating digital tools, teletherapy, and personalization for enhanced mental health outcomes. *Medicina, 61*(3), 431. DOI: 10.3390/medicina61030431 PMID: 40142242

Gomes, R. (2024). Dynamic KV-cache eviction for sustainable long-form generation. *Computational Linguistics Quarterly*, *9*(2), 201–218. DOI: 10.1162/cliq.2024.09.2.201

Goodfellow, I., Bengio, Y., & Courville, A. (2014). *Deep learning*. MIT Press.

Goodfellow, I., McDaniel, P., & Papernot, N. (2015). Making machine learning robust against adversarial inputs. *Communications of the ACM*, *61*(7), 56–66. DOI: 10.1145/3134599

Goodfellow, I., Pouget-Abadie, J., Mirza, M., Xu, B., Warde-Farley, D., Ozair, S., & Bengio, Y. (2014). Generative adversarial nets. *Advances in Neural Information Processing Systems*, *27*, 2672–2680.

Google DeepMind. (2024). *Gemini: A family of highly capable multimodal models*. Google. https://deepmind.google/technologies/gemini/

Google. (n.d.). *Coral — Edge TPU guide: Introduction*. Google Developers. https://developers.google.com/coral/guides/intro

Google. (n.d.). Coral: Production products. Google Developers. https://developers.google.com/coral#production-products

Gou, J., Xin, X., Yu, B., Song, H., Zhang, W., & Wan, S. (2025). Neighbourhood relation-based knowledge distillation for image classification. *Neural Networks*, *188*, 107429. DOI: 10.1016/j.neunet.2025.107429 PMID: 40179584

Gou, J., Yu, B., Maybank, S. J., & Tao, D. (2021). Knowledge distillation: A survey. *International Journal of Computer Vision*, *129*(6), 1789–1819. DOI: 10.1007/s11263-021-01453-z

Grassini, S. (2024). Shaping the future of education: Exploring the potential and consequences of AI and ChatGPT in educational settings. *Education Sciences*, *13*(7), 692. DOI: 10.3390/educsci13070692

Group, B. M. W. (2024). *BMC Group Report 2024* https://www.bmwgroup.com/en/report/2024/downloads/BMW-Group-Report-2024-en.pdf

Gui, J., Chen, T., Zhang, J., Cao, Q., Sun, Z., Luo, H., & Tao, D. (2024). A survey on self-supervised learning: Algorithms, applications, and future trends. *IEEE Transactions on Pattern Analysis and Machine Intelligence*, *46*(12), 9052–9071. DOI: 10.1109/TPAMI.2024.3415112

Guo, X., & Chen, Y. (2024). Generative AI for synthetic data generation: Methods, challenges and the future. arXiv preprint arXiv:2403.04190.

Gupta, A., & Sah, M. (2025). *Smart shelves: Transforming retail stocking with Internet of Things and machine learning*. Journal of Umm Al-Qura University for Engineering and Architecture. DOI: 10.1007/s43995-025-00213-1

Gupta, R., Tiwari, S., & Chaudhary, P. (2025). Computational Foundation of Generative AI Models. In Generative, A. I. (Ed.), *Techniques, Models and Applications* (pp. 23–44). Springer Nature Switzerland.

Hadi, M. U., Al-Tashi, Q., Qureshi, R., Shah, A., Muneer, A., Irfan, M., ... & Shah12, M. (2024). LLMs: A Comprehensive Survey of Applications, Challenges, Datasets, Models, Limitations, and Future Prospects.

Han, S., Mao, H., & Dally, W. J. (2016). Deep compression: Compressing deep neural networks with pruning, trained quantization and Huffman coding. *International Conference on Learning Representations (ICLR).*

Hashim, H. A. (2024). Non-Contact Automatic Respiratory Rate Monitoring for Newborns Using Digital Camera Technology and Deep Learning. *Journal of Biomedical Photonics & Engineering*, *10*(4), 040317. Advance online publication. DOI: 10.18287/JBPE24.10.040317

Hattie, J. (2009). *Visible learning: A synthesis of over 800 meta-analyses relating to achievement.* Routledge.

He, L., Fan, L., Lei, X., Fan, P., Nallanathan, A., & Karagiannidis, G. K. (2025). The road toward general edge intelligence: Standing on the shoulders of foundation models. *IEEE Communications Magazine*, *63*(9), 164–170. DOI: 10.1109/MCOM.003.2400445

He, R., Cao, J., & Tan, T. (2025). Generative artificial intelligence: A historical perspective. *National Science Review*, *12*(5), nwaf050. Advance online publication. DOI: 10.1093/nsr/nwaf050 PMID: 40191253

Herlea, D. M., Iancu, B., & Ardelean, E. R. (2025). A Study of Deep Learning Models for Audio Classification of Infant Crying in a Baby Monitoring System. *Informatics (MDPI)*, *12*(2), 50. Advance online publication. DOI: 10.3390/informatics12020050

He, Y., Zhang, X., & Sun, J. (2017). Channel Pruning for Accelerating Very Deep Neural Networks. In *2017 IEEE International Conference on Computer Vision (ICCV)* (pp. 1398–1406). DOI: 10.1109/ICCV.2017.155

Hinton, G., Vinyals, O., & Dean, J. (2015). Distilling the knowledge in a neural network. *NeurIPS Deep Learning Workshop.*

Ho, A., Hancock, J., & Miner, A. S. (2018). Psychological, relational, and emotional effects of self-disclosure after conversations with a chatbot. *Journal of Communication, 68*(4), 712–733. DOI: 10.1093/joc/jqy026 PMID: 30100620

Holmes, W., & Miao, F. (2023). *Guidance for generative AI in education and research.* UNESCO., DOI: 10.54675/PKPP3238

Holmes, W., Porayska-Pomsta, K., Holstein, K., Sutherland, E., Baker, T., Shum, S. B., Santos, O. C., Rodrigo, M. T., Cukurova, M., Bittencourt, I. I., & Koedinger, K. R. (2022). Ethics of AI in education: Towards a community-wide agenda. *International Journal of Artificial Intelligence in Education, 32*(3), 504–526. DOI: 10.1007/s40593-021-00239-1

Hossain, M. S., Rahman, M., Rahman, A., Kabir, M. M., Mridha, M. F., Huang, J., & Shin, J. (2025). Automatic navigation and self-driving technology in agricultural machinery: A state-of-the-art systematic review. *IEEE Access : Practical Innovations, Open Solutions.*

Hou, K. M., Diao, X., Shi, H., Ding, H., Zhou, H., & de Vaulx, C. (2023). Trends and Challenges in AIoT/IIoT/IoT Implementation. *Sensors (Basel), 23*(11), 5074. Advance online publication. DOI: 10.3390/s23115074 PMID: 37299800

Huang, H. (2025). *Investigating the Application of Generative Artificial Intelligence in Taxonomy* (Doctoral dissertation, The University of Auckland).

Huang, J., Wang, M., Cui, Y., Liu, J., Chen, L., Wang, T., Li, H., & Wu, J. (2024). Layered query retrieval: An adaptive framework for retrieval-augmented generation in complex question answering for large language models.

Hu, E. J., Shen, Y., Wallis, P., Allen Zhu, Z., Li, Y., Wang, S., & Chen, W. (2022). LoRA: Low rank adaptation of large language models. *International Conference on Learning Representations*, 1(2), 3.

Hu, E. J., Shen, Y., Wallis, P., Allen-Zhu, Z., Li, Y., Wang, S., & Chen, W. (2021). LoRA: Low-Rank Adaptation of Large Language Models. Retrieved from https://arxiv.org/abs/2106.09685

Hu, E. J., Shen, Y., Wallis, P., Allen-Zhu, Z., Li, Y., Wang, S., Wang, L., & Chen, W. (2022). LoRA: Low-rank adaptation of large language models. *International Conference on Learning Representations (ICLR).* https://arxiv.org/abs/2106.09685

Husom, E. J., Goknil, A., Astekin, M., Shar, L. K., Kåsen, A., Sen, S., Mithassel, B. A., & Soylu, A. (2025). *Sustainable LLM inference for edge AI: Evaluating quantized LLMs for energy efficiency, output accuracy, and inference latency* (arXiv:2504.03360). arXiv. https://doi.org//arXiv.2504.03360DOI: 10.48550

Hutto, C., & Gilbert, E. (2024). Vader: A parsimonious rule-based model for sentiment analysis of social media text. *Proceedings of the International AAAI Conference on Web and Social Media*, 8, 20.

Hwang, K. (2023). *The future of AI is "on device"* [Conference presentation]. tinyML Asia 2023.

IEEE. (2025). Advances in pruning and quantization for natural language processing. https://ieeexplore.ieee.org/document/10685352

IEEE. (2025). Software-hardware feedback loop protocols for generative workloads. IEEE Standards Association., , IEEE Standard 12207-2025.DOI: 10.1109/IEEESTD.2025.998432

Ignatov, A., Timofte, R., Chou, W., Wang, K., Wu, M., Hartley, T., & Van Gool, L. (2018). AI benchmark: Running deep neural networks on android smartphones. Proceedings of the European Conference on Computer Vision (ECCV) Workshops, 288–304. DOI: 10.1007/978-3-030-11009-3_18

Information Commissioner's Office (ICO). (2023). "Guide to the UK General Data Protection Regulation (UK GDPR)," ICO. [Online]. Available: https://ico.org.uk/for-organisations/guide-to-data-protection/guide-to-the-general-data-protection-regulation-gdpr/

Inkster, B., Sarda, S., & Subramanian, V. (2018). An empathy-driven, conversational artificial intelligence agent (WYSA) for digital mental well-being: Real-World Data Evaluation Mixed-Methods Study. *JMIR mHealth and uHealth*, *6*(11), e12106. Advance online publication. DOI: 10.2196/12106 PMID: 30470676

Institute for Research and Innovation in Intelligent Systems (IRIIS). (n.d.). *Iriis-Research/Nepali-text-corpus datasets at hugging face*. IRIIS-RESEARCH/Nepali-Text-Corpus · Datasets at Hugging Face. https://huggingface.co/datasets/IRIIS-RESEARCH/Nepali-Text-Corpus

Isosalo, A., Islam, J., Mustonen, H., Räinä, E., Inkinen, S. I., Brix, M., Reponen, J., Nieminen, M. T., & Harjula, E. (2023). *Local edge computing for radiological image reconstruction and computer-assisted detection : A feasibility study. 15*(1), 52–66.

Jabbar, W. A., Shang, H. K., Hamid, S. N. I. S., Almohammedi, A. A., Ramli, R. M., & Ali, M. A. H. (2019). IoT-BBMS: Internet of Things-Based Baby Monitoring System for Smart Cradle. *IEEE Access : Practical Innovations, Open Solutions*, *7*, 93791–93805. DOI: 10.1109/ACCESS.2019.2928481

Jeong, S., Baek, J., Cho, S., Hwang, S. J., & Park, J. C. (b). (2024). Adaptive-rag: Learning to adapt retrieval-augmented large language models through question complexity. In *Proceedings of the the Association for Computational Linguistics*. DOI: 10.18653/v1/2024.naacl-long.389

Jiang, K., Jin, G., Zhang, Z., Cui, R., & Zhao, Y. (2024). Incorporating external knowledge for text matching model. *Computer Speech & Language*, *87*, 101638. DOI: 10.1016/j.csl.2024.101638

Jiao, X., Yin, Y., Shang, L., Jiang, X., Chen, X., Li, L., & Liu, Q. (2020). TinyBERT: Distilling BERT for Natural Language Understanding. In *Findings of the Association for Computational Linguistics: EMNLP 2020* (pp. 4163–4174). Association for Computational Linguistics., DOI: 10.18653/v1/2020.findings-emnlp.372

Jin, M., Yu, Q., Shu, D., Zhang, C., Fan, L., Hua, W., Zhu, S., Meng, Y., Wang, Z., Du, M., & Zhang, Y. (2024). Health-LLM: Personalized retrieval-Augmented disease prediction system arXiv:2402.00746

Junaid, A. R., & Callixtus, I. (2024). From Complexity to Simplicity: Advancements in Large Language Model Compression.

Jurgens, D., Dimitrov, S., & Ruths, D. (2014, October). Twitter users# codeswitch hashtags!# moltoimportante# wow. In *Proceedings of the First Workshop on Computational Approaches to Code Switching* (pp. 51-61). DOI: 10.3115/v1/W14-3906

Kairouz, P., McMahan, H. B., Avent, B., Bellet, A., Bennis, M., Bhagoji, A. N., Bonawitz, K., Charles, Z., Cormode, G., Cummings, R., D'Oliveira, R. G. L., Eichner, H., El Rouayheb, S., Evans, D., Gardner, J., Garrett, Z., Gascon, A., Ghazi, B., Gibbons, P. B., & Zhao, S. (2021). Advances and Open Problems in Federated Learning. *Foundations and Trends in Machine Learning*, *14*(1-2), 1–210. DOI: 10.1561/2200000083

Kalaivani, T., Allirani, A., & Priya, P. (2011, December). A survey on Zigbee based wireless sensor networks in agriculture. In *3rd international conference on Trendz in information sciences & computing (TISC2011)* (pp. 85-89). IEEE. DOI: 10.1109/TISC.2011.6169090

Kalyan, K. S. (2023). A survey of GPT-3 family large language models including chatgpt and GPT-4. SSRN *Electronic Journal*. DOI: 10.2139/ssrn.4593895

Kang, P., & Somtham, A. (2022). An evaluation of modern accelerator-based edge devices for object detection applications. *Mathematics*, *10*(22), 4299. DOI: 10.3390/math10224299

Kashyap, R., Samuel, Y., Friedman, L. W., & Samuel, J. (2024). Editorial: Artificial intelli-gence education & governance-human enhancive, culturally sensitive and personally adaptive hai. *Frontiers in Artificial Intelligence*, *7*, 1443386. Advance online publication. DOI: 10.3389/frai.2024.1443386 PMID: 39011026

Kasneci, E., Sessler, K., Küchemann, S., Bannert, M., Dementieva, D., Fischer, F., Gasser, U., Groh, G., Günnemann, S., Hüllermeier, E., Krusche, S., Kutyniok, G., Michaeli, T., Nerdel, C., Pfeffer, J., Poquet, O., Sailer, M., Schmidt, A., Seidel, T., & Kasneci, G. (2023). ChatGPT for good? On opportunities and challenges of large language models for education. *Learning and Individual Differences*, *103*, 102274. DOI: 10.1016/j.lindif.2023.102274

Katare, D., Perino, D., Nurmi, J., Warnier, M., Janssen, M., & Ding, A. Y. (2023). A survey on approximate edge AI for energy-efficient autonomous driving services. *IEEE Communications Surveys and Tutorials*, *25*(4), 2714–2754. DOI: 10.1109/COMST.2023.3302474

Khaki, S., & Wang, L. (2019). Crop yield prediction using deep neural networks. *Frontiers in Plant Science*, *10*, 621. DOI: 10.3389/fpls.2019.00621 PMID: 31191564

Khamparia, A., & Gupta, D. (2025). Privacy-preserving generative AI in mobile healthcare systems. *IEEE Transactions on Mobile Computing*, *24*(1), 88–104.

Khan, A. T., Jensen, S. M., Rehman Khan, A., & Li, S. (2023). Plant disease detection model for edge computing devices. *Frontiers in Plant Science*, *14*, 1308528. DOI: 10.3389/fpls.2023.1308528 PMID: 38143571

Khanal, R. (2019). Linguistic geography of nepalese languages. *The Third Pole: Journal of Geography Education*, 45-54.

Khan, T. (2021). An Intelligent Baby Monitor with Automatic Sleeping Posture Detection and Notification. *AI*, *2*(2), 290–306. DOI: 10.3390/ai2020018

Khan, W. Z., Ahmed, E., Hakak, S., Yaqoob, I., & Ahmed, A. (2019). Edge computing: A survey. *Future Generation Computer Systems*, *97*, 219–235. DOI: 10.1016/j.future.2019.02.050

Kim, J. H., & Choi, Y. S. (2025). Lightweight pre-trained Korean language model based on knowledge distillation and low-rank factorisation. *Entropy (Basel, Switzerland)*, *27*(4), 379. DOI: 10.3390/e27040379 PMID: 40282614

Kipf, T. N., & Welling, M. (2017). "Semi-Supervised Classification with Graph Convolutional Networks," in *Proc. of the 5th International Conference on Learning Representations (ICLR)*, 2017.

Kitchenham, B. (2004). *Procedures for performing systematic reviews*. Keele, UK, Keele University, 33(2004), 1-26.

Koedinger, K. R., & Corbett, A. (2006). Cognitive tutors: Technology bringing learning sciences to the classroom. In Sawyer, R. K. (Ed.), *The Cambridge handbook of the learning sciences* (pp. 61–77). Cambridge University Press.

Kollig, F., Pater, J., Nova, F. F., & Fiesler, C. (2025, April). Fictional Failures and Real-World Lessons: Ethical Speculation Through Design Fiction on Emotional Support Conversational AI. In *Proceedings of the 2025 CHI Conference on Human Factors in Computing Systems* (pp. 1-15). DOI: 10.1145/3706598.3713322

Kristiani, E., Verma, V. K., & Yang, C. T. (2026). Deploying LLM Transformer on Edge Computing Devices: A Survey of Strategies, Challenges, and Future Directions. *AI*, *7*(1), 15. DOI: 10.3390/ai7010015

Kumar, A., Singh, R., & Zhao, H. (2024). Predictive thermal management for autoregressive workloads on mobile platforms. *IEEE Transactions on Consumer Electronics*, *70*(1), 88–104. DOI: 10.1109/TCE.2024.3351221

Kumar, P. (2025). Diffusion Models and Generative Artificial Intelligence: Frameworks, Applications and Challenges. *Archives of Computational Methods in Engineering*, *32*(7), 1–44. DOI: 10.1007/s11831-025-10266-z

Kumar, S., & Shastri, A. (2024). Distributed AI lifecycle management for large-scale edge deployments. *Journal of Systems Architecture*, *146*, 102932.

Kwon, W., Li, Z., Zhuang, S., Sheng, Y., Zheng, L., Yu, C. H., & Stoica, I. (2023). Efficient memory management for large language model serving with PagedAttention. *Proceedings of the 29th Symposium on Operating Systems Principles (SOSP)*, 611–626. DOI: 10.1145/3600006.3613165

Kynkäänniemi, T., Karras, T., Laine, S., Lehtinen, J., & Aila, T. (2019). Improved Precision and Recall Metric for Assessing Generative Models. *Advances in Neural Information Processing Systems*, ●●●, 32.

Lane, N., Bhattacharya, S., & Mathur, A.. (2015). DeepX: A software accelerator for low-power deep learning inference on mobile devices. *International Conference on Information Processing in Sensor Networks.*

Lauscher, A., Ravishankar, V., Vulić, I., & Glavaš, G. (2020). From zero to hero: On the limitations of zero-shot cross-lingual transfer with multilingual transformers. *arXiv preprint arXiv:2005.00633.*

LeanTaaS, Inc. (2022). *iQueue for operating room and infusion center optimization: Case studies and implementation reports*. LeanTaaS White Papers.

Lee, J., & Park, H. (2024). Hybrid collaborative inference for diffusion models in mobile and edge environments. *IEEE Transactions on Mobile Computing, 23*(5), 2779–2793.

Lee, J., & Park, S. (2025). Adaptive control policies for on-device LLMs via contextual bandits. *IEEE Access : Practical Innovations, Open Solutions, 13*, 14502–14519. DOI: 10.1109/ACCESS.2025.3421109

Lee, P. (2022). The Growing Pains of FinTech: Compliance as a Core Function. *Journal of Financial Regulation, 8*(1), 44–59.

Lewis, P., Perez, E., Piktus, A., Petroni, F., Karpukhin, V., Goyal, N., Küttler, H., Lewis, M., Yih, W.-T., Rocktäschel, T., Riedel, S., & Kiela, D. (2020). Retrieval-augmented generation for knowledge-intensive nlp tasks. In *Proceedings of the 34th conference on neural information processing systems vancouver, canada*

Li, X. L., & Liang, P. (2021). Prefix-tuning: Optimizing continuous prompts for generation. In *ACL-IJCNLP 2021 - 59th Annual Meeting of the Association for Computational Linguistics and the 11th International Joint Conference on Natural Language Processing, Proceedings of the Conference* (Vol. 1, pp. 4582–4597). Stroudsburg, PA, USA: Association for Computational Linguistics. DOI: 10.18653/v1/2021.acl-long.353

Li, Y., Liu, J., Zhang, H., Narayanan, M. B., Sharma, U., Zhang, S., . . . Banerjee, S. (2025). PalmBench: A comprehensive benchmark of compressed large language models on mobile platforms. The Thirteenth International Conference on Learning Representations. https://openreview.net/forum?id=xzSUdw6s76

Li, Y., Zhang, Y., & Sun, L. (2023). Metaagents: Simulating interactions of human behaviors for llm-based task-oriented coordination via collaborative generative agents. *arXiv preprint arXiv:2310.06500.*

Li, C., Pourtaherian, A., Van Onzenoort, L., Ten, W. E. T. A., & De With, P. H. N. (2021). Infant Facial Expression Analysis: Towards a Real-Time Video Monitoring System Using R-CNN and HMM. *IEEE Journal of Biomedical and Health Informatics, 25*(5), 1429–1440. DOI: 10.1109/JBHI.2020.3037031 PMID: 33170787

Li, C., Pourtaherian, A., Van Onzenoort, L., Tjon, W. E., & De With, P. H. N. (2020). Infant Monitoring System for Real-Time and Remote Discomfort Detection. *IEEE Transactions on Consumer Electronics, 66*(4), 336–345. DOI: 10.1109/TCE.2020.3031359

Lifelo, W., Chipeperekwa, T., & Kunda, D. (2024). Edge-based video analytics for smart cities: A bandwidth-optimized generative approach. *Journal of Urban Computing*, *8*(3), 112–129.

Li, H. T., Lin, S. C., Chen, C. Y., & Chiang, C. K. (2019). Layer-level knowledge distillation for deep neural network learning. *Applied Sciences (Basel, Switzerland)*, *9*(10), 1966. DOI: 10.3390/app9101966

Li, J., Wang, H., & Fan, X. (2023). Privacy-enhanced decentralized learning for generative models. *Pattern Recognition Letters*, *170*, 113–121.

Li, M., Lin, J., Ding, Y., Liu, Z., Zhu, J. Y., & Han, S. (2022). GAN Compression: Efficient Architectures for Interactive Conditional GANs. *IEEE Transactions on Pattern Analysis and Machine Intelligence*, *44*(12), 9331–9346. DOI: 10.1109/TPAMI.2021.3126742 PMID: 34752389

Lima, M. (2024). *Empirical evaluation of federated learning approaches for bank-account fraud detection* (MSc Dissertation).

Lin, J., Chen, W., Lin, Y., Cohn, J., Gan, C., & Han, S. (2020). *MCUNet : Tiny Deep Learning on IoT Devices. NeurIPS*, 1–15. https://arxiv.org/abs/2007.10319

Li, T., Sahu, A., Talwalkar, A., & Smith, V. (2020). Federated learning: Challenges, methods, and future directions. *IEEE Signal Processing Magazine*, *37*(3), 50–60. DOI: 10.1109/MSP.2020.2975749

Liu, D., Zhu, Y., Liu, Z., Liu, Y., Han, C., Tian, J., Li, R., & Yi, W. (2025). A survey of model compression techniques: Past, present, and future. *Frontiers in Robotics and AI*, *12*, 1518965. DOI: 10.3389/frobt.2025.1518965 PMID: 40182395

Liu, Q., He, H., Yang, J., Feng, X., Zhao, F., & Lyu, J. (2020). Changes in the global burden of depression from 1990 to 2017: Findings from the global burden of disease study. *Journal of Psychiatric Research*, *126*, 134–140. DOI: 10.1016/j.jpsychires.2019.08.002 PMID: 31439359

Liu, X., Zhang, F., Hou, Z., Mian, L., Wang, Z., Zhang, J., & Tang, J. (2021). Self-supervised learning: Generative or contrastive. *IEEE Transactions on Knowledge and Data Engineering*, *35*(1), 857–876.

Liu, Y., Ott, M., Goyal, N., Du, J., Joshi, M., Chen, D., & Stoyanov, V. (2019). RoBERTa: A Robustly Optimized BERT Pretraining Approach. arXiv [Cs.CL]. Retrieved from https://arxiv.org/abs/1907.11692

Li, Y., Bubeck, S., Eldan, R., Del Giorno, A., Gunasekar, S., & Lee, Y. T. (2023). *Textbooks are all you need II: Phi-1.5 technical report*. arXiv. https://arxiv.org/abs/2309.05463

Li, Y., Nie, J., Li, S., Jin, K., Tang, J., Zhang, Y., & Niyato, D. (2025). Intermediary Output Caching for Diffusion Model-Based Text-to-Image GenAI Services in Edge Computing Networks. *ACM Transactions on Embedded Computing Systems*, 3733106. Advance online publication. DOI: 10.1145/3733106

Li, Y., Wang, C., & Ooi, B. C. (2021). Challenges and Opportunities in Federated Learning. *IEEE Transactions on Big Data*, *7*(3), 453–462. DOI: 10.1109/TBDATA.2021.3070058

Lomurno, E. (2024). Adversarial and generative deep learning for data privacy in human-centered artificial intelligence.

Lu, C., Zhou, Y., Bao, F., Chen, J., Li, C., & Zhu, J. (2022). DPM-Solver: A Fast ODE Solver for Diffusion Probabilistic Model Sampling in Around 10 Steps. *Advances in Neural Information Processing Systems*, *35*, 5775–5787.

Luckin, R., Cukurova, M., Kent, C., & du Boulay, B. (2022). Empowering educators to be AI-ready. *Computers and Education: Artificial Intelligence*, *3*, 100076. DOI: 10.1016/j.caeai.2022.100076

Lundgren, B., & Holmström, J. (2022). Privacy and AI in education: An empirical analysis of higher education EdTech vendor privacy policies. *Education and Information Technologies*, *27*(5), 6933–6955. DOI: 10.1007/s10639-021-10892-7

Mach, P., & Becvar, Z. (2017). Mobile edge computing: A survey on architecture and computation offloading. *IEEE Communications Surveys and Tutorials*, *19*(3), 1628–1656. DOI: 10.1109/COMST.2017.2682318

Ma, D. (2022). A Survey of Deep Learning for Data Sanitization and Model Anomaly Detection in Edge Computing. *IEEE Transactions on Knowledge and Data Engineering*.

Madhu, R., Anbazhagu, U. V., Santhana Krishnan, R., Paulraj, K., Nithila, E. E., & Umesh, R. (2025). IoT-Enabled Deep Learning Framework for Smart Infant Health Monitoring. *Proceedings of the International Conference on Intelligent Computing and Control Systems, ICICCS 2025*, 420–427. DOI: 10.1109/ICICCS65191.2025.10984933

Majumdar, P., Mitra, S., & Bhattacharya, D. (2021). IoT for promoting agriculture 4.0: A review from the perspective of weather monitoring, yield prediction, security of WSN protocols, and hardware cost analysis. *Journal of Biosystems Engineering*, *46*(4), 440–461. DOI: 10.1007/s42853-021-00118-6

Makenali, S., Rokh, B., & Azarpeyvand, A. (2025). Integrating pruning with quantization for efficient deep neural networks compression. https://arxiv.org/html/2509.04244v1

Malik, P., Tiwari, S., Tomar, K., Kalambkar, K., & Yeole, D. (2024). *Drone swarm coordination using IoT for large-scale agricultural monitoring*. International Journal of Science [Available via IJSET archives/ResearchGate]. *Engineering and Technology*, *12*(6), 1–12.

Manurung, E. P., Fiumara, M., Bennin, K., & Asiedu, D. K. P. (2025). An Energy-Efficient Precision Agriculture Communication Embedded System CoAP Design. *IEEE Internet of Things Journal*, *12*(19), 39984–39990. DOI: 10.1109/JIOT.2025.3588583

Mármol-Romero, A. M., García-Vega, M., García-Cumbreras, M. Á., & Montejo-Ráez, A. (2025). An empathic GPT-based chatbot to talk about mental disorders with Spanish teenagers. *International Journal of Human-Computer Interaction*, *41*(7), 3957–3973.

Mayuravaani, M., Ramanan, A., Perera, M., Senanayake, D. A., & Vidanaarachchi, R. (2024). Insights into artificial intelligence bias: Implications for agriculture. *Digital Society : Ethics, Socio-Legal and Governance of Digital Technology*, *3*(3), 48. DOI: 10.1007/s44206-024-00142-x

McMahan, H. B., Moore, E., Ramage, D., & Hampson, S. (2016). "Federated Learning of Deep Networks using Model Averaging," arXiv:1602.05629.

Mehrabi, N., Morstatter, F., Saxena, N., Lerman, K., & Galstyan, A. (2021). A survey on bias and fairness in machine learning. *ACM Computing Surveys*, *54*(6), 1–35. DOI: 10.1145/3457607

Meng, C., Rombach, R., Gao, R., Kingma, D., Ermon, S., Ho, J., & Salimans, T. (2023). On Distillation of Guided Diffusion Models. In *Proceedings of the IEEE Computer Society Conference on Computer Vision and Pattern Recognition* (Vol. 2023-June, pp. 14297–14306). IEEE. DOI: 10.1109/CVPR52729.2023.01374

Miikkulainen, R. (2024). Generative AI: An AI paradigm shift in the making? *AI Magazine*, *45*(1), 165–167. DOI: 10.1002/aaai.12155

Ministry of Electronics and Information Technology. (2023). *The Digital Personal Data Protection Act*. Government of India.

Mir, M. S., Naikoo, N. B., Kanth, R. H., Bahar, F. A., Bhat, M. A., Nazir, A., & Ahngar, T. A. (2022). Vertical farming: The future of agriculture: A review. *The Pharma Innovation Journal*, *11*(2), 1175–1195.

Mittal, S. (2020). A survey of FPGA-based accelerators for convolutional neural networks. *Neural Computing & Applications*, *32*(4), 1109–1139. DOI: 10.1007/s00521-018-3761-1

Mohammed, A. (2025). Integrated Hybrid Renewable Energy System Optimization for Sustainable Agricultural Operations. *Process Integration and Optimization for Sustainability*, *9*(1), 367–386. DOI: 10.1007/s41660-024-00464-w

Monika, S., Battana, H., Sangeetha, M., Shaik, M., & Jawahar, M. (2024). Analysis of Maternity and Child Health Care System Integrated with IoT and ML. *10th International Conference on Advanced Computing and Communication Systems, ICACCS 2024*, 1792–1797. DOI: 10.1109/ICACCS60874.2024.10717104

Monisha, K., Kalai Selvi, H., Sivanandhini, P., Sona Nachammai, A., Anuradha, C. T., Rama Devi, S., Kavitha Sri, A., Neya, N. R., Vaitheeswari, M., & Hikku, G. S. (2023). Hydroponics agriculture as a modern agriculture technique. *Journal of Achievements in Materials and Manufacturing Engineering*, *116*(1), 25–35. DOI: 10.5604/01.3001.0016.3395

Moor, M., Banerjee, O., Abad, Z. S. H., Krumholz, H. M., Leskovec, J., Topol, E. J., & Rajpurkar, P. (2023). Foundation models for generalist medical artificial intelligence. *Nature*, *616*(7956), 259–265. DOI: 10.1038/s41586-023-05881-4 PMID: 37045921

Morabito, R., & Jang, M. (2025). Edge-native computing for privacy-sensitive AI workloads: A survey. *ACM Computing Surveys*, *57*(1), 1–34.

Motetti, B. A., Risso, M., Burrello, A., Macii, E., Poncino, M., & Pagliari, D. J. (2024). Joint Pruning and Channel-Wise Mixed-Precision Quantization for Efficient Deep Neural Networks. *IEEE Transactions on Computers*, *73*(11), 2619–2633. DOI: 10.1109/TC.2024.3449084

Moulaei, K., Yadegari, A., Baharestani, M., Farzanbakhsh, S., Sabet, B., & Afrash, M. R. (2024). Generative artificial intelligence in healthcare: A scoping review on benefits, challenges and applications. *International Journal of Medical Informatics*, *188*, 105474. DOI: 10.1016/j.ijmedinf.2024.105474 PMID: 38733640

Mudambi, S. M., & Schuff, D. (2010). Research note: What makes a helpful online review? A study of customer reviews on Amazon. com. *MIS quarterly*, 185-200.

Muir, D. R., & Sheik, S. (2025). The road to commercial success for neuromorphic technologies. *Nature Communications*, *16*(1), 3586. DOI: 10.1038/s41467-025-57352-1 PMID: 40234391

Nabil, M., Aly, M., & Atiya, A. (2015, September). Astd: Arabic sentiment tweets dataset. In *Proceedings of the 2015 conference on empirical methods in natural language processing* (pp. 2515-2519). DOI: 10.18653/v1/D15-1299

Nandhakumar, R. G., & Mohanapriya, S. (2022). Smart Baby Monitoring System using YOLO V7 Algorithm. *2022 International Conference on Information Technology Research and Innovation, ICITRI 2022*, 42–47. DOI: 10.1109/ICITRI56423.2022.9970217

Navardi, M., Aalishah, R., Fu, Y., Lin, Y., Li, H., Chen, Y., & Mohsenin, T. (2025). *GenAI at the Edge: Comprehensive Survey on Empowering Edge Devices*. In *Proceedings of the AAAI Symposium on Artificial Intelligence for Edge Computing*. AAAI Press. https://ojs.aaai.org/index.php/AAAI-SS/article/view/35586/37741

Navardi, M., Aalishah, R., Fu, Y., Lin, Y., Li, H., Chen, Y., & Mohsenin, T. (2025, May). GenAI at the edge: Comprehensive survey on empowering edge devices. In *Proceedings of the AAAI Symposium Series* (Vol. 5, No. 1, pp. 180–187). DOI: 10.1609/aaaiss.v5i1.35586

Navardi, S., Li, Z., & Zhang, Y. (2025). Model compression strategies for deploying generative AI on edge devices. *IEEE Internet of Things Journal*, *12*(4), 3451–3468.

Neupane, A., Shahi, T. B., Cowling, M., & Tanna, D. (2024). Threading the GenAI needle: Unpacking the ups and downs of GenAI for higher education stakeholders. *Journal of Applied Learning & Teaching*, *7*(2), 38–46.

Ng, D. T. K., Leung, J. K. L., Chu, S. K. W., & Qiao, M. S. (2021). Conceptualising AI literacy: An exploratory review. *Computers and Education: Artificial Intelligence*, *2*, 100041. DOI: 10.1016/j.caeai.2021.100041

Niraula, N. B., Dulal, S., & Koirala, D. (2022). Linguistic taboos and euphemisms in nepali. *ACM Transactions on Asian and Low-Resource Language Information Processing*, *21*(6), 1–26. DOI: 10.1145/3524111

Njor, E., Banbury, C., & Fafoutis, X. (2025). Fast data aware neural architecture search via supernet accelerated evaluation. *Internet of Things : Engineering Cyber Physical Human Systems*, *33*, 101688. DOI: 10.1016/j.iot.2025.101688

Nvidia (2023). *Corporate Responsibility Report Fiscal Year 2023*

O'Neill, K., & Sørensen, T. (2025). Resilient deployment of generative AI in hostile edge environments. *ACM Transactions on Embedded Computing Systems, 24*(1), 1–26.

Ogidan, O. K., Oluwagbayıde, S. D., & Ale, T. (2023). A microcontroller-Based Irrigation Scheduling Using FAO Penman-Monteith Equation. *Turkish Journal of Agricultural Engineering Research, 4*(1), 15–25. DOI: 10.46592/turkager.1170630

Olabanji, M. F., & Chitakira, M. (2025). The adoption and scaling of climate-smart agriculture innovation by smallholder farmers in South Africa: A review of institutional mechanisms, policy frameworks and market dynamics. *WORLD (Oakland, Calif.), 6*(2), 51. DOI: 10.3390/world6020051

Olabiyi, O. (2025). Deployment realism: Evaluating LLMs under physical device constraints. *International Journal of Edge Computing, 4*(1), 12–30. DOI: 10.4018/IJEC.20250101.02

Olukoya, O. (2022). Assessing frameworks for eliciting privacy and security requirements from laws and regulations. *Computers & Security, 117*, 102697. DOI: 10.1016/j.cose.2022.102697

OpenSLR. (n.d.). SLR54: Nepali speech dataset. https://openslr.org/54/

Oviatt, S., & Adams, B. (2000). Designing and evaluating conversational interfaces with animated characters. *Embodied Conversational Agents*, 319–345. DOI: 10.7551/mitpress/2697.003.0014

Oyewole, A. R., Ugwu, C. C., Adetunmbi, A. O., & Afolayan, A. H. (2024, November). A Systematic Review of Chatbot Development for Low-Resource Languages. In *2024 IEEE 5th International Conference on Electro-Computing Technologies for Humanity (NIGERCON)* (pp. 1-5). IEEE. DOI: 10.1109/NIGERCON62786.2024.10927136

Pacheco, R. G., Bochie, K., Gilbert, M. S., Couto, R. S., & Campista, M. E. M. (2021). Towards Edge Computing Using Early-Exit Convolutional Neural Networks. *Information (Basel), 12*(10), 431. DOI: 10.3390/info12100431

Pahari, N., & Shimada, K. (2024). Share What You Already Know: Cross-Language-Script Transfer and Alignment for Sentiment Detection in Code-Mixed Data. *ACM Transactions on Asian and Low-Resource Language Information Processing, 23*(7), 1–15. DOI: 10.1145/3661307

Pandey, M., Yadav, N. P., Adduru, M., & Rai, S. (2025). Creating and Evaluating Code-Mixed Nepali-English and Telugu-English Datasets for Abusive Language Detection Using Traditional and Deep Learning Models. *arXiv preprint arXiv:2504.21026.*

Pandey, C., Tiwari, V., Imoize, A. L., Li, C. T., Lee, C. C., & Roy, D. S. (2023). 5GT-GAN: Enhancing data augmentation for 5G-enabled mobile edge computing in smart cities. *IEEE Access : Practical Innovations, Open Solutions, 11*, 120983–120996. DOI: 10.1109/ACCESS.2023.3328170

Pan, Z., Lau, S. L., Yang, X., Guo, N., & Wang, X. (2023). Automatic pavement crack segmentation using a generative adversarial network (gan)-based convolutional neural network. *Results in Engineering, 19*, 101267. DOI: 10.1016/j.rineng.2023.101267

Papernot, N., McDaniel, P., & Jha, S.. (2016). The limitations of deep learning in adversarial settings. *IEEE European Symposium on Security and Privacy*, 372–387. DOI: 10.1109/EuroSP.2016.36

Papineni, K., Roukos, S., Ward, T., & Zhu, W. J. (2002). BLEU: A method for automatic evaluation of machine translation. *Proceedings of the 40th Annual Meeting of the Association for Computational Linguistics (ACL)*, 311–318. DOI: 10.3115/1073083.1073135

Parvathavarthini, S., Bhuvaneswaran, U., Arun, U. M., & Sengottayan, S. (2024). Baby Monitoring Using IOT and Deep Learning. *2024 15th International Conference on Computing Communication and Networking Technologies, ICCCNT 2024*. DOI: 10.1109/ICCCNT61001.2024.10725151

Patel, S. (2025). The Latent Space Hypothesis: Toward Universal Medical Representation Learning. *arXiv preprint arXiv:2506.04515*.

Patel, K., Shah, M., Qureshi, K. M., & Qureshi, M. R. N. (2025). A systematic review of generative AI: Importance of industry and startup-centered perspectives, agentic AI, ethical considerations & challenges, and future directions. *Artificial Intelligence Review, 59*(1), 7. Advance online publication. DOI: 10.1007/s10462-025-11435-z

Patel, M. (2025). Telemetry-aware resource management for AI-enabled wearables. *IEEE Sensors Journal, 25*(4), 3110–3125. DOI: 10.1109/JSEN.2025.122941

Patel, P., Kalyanam, R., He, L., Aliaga, D., & Niyogi, D. (2023). Deep learning-based urban morphology for city-scale environmental modeling. *PNAS Nexus, 2*(3), pgad027. Advance online publication. DOI: 10.1093/pnasnexus/pgad027 PMID: 36909824

Patel, V., Maj, M., Flisher, A. J., De Silva, M. J., Koschorke, M., Prince, M., Tempier, R., Riba, M., Sanchez, M., Campodonico, F. D., Risco, L., Gask, L., Wahlberg, H., Roca, M., Lecic-Tosevski, D., Soghoyan, A., Moussaoui, D., Baddoura, C., Adeyemi, J., & Richardson, G. (2010). Reducing the treatment gap for mental disorders: A WPA survey. *World Psychiatry; Official Journal of the World Psychiatric Association (WPA)*, *9*(3), 169–176. DOI: 10.1002/j.2051-5545.2010.tb00305.x PMID: 20975864

Pathak, R., & Singh, Y. (2020). Real time baby facial expression recognition using deep learning and IoT edge computing. *Proceedings of the 2020 International Conference on Computing, Communication and Security, ICCCS 2020*. DOI: 10.1109/ICCCS49678.2020.9277428

Paul, A., Haque Latif, A., Amin Adnan, F., & Rahman, R. M. (2019). Focused domain contextual AI chatbot framework for resource poor languages. *Journal of Information and Telecommunication*, *3*(2), 248–269. DOI: 10.1080/24751839.2018.1558378

Paula, E., Soni, J., Upadhyay, H., & Lagos, L. (2025). Comparative analysis of model compression techniques for achieving carbon efficient AI. *Scientific Reports*, *15*(1), 23461. DOI: 10.1038/s41598-025-07821-w PMID: 40604122

Perkins, M., Roe, J., Postma, D., McGaughran, J., & Hickerson, D. (2024). Game of tones: Faculty recognition of AI-generated text in student essays. *Computers and Education Open*, *6*, 100173. DOI: 10.1016/j.caeo.2024.100173

Petroşanu, D. M., & Pîrjan, A. (2024). EXPLORING COMPRESSION STRATEGIES FOR LARGE LANGUAGE MODELS TOWARDS EFFICIENT ARTIFICIAL INTELLIGENCE IMPLEMENTATIONS. *Journal of Information Systems & Operations Management*, *18*(1), 225–260.

Pimenow, S., Pimenowa, O., & Prus, P. (2024). Challenges of artificial intelligence development in the context of energy consumption and impact on climate change. *Energies*, *17*(23), 5965. DOI: 10.3390/en17235965

Piramuthu, S. (2022). IoT, environmental sustainability, agricultural supply chains. *Procedia Computer Science*, *204*, 811–816. DOI: 10.1016/j.procs.2022.08.098

Pla, F., & Lluís-F., H. (2018, June). Spanish sentiment analysis in Twitter at the TASS workshop. *Language Resources and Evaluation*, *52*(2), 645–672. DOI: 10.1007/s10579-017-9394-7

Premkumar, S., & Sigappi, A. N. (2022). IoT-enabled edge computing model for smart irrigation system. *Journal of Intelligent Systems*, *31*(1), 632–650. DOI: 10.1515/jisys-2022-0046

Prinsloo, P., Slade, S., & Khalil, M. (2022). The answer is (not always) more data: Students' rights, algorithmic decision-making, and the quest for justice. *International Review of Research in Open and Distance Learning*, *23*(4), 134–155. DOI: 10.19173/irrodl.v23i4.5907

Qayyum, A., Qadir, J., Bilal, M., & Al-Fuqaha, A. (2023). Secure and robust machine learning for healthcare: A survey on federated learning in medical applications. *Future Generation Computer Systems*, *140*, 34–66. DOI: 10.1016/j.future.2022.09.019

Qventus. (2022, January 31). *Qventus achieves major milestones as a leader in care operations automation*. PR Newswire.

Radanliev, P. (2025). Artificial intelligence: Reflecting on the past and looking towards the next paradigm shift. *Journal of Experimental & Theoretical Artificial Intelligence*, *37*(7), 1045–1062. DOI: 10.1080/0952813X.2024.2323042

Radford, A., Wu, J., Child, R., Luan, D., Amodei, D., & Sutskever, I. (2019). Language models are unsupervised multitask learners. OpenAI Blog, 1(8), 9–24. https://cdn.openai.com/better-language-models/language_models_are_unsupervised_multitask_learners.pdf

Ragnedda, M., & Ruiu, M. L. (2020). *Digital capital: A Bourdieusian perspective on the digital divide*. Emerald Publishing., DOI: 10.1108/9781839095504

Rahman, M., & Hasan, K. (2023). Defense strategies for adversarial attacks on generative AI models. *ACM Transactions on Privacy and Security*, *26*(2), 1–30.

Rajeswari, S. K. R. K. A., Suthendran, K., & Rajakumar, K. (2017, June). *A smart agricultural model by integrating IoT, mobile and cloud-based big data analytics. In 2017 international conference on intelligent computing and control (I2C2)*. IEEE.

Ramalakshmi, S., & Asha, G. (2024). Exploring generative AI: Models, applications, and challenges in data synthesis. *Asian Journal of Research in Computer Science*, *17*(12), 123–136. DOI: 10.9734/ajrcos/2024/v17i12533

Ramírez, B. G., Espejel, J. L., Díaz, M. D. C. S., & Linares, G. T. R. (2024). S\'olo Esc\'uchame: Spanish Emotional Accompaniment Chatbot. *arXiv preprint arXiv:2408.01852*.

Ramos, C., Mossman, S., & Leal, I. (2020). Evening and weekend study patterns among university students: A learning analytics perspective. *Journal of Learning Analytics*, *7*(3), 44–58. DOI: 10.18608/jla.2020.73.4

Ran, H., Guizilini, V., & Wang, Y. (2024). *Towards realistic scene generation with LiDAR diffusion models.* In *Proceedings of CVPR 2024.* https://openaccess.thecvf.com/content/CVPR2024/papers/Ran_Towards_Realistic_Scene_Generation_with_LiDAR_Diffusion_Models_CVPR_2024_paper.pdf

Rauniyar, K., Poudel, S., Shiwakoti, S., Thapa, S., Rashid, J., Kim, J., Imran, M., & Naseem, U. (2023). Multi-aspect annotation and analysis of nepali tweets on anti-establishment election discourse. *IEEE Access : Practical Innovations, Open Solutions, 11*, 143092–143115. DOI: 10.1109/ACCESS.2023.3342154

Rausch, T., Nastic, S., & Dustdar, S. (2024). Secure edge-cloud orchestration for distributed AI pipelines. *Future Generation Computer Systems, 154*, 401–417.

Reddi, V. J. (2025). Generative AI at the edge: Challenges and opportunities: The next phase in AI deployment. *ACM Queue; Tomorrow's Computing Today, 23*(2), 79–137. DOI: 10.1145/3733702

REDDY, G. C. P. (2024). Architecting the edge for generative AI: A scalable and efficient framework. *Iconic Research and Engineering Journals, 8*, 776–792.

Regmi, U. R. (2006). *The mixing of English code in Nepali public speaking* (Doctoral dissertation, Department of English Education).

Reidenberg, J. R., & Schaub, F. (2018). Achieving big data privacy in education. *Theory and Research in Education, 16*(3), 263–279. DOI: 10.1177/1477878518805308

Reimers, N., & Gurevych, I. (2019). Sentence-BERT: Sentence embeddings using siamese BERT-networks. *Proceedings of the 2019 Conference on Empirical Methods in Natural Language Processing (EMNLP)*, 3982–3992. DOI: 10.18653/v1/D19-1410

Reis, M. J., & Scrôdio, C. (2025). Edge AI for real-time anomaly detection in smart homes. *Future Internet, 17*(4), 179. DOI: 10.3390/fi17040179

Rejeesh, C. R., Joseph, A., & Kumar, A. M. N. (2025). Edge AI: Powering Real-Time Intelligence for IoT. *Journal of Applied Science, Engineering, Technology and Management, 3*(1), 01–02. DOI: 10.61779/jasetm.v3i1.0

Reuters. (2024). Nvidia unveils AI model capable of modifying voices and generating novel sounds. *Reuters Technology News.*

Reuther, A., Michaleas, P., Jones, M., Gadepally, V., Samsi, S., & Kepner, J. (2023). Distributed and edge AI: A systems perspective. *Journal of Parallel and Distributed Computing, 176*, 104–121.

Roediger, H. L. III, & Karpicke, J. D. (2006). Test-enhanced learning: Taking memory tests improves long-term retention. *Psychological Science*, *17*(3), 249–255. DOI: 10.1111/j.1467-9280.2006.01693.x PMID: 16507066

Rokh, B., Azarpeyvand, A., & Khanteymoori, A. (2023). A comprehensive survey on model quantisation for deep neural networks in image classification. *ACM Transactions on Intelligent Systems and Technology*, *14*(6), 1–50. DOI: 10.1145/3623402

Roy, B. (2025). *Edge AI and AI driven decision-making*. DOI: 10.5281/zenodo.15336448

Samuel, J., Tripathi, A., & Mema, E. (2024). A new era of artificial intelligence begins-where will it lead us? *Journal of Big Data and Artificial Intelligence*, *2*(1). Advance online publication. DOI: 10.54116/jbdai.v2i1.40

Sankaran, K., & Holmes, S. P. (2023). Generative models: An interdisciplinary perspective. *Annual Review of Statistics and Its Application*, *10*(1), 325–352. DOI: 10.1146/annurev-statistics-033121-110134

Satyanarayanan, M. (2017). The emergence of edge computing. *Computer*, *50*(1), 30–39. DOI: 10.1109/MC.2017.9

Savargaonkar, H. A., & Karandikar, A. (2024). A scoping review on the role of edge computing in search and rescue operations. *Wireless Personal Communications*, *138*(2), 989–1026. Advance online publication. DOI: 10.1007/s11277-024-11543-z

Selwyn, N. (2022). *Education and technology: Key issues and debates* (3rd ed.). Bloomsbury Academic. DOI: 10.5040/9781350145573

Senapaty, M. K., Ray, A., & Padhy, N. (2023). IoT-enabled soil nutrient analysis and crop recommendation model for precision agriculture. *Computers*, *12*(3), 61. DOI: 10.3390/computers12030061

Seshadri, K., Akin, B., Laudon, J., Narayanaswami, R., & Yazdanbakhsh, A. (2022). An Evaluation of Edge TPU Accelerators for Convolutional Neural Networks. *2022 IEEE International Symposium on Workload Characterization (IISWC)*, 79–91. https://doi.org/DOI: 10.1109/IISWC55918.2022.00017

Shah, C., & White, R. W. (2025, July). From To-Do to Ta-Da: Transforming Task-Focused IR with Generative AI. In *Proceedings of the 48th International ACM SIGIR Conference on Research and Development in Information Retrieval* (pp. 3911-3921). DOI: 10.1145/3726302.3730352

Shahi, T. B., & Sitaula, C. (2022). Natural language processing for Nepali text: A review. *Artificial Intelligence Review*, *55*(4), 3401–3429. DOI: 10.1007/s10462-021-10093-1

Shahi, T. B., Xu, C. Y., Neupane, A., & Guo, W. (2023). Recent advances in crop disease detection using UAV and deep learning techniques. *Remote Sensing (Basel)*, *15*(9), 2450. DOI: 10.3390/rs15092450

Shamsir, S., Hassan, O., & Islam, S. K. (2020). Smart infant-monitoring system with machine learning model to detect physiological activities and ambient conditions. *I2MTC 2020 - International Instrumentation and Measurement Technology Conference, Proceedings*. DOI: 10.1109/I2MTC43012.2020.9129295

Shazeer, N.. (2017). Outrageously large neural networks: The sparsely-gated mixture-of-experts layer. *International Conference on Learning Representations (ICLR).*

Shen, Y., Zhang, T., & Liu, J. (2024). Black-box adaptation of large language models for resource-constrained environments. *AI Open*, *5*, 77–89. DOI: 10.1016/j.aiopen.2024.01.002

Shimizu, T., Xu, J., & Tasaka, K. (2020). MobileGAN: Compact Network Architecture for Generative Adversarial Network. In S. Palaiahnakote, G. Sanniti di Baja, L. Wang, & W. Q. Yan (Eds.), *Lecture Notes in Computer Science (including subseries Lecture Notes in Artificial Intelligence and Lecture Notes in Bioinformatics)* (Vol. 12046 LNCS, pp. 326–338). Cham: Springer International Publishing. DOI: 10.1007/978-3-030-41404-7_23

Shi, W., Cao, J., Member, S., Zhang, Q., & Member, S. (2016). Edge Computing. *Vision and Challenges.*, *3*(5), 637–646.

Shi, W., Cao, J., Zhang, Q., Li, Y., & Xu, L. (2020). Edge computing: Vision and challenges. *IEEE Internet of Things Journal*, *3*(5), 637–646. DOI: 10.1109/JIOT.2016.2579198

Shokrollahi, Y., Colmenarez, J., Liu, W., Yarmohammadtoosky, S., Nikahd, M. M., Dong, P., Li, X., & Gu, L. (2025). *Recent advances in generative AI for healthcare applications* (Version 2). arXiv. https://arxiv.org/abs/2310.00795

Shrikumar, P. G., & Kundaje, A. (2017). "Learning Important Features Through Propagating Activation Differences," in *Proc. of the 34th International Conference on Machine Learning*.

Shwedeh, F., & Alzoubi, H. M. (2024, June). Applying Artificial Intelligence in Database Management Systems to Mitigate the Difficulties Encountered in Training Institutions' Systems. In *International Scientific Conference Management and Engineering* (pp. 177-182). Cham: Springer Nature Switzerland.

Siemens Healthineers. (2022). *AI-Rad Companion: Providing multi-modality imaging decision support*. Siemens Healthineers White Paper.

Singh, E., Pratap, A., Mehta, U., & Azid, S. I. (2024). Smart agriculture drone for crop spraying using image-processing and machine learning techniques: Experimental validation. *IoT*, *5*(2), 250–270. DOI: 10.3390/iot5020013

Singh, R., & Gill, S. S. (2023). Edge AI: A survey. *Internet of Things and Cyber-Physical Systems*, *3*, 71–92. DOI: 10.1016/j.iotcps.2023.02.004

Singh, R., & Kapoor, A. (2024). Ethical considerations for synthetic data generation at the edge. *AI and Ethics*, *4*(3), 221–238.

Singh, S., Sharma, K., Karna, B. K., & Raj, P. (2023). *Pruning and quantization for deeper artificial intelligence (AI) model optimization*. Springer., https://link.springer.com/chapter/10.1007/978-981-99-4634-1_73 DOI: 10.1007/978-981-99-4634-1_73

Sitaula, C., Basnet, A., Mainali, A., & Shahi, T. B. (2021). Deep learning-based methods for sentiment analysis on Nepali COVID-19-related tweets. *Computational Intelligence and Neuroscience*, *2158184*(1), 2158184. Advance online publication. DOI: 10.1155/2021/2158184 PMID: 34737773

Siti-Nabiha, A. K., & Jurnali, T. (2020). Institutional work and implementation of a performance measurement and management system in a developing country. *Journal of Accounting & Organizational Change*, *16*(3), 447–467. DOI: 10.1108/JAOC-07-2018-0060

Sitoula, S. (2020). Analysis of Twitter Data for Its Popularity Index and Sentiments Associated. *Zenodo*. DOI: 10.5281/zenodo.17830974

Sitoula, S., Shahi, T. B., Wibowo, S., & Neupane, A. (2025). Sentiment analysis of Nepali social media text with a hybrid deep learning model. *Social Network Analysis and Mining*, *15*(1), 85. Advance online publication. DOI: 10.1007/s13278-025-01508-w

Skouri, S., Bouadila, S., Ayed, R., Chehaibi, S., & Fteiti, M. (2025). Optimizing climate control in vertical farms: 3E analysis of thermal conditioning systems. *Energy Sources. Part A, Recovery, Utilization, and Environmental Effects*, *47*(2), 2554341. DOI: 10.1080/15567036.2025.2554341

Socher, R., Perelygin, A., Wu, J., Chuang, J., Manning, C. D., Ng, A. Y., & Potts, C. (2013, October). Recursive deep models for semantic compositionality over a sentiment treebank. In *Proceedings of the 2013 conference on empirical methods in natural language processing* (pp. 1631-1642). DOI: 10.18653/v1/D13-1170

Soji, E. S., Gnanamalar, S., Arumugam, N., Priscila, S. S., Selvam, N., & Rajest, S. S. (2024). AI-driven computer vision for intelligent home automation and surveillance systems. In *Explainable AI applications for human behavior analysis* (p. 16). IGI Global., DOI: 10.4018/979-8-3693-1355-8.ch015

Sørensen, M., Holm, F., Kristensen, A., Jensen, S., Madsen, L., Rasmussen, E., & Aline, C. (2025). Quantization as a Foundation for Deployable High Performance Diffusion Models within the Landscape of Large Scale Generative AI. *Authorea Preprints*. DOI: 10.36227/techrxiv.175624440.05705133/v1

Srisruthi, S., Swarna, N., Ros, G. S., & Elizabeth, E. (2016, May). Sustainable agriculture using eco-friendly and energy efficient sensor technology. In *2016 IEEE International Conference on Recent Trends in Electronics, Information & Communication Technology (RTEICT)* (pp. 1442-1446). IEEE. DOI: 10.1109/RTEICT.2016.7808070

Stake, R. E. (1995). *The art of case study research*. Sage Publications.

Strobel, G., Banh, L., Möller, F., & Schoormann, T. (2024). Exploring generative artificial intelligence: A taxonomy and types.

Sun, H., Xu, R., Luo, J., & Cheng, H. (2025). Review of the application of UAV edge computing in fire emergency response. *Sensors (Basel)*, *25*(11), 3304. DOI: 10.3390/s25113304 PMID: 40968850

Sun, Y., Hu, J., Wang, W., He, M., & De With, P. H. N. (2021). Camera-based discomfort detection using multi-channel attention 3D-CNN for hospitalized infants. *Quantitative Imaging in Medicine and Surgery*, *11*(7), 3059–3069. DOI: 10.21037/qims-20-1302 PMID: 34249635

Sun, Y., Shan, C., Tan, T., Tong, T., Wang, W., Pourtaherian, A., & De With, P. H. N. (2019). Detecting discomfort in infants through facial expressions. *Physiological Measurement*, *40*(11), 115006. Advance online publication. DOI: 10.1088/1361-6579/ab55b3 PMID: 31703212

Taha, M. F., ElMasry, G., Gouda, M., Zhou, L., Liang, N., Abdalla, A., Rousseau, D., & Qiu, Z. (2022). Recent advances of smart systems and internet of things (iot) for aquaponics automation: A comprehensive overview. *Chemosensors (Basel, Switzerland)*, *10*(8), 303. DOI: 10.3390/chemosensors10080303

Tang, M., Gao, R., & Guo, L. (2024). Lightweight signal recognition based on a hybrid model in wireless networks. *Telecommunication Systems*, *87*(3), 707–721. DOI: 10.1007/s11235-024-01204-8

Tao, Z., Xu, W., Huang, Y., Wang, X., & You, X. (2023). Wireless network digital twin for 6G: Generative AI as a key enabler. arXiv. https://arxiv.org/pdf/2311.17451v3

Thapa, B., & Mashayekhy, L. (2024). Multi-layer edge intelligence for autonomous vehicular systems. *IEEE Transactions on Intelligent Transportation Systems*, *25*(6), 7448–7463.

Thara, S., & Poornachandran, P. (2018, September). Code-mixing: A brief survey. In *2018 International conference on advances in computing, communications and informatics (ICACCI)* (pp. 2382-2388). IEEE. DOI: 10.1109/ICACCI.2018.8554413

Tharu, M., Pokhrel, S., & Lamichhane, B. (2023). Sentiment Analysis of Nepali COVID-19 Tweets using BERT-LSTM. *Journal of Engineering and Sciences.*, *2*(1), 49–56. DOI: 10.3126/jes2.v2i1.60393

ThinkAutonomous. (2024, October 21). 8 takeaways from Mobileye's End-To-End talk. ThinkAutonomous. https://www.thinkautonomous.ai/blog/mobileye-end-to-end

Thirunavukarasu, A. J., Ting, D. S. J., Elangovan, K., Gutierrez, L., Tan, T. F., & Ting, D. S. W. (2023). Large language models in medicine. *Nature Medicine*, *29*(8), 1930–1940. DOI: 10.1038/s41591-023-02448-8 PMID: 37460753

Tisdell, E. J., Merriam, S. B., & Stuckey-Peyrot, H. L. (2025). Qualitative research: A guide to design and implementation. John Wiley & Sons.

Tlili, A., Shehata, B., Adarkwah, M. A., Bozkurt, A., Hickey, D. T., Huang, R., & Agyemang, B. (2023). What if the devil is my guardian angel: ChatGPT as a case study of using chatbots in education. *Smart Learning Environments*, *10*(1), 15. DOI: 10.1186/s40561-023-00237-x

Tmamna, J., Ayed, E. B., Fourati, R., Gogate, M., Arslan, T., Hussain, A., & Ayed, M. B. (2024). Pruning deep neural networks for green energy efficient models: A survey. *Cognitive Computation*, *16*(6), 2931–2952. DOI: 10.1007/s12559-024-10313-0

Tokan, M., Tokan, M., Tokan, M., & F, A.TOKAN. (2024). Optimization of Battery Power Efficiency in Baby Incubator Transport Through PID-Fuzzy Control. *Jurnal Teknokes*, *17*(4), 190–196. DOI: 10.35882/7hjhwb84

Touil, S., Richa, A., Fizir, M., Argente Garcia, J. E., & Skarmeta Gomez, A. F. (2022). A review on smart irrigation management strategies and their effect on water savings and crop yield. *Irrigation and Drainage*, *71*(5), 1396–1416. DOI: 10.1002/ird.2735

Touvron, H., Lavril, T., Izacard, G., Martinet, X., Lachaux, M.-A., Lacroix, T., Rozière, B., Goyal, N., Hambro, E., Azhar, F., Rodriguez, A., Joulin, A., Grave, E., & Lample, G. (2023). *LLaMA: Open and efficient foundation language models.* arXiv. https://arxiv.org/abs/2302.13971

Tripathi, A., Samuel, J., Brennan-Tonetta, M., Nguyen, H., & Mema, E. (2025). When machines create envisioning our future with the transformative power of generative ai. *Journal of Big Data and Artificial Intelligence*, *3*(1). Advance online publication. DOI: 10.54116/jbdai.v3i1.55

Tsuji, H., Yamamoto, T., Kobayashi, M., Sasaki, K., Aso, N., & Sugiura, Y. (2025). CradlePosture: Camera-Based Approach for Estimating Neonate's Posture Based on Caregiver's Holding Behaviors. *2025 IEEE/SICE International Symposium on System Integration, SII 2025*, 434–439. DOI: 10.1109/SII59315.2025.10870587

Turner, N. (2025). *EDGE AI : Paving the Way for Intelligent, Resilient Deployments with a Systems Mindset Table of Contents. October.*

Unique Identification Authority of India (UIDAI). (2023). "Offline e-KYC Identity Verification," UIDAI. [Online]. Available: https://uidai.gov.in/en/ecosystem/authentication-devices-documents/offline-ekyc.html

United Nations Office on Drugs and Crime. (2023). "Estimated criminal money laundered annually," UNODC. [Online]. Available: https://www.unodc.org/

Vadhil, F. A., Nanne, M. F., & Salihi, M. L. (2024, April). The Powerful AI: An Exploration of Generative Artificial Intelligence Taxonomy and Applications. In *International Conference on Artificial Intelligence and its Applications in the Age of Digital Transformation* (pp. 236-250). Cham: Springer Nature Switzerland. DOI: 10.1007/978-3-031 71429-0_18

van de Ree, B. (2018). *Data Producers' Sovereignty an Exploration of Data Rights in Precision Agriculture Initiatives* (Doctoral dissertation, Eindhoven University of Technology).

Van der Burg, S., Wiseman, L., & Krkeljas, J. (2021). Trust in farm data sharing: Reflections on the EU code of conduct for agricultural data sharing. *Ethics and Information Technology*, *23*(3), 185–198. DOI: 10.1007/s10676-020-09543-1

Van Dijk, J. (2020). *The digital divide.* Polity Press.

Vaswani, A.. (2017). Attention is all you need. *Advances in Neural Information Processing Systems.*

Venkata Pavan Saish, N., Jayashree, J., & Vijayashree, J. (2025). Mathematical foundations and applications of generative AI models. *Generative artificial intelligence (AI) approaches for industrial applications*, 19-45.

Vermesan, O. (2025). Edge AI Systems Functional and Non-Functional Requirements Engineering. Generative AI Future Trends and Concepts. DOI: 10.5281/zenodo.14840306

Villat, J., & Nicholas, K. A. (2024). Quantifying soil carbon sequestration from regenerative agricultural practices in crops and vineyards. *Frontiers in Sustainable Food Systems*, *7*, 1234108. DOI: 10.3389/fsufs.2023.1234108

Villena-Román, J., Lana-Serrano, S., Martínez-Cámara, E., & González-Cristóbal, J. C. (2013). Tass-workshop on sentiment analysis at sepln. *Procesamiento del Lenguaje Natural*, *50*, 37–44.

Vindegaard, N., & Benros, M. E. (2020). COVID-19 pandemic and mental health consequences: Systematic review of the current evidence. *Brain, Behavior, and Immunity*, *89*, 531–542. DOI: 10.1016/j.bbi.2020.05.048 PMID: 32485289

Viz.ai. (2024). VALIDATE study: Utilization of the Viz.ai mobile stroke care coordination platform across healthcare systems. *Frontiers in Stroke*.

Vuruma, S. K. R., Margetts, A., Su, J., Ahmed, F., & Srivastava, B. (2024). From cloud to edge: Rethinking generative AI for low-resource design challenges. arXiv preprint arXiv:2402.12702.

Vu, T. H., Jagatheesaperumal, S. K., Nguyen, M. D., Van Huynh, N., Kim, S., & Pham, Q. V. (2024). Applications of generative AI (GAI) for mobile and wireless networking: A survey. *IEEE Internet of Things Journal*.

Walani, C. C., & Doorsamy, W. (2025). Edge vs. Cloud: Empirical Insights into Data-Driven Condition Monitoring. *Big Data and Cognitive Computing*, *9*(5), 121. DOI: 10.3390/bdcc9050121

Wall, E. (2023). *The Cost of Anti-Money Laundering Compliance*. LexisNexis Risk Solutions.

Wang, A., Sunshine, J. E., & Gollakota, S. (2019). *Contactless Infant Monitoring using White Noise*. 1–16. DOI: 10.1145/3300061.3345453

Wang, K., Chen, J., Li, H., Mi, Z., & Zhu, J. (2025). SparseDM: Toward sparse efficient diffusion models. *2025 IEEE International Conference on Multimedia and Expo (ICME)*, 1–7. Nantes, France. https://doi.org/DOI: 10.1109/ICME59968.2025.11209208

Wang, W., Chen, W., Luo, Y., Long, Y., Lin, Z., Zhang, L., . . . He, X. (2024). Model compression and efficient inference for large language models: A survey. arXiv preprint arXiv:2402.09748.

Wang, X., He, Z., & Peng, X. (2024). Artificial-intelligence-generated content with diffusion models: A systematic review. *Mathematics (MDPI).*

Wang, H., Yemeni, Z., Ismael, W. M., Hawbani, A., & Alsamhi, S. H. (2021). A reliable and energy efficient dual prediction data reduction approach for WSNs based on Kalman filter. *IET Communications*, *15*(18), 2285–2299. DOI: 10.1049/cmu2.12262

Wang, L., Bhanushali, T., Huang, Z., Yang, J., Badami, S., & Hightow-Weidman, L. (2025). Evaluating Generative AI in Mental Health: Systematic Review of Capabilities and Limitations. *JMIR Mental Health*, *12*(1), e70014. DOI: 10.2196/70014 PMID: 40373033

Wang, T., Guo, J., Zhang, B., Yang, G., & Li, D. (2025). Deploying AI on edge: Advancement and challenges in edge intelligence. *Mathematics*, *13*(11), 1878. DOI: 10.3390/math13111878

Wang, Y. C., Xue, J., Wei, C., & Kuo, C. C. J. (2023). An overview on generative AI at scale with edge–cloud computing. *IEEE Open Journal of the Communications Society*, *4*, 2952–2971. DOI: 10.1109/OJCOMS.2023.3320646

Weber, M.. (2021). "Unsupervised Anomaly Detection for Anti-Money Laundering," in *Proc. of the ACM SIGKDD Workshop on Machine Learning in Finance.*

Webster, J., & Watson, R. T. (2002). Analyzing the past to prepare for the future: Writing a literature review. *Management Information Systems Quarterly*, *26*(2), xiii–xxiii. DOI: 10.2307/4132319

Weizenbaum, J. (1966). ELIZA—A computer program for the study of natural language communication between man and machine. *Communications of the ACM*, *9*(1), 36–45. DOI: 10.1145/365153.365168

Wevolver. (2024). *Edge AI: Industry applications, NPU trends & deployment strategies.* Wevolver Engineering Report.

Williams, L., & Carter, M. (2024). Cloud-edge cooperative architectures for generative industrial analytics. *IEEE Transactions on Industrial Informatics*, *20*(3), 1551–1563.

Williamson, B., Eynon, R., & Potter, J. (2020). Pandemic politics, pedagogies and practices: Digital technologies and distance education during the coronavirus emergency. *Learning, Media and Technology*, *45*(2), 107–114. DOI: 10.1080/17439884.2020.1761641

Wilson, K. (2025). The semantic impact of search strategy modulation in real-time AI. [JMLR]. *Journal of Machine Learning Research*, *26*(102), 1102–1124. https://jmlr.org/papers/v26/25-1102.html

Winzig, J., Almanza, J. C. A., Mendoza, M. G., & Schumann, T. (2022, October). Edge ai-use case on Google Coral Dev Board mini. In 2022, *IET International Conference on Engineering Technologies and Applications (IET-ICETA)* (pp. 1-2). IEEE. DOI: 10.1109/IET-ICETA56553.2022.9971614

Xie, Y., & Fang, Q. (2025). An energy-aware generative AI edge inference framework for low-power IoT devices. *Electronics (Basel)*, *14*(20), 4086. DOI: 10.3390/electronics14204086

Xu, M., Niyato, D., Zhang, H., Kang, J., Xiong, Z., Mao, S., & Han, Z. (2023, December). Joint foundation model caching and inference of generative AI services for edge intelligence. In *GLOBECOM 2023-2023 IEEE Global Communications Conference* (pp. 3548-3553). IEEE. DOI: 10.1109/GLOBECOM54140.2023.10436771

Xu, D., Zhang, H., Yang, L., Liu, R., Huang, G., Xu, M., & Liu, X. (2025). Fast on-device LLM inference with NPUs. *Proceedings of the 30th ACM International Conference on Architectural Support for Programming Languages and Operating Systems*, 1458–1473. DOI: 10.48550/arXiv.2407.05858

Xu, G., Hao, Z., Luo, Y., Hu, H., An, J., & Mao, S. (2024). DeViT: Decomposing Vision Transformers for Collaborative Inference in Edge Devices. *IEEE Transactions on Mobile Computing*, *23*(5), 5917–5932. DOI: 10.1109/TMC.2023.3315138

Xu, M., Du, H., Niyato, D., Kang, J., Xiong, Z., Mao, S., Han, Z., Jamalipour, A., Kim, D. I., Shen, X., Leung, V. C. M., & Poor, H. V. (2024). Unleashing the power of edge-cloud generative AI in mobile networks: A survey of AIGC services. *IEEE Communications Surveys and Tutorials*, *26*(2), 1127–1170. DOI: 10.1109/COMST.2024.3353265

Xu, Y., Song, C., Sun, Y., & Yu, S. (2024, January). Advances and Challenges in Large Model Compression: A Survey. In *Proceedings of the 2024 Guangdong-Hong Kong-Macao Greater Bay Area International Conference on Digital Economy and Artificial Intelligence* (pp. 421-426). DOI: 10.1145/3675417.3675487

Xu, Y., Sun, Q., & Wang, J. (2024). Trusted execution environments for protecting edge-deployed AI models. *Computers & Security*, *133*, 103407.

Xu, Z., Xu, Y., Xu, H., Liao, Y., Yao, Z., & Xie, Z. (2025). Lightweight and post-training structured pruning for on-device large language models. *IEEE Transactions on Mobile Computing*.

Yamada, I., Washio, K., Shindo, H., & Matsumoto, Y. (2022, July). Global entity disambiguation with BERT. In *Proceedings of the 2022 Conference of the North American Chapter of the Association for Computational Linguistics: Human Language Technologies* (pp. 3264-3271).

Yang, B., Liang, R., Li, W., Wang, H., Cao, X., Yu, Z., . . . Yuen, C. (2025). Frontiers of Generative AI for Network Optimization: Theories, Limits, and Visions. *arXiv preprint arXiv:2507.01773*.

Yang, C., Yu, X., An, Z., & Xu, Y. (2023). Categories of response-based, feature-based, and relation-based knowledge distillation. In *Advancements in knowledge distillation: towards new horizons of intelligent systems* (pp. 1–32). Springer International Publishing. DOI: 10.1007/978-3-031-32095-8_1

Yang, L., Wu, C., Zhang, D., & Su, J. (2017). Early-warning threshold extraction method of agricultural SCADA server based on clustering analysis. *Nongye Gongcheng Xuebao (Beijing)*, *33*(1), 293–299.

Yan, L., Whitelock-Wainwright, A., Guan, Q., Wen, G., Gašević, D., & Chen, G. (2023). Students' experience of AI-generated feedback and differential quality across demographics. *British Journal of Educational Technology*, *52*(5), 2038–2057. DOI: 10.1111/bjet.13102 PMID: 34219755

Yan, X., Zhao, M., & Hung, P. (2024). Real-time predictive modeling in autonomous vehicles using edge-deployed generative models. *IEEE Transactions on Vehicular Technology*, *73*(2), 2210–2224.

Yao, Y., Yu, T., Zhang, A., Wang, C., Cui, J., Zhu, H., Cai, T., Chen, C., Li, H., Zhao, W., He, Z., Chen, Q., Zhou, R., Zou, Z., Zhang, H., Hu, S., Zheng, Z., Zhou, J., Cai, J., & Sun, M. (2025). Efficient GPT-4V level multimodal large language model for deployment on edge devices. *Nature Communications*, *16*(1), 5509. DOI: 10.1038/s41467-025-61040-5 PMID: 40593624

Yin, R. K. (2018). *Case study research and applications: Design and methods* (6th ed.). Sage Publications.

Yuksel, S. E., Wilson, J. N., & Gader, P. D. (2012). Twenty years of mixture of experts. *IEEE Transactions on Neural Networks and Learning Systems, 23*(8), 1177–1193. DOI: 10.1109/TNNLS.2012.2200299 PMID: 24807516

Zaheer, M., Guruganesh, G., Dubey, A., Ainslie, J., Alberti, C., Ontanon, S., . . . Ahmed, A. (2020). Big bird: Transformers for longer sequences. *Advances in Neural Information Processing Systems, 2020-December*, 17283–17297.

Zawacki-Richter, O., Marín, V. I., Bond, M., & Gouverneur, F. (2024). Systematic review of research on artificial intelligence applications in higher education: Where are the educators? *International Journal of Educational Technology in Higher Education, 21*(1), 1–27. DOI: 10.1186/s41239-024-00464-3

Zhang, S., Ma, Y., Fang, L., Jia, H., D'Alfonso, S., & Kostakos, V. (2024). Enabling On-Device LLMs Personalization with Smartphone Sensing. In *Companion of the 2024 on ACM International Joint Conference on Pervasive and Ubiquitous Computing* (pp. 186–190). New York, NY, USA: ACM. DOI: 10.1145/3675094.3677545

Zhang, H., Liu, S., & He, X. (2024). Lightweight diffusion models for real-time edge generation. *Proceedings of the IEEE/CVF Conference on Computer Vision and Pattern Recognition*, 4432–4443.

Zhang, K., Mao, Y., Leng, S., Zhao, Q., Li, L., Peng, X., Pan, L., Maharjan, S., & Zhang, Y. (2016). Energy-efficient offloading for mobile edge computing in 5G heterogeneous networks. *IEEE Access : Practical Innovations, Open Solutions, 4*, 5896–5907. DOI: 10.1109/ACCESS.2016.2597169

Zhang, Q., Chen, M., & Li, L. (2022). Edge intelligence in the AI-enabled Internet of Things: Research challenges and future directions. *IEEE Network, 36*(3), 186–192. DOI: 10.1109/MNET.001.1900340

Zhang, Q., Miller, D., & Gupta, V. (2024). The sustainability gap: Why static optimization fails for generative AI at the edge. *Sustainable Computing : Informatics and Systems, 41*, 100845. DOI: 10.1016/j.suscom.2024.100845

Zhang, R., He, J., Luo, X., Niyato, D., Kang, J., Xiong, Z., & Sikdar, B. (2025). Toward democratised generative AI in next-generation mobile edge networks. *IEEE Network.*

Zhang, X., Cao, Z., & Dong, W. (2020). Overview of edge computing in the agricultural internet of things: Key technologies, applications, challenges. *IEEE Access : Practical Innovations, Open Solutions, 8*, 141748–141761. DOI: 10.1109/ACCESS.2020.3013005

Zhang, X., Xie, G., Huang, Y., Xiong, Z., Liu, J., Cui, S., & Shen, X. S. (2025). Edge intelligence in the generative artificial intelligence era. *IEEE Wireless Communications*, *32*(6), 60–68. DOI: 10.1109/MWC.2025.3599652

Zhao, C., Liu, G., Zhang, R., Liu, Y., Wang, J., Kang, J., . . . Kim, D. I. (2025). Edge general intelligence through world models and agentic ai: Fundamentals, solutions, and challenges. *arXiv preprint arXiv:2508.09561*.

Zhao, X., Xu, R., & Guo, X. (2023, June). Post-training quantisation or quantisation-aware training? That is the question. In 2023, *China Semiconductor Technology International Conference (CSTIC)* (pp. 1-3). IEEE.

Zhou, L., Gao, J., Li, D., & Shum, H. Y. (2020). The design and implementation of xiaoice, an empathetic social chatbot. *Computational Linguistics*, *46*(1), 53–93. DOI: 10.1162/coli_a_00368

Zhou, Z., Chen, X., Li, E., Zeng, L., Luo, K., & Zhang, J. (2019). Edge intelligence: Paving the last mile of artificial intelligence with edge computing. *Proceedings of the IEEE*, *107*(8), 1738–1762. DOI: 10.1109/JPROC.2019.2918951

Zhuansun, C., Li, P., Liu, Y., & Tian, Z. (2025). Generative AI-Assisted Mobile Edge Computation Offloading in Digital Twin-Enabled IIoT. *IEEE Internet of Things Journal*, *12*(10), 13248–13258. DOI: 10.1109/JIOT.2025.3547370

Zou, H. P., Huang, W.-C., Wu, Y., Chen, Y., Miao, C., Nguyen, H., Zhou, Y., Zhang, W., Fang, L., He, L., Li, D., Jiang, R., Liu, X., & Yu, P. S. (2023). LLM-based human-agent collaboration and interaction systems: A survey. arXiv. https://arxiv.org/pdf/2505.00753

Zou, H. P., Huang, W. C., Wu, Y., Chen, Y., Miao, C., Nguyen, H., & He, L. (2025). LLM-based human-agent collaboration and interaction systems. *Survey (London, England)*.

About the Contributors

Sarbagya Shakya, a Senior IEEE member, is an Assistant Professor at Eastern New Mexico University, New Mexico, USA. He received a B.Eng. in Electronics Engineering from National College of Engineering, Tribhuvan University of Nepal in 2009 and an M.Eng. in Computer Engineering from Nepal College of Information Technology, Pokhara University of Nepal in 2014. He received his Ph.D. in Computational Science (Computer Science) from the School of Computer Science and Computer Engineering, University of Southern Mississippi, USA. He has over 10 years of experience in academia and research. His research interests include applied machine learning, deep learning, image processing, Internet of Things (IoT), Industrial IoT, Edge Computing, and TinyML, and he has published journal papers, conference papers, and book chapters in different domains on applied machine learning and deep learning.

Tej Shahi, IEEE Member, is a dedicated researcher and academic with over fifteen years of experience in teaching and research within Computer Science and information technology across Nepal and Australia. He received a B.Sc and an MSc in Computer Science with distinction from Tribhuvan University, Nepal, and a PhD in Computer Science from Central Queensland University, Australia. He was awarded gold medals by the president of Nepal for his outstanding academic achievements in his undergraduate and postgraduate studies. His doctoral research focused on the integration of remote sensing, image processing, and machine learning to optimise agricultural systems using artificial intelligence and drone technology, aiming to enhance efficiency and sustainability. His scholarly impact is evidenced by his significant presence in the academic community, including an H-index of 21 and an i10-index of 29 on Google Scholar. He is listed among the top 2% scientist by the Stanford Elsevier ranking for 2025. His research findings have been disseminated through high-quality publications in esteemed journals such as AI Review, Remote Sensing, and IEEE Transactions.

Edgar Ceh-Varela is an Assistant Professor of Computer Science at Eastern New Mexico University (ENMU). He received his Bachelor's degree in Computer Systems Engineering from the Instituto Tecnológico de Mérida, a Master's in Information Technology from the Universidad Interamericana para el Desarrollo and a Doctorate in Computer Systems in 2013 from Universidad del Sur, all from Mexico. In 2021, he obtained his Ph.D. in Computer Science from New Mexico State University (NMSU), USA. Dr. Ceh-Varela has been working in the computer science field for over 25 years. In the past years, he has published articles on applied machine learning, deep learning, natural language processing, agentic AI, wearable devices and edge computing.

Michael Cowling has been a leader in educational technology for over 20 years and was the recipient of the Universities Australia 2020 AAUT Award for Teaching Excellence (Physical Sciences & Related Studies). He is currently a Professor in Computing Technologies in the STEM College at RMIT University, where he serves as Director, Hub for Apple Platform Innovation (HAPI), an Apple-focussed teaching/research space using novel computing platforms to create dynamic new experiences. He is the President (2023 to 2025) of the Australasian Society for Computers in Learning in Tertiary Education (ASCILITE), where he is also a Community Fellow, as well as the Vice-President of the Open Access Publishing Association (OAPA). He is also a Fellow of the Australian Computer Society (ACS) and a Senior Fellow of the Higher Education Academy (Advance HE UK). Through his mantra 'pedagogy before technology', he fosters thoughtfulness in technology for students, educators and the public.

***

Laxmi Bhatt is an Assistant Professor and the Head of Department at Hillside College of Engineering, Balkumari, Kathmandu. He is engaged in teaching and academic leadership in the areas of computer science, programming, artificial intelligence, and machine learning. His academic and research interests include deep learning, medical imaging, diffusion models, and data-driven engineering solutions, with a strong focus on quality education and research-oriented learning.

Prasit Dutta completed his B.Tech in Electronics and Communication Engineering (ECE) in 2023 from S.R.M. Institute of Science and Technology. His primary research interests lie in Embedded Systems, Sensor Fusion, and the Internet of Things (IoT). He has specialized expertise in hardware-software interfacing using platforms like Raspberry Pi to create responsive monitoring environments. His work focuses on developing low-power, high-efficiency hardware architectures for the next generation of Edge Intelligence.

Naresh Kshetri received the MCA (Computer Applications) degree from University of Allahabad in 2014, MS (Cybersecurity) from Webster University in 2017, and the PhD (Computer Science with concentration in Cybersecurity) from the University of Missouri - St. Louis in 2022. Dr. Kshetri has taught several courses in Cybersecurity and Computer Science at both undergraduate and graduate levels. He joined RIT as a full time faculty of Cybersecurity in the Fall 2024. He has over eleven years of experience in teaching and research. His interests include cybersecurity, AI security, and blockchain technology. Dr. Kshetri is the Senior Member of IEEE (M '18, SM '25) and Professional Member of ACM (M '25). For a complete list of Dr. Kshetri's teaching and publications, please visit https://sites .google.com/view/nareshkshetri.

Murali M is currently working as Professor in Department of Computing Technologies, SRM Institute of Science and Technology, Kattankulathur 603203, India. He Completed his M.Tech in 2002 and Ph.D. in 2013. His research interests include Generative AI, Computer Vision, Deep Learning.

Taufik Maulana is an academic and research practitioner in Information Systems, specializing in Artificial Intelligence, Computer Vision, Edge AI, and Intelligent Information Systems. His research explores modern computer vision techniques, generative and lightweight AI architectures for edge computing, and predictive analytics for cybersecurity and regulatory compliance. He also investigates AI-driven innovation in library and information sciences, including intelligent automation, digitization, and knowledge management using machine learning, natural language processing, and large language models. His work emphasizes efficient, explainable, and responsible AI, addressing ethical, governance, and societal challenges in real-world applications.

Arjun Neupane received his PhD and Master of Information Technology (MIT) degree from University of Southern Queensland (UniSQ), Graduate Certificate in Higher Education from Griffith University and Graduate Certificate in Data Science from The University of Queensland, Australia. He has been working as a senior ICT lecturer at CQUniveristy, Rockhampton, since 2019. His main research interests include information systems, data science, machine learning, deep learning, AI, and image processing. He is interested in applying IT to solve real-world problems in different domains. He is also a member and Certified Professional (CP) of the Australian Computer Society.

Anisha Pokhrel is a Lecturer in the Computer Engineering Department who is passionate about teaching and mentoring students. Her interests lie in Machine Learning, Artificial Intelligence, and the Internet of Things (IoT), and she enjoys connecting research with real-world applications through technology-driven and research-oriented engineering education.

Jansi R completed her Ph.D. from Anna University, India, in 2022. She received her B.E. degree in Electronics and Communication Engineering from R.M.K. Engineering College, India, in 2010, and her M.E. degree in Communication Systems from SSN College of Engineering, India, in 2013. She is currently working as an assistant professor in the Department of Electronics and Communication Engineering at SRM Institute of Science and Technology. Her research interests include signal and image processing.

Naveen Kumar Ramakrishna is a technical lead and software architect specializing in applied AI systems and edge intelligence. His work spans generative AI, runtime optimization, and scalable system design, with a focus on deploying machine learning models under real-world operational constraints. He has led multiple proof-of-concept and production initiatives involving on-device AI and intelligent data platforms. His interests include adaptive inference, sustainable edge AI, and hardware-aware AI architectures.

Binastya Anggara Sekti has been a lecturer at the Faculty of Computer Science, Esa Unggul University, Jakarta, since 2016. He is actively involved in the Artificial Intelligence and Information Security Study Group. He holds a Bachelor's degree in Informatics Engineering from the Bandung Institute of Technology and a Master's degree in Information Systems Management from Trisakti University, Jakarta. Prior to entering academia, he accumulated over 25 years of professional experience as an IT practitioner in various companies across Jakarta. His work focused on developing data centers for internet service providers and delivering IT solutions for the manufacturing and oil & gas sectors. His research interests include artificial intelligence, cybersecurity, and the development of IT infrastructure.

Vandana Sharma is recognised in the Stanford list of the top 2% of scientists in the year 2024 & 2025. She is an accomplished academician and researcher, serving as an Associate Professor at Christ University's Delhi NCR Campus, India. A Senior Member of IEEE, she has an impressive publication record, with over 150 research papers in esteemed SCI and Scopus- indexed international journals and conferences. Dr. Sharma actively contributes to the academic community through various roles, including keynote speaking, session chairing, reviewing, and participating in Technical Program Committees for renowned international journals and IEEE conferences. She holds a postdoctoral degree from Lincoln University College, Malaysia.

Aayush Sinha earned his B.Tech in Electronics and Communication Engineering (ECE) from S.R.M. Institute of Science and Technology in 2023. His research interests are centered on TinyML, Edge Intelligence, and the Medical Internet of Things (MIoT). He has hands-on expertise in developing real-time surveillance hardware using Raspberry Pi and optimizing computer vision models like EfficientDet-Lite for resource-constrained environments. His work focuses on bridging the gap between traditional embedded systems and advanced AI to create low-latency, intelligent health monitoring solutions.

Sameer Sitoula has a Bachelor of Engineering in Computer Science and a Master of Technology in Software Engineering. He is currently pursuing RHD at CQUniversity, Australia. He has worked as a Lecturer and Supervisor in Nepal and completed an R&D internship at Intel Technology, Bangalore. He has strong knowledge in machine learning, artificial intelligence, and data analysis, with research publications in journals and conferences. He also has a background in management and business studies, with skills in accounting, economics, finance, and computer science. Additionally, he has experience in customer service, including client handling, bookings, and ticket management. He is a dedicated, hardworking, and quick learner with a passion for both research and practical work.

Index

Symbols

A

C

D

E

F

G

H

I

K

L

M

N

P

R

S

U

W

X

www.ingramcontent.com/pod-product-compliance
Lightning Source LLC
LaVergne TN
LVHW062336300926
849161LV00007B/1719